Householders

The Reizei Family in Japanese History

Harvard-Yenching Institute Monograph Series 61

Householders

The Reizei Family in Japanese History

Steven D. Carter

Published by the Harvard University Asia Center
for the Harvard-Yenching Institute and
distributed by Harvard University Press
Cambridge (Massachusetts) and London, 2007

Printed in the United States of America

The Harvard-Yenching Institute, founded in 1928 and headquartered at Harvard University, is a foundation dedicated to the advancement of higher education in the humanities and social sciences in East and Southeast Asia. The Institute supports advanced research at Harvard by faculty members of certain Asian universities and doctoral studies at Harvard and other universities by junior faculty at the same universities. It also supports East Asian studies at Harvard through contributions to the Harvard-Yenching Library and publication of the *Harvard Journal of Asiatic Studies* and books on premodern East Asian history and literature.

Library of Congress Cataloging-in-Publication Data

Carter, Steven D.
    Householders : the Reizei family in Japanese history / Steven D. Carter.
      p. cm. -- (Harvard-Yenching Institute monograph series ; 61)
    Includes bibliographical references and index.
    ISBN-13: 978-0-674-02453-3 (hardcover : alk. paper)
    ISBN-10: 0-674-02453-2 (hardcover : alk. paper)
    1. Reizei family. 2. Japanese poetry--History and criticism. 3. Authors and patrons--Japan--History. I. Title.
    PL713.A2C37 2007
    895.6'13--dc22

                                       2006100639

Index by the author

⊗ Printed on acid-free paper

Last number below indicates year of this printing
17 16 15 14 13 12 10 09 08 07

To Samuel George Carter

Acknowledgments

My interest in the history of the Reizei house began more than ten years ago when I was studying the writings of the fifteenth-century poet Shōtetsu, who apprenticed himself to a Reizei master in his youth. I was able to pursue my interest more fully in the autumn of 1999 at the Institute of Japanese Literature in Tokyo, where I was privileged to be in residence as a visiting scholar. Although at the time I was working on another project, it was in the reference library there that I first began reading the newsletter of the Reizei Corporation and the back matter of the *Reizei-ke Shiguretei sōsho*—a series of photostatic reproductions of texts from the house library that were capturing much attention among specialists in the field of Japanese poetry. My first thanks must therefore go to then-Director Matsuno Yōichi and the faculty of the Institute for their support, assistance, and encouragement. My discussions with members of the faculty there and with scholars who were kind enough to attend my seminar—particularly Iwasa Miyoko, Araki Hisashi, and Itō Kei—were not specifically focused on the Reizei house; but in many ways our conversations on topics such as the importance of *keiko* (training), memorization, and the mastery of convention in the practice of traditional poetry in many ways laid the foundation for the ideas that are at the heart of this book.

I also owe a debt of gratitude to my colleagues at the University of California at Irvine, most especially Susan Klein and Anne Walthall, who shared their ideas with me in discussions that helped me to formulate a useful approach to my subject matter. Not to be forgotten for the same reasons are my students David Cannell, LeRon Harrison, Helen Lee, and Toshiko Yokota.

While I was working on the book, I presented papers on topics related to the Reizei house at various places. For invaluable criticism offered on those occasions, I thank Mark McNally, Samuel Yamashita, Edward Kamens, Christian Ratcliff, and all the members of the Court Cultures Group, especially Eugene Vance. I also thank two anonymous readers for valuable comments and my editors at the Harvard University Asia Center. It goes without saying that any mistakes that remain in the book are my responsibility and should not be held against any of those who have offered criticisms or suggestions over the years.

For financial assistance that allowed me to make a number of research trips to Japan I thank the Institute of Japanese Literature, the School of Humanities at UC Irvine, the Northeast Asia Council of the Association for Asian Studies, and the Center for East Asian Studies at Stanford University, the latter also deserving thanks for providing funds to support the cost of illustrations. William Wong of the UC Irvine Library helped me considerably in acquiring materials to support my research, as did Naomi Kotake at the Stanford East Asia Library.

In the past, my research subjects—Sōgi, Ichijō Kaneyoshi, Shōtetsu, Tonna, and Bashō—have all been long dead. The Reizei house, on the other hand, is very much alive, and indeed thriving. This has meant that for the first time in my career I have had the experience of conducting live interviews. Reizei Kimiko, with whom I have been able to meet on two occasions—in the summer of 2002 and the autumn of 2005—has been agreeable, forthcoming, and helpful even in what must seem to her the most trivial of matters, such as bibliographical questions and queries concerning the proper reading of numerous names—although on the latter point she has asked me to note that no one can really be certain. I also greatly appreciate her willingness to allow me to use some family photos as illustrations. The memory of my conversation with her on the afternoon of November 16, 2005, in one of the rooms of the newly restored Reizei residence on Imadegawa Avenue in Kyoto, with the din of protests against George W. Bush—who was staying in the Gyoen just across the street—in the background, will always stay with me. She and her staff could not have been more gracious hosts.

For assistance in proofreading the manuscript I thank Daniel Sullivan, who was supported by funds from the Stanford Center for East Asian Studies, and my daughter Karen, who took a break from writing her Ph.D. dissertation to assist her father, gratis.

I cannot conclude without thanking my wife Mary for her patience and support, through thick and thin.

Contents

Reference Matter

Charts and Figures

Charts

Figures (following p. 254)

Note on Translation Format

OVER THE centuries, Japanese poems (*uta*) have been recorded in
many formats—sometimes in one line (in prose tales, for example),
sometimes in two (on poem strips, or *tanzaku*), sometimes in four (on
formal pocket paper, or *kaishi*), and sometimes in as many as eight
or nine (on screens or in the case of inscriptions). Modern editions
often record poems in a single line, including spaces to indicate the
5-7-5-7-7 syllabic breakdown that characterizes virtually all poems
until the twentieth century. But there are also editors who choose
to record poems in two lines, making a primary division between
upper (*kami*) and lower (*shimo*) halves. The fact is, then, that there
simply is no one way to put an *uta* on paper.

For the translations contained in this book, I have developed a
format adapted from the one traditionally used to record poems on
kaishi, which is the way poems were generally presented at formal
meetings—namely, three long lines and a three-syllable fourth line
(usually written in an ancient script called *man'yōgana*), as illustrated
in a *kaishi* in the hand of Reizei Tamekiyo (see Figure 1):

> *kumokiri o hedatete*
> *tōku koshiji yori ke*
> *sa mezurashiki hatsukari*
> *no koe*

"First Wild Geese of the Season"

Through the misty clouds   they have made their way
from far   along Koshi Road—
wild geese calling out in fresh voice   for the first time
this morning.

Needless to say, I have not been able to reproduce the exact sylla-
ble count or other syntactic features of the originals in most cases,
but I have tried at least to suggest their structure. For the sake of
clarity, I have used spaces to indicate line breaks according to the
5-7-5-7-7 syllable structure. Also, I have emphasized the break
between upper (lines 1 and 2 in the translations) and lower (lines 3
and 4) halves, again in an attempt to be true to dominant syntactic
structures. My hope is that all of this will create for the English
reader a sense of the "variety within sameness" that prevails in the
original poems.

Householders

The Reizei Family in Japanese History

Mencius said, "Keeping one's parents when they are alive
is not worth being described as of major importance; it is treating them
decently when they die that is worth such a description."
—*Mencius* (tr. D. C. Lau)

INTRODUCTION

Tame- Times Twenty-five

ON THE shelves of almost any sizable bookshop in Japan, next to magazines dedicated to fashion, sports, travel, cooking, and a host of other leisure activities, one will usually find a copy or two of *NHK Tanka* (formerly *NHK Kadan*), a monthly student guide for amateur students of the ancient but still popular *tanka* form of Japanese poetry. Virtually every person in Japan has studied ancient examples of *tanka* in school and thousands continue to do so as amateur poets long after they have put their history and math texts away. Latest issue in hand, men and women from all walks of life tune in weekly to the Japanese National Broadcasting program that the magazine is designed to accompany and watch a committee of teacher-poets discuss and correct students' work on the air. The academic world takes no notice of this, any more than it does of the even larger popular following accorded *haiku*, a more recent genre that is pursued as a hobby by probably ten times the number of devotees who study *tanka*. The fact is, however, that these traditional poetic forms are more a part of modern Japanese popular culture than is the form known as *shi*—a Chinese word that is now used to refer to a kind of "free verse" very much inspired by Western poetry.

At the front of *NHK Tanka* there are always ten famous *tanka*, all in conventional 5-7-5-7-7 format with accompanying photos—of the scenes described in the poems, not of the authors—chosen for a few words of appreciation by a contemporary poet. Then come essays about various topics relevant to traditional poetry; the inevitable *zadankai*, a transcript of a roundtable discussion among a group of poets; and, at the end, a listing of the poems chosen for special recognition by a group of editors. In this way traditional patterns of instruction are maintained, the chief one being that the creative process is always constrained within the dynamics of a master–disciple relationship, just as it is in the martial arts, flower arrangement, the tea ceremony, and most other traditional arts and crafts. Everything, down to the way teachers attach a few sentences of appreciative commentary to winning entries in a manner reminiscent of the ancient poetry contest, has behind it some hoary precedent. Every issue of the magazine, no matter the season, no matter whose work it presents, has as its explicit subtext the long history of the *tanka* form.

Folk mythology traces the *tanka* as a genre, which was actually known by the names *uta* or *waka* until recent times, back to the beginnings of Japanese culture, when the deities Izanagi and Izanami exchanged short poems in a scene that scholars generally take as a metaphorical representation of sexual generation. Scattered examples of the form exist in the earliest Japanese documents. It was from about the late 600s, however, that the genre seems to have firmly established itself at the imperial court and among the nobility. Thereafter it would remain a central element of court life for centuries, down until the present day. By the twentieth century it had also developed into a semi-popular form that claimed practitioners in virtually all classes and all geographical areas.

Every issue of *NHK Tanka* includes a few poems from the past, sometimes even from the distant past, chosen by a contemporary poet for brief commentary. Special favorites are the great court poets of the imperial anthologies, or *chokusenshū*, particularly the first eight of these, which abound with poems by Ki no Tsurayuki (ca. 872–945), Izumi Shikibu (fl. ca. 970–1030), Saigyō (1118–90), and other iconic figures. Ironically, however, *NHK Tanka* pays virtually no attention to the only poets of the modern world who can still make a reasonable claim to having a direct blood connection to the court tradition that sustained the genre for most of its history—the poets of the noble Reizei house.

The Reizei poets, too, follow a form of practice in which disciples submit work for critique, and they, too, issue a serial publication that includes poems by themselves and their students, along with announcements, articles by scholars, and occasional essays. The Reizei publication, however, cannot claim and does not seek a large subscription list, just as the teachers it represents cannot claim many students. The magazine itself is a slight thing, a newsletter just eight pages or so in length, with grainy black and white photos. It can make a claim, on the other hand, that the NHK publication cannot: namely, that it represents an unbroken poetic lineage that reaches back nearly a thousand years.

The name of the publication is *Shiguretei*, "The Pavilion of Showers," and it is issued directly by the Reizei family, or, more precisely, the Reizei Shiguretei Corporation. Located within the recently restored family residence on Imadegawa Avenue in modern Kyoto, the offices of this corporation bear no resemblance to the businesslike offices of NHK in the modern Shibuya district of Tokyo. Rather, work in the Reizei offices is undertaken in *tatami*-mat rooms in surroundings that cannot but remind the visitor of earlier days in what was once an imperial capital.

The family house, which sits on the southwest corner of the same city block that accommodates the campus of Dōshisha University, is not open to the public. Only several times a year is it available to outsiders, and then only to those who are enrolled students and contributors to the Reizei Corporation through their yearly membership fees. In recent years, however, a number of books, all written or edited by members of the family, have contained photos of the buildings and grounds. The house itself, which in its present form dates back to 1790, is the only surviving example in the city of aristocratic architectural traditions that in some details go back much further, some to the Heian period (794–1185). The old Courtiers' Quarter that surrounded it was essentially torn down at the end of the nineteenth century, and the same fate could easily have overtaken the Reizei residence, were it not for the quirks of fate and the extraordinary tenacity of successive generations of men and women who regarded as a sacred mission the preservation of the house, the grounds, and, most importantly, the *obunko*, or family library.

The great Kyoto fire of 1788 destroyed the family dwelling as it had stood since 1708, when it had been built to replace the original house erected in the first decade of the seventeenth century after another fire. The library, however, survived both conflagrations. For the past 400 years, it has stood on its site while all around it the city changed. One by one, other surviving residences of the nobility were leveled to make way for office buildings, stores, university lecture halls, and more modern houses. In 1917, even the front of the Reizei lot was pared down to make room for a trolley line. But the *obunko*, a small two-story building that houses manuscripts and documents on its first floor and sacred family paintings and art objects on its second, remained.

Along with the main residence, the kitchen and its storehouse, and the front gate, the *obunko* was one of the structures on the Reizei lot that was designated by the Japanese Ministry of Education in 1982 as a *jūyō bunkazai*, a rubric naming "important cultural properties" singled out for government protection and preservation. Since then, the entire house has been restored, thanks to donations from disciples and corporate sponsors. The *obunko* is not large: just a small *kura*, or storehouse, in effect, standing alone in the northeastern corner of the lot. While to the family the library itself is also a *shinden*, or "temple," that functions as an embodiment of the family deities while also housing images of other Shinto gods,[1] the more significant cultural treasures of the building lie within. For here are stored, in traditional wooden boxes, literary manuscripts and documents going back 800 years, a number of them designated as National Treasures, which thus exceed the status of the building itself.

For centuries the family kept its treasures, including various artworks, furnishings, and items of clothing, as well as literary works, hidden from public view. In fact, so important were many of the objects deemed to be treasures by the imperial family that even the male heads of the Reizei house had only limited access to them. Even as early as the Meiji period, however, the attitude of the house began to change, until finally, in 1980, pressure from scholars and the burden of paying taxes on assets that no longer produced financial dividends obliged the head of the household at the time, Reizei Tametō (1914–86), to announce to the world that some of the contents of the library would finally be opened — under the family's close supervision, needless to say — for scrutiny. Thus many priceless manuscripts, some dating back to the 1100s or before, at last became available for study. In time, photostatic copies of some of the most highly prized items began to appear in published form, while the family also allowed public display and photographic documentation of those items and some others of cultural interest. This required the family to take on a new identity, as a corporation backed by modest support from the national government and donations from the corporate elite. What had been a sleepy and rather obscure little com-

---

1. Reizei Fumiko, *Reizei Fumiko ga kataru Kyō no miyabi*, pp. 127–33.

pound dwarfed by the larger structures surrounding it on Imade-gawa Avenue now became a place of constant, although still largely quiet, cultural activity.[2]

It should be stressed that relatively few of the old manuscripts that emerged from the family library were truly unknown. Unless one counts some of the materials from the late Edo period, many of which have not yet been revealed, few of the Reizei treasures represent a textual "discovery" in the usual sense of that term.[3] What distinguishes them in most cases is not new content but the fact that they were actually written out by men such as Fujiwara no Shunzei (1114–1204) and his descendants in ancient days. The Reizei do not claim to have a new play by the Bard, then, so much as one in his own hand. In this sense, the contents of the library boast the authority of lineage more than anything else. As recent exhibitions have made clear, the *obunko* is as much a museum as it is a library.

Knowing this, the family still withholds much from public view and maintains the library as a sacred space. When the restoration project required moving the sacred objects on the second story next door to another structure in 1997, the Shinto Priests of Kami Goryō Shrine insisted that the transfer take place at night (although in the end they had to settle for twilight, since there was no electric lighting in that part of the compound) and that the objects be handled only by men, while the women, including Reizei Fumiko (b. 1916), who had served as *de facto* head of the house for some time, stood looking on from the garden. Even now the second story is off limits to all but the head of the household on prescribed days of the year. As Fumiko said in 1999, "I think the Reizei is a difficult house, truly fussy about everything."[4] Despite all of her labors for the family over the years, she notes that the first time she ever entered even the first story of the *obunko* was in 1981, when the decision to "open" the place up virtually demanded her entry. Even two decades later

---

2. For more details, see pp. 344–57 below.

3. A few exceptions are the partial text of a late Heian poetry collection called *Genyōshū* (1256); a personal poetry collection of Fujiwara no Tameie; and a gazetteer entitled *Bungo no kuni fudoki*. All of these are truly discoveries since other manuscripts of them — at present, at least — do not exist.

4. Reizei Fumiko, *Reizei Fumiko ga kataru Kyō no miyabi*, p. 132.

she admitted that the place for her was rife with things she reveres but in fact cannot claim to know much about.[5]

Yet what has recently been opened to view does make it possible to tell the Reizei story in a more comprehensive way than has ever been possible before. Particularly important in this connection are the colophons to a variety of texts and an array of documents dealing with family possessions and properties, which have been the subject of articles by a number of Japanese historians. Together with poetry collections and critical writings by members of the Reizei house and their disciples that have only appeared in modern editions in the last several decades, these new materials give us a history as complete as any we have for a family of noble Japanese lineage. That history is not grist for the tabloids; in fact, for all their noble blood ties, the recent members of the family seem practically indistinguishable in their private lives from countless other members of middle-class merchant families in the same city—an affiliation that in many ways the Reizei seem to embrace. Yet, whatever its quotidian preoccupations, the family remains linked to a larger narrative. This is what impresses the researcher: not so much the stories of the individual members of the house over the years, although some of them are fascinating in themselves, but the story of the Reizei house as a cultural institution, bits and pieces of which are scattered throughout the family archives.

One thing recent publications by the corporation and research on other documents conducted by Japanese scholars make clear is that the Reizei house has participated—though never as central political figures—in virtually every important event in Japanese history since around 1150, from the Genpei War of 1180–85, to the various "disturbances" of the next few centuries, the founding of the Tokugawa regime in the early seventeenth century, the Meiji Restoration, and even the "bubble economy" of the 1980s. In this sense, the story of the Reizei family is in some ways a history of Japan—a story that involves emperors in virtually every generation, along with other members of the nobility; the Kamakura shoguns, the Muromachi shoguns, and the Edo shoguns; the warlords of the period of the fourteenth and fifteenth centuries and of the Sengoku period, as well as the great daimyo of Tokugawa times; Confucian scholars,

―――――――

5. Ibid., pp. 127–33.

Nativist philologists, and academics of the great universities of the twentieth century; Buddhist clerics and Shinto priests; merchants, shopkeepers, bankers, industrial giants, and multinational corporations. It is also a history of the city of Kyoto, with which the family's identification is now as strong as ever, but also of Kamakura, the port city of Sakai, of castle towns such as Sunpu in Suruga, and of Edo and Tokyo.

Finally, and most fundamentally, though, the story of the Reizei house is a history of a particular kind of poetic practice that shares a great deal with other traditional Japanese art forms, most prominently traditional painting, the tea ceremony, and calligraphy. Now that the details of the story—especially details of family history in the Edo period and on into the twentieth century—have become more readily available for analysis, it is a history that asks to be told. No doubt scholars will be poring over the contents of the family collections for generations to come, occasionally coming up with new information. Most of what comes forth, however, will be in the nature of footnotes to a narrative that is already accessible in its contours. For while we often refer to the heads of the Reizei house as poets, they were in fact less poets in any modern (and inevitably romantic) sense than they were teachers for whom individual poems generally meant much less than what one might call the poetic enterprise, what usually goes by the term *michi*, or Way. It is their dedication to this Way that has sustained the lineage, forming the core of its collective identity down to the present day as well as the core of the story that will be told here.

As Adam Nicolson says in his book on the making of the King James Bible, modern people "trained up on centuries of individualism" have a hard time appreciating collective work in the arts (or— to characterize more adequately the ambitions of those writing in almost all genres of Japanese poetry until the twentieth century— work done by individuals as part of a larger collective effort). "Isn't the beautiful, we now think, to be identified with what is original, the previously unsaid, the unique vision of the individual mind? How can a joint enterprise . . . produce anything valuable?"[6] Clearly for the Reizei house, its many disciples, and many artists in countless other forms, however, such a prejudice did not exist. For, as Eiko

---

6. Nicolson, *God's Secretaries: The Making of the King James Bible*, p. 69.

Ikegami has recently argued, rather than "an individualized modern notion of arts and literature," many Japanese forms of aesthetic expression have assumed "an interactive process as their most meaningful aspect."[7] Moreover, a narrative that places individual poets in a continuum goes further toward elucidating why and how this came to be true in the case of the courtly poetic tradition than could the analysis of individual poems by even the most highly regarded poets of the Reizei lineage. In that sense, my hope is that this book will be first and foremost a history of the house as a house — rather than just of the various individuals who bear its name — and the poetic enterprise to which that house was dedicated.

THE NARRATIVE that follows consists of ten chapters and a conclusion that trace the story of the Reizei house chronologically from its beginnings in the 1200s up until the early years of the twenty-first century, from the time of Tameie (1198–1275) and his son Tamesuke (1263–1328), that is, through the times of Tamemasa (1361–1417), Tamekazu (1486–1549), Tamemura (1712–74), and ultimately to the time of the current head of the lineage, Tamehito (b. 1944). If the repetition of *Tame* in every name for over 20 generations seems tedious, one must recall that in the matter of choosing names, noble houses tended to stress continuity. For the Reizei, in other words, naming presented an opportunity to link heirs in time and to emphasize collective over individual identity.

My chapter titles, however, are meant to trace the complementary journey of the house in space, from its beginnings on the slopes of Mount Ogura west of ancient Miyako to its current address on Imadegawa Avenue in the modern city of Kyoto. In every generation the Reizei have been faced with the same basic economic challenge: to find ways to parlay their social and cultural capital — their pedigree, their rank, their stores of knowledge, texts, and artifacts and the status those things conferred — into financial support to sustain itself in its practice of the poetic Way. Despite the strong affiliation of the lineage with Kyoto, the demands of working in the cultural marketplace have often involved even the heads of the house in travel: to Kamakura in the beginning, then to "little Kyotos" in provinces such as Noto and Suruga, and finally even to Edo, capital of the

---

7. Ikegami, *Bonds of Civility*, p. 7.

Tokugawa shoguns. While the forward movement of the Reizei story through time may seem unilinear, then, their journey in space symbolizes the many detours and bypaths they traveled along the way and in that sense it disturbs the narrative enough to remind us that it is indeed a narrative.

After the epilogue I have included a selection of 100 poems by poets affiliated with the Reizei house, from the earliest times to the present, with brief commentary. In the course of my narrative I also refer to many poems, and include some rhetorical and stylistic analysis when it is relevant to the issues at hand in the larger story. In order to give a full picture of Reizei practices, however, I felt that it was necessary to include a more substantial selection of what those practices were aimed at producing—namely, poems. Again, I have organized them in chronological fashion, beginning with Fujiwara no Michinaga (966–1027), the great mid-Heian politician to whom the Reizei (and many other noble lineages) traced their origins, and ending with Kimiko (b. 1947), who bears the name Reizei in its twenty-fifth generation. In keeping with a philosophy that emphasizes ongoing process over product, I have selected poems that I see as representative of the general ideals of the house rather than poems that might be characterized as somehow eccentric or unusual.

ONE

Mount Ogura

WE KNOW from a host of sources, not the least his own diary, that from his 40s onward Fujiwara no Teika (1162–1241) had a cottage somewhere on the slopes of Mount Ogura west of Kyoto. Scholars do not agree, however, on precisely where it was located. One group advocates the precincts of Nison-in Temple; another argues for the environs of a neighboring temple, the Jōjakkōji; still another insists on the area around present-day Rakushisha, residence of the haiku poet Mukai Kyorai (1651–1704) during the late 1600s; and finally, another faction points to a site just a short walk from the outer gate of Nison-in, now occupied by upscale suburban homes.

The last of these places is favored as the site of Teika's hideaway by the Reizei family.[1] More specifically, the Reizei point to Enri Cottage—pronounced Onri by some—as the site where their illustrious ancestor retreated from the noise and bother of the city. A plaque bearing the name by which Teika's cottage came to be known—Shiguretei (or, alternatively, Shigure no Chin), meaning "Pavilion of Showers"—still hangs from the eaves of the small Buddhist nunnery, founded in the late nineteenth century, that now occupies the spot. After Teika's death, so the story goes, the cottage passed to his son, then to the son's granddaughter, and then into other hands, and was allowed to molder away until the family restored it in the 1700s, only to suffer ruin again before it was taken over by Tenryūji for use as a nunnery. The plaque was donated by Tametsugi (1881–

---

1. Reizei Kimiko, "Shigure no chin," p. 2.

1946), twenty-second head of the Reizei house. Close by is a stone cistern that, according to tradition, provided Teika with the water he needed to grind ink for the recording of his poems. There is a grave marker there as well.

Some of the most eminent scholars politely part company with the Reizei family on the issue of the most likely location of Teika's retreat, most concluding that the Enri Cottage is actually the site of the much more substantial dwelling of Teika's son and heir, Tameie.[2] There is little heat in the disagreement, however: the family is quick to point out that as the site of both Teika's cottage and the residence of Tameie and the wife of his last years—known now as the Nun Abutsu (d. 1283)—all of the Ogura area is hallowed ground.[3] Any trace of the original buildings went to dust ages ago, in any case, but the natural beauties of Mount Ogura and its environs, which no doubt attracted Teika to the area in the first place, remain, as do his progeny. This, rather than any remaining foundation stones, is what brings the family to the area when they wish to celebrate his poetic legacy. Although property is important in supporting the claims of the family, the greatest treasure of the Reizei house—the foundation of its identity, as any number of heirs have insisted over the past eight centuries—is its long history of service to the imperial court and beyond that to the elements of court culture that were later to become synonymous with "Japanese civilization."

AS IS the case with most lineages associated with the imperial court, the story of the Reizei family begins in the last years of the Heian period. Kyoto was one of the largest cities in the world at that time, a true metropolis of nearly a million inhabitants, which was crowned by the imperial palace compound itself, a broad complex of buildings and gardens symbolically located between First and Second Avenues in the north, surrounded by the homes of the high nobility scattered around it and throughout the rest of the city, mainly to the east and the south.[4] For any nobleman, Heian Kyō, or Miyako, as it was commonly known, was the epicenter of high culture.

----

2. Imatani, *Kyōgoku Tamekane*, pp. 7–10.

3. Reizei Fumiko, "Fujiwara no Teika-kyō nanahyakugojūnenki," p. 2.

4. Souyri, *The World Turned Upside Down*, p. 10, estimates the population of the Kinai, or home provinces, at around 1.4 million at this time.

From early on, the western half of the city proper lagged behind in development, becoming an abode for badgers and foxes, in the parlance of the time. But this does not mean that the city was anything but a lively place. Already villas and temples dotted the Eastern Hills across the Kamo River, as well as the meadows of Saga further to the west. The Heian period was, generally speaking, a peaceful and prosperous time for the court elite, who could trace their history back hundreds of years through a long succession of emperors, and who held deeds to much of the revenue from tax-free estates all over Japan, especially in the rich Home Provinces around the capital.

It was during Heian days that the parent lineage of the Reizei family came into being, specifically during the time of a courtier named Nagaie (1005–64) of the Northern Fujiwara clan. Born the sixth son of Michinaga, one of the most powerful political figures of the early eleventh century, Nagaie was only moderately successful in obtaining high offices, rising only to major counselor of senior second rank. Such was usually the fate of younger sons in a patriarchal system that operated upon the principle of primogeniture. But as a talented poet in the native *uta* form, Nagaie was nevertheless able to establish a reputation that he left to his descendants as a sort of legacy. Little could he have known, however, that one of his descendants — Tametō, twenty-fourth head of the house, speaking nearly a millennium later, in 1982 — would look back on his poetic contributions as the foundation of a veritable dynasty: "As anyone with experience in the study of Japanese literature will know, our lineage has served the imperial family as leaders in the Way of Poetry for generations, ever since we received from Emperor Go-Reizei an imperial directive to make the Way of Poetry the special domain of the house."[5]

Exactly when — or indeed if — Go-Reizei (1025–68; r. 1045–68) issued this command to Nagaie we do not know. However, records reveal that from the mid-eleventh century on, his descendants did in fact dedicate themselves to poetry in the *uta* form, which along with other arts such as Chinese poetry, calligraphy, and music would remain a central interest of court culture until modern times. As in other similar situations, the imperial court and the arts had a symbiotic relationship in which each provided a sense of legitimacy to the other.

---

5. Reizei Tametō, "Kadō no shinan ni ikiru," p. 2. See also Reizei Fumiko, *Reizei Fumiko ga kataru Kyō no miyabi*, p. 184.

By the thirteenth century, the northern Fujiwara clan would split into many branches that constantly vied among themselves for offices. Most prominent among these were the lineages of Michinaga's eldest son, Yorimichi (992–1074), which would eventually be called the Five Houses of the Regency. They would dominate the upper levels of the court bureaucracy: the offices of Chancellor, Regent, and Ministers. Below them in the order of things came many lesser branches of the Fujiwara, the Murakami Genji, and a few other families of ancient pedigree. Over time, these lesser families tended to become associated with particular arts and occupations that became the justification for their continued presence at court. For some, the specialty was the lute (*biwa*), for others, ritual, or court costume, or calligraphy. For the descendants of Nagaie, the "occupation of the house" (*kagyō*) would be Japanese poetry.

The identification of Nagaie's lineage with court poetry was thus established early in court history. The name Reizei, however, would come much later, to one of the grandsons of Teika who lived for a time in a house that fronted on Reizei Street in Kyoto. Nagaie was known instead by the name Mikohidari, which derived from one of his residences that had formerly been the home, near the intersection of Sanjō Bōmon and Ōmiya Streets, of an imperial prince (*miko*) who had served as Minister of the Left (*hidari*). In fact, this name was the one that would be used by many generations to come in referring to the senior branch of the house; and it is still this name that is often used by historians speaking of the immediate descendants of Nagaie, from his son Tadaie (1033–91), to his grandson Toshitada (1073–1123), his great grandson Toshinari (also read Shunzei), and his great-great grandson Teika.

Both Nagaie's heir and his heir's heir were poets whose place at court to some extent depended on their literary talents, in addition to their skill as politicians. Likewise, Toshitada, though never obtaining even Nagaie's modest offices, managed to get close to various imperial patrons and to maintain a position among other poetic houses. It is with Shunzei, though, that most accounts of the origins of the Reizei house begin in earnest, partly because the same is true of accounts of medieval court poetry in general.

One reason for the success of Shunzei, born in 1114, is that he lived a very long time, until the age of 91 by the traditional count. His accomplishments as head of the house could never have been realized, however, without great poetic talent and a measure of good luck. His were turbulent times, after all, which many did not survive, no matter what their abilities. First were the political upheavals of the time, most readily symbolized by the Hōgen Disturbance of 1156, the Heiji Disturbance of 1159, and the Genpei War of 1180–85, each of which offered ample opportunity for misfortune or self-destruction. Then there were the natural disasters, including the Kyoto fire of 1177, the whirlwind of 1180, the great earthquake of 1185, and hosts of famines, epidemics, and other calamities. Along with all these events came political and economic reverses for the old noble families that left many greatly diminished in stature.

A century before, the Fujiwara had still reigned supreme in the capital, dominating almost all government institutions and garnering for itself the lion's share of the income of the provinces through private estates. But in the last years of the eleventh century a succession of strong Retired Emperors had begun to challenge Fujiwara hegemony, building an equally strong base for themselves, likewise on the foundation of tax-free estates. Then had come the rise of the Taira, a warrior clan that managed to take over the highest government offices while Shunzei was in his late 40s, only to lose power themselves to forces from outside the capital—the Minamoto alliance of the East Country. After defeating the Taira and their supporters in combat, the Minamoto established a new military government in Kamakura, effectively putting an end to the dominion of the court aristocracy. Rather than simply usurping the old courtly offices or attaching themselves to noble patrons, the Minamoto created new offices and filled them with men whose allegiance was to themselves and their vassals first of all, and to their own economic interests.

The leader of that military coalition, Minamoto no Yoritomo (1147–99), was no revolutionary in the usual sense of the term, however; he never seems to have contemplated doing away with the imperial system completely. Instead, he immediately put on the throne a new emperor, from the established lineage, surrounded as always by court officers of the old aristocracy, whom he provided with modest support as part of a plan designed to return the country to normalcy. The long-term implications of this shift in political control were therefore perhaps not immediately obvious to either the old nobility or the military aristocracy. Yoritomo and his retainers were in fact rather generous with many noble families, whose prestige in cultural matters they recognized. Before long Yoritomo was even mimicking the nobility by trying to place two of his daughters in the imperial harem, no doubt hoping to become the grandfather of an emperor in the tradition of Fujiwara no Michinaga and, more recently, the leaders of the Taira clan.

After the end of the Genpei War, the noble houses were therefore stripped of some of their political power, but still retained much of their wealth and their traditional place at the apex of the social hierarchy. New officials appointed by the Kamakura shogun now became involved in the details of practical administration at the provincial level; but still the nobility claimed considerable revenues from provincial estates, and they still retained their offices and some actual jurisdictional control, especially in Kyoto and its environs. Government thus became a joint venture, involving both the old elite and the warriors of Kamakura, with the latter decidedly in control in the East Country but the former still very powerful in the provinces around Miyako. Needless to say, the imperial family remained at the center of politics. As before, the emperor was a figurehead of considerable symbolic power and substantial wealth, which those around him—whether from the old nobility or the new military aristocracy—sought to draw upon for their own purposes.

It is not true, then, that the imperial court after 1185 was reduced to a small community of antiquarians whose primary concern was the maintenance of the few privileges it had left. Some of the old houses, with the assistance of patrons in the rising military aristocracy, were still able to amass great wealth and to wield real political power. In addition, many old lineages still had longstanding ties with local constituencies in large temples and shrines and estates, especially around Kyoto. More importantly, the court families still boasted a great store of specialized knowledge and artistic competence that helped them function effectively in the theater of cultural power. Nowhere was this more apparent than in poetry in the native *uta* form, which had attracted devotees outside the court from long before. Even in the new order of the Kamakura shogunate, then, the poetic houses—the Mikohidari conspicuously among them—had a place.

BY THE end of the Genpei War in 1185, Shunzei was already the premier poetic figure of an elite society in which poetry thus continued to play a central role. The most prosperous houses, from the imperial house on down, were still holding poetry contests, commissioning anthologies, sending poetic works to shrines and temples as votive offerings, and calling in tutors to train their children in the craft of composition and niceties of poetic ritual. Poems were used in private correspondence, to offer congratulations or condolences, to petition the gods and buddhas for favors, and to celebrate important occasions, public and private. Moreover, poetry in Japanese was by this time becoming an important art form in its own right, a discourse of its own, supported by many practitioners at all levels of literate society. In this world, Shunzei, after long years of competition with rivals, reigned supreme as scholar, arbiter of taste, and patriarch of what was called the Way of Yamato Speech (*yamato no kotonoha no michi*), complete with all the religious connotations such phrasing implied. Later generations would apotheosize him for their own reasons; but in his own day the aura around him already shone.

Shunzei pursued his career, however, in the secular world until the end. Most standard histories note that he was not even as successful in gaining high rank and office as his own father had been, who was a middle counselor of junior second rank at the time of his death. To counterbalance this, however, one must not forget that Shunzei had been marvelously adept in an equally important area: the gaining of financial support for his family through ties of patronage. As in the realm of poetry, in the socioeconomic world Shunzei was a careful strategist. One measure of his success was that he had been able to place so many of his children in secure livings. In all, genealogies show that Shunzei had at least 23 children. Of his ten sons, only two—Teika being one of them—stayed in the lay world. The others all became priests at temples in the Home Provinces, where they served as part of a large and very useful family network. But it was in the placing of Shunzei's female progeny that his skill as head of a noble household became most apparent. For all thirteen of his known daughters stayed in the lay world in one way or another, ten going into service in the salons of members of the imperial family, with a few of those and others going on to marry prominent courtiers. For centuries, astute courtiers had used their daughters to provide opportunities for their sons and grandsons; Shunzei did the same.

In order to be in a position to place his children so well, Shunzei had worked very hard, and not under the easiest of circumstances, particularly in his youth. Losing his father at the age of ten, he had been placed in the care of another branch of the Fujiwara for some years. As the heir of a poetic house, he studied calligraphy, the Chinese classics, the Japanese classics, and poetic lore. Fujiwara no Mototoshi (1060–1142), one of the leading literary lights of the day, became his teacher, instructing him in literary history as well as poetic composition and involving him in events where he could show his mettle. Almost immediately his talent became apparent, impressing not only his teacher but other participants in courtly poetic affairs. As he gained experience, Shunzei showed promise both artistically and socially — a crucial combination in court society, where artistic talent was generally tried in social settings. In the early medieval era, and for that matter through the late medieval era and on into the Edo period, poems might be composed in private, but they were almost always "aired" at some public event that demanded ritual knowledge, social skills, and political savvy — all three of which Shunzei seems to have displayed from his earliest days. Eventually Shunzei's performance attracted the notice of Emperor Sutoku (1119–64; r. 1123–41) and later Emperor Go-Shirakawa (1127–92; r. 1155–58), whose patronage was an undeniable factor in his success at court. Yet he seems to have stayed out of partisan political conflicts as much as possible, no mean accomplishment given the complex state of affairs at the time. In poetic matters, he was a formidable competitor, but unlike some others he succeeded in avoiding the kinds of political entanglements that could swiftly bring an end even to a poetic career.

So Shunzei's ability to negotiate the perilous straits of court life showed itself early on. In one crucial way, though, he was undeniably helped by what can only be attributed to chance — namely, his longevity. In his early 60s he had been seriously ill, taking the tonsure as a lay monk at the age of 63 to prepare for the next life. But he lived on, while his greatest rival, a man named Kiyosuke (1104–77) of the Rokujō poetic house, died just a year later, at the age of 74, in 1177. It was during the nearly three decades by which he survived Kiyosuke that Shunzei became the unquestioned leader in poetic affairs in the imperial capital. Not long after Kiyosuke's death, he became tutor to the regental Kujō house, the spectacular rise of which in the 1180s would greatly assist his own. Thereafter, Shunzei was a fixture at poetry contests and other gatherings sponsored by that house, where he acted the part of teacher and judge. In this he set a pattern of practice for his descendants to follow, for whom the seeking out of patrons would be a fundamental element of poetic practice.

Shunzei's crowning literary achievement came in 1183, when, during a brief lull in the fighting during the Genpei War, he was asked to serve as sole compiler of a new imperial anthology. This was the seventh such collection, the first, *Kokinshū* (Collection of Ancient and Modern Times) having been compiled by the courtier Ki no Tsurayuki and his cohorts back in 905. In more recent years, other lineages, mostly of Fujiwara affiliation, had seen their leaders selected as compilers. This was the first time, however, that the Mikohidari had been so honored. Furthermore, since the last entry in the series had been commissioned from the father of Shunzei's rival Kiyosuke, the choice of a man of Nagaie's lineage was of great political significance, representing the fulfillment of an ambition going back several generations.

One might think that a poet presented with such an opportunity would attempt something new and revolutionary. But the format of imperial collections was not a matter of choice. To enter the ranks of the compilers of the past was rather to accept the power of precedent, which dictated both the ritual activities associated with its compilation — which Shunzei followed scrupulously, aided by his son Teika — and the organization of the poems in the collection. Shunzei's anthology was therefore not in a sense Shunzei's anthology at all, but a product of long tradition that it was his purpose to honor, as is apparent in its conventional design, which presented poems in books on spring, summer, autumn, winter, love, and miscellaneous topics such as travel, congratulation, and lamentation. He listed poems not by historical period or authorship but instead by their conventional topics (*dai*), which were arranged in a prescribed order — snow following autumn leaves, for instance, and "Lovers Meeting" after "Loving in Secret." In this way, the anthology would display what was perceived as the natural order of things, combining the talents of many individuals to create a sequence of poems that in the end represented a unified whole meant to honor the current emperor and those around him. Poems from some earlier periods were chosen, so that the finished work would bring into clear relief the poetic accomplishments of the court throughout its long history. Shunzei even went so far as to place the following poem by one of his rivals, Minamoto no Toshiyori (1055–1129), first in the collection, explaining to his dismayed supporters, "When I was choosing poems . . . I didn't look at the names, but looked at the poems."[6]

---

6. Quotation from *Kensai zōdan*. See Carter, "Chats with the Master: Selections from *Kensai Zōdan*," p. 315.

Written on the first day of spring

On spring's first morning   I look out
across the fields   of Ashita Moor —
to where on this very day   the mists begin
to rise.[7]

haru no kuru / ashita no hara o / miwataseba / kasumi mo kyō zo / tachihajimekeru

One may attribute such a gesture to Shunzei's sense of fair play, of course; but everything we know about the institutions of poetry in his time says that we should also see the head of the Mikohidari acting as the agent of a discourse larger than himself — a set of practices and conventions animated by powers much larger than his own. Toshiyori's poem was an excellent treatment of its theme: sufficiently lofty in tone, sufficiently dignified in imagery, sufficiently decorous in aural effect, and also showing things as they should be according to the court calendar, with mists (*kasumi*), the first harbinger of spring, beginning to spread over the fields on precisely the right day, the first day of the new year. It was these qualities more than anything else that recommended it for so signal an honor.

Putting an imperial collection together was a difficult task at any time, and more so during times of warfare. The larger structure of the work was already decided, but which poems to choose was largely up to the compiler, with input from patrons. But Shunzei had a lifetime of experience in poetic practice that must have served him well as preparation for choosing appropriate poems and deciding upon their proper placement in the pre-ordained sequence. In addition, he had the teachings of Mototoshi, which included not just composition but study of the works of past masters. He evidently also had a sizable library — much of which would later end up in the storehouse of the Reizei house — containing copies of personal collections, poetry contests, and other manuscripts that he had been collecting for years — along, perhaps, with resources that he had inherited from his father, or for that matter, his mother, who could trace her genealogy back to the Mother of Michitsuna (fl. ca. 954–74), author of *Kagerō nikki* (Gossamer Diary, late tenth century), which was already a court classic. In every way he was in a good position to proceed.

Shunzei completed work on the anthology in the fall of 1187, after the war cries of recent years had finally faded into the past. A new

---

7. *Senzaishū*, poem no. 1.

emperor, known to us as Go-Toba (1180–1239; r. 1183–98), was on the throne, and the attitude at court was optimistic. The collection, which he titled *Senzaishū* (Collection of a Thousand Years), contained nearly 1,300 poems, mostly by poets of the present and the recent past. With the exception of a few archaic forms at the end of the collection, all the poems were in the *uta* form, and virtually all the poets were courtiers or people with strong courtly ties, such as Saigyō. Needless to say, the talents of Shunzei's primary patrons in the Kujō house, as well as his own forebears and other supporters, were well represented in the collection when he presented it for imperial review in 1188.

Although at first he modestly attempted to restrict the number of his own poems to only a dozen or so, Shunzei was prevailed upon by his sponsors to add to that number. In the end, 36 of his poems were included. Among them was one that he regarded as among his very best. It serves as well as any of his works to display the chief features of his style.

> "Autumn"
>
> As evening descends   the autumn wind
> on the fields   pierces to the quick:
> a quail cries from the deep grass   of Fukakusa
> Village.[8]
>
> *yū sareba / nobe no akikaze / mi ni shimite / uzura naku nari / fukakusa no sato*

While it was placed in one of the autumn books of the new anthology, the poem is not straightforward natural description, and it seems to hint at something behind the surface in a way consistent with the author's ideal of *yūgen*, or "mystery and depth." As any educated courtier would immediately know, that something is in fact a famous poetic exchange, recorded in *Tales of Ise*, between the legendary Ariwara no Narihira (825–80) and a woman whom he is leaving behind in a place called Fukakusa, "Deep Grass"—a woman who vows to spend her time calling out like a forlorn quail awaiting her hunter's return. Shunzei's poem, through a technique called *honkadori* ("allusive variation," or the building of a new poem around a line or lines from a well-known older one), therefore gestures toward a story in one of the primary texts of the courtly poetic tradition, and toward a past that would serve as a kind of golden age in the courtly imagination. Not by chance, the poem also makes an important claim: that

---

8. Ibid., poem no. 259.

its author is one who has the proper knowledge and sensibility to respond to everything the call of the quail implies. That the poem was not written at Fukakusa but in his own chambers, for a small anthology solicited by a patron, makes the point even more clear.[9] One of his critics complained that the line "pierces to the quick" contravened the ideal of understatement.[10] Later generations have tended not to agree. The poignancy of the poem's emotional content, along with its sonorous phrasing and skillful combination of sensory images — the sight of the grassy fields, the cold touch of the autumn wind, and the sound of the quail — have sustained it as one of the most oft-quoted poems in the classical canon.

As noted above, records stress that in making selections for *Senzaishū*, Shunzei attempted to be fair.[11] In addition to poems by his patrons and friends, he also included 20 poems by his old opponent Kiyosuke, for instance. Without representation of all factions the collection could not have been deemed complete as a record of its era, which was one of the primary functions of such collections. Yet Shunzei did hold unflinchingly to one standard: to be included in a court project, a poem had to be elegant in statement and serious in tone. Playfulness could be tolerated, but not if it crossed over the line into frivolousness, that is, play for the sake of play alone. Poetry was for him no hobby but a serious and essentially religious Way (*michi*), and one that he hoped to pass on as a vocation to his heirs in the Mikohidari house. His activities as a collector of manuscripts, his painstaking care in the composition and recording of judgments for poetry contests, his careful training of his son and heir in all the facets of poetic practice, his authorship of a meditation on the history of the *uta* form (*Korai fūteishō*, Notes on Poetic Style, Past and Present, 1197) designed to instruct young poets in their tradition — all of these things show that Shunzei, however neoclassical in his attitudes, was also a forward-thinking man. As the first member of his lineage to be honored with the responsibility of putting together an imperial collection, he wanted above all to create a tradition for the descendants of his own house. Even his work in the definition of aesthetic ideals is probably best understood as at least partly dedi-

---

9. The poem was written for the *Kyūan hyakushu* (1150).

10. The poet was Shun'e (b. 1113). Quoted in Brower and Miner, *Japanese Court Poetry*, p. 270.

11. See Carter, "Chats with the Master," pp. 314–15; also notes 82 and 83.

cated to that goal. Later theorists from Teika to Shinkei (1406–75) and Zeami (ca. 1364–ca. 1443) would look to Shunzei as one of the founders of medieval aesthetics, but countless others in at least half a dozen sub-lineages would also revere him as the patriarch of their order and the one who established their patterns of practice.

As the years accumulated, so did Shunzei's accomplishments. The postwar era brought a true florescence of the arts, especially after Emperor Go-Toba left the throne in 1198, becoming Retired Emperor and freeing him from the many ritual duties incumbent upon those who occupied the position of emperor. A true connoisseur of all the courtly arts, Go-Toba gathered around himself the best talents of the day. Under his supervision, and with money provided from provincial proprietorships (*chigyōkoku*) under his direct control, the Imperial Palace Compound was rebuilt, and numerous new palaces—he was to live in 18 different residences during his 23 years in office—were constructed, all of which served as venues for cultural display. With Go-Toba's patronage, Shunzei took on the role of arbiter of taste in poetic matters, serving as judge for poetry contests and in general acting the part of tutor in poetry to the court.

Another of Shunzei's accomplishments during these years was his preparation of his son, Teika, to be his heir. To anyone in court society, where inherited position could only be maintained through constant effort, this was a primary obligation. Shunzei's eldest son, Nariie (d. 1220), while remaining on the roster of court officials, had been passed over as heir because of his lackluster showing as a poet. It was therefore all the more crucial to the welfare of the entire family that Teika, who did show signs of talent, should be given every opportunity to succeed. Following common practice, Shunzei had given up his own court post as Master of the Right Capital late in 1175 in order to make a place on the upper roster for his heir, who was immediately advanced to the office of Gentleman-in-Waiting (*jijū*). In the coming years, Shunzei also arranged for his son's service in the entourage of Go-Shirakawa and then Emperor Takakura (1161–81; r. 1168–80), for his placement as a ward in the house of the powerful Fujiwara no Muneie (1139–89), for his marriage to the daughter of another powerful courtier, Fujiwara no Sueyoshi (1153–1211), and for his appointment as *keishi*, or steward, in the Kujō house. In every way possible, the old man thus sought ways to attach his son to powerful patrons. In court society, even "inherited" offices and estates had to be fought for constantly, through effective service and skillful politicking, since there were never enough positions to go around. Far from retiring to a cottage in the mountains for his final years, which would have seemed a natural course for one of his advanced age, Shunzei thus remained very much in the world. Quick tempered and evidently not blessed with his father's social skills, Teika was a trial to his father in many ways. But as a poet he was already, as the equally arrogant Emperor Go-Toba would later grudgingly admit, "in a class by himself."[12]

When Go-Toba chose Teika as one of the compilers of a new imperial anthology in 1201, Shunzei had good reason to rejoice. Now in middle age with children of his own, living in a new home on a street named Reizei just north of Nijō Avenue in the northern section of the capital, Teika gave every sign of having established himself as worthy to inherit the Mikohidari name. Recently advanced to the office of middle captain in the Imperial Guards, with the rank of senior fourth, lower grade, he was very much a part of the hierarchy and appears to have been diligent in his duties, literary and otherwise. Having assisted his father in the compilation of *Senzaishū*, he was also well prepared to undertake what Go-Toba asked of him. That he was not sole compiler, but only one among half a dozen who had been called into the Poetry Bureau, was a frustration that had to be borne. Shunzei himself had not been able to achieve his vaulted status until his late 60s; in 1201 Teika was only 40.

SHUNZEI DIED in the Eleventh Month of 1204, having never seen the final form of the new imperial anthology, which was called *Shin kokinshū*, or "New Kokinshū," in an obvious attempt to claim that Go-Toba's era should be regarded as a new golden age similar to the time of *Kokinshū* 300 years before. When the collection was presented for imperial review in the Third Month of 1205, however, it testified to his place in the scheme of things. Seventy-two of his poems appeared in its pages, more than those of any other poet save the monk-poet Saigyō and senior members of the Kujō house, the latter being some of the primary patrons behind the project. And there was much more to his legacy. Not only had he produced some of the most highly regarded poems of the century himself, but he played a major part in elevating the *uta* form into the most prestigious of courtly arts and in raising the practice of that form into a *michi*, or Way, with all the

---

12. Brower, "Ex-Emperor Go-Toba's Secret Teachings," p. 38.

sacral connotations of that word. He had not started this process, to be sure; credit for that must go to earlier generations, including that of his teacher, Mototoshi, as well as to his rivals in the Rokujō lineage. The notion of setting apart certain secular activities as semi-religious "Ways" was a general trend of the time that had more to do with the power of Buddhist conceptions and socioeconomic pressures than with the efforts of any single individual. The significance of Shunzei's advocacy, however, cannot be denied. His descendants would be dedicated to poetry not only as the occupation of their house but also to the maintenance of traditional poetic practices at court as a Way of religious devotion founded in Nativist mythology and Buddhist doctrine—a Way that if pursued according to proper precedents promised the protection of the gods and buddhas.

Of course there was self-interest in this elevation of poetry into a semi-religious Way for Shunzei and his heirs, who would serve as tutors of the Way to various constituencies for the next 800 years. Just as surely as the establishment of a new poetic tradition at court served the demands of the larger culture, it also served the needs—the economic needs, that is—of the Mikohidari house. Still, Shunzei was more responsible for the ultimate advancement of poetry at court, and its recognition as a field of practice in the broader social arena, than any other figure of his time. This was partly because of his tireless promotion of the form; yet it was also because his own style and the ideals it represented answered so well the demands of the day as felt by those trying to create a foundation for a new era in court history in which the status of the arts would be, if anything, more important than before. For while highly "literary" in its reverberations, Shunzei's style was not erudite or obtuse, not haughty or exclusive. As Go-Toba would say years later, "I recall [his] poetry as gentle and evocative, infused with deep feeling, and moving in its sensitivity."[13] Shunzei's rivals in the Rokujō house were scholars, first of all, and their style was at times pedantic, their attitudes bookish and, to that extent, rather narrow in their appeal. Of Kiyosuke's poems, the most that Go-Toba could say was that some were "pleasingly archaic."[14] Shunzei's emphasis on training the sensibility, rather than on scholastic learning—especially Chinese learning and the study of ancient Japanese texts such as *Man'yōshū* (Collection of

---

13. Ibid., p. 36.
14. Ibid.

Ten Thousand Leaves)—seemed to make the composition of poetry in Japanese a less formidable and more enjoyable task, indeed, something somehow natural for anyone claiming a refined sensibility.

Shunzei had put the matter succinctly in the short Japanese preface he attached to *Senzaishū*:

Learning the Way of the *uta* does not mean extensive learning in the writings of Cathay or Japan, nor does it mean comprehending the Buddhist Law ensconced deep in the recesses of Deer Park and Vulture Peak; rather it is simply to allow words to express the thoughts of one's heart, using nothing but the 47 characters of the *kana* syllabary. Anyone who strings together 31 syllables has plumbed the depths of the Eightfold Clouds and entered into the inner precincts amidst the many isles of Yamato.[15]

Deer Park and Vulture Peak were places where the historical Buddha had delivered famous sermons. Here, however, they serve as little more than metaphors for the obscurities from which Shunzei wants Japanese poetry to be free. In the very next sentence he equivocates somewhat, adding that no one should conclude that composing *uta* is easy. "Something that gets harder as you hack away at it, gets loftier as you look up at it—that is the Way of Japanese Poetry."[16] Inevitably, the tension between book learning and practical training in composition would remain, with certain kinds of knowledge serving the poetic houses as a needed form of distinction. But still Shunzei suggested that participation in the world of poetry was possible without a Doctor of Letters, even for interlopers from the East Country. His accomplishment was therefore to have made poetry—poetic composition, that is—more accessible and therefore to broaden the borders of poetic practice.

As a poet, Teika was much influenced by his father—in matters of style, too, but most especially in his attitude toward the Way. At the end of one of his treatises on the art for a high-placed student, he would later write: "My father warned me never for a moment to compose poetry in other than a formal sitting position."[17] If poetry was in some sense the family business, Teika had learned from his father that it was a serious one that demanded religious dedication, as well as a social one that required proper comportment. But he too would in time stress the accessibility of the tradition to all—among

---

15. *Senzaishū* preface.
16. Ibid.
17. Brower, "Fujiwara Teika's *Maigetsushō*," p. 423.

the basically literate, that is—who were willing to dedicate them-
selves to the rigors of training.

After Shunzei's death Teika strove valiantly to maintain the pro-
per posture at court, which was still the only true venue for a man
of his aspirations. His dedication to the family was also complete,
as it had to be for the next generation to maintain its place in the
scheme of things. Yet it must be said that Teika was unlike Shunzei
in many ways. Perhaps this is one reason why he cautioned in the
same treatise that a teacher must always remember that "to insist
that a person who has no disposition for it compose in a certain style
that the teacher prefers simply because he happens to find it per-
sonally congenial" is to "do damage" to the Way of Poetry.[18] If later
medieval traditions are to be believed, Teika called himself a versi-
fier (*utazukuri*) who "assembled" poems, rather than a true "poet"
(*utayomi*)—a designation he reserved for his father, Saigyō, and a
few others.[19] Certainly Teika was a more cerebral poet, especially
in his youth, when poems like the following earned him puzzled
looks from some at court.

> "Praying for Love"
>
> The years, too, passed by   while my prayers
> ended empty   —null as that bellsound
> that signals from Hase's peak   an evening somehow
> far away.[20]
>
> *toshi mo henu / inoru chigiri wa / hatsuseyama / onoe no kane no / yoso no yūgure*

Careful attention to the conventional topic (*dai*) of this poem
resolves its obscurities swiftly: it presents a lonely man, his prayer of
winning the heart of a lover unanswered over the years, who listens
to a distant temple bell announcing an evening that promises assig-
nations for others but not for him. Thus it is a rather roundabout
statement of the theme of unrequited love. When this poem was en-
tered in the famous *Roppyaku-ban uta-awase* (Poem Contest in Six
Hundred Rounds, 1193), Shunzei had awarded it the win in its round,
over a poem by Ietaka. In doing so, however, the father commented
that his son's poem was "full of feeling, but perhaps shaky in its

---

18. Ibid., p. 420.
19. Carter, "Chats with the Master," p. 306; also note 35.
20. *Shin kokinshū*, poem no. 1142.

phrasing."[21] The words of the poem did not flow smoothly, nor did its logic, at least on the surface. Moreover, phrases such as *yoso no yūgure* (an evening described as "far away" because it calls other lovers to meet) must have seemed obtuse. Even in criticizing his son, though, Shunzei managed to do him honor. For as scholars point out, his characterization brings to mind Ki no Tsurayuki's description of the great early court poet Ariwara no Narihira as one likewise given to producing poems whose form seemed overpowered by an abundance of feeling.[22] Even in his excesses Teika had the intelligence to follow illustrious models. Far from dismissing him for his adventuresome spirit, Shunzei seems to have appreciated his son's creativity.

Teika's temperament, on the other hand, was less easy to admire. Here, too, Teika seems to have been very different from his father, whom the records reveal as above all a circumspect man. In 1185, the young heir of the Mikohidari house was actually banned from court service after physically assaulting another courtier. After several months, Shunzei managed to secure a pardon for his son, and no such incident occurred again. But still Teika spoke his mind too often and too vociferously. To sum it up in one word, he seemed at times to lack precisely what someone in his position could least afford to lack — tact. It was this that offended many at court, including Go-Toba, whose opinion of the poet, written many years later, could hardly be more frank:

The way he behaved, as if he knew all about poetry, was really extraordinary. . . . He was utterly oblivious of others and would exceed all reason, refusing to listen to anything other people would say. In general, the tenor of his Lordship's critical viewpoint was that he would never take into consideration any extenuating circumstances of time or occasion in his judgment of a poem, and because he himself was incapable of a relaxed, casual attitude toward poetry, he would scowl angrily even when people praised one of his poems, if it happened to be one of which he was not particularly proud.[23]

Teika was evidently too much the perfectionist for Go-Toba's taste. Less so than his father, at least in public venues, the new heir of the Mikohidari line seemed unwilling to think of poetry as a courtly

---

21. Kubota Jun, *Ransei ni hana ari*, pp. 99–100.
22. Ibid., p. 100.
23. Brower, "Ex-Emperor Go-Toba's Secret Teachings," p. 38.

appurtenance, another amusement to which the Retired Emperor devoted only a portion of his time and energy. One might even say that Teika seemed to regard himself as the head of a poetic house first and an imperial attendant second, an attitude that would affect his descendants — or at least some of them — for centuries to come. Whereas portraits of Shunzei generally show him wizened and beatific, in monk's garb, with a serene expression on his face, portraits of Teika — perhaps influenced by Go-Toba's description — show a rotund, middle-aged man in full court garb, with a severe and haughty countenance made more so by a string moustache and a goatee.

Despite all this, Teika managed to succeed at court, where haughtiness was hardly unusual. Even before his father's death, he had become a judge and a tutor, eliciting interest even from master poets such as Saigyō; in time he attracted the interest of many powerful students among the court nobility and the military elite, including the shogun Minamoto no Sanetomo (1192–1219). Records do not always give us details about the services he provided for students. However, various manuscripts show that among his duties was the perusal of poems handed in for critique, which might involve only the penning in of *gatten*, or complimentary marks, next to praiseworthy poems but could also entail rewriting, commentary, and so forth.[24] No doubt some high-ranking students also consulted him for advice on poems to be submitted for public events. What payment was rendered in return for such services is also unclear, although one can assume that some form of remuneration — in the form of gifts and favors, from someone like Sanetomo — was received. In Teika's time wealthy and powerful patrons were still much more important than direct revenues from teaching. Only centuries later would such transactions be institutionalized, with students providing a vital source of support for the house.

As the years went by, Teika continued to be active in poetic affairs of all sorts and to make modest advances in court rank and office. In 1211, he finally entered the ranks of the senior nobility (*kugyō*), when he was advanced to junior third rank. At this point he established his own *mandokoro*, or administrative office, taking on two stewards of his own in the same way the Kujō, whose patronage he still enjoyed, had taken him on decades before. For the next 30 years he would serve as a poetic figure in a position similar to that of his father.

---

24. Murayama, *Fujiwara Teika*, p. 315.

With Go-Toba, however, Teika's relationship remained strained. In his diary, he was critical of Go-Toba's extravagant habits, although of course he could not afford to make such feelings public.[25] It did not help matters when in 1213 Go-Toba confiscated incomes from part of one of Teika's estates and gave it to one of his favorites — an action that the Mikohidari were able to reverse only years later.[26] The relationship between the two men came to an impasse in the Second Month of 1220 when Teika was barred from palace attendance over what the Retired Emperor perceived as an insult. But in the end even this actually worked to Teika's benefit when it removed him from any suspicion of involvement in the disastrous Jōkyū Rebellion of the very next year, in which the Retired Emperor called upon loyalists to rise up and overthrow the shogunal government. The plot was probably doomed from the beginning, but the men around Go-Toba were too timid to share their frank opinions about chances for success. Within a month, an invading army of nearly 200,000 warriors from the East Country overcame the forces of the Retired Emperor, and he and his sons were sent into exile. In addition, a number of high-ranking courtiers were beheaded and as many as 3,000 estate rights were confiscated. Although many of the rights were restored to their owners almost immediately, a precedent had been set: in these and other matters, the Kamakura government would now demand direct oversight of Kyoto affairs. To make their intentions known, the warrior government sent two of its own generals to serve as deputies at a place called Rokuhara, right in the middle of the imperial capital. While always stopping short of abolishing existing court institutions and procedures, in the coming years Kamakura would come to dictate almost all important decisions, even including questions of succession in the imperial house.

BUT ALL of this would take time. When troops from the East Country established order again in the summer of 1221, many in the old capital felt only relief. Teika's family, too, had been affected when Taira no Yasunori, one of his wards (*yōshi*) who had gone into Go-Toba's service, was obliged to commit suicide for his complicity in the af-

---

25. Imatani, *Kyōgoku Tamekane*, p. 18.
26. Smits, "The Poet and the Politician," p. 435.

fair.[27] The immediate family, however, came through unharmed. Evidently there was some talk of Teika's son Tameie, a favorite of Go-Toba, accompanying the deposed sovereign into exile, but his father no doubt forbade it.[28] While correspondence between the Mikohidari and the exiled sovereign continued, Teika stopped short of showing any public support. Imperial patronage was in these days still crucial to success at court; but members of the Mikohidari were like other noble houses in opting for their own survival — and the survival of the culture they represented — when a choice had to be made. No members of Teika's household were packed off to the provinces under censure; no Mikohidari estate rights were appropriated. His home on Reizei Street came through the siege unscathed. Go-Toba would die in exile nearly 20 years later on the rugged island of Sado in the Japan Sea, while one of his nephews served as emperor and the Mikohidari house continued to prosper and expand in Kyoto. In the early autumn of 1222, in fact, Teika was advanced to junior second rank, a promotion that illness and premature retirement had kept beyond his father's grasp. Far from suffering reverses as a result of the disturbance, the Mikohidari emerged perhaps stronger than before.[29]

One reason for Teika's success after the Jōkyū Rebellion was again simply luck, this time luck in marriage. For reasons that remain obscure, his first marriage had ended in divorce, probably sometime in his early 30s. But the woman he had married in 1194, a daughter of then Major Counselor Fujiwara no Sanemune (1144–1212), stayed on, and in the years to come her connections accounted for her husband's rise at court probably more than any other factor. Sanemune himself rose to the lofty office of Palace Minister before taking the tonsure and going into an elegant retirement, then turning over the fortunes of the family to his son Kintsune (1171–1244), founder of the Saionji lineage of the Northern Fujiwara and the man who betrayed Go-Toba to the shogunate before the rebellion. In the summer of 1222, Kintsune vaulted over the offices of Minister of the Right and Minister of the Left to become Chancellor, an office second only to that of the Regent. Although he resigned from his offices soon thereafter, he would remain a power behind the scenes for years to come. From

---

27. Ishida, *Fujiwara Teika no kenkyū*, p. 70.
28. Akase, "Reizei-ke no so, Tameie to Abutsu-ni," p. 95.
29. Imatani, *Kyōgoku Tamekane*, p. 20.

that time on one of the most powerful men in the government in Kyoto was Teika's brother-in-law.

In a letter he wrote to a friend in 1222, after his promotion to second rank, Teika revealed that he knew precisely how crucial Kintsune's success was for his own future. "Second rank is the highest rank a courtier can achieve. If not for the disturbance in the world, how could I ever have attained it?"[30] At any one time, only two dozen or so courtiers in active service held such high positions in the hierarchy, and no one could achieve such distinction without political support. It is not surprising, then, that the next decade would be one of the most secure periods of Teika's life. Before, he had benefited from the ascendance of the Kujō, who were still a force to be reckoned with in the capital; now he was assisted by the rise of the Saionji. When Kintsune held events at his spectacular new Kitayama pleasure villa, which was said to rival the estate of his ancestor Michinaga in splendor, Teika was often there in attendance; when the poet needed favors or financial assistance to maintain a proper lifestyle for himself and his family, it was to his brother-in-law that he turned first of all.

Over and above these benefits, Teika's second wife also produced children, one of them being Tameie, who would in time become the poet's heir. Like Shunzei, Teika managed to place his children—he had at least ten that we know of—where they could prove advantageous to the house. One daughter went into service with Go-Toba early on and then entered the entourage of Emperor Go-Horikawa (1212–34; r. 1221–32), evidently taking a younger sister with her; another became the consort of Saionji Kinsuke (1223–67), Kintsune's grandson. The maintenance of a family network was another responsibility of the heir of any courtly lineage and Teika seems to have taken these responsibilities as seriously as his literary ones.

The most that daughters and younger sons could do, however, was to make connections; the ultimate fate of any noble house was in the hands of its primary heir. Here Teika faced disappointment, for as virtually every source says that makes any note of Tameie at all, Teika was not always happy with the boy in his youth. What made matters worse was that Teika had already been disappointed by his eldest son, Mitsuie (b. 1184), whose lack of basic intelligence had forced him finally to write to an acquaintance, "Never again

---

30. Murayama, *Fujiwara Teika*, p. 76.

will I recommend this oafish son of mine for anything."[31] No doubt the situation was not easy for Mitsuie either, as he does more than hint at in one of his few recorded poems.

> Up the mountain   on my father's
> snowy path   I will never go—
> but oh that to the foothills   I could at least
> make my way![32]
>
> *tarachine ya / oyobanu yama no / yuki no michi / fumoto dani mo / nao ya oyobamu*

A poignant complaint—but not one that Teika was prepared to hear. The simple fact was that Mitsuie's literary efforts showed no promise. Nor did he show any aptitude for administering the affairs of the house. When Teika's diary mentions him it is with undisguised frustration: he is always lazy, irresponsible, an embarrassment. He went only as high as junior fifth rank—the fate of most younger sons but also, evidently, of elder sons who failed to impress. Mitsuie seems to have taken the tonsure at about the time of the Jōkyū disturbance and is seldom mentioned in records thereafter. Even by Teika's day, the fortunes of the Mikohidari house were so synonymous with performance in poetic affairs that a young man who failed in that area was left with no place.

There is no sign that Teika thought of Tameie as a dullard from whose basic incompetence the court, and the family, had to be protected. After undergoing his initiation rites (*genpuku*) at age eight (with his uncle, Kintsune, trimming his hair and his grandfather, Sanemune, performing the ceremonial capping—all done at Sanemune's mansion), the boy entered the court ranks, and in fact ascended rapidly. By the age of twelve he was made lesser captain; then, early in 1213, he was appointed to serve among the personal attendants of Go-Toba, whose affection for him was obvious. At first, Teika was overjoyed at his son's good fortune. "My whole life I've been unlucky," he wrote in his diary, "but now the clouds clear from my countenance, thanks to my son."[33] Before long, though, his joy

---

31. The statement was made to Kujō Yoshisuke (fourth son of Kanezane; 1185–1218). Murayama, *Fujiwara Teika*, p. 280.

32. Tsukamoto, "*Meigetsuki*: hito no ko no chichi, Teika," p. 21. *Fuboku wakashō*, poem no. 7292.

33. *Kundoku Meigetsuki*, vol. 3, pp. 235–36.

turned to vexation. One of the most oft-quoted passages in his diary, from the Fifth Month of 1213, explains why:

In recent days, noon and night, he plays kickball, I hear. Just at a time when His Two Majesties favor the game, he has the bad luck to become a constant attendant. . . . He never looks at a book, and the few things he read when he was seven or eight he has entirely forgotten. Again, the bad luck of the house sets to work.[34]

Along with archery, kickball (*kemari*) was considered a proper "courtly" sport, with traditions of its own that could be traced back into the distant past. As legend had it, the name Fujiwara — "Wisteria Field" — had in fact been given to the courtier Kamatari (614–69), founder of the lineage, when he went after a ball into a patch of wisteria. Participants dressed in fine robes usually played the game, which involved kicking a leather ball back and forth, with the aim of keeping it in the air for as long as possible, before an audience of court lords and ladies in the courtyard of some fine mansion. To be invited to participate in such events was therefore evidence that Tameie was popular among his patrons, as well as talented athletically. Furthermore, even Teika's diary admits that the boy's fascination with the game was more a product of his adolescent desire to please his patrons than his own interest.

Yet Teika continued to complain about Tameie's lack of dedication to what he considered the true family vocation. Personal prejudices aside, no one could claim that kickball was considered as serious an art form as music or poetry. More to the point, it was not the family tradition that Toshitada, Shunzei, and he himself had done so much to build. The manuscripts that several generations had collected with such care would be of little use to an athlete. Kickball was fine, as far as it went, then; but not if it conflicted with the boy's proper apprenticeship in poetry.

So just as Shunzei had had to worry about Teika, now Teika had in turn to worry about Tameie, although for different reasons. Teika had been too temperamental; Tameie, it would seem, was not temperamental enough — a pleaser anxious to do the bidding of his patrons, regardless of the long-term interests of his own house. The young man continued to make his way up the court ladder, but even by age 20 showed no real talent for poetry, at least in his fa-

---

34. Tsukamoto, "*Meigetsuki*: hito no ko no chichi, Teika," 1956, p. 20.

ther's eyes. In the end, Teika's chastisements, probably along with other factors we know nothing about, precipitated a crisis that is described in a miscellany written by a later poet, probably on the basis of conversations with later heirs of the family.

When Tameie was young he was not proficient in the Way. Even though he had connections in the world as heir of his father and grandfather, he made no progress. Having determined to abandon the lay world, he went to Hie Shrine to bid his leave. Around that same time, he visited Reverend Jichin to tell him of his intentions and say farewell.

"How old are you?' the Reverend asked him.

"Twenty-five," Tameie replied.

Then Jichin said, "You are not yet at the age when things have become clear. You should put your decision off, and decide only after you have accumulated more experience in practice."

Following this advice, Tameie gave up his plan to leave the world and composed a thousand poems in five days. After finishing the task, he showed them to his father, who looked at the ten poems on the topic, "The Beginning of Spring" and said, "Well, if you can produce poems as good as these, then things look good." After reading through all the poems, he told him to show them to Ietaka. In time, Tameie became Master of the Way and further improved on the heritage of his fathers — all thanks to Reverend Jichin.[35]

There are other versions of this story, some of which differ in a few particulars. But there are reasons to believe the gist of it. In every telling it is Jichin (1155–1225), one of the sons of Teika's patron Kujō Kanezane (1149–1207) and a major poet himself, who advises Tameie to put off his decision to give up the fight; in every telling the incident involves a visit to Hie Shrine, which is known to have been important to members of the Mikohidari lineage. Furthermore, we do indeed have a thousand-verse sequence by the Mikohidari heir written around this time — in the Eighth Month of 1223 — that boasts some "complimentary marks" by Teika and Jichin himself. In all, then, the story is probably not just family mythology, even if one wants to suggest that other factors, such as the recent fall of his patrons, Go-Toba and Juntoku (1197–1242; r. 1210–21), must also have contributed to Tameie's disaffection at the time.[36] For whatever reason, the years after the Jōkyū Rebellion seem to have been a watershed for Tameie as well as for his father. After 1223 Tameie's performance as a poet never again seems to have given his father serious cause for concern.

---

35. The poet is Tonna (1289–1372). See Tonna, *Seiashō*, p. 99.

36. Imatani, *Kyōgoku Tamekane*, p. 24.

For the rest of his life, he dedicated himself to the Way of Poetry, although he left a tradition of involvement in *kemari* that his descendants would make use of in later days.

One sign that even a few years before all this Teika had not given up on Tameie completely was the marriage he had arranged for him, probably in 1220 or 1221. The usual strategy would have been to search out an appropriate match among the younger daughters of the high nobility. But in recent years, many courtiers had begun looking to more prosperous quarters for marriage partners, one notable example being Teika's patron Fujiwara Kintsune, who had used marriage as a way to ally himself directly with Minamoto no Yoritomo.[37] The new military aristocracy, comprised of men from the provinces, many of whom claimed courtly lineage of one sort or another, were often anxious to make connections with the old elite. In turn, they had two things the court families of course needed: full coffers and political influence.[38]

One such figure was Utsunomiya Yoritsuna (1178–1259), a warrior claiming ancient Fujiwara lineage who had been among the direct retainers (*gokenin*) of the shogun. A warrior clan whose base of power was located northeast of Kamakura in Shimotsuke Province, the Utsunomiya were one of the most powerful families in the East Country. Political troubles had forced Yoritsuna, along with 60 of his personal retainers, to take the tonsure in 1205, renouncing all future political ambitions. Many men in such a situation would have retired to a hermitage in Kamakura. But Yoritsuna, going under the Buddhist name Renjō, had received a courtly education and was an ardent poet; furthermore, he was a disciple of the priest Hōnen (1133–1212), founder of the Pure Land sect, who wanted to have immediate contact with his teacher and fellow disciples in Kyoto. So to Kyoto he had come, in 1208, establishing a home in the city not far from Teika's and a spacious villa on the Saga Plain.

Court families were quick to make Renjō's acquaintance. By what means the connection with Teika was made we cannot say. As a follower of the Way of Poetry, however, Renjō would have known Teika by reputation. The birth of Tameie's first son, Tameuji (1222–86), in 1222, to Renjō's daughter cemented the relationship. Two more sons

---

37. Kintsune married the daughter of Yoritomo's *imōto muko*, Ichijō Yoshiyasu (d. 1198). Saneuji was thus both a Fujiwara and a Minamoto.

38. Murayama, *Fujiwara Teika*, p. 82.

were born within a few years. All would grow up under Renjō's care-
ful eyes, benefiting greatly from his wealth and political affiliations
while also being tutored by their father and grandfather in poetry.

BY THE mid-1220s, then, the Mikohidari house was prospering in every
way. In 1226, Tameie was appointed a consultant of junior third rank,
entering the ranks of the high nobility and putting him in a position
to take over Teika's position as leader at court poetic events. Teika
himself was finally appointed a middle counselor of senior second
rank in the First Month of 1232, at the age of 71. At the end of that
same year he resigned his offices, and less than a year after that he
took the tonsure with the name Myōjō.

Even after retirement, however, Teika was still involved in poetic
affairs. In fact, one reason for his decision to leave the lay world
may have been that in the summer of 1232, after several years of dis-
cussions on the matter involving the regent Kujō Michiie (1193–1252),
he had received an order from Emperor Go-Horikawa, the fifth
emperor he had served, to prepare for another imperial anthology.
This project would not come from a Poetry Bureau—he would be
sole compiler, putting him in precisely the same situation that
Shunzei had been in back in the mid-1180s: a lay monk honored with
an assignment that would be the culmination of his poetic career.
Evidence shows that for many years and following his father's lead,
Teika had been collecting the personal anthologies of poets, past and
present, in preparation for just such a task.[39] Although not without
his usual grumblings, he set to the task immediately and made rapid
progress. Since well before the date of the formal commission, he
had been working on the project and within a few months he was
able to present the emperor with a draft preface for the work and a
table of contents. During the compilation of *Shin kokinshū* 30 years
before, progress on the work had been hampered by the compli-
cations of working with other compilers and Go-Toba. Now he could
proceed relatively unfettered. Besides, his ultimate goal was to
secure the privilege of compiling such works for the heads of his
own house—exclusively—into the future. However difficult the
labor, which as always involved political interference, he wanted

39. Hashimoto, "Chokusenshū senshin to shikashū," and Tanaka Noboru,
"Reizei-ke ga tsutaeta kotenseki," p. 127.

to push the example of the *Shin kokinshū* into the past and establish a sure foundation for his own heirs.[40]

The sudden death of Go-Horikawa in the Eighth Month of 1234, at the age of only 23, was a shock to Teika. Thinking that this unhappy event spelled the end of the project,[41] Teika took his working manuscript of the imperial anthology out into his garden the day after the sovereign's death and burned it—a drastic action but one in keeping with the character of a man who seems to have thought of himself as, despite all his good fortune, doomed to bad luck. There were rumors that Go-Toba's vengeful spirit was responsible for the young sovereign's death; no doubt Teika feared that he might be cursed as well. Over time, however, the Imperial Regent and others prevailed upon him to relent, and in the Third Month of 1235, the collection, bearing the unassuming title *Shin chokusenshū*— "New Imperial Anthology"—was complete. On the twelfth day of that month, a fair copy was presented to Kujō Michiie in the hand of Yukiyoshi (b. 1179) of the Sesonji house, who were experts in calligraphy in the same way that the Mikohidari were experts in poetry. The courtly project was complete.

In fitting tribute, the anthology began with a poem by the deceased emperor, one of five of his works included in the final product. In addition, there were 35 poems by Shunzei, 6 by young Tameie, and many poems by Teika's patrons in the Kujō and Saionji families, while poems by Go-Toba and his sons were excluded—on the insistence of Michiie, who had the right of approval over the project—altogether out of deference to the sensitivities of the shogunate. But that kind of favoritism was only to be expected in a courtly work. Teika had restricted his own number to only 15 poems, a total far fewer than the 46 he had been allowed in *Shin kokinshū*. On that count, no one criticized him. But there were those who did complain that Teika's labor gave too much space to people like Renjō, who were not courtiers in the strictest sense of the term. Some went so far as to dub the work "The Uji River Collection." The connection of the Uji River with war-

---

40. See Kobayashi, "Tameie, Tameuji, Tameyo."

41. As Kubota Jun notes, Teika probably had in mind the precedent of Fujiwara Kiyosuke, whose imperial anthology project had never come to fruition because of the death of Emperor Nijō in 1165. See Kubota Jun, *Ransei ni hana ari*, p. 237. See also Smits, "The Poet and the Politician," p. 452.

riors went back to a famous poem attributed to the *Man'yō* era poet
Hitomaro (fl. ca. 680–700).

> Like waves that ripple   'round the stakes
> of fishing weirs   in Uji, river
> of the sovereign's mighty men —   so I wander
> on my way.[42]
>
> *mononofu no/yaso no ujikawa no/ajiroki ni/isayou nami no/yukue shirazu mo*

Teika's warrior connections could not be denied. The second
shogun, Sanetomo, who had been cut down by an assassin in 1219,
had been his student; for that matter his patrons the Kujō had been
very much allies of the shogunal government, as were his in-laws
the Saionji. Lastly, his strong ties to Renjō were a matter of public
knowledge. His only response to the criticisms was therefore stoical
silence. In a world in which patronage was the most fundamental
means of support, to gain the backing of those in power was the only
hope of success, after all. Those who voiced such criticisms could
easily be dismissed as enemies of the house, who were probably jeal-
ous of its exalted position.

Later heirs, including those of the Reizei family, would argue heat-
edly over the question of which anthology, *Shin kokinshū* or *Shin
chokusenshū*, represented the essence of Teika's poetics. In modern
times, the former collection is much more popular among scholars
and critics. But the earlier work had been a collaborative effort, while
the later was in some ways Teika's own, and very much a product of
his mature years. It seems fairly clear that he meant the *Shin chokusen-
shū* as a distillation of a lifetime of thinking about Japanese poetry. It
is significant, then, that for his own entries he chose not the more
conceptually complex and philosophically engaging poems of his
early years, but poems like this one, written in 1232:

> On "A Distant View," from a 100-poem sequence composed
> at the home of the Regent-Minister of the Left
>
> Out through the gates   of the Palace
> of Many Stones   I come, every night —
> to confront, though unawaited,   the moon on
> the mountain rim.[43]
>
> *momoshiki no/tonoe o izuru/yoi yoi wa/matanu ni mukau/yama no ha no tsuki*

---

42. *Man'yōshū*, poem no. 266.
43. *Shin chokusenshū*, poem no. 1168.

Significantly, the poem presents a courtier, finished with his duties in the imperial palace, coming out of the gate to be greeted—not unexpectedly, perhaps, but without conscious anticipation—by the beauty of the moon. Court service first, aesthetic pleasures second? As a later courtier would declare, "For the nobility, the Way of Imperial Appointment is primary; for them poetry is only a worthy amusement."[44] Even if such an interpretation goes too far, the poem does remind us that even after gaining a reputation as a poet, Teika spent much of his time as an imperial attendant or as a retainer of higher-ranking families. The truth is that for the older Teika, poetry was a vocation, but only in the context of his larger career as a member of the imperial court, which is to say that his dedication was not to poetry in some abstract sense but to the practices of a particular tradition.[45]

Most of the other poems by Teika in the new anthology, as well as those he chose to represent other poets, are equally courtly in their references. This had not been so true of the poems in *Shin kokinshū*, which, while certainly a product of courtly events, often gestured toward other realms, real and imaginary. For courtiers of Teika's time, *Shin chokusenshū* was less obscure, more polished, more unified in tone and sensibility and hence a more proper model for their own study. Compared to his poem on Hase's far-off bell sound, the poem on leaving the palace on a moonlit night is syntactically smoother, as well as more transparent in its reasoning. In his maturity Teika had come to value what he called the quality of *ushin*, or depth of feeling, more than rhetorical virtuosity or syntactic ambiguity; poems that maintained a proper balance between flower (*hana*) and fruit (*mi*), he said in a treatise.[46] Perhaps he was implying a criticism of the excesses of Go-Toba, whose extravagant regime had ended in violence and a period of real diminution for the noble families. The new anthology, more than its predecessor, in any case, seemed to argue for restraint.

---

44. The quotation is from the Edo period poet Sanjōnishi Sanenori (1618–1701). See *Waka kikigaki*, p. 844.

45. See Kobayashi, "Tameie, Tameuji, Tameyo," and Tanaka Noboru, "Reizei-ke ga tsutaeta kotenseki," for details on the ultimate priorities of Shunzei, Teika, and later heirs of the house.

46. Brower, "Fujiwara Teika's *Maigetsushō*," pp. 414–15.

TEIKA NO doubt thought of *Shin chokusenshū* as his last major poetic project. He was now 74 years old, and the chances of another imperial anthology being ordered in his lifetime were remote at best. By this time he was composing little poetry. Instead his days were spent collecting manuscripts for his library, studying, collating, and editing court classics, and copying out Buddhist sutras in preparation for the life to come. The more humdrum affairs of the Miko-hidari house had effectively been passed to his son.

Midway through 1235, however, Teika received a request that would alter the canon of Japanese poetry. It came quite innocently, from Renjō, Tameie's father-in-law. Teika records the matter very straightforwardly in his diary entry for the 27th day of the Fifth Month of that year.

> I know nothing about calligraphy, but the Lay Monk is very persistent in his requests for *shikishi* for the sliding door-panels of his villa in Saga. They would turn out very unsightly, I knew, but I pushed ahead, took up my brush, and then sent the results off. I chose one poem each from antiquity on, beginning with Emperor Tenchi and going as far as Ietaka and Masatsune.[47]

Just a few weeks before, Teika had spent a few days as Renjō's guest at the Chū-in, the latter's spacious Saga villa, located not far from his own retreat on Mount Ogura. Tameie had been there, too, along with several other courtiers. The group had composed a linked verse sequence — a new genre that was one of the favorite pastimes of Teika's last years — and chatted amiably about various matters. After ten days, though, Teika seems to have tired of the place, which he worried was not good for his health. "My observation over the years is that those who spend time near the water in summer often come down with malaria. Then there is the danger of dropsy . . . so I informed my host that I would be returning to the city."[48] His own house on Kyōgoku Avenue in the city had no pond and no streams, and thus seemed to pose no threat to his frail constitution.

Though Teika says nothing about it in his earlier entry, he and Renjō had no doubt discussed the history of Japanese poetry during

---

47. *Kundoku Meigetsuki*, vol. 6, p. 175. Quoted in Matsumura, *Hyakunin isshu*, p. 25.

48. *Kundoku Meigetsuki*, vol. 6, p. 171. See Matsumura, *Hyakunin isshu*, pp. 24–26.

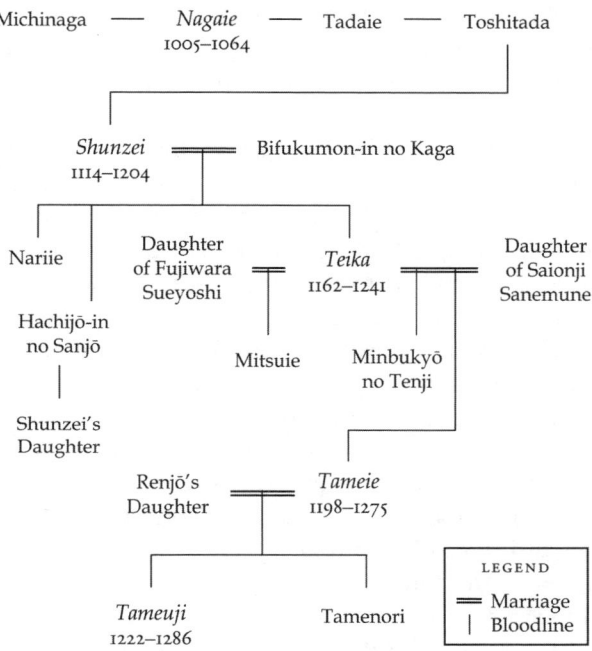

Chart 1 The Origins of the Mikohidari Lineage

his visit. The request for poems in Teika's hand, on square *shikishi* paper, may even have come when he was still at the villa. His reluctance to proffer *shikishi* in his own hand, which was indeed probably "unsightly" by the standards of his time, is not surprising. But he did so, no doubt assuming that his little primer would be hidden away and forgotten.

As any student of Japanese culture knows, it was not. For the little anthology he put together for Renjō, which came to be known as *Hyakunin isshu* (*One Hundred Poems by One Hundred Poets*) would go on to become the single most widely read work in the history of the *uta* form.[49] Other poets would follow it with scores of other

49. For an explanation of the complex manuscript history of the little anthology, see Matsumura, *Hyakunin isshu*. Recent research suggests that it was the sequence titled *Hyakunin shūka* (One Hundred Poems of Excellence by One Hundred Poets) that Teika produced for Renjō, then producing another sequence—different only in that it contained poems by the exiles Go-Toba and Juntoku—to adorn the walls of his own retreat, which would

100-poem collections, with titles such as "The New One Hundred Poems by One Hundred Poets," compiled by a shogun in 1483; "One Hundred Poems by One Hundred Warriors" of 1660; the seventeenth-century "One Hundred Poems by One Hundred Women"; the "One Hundred Poems by One Hundred Eccentrics" of 1852; and — in the fall of 1999 — "The *New* New One Hundred Poems by One Hundred Poets" (*Shinshin hyakunin isshu*), compiled by the popular novelist and scholar Maruya Saiichi. But none of these would gain anything close to the prominence of the little anthology Teika put together in a few weeks in 1235. Probably the main reason for the work's popularity in the medieval period was that it offered such a handy introduction to the *uta* for students. However unintentionally, Teika had produced a textbook. For serious poets the imperial anthologies were of course preferable as primers, but Teika's selection was just the thing for beginners. The poems he had chosen displayed all the rhetorical features of the court tradition and clearly reflected the attitudes of his mature years. That short verse-by-verse commentaries would later be appended to the collection, making it a true textbook, thus comes as no surprise; such commentaries were written for *Kokinshū* and other imperial anthologies, too. However, no other poetic text can claim to have later become part of a card game — a game that is still played at New Year's all over Japan.

AFTER FULFILLING his obligation to Renjō, Teika returned to the interests of his final years: books, sutras, and his garden. His grandsons by Tameie, now in their teens, visited from time to time. The eldest of them, Tameuji, was made a middle captain in 1237, and was evidently a serious young man, unlike his father at the same age, although he too seems to have been skilled at kickball.[50]

Tameie himself had achieved the office of middle counselor in 1236, at the age of 39. No doubt the patriarch of the Mikohidari lineage was pleased. When Tameie was appointed a major counselor in the Second Month of 1241, Teika must have been overjoyed. No one in the Mikohidari lineage had reached those heights since Tadaie, more than 160 years before. So, despite his father's years of fretting, the young kickball enthusiast had done well for himself after all.

---

explain why early on *Hyakunin isshu* was known as *Ogura sansō shikishi waka* — Poems on *Shikishi* from the Mountain Retreat at Ogura.

50. Kaneko, "Fujiwara Tameuji no shōgai," p. 41.

He was clearly being recognized as a fine poet—less imaginative than Teika had been at the same age, to be sure, but in that he was only following his father's advice. He was already performing well as de facto tutor to the court, which was the distinction that Shunzei and Teika had most wanted for their heirs.

Teika died in the summer of 1241, at the age of 80. Plagued with various ailments from his teens on, he had expected to expire long before. When the end finally came, he left the family in as strong a position as could be hoped for—certainly as strong as when Shunzei had passed on in 1204. With Renjō and the Saionji as patrons and Tameie hale and hearty, the future of the lineage looked secure.

Teika's literary legacy was in most ways as impressive as his father's and similar in its particulars. He too left teachings on poetic ideals such as *yūgen* ("mystery and depth") and *ushin*, in addition to over 4,000 of his own poems, which embodied his ideals. Equally important, he left a tradition of poetic practice in the form of treatises, instructions to heirs and disciples about everything from composition to etiquette and ritual, and a network of social affiliations—all of which were necessities for anyone attempting to compete in the poetic culture of the court. Moreover, the textual trove he left his children and grandchildren was truly voluminous. His diary, which he had begun at 19 and continued to keep until he was 74, contained little of what moderns expect from such a work—some complaining but no soul-searching and few confessions; yet it would be used as a reference work for future heirs whenever they wanted information about what clothes to wear for a courtly event or the order of things for a family ceremony, just as he intended. He also left a handful of critical writings and an impressive collection of manuscripts, many of which he himself had received from Shunzei. As might be expected of the head of a poetic household who wanted to put his descendants in a good position to compete at court, he had collected personal poetry anthologies in particular: the sort of texts that would be useful in the compilation of future imperial collections. No doubt he thought of that specific responsibility as one of the most fundamental duties—and callings—of the Mikohidari house.[51] But he also left behind other texts, especially those in which poetry figures prominently, including *The Tale of Genji*, *Tales of Ise*, *Tales of Yamato*,

---

51. Kobayashi, "Tameie, Tameuji, Tameyo." See also Hashimoto, "Chokusenshū senshin to shikashū."

The Tosa Diary, and *The Sarashina Diary.* Indeed, his manuscripts are some of our earliest extant copies of these court classics. Along with other texts, especially sutras, these treasures went to Tameie in seventeen boxes, forming the nucleus of what would later become the Reizei Library. In the days before printing, it was only with such textual assets that a poetic house could even hope for success.

Teika was also able to leave his son wealth in other forms. His diary shows that at one time or another he held the rights to incomes from at least sixteen different estates. Most of these were temporary in nature, assigned to him along with offices and usually coming from patrons in the Kujō or Saionji families. But he also had four deeds of his own to pass on to his son: one to revenues from the Yoshitomi Estate on the southeastern shores of Lake Biwa, one to Koazaka Estate in Ise, and two others to estates in Harima, called Koshibe and Hosokawa. Though the history of each of these hold- ings is complex, in every case Teika received them from relatives — his father, his mother, and an older sister. The ultimate authority over these properties rested in the hands of wealthy patrons who acted as guarantors and protectors, to whom Teika had often ap- pealed for help in various matters. As time went on, the need to provide policing and to exert some sort of force against interlopers and recalcitrant locals only increased, making the management of family assets a constant concern. From each of these sources, how- ever, Teika had received various forms of income: rice and other kinds of produce, livestock, laborers, timber, and so on. However generously treated by patrons, no noble family of the Kamakura age could get along without its own independent revenues. Tameie was fortunate that his father was able to pass on clear deeds to such prosperous and basically secure holdings. The Hosokawa Estate, for the administration of which Teika had received — from his student, Shogun Minamoto no Sanetomo — a special exemption from inter- ference by even shogunal estate stewards (*jitō*), would be of particu- lar importance for the family in the years ahead.[52]

In addition to estates, Teika also deeded his son several houses. After leaving his father's home on Fifth Avenue in his late 20s, Teika had lived in places we know by the names of the streets they fronted on — Bōmon, Takakura, Ninth Avenue, all within the city. Why he moved from the first two houses and what happened to them after

---

52. Fujimoto, "Shōen to Reizei-ke," pp. 221–54.

his departure is unknown. But it appears that he left the house on Ninth Avenue in about 1210, perhaps turning it over to one of his elder sisters, who is known to have lived there later. His next house was located on Reizei Street, north of Second Avenue. He stayed in it for over a decade, through various remodelings, as his family grew in size. From around the time of the Jōkyū Rebellion, however, he turned the Reizei house over to Tameie and moved to a site on First Avenue at Kyōgoku, the eastern border of the city, running along the Kamo River.[53]

Teika's diary gives little description of his early houses but goes into considerable detail about the Kyōgoku house in the context of describing remodeling that he had done in 1226. From those entries we learn that the lot was not large—certainly nothing like the huge city estates of the Retired Emperors such as the Kan-in or Rokujō Palaces, diagrams of which are routinely used to represent the features of *shindenzukuri* architecture in history books. Palaces of that size routinely occupied several full city blocks, with a main *shinden* hall in the center connected to numerous annexes by roofed walkways and large garden spaces, complete with streams, gazebos, and artificial ponds. Teika's lot, even after he added onto it through purchase of adjoining properties to the south, probably never amounted to much more than a quarter of a city block. Rather than an expansive complex of connected pavilions, it contained only one main hall, with no annexes. Even after adding an entry corridor (*chūmon-rō*) and some outbuildings—a carriage shed, a guards' quarters, and a small chapel—the place was modest in proportions and furnishings. The only luxury Teika allowed himself was a fine garden of shrubs, evergreens, and various flowering trees, which he alludes to affectionately.[54]

Besides these dwellings in the city, Teika by middle age also had a few small houses here and there, for times when the directional taboos prohibited him from staying in his primary houses. He also had, for a time at least, a cottage in the northern suburb of Sasaki and the cottage at the foot of Mount Ogura in Saga, near Renjō's Chū-in villa. The latter cottage, mentioned at the beginning of this chapter, would come to be known as "The Pavilion of Showers,"

53. Ishida, *Fujiwara Teika no kenkyū*, pp. 77–96.

54. Nakamura, "Kugyō no ie, suki no ie," pp. 182–86. See also Tsunoda, "Fujiwara Teika no Ichijō-Kyōgoku tei."

probably because of poems like the following by Teika, which his
son would eventually put in an imperial anthology:

"Autumn Morning"

Mount Ogura   in the season
of showers: where every morning
they were fainter yesterday   — those autumn leaves
all around.[55]

ogurayama/shigururu koro no/asa na asa na/kinō wa usuki/yomo no momijiba

Though benefiting from the natural beauty of the area, the cottage
itself was no doubt small and quite rustic. The grounds, however,
appear to have been spacious, much more so than those around his
home in Kyoto.[56] From about 1199 on, Teika used the place as a re-
treat to escape the noise and bustle of the city. When he first moved
in, there was a memorial hall there to the memory of the wife of
Taira no Munemori (1147–85) on the property, erected after her death
in 1179 and maintained by her family, from whom it is most likely
that Teika purchased the place, through the offices of one of his
sisters.[57] There were other graves nearby as well, including that of
his ancestor, Tadaie, which had been memorialized in a poem by the
latter's son included in *Shin kokinshū*:

Written near the grave of Major Counselor Tadaie on
Saga Moor, when he was on his way to visit Hōrinji

Ever wet with dew   are the fields
of Saga Moor   — and more so today
as I drench the sleeves of my robe   seeking out
ancient remains.[58]

sarade dani/tsuyukeki saga no/nobe ni kite/mukashi no ato ni/shiorenuru kana

The Saga cottage went to Tameie, who also inherited the nearby
estate of his father-in-law in a few years. How much he used Teika's
old haunt is not known, but odds are that he lived in the cottage very

---

55. *Shoku gosenshū*, poem no. 418; also *Shūi gusō*, poem no. 2289.
56. See Takenishi, *Hyakunin isshu*, p. 18. Takenishi quotes an article that
appeared in the *Chūnichi shinbun* (July 15, 1983) in which Tsunoda Bunpei
estimates the size of the Chū-in estate at 8,168 *tsubo*.
57. Matsumura, *Hyakunin isshu*, p. 27.
58. *Shin kokinshū*, poem no. 785.

little.[59] The support he received from Renjō probably accustomed him to a level of wealth that his father had seldom known. Still, the Reizei residence, remodeled many times to accommodate the needs of his growing family, continued to serve as his primary home for many years to come. Teika's Kyōgoku residence also stayed in his hands, eventually going to Tameie's own heirs.

As CUSTOM dictated, Tameie resigned as major counselor to mourn his father in 1241. For nearly a decade thereafter, his name stayed on the list of former court officials. Then in 1250 he was appointed head of the Ministry of Popular Affairs, an office that his father had held and which would become almost hereditary with his descendants. During all this time he was more active than ever as a poet, holding a central place in the coterie around Emperor Go-Saga (1220–72; r. 1242–46), one of the most literary of all medieval emperors. It was no surprise, then, that in 1248, a command should come to Tameie to serve as sole compiler of a new imperial anthology. For the next three years and more he worked on the project, which he presented for review under the title *Shoku gosenshū* (Later Collection, Continued) at the end of 1251. As the product of the head of the Mikohidari household, acting alone and without interference from other compilers, it would be ranked with Shunzei's *Senzaishū* and Teika's *Shin chokusenshū* as a Mirror of the Way. In order to enunciate the dominant position of the house at the time, he chose for the first poem one by his grandfather, Shunzei:

> Written on the idea of Spring arriving in the midst of the old year
>
> Has spring come, then,   before the old year
> is done?   In the mountains
> of Yoshino, haze hovers   above peaks still white
> with snow.[60]
>
> *toshi no uchi ni / haru tachinu to ya / yoshinoyama / kasumi kakareru / mine no shirayuki*

The message of this choice was of course clear: as head of the Mikohidari lineage, Tameie was asserting proprietorship. To use one of his own poems, or even his father's, might have been going too far.

---

59. The headnote to a poem in *Gyokuyōshū* (no. 2600) indicates that by the early 1300s the Saga retreat was in the hands of Nijō Michihira (1287–1335).

60. *Shoku gosenshū*, poem no. 1.

But so unassailable was Shunzei's reputation that no one would dare to find fault.

A few years after finishing the imperial project, Tameie fell ill and took the tonsure; but like Shunzei, he lived on, though he was never again robust. When his patron Saionji Saneuji (1194–1269), son of Kintsune, arranged for another order to compile an imperial anthology less than a decade later, in 1259, he was reluctant to sign on. Through Saneuji, he tried three times to decline the honor, complaining that he had left the world and that he was in ill health and suggesting that the honor should go instead to his heir Tameuji, who was now 38 years old and a middle counselor. But in the end the head of a poetic house could not refuse such an order. He returned to his library and began the process of sifting through manuscripts. Choosing the poems was a time-consuming and tedious process, especially since so many petitioners came to beg recognition for themselves, their children, and their ancestors. Headnotes had to be checked for accuracy to be sure that attributions and dates were correct, that offices were correctly noted, and so forth. At every stage the process was hemmed in with rites and precedents.

From the beginning, then, progress on the project was slow. Tameie may not have realized, however, that his hesitation had given his rivals time to act. Like any other artistic field, the field of court poetry was a site of contest; there were always competitors ready to take advantage of any opportunity to assert claims. Chief among Tameie's rivals was one of Teika's own former students, a man named Hamuro Mitsutoshi (1203–76), now tonsured under the sobriquet Shinkan. Since the mid-1240s Shinkan had distanced himself from Tameie and had made alliances with a number of other like-minded poets. Recently, Shinkan had even gone to Kamakura, seat of the shogunate, where he found many young poets eager for his instruction. His chief triumph there was enlisting as his disciple Prince Munetaka (1242–74), a son of Go-Saga who was serving at the time as shogun—the first imperial prince to do so. With the shogun behind him, Shinkan now demanded to be included as a compiler. There were others ready to make the same demand as well, most of them his comrades in opposition to Tameie. Among these were Rokujō Yukiie (1223–75), of the old Rokujō lineage that had been rivals since the time of Shunzei, and Kujō Motoie (1203–80), a son of Yoshitsune (1169–1206), Teika's great friend and benefactor.

Tameie protested against the interference of men that he deemed interlopers. He had put together the last imperial anthology by himself, he proclaimed, and, despite his initial reluctance was competent to do so again. No doubt he remembered his father's grumbling about the difficulties of government by committee at the time of *Shin kokinshū* and wanted no part of such an arrangement. Nevertheless, when his opponents declared that they too were from old poetic houses, some of whose ancestors had participated in the compilation of *Shin kokinshū*, Go-Saga acceded to their requests.[61]

So all of Tameie's efforts — and all of Teika's — to put the precedent of *Shin kokinshū* behind them had failed.[62] Like it or not, they would have to share the honor of serving as compiler with other houses. To withdraw altogether would set a bad precedent for the future; the idea of an anthology with no Mikohidari involvement at all was unthinkable. Shinkan, Yukiie, Motoie, and Kujō Ieyoshi (1192–1264), another former student of Teika's, were thus added as compilers in the Ninth Month of 1262. Two other men, both evidently allies of Shinkan's, were assigned to do clerical work.

Just how acrimonious things became during the next period is suggested by an anecdote recorded later:

Once, the Lay-Monk Minister of Popular Affairs Tameie was passing by the house of the Lay-Monk Controller Shinkan and saw a carriage decorated with sparrow crests parked there. When he had a servant go and ask whose carriage it was, he was informed that it was the carriage of the Governor of Hyūga, Lord Kaneuji. This made Tameie so furious that after returning home he went directly to the Poetry Bureau and cut from the anthology the three poems by Kaneuji that had been selected for inclusion.[63]

Minamoto no Kaneuji (d. ca. 1278) was not just one of the hopeful poets of the day, but librarian in the Poetry Bureau itself. That only one of his poems appeared in the anthology is an indication that the story may not be apocryphal. The battle lines were drawn, and for those who crossed them there were risks — a lesson that later generations would all have cause to learn well.

Somehow, though, the process continued, probably with Tameuji doing much of the work for his father. After years of haggling, especially between Tameie and Shinkan, the anthology, called *Shoku kokin-*

---

61. Kubota Jun, *Ransei ni hana ari*, p. 406.
62. Kobayashi, "Tameie, Tameuji, Tameyo," pp. 79–80.
63. Tonna, *Seiashō*, p. 93.

shū (*Kokinshū,* Continued) was finally complete in the last month of 1265, nearly six full years since the command for the work had been issued. A formal banquet, modeled directly on the one held to celebrate the completion of *Shin kokinshū* in 1205, was held in the Third Month of 1266. Prince Munetaka ended up with more poems — 67 in all — than any other poet. Tameie, too, was well represented, but the sight of 30 poems by Shinkan must have marred the moment.

Ironically, however, in the summer of 1266 the shogun Munetaka was deposed. The official charge against him was, predictably, plotting against the government, though in reality the leaders in Kamakura probably just wanted to replace the 25-year-old shogun with a younger and more manageable figurehead. So Munetaka's two-year-old son Koreyasu (1264–1326) took his place, which of course meant that practical decisions were turned over to the Hōjō house, who served as shogunal regents. Disabling the opponents of the Mikohidari was probably the furthest thing from the minds of the Kamakura oligarchs, but in effect this is what they did. With Munetaka in seclusion, Shinkan effectively went into hiding, leaving Tameie and his heir as unchallenged leaders in the poetic circles of the capital.

By this time Tameie was living in Saga in a retirement much more comfortable than Shinkan's, his days dedicated to study of the court classics and Buddhist devotions. As Teika had done in his last years, he too put together his poems into a personal anthology that he would pass down to his progeny. According to a later document, he took care, however, not to make one of the mistakes that — in his judgment — his father had made.

My later father's poems were superb, of course, but if descendants who know nothing about poetry should put them into anthologies indiscriminately, there are many bad poems among them. My own poems are stupid by comparison, but even if such descendants should put them in anthologies, I have taken care not to leave behind any poems that are all that bad.[64]

Usually this quotation is adduced to document Tameie's conservatism as an individual, which it indubitably reveals. At the same time, however, it should be noted that it also shows a strong sense of responsibility toward the future of the house and of the imperial court. As head of the Mikohidari lineage and the compiler of two imperial anthologies himself, Tameie knew that in the future his

----

64. Ibid., p. 114.

poems would inevitably be included in later similar projects, and it was with that ambition clearly in mind that he passed them on. His care in cutting out any poems not appropriate for such a venue was surely meant as a lesson to his heirs and students. Teika had perhaps not been so conscious of the precedents he was setting, but for Tameie, operating in the salons of the late thirteenth century, such naiveté was no longer possible. In this sense, his stance was a rational one that emphasized the nature of poetry as an ongoing enterprise dependent more on discipline than on individual genius, the latter being something that in any case could not be taught.

Tameie probably gave manuscripts of his own poetry collections to Tameuji as soon as he produced them. Likewise, he had probably passed on the secret teachings of the house orally, as was the custom, to Tameuji long before.[65] His estate rights, too, had already been turned over to his heir. Exactly when he let go of his houses we do not know, but at some point the house on Reizei Street went to Tameuji, and Teika's old house on Kyōgoku to Tamenori (1227–79), a second son also by the daughter of Renjō. One result of Tameie's wealth and successes at court was that his descendants all wanted to remain in the lay world rather than go to monasteries. Far from thinking of retirement, Tamenori had married the daughter of a steward in the Saionji house, and was clearly ambitious. The jealousy between the brothers was palpable, and no doubt worrisome to their father. But such rivalries were to be expected in noble families, where success served to raise expectations even for younger sons.

Tameie never hesitated in his choice of Tameuji as his heir, however. His eldest son now had two sons of his own by a daughter of Asukai Norisada (1210–66), the son of Teika's disciple Asukai Masatsune (1170–1221), who was himself heir of a household that also specialized in both poetry and kickball. Thus the tradition of marriage alliances continued. No doubt the rivalries would as well, but Tameie was now beyond all that, or so he thought. He too wrote poems — many more than his father had, in fact — on the melancholy beauties of Mount Ogura. The following four poems, all written between 1264 and 1268 on different occasions and in different seasons, are remarkably similar in tone.

––––––––

65. See Satō, "Kagaku to teikin to karon — Tameie karon kō," for a study of the house teachings during these early years.

"Spring Moon," for a three-verse session held on the death
anniversary of Retired Emperor Go-Toba [in 1264]

At the best of times   my cottage
on Mount Ogura   is in the shadows—
and more so when the mists   obscure the rays
of the spring moon.[66]

sarade dani / yado wa ogura no / yama tote ya / honoka ni kasumu / haru no tsuki kage

"Mountain Home," written for a poem sequence on the 11th day
of the Twelfth Month [of 1266]

So accustomed am I   to the wind
in the pine trees   at Mount Ogura
that my dreams of the city   drift ever
farther away.[67]

ogurayama / matsu fuku kaze wa / kikinarete / miyako no yume zo / tōzakariyuku

"Deer," from a sequence of 28 poems [written
in early spring, 1267]

Through all the years,   when autumn
appears again   at Mount Ogura,
always there is the same feeling   in the call
of the stag.[68]

aki o hete / ogura no yama ni / tatsu shika wa / onaji kokoro ni / ne koso nakarure

"Pine Tree at a Mountain Home," from a 100-poem
sequence composed at leisure [in 1268]

At Mount Ogura   I hide away
in the dark   beneath the pines—
myself an aging tree,   growing older
all the time.[69]

mi o kakusu / ogura no yama no / matsu no kage / onaji oiki ni / furimasaru kana

These poems show that while not as imaginative or as broad-ranging
as his father's, Tameie's work was perhaps more serene. Composi-
tion on prescribed topics (*dai*) demanded first that the poet give
proper attention to the topic itself, seeking to articulate something
of its essence, which was sometimes defined as simply the history
of its treatment in earlier poems and sometimes in more philosophi-
cal terms. The challenge was thus to engage the poets and poems

---

66. *Fujiwara Tameie zenkashū*, poem no. 4508.
67. Ibid., poem no. 4912.
68. Ibid., poem no. 4959.
69. Ibid., poem no. 5228.

of the past: to participate, again, in a common enterprise. Each of Tameie's poems manages to do this by employing subtle variations on established conventions of treatment while also conveying the kind of emotional resonance that Teika gave the name *ushin*. There can be no doubt that those who knew the Mikohidari connection to Mount Ogura—treated appropriately as misty, shady, remote, and forlorn—must also have appreciated the more personal dimensions of Tameie's reflections. For him the site was probably a refuge of sorts, but one that was connected to the onset of old age and decline.

With Shinkan and his rivals in the Rokujō house well out of the way, the heir of the Mikohidari fortunes was in a position Teika had never achieved. Wealthy and secure, Tameie could have faced the future with confidence and only the highest of aspirations for his growing progeny. Yet there were worries. Even a decade before, in 1253, he had brooded over not his own fate so much as the fate of his children, not knowing how well his fears would be justified.

"Lament"
The troubles I face   as I myself
take on years   are quite forgotten
as I grieve about my children   in a world
yet to come.[70]

nageku beki / mi no oiraku wa / wasurarete / nao ko no yo nomi / omou kanashisa

Just what about the "world yet to come" so worried Tameie we cannot know, if indeed there were any specific personal concerns behind the poem at all. No headnote or other source mentions anything specific. But we can be sure that Tameie's own experience had taught him how competitive life at court could be. Factionalism and strife were virtually inevitable and were almost sure to be as much a part of life for his heirs as they had been for him. Furthermore, whatever his own fate as the son-in-law of a wealthy patron, there could be no denying that many court houses had lost much in recent years. However conventional, then, the ironic pose Tameie strikes— of an old man who has reached the point where he no longer worries about himself but still worries over the future of his children— reveals sentiments that are completely in character for the head of a noble house.

---

70. Ibid., poem no. 2895.

TWO

Kamakura

LIKE MOST literati of his high station, Fujiwara no Tameie constantly sought to borrow manuscripts for his library, which had to be copied by hand, as did his own poetry and other writings. This required experience as well as special knowledge of both calligraphy and literature. To read one character for another, to inadvertently translate a phrase into more modern form, to garble a passage, to skip a word or two—these were mistakes that an untrained hand could make in an instant. For day-to-day correspondence or trivial household matters, young people of middling education would do; not so for the copying of long sought-after literary treasures. A meticulous and experienced hand was required for this kind of work. Hence the need for highly trained copyists.

The need for such a helper in the early 1250s brought to Tameie the woman who is rightly credited as the true founder of the Reizei house, known to us by her Buddhist name, Abutsu. Initially, probably around 1253, she had been introduced to one of Tameie's daughters as a person qualified to serve as copyist for *The Tale of Genji*.[1] That daughter, known as Dainagon no Suke (1233–63), had studied poetic composition under Teika. No doubt she and the new copyist, who was also a gifted poet, first became acquainted through such common interests. In the natural course of things, the new helper was introduced to Tameie, whom she would serve as scribe—and eventually much more—for the remainder of his life.

---

1. Akase, "Reizei-ke no so, Tameie to Abutsu-ni," p. 110.

She had been born about 1225, probably into an aristocratic lineage, although records do not make her origins entirely clear.[2] In her mid-teens she was sent into the service of an imperial princess named Ankamon-in (1209–83) who sponsored a salon where two of her sisters were apparently also in service.[3] She was highly literate, as the close attendants of such a figure would have to be. Long before, ladies-in-waiting in the courts of high-ranking women had established a tradition of literary service that provided a model for later aspirants. Murasaki Shikibu, the author of *The Tale of Genji*, the great poet Izumi Shikibu, and other ladies-in-waiting such as Sei Shō-nagon and Akazome Emon (early eleventh century) had provided services to earlier salons in the same way. The same patterns held in the 1300s. Like those famous women, Shijō (or Uemon no Suke) — the name by which the woman went in Ankamon-in's entourage — came from the middle class of Kyoto society and had evidently received the sort of education that would allow her to rise in court circles, probably with the end goal of becoming the wife of a courtier. She was thus participating in a tradition as old as Tameie's own.

We know little of Shijō's career in Ankamon-in's chambers, except that not too long after beginning service there, as if living out the plot of a court romance, she fell in love with a high-ranking man whose ardors soon cooled. She would later describe this incident in her life in a short prose confession of sorts. *Utatane* (Fitful Slumbers) became a minor classic only later, after her reputation was made in other ways; it is doubtful that it was widely circulated during her own life.[4] But looking at it now one sees that, in addition to being a good story-teller, Shijō was already a fine stylist and an accomplished poet who knew the canon of Japanese literature. Like many young women of her class, she had evidently been groomed to literary service and even after her misfortune was probably looking for a proper situation.

After leaving the salon of Ankamon-in, Shijō spent some years that are largely unaccounted for, ending up for a time in Hokkeji, a nunnery in Nara, the ancient capital south of Kyoto in Yamato Province. While there, she became pregnant and had to leave the temple, returning to the lay world but continuing to live nearby. Some sources

---

2. Ibid., pp. 108–9.

3. Tabuchi, *Abutsu-ni to sono jidai*, p. 126.

4. Wallace, "Fitful Slumbers: Nun Abutsu's *Utatane*," offers a full translation of the text.

indicate that she married at that time, others only that she was in-
volved in an affair. Whatever the case, she gave birth to a daughter
and later to at least one other child and probably another. Later por-
traits depict her as a very beautiful woman and the record leaves little
doubt that she had many suitors.[5]

Evidently while she was at Hokkeji, Shijō came to the attention
of Tameie's daughter.[6] When she began her copywork for Tameie
she was probably in her late 20s, more than 20 years his junior and
probably still attached to another man. Over time, however, she
became his secretary, his disciple, and in the end his chief female
companion, producing at least three children. The first, known to
us only as the monk Jōkaku, was born in 1258; later, in 1263, came
Tamesuke; and two years after that, Tamemori (1265–1328). By the
time Tameie was writing his elegiac poems on Mount Ogura, she
was a fixture in his house.

There was nothing unusual in the relationship. Tameie and his
former primary wife (*shōshitsu*) evidently had separated some years
before, making Shijō a "second wife" and not a secondary wife—
a point on which many early sources have apparently been confused.[7]
Shijō was from a proper background, literate, and no doubt a good
companion and a help to Tameie in his studies. Those facts were
enough to justify her new place in the house. Furthermore, she and
her boys seemed to fill the void left by the loss of the daughter
who had introduced Shijō into Tameie's household—who had died,
not long before Tamesuke's birth. Apparently she had been Tameie's
favorite among his children, and there is even some evidence to
suggest that he believed young Tamesuke was her reincarnation.[8]
Tameie wrote a group of poems in the daughter's memory titled *Aki
no omoi no uta* (Poems on Autumn Musings), which is one of the
texts—in this case not known before—recently discovered on the
shelves of the Reizei *obunko*.[9]

As the years went by, Shijō made it known that she did not think
of herself as a mere concubine of Tameie's declining years. Early on
in the relationship, she had lived in a separate residence located

5. Tabuchi, *Abutsu-ni to sono jidai*, pp. 93–112.
6. Akase, "Reizei-ke no so, Tameie to Abutsu-ni," p. 110.
7. Tabuchi, *Abutsu-ni to sono jidai*, p. 152.
8. Fujimoto, "Shōen to Reizei-ke," p. 239.
9. See Tanaka Noboru, "Reizei-ke ga tsutaeta kotenseki," pp. 147–48.

not far from the palace of her former patron, Ankamon-in. By 1267, however, evidently she was living at Tameie's Chū-in villa (also read Nakano-in). By then it was obvious to Asukai Masaari (1241–1301), a visitor to Tameie's Saga villa in the autumn of that year, that Shijō was a central part of the old man's life. Masaari was the son of Asukai Norisada (d. 1266), whose daughter was Tameuji's wife and the mother of his heir, and thus in close contact with the main Mikohidari house. Perhaps for that reason, Shijō took his visit as an opportunity to make her position clear, knowing that what she said would be dutifully reported to Tameuji, Tameie's eldest son and heir.

Masaari, who came from an important poetic house, visited Tameie in Saga to ask him questions about poetic lore—first of all, about *Kokinshū*, which as the head of a poetic house Tameie had been studying since his childhood. Poets were expected to memorize the first of the imperial anthologies and to use it as a model; and Tameie had received secret teachings on the text—interpretations of poems, proper readings of obscure passages, lore about poets, and so forth—that any enterprising poet would covet. In the brief diary account that he left of his visit, however, Masaari dwells on the details surrounding the old man's lectures on *The Tale of Genji*, for which Shijō, somewhat to Masaari's surprise, acted as lector. Nearly a century before, Shunzei had recommended reading Murasaki Shikibu's tale as essential for anyone wishing to develop a properly courtly sensibility.[10] Teika, too, had been a scholar of the tale, leaving behind what is still today one of our earliest and best manuscripts—the so-called *aobyōshi* rescension, which he had produced after years of exhaustive textual study. Now Tameie was following in the family tradition by offering his lectures, which probably consisted of brief exegeses of bothersome passages from the tale.

Masaari seems to have been most impressed, however, by Shijō's role in the proceedings rather than by Tameie's lectures. His entry for the 17th day of the Ninth Month, for instance, has this to say: "As lector, the female master of the house was called in. She read from within the blinds. It was fascinating. Her way did not resemble the way ordinary people read; she must have had training."[11]

---

10. Shunzei says this in his "words of judgment" appended to round 506 of *Roppyaku-ban uta-awase*.

11. Hamaguchi, *Asukai Masaari nikki chūshaku*, pp. 48–49.

Masaari's account goes on to relate how after the lecture, when saké was being served, Shijō, whom he again calls the "female master of the house" (*onna aruji*) summoned him to her curtains. There she went on about how Tameie was the grandson and son of compilers of imperial anthologies and himself a compiler, but that, sad to say, many people these days did not seem to credit such things— although she was quick to add how certain she was that Masaari, as the grandson of one of the compilers of *Shin kokinshū*, would be not among that number. Masaari concludes the section by saying, "The male master of the house, a sensitive man and getting on in years, got very drunk and fell to weeping." Abutsu was anxious to get across two messages: that Tameie was not getting the respect he deserved, especially from his heir, Tameuji, and that she claimed literary credentials herself.[12]

Our primary source for the next few years in the story of Tameie and Shijō is another of Tameie's sons by Renjō's daughter—one Genshō (1224-1303), by this time a monk for several decades—who is anything but objective when it comes to his opinion of the goings-on at the Saga villa. From Genshō's perspective, Shijō was an interloper out to take advantage of Tameie in his dotage. She was relentless, he notes, in pursuing special favors for the sons of his declining years, at times even interfering in poetic affairs. Her ultimate goal, as Genshō sees it, was to appeal to the old man's emotions, asking him to think carefully about the welfare of her sons after his own death. Tameuji was narrow-minded, she said; he could not be trusted to care even for his own full brothers, let alone Tamesuke and Tamemori. Then came the final barb: if Tameuji is so lacking in sensitivity, should not Tameie be teaching the Way of Poetry to sons with more sympathetic hearts?[13] Since the time of Shunzei, the Mikohidari house had stressed over and over again that poetry came from the heart. To accuse Tameuji of being insensitive was therefore also to impugn his qualifications as a poet and as head of the house.

Independent evidence shows that Tameuji did have little use for his younger brother, Tamenori; nor had things been cordial between Tameuji and his father for some time, especially since the old man had gone into retirement. However, one need not believe that this was all a result of Shijō's machinations to accept that she made good

12. Ibid., p. 49.
13. Quoted in Yanase, *Kōchū Abutsu-ni zenshū*, pp. 265–67.

use of the opportunity the situation offered. Tameuji, it may be imagined, had indeed neglected his father somewhat since the latter's retirement and his mother's departure; and he probably did think of his brothers—particularly those still in lay life, who were in some ways a threat to him—as nuisances at best. Meanwhile, Tameie had grown very attached to the children of his old age. One is tempted also to think that Tameuji was made uneasy by Shijō's talents as a poet, which were at least the equal of his own, although in such a male-dominated society it is hard to believe that she could have been perceived as a real threat to him on that score. In any case, as Tameie's health declined, the stage was obviously being set for the sort of conflict that is familiar to any student of aristocratic life.[14]

No doubt Tameuji, now in his mid-40s and serving as a major counselor at court, was scandalized by what he heard from Masaari and others. He had male children of his own—Tameyo (1250–1338), Tameo (precise dates unknown), and Tamezane (1266–1333)—to provide for, all of them still in the lay world and expecting careers at court. All signs are that he had no patience for Shijō and her campaigning, and little sympathy for his aging father. His initial response, however, was probably to ignore them as much as possible, that is, until Tameie, with Shijō's active encouragement, began to revise his will. As a court official, Tameuji was at the peak of his power and probably had many sources of income, including temporary revenues from some offices, gifts and fees from patrons, and perhaps even overt help from the estate of his grandfather, Renjō. But he knew that the future of his house would clearly be in jeopardy without the estate rights that had served as its financial foundation for the past century.

At first, in 1269, Tameie asked his heir only for the rights to one estate, Koshibe in Harima Province, which he asked to be signed over to Tamesuke as a source of support for a modest career at court. However reluctantly, Tameuji agreed to this, with the proviso that the rights would return to the main house if Tamesuke ended up with no male progeny—all in accordance with prevailing custom. But in subsequent years Tameie wrote out a number of documents, all addressed to Shijō—who had by this time taken the tonsure as Abutsu—that revoked more unreservedly the terms of his earlier bequest of all his goods and properties to Tameuji. To these documents Tameuji did not—probably would not—add his seal. So intense was his reaction

---

14. Akase, "Reizei-ke no so, Tameie to Abutsu-ni," pp. 114–18.

to the prospect of the loss of revenues from Yoshimi Estate, in fact, that he begged his father to relent, and got it back. In return, though, his father was adamant about granting to Tamesuke the rights of proprietorship (*ryōke*) and stewardship (*jitōshiki*) over Hosokawa Estate. As noted earlier, the *jitōshiki* had been granted to Teika by the Kamakura government in reward for his service to the shogun Sanetomo in a gesture both rare and lucrative. Hearing that his father had turned over revenues that provided Tameie with more than half of his annual income to a child not yet into his teens and as yet totally unproven in court circles, Tameuji can only have concluded that his father had taken leave of his senses.[15]

There is much to suggest, however, that Tameie was entirely in control of his faculties but just very angry with his heir, and not just over the question of how the sons of his old age would be supported after his death. A hint as to his state of mind comes in a letter to Shijō dated 1273, and is not about lands but books, specifically Teika's diary, *Meigetsuki*[16] (Record of the Full Moon):

The diary . . . is thought by others to be of no importance, but I consider it my most precious possession. My other children and grandchildren care nothing for it, having no inclination at all to look at such a thing. Consequently, I bequeath it to Tamesuke. Tell him to memorize what it says about the conduct of activities at court and learn how people should comport themselves on public occasions. . . .[17]

Ironically, Tameie, who had not been quite studious enough to impress his father as a young man, now felt the same way about his eldest son. Tameuji did not understand the Confucian virtue of filial piety; he was not concerned enough about the family's glorious past and what it would take to sustain that legacy into the future. Some other documents also indicate that Tameie had never been overly impressed with Tameuji's poetic talent, although the central issue was probably less literary than emotional.[18] No one could argue that reading *Meigetsuki* would improve one's performance as

---

15. For a summary, see Fujimoto, "Shōen to Reizei-ke," pp. 238–54. See also Akase, "Reizei-ke no so, Tameie to Abutsu-ni," pp. 115–18, and Atsuta, "Reizei-ke ryō no seiritsu," p. 7.

16. Here I give the standard pronunciation for the title. I should note, however, that the Reizei prefer *Meigekki*.

17. Brower, "The Reizei Family Documents," p. 448.

18. Kaneko, "Fujiwara Tameuji no shōgai."

a poet; but still, Teika's scribblings were tied up with the identity of the house and as such, Tameie felt, deserved more respect.

The letter bequeathing Teika's diary to Tamesuke was written in the Seventh Month of 1273. Just a few months before, beginning on the 21st day of the Fourth Month, Tameie had taken Tamesuke and Tamemori along on a pilgrimage to Hie Shrine. This was no casual visit: the group spent 100 days there, doing devotions and no doubt discussing the Way of Poetry. Tamesuke was only ten years old at the time, but already he had been studying composition, with his mother and his father, for at least five years, having been given as an encouragement a copy of the *Sandaishū*—the *Three Collections,* referring to the first three imperial anthologies—at the age of three. Evidently he showed more promise, perhaps, than had Tameuji at that age. Fifty years before, in connection with a pilgrimage to the same shrine, Tameie had made the decision to dedicate himself more seriously to the family Way established by Shunzei and Teika. Now he was hoping that with the help of the god, Tamesuke, the older of his young sons, would be able to do the same.

The bequest of Teika's diary makes it clear that Tameie was thinking about a career for Tamesuke at court, the only place where the information in the diary would be truly useful. The boy had been given his first court rank at the age of two and was serving as gentleman-in-waiting of junior fifth rank by the age of seven: not the most auspicious of starts, but still one that gave reason for hope. But the nature of the rest of Tameie's provisions, which amounted to turning over all of his treasured manuscripts, makes sense only if he had hopes for the boy as a poet. Conceivably, Tameuji already had copies—although perhaps not originals—of many of the texts in the family library. Tamesuke, on the other hand, would need such resources to be able to compete in the poetic world, which is what Tameie wanted to make it possible for him to do.[19] In any case, even in the 1200s originals had more value than copies.

Further evidence of Tameie's hopes for Tamesuke comes in the form of a primer he wrote around this time. The title of the work, *Eiga no ittei* (The Foremost Style of Poetic Composition), is prosaic indeed. The work does not claim to have much to say to advanced

---

19. Akase, "Reizei-ke no so, Tameie to Abutsuni," p. 118. See also Fujimoto, "Kami Reizei-ke to Shimo Reizei-ke," p. 4.

poets. From the first sentence, it is written in an avuncular tone that makes it easy to imagine Tameie addressing his son directly:

The composition of poetry does not necessarily depend upon talent and learning. However, although it has been said that poetry comes from the heart, without practice it is impossible to gain a reputation for skill. It may happen that a man will compose a superior poem spontaneously, but later, when he has written something inferior, his former high reputation will be sullied and people will speak ill of him, asking from whom he had obtained his earlier verse. When that happens to a man, he may become discouraged and give up poetry altogether. Such a thing can lead only to the decline and ruin of this art. Consequently, first you must learn certain essential matters and then give expression to your own thoughts and feelings in each of your poems.[20]

His own father had told Tameie that poetry comes from the heart, not from learning (*saigaku*).[21] But in catechizing his own child, Tameie evidently felt the need to elaborate, as well as to expand on specific features of practice rather than on abstractions. The rest of the work deals, in textbook format, with fundamentals such as the necessity of properly understanding the fixed topics (*dai*) on which almost all poems were written at the time, the importance of creating poems that sound smooth and polished when read aloud, the need to avoid using "extra syllables" (*jiamari*) in most circumstances, the proper handling of "borrowed lines" from older poems (*honkadori*), and so on. At the end, Tameie even gives a list of phrases that are so strongly identified with particular poems of the past that "they must on no account be employed again."[22] Throughout, the emphasis is on the mastery of craft rather than on individual creativity, on the development of a disciplined imagination rather than on a search for unfettered originality. It is thus a primer on practice and not a work of critique or interpretation, and as such was aimed at young practitioners of the art, first of all.

Teika's *Maigetsushō* (Monthly Notes, 1219) was probably also intended for a beginning student and says some very similar things.[23]

---

20. Brower, "The Foremost Style of Poetic Composition," p. 399.

21. See Carter, "'Seeking What the Masters Sought': Masters, Disciples, and Poetic Enlightenment in Medieval Japan," p. 42.

22. Brower, "The Foremost Style of Poetic Composition," p. 426.

23. "To produce an ill-conceived poem not only becomes a source of misery by inviting the scorn of others, but can also cause a person to grow tired of poetry and may even lead to the decline of the Art itself." Brower, "Fujiwara Teika's *Maigetsushō*," p. 413.

But whereas the earlier work included extended philosophical passages, Tameie's handbook includes long lists of exemplary poems and concrete advice for poets who had to face the daunting challenge of performing in the public arena of the court—which was where poets would ultimately be tried, tested, and either succeed or fail. For such poets, Tameie's caution was "never [to] produce anything that is extremely bad."[24] Whereas he ends on a more positive note, saying that a poet should aim for phrasing and conception "that sound new and unusual,"[25] the overall message of the text is more cautious. Prepare well through constant practice, the Patriarch declares, and then when put on the spot always think things through, be careful—that last phrase being one that he recommended for poets to keep in mind even into old age. No doubt this would be the best advice for Tamesuke as he began to put himself and his work on display before his peers. Tameie knew that his father's own early poems had provoked controversy, which was something that a poet in his young sons' situation could not afford to do. Scholars who dismiss Tameie's advice as no more than evidence of his conservative stance on stylistic issues have therefore missed one of the primary purposes of the text, which was to prepare students for the practice of a profession, for participation in a discourse that demanded very specific kinds of competence.

It was for this reason that Tameie's primer would be so highly regarded by later generations of the Reizei house. Again, Tameie seemed to be following the lead of his father, whose *One Hundred Poems by One Hundred Poets* was held in similar high esteem. Tameie's "how-to book" was likewise useful for those seeking an entrée into the world of court poetry via the advice of not just a prominent poet but also an experienced teacher.[26] For decades he had played the role of tutor to young men of other families, and in his final years he was doing the same for Tamesuke and Tamemori, whose days under his tutelage were now numbered. A handbook was something they could turn to even in his absence for practical

---

24. Brower, "The Foremost Style of Poetic Composition," p. 429.

25. Ibid.

26. Iwasa Miyoko argues that Tameie set out to create a "system that would allow anyone following it to compose poems." See Inoue, "Reizei-ke no rekishi 3: Tameie, Abutsu-ni," p. 5.

guidance and support in how to pursue the Way of the Mikohidari house.

Tameie continued to tutor his younger sons and also other students. Included among these were his grandson Tamekane (1254–1332) and granddaughter Tameko (d. 1316?), children of his second son, Tamenori, who also could expect little encouragement from the main house.[27] Moreover, it is clear that in his relations with his grandchildren he was not holding anything back, passing on secret teachings on the *Sandaishū* and in 1274 having them move into his house for a time in order to complete their apprenticeships.[28] Meanwhile, Abutsu, too, continued to instruct her sons, preparing them for the profession of poetry and for court service. No doubt Tameuji was incensed at these affronts to his honor as head of the house: his own father's home was becoming a meeting place for the opposition.

But Tameie was well into the decline that would carry him off, and neither side wanted a public confrontation. Tamesuke was too young to take on adult responsibilities, as both Tameie and Tameuji must have known. Tameuji, on the other hand, was a central figure in the coteries around the various members of the imperial family and the highest noble houses. For the time being, the latter's position as head of the senior lineage was unassailable. He was an experienced poet—both artistically and socially—with whom Tameie had shared much. Furthermore, any sort of public scandal could easily lead to something that would bring embarrassment to the family, a fate that Tameie had warned against explicitly in his primer. When there was talk of a new imperial anthology in 1274, Tameie was therefore quick to put forward Tameuji, who was after all head of the Mikohidari house, as compiler.[29] His affection for Abutsu and his younger sons aside, he would do nothing to fundamentally jeopardize the position of the house that his ancestors had worked so hard to build. Tameuji was a competent poet, a responsible official, and undeniably the only member of the family in a position to undertake a task so crucial to the welfare of the house. This in itself is enough to show how aware

---

27. Huey, *Kyōgoku Tamekane*, p. 22.

28. See Tabuchi, *Abutsu-ni to sono jidai*, p. 248, and Imatani, *Kyōgoku Tamekane*, pp. 40–41.

29. Katayama, "*Shoku shūiwakashū*," p. 410; see also Kobayashi, "Tameie, Tameuji, Tameyo."

Tameie was that the practice of poetry, however grounded in aesthetics at one level, had a political dimension that could not be denied.

ONE WONDERS what would have happened if Tameie had lived to the age of Shunzei, seeing Tamesuke into his majority. But he did not. In the Fifth Month of 1275 he died, leaving the fate of Tamesuke and the final disposition of his various holdings undecided. As was customary, Tamesuke briefly vacated his post as gentleman-in-waiting to mourn his father. When he was reappointed several months later, it was under the darkest of clouds. No doubt most people at court thought that his cause — in the imperial court, in any case — was lost. Now that Tameuji had male heirs of his own, the oldest in his mid-20s and already serving as a middle captain at court, there was no point in waiting in the wings on the chance that scandal, illness, or death might make ascension to the head of the household possible.

In such predicaments, the standard course was for young men to take the tonsure and give up hopes of secular careers, opting for a quiet life in some temple compound. Forsaking court life, however, did not mean forsaking poetry and polite society altogether. Many men had gone on to considerable prominence in poetic circles after appeasing their family superiors by relinquishing claims to high rank and office. One can only imagine that some around them encouraged Abutsu's sons to do the same.

Left to himself, Tamesuke might have been forced to take that course and give up on maintaining a lineage of his own. But he was not alone, and anyone who counted him out was underestimating the resourcefulness and tenacity of his mother. After her husband's death, Abutsu dedicated herself to prayers for her late husband's soul but also to preparing her son for a career at court. Before dying, Tameie had told her to pursue her son's interests aggressively, and apparently she was ready to do so.[30] Almost immediately, for instance, she again noised it about that Tameuji had been an unfilial son, never properly attentive to his father's wishes. When, predictably, Tameuji countered by refusing to recognize the validity of the letters she had in Tameie's hand granting her son estate rights and manuscripts, she began the long process of seeking a settlement through the authorities.

---

30. Atsuta, "Reizei-ke ryō no seiritsu," p. 6.

As fate had it, a formal order for an imperial anthology finally came to Tameuji at about this same time. It was his first. As if to emphasize his dominance, no other compilers were named, not from other poetic houses, and not from other branches of his own—putting him in the same company as Shunzei, Teika, and his father. When 100-verse sequences were solicited from major poets of the day, all Tameie's relations were included in the group—Abutsu herself, Tamesuke, Tamenori and his children, Tamekane and Tameko, and even Tameaki (ca. 1230s–after 1295), another son of Tameie by still another wife.[31] But when the anthology was made public in late 1278 it was obvious that it was a partisan effort that gave generous attention to Tameuji's patrons, his in-laws in the Utsnomiya family, and his own sons while almost entirely passing over his younger brothers and nephews. As if in a final act of protest, Tamenori—Tameuji's younger brother, who had spent most of the previous 50 years in a feckless attempt to make a place for himself in an inhospitable world—died in the Fifth Month of 1279, cursing Tameuji for years of rejection. When his mother, who was also the mother of Tameuji, died later that same year, the last impediment to open warfare between the senior and junior branches of the Mikohidari house had been removed.[32]

The battle lines were as clearly drawn as in any court poetry contest. On one side were Tameuji and his immediate family and all of his patrons at court, including the reigning emperor, Go-Uda (1267–1324; r. 1274–87), and Retired Emperor Kameyama (1249–1305; r. 1259–74). On the other were Abutsu, her sons Tamesuke and Tamemori, and a host of other disaffected parties. These included most prominently Tamenori's son, Tamekane, an energetic and talented young man who, as noted above, had studied under Tameie and was already making a name for himself at court. Records do not disclose at this point how many other friends Abutsu could count among the nobility. Tamekane had inherited his father's relationship with the Saionji family, for whom he was effectively serving as a retainer, according to a trustworthy contemporary source.[33] It is also certain that Former Regent Sanetsune (1223–84), of the high-ranking Ichijō line, was at least friendly toward Abutsu. Though hardly in the

31. Inoue, *Chūsei kadanshi no kenkyū, Nanbokuchōki*, pp. 6–8.
32. Kaneko, "Fujiwara Tameuji no shōgai," p. 46.
33. Huey, *Kyōgoku Tamekane*, p. 22.

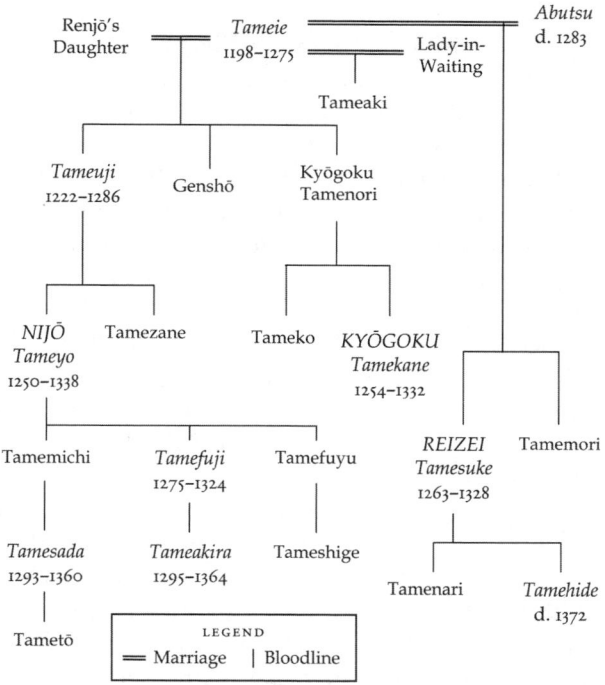

Chart 2 The Nijō, Kyōgoku, and Reizei Lineages

majority, then, Abutsu was not without allies. Not all of those choosing to affiliate with one side or the other were truly concerned about poetry, of course. Some alliances were purely political, resulting from positioning on other issues, including most specifically succession disputes in the imperial family.

Records show that even after Tameie's death Abutsu stayed on in the capital. From the beginning, however, she must have known that she could not win her case in Kyoto, where her appeal would ultimately go to the Retired Emperor, who was one of Tameuji's patrons. When she sent up her suit, it was probably with little hope of victory and only as the first step in what was sure to be a drawn-out process. When her suit was summarily dismissed, she made plans to go to the East Country and take up her cause before the military government, which had final jurisdiction in cases involving *jitō* rights of the sort Teika had been granted by Sanetomo years before. There were precedents for such a strategy. Both Shunzei's granddaughter—known confusingly as Shunzei's Daughter—and Tameie's first wife had presented suits in Kamakura. Just 30 years earlier, the widow of a man named Koga Michimitsu (1187–1248) had been embroiled in a conflict with Michimitsu's heir Michitada (1217–50) that was in almost every respect identical with what was transpiring between Abutsu and Tameuji. That Abutsu would have heard of such matters seems certain.[34]

Abutsu left for Kamakura midway through the Tenth Month of 1279, prepared to take her chances with the Hōjō regents, whose legal policies were apparently more likely to tolerate overturning a previously established will. Tamesuke, who was now a court official for whom an absence from official duties would be ill-advised, had to stay in Kyoto, living in the house on Reizei Street that would thereafter give his lineage its name. Tamemori did the same. No doubt there were friends of the family among the nobility who would look after the young men while Abutsu went to fight their cause.

It took her two weeks to make the trip, which she undertook mostly on horseback with only a small samurai escort. The record she left of the journey — titled *Izayoi nikki*, (The Journal of the Sixteenth Night Moon) — was probably written based on notes made along the way. It would become her most widely read literary work, although again only in later years. As was conventional in such travel journals, which by this time formed a growing genre, she used it primarily to memorialize famous historic sites with her own poems: places with storied names such as Meeting Hill, Eight Bridges, Sleeve Port, Swift River, and, of course, Mount Fuji. But from the beginning she also made it clear that her journey had a very specific purpose. Although only obliquely, she in fact attacks Tameuji in the first sentence by suggesting that he was evidently not acquainted with a certain old Chinese text — *The Classic of Filial Piety* — that according to legend had been hidden in a wall in the home of Confucius: "Young people of our day never even dream that the title of that book taken from a wall long ago might somehow apply to them. Likewise, the injunctions my husband left behind, though clear and constant as the flutter of kudzu leaves, have all been for nought."[35]

The "injunctions" (*isame*) Abutsu alludes to were of course the contents of Tameie's letters to her, which were as clear in their intent, she intimates, as the pale green, almost white undersides of kudzu leaves fluttering in the wind. By saying that they were "for nought"

---

34. Tabuchi, "Nyōbō kajin no ie ishiki: Abutsu-ni made," pp. 20–21.
35. Yanase and Takei, *Izayoi nikki, Yoru no tsuru chūshaku*, p. 5.

she refers directly to her recent treatment by the Kyoto tribunals. In the next sentences she goes on to complain of her rejection by both the offices of the emperor and his "loyal ministers" in the Rokuhara Shogunal Headquarters and then expresses her commitment nonetheless to honoring the command of her husband as stated in his final words: "Support the Way; nurture my children; pray for me in the next life."[36] It was Tameie's final words, she suggests, that kept her from doing what many women would have done in the same situation and abandoning her sons for a life dedicated wholly to Buddhist devotions. Instead, she banished from her mind all hesitation, realized the futility of staying on in Kyoto, and determined "to yield to the enticements of the sixteenth-night moon"[37] beckoning her to Kamakura and a chance to win the privileges her sons would need to compete in the aristocratic arena.

EVEN TODAY, Kamakura presents a contrast to Kyoto in almost every way. Kyoto sits in a broad basin, some miles across, virtually surrounded by high, wooded mountain ranges; Kamakura follows the contours of a half-dozen narrow valleys, each separated from the other by what must be called low hills by comparison. Kyoto is at the confluence of several major rivers, while in Kamakura there are only streams. Kyoto is well inland; Kamakura verges on the sea.

There must have been many other contrasts in the late 1200s, when Abutsu arrived there. Kyoto was an old city, by any measure, whose population was in the hundreds of thousands. Kamakura was an upstart with a population of only 75,000 or so, whose history as a cultural center could be traced back only to the middle of the previous century.[38] It was then that a precursor of Minamoto no Yoritomo had established a residence for himself in the Kamegayatsu area, probably because the site was near the crossroads of two thoroughfares, one going east, the other west. Already at that time several temples, including the Sugimotodera, were located along the roads, and not far away in the village of Yuinohama was a local branch of the Hachiman Shrine of Iwashimizu back in the Home Provinces. But the truly crucial event in the city's development had come only

---

36. Ibid., p. 6.
37. Ibid.
38. Ishii, "The Distinctive Characteristics of the Environs of Kamakura as a Medieval City."

in the 1180s, when Yoritomo had chosen the site as his stronghold. Establishing his headquarters on a rise at the end of the largest of many valleys that open toward the sea, he also moved the shrine, which would thereafter be known as Tsurugaoka Hachiman Shrine, from the coast to the same site, claiming it as the tutelary shrine of the Minamoto clan. Then he built a broad, straight avenue from Yuinohama leading up the shrine compound, which would become the center of a new city that was in essence a fortress.[39]

In the years to come, Yoritomo's family and retainers had come to live in Kamakura, as had his in-laws of the Hōjō family, who after his death dominated the office of regent in the warrior government. In addition, more temples and shrines—the Shōchōjū-in and the Yōfukuji to begin with, and later the Jufukuji, the Daijiji, and Amidist temples such as the Kōmyōji—were built there, often under the direct sponsorship of the shogunal government. The growth continued after Yoritomo's death, as the Hōjō family, the true rulers of the Kamakura government, continued to use the city as its base of operations during the shogunal tenure of Teika's student Minamoto no Sanetomo and his successors. By mid-century, the place had become the preeminent city of the eastern seaboard, boasting a large population of perhaps 40,000—warriors, servants, artisans, shopkeepers, and priests of every sect and persuasion.[40] Especially after the Hōjō regents decided to appoint men from Kyoto—first from the high nobility and then from the imperial family itself—as shoguns, the influence of court culture on the seat of the military government was great. So, despite its strong affiliations with the warrior elite, the shogun's capital was not completely foreign territory to people of the imperial court. Visitors from the Home Provinces were commonplace.

Abutsu arrived in the East Country at the very end of the Tenth Month of 1279. The place where she ended up living, she notes in *Izayoi nikki*, almost half of which describes her life after arriving in Kamakura, was called Tsukikagenoyatsu, The Valley of Moonlight. It was an elegant name for what she describes as a rather dreary place: "The place where I live in the East Country is called The Valley of Moonlight. It is at the foot of a hill, close to the shore,

---

39. Ibid.

40. Pierre Francois Souyri gives the population in the early 1400s as about 50,000. Souyri, *The World Turned Upside Down*, p. 99.

and terribly windy. Standing next door to a mountain temple, it is a peaceful place, but very forlorn, where the sound of the waves and the wind in the pines never stop."[41]

Scholars take the "mountain temple" as a reference to Gokurakuji, a temple of the Ritsu sect that had been founded just 20 years before. Located down the coast road to the west of Tsurugaoka Hachiman Shrine and the government compounds that surrounded it, the site must have been exactly as she describes it: peaceful but somewhat isolated and close enough to the sea to be troubled by tidal winds. Who provided the nun with these lodgings we do not know, but her rooms can only have been more rustic than those she had been accustomed to in Kyoto.

Abutsu consoled herself with prayers for Tameie's salvation and an active correspondence with family and friends back in the capital. A poem sent to a lady she had known years before during her service to Ankamon-in reveals her disconsolate feelings as the year 1279 drew to a close and she thought of "the cloudy realms"—a metaphor for the imperial palace—that she had left behind.

> My spirits fading,   I gaze off
> into a sky grown dark   as my mood—
> to where in those cloudy realms,   far away, it starts
> to snow.[42]
>
> *kiekaeri / nagamuru sora mo / kakikurete / hodo wa kumoi zo / yuki ni nariyuku*

The unnamed lady replied speedily, as did many others, throughout the months of the new year. In summer, mail service was interrupted for a time by a disturbance on the road from Kyoto caused by warrior monks of the great Tendai monasteries of Mount Hiei and Miidera. Finally, though, a large bundle of letters came in the Eighth Month. Among them was one from Tamesuke, who enclosed a set of 50 of his poems for her to look over, critique, and return. Ever the tutor, she "marked" 18 of his compositions as excellent, and jotted in replies to a few of the poems that were obviously personal in their overtones. At the end, she appended a poem encouraging him to continue on the Way, speaking for his father.

> "If he could see this,   ah how happy
> he would be!"   I cannot but muse—

---

41. Yanase and Takei, *Izayoi nikki, Yoru no tsuru chūshaku*, p. 188.
42. Ibid., p. 200.

daring then to take his place   and weep aloud
for joy.[43]

kore o miba/ika bakari ka to/omoitsuru/hito ni kawarite/ne koso nakarure

No record survives to tell us so, but Abutsu must have begun her appeals to the Kamakura authorities soon after her arrival. Her journal ends, however, in the Eighth Month of 1280, without another overt mention of her practical purposes for leaving her sons behind in Kyoto. No swift conclusion to her case was likely. Her stay in the East Country, which she and her sons had perhaps hoped would be of short duration, would drag on for months and then years.

No one can say exactly why Abutsu's pleas did not receive a more timely review. It is certain, however, that the government in Kamakura was busy with other things, most especially with the threat of another invasion by the Mongol armies that had already conquered China and Korea and were threatening Japan. In the winter of 1274, an armada of 900 ships had overrun the islands of Tsushima and Iki and then attacked Hakata on the mainland of Kyushu. The attackers had been defeated then, thanks largely to the timely—miraculous, say the witnesses of the time—intervention of a storm that destroyed much of the enemy fleet. Since then, the government had sent several envoys coming with demands of fealty to Khubilai Khan back with their heads in their hands—literally—and hardened defenses along the coastlines where a new attack was most likely to occur. This was an expensive proposition, however, that put strain on both government institutions and on bonds of loyalty with warlords who had to bear the cost of defense with no hope of booty at the end.

Nearly two years after Abutsu arrived in Kamakura, the Mongols mounted another invasion, in the summer of 1281. This time, the armada was even larger, totaling more than 4,000 ships and 140,000 men. The Japanese troops, helped by ramparts erected in advance, held back the assault for several months, but again it was only the fortuitous arrival of a typhoon that won the day. Needless to say, the whole episode left the government in a permanent state of unease. Today we know that the Mongols would never again attempt to take the Japanese islands, but the government at the time knew no such thing. For years to come it felt obliged to maintain readiness on the Kyushu coastline and to stay ready to repel another alien

---

43. Ibid., p. 258.

force. No doubt talk in the government chambers in Kamakura was of little else.

Whether because of other factors or because of the Mongol threat, Abutsu had still by the fall of 1281 heard nothing about her case. Not one to sit idly and wait, she had begun in the summer before to take her case before a still higher court—the native gods. In all, over the three-year period ending in the First Month of 1282, she would send 100-poem sequences as votive offerings to ten of the great Shinto shrines of the East Country. Native poetry had its mythical origins in the words of the gods, she knew, and the custom of asking for their help in poetic matters was a time-honored one. For each of the sequences, she wrote on the same set of topics, which are no different from those used in more secular settings—"Haze" and "Warblers," in spring, "Plovers" and "Ice" in winter, and so on. The point of the exercise was more to put one's best work forward as an offering than to plead one's case directly through the content of the poems. When the topic allowed it, however, Abutsu did manage to work in a more personal statement. In a poem on "Showers" presented to Ima Hie Shrine, for instance, the emotion expressed seems clearly her own:

> While to the rain   I add my showers
> of tears,   I would ask this:
> Is the empty sky above   also troubled
> in its thoughts?[44]
>
> *towaba ya na / namida to tomo ni / shigure shite / munashiki sora mo / mono ya omou to*

Poems presented to shrines of course became shrine property, but no doubt many poems like this one from the sequences were soon being repeated by Kamakura literati—friend and foe alike—who knew the reasons behind Abutsu's journey. She had raised a strong voice in Kyoto and she would continue to do so in Kamakura.

There were of course fewer places to hear that voice—poetically, that is—in the East Country. But it should not be supposed that poetry had no part in the cultural life of Abutsu's new home. Just as in the imperial capital, salons tended to form there around important personages. In Kamakura, this meant first the man holding the office of shogun. As noted above, in the early years, these men had been descendants of Minamoto no Yoritomo; then the office had gone to

---

44. Yanase, *Kōchū Abutsu-ni zenshū*, p. 353.

courtiers of the Kujō lineage; and more recently imperial princes had been appointed to the post, at the insistence of the Hōjō regents. All who held the office were encouraged to pursue interests in the courtly arts as a way of maintaining identification with traditional symbols of power. In turn, they too proclaimed poetry, along with calligraphy, kickball, and music, as among the necessary accomplishments of high-ranking military men.[45] Sanetomo, as mentioned earlier, had studied with Teika; indeed, so intense was his interest in literature, both Chinese and Japanese, that he had gone so far as to establish in Kamakura a government office, the Gakumondokoro, or Scholarship Office,[46] devoted to the idea of encouraging study among the members of his entourage. Since 1210, the shogunate, meaning really the Hōjō clan first of all, serving in their capacity as regents to the holder of the ultimate office, had been sponsoring its own poetry meetings, all conducted according to the etiquette of such meetings in Kyoto. In time many warrior families were also holding their own meetings and contests. Along with the names of Tameie's in-laws in the Utsunomiya family, poetic records of the time list names such as Gotō, Shimazu, Naitō, Wada, Tō, Sasaki, Nikaidō, and Ashikaga. Already some of these names had appeared in imperial anthologies; many more would do so in the future.

On the same lists are also found many noble names. Some were of priests serving in positions in the many prosperous temples and shrines of the area, such as Tsurugaoka Hachiman Shrine, where one Ryūben (1208–83), a son of the Middle Counselor Shijō Takafusa (1148–1206) who was also a devotee of _uta_, spent 50 years as head priest. Many more, however, were courtiers per se who ended up in Kamakura, some for reasons similar to Abutsu's. Among these there were those who came to stay, partly because they saw opportunities for gaining wealth and power in the East Country that might not be possible in Kyoto.[47] Ōe no Hiromoto (1148–1225), a descendant of the great Heian period scholar Masafusa (1041–1111) of that same lineage, had led the way by putting his scholarly and administrative talents to work for the shogunal government in 1184. A whole train of expatriates had followed, many of whom also became centrally involved in the world of poetry at the same time. Then there were

45. Yonehara, _Sengoku bushi to bungei no kenkyū_, p. 6.
46. Tonomura, _Kamakura no kajin_, p. 50.
47. Ibid., p. 124.

men such as Asukai Norisada, father-in-law of Tameuji, and his son Masaari, the young man who had visited Tameie and Abutsu in Saga some years before. As experts in both poetry and kickball, the Asukai found their talents much in demand in Kamakura, perhaps even more so than back in Kyoto, where the competition was more intense. Norisada himself had spent 40 years in Kamakura, from 1225 until his death in 1266, and Masaari also lived there much of the time in a house in Izumigayatsu, where he held poetry meetings of his own. These were only a few of the scores of courtiers who spent long periods of their lives in the warrior capital. As might be expected, many married their sons to the daughters of wealthy warlords, making for even stronger bonds in the future.[48]

So Abutsu was able to bide her time usefully while waiting for a hearing on her petition before the shogunate. Political affiliations doubtless made her unwelcome in some quarters, since Tameuji too had his supporters in Kamakura, particularly among the members of the Utsunomiya clan. But there was ample room for her to maintain an active profile, thus exercising her talents and keeping her claims as the representative of Tamesuke before the public. Holding study classes on both *The Tale of Genji* and poetry, she rapidly became well known in literate society.[49] One comic poem written by a partisan of the Hōjō family to Tameuji describing her, with some sarcasm, as "the old nun—here so long—who just keeps hanging on" is further evidence that she was making her presence known.[50] Her association with Tameie and her own considerable knowledge of poetry, court classics, and court lore made her a figure to be reckoned with.

All indications are that Abutsu still maintained constant contact with Tamesuke and Tamemori in the capital. Certainly other poets must have come for critique, and the sons may even have visited her occasionally, although the records do not say so explicitly. Her concern for their future is apparent in everything we do know about her life in Kamakura. One of her last acts, in fact, was to write a primer of poetic composition whose primary audience—in addition to the

---

48. Ibid.

49. Tabuchi, in *Abutsu-ni to sono jidai* (p. 175), quotes from a polemical essay by Imagawa Ryōshun to substantiate this point.

50. Tonomura, *Kamakura no kajin*, p. 280. The author was the priest Kōchō, a son of Fujiwara Sanefumi (of the Hachijō lineage), who had gone to a member of the Hōjō clan as a ward and lived in the East Country.

unnamed person of substance who may have been its first reader —
can only have been her heirs. In later history it became known as
Yoru no tsuru (A Crane in the Night), but the only title attached to
it in its earliest form was probably "The Teachings of Abutsu the
Nun." As far as we know, it became a sort of last testament.

Abutsu begins her essay by saying that there are already many
treatises and handbooks available for aspiring poets — probably re-
ferring to the works of Teika and Tameie, and beyond them to the
more pedantic works of the Rokujō poets — which she recommends
as obvious sources for the preliminary stages of study. Her task,
she says, will be to concentrate on a few matters of particular impor-
tance learned over many years, as she says, "as I shared the company
of someone well-regarded as a poet" — an unvarnished allusion to
Tameie.[51] Among these matters are some already dealt with in *Eiga
no ittei*, such as the proper treatment of topics, allusive variation, and
so on. Rather than simply repeating his advice, however, she gives
practical examples meant to illustrate the importance of going be-
yond what convention might suggest.

When composing on compound topics in the love category, it seems that true
adepts (*jōzutachi*) rely on indirect expression rather than revealing the ration-
ale (*kotowari*) of the topic overtly. As I recall, for instance, this is a poem on
"Meeting Once, but Not Again," by the Kyōgoku Middle Counselor [Teika].

> As the colors fade   on the fall leaves
> of Mino,   I cross Naka Pass —
> growing ever farther away   from the Gate
> at Meeting Hill.

> *iro kawaru / mino no nakayama / aki koete / mata tōzakaru / ausaka no seki*

He wrote many poems in this way. If I were to compose on the same topic, I
fear I would end up with something like, "to meet once and not again — / ah,
what a painful kind of love."[52]

Here Abutsu says little that presages the distinctive features of the
Reizei approach to poetic composition that would emerge in the work
of her son and his descendants, except perhaps for a positive attitude
toward rhetorical skill (*jōzu*).[53] On the other hand, she is consistent

---

51. Yanase and Takei, *Izayoi nikki, Yoru no tsuru chūshaku*, p. 352.

52. Ibid., p. 361. Teika's poem in no. 1470 in *Shūi gusō* and also appears as
no. 1232 in *Shoku kokinshū*.

53. See pp. 98–99 below.

with Tameie—and also Shunzei and Teika—in insisting on subtlety and on emphasizing the display of sensibility rather than knowledge as the goal of composition.

The same basic pattern is repeated throughout the essay. First she cautions against the use of archaic words or phrases too closely associated with recent poets—again following a theme of Teika and Tameie—but then also suggests that there is really no reason poets of the present cannot be as good as those of the past. What she wants to communicate, in slight contrast to Tameie in his primer, is that her sons should study from the past but also look forward to the future as participants in a still-vibrant tradition. "Between the past and the present," she says, "there really should be no difference."[54] At the heart of her essay, however, is a desire to present the Way of Poetry as a sacred Way, analogous to the Buddhist Way she knew so well from the sutras she had been reading in Tameie's memory for years. Just as monks and nuns have scriptures, you have the old anthologies, she tells her students: look there for guidance.

Abutsu knew that after her death Tamesuke and Tamemori would likely have no teachers but the old books to guide them. Her advice was therefore for them to make the Way of Poetry truly the substance of daily life, turning all experience into instruction.

One who would compose *uta* should put proper feeling (*nasake*) concerning the happenings of life (*koto ni furete*) first of all: coming to know the sadness of things, clearing one's mind, and inscribing in one's eyes and heart the scattering of the blossoms, the falling of the leaves, the colors that dew and showers bring on in the various seasons. Then in everyday life (*tachii ni tsukete*), you must keep your mind on the question of how to render this into poetic conception (*uta no fuzei*).[55]

These sentences present classic doctrine that can be traced back to the *Kokinshū* preface where the composition of poetry is described as putting into words the feelings aroused by the events of life. But in encouraging poets to keep their minds on poetic composition in everyday life—literally, "whether standing or sitting"—she is also encouraging an approach that makes poetry the very substance of life. One cannot help thinking that it was meant particularly for her sons, whom she wanted to carry on in a family Way that she knew would

---

54. Yanase and Takei, *Izayoi nikki, Yoru no tsuru chūshaku*, p. 403.
55. Ibid., p. 411.

demand daily practice and dedication. Economic conditions would not allow her sons to model their lives on their father's. To maintain their place in the scheme of things, they would have to be teachers, arbiters, masters of the Way of Poetry. For them, especially, the question of how to render experience into poetic expression, and in that sense to be dedicated experts, would be crucial.

At the essay's end, Abutsu describes herself in self-deprecating terms as "an old, rotting tree in a valley," who would not compare her own poetic abilities to those of the great court ladies of old. Yet anyone looking at her life must conclude that her actions were fundamental in establishing a foundation for what would become the Reizei house. Tameie had left his sons his own primer and tried to leave them his books and estates, as well as a social network. But in addition to her travel record and confessional tale, Abutsu too left her teachings on poetry and on *The Tale of Genji*, becoming the first woman in the history of the courtly tradition ever to do so, in written form, at least. And she too left a social network, along with as many of the books as she could keep from Tameuji's reach. Finally, she left them an example of tenacity and patience that future generations would see as an inspiration in their own struggles in the literary field.

It must be noted, though, that when Abutsu died, on the 29th day of the Fifth Month of 1283, nearly four years since coming to the shogunal seat, she still had not been able to accomplish her chief mission. Tameie's estate rights had still not been restored to her progeny. Some early texts indicate that she died in Kyoto, but recent scholarship argues that she was probably still in the East Country, still awaiting a decision on her suit against Tameuji. A stele erected in the Taishō period marks the spot near Gokurakuji where her house supposedly stood; and there is a small memorial stele in a tiny grotto beside a road in the outskirts of the city that claims to mark her grave but that also dates from fairly recent times.[56]

Reizei Tamemura, writing more than 400 years later, saw Abutsu's place in the history of the Reizei lineage clearly, going so far as to append the honorific suffix *kō* to her name—making her "Lord Abutsu" (Abutsu-kō):

Abutsu devoted herself to Tameie and helped him along the Way for many years, taking charge of the manuscripts of the house, which were then

---

56. Ueno Takeshi, "Gokurakuji to Tsukikage no yatsu," p. 5.

passed down from Tameie to Tamesuke. We revere Lord Abutsu greatly because it is entirely owing to her that we now have in our house all the texts we possess, from books in the hands of Shunzei, Teika, and Tameie, to the secret teachings on *Kokinshū*, and *Meigetsuki*."[57]

The estates she had been unable to retrieve were from the beginning destined to pass from family hands in later years in any case: that was the nature of property in court society. The future of the family, Abutsu had the foresight to see, would be dependent on its surest link to the past—its poetic traditions and its books.

It must have felt like a near death-blow to Tamesuke when in the Sixth Month of 1286 the Retired Emperor decided in favor of the senior house on the issue of who had claim on the proprietary rights (*ryōke-shiki*) to Hosokawa Estate and also ordered that the Mikohidari collection of manuscripts be turned over to the Nijō. But Tamesuke was not ready to give up, even if proceeding meant using deception. Securing revenues from Hosokawa Estate was beyond his power, but he could resist turning over the manuscripts that his father had left to him in order to give him a chance to succeed as the head of branch of the Mikohidari at court. In order to comply outwardly with the order of the Retired Emperor to turn over Tameie's library, which Kameyama probably thought of as much the property of the court as of any one lineage, he therefore sent Tameuji some manuscripts of little value, holding back the real treasures.[58] These his mother had probably left in the safekeeping of some ally—perhaps Ichijō Sane-tsune, a former imperial regent whose status would provide a barrier against hostile inquiries.[59] Tameuji, who, as Tameie had said, seems not to have paid as much attention as he should have to his father's library, probably did not know exactly what his half-brother possessed and was helpless to prove that anything had been kept back.[60]

---

57. Miyabe no Yoshimasa, *Yoshimasa Kikigaki* (Yoshimasa's Notes), p. 689.

58. Ogawa ("Kadōka no hitobito to kuge seiken," p. 196) argues that the expertise of the various houses in courtly arts and disciplines was probably perceived of as necessary for proper governance and thus not simply a matter of "private" property or expertise. See also Inoue, *Chūsei kadanshi no kenkyū, Nanbokuchōki*, pp. 214, 428.

59. See Inoue, *Chūsei kadanshi no kenkyū, Nanbokuchōki*, pp. 214, 428.

60. An old story told by Kitabatake Chikafusa (1293–1354) in the mid-1300s accuses the Reizei of turning over forgeries to the senior house—stored in two boxes, one inlaid with the image of a cormorant and the other with the image of a rabbit—the contents of which Tameuji knew nothing about. See Brower

So a court order was not enough to make Tamesuke give up the fight. If he had learned anything from his mother, it was perseverance. Since the question of the more valuable *jitōshiki* had yet to be decided by the officers of the shogun, the heir of the Reizei house now had to steel himself for the coming competition. So important was this issue to Tameuji that he left for Kamakura immediately after receiving news of the decision in Kyoto. He was no stranger there, having family ties in the Utsunomiya house and numerous students and friends among the shogun's attendants. All in all, he was as beholden to military patrons as the Reizei were, and he may in the end have spent more time in Kamakura than Abutsu did.[61]

No doubt the head of the Mikohidari house fully expected another decision in his favor. He had come all the way to Kamakura to secure it, after all, and was using his many connections to that end. But in another ironic twist Tameuji too died, in the Ninth Month of that very year, on the 14th day, before ever hearing the outcome of the case. A few scant remarks in some earlier records, some traceable to Abutsu, record that he had had various bouts of sickness in the past, beginning back when he was a child.[62] Whether anticipated or not, death came for him when he was only 65. In his anger at Abutsu, he had gloated that her early death at around 60 was the work of the gods who were punishing her for defiance of the leader of the house. Tamesuke and Tamemori now could gloat in turn. Tameuji's son and heir, Tameyo, a 36-year-old consultant of the third rank at the imperial court, was already far senior to Tamesuke, a mere 21 years old and languishing at senior fifth rank. On equal ground or not, it was now up to Tamesuke to pursue the suit into the next generation.

---

and Miner, *Japanese Court Poetry*, p. 351. More recently, however, inconsistencies in that story and textual evidence have led scholars to the conclusion that the texts in question — *Sangoki* (A Record of Thrice Five Nights), *Gukenshō* (Notes on My Foolish Views), *Guhishō* (Notes on My Foolish Secrets), and *Kirihioke* (The Paulownia Brazier) — all attributed to Teika and all widely circulated in the late medieval era, were not forged in that context but rather out of a desire on the part of some East Country poets to bolster their authority through the concoction of new "secret" teachings. See Klein, *Allegories of Desire*, pp. 52–53 and 95–99, and Atkins, "Fabricating Teika."

61. Kaneko, "Fujiwara Tameuji no shōgai, pp. 46–47. See also Ogawa, "Kadōka no hitobito to kuge seiken," pp. 206–7.

62. Kaneko, "Fujiwara Tameuji no shōgai," p. 38.

THREE

Wisteria Valley

AS LONG as his mother was able to represent the cause of the house in Kamakura, Reizei Tamesuke appears to have stayed in Kyoto, where he tried to maintain a proper profile as an heir of Teika and Tameie. After his mother's death, however, he traveled east to arrange for the disposition of her property and belongings. Within several years he was spending a good deal of time there, taking her place as a lobbyist with the shogunate. This meant being absent from the court, of course; but in the current political situation he had little hope of further advancement in the imperial ranks in any case. His nephew and ally, Kyōgoku Tamekane—who was ten years his senior—had almost gone to Kamakura in his teens, when prospects in the capital had not looked good.[1] Perhaps he now encouraged Tamesuke to follow the same course.

Evidence shows that Tamesuke retained a house in Kyoto, probably for all of his life—a place located on Reizei Street, from which his lineage would get its name. He also had possession of Tameie's old Chū-in Estate in Saga, at least for a time.[2] Throughout his life he would often travel back to the capital, many times staying for months at a time. After 1286 or so, however, it was in the shogun's capital in the East Country that he became prominent as a poet.

In Kamakura, Tamesuke had a house in an area called Fujiga-yatsu—"Wisteria Valley"—near Jōkōmyōji Temple, perhaps on land

---

1. Imatani, *Kyōgoku Tamekane*, pp. 40–41.
2. Atsuta, "Reizei-ke ryō no seiritsu," p. 7.

granted him from patrons of the Akabayashi house.[3] Across the narrow valley was the Jufukuji, a Zen temple founded in 1200 by the renowned Zen monk Eisai (1141–1215) under the sponsorship of Hōjō Masako (1157–1225), whose grave marker was located behind the temple, next to that of her husband, shogun Minamoto no Yoritomo; closer by was a temple founded at Yoritomo's request by the equally famous monk Mongaku (1139–1203). Whereas it was only a few minutes as the crow flies from the shogunal offices near Tsurugaoka Hachiman Shrine, the site was separated from the center of the city by steep hills and was in that sense somewhat isolated. Nevertheless, this did not keep people away. Before long, Tamesuke was holding poetry gatherings there, probably involving literati friends of his mother. With her usual perspicacity, Abutsu evidently had set up a network of supporters to help him ease into poetic practice in the stronghold of the shogunate.

Maintaining dwellings in both Kyoto and Kamakura must have been an expensive proposition. His ability to do so at all leads one to suspect that his father and Abutsu had managed to pass on some additional financial resources for his support as well. Although in 1289 Tamesuke won another round in the family suit over the *jitō* rights to Hosokawa Estate, the senior house would not let the matter rest: Tameyo, Tameuji's heir, filed a countersuit that overturned the 1289 decision in 1291, and only in 1313 would a final judgment in favor of the Reizei claims to the *jitō* rights come down. In the meantime, Tamesuke had to rely on whatever other incomes he had, the generosity of patrons, and revenues from literary services. The colophons to various texts suggest that already he was making use of the texts he had inherited from his father, lending copies of some prized texts out, no doubt for fees and favors, and adding to the collection whenever possible. One record indicates that he was very careful in his lending strategy, requiring an oath from the lender not to allow anyone else to make a copy without his explicit permission.[4] This was a practice that would continue for centuries to come, indeed, down to the twentieth century: the library was not a lending library but a

---

3. Ueno Takeshi, "Jōkōmyōji to Tamesukebo," p. 5. The Akabayashi descended from Hōjō Nagatoki (1230–64), a student of Tameie. Various sources make it clear that members of the Akabayashi house were among Tamesuke's supporters in the East Country. A grave marker for Tamesuke, erected in the mid-Edo period, stands on the hill that rises behind Jōkōmyōji.

4. Inoue, *Chūsei kadanshi no kenkyū, Nanbokuchōki*, p. 72.

family safe of sorts, access to which had to be restricted if it was to retain its value. It was as such that it gave a special status to those who owned it. Assuredly, this status had purchase in Kyoto first of all; but Tamesuke soon learned that it could serve as capital in Kamakura as well, even for a junior branch of the Mikohidari house. While never giving up on the ambition of advancing in rank and office, he resigned himself to long periods of separation from the day-to-day events of court life.

In Kyoto, too, developments were not entirely unfavorable, at least for a season. Some years before, a succession dispute between the sons of Emperor Go-Saga had split the imperial line into two competing lineages, called the Daikakuji and the Jimyō-in after residences near Kyoto where their originators resided. Not surprisingly, the split had polarized the court families as well, who tended to line up on one side or the other according to their affiliations and perceived advantage. Tameyo, a close confidant of Kameyama of the Daikakuji side, of course made his place there, and prospered accordingly under the reign of Kameyama's son, Emperor Go-Uda. Predictably, though, when Go-Uda stepped down in 1287 to make way for the ascension of a candidate from the Jimyō-in line—in keeping with the terms of a political arrangement worked out by the Kamakura government—the opposition rose to the occasion.

In the field of poetry, the champion of the Jimyō-in cause in Kyoto was again Tamekane, the son of Tamenori, who had studied at Tameie's knee along with his uncle Tamesuke in the old days. Since 1280, Tamekane had been serving as poetic tutor to the crown prince, and now that his patron—Hirohito, known more popularly by the name Fushimi (1265–1317; r. 1287–98)—had ascended as emperor, he made every attempt to take advantage of the situation for his own house. Partly because of his own intellectual interests and partly out of a desire to distance himself from his competitors on the Nijō side of the family, Tamekane advocated a progressive style influenced greatly by his study of Buddhist texts, ancient Japanese poetic anthologies such as *Man'yōshū*, and the more innovative works of his great-grandfather, Teika. Tameyo of course did everything he could to obstruct these advances, but with the emperor standing behind him as a patron, Tamekane proved hard to impede. When Go-Uda stepped down as emperor, so did Kameyama as senior retired emperor (*jisei no kimi* or *chiten no kimi*), ceding that position to Go-Fukakusa (1243–1304; r. 1246–59), founder of the Jimyō-in line. In a matter of months the political situation shifted in favor of Tameie's disaffected sons and grandsons, although evidently not to the extent that Tamesuke felt ready to return to the capital permanently.

As might be expected, the party newly in power, knowing that its tenure could be only temporary, acted swiftly. Tamekane lobbied for promotions in court rank and office, which he received, rising two full steps in rank and proceeding from middle captain to middle counselor in a few short years. On several occasions he was designated as special envoy for Fushimi at important celebrations, raising his profile at court. Most significantly, he was able to gain from his patron sponsorship of poetic events over which he could preside — contests, dedicatory sequences, and so forth. Poetic activities crowded the calendar at Emperor Fushimi's court, and by 1293 the emperor was ready to issue a command for an imperial anthology, the crowning event of any reign for poets and their patrons.

As senior heir of the Mikohidari house, Tameyo had to be included among the compilers; not to do so would be to put in question the foundations of aristocratic society. But to counterbalance the latter's influence, Fushimi appointed three others to share the duties and the honors: a member of the Asukai family, a member of the Kujō family, and his favorite, Tamekane. Not to be excluded, Tamesuke, in the early summer of 1294, went up to Kyoto in person to petition the emperor to be added to the list, with Tamekane's endorsement and perhaps his outright encouragement. His arguments were straightforward: first, that he had received both books and teachings directly from Tameie, and second, that he had practiced the Way for years — a clear reference to his role as tutor, teacher, and master of ceremonies in the East Country. Against the inevitable charge that he was not in the capital most of the time and in that sense not a proper courtier, he replied that this had also been true of Asukai Masatsune, one of the compilers of *Shin kokinshū*, and that, besides, in Kamakura he was "in service" to the shogun, who was after all an imperial prince.[5] The tone of his petition was importunate, to say the least. To everyone — especially to Tameyo and his heirs — it was apparent that the anthology project represented an attempt by the opposition to defy the authority of the main house.

From the beginning, then, progress on the project was hampered by bickering among the compilers and their constituencies. Rather than showcasing the glory of Emperor Fushimi's reign, events

5. Ibid., p. 30.

served only to reveal dissensions within the Mikohidari house. Ostensibly, the arguments were over ceremonial or literary matters, such as "What month should be chosen for the handing down of a formal command?" "What previous anthology should be taken as a model?" and "What, if any, poems from the *Man'yōshū* should be included?"[6] But the motives behind the controversies were political as much as they were philosophical. Indeed, the political posturing incident to the project may be said to have brought the conflict in the house out into the open as nothing had ever done before. In response to Tamesuke's request to be added as a compiler, in a letter to the emperor Tameyo dismissed his uncle from the East Country as a pretender to authority and put forward his own eldest son, Tamemichi (1271–99), as a candidate instead.[7] At the same time, he began to solicit help in his campaign from other members of the family more friendly to his cause, most specifically Genshō, whose attacks on Abutsu, alluded to above, may have been written around this time.

Although the records do not say exactly when, by sometime in 1295 it appears that Tamesuke returned to the East Country with the future of the anthology still unsettled, as it would remain for some years, during which time one of the chosen compilers fell ill and other obstructions, natural and manufactured, arose. Even with the assistance of Tamekane, life in the capital had doubtless been difficult for the head of the Reizei house. In Kamakura, on the other hand, he had a client base and his services were in high demand. Since 1289, a younger brother of Emperor Fushimi, Prince Hisaakira (1276–1328), had been serving as shogun. Needless to say, a man from such a background was bound to be interested in the courtly arts. He even set up a Poetry Bureau of his own in Kamakura, where he held frequent poetic gatherings for his retainers, mimicking events in Kyoto.[8] It is no surprise that Tamesuke, as head of a Mikohidari lineage, should in this context be looked to for leadership. His years of instruction under Tameie and his library sources made him a valuable resource, especially in public settings, where everything—the seating order of participants, forms of address, placement of furnishings, ways of reading poems aloud, even the type of paper used to record events—was dictated by precedent. Speaking of another poet

---

6. Huey, *Kyōgoku Tamekane*, pp. 30–33.

7. Ibid., p. 33.

8. Inoue, *Chūsei kadanshi no kenkyū, Nanbokuchōki*, p. 67.

in a similar situation, a high-ranking courtier would later make a telling comment: "One didn't think of him as having inborn talent, but he was particularly good at composing poems for formal occasions (*hare no uta*) . . . and he had committed all the poems of *Kokinshū* to memory. One thought of him as truly a man of the Way."[9]

The evidence of his poems shows that Tamesuke *did* have some poetic talent, but the passage is significant in hinting that what was expected of men of the poetic houses was professional competence rather than artistic excellence. Thanks to his training, Tamesuke could produce a proper poem on demand; more importantly, he could offer his patrons and students a fund of knowledge — of history, of technique, of etiquette, of convention. Rather than a "poet" in the more modern sense of that term, then, he was a literatus whose profession was to provide services in the field of poetic discourse — which would likewise be the calling of generations of the lineage after him. The texts in his library and the knowledge and expertise he possessed as a "man of the Way" — a phrase that is used interchangeably with "house man" (*ie no hito*), referring directly to the heirs of poetic houses[10] — were his greatest assets. As one who knew the protocols for various kinds of gatherings, as well as the canon and literary history, a man of his experience was indispensable to the proper conduct of gatherings. When the shogun, or for that matter any person of prominence in the area, planned meetings or commissioned sequences, it was Tamesuke who was consulted on the choice of proper topics, the sending of appropriate letters of invitation, and everything else.

In this sense Tamesuke was fast becoming a literary jack-of-all-trades, available as private tutor in all forms of Japanese poetry, lecturer on the court classics, and master of ceremonies for poetic events, public and private. One record, for instance, says that he invited guests to his house for what can only be characterized as graduate seminars, following a custom inaugurated by his mother:

At his Fujigayatsu residence, he would have people choose poems that they liked from the first eight imperial collections — six poems taken from the seasonal books, love, and miscellaneous topics — and then lead discussions on their merits. Or again, he would have people choose by lot chapters from *The Tale of Genji*, which they would then write about, thereafter discussing good and bad points under his supervision. This was done in

---

9. Nijō Yoshimoto, *Kinrai fūtei*, p. 185.
10. Ibid., pp. 183–85.

order to encourage people to examine things carefully. His mother had held similar events, at which even people of learning such as Saien were present.[11]

From this passage we learn that in addition to teaching composition to his students, which was still his first obligation as a man of the Way, Tamesuke was running a kind of school for more advanced students. Whether anyone as learned as Saien — the Buddhist name of a prominent member of the local Utsunomiya clan — attended his classes is unknown, but various documents show that his efforts were being rewarded. Not surprisingly, he was even looked to as an authority on the rules and conventions of composition in *renga*, or linked verse, a newly developing form that was very popular among his warrior patrons.[12] As a master of the *uta* form, his dedication was to that form first of all, but when his services were requested in linked verse gatherings he could not very well turn away.[13]

Tamesuke's own younger brother, Tamemori, seems also to have spent most of his time in Kamakura after Abutsu's death. He too was estranged from the main house. Indeed, it appears that once again Kamakura had become a center for the opposition, just as it had been in the days of Tameie's rival, Shinkan. Records show that Tamesuke's half-brother Tameaki, for instance, was living in a cottage there, where he had a small salon of his own; also present, at least some of the time, was Tameuji's son Tamezane.[14] Clearly these younger sons too were finding Kamakura a good arena for their special talents. In addition to providing instruction and other services to Kamakura literati, they were also involved in writing treatises that they claimed represented the "true teachings" of the Mikohidari lineage, some of them involving esoteric religious traditions of questionable derivation but undoubted appeal.[15] As the owner of a thoroughly authentic collection of manuscripts, Tamesuke had less need to be as involved as others in these kinds of activities. We do know from later sources, however, that he was among those who passed on "secret" oral traditions on *Tales of Ise* and thus was active in all dimensions of literary

---

11. Imagawa, *Nigonshō*, p. 83.

12. Kidō, *Rengashi ronkō*, vol. 1, pp. 197–202.

13. Imagawa Ryōshun, a later Reizei partisan, records an anecdote in which Tamesuke chides his own son for wasting a good idea in a linked verse session rather than saving it for his *uta*. See Imagawa, *Rakusho roken*, p. 100.

14. Inoue, "Reizei-ke no rekishi 5: Tamesuke no shūhen to Tamehide," p. 4.

15. See Klein, *Allegories of Desire*.

discourse in Kamakura.[16] Clearly, traffic in manuscripts and secret teachings was becoming a lucrative business. Members of the Asukai, Rokujō, and other "poetic" families also came to the coastal city to ply their trade in a thriving market.

So the shogunal seat was a place where anyone with a valid pedigree could lead an active life as a literatus, as active, in fact, as Tamekane's had been back in Kyoto—although certainly not as prestigious or profitable. To be tutor to the shogun and his hangers-on in Kamakura was one thing; to be tutor to the emperor in the capital city was quite another. Whereas Tamesuke was becoming a literary tradesman of sorts, Tamekane was living the life of an aristocrat as a high officer of the court with stipends to support his lavish lifestyle and little need to "take in students" or employ himself as a master of ceremonies anywhere but in the imperial chambers. By the mid 1290s he was in fact becoming so conspicuous a force in poetic affairs that the main Mikohidari house felt the need to put up a defense against him. Titled *Nomori no kagami* (The Field Guard's Mirror), it was written in 1295 by an unidentified partisan of Tameyo and the senior line, and circulated widely among interested parties. Tellingly, its main subject is not the virtues of Tameyo but the excesses of Tamekane, who is portrayed in its pages as an enemy to all things orthodox. Specifically mentioned are his departures from traditional aesthetic ideals, his impatience with accepted standards of diction, his dismissal of the *Kokinshū* as the only valid model for court poets, and, by extension, his failure to kowtow to the orders of his seniors in the Mikohidari lineage.[17] Genshō's attack had been more limited in scope; the new assault was longer, more thorough, and articulated distinct philosophical differences, however transparently political the motivations underneath.

No doubt Tamekane was little bothered by the fulminations of the Tameyo faction as long as he had the favor of Emperor Fushimi. Ten years Fushimi's senior, he obviously thought of himself as a protector of sorts and as the leader of the imperial poetry salon, which sponsored numerous events, from small gatherings to large poetry contests. Ironically, however, it was this intense loyalty rather than anything explicitly literary that would soon lead to Tamekane's downfall—his first, that is; there would be another rise and fall to come. What specific act, if there was just one, resulted in his censure

---

16. Ibid., pp. 106, 261–64.
17. *Nomori no kagami*, pp. 67–81.

is not clear. What we do know is that in the First Month of 1298 he was arrested by policemen from the shogunate's Kyoto head-quarters at Rokuhara, who detained him for several months before sending him off to a very cold exile on the island of Sado in the Japan Sea. After the Jōkyū Disturbance, Emperor Juntoku had spent time as an exile in the same place.

Tamekane would spend the next five years on Sado. Like most offenders of his rank sent into exile, he was not put in a jail cell but was allowed to live freely in his rustic surroundings, usually sur-rounded by guards. There is no consensus among scholars as to precisely what the real offense was that demanded such punishment. The official charge of "plotting against the shogunate" was invoked so often and so cynically at the time that it is hard to take seriously, even allowing that sentiment against the military government was widespread at court. Most likely, Tamekane's mistake was being too vocal a supporter of the Jimyō-in line at a time when a rotation to the Daikakuji was imminent. It was probably Saionji Sanekane (1249–1322), great grandson of Teika's patron Kintsune and current Kamakura Liaison Officer (*tensō*), who made the final decision to neutralize Tamekane. Although the two men were on the same side in many poetic matters, Sanekane was a politician first and last. After Tamekane's departure, Sanekane quickly obliged Fushimi to give up the throne to his son, who set up a young member of the other lineage as Crown Prince, preparing for a proper transition to a period of Daikakuji rule. The lesson in all this was one that Tamekane should have understood as the heir of Shunzei and Teika—namely, that poets became too directly involved in politics only at their peril.

Tamekane's exile meant the end of any hopes for completion of the imperial anthology that had been ordered back in 1293. He had already done a great deal of work on the project, in the way of collecting materials, at least; but factional strife had impeded any formal progress. When Go-Fushimi (1288–1336; r. 1298–1301) was re-quired to abdicate in the First Month of 1301, turning over the throne to Go-Nijō (1285–1308; r. 1301–8) as Emperor and Go-Uda as senior Retired Emperor, Tameyo and his supporters were again in the as-cendant. Before the end of that year Tameyo was called as compiler of a new anthology, which was presented for imperial accolades by the end of 1303, complete with just over 1,600 poems in 20 books, mostly by partisans of the Nijō cause.

Along with many others, Tamesuke was asked to hand in a 100-poem sequence to serve as raw material for the collection. In it he included poems like this one that reveals the influence of Tamekane:

"Summer Moon"

Gazing out, I wait   for it to rise
from thick forest   on a near hillside —
the moon casting its light   on my garden
from afar.[18]

machiideshi / hayama no ko no ma / shigeriaite / kage tōku naru / tsuki no niwa kana

Not surprisingly, however, it was not poems of this sort but plainer efforts that Tameyo chose for the anthology, such as the following poem on the topic "Year's End":

If only I knew   the new year
would bring an end   to all my troubles,
then I would be more eager   for the springtime
to begin.[19]

waga mi yo no / uki mo hate aru / toshi naraba / chikazuku haru mo / isogare ya sen

By Nijō standards, Tamesuke's melancholy treatment of its topic no doubt came across as a courtly poem in ways the more purely imagistic poem on the summer moon did not. If the Reizei were represented in the imperial project, then, it was in a way that on the surface may have seemed conciliatory but that could also be seen as an assertion of Tameyo's authority over all branches of the house.

How Tamesuke reacted to this we do not know. The only thing we can be certain about is that he must have been pleased to be included in the pages of the anthology, where he saw four of his poems listed. While siding with Tamekane on some issues, the survival of his own lineage had to be Tamesuke's primary concern, and inclusion in an imperial anthology was still the greatest honor that could come to a court poet, and one that conferred a kind of legitimacy upon him as the head of a noble lineage, however junior. As one scholar has remarked, when it came to hope of representation in such projects, most poets were entirely willing to write in any style that promised favor.[20] This was less true of poets in the poetic houses, perhaps, who had more vested interests in maintaining

---

18. *Kagen hyakushu* 25. Cf. poem 77 in *Fujigayatsushū*.
19. *Kagen hyakushu* 60. Cf. poem 192 in *Fujigayatsushū*.
20. Kobayashi, "Kyōgoku-ha kajin to wa ika naru hitobito o sasu ka."

philosophical differences. But for a poet in a junior lineage any opportunity for participation in the most prestigious of courtly poetic venues was no doubt welcome.

RATHER THAN the new imperial anthology, however, it is the headnotes to poems in two other and somewhat later collections, both compiled by people close to Tamesuke in Kamakura, that provide us with our most important sources for his activities during the time of Daikakuji ascendancy at court, which would last for nearly a decade. Both compilations—one called *Shūifūtei wakashū* (Poems in the Style of the Gentleman-in-Waiting, before 1308) and the other *Ryūfū wakashō* (Poems in the Willow Style, 1310)—belong to the genre called *uchigiki,* "preparatory" collections that were probably intended to serve as resources for imperial anthologies in the future. Put together between 1308 and 1310 but in the beginning probably circulated only among intimate members of Tamesuke's circle, the collections are similar to imperial anthologies in structure, and contain poems by the usual range of poets, especially the three patriarchs, Shunzei, Teika, and Tameie. In this sense they are little different from many other small anthologies compiled by other poets hoping for eventual representation in imperial projects. The most distinctive trait of both works, however, is that they include so many poems by Kamakura poets. These include Tamesuke himself, of course, but also the shogun Hisaakira, Tameaki and Tamezane, and a host of other students and patrons of the Mikohidari factions in the East Country. Significantly, Shinkan and his group of malcontents had put together several such works in Kamakura decades before; now it was the turn of Tamesuke and his allies.[21] In this sense, the anthologies were clearly meant to "represent" the salons of the shogun in the present rather than simply to provide raw material for the future. Once again, the younger sons of the house were proclaiming their independence. Tameyo and his supporters back in Kyoto, who must have learned of the existence of the new collections early on, no doubt thought of them as opposition statements.

The poems recorded in the anthologies themselves bear out this characterization. Many, like the following by Tameaki, exhibit rather vividly the growing influence of Tamekane's ideas in their focus on delicate moments of change in an imagined landscape, depicted "as is" with no overt editorializing.

---

21. Tonomura, *Kamakura no kajin*, pp. 168–74.

"Evening Mist"

At the bay's far edge,   again the setting sun
appears   — sinking into the waves;
evening mist hangs on the beach   above a stand
of pines. [22]

ura tōki / nami ni irihi wa / arawarete / yūgiri kakaru / iso no matsubara

It was probably with such scenes in mind that a few years later Tameyo accused Tamekane and his followers of betraying the ideals of his ancestors with poems that "do no more than describe a scene right before one's eyes, with the commonest of words." [23] Of course Tamekane had a different goal in mind: what in his one critical work he characterizes as an attempt to "harmonize" with the landscape and "become at one with the very spirit of heaven and earth." [24] But this was too abstract for Tameyo, who wanted more from a poem— specifically, more courtly language and some overt reference to the sensibility at work in creating the proffered scene, or in other words, a sign that the poem was avowedly "poetic" in its conception. To him poems such as those above, which displayed no classical figures of speech, no traditional wordplay, indeed, little indication whatsoever that the mind at work is the manifestation of a "courtly" sensibility, were hard to distinguish from prose.

For Tamesuke to display his support for Tamekane's ideals so openly must have offended Tameyo as head of the Mikohidari lineage. Equally offensive were the poems that openly express the disgruntlement of those who felt they had been banished from their rightful home. Even a Nijō partisan such as Genshō offered statements that hinted at disaffection:

"Autumn Lament"

A no-account am I,   of no more standing
in the world   than a drop of dew —
giving up on claims and still   finding nowhere
to abide. [25]

to ni kaku ni / kazu ni mo aranu / tsuyu no mi wa / sutete no nochi mo / okidokoro naki

---

22. *Shūifūtei wakashū*, poem no. 109.

23. *Enkyō ryōkyō sochinjō* (Suits between Two Lords of the Enkyō Era), p. 73.

24. Kyōgoku, *Tamekane-kyō wakashō* (Lord Tamekane's Notes on Poetry, 1287), p. 155.

25. *Shūifūtei wakashū*, poem no. 458.

Such complaints could be explained away, since monks—and lay people, for that matter—had been writing such lamentations for centuries, many of which even appeared in imperial anthologies. In this sense, alienation was in fact a conventional topic, a "subject position" that any poet had to be able to occupy. The following lament by Tamesuke's younger brother Tamemori, written under his Buddhist name Kyōgetsu, must on the other hand have been more difficult to dismiss. It expressed resentment with little equivocation over circumstances that all would recognize as anything but generic.

> Written when he was living in the East Country,
> after leaving the world
>
> So hard was life there   that I gave up
> and came away   —I remind myself.
> In the moonlight, though, how I long   for those autumns
> back home![26]
>
> *sumiwabite / ideshi kata to wa / omoedomo / tsuki ni koishiki / furusato no aki*

More than two decades had passed since the younger sons of the Mikohidari line had taken up residence on the eastern seaboard; but still, for Tamemori and Tamesuke Kamakura would never be Kyoto. Giving up on advancement at court, Tamemori had taken the tonsure; and only in 1308, at the age of 46, had Tamesuke finally been advanced to junior third rank, with the office of consultant. The promotion put him among the upper echelons in Kamakura, where his status and talent made him the most prominent local poet. The only proper dwelling for a court poet, however, was the ancient capital, to which permanent return must have remained a cherished hope.

WHAT IN the beginning must have seemed an opportunity to return to Kyoto permanently had in fact come in 1308, when Prince Hisaakira was deposed and a new imperial prince was sent to take his place. To legitimate the act, a charge against the shogun was manufactured, but it was common knowledge that this was a mere expedient. The truth is probably that the Kamakura authorities again wanted a younger and more manageable man in office.[27] Whereas one of his infant sons became the new shogun, Hisaakira was allowed to return to Kyoto and "retire" into the life of a literatus. It goes without saying that many members of his court went with him,

---

26. *Ryūfū wakashō*, poem no. 84.
27. Inoue, *Chūsei kadanshi no kenkyū, Nanbokuchōki*, p. 202.

including, it would seem, Tamesuke, one of whose daughters had recently been taken into Hisaakira's harem, making the Reizei heir a relative as well as the shogun's official tutor in poetry.[28]

There were other reasons to spend time in the capital. In another rotation, a son of Fushimi had ascended as emperor in 1308, with Fushimi himself now taking over the position of senior Retired Emperor and reigning sovereign. With this turn of events, Tamekane, who thanks to his patron's lobbying had been allowed to return to the capital in 1303, immediately began to make plans to take up where he had left off in working toward a new imperial anthology. Rather than being a mellowing influence, the years of exile had evidently served to embolden the head of the Kyōgoku house, who was now in his 50s and as self-assured as ever. By the end of 1310 he had been appointed a major counselor of senior second rank, the highest rank heirs of the Mikohidari rank could expect, and he was as fully involved in Kyoto politics as he was before his trip to Sado. Tameyo's heir Tamefuji (1275–1324) was by comparison only a consultant of junior third rank.

Tamekane's request to take up again the once-abandoned anthology project of course put new fire into the old controversy. No sooner did the plans become public than Tameyo filed a suit with both Fushimi and the shogunate protesting the proposal as rightful heir of the Mikohidari lineage. Two of the original compilers had died, he argued; and how could a man who had been exiled as an enemy of the state be preferred for such an honor over the legitimate heir of the senior line of the same house? A few of his remarks, which we have only in summary form as quoted in a document dated several generations later, reiterate earlier attacks on Tamekane's style as unorthodox in terms of the traditions of the house. Mostly, though, his attacks, which came in the form of a number of suits, concentrate on the issue of authority, which Tameyo claimed to have as a matter of public record.

From the age of fifteen, I studied under my grandfather in order to gain practice in the Way of the house . . . during which time I received the teachings on the *Sandaishū* and all the lore on compiling anthologies. Even on occasions when visitors came to receive the teachings, I was invited to listen in. When he was on his deathbed I received the teachings on the *Sandaishū* again. Can it be that Tamekane is really not aware of all of this? My late father studied under his forebears for 50 years, and I studied under my own

28. Imatani, *Kyōgoku Tamekane*, p. 171.

late father for more than 30 years myself, attending to his every need and never ceasing to talk about the family Way. These are things that everyone knows.[29]

Occasionally, the exchanges between the two men involved more philosophical issues, but for the most part the vocabulary of the debate was unabashedly political. Tamekane could of course also claim to have studied for years under the patriarchs — indeed, under Tameie. But in the end the substance of the exchanges had little to do with the outcome of the conflict, which was decided in Tamekane's favor for the simple reason that it was his great patron, Fushimi, who as reigning sovereign had final say in the matter. Such suits were routine at court, where strife between close family members over office, property, and privilege was a fact of everyday life. Usually the subject was more worldly on its surface, with suits over appointments to offices, estate rights, and other forms of property or income being the most common, but the tactics were the same.

The exchanges between Tamekane and Tameyo say relatively little about Tamesuke, except to indicate that he was considered a friend to the Kyōgoku cause. Tameyo does refer to Abutsu's suit over the estates as a "betrayal" of the house[30] and sees her as one source of some of Tamekane's "mistaken" ideas.[31] One value of the document is therefore that it shows how clearly the senior house thought of Tamesuke as one of Tamekane's allies, as Tamesuke must also have thought of himself. The political situation required such alliances, and at this late date there could be no going back. If nothing else, the statements presented to Fushimi by the rival faction make it clear that the divisions were over secular interests, first of all, making any attempt at literary rapprochement pointless.

So after nearly two decades, work on an anthology representing the Fushimi faction was resumed — predictably, given the politics involved. Also predictably, Tamesuke quickly asked to be added to the list of compilers, just as he had two decades earlier, and again with Tamekane's endorsement. Probably to forestall further countersuits by Tameyo, Fushimi denied Tamesuke's request to be appointed a compiler, instead giving Tamekane sole authority for the project in the Fifth Month of 1311, at which point Tameyo protested by with-

---

29. *Enkyō ryōkyō sochinjō*, pp. 70–71.
30. Ibid., p. 71.
31. Ibid., pp. 76–77 and p. 81.

drawing from attendance at court — but to no avail.[32] In a last-ditch attempt, Tamesuke also sent appeals to several highly placed warrior patrons to intervene on his behalf, but with no success. Appointing Tamesuke would doubtless again have opened to debate the question of participation by other factions, leading to more conflict and more delays. Tamekane did show his goodwill, however, by allowing his uncle an informal role in the project. For the first time, the son of Abutsu was allowed some participation in preparation of an imperial anthology.

In the meantime, and not by coincidence, Tamesuke was finally making advances in rank. By the time the finishing touches were put on the new imperial anthology in 1313, he had been elevated to junior second rank, although he no longer held office. In the anthology, which was titled *Gyokuyōshū* (Collection of Jeweled Leaves), fourteen of his poems were included, putting him almost on a par with Tameuji and well above Tameyo, who was represented by only ten. Also included were the other members of the East Country salons: Abutsu, Tamemori, Tameaki, Tamezane, Tamesuke's daughter (precise dates unknown), along with Tamemori's, and even some of his patrons. That the anthology was so large — it contained 2,800 poems, nearly twice as many as most Nijō anthologies — may have diminished the honor of inclusion in some minds, and it was attacked by the opposition on these and other grounds. Still, the very fact of the anthology's existence must have felt like a triumph to the junior lines of the house. One reason for the inclusion of so many poems was that the compiler knew that another opportunity might not be offered again.

LATE IN 1313, Retired Emperor Fushimi took the tonsure, with Tamekane accompanying him. But, for Tamekane, at least, this step did not signal a withdrawal from worldly affairs. As poetry tutor to Fushimi's son, the reigning Emperor Hanazono (1297–1348; r. 1308–18), he continued to be active in literary affairs, and he was tireless in pursuing advantages for his supporters. Once again, however, he found himself alienated from Saionji Sanekane and other powerful courtiers, who would tolerate his excesses only so long. The final straw came in the Fourth Month of 1315, when Tamekane made a grand progress to the old capital at Nara, to visit the Kasuga Shrine, titular shrine of the Fujiwara clan. Along with him went a large entourage of supporters,

---

32. Inoue, *Chūsei kadanshi no kenkyū, Nanbokuchōki*, p. 154.

including many courtiers, Tamesuke among them. As might be expected, there were sutra readings, kickball matches, banquets, and poetry meetings, all done in high style. The specific offense that is usually noted in attempts to explain the reaction of Sanekane and others is that at one of the events Tamekane arranged to have participants sit in rank order, with himself in a seat alone at the center — precisely as if he were regent or chancellor rather than a major counselor.[33] There can be no doubt that the offense was in fact just such a display of arrogance, although the formal charge was listed as plotting against the shogunate once again.[34]

In the end, then, neither Fushimi nor Hanazono could protect Tamekane from the anger of his superiors. Late in that same year Tamekane was arrested by shogunal officers and again taken to Rokuhara; early in the new year he was sent packing, this time to Tosa — a balmier place than Sado, but just as far away from the affairs of the court. Although years later he was allowed to move closer, as far as Izumi Province, he would never see Kyoto again. His heir, a young grandson of Tameuji named Tamemoto whom he had adopted because he was childless himself, was stripped of his offices and went into retirement along with most other partisans of the Kyōgoku cause.

As noted above, Tamesuke had been among those who accompanied Tamekane to Nara, where he in fact served in the capacity of lector (*kōji*) at a grand poetry gathering. It appears, however, that he was not named among the "conspirators" against the government. One reason may well be that he still had high-placed friends in Kamakura who could protect him from such accusations. It was clearly in Kamakura that he was spending most of his time, making trips to Kyoto only for specific events. The reasons for this remain unclear, since we know that for years his desire had been to return to the imperial city and to take up his place at court. A brief note in one document, however, probably hints at the primary motive for his continued residence in the provinces, even after the ascension of the Jimyō-in line. Dated 1310, the source simply says that he had to return to the East Country for financial reasons.[35] By this time he had been living in Kamakura for nearly a quarter of a century, after all; many members of his extended family still lived there, as did many friends.

---

33. Huey, *Kyōgoku Tamekane*, p. 61.
34. Ibid.
35. Inoue, *Chūsei kadanshi no kenkyū, Nanbokuchōki*, pp. 151, 203.

More importantly, Kamakura was home to most of his primary pa-
trons and disciples.[36] Whether he himself had more formal financial
interests there, in the form of estates or other revenue-producing en-
terprises, is not known. Yet there can be little doubt that Kamakura
was his economic base. Back in Kyoto, the main house dominated
events involving the Daikakuji line of the imperial house, where he
could never be on an equal footing. Jimyō-in circles were more ac-
commodating, perhaps, but there too he remained a junior member.
Among the elite of the imperial ranks, then, he could never be more
than a lowly retainer, whereas in Kamakura he was the leader of the
most powerful poetic coterie of the East Country.

The ultimate proof of Tamesuke's stature in the shogun's capital
is that even after finally winning the suit against the main house over
the Hosokawa Estate in 1313, he stayed there rather than returning
to the house on Reizei Street in Kyoto. Likewise, he remained there
after being made middle counselor in the summer of 1317, resigning
from that office only six months later. By this time his heir, Tamenari
(d. 1330; name also read Tameshige), was on the imperial roles, and
perhaps living in Kyoto at least some of the time. Now in his late
50s, Tamesuke appears to have transferred to his son any hopes he
had left for triumphing in the chambers of the emperor's court.

Even after Tamekane's banishment and the enthronement of a
Daikakuji emperor—Go-Daigo (1288–1339; r. 1318–39), who took office
in 1318—there was evidently no thought of repairing the rift with the
main house. Now that Tamesuke was a duly recognized poet, with
powerful patrons of his own, there was less practical reason to do
so. When a new imperial anthology was being planned in 1318, he
was asked to present a 100-poem sequence; and in other ways, too,
his place in the scheme of things was recognized. As a Reizei disciple
later explained, however, there seems to have been no thought of
naming him as a compiler: "Tamesuke was quite skilled and had
been handed down all the writings, but he had gone to Kamakura . . .
and because he was not residing in the capital, he was not made a
compiler."[37]

Evidently, to be skilled—the Japanese word is *jōzu*, a term that
implied rhetorical virtuosity and imagination but also a certain lack

---

36. Ibid.

37. See the headnote to poem 524 in *Ungyokushū* (Collection of Jeweled
Clouds, 1514). The author is Junsō (precise dates unknown), a disciple of Kido
Takanori (1434–1502), who in turn studied with various Reizei masters.

of restraint—was not enough for success at court.[38] The Reizei heir's affiliations with the provincial city could not be escaped. Besides, political differences had by this late date hardened into differences over matters of diction, style, and aesthetic ideals. Both factions were elitist and conservative by modern standards, but the main house adhered to more rigid rules in virtually all areas, while Tamesuke and his cohorts allowed themselves more latitude in choice of topics, images, and tone. Five of Tamesuke's poems were included in the anthology, but all were conventional works that did not truly represent the breadth of his own style. Now in his late 50s with a distinguished record, he cannot have been pleased with the situation, but that was politics.

That Tameyo still thought of his uncle as the enemy is evident in the former's only extant critical work, *Waka teikin* (Courtyard Teachings on Japanese Poetry), which he wrote around 1326. There he attacks one particular poem from the recent 100-poem sequence as uncourtly:

> "Spring"
>
> Deep into springtime,   they dam up
> the waters   of nearby marshes—
> and then dress the seedling beds   with grasses cut
> in the fields.[39]
>
> *haru fukaki / nosawa no mizu o / sekitomete / kusa kariiruru / oda no nawashiro*

Had this poem been composed extemporaneously for an informal gathering, it might have escaped criticism. But in the world of poetry, differences in venue mattered, as a man of the Way was supposed to know. Traditionally, poems written for meetings in the imperial palace, formal poetry contests, dedicatory sequences, memorial services, and so forth—poems known as *hare no uta*—were expected to adhere to standards of diction and decorum that might be relaxed in private correspondence or at more intimate gatherings in individual homes, where one of the purposes of composition was experimentation and training (*keiko*). As an entry in a poem in a 100-poem sequence solicited in preparation for an imperial anthology, therefore, Tamesuke's rustic scene was to Tameyo's mind an affront to stan-

---

38. The same term would later be used to describe the work of Shōtetsu, who was also affiliated with the Reizei school. See *Karasumaru Mitsuhide-kyō kuden*, p. 516.

39. Nijō Tameyo, *Waka teikin*, p. 134. *Bunpō hyakushu*, poem no. 156.

dards set down by Teika years before, when the patriarch advised against using "words that are too close to the common and vulgar usage, or effects that are rough and frightening."[40]

Of the final lines of this poem someone said, "Surely this is entirely too close to the common and vulgar." When I asked around about what sort of thing actually goes on out in the country, I was told that indeed people put compost in when preparing paddies. If that is the case, then the image is a crude one indeed. No one who had received the teachings of the house and heard its secret lore would produce such a thing. The author must not have known what he was about.[41]

There was little subtlety in this posturing. The "someone" was of course Tameyo himself, whose claim to have to ask elsewhere about "what goes on in the country" was a sharp jab at Tamesuke and other members of the family who—not by their choice, he knew—spent so much of their lives outside of the capital, where they witnessed sights a high-ranking courtier would be less likely to see. Once again, though, the attack at the end came down to a claim of superior authority. The image of farmers working in the paddies might have offended some, no doubt; but what really rankled was the fact that Tamesuke would present such work in a formal sequence as a representative of the Mikohidari house. In the next lines, the head of that house made the charge more explicitly than ever before:

There are some who, hoping to make a name for themselves off in the provinces, revile against the legitimate heads of the house, or claim, "I alone am the one who has received the house's secret teachings." Again, there are those who say groundless things in an attempt to gain credence with their disciples, or say that the current Master is a feeble poet who, when it comes to works of real power or any resonance, can neither adequately judge the works of others or produce anything comparable himself. Countless others believe such charges.

Yet how profoundly deluded these people are! For would it be proper for the head of a household—after giving up rights to estates passed down for generations and instead accepting commissions from the court to compile imperial anthologies—to even consider dispensing things that it keeps most secret to illegitimate sons?[42]

"Illegitimate sons" may be too strong a translation for the Japanese word (*soshi* or *shoshi*) Tameyo uses here, which means any son

---

40. Brower, "Fujiwara Teika's *Maigetsushō*," p. 410.
41. Nijō Tameyo, *Waka teikin*, pp. 134–35.
42. Ibid., p. 135.

other than the recognized heir. There can be no doubt, however, that Tameyo's purpose was to declare his own status as *chakushi*, or legitimate heir, while dismissing Tamesuke and Tamekane—whom Tameyo had attacked in the same way—as pretenders to the family name who should never be asked to undertake the most fundamental duty of the house at court; the compilation of an imperial anthology.[43] All members of the lineage still signed themselves Fujiwara on official documents, of course; but the traditions of that same clan allowed only one man at any one time to serve as heir of the Mikohidari line. Behind the attack is Tameyo's knowledge that his uncle did have many of his grandfather's books, and that the main house would probably never get its hands on them. Likewise, the main house had finally failed in its attempts to secure the rights to Hosokawa Estate. For such "family treasures" to be in the hands of opponents was therefore more than a cause for chagrin.

Despite all of this, at the time he wrote the words above, Tameyo was indisputably the premier poetic figure of the capital, a master with disciples at all levels of court society. Following a predictable pattern, he had managed years before to send one of his daughters— Tameko—into the harem of a future emperor (Go-Daigo) when the latter was still Crown Prince; and she had produced four children, including Princes Muneyoshi (b. 1311) and Takayoshi (1311–37), who would play crucial roles in political events to come. Unfortunately, Tameko herself had died, probably after giving birth to the second of her princes in 1311. The relationship between the Nijō house and Go-Daigo, however, remained strong. Go-Daigo, who had taken office in 1318, was already proving to be an energetic leader, and a man who was truly interested in intellectual matters, especially statecraft, and in the courtly arts. With such a patron, Tameyo had no doubt felt little need to fear detractors in the provinces.

Furthermore, Tamesuke was far away in Kamakura most of the time, not yet tonsured but already in a kind of retirement. Only one other time, in fact, would he get involved in an open conflict with Tameyo. Revealingly, it was again a conflict in which the library

---

43. Ishida Yoshisada argues that the attack here was aimed at Tamesuke, Tamezane, and Tamekane—all renegades from Tameyo's point of view; Inoue argues for Tamesuke and Tamekane. See Inoue, *Chūsei kadanshi no kenkyū, Nanbokuchōki*, pp. 278–79. Tameyo's dismissal of Tamekane as likewise a *soshi* is recorded in *Enkyō ryōkyo sochinjō*, p. 67. See also Huey, *Kyōgoku Tamekane*, p. 166.

became a crucial player—and one that tells us more than any other
event how much cause the main house actually had to resent the
Reizei. The incident happened in the spring of 1328, in Emperor Go-
Daigo's chambers, to the eventual embarrassment of Tameyo. At the
time, evidently Go-Daigo was studying old poetic texts, or perhaps
collecting the same for his own library. In this connection, Tameyo
was asked something about *Korai fūteishō*, a work of poetic criticism
and history by Shunzei, and replied that that text was probably not
really by Shunzei at all, implying that it was either an outright forgery
or a case of mistaken attribution. Whether this means that the Miko-
hidari did not have a copy of this seminal text, which is now consid-
ered one of the primary critical texts of the medieval poetic tradition,
or that the one they had was a copy with a questionable colophon,
we do not know. But we do know that Tameyo's claim soon came
to the ears of Tamesuke, who must have been in Kyoto at the time.

Seizing the opportunity, Tamesuke quickly went to his boxes
and took his prized copy of the work in Shunzei's own hand, with
appropriate signatures, to the imperial palace to show Go-Daigo
how wrong his rival was.[44] Evidently Tameyo did not challenge the
authenticity of the text once the emperor had had a chance to see
it with his own eyes. Just as Abutsu and Tamesuke had eventually
prevailed on the issue of the estates promised them by Tameie, they
now could count another triumph made possible by the boxes of
books left to them by Tameie, which they had carted around from
place to place over the last 40 years. Tameyo withdrew to his fine
mansion, still Go-Daigo's favorite, still a former major counselor of
senior second rank, still head of the Mikohidari house, of course—
still in the superior position, for all that. But he must have been
mortified that his uncle would choose to subject him to such public
humiliation. More importantly, he must now have realized that the
main house would ever after have to be careful about what pro-
nouncements it made about its own textual heritage. Despite all his
claims to hold the "secrets" of the house, it was now clear to all that
there were some things he did not possess, even including texts by
so seminal a figure as Shunzei. Writing the Reizei off as "illegiti-
mate" would not be so easy any more.[45]

---

44. See Kobayashi, "Karonshi no yami," pp. 24–25 and Akase, "Reizei-ke
no so, Tameie to Abutsu-ni," p. 119.

45. Kobayashi, "Karonshi no yami," pp. 30–32.

SO TAMESUKE scored another victory—thanks to his possession of a manuscript, it should be added, that in the late twentieth century would assist in "saving" the house again when it was named a National Treasure by the Japanese government.[46] But he did not have long to savor it, for in the Seventh Month of 1328, he died, probably in Kamakura, though one source says in Kyoto—just as in the case of his mother.[47] Although records say nothing about the cause of his death, there are some signs that it was not unexpected, the chief being that he had for some time been signing over his deeds for various estate rights to his heirs as part of his legacy.

Although also leaving his heirs the manuscripts that had been such an asset to him, Tamesuke left behind no critical writings of his own, probably thinking that it was enough to have given them a lifetime of daily instruction and the primers—*Eiga no ittei* and *Yoru no tsuru*—written by his father and mother. Moreover, his poems remained to represent his philosophy, which was based on the idea of embracing all the styles defined by Teika. This was no doubt what had served him best as the leader of the Kamakura coteries, to whom he was not just a poet but a teacher and guide in all kinds of venues; and it was this example that would be his chief poetic legacy to later generations of the Reizei line. In this sense, Tamesuke was clearly not a member of the Kyōgoku faction, or not simply so—a point worth emphasizing since so many times literary histories note nothing more about him than his close relationship with Tamekane.

This is not to deny that he was an ally of the Kyōgoku cause politically, or even that he was unsympathetic to Tamekane's aesthetics, which by all accounts allowed for more stylistic experimentation than did the approach of the senior house. It is to suggest, on the other hand, that Tamesuke was aware of his status as the head of his own lineage and of the connection of his lineage back to the poetics of Shunzei, Teika, and above all his own father, Tameie. One is not surprised, therefore, to find poems by the Reizei heir that clearly qualify as examples of the style of "deep feeling" (*ushin*), but that also follow Abutsu's advice about relying on producing interesting conceptions rather than straightforward description:

---

46. See pp. 344–47 below.
47. Inoue, *Chūsei kadanshi no kenkyū, Nanbokuchōki*, p. 326.

Autumn: "Autumn Leaves"

What sense would there be   in urging on
the showers?   — knowing as I do
that when the leaves are myriad-dyed   autumn will be
at its end.[48]

shigureyo to / nani isogiken / momijiba no / chishio ni nareba / aki zo tomaranu

Winter: "Snow"

Before the new day dawns   even more
will have fallen   — as I too continue
gazing out from lamplight   into a garden
white with snow.[49]

akuru made / nao zo furisou / tomoshibi no / kage yori mitsuru / niwa no shirayuki

Such topics could easily have evoked the kind of "objective" scenes favored by Tamekane, but instead Tamesuke treated his topics in ways that portrayed not just scenes but imagined emotional reactions to those scenes. While in no way repudiating the other approach, such poems—and there are many like them among the poems he left—provide evidence that the head of the Reizei house wanted to claim all the traditions of his lineage and not just part of them.

This attitude comes across clearly in Tamesuke's personal anthology, *Fujigayatsushū* (also read *Tōgokushū* and sometimes *Fujidanishū*), which also contains poems such as these that are reminiscent of the highly evocative poems of the *Shin kokinshū* age:

Spring: Written on "A Dream in Spring," for a poem contest
at the house of Former Major Counselor Tamekane

Pillowed on my arm   on a night
of blossom scent   and moonlit haze,
I see a dream that all too soon   parts from me
and goes away.[50]

hana kaori / tsuki kasumu yo no / tamakura ni / mijikaki yume zo / nao wakareyuku

Autumn: "Autumn at Mount Takase"

So far from any town,   there is no one
to hear   the call of a stag
sounding out high and clear   on Takase's
autumn wind.[51]

sato tōmi / kiku hito nashi ni / saoshika no / koe wa takase no / yama no akikaze

---

48. *Fujigayatsushū*, poem no. 162.
49. *Kagen hyakushū*, poem no. 58.
50. *Fujigayatsushū*, poem no. 45.
51. Ibid., poem no. 110.

Of the 309 poems in Tamesuke's personal collection, relatively few connect so clearly back to the age of Go-Toba's court. Taken together, however, the poems recorded there do show an attempt by their author to engage fully with the tradition he had inherited. In addition to most of the poems of the 1303 sequence, his collection includes many poems from earlier in his career—beginning in 1292— as well as some from as late as 1323. Although compiled by descendants after his own death, the collection boasts explanatory head-notes that reveal much about both the range of his poetic works, as well as the range of his larger *work* in the literary field.[52] That more than half of the poems he left to posterity were composed for formal, public events (some in Kyoto but many also in Kamakura) held when imperial anthologies were being planned (in 1293–94, 1303–4, and 1319), for example, is evidence of how important such occasions were in the lives of poets. It is also noteworthy that most of the poems in the collection were composed on prescribed topics (*dai*), attesting to the dominance of this form of composition in both formal and informal settings, and evidently in Kyoto and in the provinces. Finally, headnotes show that Tamesuke was involved in all the standard sub-genres of the day—poetry contests in the chambers of the shogun and several emperors, numbered sequences (ranging from three poems to a thousand) commissioned by patrons, poems for memorial services, poem offerings to shrines, poems inscribed on standing screens, poems written extemporaneously, poems written on topics chosen by lot, and finally poems written for amusement for sequences with titles such as "One Hundred Poems on Birds," "One Hundred Poems on Plants," and so forth.

Tamesuke's anthology is therefore like many others of its day compiled in Kyoto. However, in one way—a way that tells us something important about the nature of his poetic practice—his collection is distinctive: namely, in the prominence it gives to poems in one way or another related to the topic of travel. This topic had become conventional long before, of course, and one section of his anthology—poems 193–210—predictably records poems written on such topics for poetry contests and other events. But other poems in which travel is a sub-theme are scattered throughout the collection.

---

52. References in various collections indicate that Tamesuke himself may have left both a personal anthology and a travel record, but *Fujigayatsushū* as we have it now was put together sometime in the late Muromachi period, probably by one of his descendants. See Kazari, "*Fujigayatsushū* ni tsuite."

There are 24 poems introduced with the headnote, "From among his poems on famous places," for instance, as well as several more on topics that involve references to such places—including the one he wrote on "Autumn at Mount Takase," quoted above. Furthermore, headnotes tell us that 30 of the poems in his collection come from a 100-poem sequence titled *Kaidō yadotsugi hyakushu* (One Hundred Poems Written at the Station Stops of the Coastal Road). To anyone acquainted with his career, that he should have produced such a sequence comes as no surprise. In his time Tamesuke had traveled the coast road as frequently as had any other person of his class, no doubt, and headnotes show that many of the poems in the sequence, and others such as the following, were indeed written while he was on the road between Kyoto and Kamakura:

> Travel: When he was going down to the East Country, he was in the Hakone Mountains, taking a road for the first time. He asked someone about some particularly high peaks looming in the distance and was told they were peaks they had already crossed.
>
> How little they seem   like places
> already crossed!   Those Hakone peaks
> rising high above the clouds   that rise high
> above the trees.[53]
>
> *moto koeshi / michi to mo miezu / hakoneyama / kozue no kumo ni / amaru takane wa*

At court, many poets knew travel primarily from famous poems rather than from actual experience. Indeed, Tameie had counseled that when writing on places with a long literary history, poets should follow precedent: "In the present age, pine trees grow no longer along the coast at Ōyodo, and waves break no more against the pines of Suminoe. Even so, you should still follow the old familiar treatment."[54] Since Tameie had also said that when "on the spot" one could base one's poem on actual scenery,[55] his son was not transgressing any rule by writing poems inspired more by direct experience than by book learning. In writing such a large number of poems based on actual journeys, however, Tamesuke did depart from the standard pattern of his time.

The easy explanation for this feature of Tamesuke's work is, again, that he traveled more than other poets did. What is less easy to ac-

---

53. *Fujigayatsushū*, poem no. 210.
54. Brower, "The Foremost Style of Poetic Composition," p. 407
55. Ibid., p. 406.

count for is why he wrote so many poems about places that were not famous—including many that had never been the subjects of earlier poems. Among the places written about in *Kaidō yadotsugi hyakushu*, for example, are places like Hamabe, Odawara, and Hizaka, to name a few, that appear in none of the standard lists of *utamakura* prior to his time and in few thereafter. These poems were thus descriptive by necessity and often presented scenes that, like the following one written on what at the time was an obscure beach in Tōtōmi, seem strikingly original, especially when compared to contemporary poems about truly famous places:

> "Shirasuga in Tōtōmi"
>
> Waves, I first thought,   rushing in to cover
> white sand.   But no—seagulls
> in numbers beyond counting   on a sandspit
> just off shore.[56]
>
> *masago kosu / nami ka to mireba / kazu shirazu / kamome mureiru / oki no hanaresu*

As Sakai Shigeyuki has shown, Shirasuga, located on the coast in what is now Shizuoka Prefecture and later one of the famous 53 stops on the Tōkai Road, was found nowhere on the lists of famous places or in diaries before Tamesuke's time, except for a collection of "banquet songs" (*enkyoku*) compiled in the 1290s.[57] In itself, this fact may seem of limited interest, but when one considers what the presence of poems about such obscure places may reveal about Tamesuke's activities as a poetry master, a new vista opens to view. For, as Sakai argues, the most likely explanation for why Tamesuke wrote poems at places not chronicled in past poetry was that he had acquaintances there, indeed, probably disciples.[58] Other sources corroborate that other poets of the time were feted by followers in towns along the seaboard,[59] and there is no reason to believe that Tamesuke—a man of noble lineage, courtly office, and acknowledged literary status—would not have been greeted in the same way.

Headnotes in his anthology contain references to a number of important people of the East Country who were both students and patrons: first of all, the Shogun-Prince Hisaakira, of course, but also Gen'e (d. 1307), son of shogun Kujō Yoritsune (1218–56) and chief

---

56. *Fujigayatsushū*, poem no. 284.
57. Sakai, "Reizei Tamesuke no *Kaidō yadotsugi hyakushu* ni tsuite," pp. 33–34.
58. Ibid., p. 41.
59. Ibid.

priest of the Tendai sect; Hōjō Sadatoki (1271–1311) and other members of that powerful clan; and the Zen priest Musō Soseki (1275–1351). Other sources tell us that he was also a teacher to Ta'a (1237–1319), head of the Ji (Time) sect of Buddhism, and to the *renga* master Gusai (d. 1376). However, with the exception of Fujiwara Nagakiyo of Katsumata (precise dates unknown) in Tōtōmi — who was prominent enough as a poet to be represented in *Gyokuyōshū* — Tamesuke's collection contains no references to lesser figures. Yet this does not mean that he had no disciples among the ranks of the warrior class, who as residents in the regions along the coastal roads would have enjoyed any attention paid to them by a poet of Tamesuke's stature. Behind his travel poems, then, we find evidence of another pattern set by Tamesuke for coming generations of the family, whose relationships with disciples far from Kyoto would be of crucial importance in maintaining their position in the literary field.

TAMESUKE WAS 66 at the time of his death, more than a decade younger than his nephew, Tameyo, who was still very active at court at the advanced age of 79. Among the many factors impinging on the success of any courtly lineage, none were so intractable as illness and death, which in a moment could change fortunes — and political alliances — irrevocably. Ill health and premature death would plague the Reizei lineage, in particular, for centuries to come.

As if to emphasize this point, less than two years later Tamesuke's heir, Tamenari, died as well. A captain in the Guards' Office at court, he had been representing the next generation of the Reizei lineage ever since his father had resigned his offices in 1317 and was already quite active as a poet. Judging from a poem by him in *Gyokuyōshū*, however, it appears that he may have spent a good deal of time in the East Country himself.

> Beneath autumn skies   along the East Country
> Road,   I remember
> seeing in the capital   the moons of summer
> and spring.[60]
>
> *azumaji no / aki no sora ni zo / omoiizuru / miyako nite mishi / haru natsu no tsuki*

It also appears that Tamenari too may have been troubled by illness for some time — or at least this is what seems to be suggested by the decision of his father, just before his own death, to sign over

---

60. *Gyokuyōshū*, poem no. 1979.

estate rights and the family library not to Tamenari but to his own younger son Tamehide (d. 1372), a young man still in his late 20s and only at the level of fifth rank.[61] Again, what lurks behind the records is no doubt ill health, first in the case of Tamenari but probably again in the case of Tamenari's nameless son and heir, who had died young. Thus, with little preparation, it was young Tamehide, whom Tamenari had formally adopted as his heir, who became the head of the Reizei house in 1330. To make matters worse, Tamesuke's brother Tamemori and his chief patron, Prince Hisaakira, had also died in 1328, leaving the young heir of the Reizei fortunes bereft of support from the two men besides his father who would have been in the best position to give it.

It would be hard to imagine a more difficult situation for a young man charged with continuing the traditions of a noble house, where there were always too many competitors for every office. In Kamakura and along the coastal road, the lineage still had powerful supporters, and apparently a strong financial base. But it appears that Tamenari's widow was reluctant to give up her husband's revenues, leading Tamehide to appeal for help to the imperial court—in order to preserve, he says, the precious treasures of the family library.[62] In terms of human resources, Tamehide was virtually bankrupt. Within the space of a few years, his father, his elder brother, and his uncle had left him, while his natural ally Tamekane was still in exile, and his chief competitor, Tameyo, was by contrast healthy despite his advancing years. Shunzei, first patriarch of the house, had lived into his 90s, and it appeared that Tameyo would do the same. Furthermore, Tameyo had a long list of ambitious sons and grandsons who were poised and ready to take his place in the court hierarchy. Despite Tamesuke's successes, his heirs were thus scarcely better off than he had been when Abutsu had died nearly 50 years earlier, in terms of the ultimate desire of any noble poetic lineage—acceptance and success at the imperial court.

---

61. Inoue, "Reizei-ke no rekishi 5: Tamesuke no shūhen to Tamehide," p. 4.
62. Atsuta, "Tamehide no futatsū no hōshijō," pp. 6–9.

FOUR

Miyako

HOWEVER GRAVE Tamehide's personal challenges must have seemed, they paled before what would happen just the year after he took over as head of the Reizei house—1331, the year of the Genkō Disturbance. Not since the rebellion of Go-Toba more than 100 years earlier had the imperial family, the noble lineages, the great monasteries and shrines, and the high-ranking military clans faced such a crisis.

As in the case of the Jōkyū Disturbance, the catalyst was an ambitious emperor and his cohorts. Ever since coming to power in 1318, Emperor Go-Daigo had been seeking ways to bolster his power as sovereign. This was no small task in a multi-layered system dominated by the reigning retired emperor, the local shogunal authorities in Rokuhara, and ultimately by the Hōjō regents in Kamakura. In 1321, he had made some progress toward his goal by persuading his father, Go-Uda, then reigning retired emperor, to cede control to him. Immediately, Go-Daigo gathered around him a cadre of capable courtiers, chosen not only for their pedigrees but also for their administrative skills and acumen. With them, Go-Daigo undertook a serious study of history and political philosophy and proceeded to revamp various institutions and offices with the goal of making them respond better to his directives. At the same time he sought alliances with various religious establishments and warrior families. The goal, of course, was the reestablishment of more direct imperial rule.

The first stage of the rebellion had taken place in 1324. Evidently by then things had even advanced to the point that a day in the Ninth Month had been chosen for an attack on the Rokuhara headquarters of the shogunal government. Unfortunately for Go-Daigo and his backers the plot was betrayed from within, and before the agreed-upon day came, two of Go-Daigo's advisors, both from the Hino family, were arrested as ringleaders. To avoid arrest himself, Go-Daigo sent another member of his entourage—Madenokōji Nobufusa (b. 1258)—as an imperial envoy to Kamakura, in order to proclaim the sovereign's innocence. It is hard to believe that anyone credited Nobufusa's protestations, but the Kamakura government took no action against Go-Daigo. Perhaps to avoid the possibility of a true uprising under the emperor's banner, the officers of the shogunal government had put the blame on one of the Hino men—Suketomo (1290–1332). He was sent into exile, and apparently for a time things settled down. That is, until 1331.

Go-Daigo had never given up his ambitions. By 1330, in fact, another plot to return him to direct rule was evidently well underway. Again, though, before any military action had been taken, in the Fourth Month of 1331, someone from within the emperor's own circle leaked the news to the shogunate—out of a desire to protect him from himself, some accounts say. This time Hino Toshimoto (d. 1332) was arrested and charged with sedition. Rather than send an envoy to proclaim his innocence, though, Go-Daigo now chose to flee to Nara and on to Kasagidera, south of Kyoto, where he sent out a call for troops to rally to his cause. His hope was that his lobbying would produce enough allies to carry his plans forward. There were always disenchanted samurai around who, either because of grudges against the Kamakura government or pure self-interest, were ready to support a coup attempt.

In the beginning it appeared that Go-Daigo had calculated correctly. Sympathizers among the military clans did respond, with considerable effect. But it was not long before Rokuhara forces, augmented by shogunal troops from the East Country, laid waste to the emperor's stronghold. In the Ninth Month of 1331, Go-Daigo managed to escape to a place in Yamashiro, only to be betrayed by locals and turned over to representatives of the shogunate. To signal that there would be no going back, the shogunate quickly installed a new emperor from the Jimyō-in line—known now as Kōgon (1313–64; r. 1331–33)—on the throne. In the Third Month of 1332, Go-Daigo was sent into exile on the island of Oki in the Sea of Japan. The Hōjō regents appeared to have succeeded in disposing of another rebellious sovereign.

Other emperors had been sent into exile and stayed there, Go-Toba being the most obvious case. But Go-Daigo was perhaps a more determined leader, and certainly he had more support than his forebear had had a century before. A number of courtier-chieftains, such as Kitabatake Chikafusa (1293–1354) and Chigusa Tadaaki (d. 1336), continued to foment revolt against shogunal authority even after his banishment. To put down the uprising permanently, the shogunate sent a large army—at least 50,000 men—to the ancient capital in the First Month of 1333. As if in response, just a month or so later, Go-Daigo broke free from his prison—in a daring escape, accompanied by only one retainer—and made his way to Hōki on the mainland. From there he commissioned Chigusa Tadaaki to lead his forces in an attack on the shogunal guard in Kyoto. There the fighting was fierce, leaving some sections of the city in ashes. Even parts of the palace, including a storehouse filled with imperial treasures, were destroyed.

In response to these developments, the shogunate sent one of its chief generals, Ashikaga Takauji (1305–58), at the head of a large army to take charge of its expedition against the royalists. Ironically, this would prove to be its own undoing. For on the way to Kyoto, at a shrine in Tamba Province, Takauji turned against the shogunate and announced a pact with Go-Daigo, proclaiming a restoration of his own warrior lineage—the Minamoto—at the same time. Then he swiftly overcame not Go-Daigo's forces but the shogunal troops at Rokuhara in Kyoto.

The chief officeholders of the shogunal government in Kyoto had time to get away, fleeing east with Emperor Kōgon and two retired emperors, with the aim of finding shelter in Kamakura. Finding their way blocked by armies loyal to Go-Daigo, however, the representatives of the shogunal government soon realized that all hope was lost. Rather than capitulate, they locked themselves up in Rengeji Temple, where more than 400 of them committed suicide. The sovereigns were taken into custody and returned to Kyoto, where they were held in a kind of house arrest. Meanwhile, Takauji dispatched a large force, headed by Nitta Yoshisada (1301–38), to attack Kamakura. In the Fifth Month of 1333, the Hōjō were defeated, bringing an end to the Kamakura shogunate. Takatoki (1303–33), last of the shogunal regents, also ensconced himself in a temple, along with several hundred family members and retainers, and disemboweled himself.

Thus a new era had begun. In fact, though, the fighting was far from over. From the start the pact between Ashikaga Takauji and Emperor Go-Daigo was a fragile one at best. Both men wanted to exercise power. A sign of the trouble to come came in the Sixth Month of 1333, when the emperor appointed as shogun his own son, Prince Moriyoshi (1308–35), rather than Takauji. At the same time, the emperor began restructuring the government, creating a new hierarchy with himself at the top as undisputed monarch. Plans for reconstruction of the imperial palace, burned in 1219 and never rebuilt, were drawn up, and money solicited. In every way, Go-Daigo made it clear that he intended to share power with no one. He would be sovereign in name and deed and the ancient word *Miyako* would once again refer to an imperial capital.

The first decisive break between the emperor and Takauji came in the Eighth Month of 1335, when Takauji left the capital at the head of an army to put down an uprising from Hōjō holdouts in Kamakura. That in itself, of course, was no crime: he was after all the putative head of the emperor's army. The problem was that he departed without the emperor's order, ignoring the fact that Go-Daigo had appointed Prince Moriyoshi to undertake that very task. Takauji defended his decision by declaring that several of the provinces of the East Country in danger were his own domains (*chigyōkoku*), which he felt he had to protect from any possibility of a resurgence of Hōjō power. Go-Daigo, however, was not convinced.

Joining forces with his brother, Tadayoshi (1306–52), whom he had left in charge in the East Country, Takauji defeated the Hōjō holdouts. For this Go-Daigo rewarded him with junior second rank—a great honor, perhaps, but one that also could be seen as reducing him to the status of one of the emperor's courtiers. That Takauji then refused Go-Daigo's command to return at once to the capital is perhaps best understood as a signal to the sovereign that he would not be ordered around. Staying on in Kamakura, Takauji began to hand out rewards to those who had assisted him in recent battles. Upon hearing of this obvious challenge to his authority, the emperor dispatched an army to subdue the East Country and bring Takauji down.

The year 1336 was one of constant fighting between the armies of Takauji and the emperor. First the Ashikaga general won, wiping away all resistance to his army as he made his way south toward Kyoto; then a counterattack obliged him to abandon the city and retreat down the coast of the Inland Sea, all the way to Kyushu. In the process, he appropriated Kōgon as retired emperor in an attempt to gain the favor of Heaven—and some more allies—for his cause. Late in the year, there was a brief rapprochement. Again Go-Daigo promoted Takauji, this time to the high office of major counselor. As soon as it became clear that Takauji had no intention of assisting in any true imperial restoration, however, Go-Daigo fled to the mountainous region of Yoshino, south of Nara. There he set up what would be called the Southern Court, which while seldom strong enough to offer real opposition, would last until 1392. For his part, Takauji placed one of Kōgon's sons on the throne and, in the Eighth Month of 1338, finally got his wish to be made shogun. Rather than in Kamakura, he set up his offices directly in the northernmost district of the city, where he could maintain a watchful eye on the court. His vassals also quickly established residences in the city, changing the character of the place—and of course of Kamakura, which they left behind—forever.

EVENTS SUCH as these could leave no court family unscathed. Among high-ranking courtiers, a number were executed. One of these was Saionji Kinmune (1310–35)—great-great-great-great grandson of Teika's benefactor, Kintsune—who as head of a lineage loyal to the Hōjō was taken prisoner and eventually beheaded. On the other side, Hino Suketomo and Hino Toshimoto, Go-Daigo's faithful advisors, were likewise put to the sword. Needless to say, the conflicts of the time also split many families, some following Go-Daigo and others Takauji. Some members of the highest lineages ended up staying with the Southern Court as it roamed around the hinterlands in search of a permanent shelter that would never be found.

Tameyo, senior member of the Mikohidari lineage, which by this time was being referred to as the Nijō house, came through the years of turmoil unharmed. In 1329, before all the trouble began, he had taken the tonsure and withdrawn somewhat from worldly affairs, leaving the protection of house traditions to his heirs. His family, on the other hand, was another matter. His grandson, Tameakira (1295–1364), for instance, was taken prisoner by shogunal police in 1330 and nearly put on the rack because the authorities thought that he must know something of the plans of Go-Daigo, in whose court he served. In the end, he was saved, so the story goes, by the following poem, which so impressed his captors that they let him go:

Who would have thought   — that one day
I would be asked   not about the Way,
but about the unhappy affairs   of this cruel world
of ours?[1]

omoiki ya / waga shikishima no / michi narade / ukiyo no koto o / towaru beshi to wa

Tameyo's fifth son Tamefuyu (1305?–35), another of Go-Daigo's circle, was given no such opportunity to save himself. Serving in the army sent by Go-Daigo against Takauji, he died in battle at Takenoshita, in the mountains of Hakone, in the Twelfth Month of 1335. This was the third of Tameyo's sons to precede him in death: Tamemichi, his oldest, had been taken by illness in 1299; his second son, Tamefuji, by illness in 1324; and now Tamefuyu. Furthermore, Tameyo's daughter Tameko, consort to Go-Daigo, had also died, as had her son Takayoshi, who after years spent in exile killed himself in order to avoid capture at the fall of Kanezaki Castle. Muneyoshi was still alive, as far as anyone knew, wandering through the provinces with the Southern Court. So the losses to the senior line of the Mikohidari house had been great.

One effect of the death of Tamefuyu was predictable. Already the passing of Tamefuji had nearly split the house into two factions: those following Tameyo's first son's heir, Tamesada (1293–1360), and those following the sons of Tamefuji. Still at work, in other words, were the same forces that had divided the descendants of Tameie 40 years earlier, creating the Nijō, Kyōgoku, and Reizei lines. On various occasions, Tameyo had been forced to intervene personally to keep the peace. Now further dissension was virtually inevitable. When Tameyo died in 1338 at 89, it was still not clear which faction would triumph. Tamesada, the son of Tameyo's own first son, Tamemichi, was perhaps the most dominant figure, as he should have been by the rule of primogeniture; but Tameakira, the heir of Tamefuji, who had served as head of the lineage during Tamesada's minority, was apparently always ready to challenge his cousin's authority, as an incident of the time attests: after relations between Tameakira and Tamesada became strained, Tameakira would go around to various gatherings with his copy of *Kokinshū* in his breast

---

1. The incident is recorded in *Taiheiki*. See McCullough, *Taiheiki*, pp. 32–33. Translation of the poem is mine.

pocket, lecturing on proper pronunciations and then proclaiming, "This interpretation is the one *I* received!"[2]

Since at least the time of Teika, *Kokinshū*, the first of the imperial anthologies of *uta*, had been the single most highly-regarded text in the poetic canon. It is not surprising, then, that Tameakira should be displaying his copy of the anthology—along with the teachings he had received concerning pronunciation of problematic words in the text, which were some of the earliest "secret" teachings in the poetic tradition—as a way to bolster his authority in the poetic field. Once again, library resources were being pressed into service in literary debates.

After Tameyo's death, then, internal conflicts left the senior Mikohidari line in a somewhat weakened position, despite their many allies and patrons at all levels of literate society. Moreover, the defeat of Go-Daigo's cause also dealt a blow to the Nijō house. For as things turned out, it was a Jimyō-in emperor that Takauji put on the throne, with Kōgon acting as reigning retired emperor. In comparison with 30 years before, the imperial prerogative was of course much reduced, for Kōgon obviously owed his appointment to Ashikaga Takauji, and was entirely dependent on the new shogunate for his support. But in Kyoto and the Home Provinces, at least, the imperial court was still an institution of great symbolic force—a force that Takauji was anxious to put to use. Poetic activities thus commenced even as the fighting was still going on. Like most men of his station, Takauji had been composing poems since childhood, succeeding well enough to see one of his compositions included in the sixteenth imperial anthology, *Shoku goshūishū* (Later Collection of Gleanings, Continued), in 1326, at the age of 22. That he would become a patron of poets was obvious to all concerned. The great fear of the senior lineage of the Mikohidari house was that he would first and foremost be a patron of Kōgon, who had strong ties to Kyōgoku Tamekane.

If the triumph of Takauji was a mixed blessing for the family of Tameyo, then, it was better news for adherents of the Jimyō-in line. Retired Emperor Hanazono, son of Fushimi, was still alive, biding his time; so was Fushimi's empress, Eifukumon-in (1271–1342). Likewise, Tamekane's adopted heirs Ōgimachi Kinkage (1297–1360) and Tamemoto (precise dates unknown) had been waiting decades for a return to favor. Through all their years out of power, the Kyōgoku faction, though few in number compared to their adversaries, had

---

2. Imagawa, *Nigonshō*, p. 82.

been waiting for a change of regime. While not entirely critical of Go-Daigo's designs, from which they too would have benefited, their policy had been to keep their own counsel. They were thus in a position to fill the void when a new emperor had to be found.

The resurgence of the Jimyō-in was in turn a godsend for Reizei Tamehide. We know little about his movements during the war years. A later record says that some time during the disruption, his estates, including the one Abutsu and Tamesuke had fought so long to secure against the suits of the main house, were confiscated by warrior barons, as were so many noble estates when the central power structure was preoccupied with its own survival.[3] In addition to economic privations, he may also have experienced firsthand the horrors of battle as Kamakura fell in the summer of 1333. Many of those who slit their bellies rather than submit themselves to the indignities of capture were men he had sat with in poetry gatherings for years.

After the defeat of the Hōjō and the departure of the Ashikaga and its many vassals, the eastern capital was a forlorn place. Temples and shrines remained, as did some local warrior clans, but the offices of the shogunate were burned-out shells. In the space of a few years, opportunities for service as a literatus had diminished conspicuously. Tamehide too had a copy of *Kokinshū*, indeed, one dated 1226 in Teika's own hand that, as one of the earliest extant texts of that classic, would be classified a National Treasure by the Japanese government in the 1980s. After the fall of the shogunate, however, there were fewer patrons in Kamakura for such a treasure to impress. By 1334, records hint that Tamehide was already in Kyoto, hoping to find a market for his talents there. For the time being, progress at court was unlikely, but the new regime in Kyoto offered more of a future than did the deserted capital of the old order.

Tamehide had one advantage over many others in Kyoto, namely, that he was already acquainted with Takauji.[4] As noted above, the Ashikaga chieftain's interest in poetry had brought the two men together in Kamakura. This no doubt explains why in the Ninth Month of 1336, Tamehide was among the few courtiers involved in a dedicatory sequence presented at Sumiyoshi Shrine as a prayer for

---

3. See Atsuta, "Tamehide no futatsū no mōshijō," and Atsuta, "Bannen no Tamehide."

4. Atsuta, "Tamehide no futatsū no mōshijō," p. 7.

victory in coming battles led by Takauji and his brother Tadayoshi.[5] Unfortunately, this connection did not lead to immediate recognition at court, where he was still only a gentleman-in-waiting (*jijū*) of fifth rank. But when Takauji became secure in his new position, Tamehide had every right to expect the shogun's favor.

Just at the point when Tamehide seemed to be poised for success at court, however, he dropped almost completely out of sight—and not for a short time, but for a period of nearly six full years, from 1338 until 1344. As always, gaps in the record are hard to explain. In this case, though, an answer to the question of why there are so few mentions of him during at least some of these years is answered by a letter recorded in the diary of a prominent courtier from the intercalary Ninth Month of 1346. At the time, planning for the formal "airing" of a set of 100-poem sequences was underway, and Tamehide had been nominated to serve as lector by Retired Emperor Kōgon. Evidently there were some who thought he was not up to the task: "Tamehide is to serve, it seems. But his voice is very frail, and he is not experienced. Since his illness, his eyesight is poor, of course, nor does he hear too well. One wonders how he can perform as reader."[6]

Despite reservations of this sort among some of the participants, Tamehide was allowed to undertake his appointed role just a few days later—although according to the same courtier, "His voice was so faint that one couldn't hear him."[7] Undeniably, the heir of the Reizei house was still recovering from a severe illness. As recently as the Second Month of that same year he had begged off attending a Jimyō-in poetry gathering, pleading that he was indisposed.[8] The formal reading of the sequences was evidently too important an opportunity to miss, but fulfilling his duties appears to have been a physical challenge. Later records suggest that he was left with a chronic condition that would plague him for the rest of his life.

So participation in the event of autumn 1346 revealed the effects of his illness; but it also marked his return to activity, evidently inspired at least partly by the prospect of a new imperial anthology—the compilation of which was always a central concern for all branches of the Mikohidari house. It was for the collection, indeed,

---

5. Inoue, *Chūsei kadanshi no kenkyū, Nanbokuchōki*, pp. 382–84.
6. Ibid., p. 448.
7. Ibid.
8. Ibid., p. 446.

that the 100-poem sequences had been commissioned. Talk about the project had begun in 1344, with Takauji's blessing. In a rare departure from precedent, the new anthology, which would be called *Fūgashū* (Collection of Elegance), was announced as the work not of "commissioned" courtiers but of Retired Emperor Kōgon himself, with considerable input by Hanazono, now designated *hōkō*, or Priestly Retired Emperor. Doubtless the primary reason behind this decision was that poetry was so important to the sovereigns themselves, who aimed at a return to the glory days of the Jimyō-in salons of 30 years before, the time of Fushimi and Tamekane. But that Tamekane's Kyōgoku line was now defunct was also a factor, which would have made it difficult to appoint as compiler anyone from the court ranks except a member of the main Mikohidari house. For some ritual functions, such as the formal banquet celebrating the project, the emperors did allow members of the main house to take charge: not even politics could be allowed to get in the way of proper attention to the requirements of ritual, in which the main house had experience.[9] To appoint a descendant of Tameyo as compiler, however, would have been to give up too much; and appointing Tamehide to such a responsibility was evidently out of the question, probably because he was still only at fourth rank and not experienced at court. Thus no courtier was given chief responsibility for the project. On the other hand, a Poetry Bureau was established, complete with fellows (*yoriudo*), among whom were Tamekane's heirs Kinkage and Tamemoto, and Reizei Tamehide. This was the first time a member of the Reizei lineage had ever been so honored.

Records do not reveal what duties Tamehide performed during his tenure as fellow. A contemporary reports that Tamehide told him that during this time, "I went to the Hagiwara Palace and often talked with the retired emperor."[10] Knowing Hanazono, one must assume that the men talked a great deal about poetic history and philosophy. Most of Tamehide's responsibilities, however, were probably clerical, with larger questions of selection and design being left to the sovereigns themselves. In addition, however, he probably had a say in which poems from the Reizei line were chosen. In all, 60 poems by various members of the lineage were included in the collection, the lion's share coming from Tamesuke (honored with

9. Ibid., p. 453.
10. Tonna, *Seiashō*, p. 117.

18 selections), Abutsu (14), and Tamehide himself (10). Some of them, such as the following one by Tamehide, show an explicit debt to Kyōgoku Tamekane, who had of course been a teacher to Hanazono and a political ally of Tamesuke:

> Autumn: From among his poems on "The Moon"
>
> Mist clears away   and reveals mountain
> slopes   far in the distance;
> carrying moonlight downstream   are the waves
> of Uji River.[11]
>
> *kiri haruru / tō no yamamoto / arawarete / tsukikage nagasu / uji no kawanami*

As was nearly always the case by the era in question, this poem was composed on a fixed topic and therefore was not intended to describe "actual" experience but rather to present an idea — and in a way that was slightly new, following advice set down by Tameie generations before.[12] It is anything but coincidental that in order to do so, Tamehide chose a conception at the pivot of the poem in which haze clears away to reveal moonlight. Such transformations of the landscape involving the play of light, suggesting a moment captured in the forward movement of time, were a staple of Kyōgoku poetics.

It should be stressed, however, that even in *Fūgashū* Tamehide was also careful to present himself as the heir of Teika and his style of "deep feeling" (*ushin*), which is apparent in a poem that plays on the old tension between cherry blossoms and the wind:

> Spring: From among his poems on "Blossoms"
>
> Blooming everywhere,   with no sign
> of scattering: cherries at their height.
> I would not begrudge a breeze —   just enough to bring
> their scent.[13]
>
> *sakimichite / chirubeku mo aranu / hanazakari / kaoru bakari no / kaze wa itowazu*

Many years later, Tamehide would be quoted as saying, "To adhere to only one style constricts the Way."[14] This would become a refrain, perhaps *the* refrain, of Reizei pronouncements on the practice of poetry, expressing not so much commitment to any style as to an

---

11. *Fūgashū*, poem no. 619.
12. Brower, "The Foremost Style of Poetic Composition," p. 429.
13. *Fūgashū*, poem no. 166.
14. Imagawa, *Shisetsu jikenshū*, p. 215.

attitude. Indeed, the poems he chose for *Fūgashū* show that Tame-hide was skilled in all styles, as experience as a teacher among the novices of the East Country no doubt had taught him to be. If there is any feature that can be said to dominate his work, it is perhaps the same penchant for rustic scenes—especially travel scenes—that characterized the work of his father and that would become a the-matic tradition for the Reizei house. In this context, however, it is worth remembering that just as surely as *Fūgashū* was a Kyōgoku project, a sort of *Gyōkuyōshū II*, it was therefore *not* a Reizei project in any meaningful sense of the word, as one would expect given that less than three percent of its poems would finally be by members of that lineage. The fact that scholars perpetuate the idea that the Kyōgoku and Reizei houses were supposedly identical in stylistic terms by using terms like "the Kyōgoku-Reizei style" should not be allowed to obscure the truth of the matter, which is that while poets like Tamehide were skillful at producing poems in the manner of Tamekane and his coterie when occasion required it, they also composed in a range of styles when they had either the inclination or the need to do so. For them, poetry was not a matter of any one narrowly-defined style, but instead a realm of practice that required versatility (*jiyū*) first of all.[15] It is not by coincidence that whereas later Reizei critical writings and transmissions frequently refer to the critical writings of Teika and Tameie, never once do they refer in any explicit way to Tamekane's one critical treatise, *Tamekane-kyō wakashō* (Lord Tamekane's Notes on Poetry).

Nevertheless, the *Fūgashū* years were a true contrast to the previ-ous decade for Tamehide and his family. A note from one of his students at the time corroborates the impression that for the first time ever a Reizei man was being accepted in poetic circles as more than an outsider:

In the late 1340s, poetry meetings to compose 100-poem sequences were held three times a month, with Major Counselor Tamesada doing the marking, and offering criticism. Those attending were all men of reputation. From the houses, Lords Tametada and Tamehide were regulars. Lord Tameakira also joined them sometimes. Tonna, Keiun, and Kenkō were also regulars, who expressed their opinions.[16]

---

15. Inoue, "Reizei-ke no rekishi, Ōchō kara chūsei e," pp. 105–6.
16. Nijō Yoshimoto, *Kinrai fūtei*, p. 183.

Some scholars are dubious about the scenario presented in this account, arguing that it seems unlikely that Tamehide and his political rivals from the Nijō house were "regulars" at such events.[17] Yet other sources attest that the author of the statement—the courtier Nijō Yoshimoto (1320–88), heir of a different and much more prestigious noble house that was also, confusingly, called Nijō—did indeed have relationships with all the poets he mentions, and we know that rivals had met in former times and would do so in later times as well. Rather than for submission as raw material for an imperial anthology, 100-poem sequences composed at *tsukinamikai*, or "monthly meetings" held at various houses, were considered a kind of composition practice (*keiko*) through which poets could test their mettle—and propound their views. The meetings held by Tamesada, current head of the main house, involved only the most highly regarded poets, including his courtier cousin Tameakira and Tameyo's prominent commoner disciples—the monks Tonna (1289–1372), Keiun (precise dates unknown), and Yoshida no Kenkō (b. 1283). For Tamehide to be a regular member of the salon is a testimony to his talent and prominence. Unfortunately, no record of the poetry composed for these events has survived, leaving us no hint of Tamesada's opinion about his cousin's poems. That he was invited to participate at all, however, indicates that he was now part of the establishment. After nearly half a century, the dream of Tameie and Abutsu had finally been realized.

The *Fūgashū* achieved final form only in 1349. Eifukumon-in had died in 1342 and Hanazono too passed away, in 1348, before the collection was completed. Thus those with connections to the glory days at Emperor Fushimi's court did not live to see their persistence materialized in the form of a second monument to the Kyōgoku style. For this and other reasons, *Fūgashū* has always been considered a dark and melancholy work, dominated by poems like these—the first by Kōgon, the second by Hanazono—that hint at loneliness and loss:

Spring: From a 100-poem sequence

Even the frog's voices   as they call
from the water   sound worn and old;
at a pond surrounded by trees   spring approaches
its end.[18]

minosoko no / kawazu no koe mo / mono furite / kobukaki ike no / haru no kuregata

---

17. See volume 10 of *Karon kagaku shūsei*, p. 382, note 4.
18. *Fūgashū*, poem no. 266.

Winter: On the feeling of winter dusk

Well into dusk   still there is light
in my garden—   but only from snow;
inside it is darker still   next to my small
box of coals.[19]

kureyaranu / niwa no hikari wa / yuki ni shite / oku kuraku naru / uzumibi no moto

An old pond at spring's end, a man looking out into snowlight from the dark on a cold winter night—these are dreary images, to be sure. A close reading of *Fūgashū*, however, reveals that such images do not dominate the collection so completely as many literary historians suggest. The poems by Tamehide quoted above on the wind in the blossoms and moonlight shining on river waves, for instance, could hardly be called stark. The first poem in the anthology by a poet of the Reizei lineage—number 24, by Tamesuke, which we can assume was chosen either at Tamehide's suggestion or with his permission—is in fact celebratory in mood, as is the case with the majority of the poems selected for inclusion in the imperial anthology.

Spring: On "Spring Morning," from a poem-contest held at the home of Former Major Counselor Tamekane

Where first light of day   shimmers high up
on the peaks,   the skies are clearing—
while down below the pines   the slopes are hidden
by haze.[20]

izuru hi no / utsurou mine wa / sora harete / matsu yori shita no / yama zo kasumeru

Again, this poem may be characterized as in the Kyōgoku style syntactically and in the way it treats a moment of change in the natural landscape. It does not, on the other hand, articulate the sort of somber mood often attributed to the second and last anthology of the Jimyō-in lineage. Any imperial anthology was a memorial, after all, and thus obliged its compilers to fill it with images that were on the whole positive and affirming. Even if many poems by Hanazono and Kōgon, both of whom were operating under the influence of Chinese art and poetry of the Song dynasty, may be characterized as melancholy, the same cannot be said for the entire anthology.

19. Ibid., poem no. 878.
20. Ibid., poem no. 24.

ANOTHER SERIES of political upheavals in the early 1350s soon threatened Tamehide's hard-won position in the capital city. The initial conflict was between Ashikaga Takauji and his brother Tadayoshi, but as matters progressed the imperial line inevitably became entangled. In the midst of the maneuvering that always accompanied such conflicts, Takauji repudiated his ties to the Northern Court and invited the forces of the Southern Court to return to Kyoto, which they did early in the next year, only to be chased out again in a few weeks. Over the next five years, similar incidents occurred again and again. At last, in 1355, an apparently permanent truce was established, with Go-Kōgon (1338–74; r. 1352–71), son of Kōgon, on the throne of the Northern Court, which had returned to power in Kyoto, backed by the shogunate. Again, though, the noble families had gone through a period of crisis that had left them bloodied and worn. As might be expected, during the fighting there were few formal poetic events at court. True to the pattern of the past, however, the upheaval was followed by a renewal of interest after peace returned. A flourishing artistic environment was always considered a sign of political order.

Despite his status as heir of the Jimyō-in line, Go-Kōgon was by education an adherent of the Nijō cause mostly due to the influence of his advisors, particularly the regent-literatus Nijō Yoshimoto, already mentioned above. In his early years, Yoshimoto had written poems in the Kyōgoku style, participating in many events with Tamehide during the Jimyō-in revival that produced *Fūgashū*. Years of political turmoil and warfare, however, must have made adherence to a narrower sense of orthodoxy—and to the claims of senior houses—seem the safest way to proceed. To sanction a style highly criticized by the senior members of a court lineage now must have appeared unwise. So Yoshimoto began to refer to the style of Fushimi and his descendants as *ifū*, "unorthodox."[21] By doing so, he even succeeded in convincing Takauji to take a turn toward the plain style of Tamesada. Obviously, this put the Reizei line, whose recent political alignment with the Kyōgoku house could not be denied, in a subordinate position again. For centuries to come, members of the senior house and their supporters would employ the word *ifū* in their attempts to dismiss their Reizei cousins from proper consideration.

Despite all this, Yoshimoto apparently did not consider Tamehide a foe. Still the two met in gatherings, and were cordial. Furthermore,

---

21. Nijō Yoshimoto, *Kinrai fūtei*, p. 188.

Emperor Go-Kōgon also extended his patronage to the Reizei on a number of occasions, beginning in the mid-1350s, even rewarding Tamehide with some new estate revenues.[22] Even some members of the main house maintained friendly relations with the Reizei heir. Most notable among these was Tameakira, the heir of Tameyo's son, Tamefuji. But things were different with Tamesada, head of the Nijō house and a major counselor at court. As noted above, Tamehide had been a regular visitor at Tamesada's house a decade earlier, but the relationship had evidently deteriorated over time. When Tamesada was putting a new imperial anthology together in the late 1350s, Tamehide was so disaffected that he refused even to submit any of his poems for review, a sign that the men were not even on speaking terms. This intransigence would become a tradition of the house: in the future, too, the family would remain steadfast when it came to maintaining the pride of the lineage, even when doing so meant short-term censure and economic hardship. One of his students would later note that Tamehide was perhaps not aggressive enough for the game of court politics, lamenting that "the late Lord Tamehide was of a modest disposition, and was late to make a name for himself."[23]

When it came to his position as heir of the Reizei hopes, however, Tamehide apparently did have the courage and political strength to take a stand. That he could afford to do so is one measure of the stature the Reizei had been able to achieve in Kyoto. The dominance of the Nijō faction at court kept him from advancing rapidly in rank, as a proxy lament by his son written around this time reveals:

> Miscellaneous: A poem on the topic, "Lament, with Mountain as an Image," written back when Former Consultant Tamehide was still only at fourth rank
>
> Still in the shadows   of the scrub oak
> on the slopes   of Status Mountain,
> I face the pathway ahead —   my progress
> ever so slow.[24]
>
> *kuraiyama / mada shiishiba no / kage nite / waga noberu beki / michi wa isogazu*

---

22. Atsuta, "Bannen no Tamehide," refers to documents that show the emperor confirming estate rights in Suruga, Tōtōmi, and Awa, also noting that Tamehide was among those who accompanied the emperor in his flight from the capital in 1352, along with Yoshimoto.

23. Imagawa, *Nigonshō*, p. 81.

24. *Shin shūishū*, poem no. 1746.

Yet, notwithstanding the frustration expressed here, numerous records indicate that Tamehide was prominent and well respected even by those who might have in some sense considered themselves adversaries. The monk-poet Tonna, for instance, welcomed Tamehide to his famous cottage near Ninnaji on numerous occasions; and records also show correspondence with Yoshida no Kenkō, another of Tameyo's disciples. All of this remained true despite his tendency to produce poems that must have offended Nijō tastes, as in the case of one recorded later by a disciple. Although no topic for the poem is recorded, it seems safe to place it in the travel category, though whether written on the road or in a gathering we cannot know.

> Buffeted and blown   as I climb
> Kiso Slope   against morning wind
> I draw my arms into sleeves   soon chilled through
> by driving snow.[25]
>
> *furifubuku / kiso no misaka no / asakaze ni / yagate shimitsuku / yuki no makurite*

Adherents of Nijō poetics no doubt would have condemned such a poem as too rustic, as they had in the case of Tamesuke's poem about peasants dressing rice paddies. That Tamehide was composing such poems is evidence that despite hardships he was holding fast to the more broad-minded credo of his lineage.

No doubt one reason for the continued success of Tamehide in the Kyoto market was that many wanted access to his library, which was known to hold treasured texts not available elsewhere.[26] In an age before the advent of printing, the importance of such a resource cannot be overstated. But it also appears that these disciples of Tameyo had long before formed relationships with Tamehide that more recent political developments were not powerful enough to break. Factoring friendship and long-term association into the calculus of political affairs is no easy matter, but their significance cannot be entirely discounted.

In 1360, Nijō Tamesada died, while Tamehide, though still ill much of the time, lived on. For the next twelve years, until his own death, he would by virtue of his pedigree and well-tested competence be one of the most important poetic figures at court, acting the time-worn part of judge and arbiter in poetic affairs. During this time there

---

25. The poem is recorded by Imagawa Ryōshun in *Rakusho roken*, p. 115.
26. Inada, *Waka shitennō no kenkyū*, p. 119

would be turmoil again in the world of politics, with the armies of the Southern Court even holding the capital for a few weeks again in 1362. Thereafter, the royalist cause remained strong only in Kyushu, however; and with the reign of Shogun Ashikaga Yoshimitsu (1358–1408), who took office in 1368, the Muromachi shogunate entered its most stable and prosperous period. Through all this time, Tamehide retained his place. In the late 1360s, in fact, records indicate that he was serving as tutor to the shogun Yoshimitsu's predecessor—Yoshiakira (1330–67), who had inherited that office upon Takauji's death in 1358. Even after the imperial salons fell under the sway of the main house again, Tamehide retained a strong position in the *buke kadan*—the salons of the military elite. In coming years, as the power of the imperial house declined, it would be the *buke kadan* that provided real financial support for all the courtly arts, from music and kickball to poetry.[27] Already in the era of *Fūgashū*, Ashikaga patrons had been among the most important patrons of poetry, and their influence would only increase in time. Even imperial anthologies would be compiled upon their order—relayed through the emperor, of course—and financed by their largess.[28]

In order to memorialize his tenure as shogun, Ashikaga Yoshiakira issued an order to Nijō Tameakira to compile a new imperial anthology in 1363. Having been passed over as compiler again, Tamehide cannot have been entirely pleased with Yoshiakira's plan. But he and Tameakira were still on good terms, evidently; there would be no refusal to participate in the project this time. Quite to the contrary, in fact, Tamehide apparently cooperated fully on the anthology, which would include eight of his poems in the end, a better representation than the family had enjoyed in any other Nijō anthology. When Tameakira, at the end of the next year, died before actually completing the project, a rare opportunity for rapprochement with the main house was presented, which Tamehide accepted. For Tameakira had no heir, and none of the other Nijō adherents was in a position to undertake the ceremonial work necessary to bring the project to completion. Tamesada's heir was too young; and Tameakira's brother Tametada (d. 1373) had been too involved with the Southern Court in recent years to make him an acceptable can-

---

27. Inoue, *Chūsei kadanshi no kenkyū, Nanbokuchōki*, p. 648. See also Huey, "Warrior Control over the Imperial Anthology."

28. See Huey, "Warrior Control over the Imperial Anthology."

didate to the shogunate. To complete the compilation process, the monk-poet Tonna was called in, since that part of the work presented no social problem. As a commoner, though, Tonna could not undertake the ritual of presenting the anthology for imperial review, and not to present it for such recognition would mean that the work could never be accepted as a truly "imperial" anthology. The ready solution, dictated by precedent, was to adopt an heir for Tameakira, posthumously, in this case. The one chosen for the honor was none other than Tamehide's son, Tamekuni (precise dates unknown). When the nineteenth imperial collection was presented to the emperor on the thirteenth day of the Twelfth Month of 1364, it was Tamehide's son who did the honors as a middle captain in the Guards, senior fourth rank.

One by-product of Tamekuni's adoption was that he also inherited the office of steward (bugyō) of the Poetry Bureau, which was located on Fifth Avenue in Kyoto, where the actual day-to-day work of the project was evidently taking place and where Tamehide occasionally held poetry gatherings.[29] Although the exact contents of the library there are not known, they must have been of considerable value. In this way Tamehide was able to get his hands on most of the manuscript holdings of the senior Mikohidari lineage—with no need, it appears, to reciprocate. Furthermore, the prominence he gained through the incident seems to have helped pave the way for progress in office and rank. He became a middle counselor at the end of 1366 and received promotion to junior third rank immediately thereafter. In order to secure these and other favors, including reconfirmation of some estate rights after a suit with the senior house, he was evidently able to secure the intervention of various well-placed disciples, including Nijō Yoshimoto, and ultimately Sasaki Dōyo (1306–73), one of the most powerful warlords of the era.[30]

Tamehide did not stay in office long, resigning in the Fourth Month of 1468. The chief reason that he stepped down so soon was the death of Ashikaga Yoshiakira just a few months before, whose

---

29. Along with the office came rights from at least one estate. See Atsuta, "Tamekuni to Tamemasa," p. 7. Imagawa in Rakusho roken (p. 107) mentions a poetry gathering held at the Gojō Wakadokoro, although he mentions no particular date.

30. Inoue, Chūsei kadanshi no kenkyū, Nanbokuchōki, p. 633, and Atsuta, "Tamehide no futatsu no mōshijō, p. 8.

passing had sent many followers into holy orders, as was the custom. However, Tamehide did not take that step, and remained as active as ever at court, participating in poetry gatherings at the palace and also holding his own "monthly meetings." Now that Tameakira was gone, Tamehide's relations with the main house—represented by Tamesada's son, Tametō (1341–81)—were again strained. But the difference in age and experience between the two men was enough to give him the edge in most circumstances. In 1371 Tamehide was promoted to junior second rank.

In the summer of 1372, Tamehide passed away, no doubt a victim of the illness that had plagued him for decades. After his recent accomplishments, one would think that he could have died a satisfied man. One source, however, indicates that the situation at his death was worrisome. After noting his demise, the writer adds: "His son, Lord Tamekuni, took the tonsure, suddenly, last year; so Tamehide's young grandson will inherit. The library has been entrusted to Sasaki Takahide, junior assistant in the Ministry of Civil Affairs. This was done in order to keep the library intact, it is said. Takahide is among the foremost disciples of Tamehide's house."[31]

No record says anything about why Tamekuni took the tonsure. If it was due to illness, he must have recovered, since he is noted as a participant in poetic activities, sporadically, that is, for the next 30 years. Whatever the reasons behind his decision, it had a profound impact on the house, since a tonsured man could no longer hold political office or be directly involved in court affairs. His son Tamemasa was only twelve years old in 1372, and not in a position yet to compete against the senior house. Fortunately, he had behind him men like Sasaki Dōyo's son and heir Takahide (d. 1391), who could protect his interests for a time. As the author of the note above recognized, the Reizei heir still had the family library, the resources of which Tamehide had managed to augment. No doubt it was Tamehide who had arranged with Takahide to protect the house manuscripts against predators. Beyond that, however, all of Tamehide's attempts to gain a better position for his lineage in the literary field were in jeopardy.

UNDER THE reign of Ashikaga Yoshimitsu, the Muromachi shogunate would enjoy a rare era in which the authority of the central government was little challenged. The soldiers of the Southern Court who

---

31. Inoue, *Chūsei kadanshi no kenkyū, Nanbokuchōki*, pp. 660–61.

occupied the streets of Kyoto in the last days of 1362 had been the last that would ever do so. Kitabatake Chikafusa and the other stalwarts of the royalist movement were long gone, and the death in 1368 of Emperor Go-Murakami (1328–68; r. 1339–68), Go-Daigo's heir, along with the capitulation of Kusunoki Masanori (precise dates unknown) the following year, had put an end to any hope of reasserting their power in the Home Provinces. Go-Murakami died in Sumiyoshi in Settsu Province, on the coast, and he had several successors, whose offices continued to exist at Amano in Kawachi Province. But the Southern forces in the area were too small to present any real threat to the shogunate in Kyoto. Surrounded by strong and capable advisors, the young Ashikaga Yoshimitsu could claim a firmer hegemony than any ruler since before the rebellion.

Yoshimitsu's advisors are known by a host of names: Hosokawa, Hatakeyama, Shiba, Isshiki, Nikki, Shibukawa, and so on—names that come up repeatedly in historical records for the next 100 years and more. However, all were offshoots of the Ashikaga line, which in turn traced its roots back to the ancient Minamoto clan. Just as courtiers with names as various as Kujō, Saionji, and Tōin actually identified themselves as Fujiwara in official documents, so most of the leaders of the shogunate claimed common descent from a prestigious ancient clan. When Ashikaga Takauji had turned against the Kamakura shogunate back in 1333, it had been his avowed intent— some say inspired by an old prophecy—to restore the Minamoto to power after more than 100 years of rule by the Hōjō, who claimed descent from the rival Taira clan. By the time of Reizei Tamehide's death in 1372, it appeared that Takauji's hope had been realized. Virtually every high post in the shogunal government was held by a member of the Ashikaga lineage, most of whom also served as *shugo*—shogunate-appointed governors—over the largest and most wealthy provinces all around the capital, along the Inland Sea, and in the East Country.

Yet even after all the years of fighting, one area remained that was still largely under royalist control—Kyushu. There Prince Kaneyoshi (d. 1383), another of Go-Daigo's sons, had enough strength to keep shogunal troops at bay. The forces at his disposal were not large, especially after the defeat of royalists in Settsu Province in the early 1360s. But he had made strategic alliances with local clans, in particular the Kikuchi. Until he and his followers could be overcome decisively, the Ashikaga shogunate could not feel entirely secure. Among other things, there was concern that the Southern Court might make a pact with the Ming Dynasty in China as a tributary state, which was an opportunity Yoshimitsu wanted to reserve for himself.

The man sent by the shogunate to subdue Prince Kaneyoshi was another member of the Ashikaga clan, bearing the surname Imagawa because of the lineage's association with an estate of that name (in Mikawa Province) generations earlier. Traditionally, the Imagawa had served as *shugo* on the eastern seaboard, in the provinces of Tōtōmi and Suruga. Sadayo (1326–1420), current head of the house, had himself served in the leading councils of the shogunate and as *shugo* of Yamashiro Province—the area surrounding Kyoto itself— until the death of Ashikaga Yoshiakira in 1367. Then, along with scores of the deceased shogun's other close followers, he took the tonsure as a display of fealty to his lord. Thereafter he was known by his Buddhist name, Ryōshun. It was he who was dispatched as governor general of Kyushu in 1371, with the explicit order to subdue the royalist forces permanently. He was 45 years old and already a seasoned commander.

Ryōshun's departure obviously affected the members of his own clan and the shogunate most directly. But also affected were the family of Reizei Tamehide, who had counted the Imagawa scion as one of his chief disciples for years. From early on the Imagawa clan had been involved in literary matters, and Ryōshun was a true believer in the ideal of *bunbu* (dedication to both letters—*bun*—and the martial life—*bu*) and a connoisseur of both *uta* and *renga*. Some time in his early 20s—which would mean in the late 1340s, roughly the *Fūgashū* period—he had met the Reizei heir and become a disciple. Later he described his decision to support the Reizei cause in nostalgic terms:

I determined to become a disiciple of the Reizei house because of this poem by Lord Tamehide, on the topic "Autumn Rain":

> A hard thing it is   to find a friend
> of true feeling   in this world of ours.
> Alone, I listen to the rain   through a long
> autumn night.

> *nasake aru / tomo koso kataki / yo narikeri / hitori ame kiku / aki no yosugara*

For some reason, this poem impressed me, and I became a disciple.[32]

---

32. Imagawa, *Rakusho roken*, pp. 108–9.

We do not know precisely when this poem was composed, or under what circumstances. Since a conventional topic is mentioned, it is safe to assume that it was composed at a gathering of some sort, most likely an event sponsored by the shogunate or one of its generals, or perhaps a monthly meeting of the Reizei house. We do know that for the next 20 years, Ryōshun would be one of the Reizei house's staunchest supporters. We also know that he would use his position as a close vassal of first Ashikaga Takauji and then the latter's heir Yoshiakira to gain advantages for his noble teacher.

When Ryōshun left for Kyushu in 1371, Tamehide could not have known that he would leave the fortunes of the house to Tamemasa so soon, any more than he could have known that Ryōshun would be away in Kyushu for nearly a quarter of a century. During that time, Ryōshun would perform admirably as a general and put an effective end to the remnants of the Southern cause, winning accolades from his compatriots in the shogunal ranks. Under his administration, the many leaders of the various Kyushu clans were converted from enemies to allies of the Imagawa and the Ashikaga regime. Even when busy with military matters, however, Ryōshun continued to compose poems and to sponsor an active literary salon among his own generals and local aspirants to high culture. So far away, however, he could be of little help to the son of his old teacher. Although we can assume that there must have been some correspondence between the two men, there is no record of any face-to-face meeting until Ryōshun was called back to the capital in 1395.

Much had changed in the capital during Ryōshun's absence. Most obviously, the long conflict between the Northern and Southern Courts had come to an end when the shogunate put together a deal acceptable to the last emperor of the royalist cause, Go-Kameyama (d. 1424), a grandson of Go-Daigo, in the last days of 1392. Almost immediately, the warrior government began to renege on its promises to the Southern holdouts, now housed in Daikakuji Temple in Saga, just outside the capital, but the will to fight was gone. Eventually, Go-Kameyama did flee the capital and tried to raise troops again in Yoshino, but fruitlessly. In coming years, malcontents who raised the standards of princes of the Southern line in revolt against the government did so without any success. The period of divided rule was over. Even diehards of the old cause such as the courtier-poet Kazan-in Nagachika (1345?–1429) returned to the capital in the early 1390s and began to participate again in poetic events there, whether sponsored by the imperial court or the shogunate. Ashikaga Yoshi-mitsu, only a boy back in 1371, was now a mature man and probably the most able leader the Ashikaga line had or ever would produce; and he was a patron of the arts par excellence.

Yet there had been great changes on the Nijō side as well, of which Ryōshun cannot have been unaware. Of the four lines descending from Tameyo, Tamefuji's line had died out completely, as had Tame-michi's long before; and the remaining lines, descending from second son Tamesada and fifth son Tamefuyu, were not in the best of shape. Only one imperial anthology had been compiled during the previous two decades, and it had nearly been abandoned when the man called as its compiler—Tametō, whom records refer to as a lazy drunk who managed to do nothing on the project for six full years—died before it could be completed.[33] As had happened in the past, another descendant was called in to complete the project. But when that man, Tameshige (1325–85), in turn died in 1385, only his son, Tamemigi (d. 1399), was left to carry on the family name. In this sense, when Ryō-shun returned to Kyoto, the Nijō house was at its nadir as a courtly lineage.

If the bloodline was nearly defunct, however, the traditions it represented—which had become associated with the ideal of ortho-doxy—were not. Tameyo, it will be remembered, had nurtured many disciples among both the nobility and the commoners, some of whom now had established poetic houses in their own right and had over time gained great status in literate society. First of these was the Asukai house, a branch of the Fujiwara descended from the same man who had labeled Abutsu "Lady Master" in Tameie's final days. The Asukai could trace their authority back to Teika, had ties to the Nijō through marriage, and had a long history in the tradition of *kemari* (kickball) as well. At court, the current head of the Asukai family, Masayori (1358–1428), was a trusted member of Yoshimitsu's circle. Then there were the progeny of the cleric Tonna, the most prominent of Tameyo's commoner disciples. After a distinguished career, Tonna had left his own texts and teachings (and properties) to his son Kyōken (precise dates unknown), who retained his father's famous cottage at Ninnanji and had hereditary rights to a cloister in the Ninnaji complex called the Jōkō-in. Both the Asukai and Tonna's heirs were skillful politicians who had managed to make a place for

---

33. Inoue, *Chūsei kadanshi no kenkyū, Muromachi zenki*, pp. 24–25.

themselves in the new order. Furthermore, there were also many disciples of the Nijō house among other noble houses at court and the military aristocracy, not to mention Buddhist monasteries and Nativist shrines.

So despite his pedigree Tamemasa faced firm opposition on a number of fronts. It may be that he also had his grandfather's demure temperament, which may have kept him from pursuing his own interests aggressively.[34] Ryōshun, on the other hand, could not be described as reserved by any standard. After the military campaigns he had fought in Kyushu, literary debates must have seemed like parlor games. At first, even after his return to Kyoto, his time was often taken up with secular matters. When political reversals made it advisable for him to withdraw from the fray in 1400, however, he committed himself completely to literary concerns, which included the advancement of Tamemasa's career. Although in his mid-70s, Ryōshun was still fit and energetic and gave no sign of flagging in his devotion to the Way. He no longer took part in many public events but remained active in private poetry gatherings and spent most of his time in study, research, and reading religious texts. In a word, he took up the life of a *suki*, or connoisseur of the arts, although the standard English translation of the word carries connotations that are perhaps too frivolous, for there was nothing casual about Ryōshun's commitment to poetry or to the success of the Reizei house.

ONE OF Ryōshun's tactics was to lobby from behind the scenes for appointments and promotions for the heir of the Reizei fortunes. On the surface, Tamemasa's rapid progress at court makes it seem that Ryōshun's efforts were immediately successful. In 1398, Tamemasa was elevated to junior third rank; the next year he was made a consultant. Furthermore, from around this time he seems to have begun serving as judge for dedicatory poetry contests held monthly at Kitano Shrine, under the auspices of the shogun—another sign that his authority was being recognized.[35] In fact, though, another

---

34. Atsuta, "Tamemasa to shōen," (pp. 5–6) deals with documents that show Tamemasa had lost rights to several of the estates in Suruga, Bizen, and Awa that Tamehide had worked so hard to secure a generation before.

35. Imagawa, *Nigonshō*, p. 80.

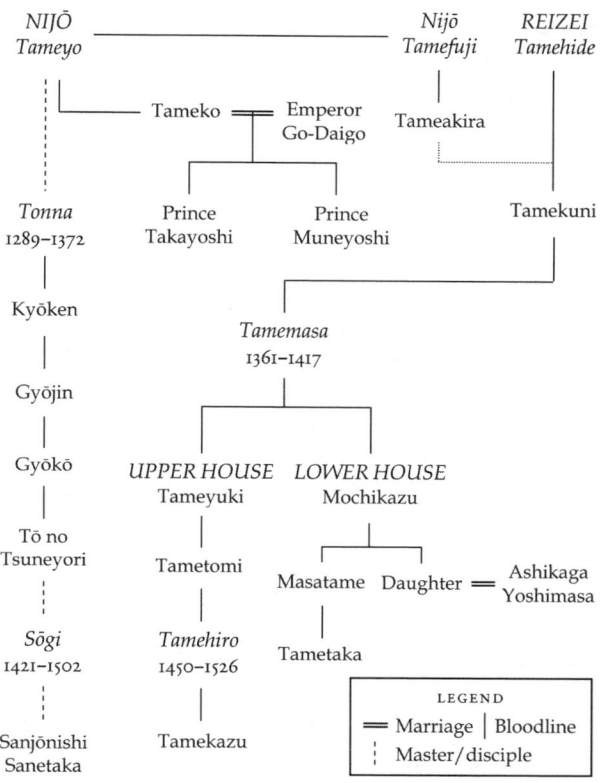

Chart 3 Competing Lineages, 1300–1550

factor may have been more directly involved in these promotions, namely, the death of Nijō Tamemigi around this same time. The only explicit record we have of the event comes from 80 years later, but there is no reason to doubt it. It is chilling in its brevity: "Tamemigi, a man of the Nijō house, was on pilgrimage to Ishiyama when the late Roku-on Consultant had him killed. That was the end of the Nijō line."[36] What turned Ashikaga Yoshimitsu—the Roku-on Consultant—against Tamemigi is not mentioned, but other documents make it clear that he had managed to get one of the shogun's serving women pregnant and then compounded his crime by plotting to murder her before the truth came out.[37] In any case, Tamemasa's rapid rise after 1400 (he became a middle counselor in 1402 and began

36. Inoue, *Chūsei kadanshi no kenkyū, Muromachi zenki*, p. 31.
37. Inoue, "Reizei-ke no rekishi, Ōchō kara chūsei e," p. 115.

appearing regularly at poetic gatherings at the imperial palace) must therefore partly be attributed to his status as the senior survivor of the Mikohidari lineage. Later records make mention here and there of other descendants of Tameyo, but all were younger sons who for one reason or another apparently were not in a position to truly take up the standard of the main house, especially now that Tamemasa had Ryōshun behind him. By the beginning of the fifteenth century, then, only the Reizei could claim direct descent from the patriarchs — in a world where such things still mattered.

Thus more than Ryōshun's lobbying went into Tamemasa's success at court: his pedigree was still his greatest asset. That Ryōshun felt some urgency in the cause even after Tamemigi's death, however, is attested to by a whole series of essays, written between 1403 and 1412, all of which in one way or another attack the Nijō "school" — meaning the Asukai and Tonna's descendants — while championing the Reizei as the legitimate heirs of Shunzei and Teika. Ironically, Tamesuke and Tamehide left no critical or scholarly writings behind, nor would Tamemasa himself. That task fell to Ryōshun, a soldier who was known for his behind-the-scenes maneuvering but who also knew the value of frontal assault.

The first of Ryōshun's essays was written in 1403 and was addressed directly to the Poetry Bureau, probably meaning the office of the Nijō house, although it is unclear just who headed this bureau at the time. The work is titled *Nigonshō* — which may be roughly translated as "Notes on Two Kinds of Words." The gist of the first long passage of the work is that, in Ryōshun's opinion, at least, the Nijō position on diction, which allowed only for the use of vocabulary sanctioned by precedent, was too narrow: "One must question a teaching that says, 'Use ancient words, and none else.'"[38] This was an old argument, and not one that could be expected to move the descendants of Tameyo. As noted before, by this time even Retired Emperor Fushimi had been ruled a deviant on this and other counts. Among the elite, crises nearly always inspired retrenchment. Rather than narrowly philosophical or even pedagogical, Ryōshun's purposes must therefore be seen as more partisan and polemical. Most scholars in fact argue that his assaults were not meant only for his opponents, but for Tamemasa himself, whom the old man wanted to encourage not to abandon the central tenet of the Reizei house —

---

38. Imagawa, *Nigonshō*, p. 65.

which can be described as open-mindedness — out of a desire to be accepted among other poets at court.[39] The last half of the document as we have it now, in fact, was probably presented to Tamemasa directly, appealing to him not to be overly influenced by the works touted by many of his contemporaries. In particular, Ryōshun attacks Tonna, or, to be more precise, those who hold that poet up as a model:

Tonna especially seems able to compose in only one style. Yet would it not be a dubious course to follow only that style, and conclude that we should learn nothing but that style, proscribing the other nine of the ten styles established since long ago? The styles of Tameyo and Tamekane are as different as black and white; and their teachings, as we have received them, are also entirely different. I have no doubt myself that this is because each adhered to only one syle. The teaching of the Fujigayatsu Lord did not say to stop at one style; from ancient times to the present, he said, the style of the disciple does not resemble that of his teacher, nor do the poems of the son resemble those of his father.[40]

The Fujigayatsu Lord refers to Tamesuke, whose dwelling in Kamakura, as noted earlier, was in the area known as Fujigayatsu, Wisteria Valley. What Ryōshun is saying to Tamemasa is therefore that he should hold fast to the teachings of his own ancestors first of all and not the Nijō style, or for that matter the Kyōgoku style, both of which are portrayed as too confining and as based on an incomplete understanding of the Mikohidari heritage. This is what is required to be true to the ideals of the true patriarchs, Shunzei, Teika, and Tameie, next to whom Tonna and his progeny were no more than interlopers. Ryōshun had of course known Tonna himself in the old days. The implication is that back then a man with no pedigree would not have been able to rival a noble house in influence, as Tonna's grandson Gyōjin evidently was able to do in the early 1400s. In fact, Ryōshun even claimed that in his last days Tonna had become a disciple of Tamehide, recognizing the latter's authority after the decline of Nijō fortunes.[41]

The historical record includes no reply to Ryōshun's barrage against commoner poets of the Nijō persuasion. When five years later he wrote another essay, this one titled *Shisetsu jikenshū* (The Master's Teachings and Some Views of My Own), his tone was somewhat less

---

39. Inoue, *Chūsei kadanshi no kenkyū, Muromachi zenki*, pp. 51–53.
40. Imagawa, *Nigonshō*, p. 78.
41. Ibid., p. 80.

confrontational. But an expanded version of his earlier encourage-
ment of the "ten styles" shows that his position had not changed.

In Japanese poetry there are ten styles; from these one should not depart. Any
of these styles will do. Just start with the one style you have mastered well,
be diligent in practice, and then one by one study composition in the remain-
ing nine styles — that is what I was told. Therefore one should not dismiss any
style as bad just because it doesn't suit you or seems difficult for you to learn.
A master adapts to all styles. Someone born with a tendency to be coarse
in speech should commit in his heart to try to make every poem graceful and
refined, just as someone who has no natural gift for poetry and seems to
be weak should put strength into his efforts, composing with energy.
    I was instructed that to favor only one style is to constrict the Way. Tameyo
taught that poems should be composed with elegance, smoothly — and only
in that way, whereas Tamekane's teaching was to compose in grand tones,
with an abundance of words, of any sort, just as one pleases. Tamesuke's
instruction was rather that, no matter which of the styles, one should build
on the one you have mastered and then proceed to try your hand at the idioms
of the others. Since long ago, disciples' poems have always differed from
those of their teachers; nor do the poems of the son resemble those of the
father. Therefore one should follow what comes naturally, I was told.[42]

As a way of driving his point home, Ryōshun appends to this
statement four examples each of poems in the ten styles. All are
poems by old masters of earlier ages — Ki no Tsurayuki, Toshiyori,
Saigyō, Shunzei, Ietaka, and so forth — most of which had been quoted
in earlier critical texts by the patriarchs. If these poets composed in
all styles, he implies, why should poets of the present age not do
the same? Ryōshun's readers would have known that Teika himself
had categorized poems into ten styles (*jittei*) and that it was ludicrous
to suggest that in stressing the fundamental importance of *ushin*
("deep feeling") — which he did, there could be no mistake — the patri-
arch had intended to discount entirely the other nine.[43] As noted in
Chapter 1 of this book, Teika himself had in fact warned one of his
students about precisely what Ryōshun accused Tonna of doing. "It
would result in terrible damage to the Art of Poetry," he had said,
"to insist that a person who has no disposition for it compose in a
certain style that the teacher prefers simply because he happens to
find it personally congenial to himself."[44]

---

42. Imagawa, *Shisetsu jikenshū*, pp. 214–15.
43. Brower, "Fujiwara Teika's *Maigetsushō*," p. 414.
44. Ibid., p. 420.

The next of Ryōshun's essays, written in 1409, was not addressed to Tamemasa but to Ryōshun's own son, under the unambiguous title *Ryōshun isshiden* (Ryōshun's Teachings to His First Son). In content, it is quite different from the earlier works, more informal in tone, more focused on practical advice than on polemics, and doubtless it did not have the sort of broad circulation that the earlier essays—or at least their contents, in reported form—must have had. Nevertheless, the advice it contains on how to pursue the Way of Poetry is probably little different from the advice he gave Tamemasa. From beginning to end, the focus is on the importance of *keiko*, a word that may be translated as "training," meaning both preparation and ongoing engagement in poetic activities. The word had ancient origins, but it was during this period that it gained a truly central place in poetic discourse:

When it comes to *keiko*, one is instructed by one's father or teacher in the beginning, composing according to their direction even when one doesn't understand. One can be called a connoisseur [*suki*] only later, when one composes with more self-assurance. One who has become a connoisseur will not abandon the Way.

During one's apprenticeship, one cannot compose poems as well as one would like: you are jealous of a friend who is praised for having composed a fine poem, you become resentful, and at that time you may even abandon the Way. But this is before one has become a connoisseur. A serious person, whose heart is pure, will not take offense when jeered at or laughed at, and not be overly grateful when praised. One must by all means continue training until becoming a connoisseur. While one is thus engaged in apprenticeship, one should not spend too much time with friends who are not connoisseurs. This is true not only in poetry: for one should avoid bad friends in general, I was told.[45]

If the tone here is chatty and paternalistic, it is probably by design: Ryōshun's pose is that of a master sharing his wisdom with a disciple much as he would in the relaxed moments after some poetry gathering. However relaxed, though, the image of himself that he projects, as in the following passage, is intended to instruct:

There are days when one produces poems easily but also days when one just cannot. This is something that after more than 80 years of practice I have come to understand. In other words, at a time when one is looking through collections, savoring great poems in tranquility, conceptions come to mind

---

45. Imagawa, *Ryōshun isshiden*, p. 179.

and words flow smoothly, whether one is composing for a gathering in advance or on the spot. But at a time when one is distracted by other matters, the poems come to mind more slowly. . . . And when a poem doesn't come to mind, even a master may get down on occasion. But a true connoisseur will keep on composing, even in the midst of war or grief.[46]

No doubt Ryōshun himself had on many occasions kept on composing poems even in the midst of campaigns while in Kyushu. That is what dedication to poetry as a Way required: religious devotion, the discipline that comes from constant training. One of the central messages of Ryōshun's instructions to his son—and to Tamemasa, of course—was that poetry was something elemental, dedication to which brought its own rewards.

In 1412 Ryōshun produced the last of his essays, *Rakusho roken* (Revealing Scribblings). At the end of it he noted that he was writing in response to attacks against Tamemasa by certain "commoner poets," probably alluding again to Tonna's descendants, who must have felt threatened by the revival of Reizei fortunes and by Ryōshun's own diatribes of the preceding few years. After confessing that in his old age, Japanese poetry had been the only friend to offer him comfort, Ryōshun lamented the jibes against Tamemasa's poems circulating at the time and once more did his best to set the record straight.

On the Houses of Japanese Poetry: From Lord Shunzei to Lord Teika there was one lineage, which after Tameie's day split into the three houses of Tameyo, Tamekane, Tamesuke. Even then, the Reizei inherited the house and its secret books; that is something the whole world knows. Now, the lineages of Tameyo and Tamekane have virtually died out, their last branches coming to a final end with Lord Tameakira and Lord Tameshige, which is a sign that they must have lost favor with the gods.[47]

After thus disposing of the Nijō—or averring that the gods had done so—Ryōshun goes on to praise Tamemasa and attack Tonna, again, as an interloper whose elevation to hero status he depicts as a travesty:

Perhaps because he has a natural talent for new styles, each of Lord Tamemasa's poems sounds fresh; and he never writes to gain the praise of men but always with the intent of expressing something from deep in his own heart. . . .

---

46. Ibid., p. 188.
47. Imagawa, *Rakusho roken*, pp. 89–90.

In recent years, there are those who think of Tonna as some kind of sage of poetry, and focus their attention entirely on his personal anthology, *Sōanshū*, either praising it or stealing from it. But Tonna was capable of composing in just one style and wrote nothing at all in the others. How can we say that it is only Lord Tamemasa whose style is lacking? The adepts of old, too, gained in merit after taking on years, gaining fame and producing famous poems. Whom can one name that was skillful from youth on up? As long as one remains within the ten styles, one should study the style that suits one the best and comes most naturally. And who has the right to criticize? If one doesn't think well of Lord Tamemasa's style, one doesn't need to study it. But as long as the Way of Poetry continues in the house, he is the one people should ask about the teachings on the *Sandaishū* and the proper way to compose poems.[48]

After all the rhetoric, it is the last sentence of this passage that is the most crucial to Ryōshun's argument. For despite all the claims about the excellence of Tamemasa's poetry, Ryōshun knew that in the end artistic talent was not sufficient for success at court, however necessary; other kinds of capital, social and cultural, were equally important. In the case of the Reizei, that meant the authority of lineage and the texts in the family library, including early texts of the *Sandaishū* and a host of others to which outsiders had no access without permission, along with "oral transmissions" (*kuden*) passed down from generations before—without the latter of which Ryōshun argued, no one could claim true status in the field. Even access to written commentaries was not enough:

Because nowadays people are able to look at the commentaries on their own, they don't seek out the oral transmissions, mistakenly thinking that they need not ask about the teachings of former sages and masters of today. But understanding of *Man'yōshū*, in particular, demands the perspective of the oral transmissions.[49]

Such statements seem so self-serving that it is easy to discount them as pure propaganda. If so, however, it needs to be emphasized that the propaganda was clearly succeeding, as one might expect it to in a highly hierarchical and status-conscious society. For all the evidence suggests that, precisely because they bolstered the authority of various houses and traditions, the passing on of "secret teachings" from masters to disciples was by this time becoming the ultimate form of licensing for most artists. Tonna had known this,

------

48. Ibid., p. 91.
49. Ibid., p. 92.

as evidenced by the care he took in gaining instruction under Tame-
yo and later Tamehide; and his heirs, Ryōshun implied, should be
aware of it too. Among all the poets of the day, only Tamemasa
could claim a direct relationship with the founders of the medieval
poetic tradition, by bloodline, textual inheritance, and direct instruc-
tion, especially after Tamehide had managed to gain access to the
Nijō manuscripts by adopting his son into the Nijō line.

The precise content of the Reizei oral transmissions is impossible
to know in great detail, since the whole point of such transmissions
was that they should pass only from master to disciple, and only
in oral form—at least in the early years of the practice. Ryōshun's
singling out of eighth-century *Man'yōshū* as a text that could not be
interpreted properly without instruction, however, hints that some
of the teachings involved issues not of semantic "interpretation" so
much as issues of proper pronunciation, which in the case of that an-
cient text were legion. The same conclusion is suggested by anecdotes
such as the one noted above involving Tameakira carrying around
a treasured manuscript of *Kokinshū* to gatherings in order to support
arguments about the proper vocalizing of problematic words. Other
hints about the content of the transmissions are available in the afore-
mentioned *Reizei-ke waka hihi kuden* (Secret Poetic Transmissions of
the Reizei House), which, although dating from a later time in written
form, contains not only items attributed to Shunzei and Teika—all
traceable to extant sources from earlier times—but also one attributed
to Tamemasa himself: "When recording a poem on a poem strip,
one should not ink one's brush before beginning the lower half of
the poem. This was the teaching of Lord Tamemasa."[50]

Here we see that the teachings involved not only philological
problems but also ritual practices, which seem to have differed be-
tween lineages. All houses recorded poems on strips of paper—
tanzaku—in two lines, breaking the poem into its upper and lower
halves (*kami no ku* and *shimo no ku*). Yet even in so seemingly trivial
a practice, evidently the houses had evolved distinct traditions. The
teaching of poetic composition to disciples no doubt still remained
the primary activity of the Reizei heir, but those same disciples
needed to be catechized in both knowledge and practices in order
to participate fully in poetic culture. Ryōshun's point, which we
can be sure was not lost on those who read or heard the arguments

---

50. *Reizei-ke waka hihi kuden*, p. 221.

propounded in *Rakusho roken*, was that, as the direct heirs of the patriarchs of the Mikohidari line, the Reizei and their traditions had the greatest claim to authority now that the Nijō house was gone.

IN THE Third Month of 1415, as if in recognition of Ryōshun's insistence that Tamemasa was the only legitimate heir of Japan's premier poetic house, the Reizei heir was promoted to the office of major counselor, becoming the first member of the Reizei lineage ever to attain that lofty post. Already honored with the post of Minister of Public Affairs, this put him on a par with earlier Mikohidari heirs, from Teika to Tameyo. Then he was honored with the request to present a 1,000-poem sequence of his poems to the new shogun, Yoshimochi, which he submitted later the same year. Finally, the poet Shōtetsu (1381–1459) records that during the next few months, the rights to both Hosokawa Estate and Ono Estate—which had been lost by the family half a century before, in the confusion following Go-Daigo's rebellion—were returned to the Reizei by shogunal edict, along with a promise to enforce demands for revenue. For years the house had been petitioning for the return, with some success, but with Yoshimochi's support the rights were now secure, at least for the time being.[51]

Thus after more than 100 years, the full ambition of Tamesuke finally came to pass: the Reizei lineage was recognized as the rightful heir of Tameie, with all requisite honors, privileges, and resources. So flush was the house, in fact, that Tamemasa began to contemplate plans to divide it into two branches between his two sons, both of whom showed poetic talent. The first, Tameyuki (1393–1439), was already on the roster at court, while the second was only in his early teens and had not yet had his coming-of-age ceremony. Such "splits" were not uncommon in noble families, even in the late medieval period. One example is the Hino lineage, which thanks to its close association with the Ashikaga shoguns, who generally took their wives from that clan, was able to spawn not just one but two separate sub-lineages—the Yanagiwara and the Karasumaru. Wealth was a prerequisite for such an action, of course; but equally important was talent, just as it had been when Tameie chose to divide his own lineage a century or more before. For a father to contemplate such an action meant that he saw great potential in the younger son, so much so that he could not bear to see him off to some temple, which

---

51. Atsuta, "Tamemasa to shōen," pp. 7–8.

was the usual fate of all but the eldest son in a noble house at the time.[52] In this case, there is no sign that there was bad blood between Tamemasa's sons: the separation would be an amicable one in which the elder took the main estate rights (many of which we have no record of) and the library inherited from Tameie as his birthright, while the younger got the Hosokawa Estate, half the Ono Estate, the library inherited from the Nijō line at the time of Tamekuni, and a treasured portrait of Abutsu.[53] In addition, the younger son was given the honor of using one of the characters from the name of the shogun—Ashikaga Yoshimochi (1386–1428)—to use in his own—*Mochi*kazu (1402–54; later changed to Mochitame). With such a foundation in both material and social capital, Tamemasa looked forward to a future in which the Reizei would finally rule in poetic matters in the capital city.

The next event in the saga of the Reizei family—Tamemasa's death at the very hour of his triumph—seems almost predictable. He died, suddenly it would seem, in the First Month of 1417, at only 57. Despite all of his efforts, then, the Reizei house again had to be entrusted to young men without paternal support, always a risky proposition in a hierarchical society where the connections of senior officials were nearly always a factor in promotions and favors. Tameyuki was not yet 30, and the younger son had not even attained his majority. Fortunately, both were well liked by Ashikaga Yoshimochi. The heirs of the Asukai lineage and Tonna, however, were older, more seasoned, and they too were in the shogun's good graces. Once again, the years ahead promised only uncertainty for the Reizei house.

Scholars disagree about the date of Imagawa Ryōshun's death. Almost certainly, though, he passed on in his late 80s, before or not long after Tamemasa. So the Reizei would have to go on without his help as well. The old warrior's son, though active as a poet in Suruga Province, would never become a force in Kyoto. Yet Ryōshun's legacy to the Reizei house, in the form of his essays, would continue to perform service in the years to come. It is tempting, in fact, to assume that it was Ryōshun rather than members of the house per se who actually defined what is called "the Reizei style." But *Reizei-ke waka hihi kuden*, recorded by some member of the house in later times, shows that the old soldier's arguments were probably

---

52. Atsuta, "Shimo Reizei-ke no bunritsu," p. 7.
53. Reizei Fumiko, *Reizei Fumiko ga kataru Kyō no miyabi*, p. 191.

very much in keeping with instructions passed down from Tame-suke. Unlike Ryōshun's works, *Reizei-ke waka hihi kuden* was not a widely circulated text but rather a manual written for a specific student, recording some of the teachings that were passed on only to disciples. But there we find a statement about the ten styles that is remarkably similar to Ryōshun's:

In Japanese poetry, one should for the most part aim for the broad Way, attempting all of the ten styles. For each person to think only of the style he has mastered as good and dismiss as bad other styles that seem too lofty or difficult—that would be terribly constricting. Tamesuke said, "Among the ten styles, no matter which one it is, one should first learn to compose in the one that suits one's heart and thus has been able to master; thereafter, if one will attempt all ten styles, one will develop strength and become adept. It is impossible to determine which of the styles of poetry is above the rest. A good poem, in whatever style, is simply good; a bad poem, in whatever style, is simply bad."[54]

So Ryōshun's progressive attitudes may in fact have been in-herited from his Reizei teachers, whose poetry reflects precisely the same opinions. Of course one must be careful in calling these atti-tudes "liberal" in the modern sense of the word. By definition, the noble houses of the imperial court, no matter what their area of specialization, were elitist and conservative. Ryōshun's own insis-tence on the importance of pedigree and textual lineage is proof enough of that. One can justifiably claim, however, that by com-parison with their rivals of the Nijō tradition the Reizei were more open-minded on matters of diction and style and more well disposed toward new ideas in general. A statement by a poet writing some years later confirms the general impression succinctly: "In general, the Nijō house is so intent on avoiding anything unorthodox that they proscribe even the least bit of ingenuity. In the Reizei house, however, they try to put something unexpected in every poem, so that when one hears the poem it is as if one has suddenly been startled awake."[55]

Accounting for this is no easy matter. Certainly, at some level, the individual predilections of Tamesuke, Tamehide, and Tamemasa must have played a role in establishing the "house style" (*ie no kaze*).

---

54. *Reizei-ke waka hihi kuden*, pp. 217–18.
55. From *Tsuribune*, an early sixteenth-century *waka* treatise. Quoted in Hamanaka and Nagasaki, *Kōdō suru josei, Abutsu-ni*, p. 190.

Likewise, the position they took vis-à-vis the main house may be explained largely by the practical need to distinguish themselves from their competitors: as in so many political and ideological disputes, opponents often took up their "positions" less for positive than for negative reasons. In such battles, to enunciate difference was the whole point. Rather than attributing the broad-mindedness of the Reizei poets solely to such factors, however, one should at least mention the influence of their place in the literary field of the day—a place outside Kyoto, especially in the early days, in a market where the courtly orthodoxy and scholasticism of the senior house might have been a hard sell. Relatively few of Tamesuke's students among the warrior elite of Kamakura could boast the sort of education that courtiers in Kyoto took for granted. When it came to composing poetry, these men wanted to do things the proper way—which is why they valued the services of the Reizei house in organizing and directing poetic events. Furthermore, they wanted the poems they produced to be acceptable in courtly terms. However, they did not know the literary canon as well as the Kyoto elite did, and they could not be expected to recognize allusions so readily; they may well have found themselves quite naturally on the side of Ryōshun in the debate over "poetic" vocabulary. In this context, then, one can see how patrons of Reizei in the East Country would be attracted by another statement from *Reizei-ke waka hihi kuden*: "The most fundamental of styles is based on describing things just as they are, with no adornment."[56] The warrior ethic was based on simplicity and directness—ideals that the Reizei approach seemed to validate.

Of course critical principles are not always clearly manifested in poems. But, in the case of the early Reizei poets, there does seem to have been general agreement between dogma and practice. This is particularly evident in the poems of the 1,000-poem sequence Tamemasa presented to the shogun in 1415, which is our most substantial record of his poetic work. As noted above, this sequence was commissioned by the shogun, and as such included only well-polished verses; nothing experimental or haphazard could be allowed in so formal a collection. Furthermore, all of the poems are on the usual

---

56. *Reizei-ke waka hihi kuden*, p. 216. A similar injunction is found in *Yakumo mishō* (ca. 1242?), a primer written by Retired Emperor Juntoku. See supplementary note 37 in *Reizei-ke waka hihi kuden*, p. 349.

dai, or fixed topics, many in fact on topics that had been in use for at least 300 years. If conventional in that sense, however, Tamemasa's offering to Ashikaga Yoshimochi does display broad mastery of many styles, as recommended by Ryōshun, Tamehide, and Tamesuke. Long after his own untimely death, the 1,000-poem collection would serve as a handbook for heirs of the house and their disciples. More than 300 years later, for instance, Reizei Tamemura, when asked who of those in the Reizei lineage were particularly excellent as poets, he would list only three as "poets of real power" (*chikara mo aru onsakusha*), among them Tamemasa.[57]

However insistent Reizei texts are on the importance of mastering the ten styles defined by Teika, in actual practice there is little evidence that they attempted to mimic those styles in any precise way. Instead, the textual record shows that "ten styles" was a kind of shorthand for general variety in conception, vocabulary, diction, subject matter, and tone—a kind of variety that they felt was lacking in poems inspired only by the ideal of *ushin* as defined by their opponents in the Nijō camp. Thus while it may be difficult to single out poems from Tamemasa's collection as examples of, say, Teika's *yūgen*, one can nevertheless point to poems that in their richness of imagery, intricacy of conception, and evocativeness are at least reminiscent of the works of the *Shin kokinshū* era:

> Spring: "Dawn Moon in Spring"
>
> Ever more heavy,   the moon sinks
> to the bottom   of the spreading haze—
> as a bellsound rings out, clear   in a sky opening
> to dawn.[58]
>
> *tsuki wa nao / kasumi no soko ni / omoritsutsu / kane no oto sumu / akegata no sora*
>
> Love: Love, with "Pine Crickets" as an Image
>
> How forlorn it seems   to listen as the vows
> one made   fade into darkness—
> with the calls of pine crickets   showering down
> near the eaves.[59]
>
> *kikiwabinu / tsuraki chigiri no / kakikurete / nokiba shigururu / matsumushi no koe*

---

57. Miyabe no Yoshimasa, *Yoshimasa kikigaki*, p. 686. The others are Tamehide and Tamehihro.

58. Reizei Tamemasa, *Tamemasa senshu*, poem no. 81.

59. Ibid., poem no. 745.

The components of the first poem, both visual and aural, combine to make a shadowy landscape full of symbolic potential rather than presenting any kind of straightforward description. Much the same can be said of the scene of crickets' voices "showering" down in the night, pushing all thoughts of love into the darkness. If nothing else, then, these poems reveal that Tamemasa was truly a student of the patriarchs who could produce poems in a broad range of registers. The fact is borne out also by the following example, which displays a complementary dimension of his craft:

Spring: "Plum Blossoms Next Door"

I had not thought   to be gazing
at flowers.   But across the fence,
between yards, blossoming high: branches of flowering
plum.[60]

hana min to / shirazarikeri na / nakagaki no / hedate ni takaku / sakeru ume ga e

As is so often the case in court poetry, this poem presents a moment of aesthetic enchantment that in turn validates the poet as a person of proper sensibility, the sort of person who is prepared by temperament and training to appreciate beauty when it suddenly appears. If the earlier poems seem close to the more evocative poems of Teika's early years, however, this one is more witty and cerebral and shows that Tamemasa was indeed committed to "aiming for the broad Way."

To give his Nijō critics their due, however, it must also be admitted that apparently these are not the styles Tamemasa prefers. For a much larger proportion of the poems of the 1,415 reveal less of a debt to Teika than to the "unorthodox" style of *Gyokuyōshū* and *Fūgashū*, which, to the consternation of his Nijō rivals, Tamemasa doubtless accepted as a legitimate strain within the court tradition:

Summer: "The Winds of an Evening Shower"

As a raucous wind   blusters through a grove
of trees,   birds rise into flight;
passing roughly —   an evening storm roiling in
the summer sky.[61]

kaze sawagu / hayashi no tori mo / tachiukare / araku zo suguru / yūdachi no sora

---

60. Ibid., poem no. 62.
61. Ibid., poem no. 289.

Autumn: "Moon in a Grove of a Trees"

From the treetops   of a grove chilled
by the moon   I hear something:
beneath the snow falling down —   the call
of a night crow.[62]

tsuki sayuru / mori no kozue ni / kikoyu nari / yuki no shita naru / yogarasu no koe

No doubt Nijō Tameyo would have been critical of both these poems, the first for its confusion of images ("A poem on the topic 'Evening Showers' should focus on rain and not on birds!") and the second for the neologism "night crow" (*yogarasu*), a colloquialism that from the orthodox point of view was not appropriate in poetry. That Tamemasa chose to include in a collection presented to the shogun such offenses against the stricter conventions of the main house shows that Ryōshun's encouragements had had their desired effect. Tamemasa had become a standard-bearer for what over time had become the traditions of his own house.

This same fact is even more apparent in a host of poems that quite openly depict scenes from everyday life of the sort found so often in poems by Tamesuke:

Spring: "Lark Along the Road"

A farmer's plow   must have left some earth
unturned   out on the meadow:
from the paddy dike ahead   a lark raises
its voice.[63]

suki ireshi / noda no shibafu ya / nokoruran / yukute no tsutsumi / hibari naku nari

Winter: "The Road at the End of the Year"

As the old year wanes,   people are busy
as can be: meeting on the street,
they speak but a word or two   and then go their
separate ways.[64]

toshi no kure / sa zo isogashi to / au hito no / tada hitokoto ni / yuki wakarenuru

In *Nigonshō*, Ryōshun had noted that the main house criticized Tamesuke's poems as lacking in "loftiness" (*take*).[65] Perhaps they would have characterized Tamemasa in the same way. Rather than viewing

---

62. Ibid., poem no. 410.
63. Ibid., poem no. 91.
64. Ibid., poem no. 594.
65. Imagawa, *Nigonshō*, p. 80.

pastoral vistas from afar, the speaker of these poems describes quo-
tidian reality—and from up close. Where the impetus behind such
quotidian scenes comes from is hard to say. The most immediate
possibility is Zen Buddhism, an interest in which Tamemasa may
have inherited from Tamesuke, who is known to have studied with
the great monk Musō Soseki. Wherever the stance derives from, it
is one of the most outstanding features of his poems, and one that
again contrasts sharply with the approach of the Nijō house. The
poem about a lark singing near a recently plowed field, for instance,
must have raised eyebrows in the same way Tamesuke's poem about
grass cut for fertilizer had long before. And anyone with a proper
poetic training knew that people in poems do not stop to chat right
out on the street, even if only exchanging a word or two.

A final example from the sequence must have evoked a similar
reaction. This one is on the common topic of *kinuta*, or robes being
cleaned on a fulling block, a topic that in countless earlier poems
evokes the image of a lonely wife waiting in solitude for her man
to return. What Tamemasa does with the topic is almost plebian by
comparison:

> Autumn: "Robes Beaten in the Night"
>
> As evening falls,   friends from
> all around come   and gather to talk:
> noises rising with the sound   of mallet
> on fulling block.[66]
>
> *yoi no ma wa/atari no tomo mo/yorikite ya/hitooto shigeku/koromo utsuran*

Again, the scene Tamemasa presents is not remote but immediate:
the voices of people chatting in the evening, mixed with the crack
of a mallet striking the fulling block. Imagining the scene one cannot
help but remember that Tameie—at least according to the report
of the Reizei nemesis Tameyo—had criticized a poem by the *Shin
kokinshū*-era poet Kujō Yoshitsune because it suggested that his
own wife was fulling the robes, something no woman of high rank
would ever do.[67] Furthermore, Tamemasa's poem does much more
than that. Not only does it refuse to end on a note of refined melan-
choly; it creates a plebeian scene of friends gathering together in the
evening to enjoy one another's company. Rather than pathos, then,

---

66. Reizei Tamemasa, *Tamemasa senshu*, poem no. 451.
67. Nijō Tameyo, *Waka teikin*, pp. 133–34.

the scene offers something akin to conviviality. Once again, the poem seems to suggest a basis in lived experience, or at least the willingness to allow a broader range of experience into the world of *uta*, as if everyday experience might be valuable in and of itself. No doubt Nijō poets had witnessed such things as well; even life in the capital was not entirely removed from the activities of everyday existence. But they chose, as a matter of principle, not to write so directly about the stuff of normal experience. In this sense, the poems of Tamemasa's 1,000-verse sequence, a copy of which went into the house library as a legacy to generations to come, lived up to Ryōshun's praise of them as fresh and new.

FIVE

Muromachi, Sakamoto, and Beyond

RECORDS FROM the mid-fifteenth century tell us that at that time Reizei Mochikazu was living near the intersection of Konoe and Muromachi Avenues and that his elder brother Tameyuki was not far away, although the precise location of his residence is not known.[1] Nearby was the Tsuchimikado Palace, residence of the emperor, as well as the palace of the retired emperor. Proximity to these important symbolic sites was an unequivocal marker of status in noble society.

Of course the huge compounds of the shogun and his strongmen, many of which were located in the same area, dwarfed the houses of even the most powerful nobles. Yet to be able to maintain a residence anywhere in the northern reaches of the capital city—an area known by the name Muromachi—was a privilege afforded only to those with high lineage and the resources to support a sizable household. That the brothers were living there at all shows that they were somehow able to maintain a courtly lifestyle, though both were still only at fifth rank and far from realizing the potential of their birthright.[2] The men seem to have had a cordial relationship, based partly on common interest. Allusions to the Reizei Poetry Bureau and scattered references in contemporary documents to various events and activities indicate that they were practicing their house specialty as their father had taught them to do, teaching disciples poetry composition and passing on the oral transmissions to qualified candidates;

---

1. Carter, *Regent Redux*, p. 132; Inoue, *Chūsei kadanshi no kenkyū, Muromachi zenki*, p. 138.

2. Inoue, "Reizei-ke no rekishi 8: Tamemasa, Tameyuki," p. 5.

acting as leaders at various gatherings, including their own *tsukinami-kai*, or monthly meetings; and putting the resources of their libraries to use.

As might be expected, there were ups and downs. During the reign of Ashikaga Yoshinori (1394–1441), for instance, the Reizei brothers appear to have been under a kind of censure, having offended him in some way that the records do not disclose.[3] The most open sign of the shogun's disfavor came in 1433, when there were rumors about the possibility of a new imperial anthology. As direct heirs of Teika and Tameie, Tameyuki and his brother must have assumed that the time had finally come for the Reizei to take their rightful place in history as compilers of a memorial to their age, which is surely what Tameie, Tamesuke, and Tamehide had planned for in times past. When the announcement was made, however, the man honored with the appointment instead was Asukai Masayo (1390–1452), who would be assisted by Gyōkō (1391–1455), a descendant of Tonna. The Reizei men were not even offered the honor of serving as co-compilers or librarians, and when the anthology was finished six years later, only two of Tameyuki's poems were included, and not a single one by Mochikazu. In the meantime, the shogun had stripped Tameyuki of all incomes from the Ono estate, in response to Reizei refusals to share documents with Masayo.[4]

We know about Tameyuki's punishment from *Kanmon nikki*, the diary of the father of Emperor Go-Hanazono (1419–70; r. 1428–64), who had ascended in 1428.[5] Remarkably, however, other records reveal nothing to suggest that either Tameyuki or Mochikazu was ever put under house arrest or otherwise restricted in their movements around the city. Indeed, an amazing feature of the story is that both seem to have continued to perform many of their usual literary functions, as evidenced by four manuscripts containing poems by Mochikazu for the years 1429, 1432, 1434, and 1437. Whereas the four documents deserve some attention as the first texts that can be called "personal anthologies" of any member of the Reizei lineage,[6] they are equally interesting as records of the life of the house during a time of distress.

---

3. Brower and Carter, *Conversations with Shōtetsu*, pp. 44, 48, 64–65.

4. Inoue, *Chūsei kadanshi no kenkyū, Muromachi zenki*, pp. 110–17. See also Brower and Carter, *Conversations with Shōtetsu*, pp. 54–55, 57.

5. Brower and Carter, *Conversations with Shōtetsu*, p. 57.

6. As noted above, Tamesuke's *Fujigayatsu wakashū* was actually compiled long after his death, with poems from other sources.

The most noteworthy feature of the last three texts is that they contain virtually no mention of activities at the imperial court: no attendance at poetry gatherings or rituals in the imperial palace or at the residence of the emperor's father. As noted earlier, Mochikazu had been a regular in the salon of Retired Emperor Go-Komatsu (1377–1433; r. 1382–1412). Reflecting this fact, the 1429 record, which includes nearly 400 poems, many with headnotes that provide information about where and when they were composed, notes numerous gatherings in the retired emperor's chambers. Sometimes Mochikazu was in attendance, evidently as one of the courtiers assigned to be "on watch" (*kobanshū*) in Go-Komatsu's precincts; on other occasions, he was among those particularly invited to the sovereign's monthly poetry meetings or special banquets. After Go-Komatsu's death, however, Mochikazu's invitations to such activities appear to have ceased. Likewise, neither brother participated in shogunal meetings after the announcement of plans for a new imperial anthology.[7]

Yet the later collections of the 1430s show that, despite being excluded at court, the Reizei were still holding their own monthly meetings religiously, usually on the 16th day of each month, at the Reizei Poetry Bureau. Who attended these meetings is not recorded for the most part, but as such meetings were primarily for family members and disciples, we can assume that generally the brothers and their progeny, as well as some family retainers, were there. Almost certainly, the number also included some women from the household, among them nameless daughters who would contribute greatly to the family fortunes in days to come. Headnotes to the poems indicate that the meetings were held according to established precedent, with attendees bringing poems on pre-assigned topics with them for formal "airing" (*hirō*), after which the group would turn to extemporaneous composition (*tōza*). As senior member of the line, Tameyuki probably had the responsibility of choosing topics and assigning other members to serve as lectors and scribes.

Another activity noted in the collections of 1432, 1434, and 1437 are visits to various shrines in the Kyoto area, most notably Kitano Shrine, located just west of the city. Dedicated to the god of scholarship, Sugawara no Michizane (845–903), this shrine was a major site of worship for all literati and served as a place to offer up prayers for success, for redress, and so on. No doubt during the days when the house was suffering under censure, Tameyuki and Mochikazu

---

7. Inoue, *Chūsei kadanshi no kenkyū, Muromachi zenki*, pp. 582–85.

visited there often to plead their case to the god. Mochikazu's visits to other shrines and temples at Kurama, Ishiyama, and Tamatsushima may have been similarly motivated. His pilgrimage to Niitamatsushima Shrine on Fifth Avenue, a small shrine dedicated to the memory of Shunzei, almost certainly must have been inspired by hope for favor from the founding patriarch of the Mikohidari line.

The collections also show evidence that, in addition to making pilgrimages to religious sites, the brothers traveled for more secular reasons or to admire the blossoms or fall leaves. Also noted is their ongoing correspondence with patrons, some of them among the military elite who evidently felt free to communicate with a house supposedly under censure. While hardly evidence of an extravagant lifestyle, then, it appears from Mochikazu's collections that despite political losses and financial hardship, even the lower house was somehow able to maintain itself as an institution. Not coincidentally, Mochikazu in fact notes that the house was careful to keep the memory of the patriarchs alive and in the public eye by visiting appropriate sites and composing poems on the death anniversaries of Shunzei, Teika, and Tamemasa, the latter at the Poetry Bureau. Thus it is apparent that even in the absence of direct support from either the shogun or the imperial family, the Reizei were able to find a market for their services in literate society — meaning the noble houses, the military aristocracy, and religious establishments, all of which held poetry gatherings that required the expertise of specialists. In 1439, Tameyuki died, still only a middle captain of fourth rank, but the younger brother was still able to keep the Reizei Way alive.

In the summer of 1441, Ashikaga Yoshinori was assassinated, bringing to an end a difficult period for many noble houses. The warrior leaders of the various clans that made up the shogunal councils acted quickly to choose a young man as shogun and issued orders of amnesty for all at court who had suffered the murdered shogun's displeasure. For the government, the death of the shogun was an opportunity to put the affairs in the hands of more stable men, men who would interfere less in the internal affairs of their own clans, first of all, but also men who could return the atmosphere of the capital city to a state of calm.

Naturally, there were many among the court aristocracy eager to return to their places of prominence. Among these were of course the leaders of the Reizei house, Mochikazu and young Tametomi (1426–97), Tameyuki's heir. Also prominent in the revival were Ichijō

Kaneyoshi (1402–81), head of one of the five houses of the regency and an important scholar, who had been under a cloud during much of Yoshinori's reign, and the poet Shōtetsu, a disciple of Ryōshun and Tamemasa, who was the most prominent *jige* poet of the time. An old-fashioned poetry contest at Kaneyoshi's house, patterned on events from earlier and more prosperous days, was held earlier in 1443 as a kind of "coming out" for many who had been in disfavor. Shōtetsu was there, as were Tametomi and Mochikazu; so was Tonna's heir Gyōkō, partisan of Nijō traditions. But Asukai Masanaga (precise dates unknown) chose not to attend the event, instead sending his entries in for consideration in absentia. In all, the contest was interpreted as a declaration of the return of the Reizei to active participation in poetic life at court.[8] While not "public" in the modern sense, poetry contests were highly "publicized" events that functioned as displays of power and patronage.

The next two decades were a time of renewal for the Reizei. Beginning in 1446, they were again invited to poetry gatherings at the imperial palace, after a decade of spotty attendance. There they participated regularly alongside the Asukai, in time taking on some leadership roles. Although we have no direct evidence of monthly meetings held by Tametomi, we do know that Mochikazu held his own monthly gatherings on the 21st day of each month—separately from those of the upper house, we may assume. Furthermore, we know from an entry in a diary of the time that Mochikazu passed on the house teachings concerning the proper conduct of poetry meetings to middle-ranking courtiers, who also brought him poems for critique.[9] So he too practiced according to patterns set down by previous generations, as poet, judge and critic, and tutor. With the support of Ichijō Kaneyoshi, Mochikazu was advanced to junior fourth rank, upper grade, in 1442. By 1449 he was promoted to junior third rank and made a consultant. Perhaps as a clear avowal of his identity as a member of the Reizei house, he changed his name from Mochikazu to Mochi*tame*, connecting himself to a long line of ancestors. Even when participating in a poetry gathering at the imperial palace for *tozama*—"outsiders," whose number included the young shogun Ashikaga Yoshimasa (1436–90) and some high-ranking clerics, as well as Ichijō Kaneyoshi, Mochitame's nephew Tametomi,

---

8. *Saki no sesshō-ke uta-awase.* See Inoue, *Chūsei kadanshi no kenkyū, Muromachi zenki*, pp. 138–41.

9. Inoue, *Chūsei kadanshi no kenkyū, Muromachi zenki*, p. 138.

Gyōkō, and Asukai Masanaga—it was therefore very much as an insider and as part of the elite circle of poets surrounding the emperor and the shogun.

> On "Snow in the Pines," from a 50–poem sequence composed
> on the 18th day of the Sixth Month for the first Outsider Gathering
> of the year
>
> A withering wind   turns my eyes
> toward what the sound   left in its wake—
> snow-covered pine boughs   that are gently
> swaying still.[10]
>
> *fukishiori / oto seshi kaze no / ato ni mata / shizuka ni nabiku / yuki no matsugae*

Tametomi too made steady progress in the ranks, likewise receiving support from Kaneyoshi, who took Tametomi into his employ as a *kerai*, or house steward, following a pattern set by Teika and Tameie centuries before. Tametomi's older sister was made the wife of Kaneyoshi's heir, Norifusa, further cementing the relationship between the two houses and showing the important role still played by patronage in court culture.

Mochitame fell ill in 1454, and when it became apparent that he would not recover, he was granted junior second rank and promoted to major counselor. As had happened so often before, this left a Reizei heir—his son Naritame, later known as Masatame (1445–1523)—in a vulnerable position. Only ten years old, the young man was not judged mature enough even to be entrusted with the secret teachings of the house, which were instead given to his older sister. But that sister, known as Tō Dainagon no Tsubone (precise dates unknown), turned out to be a gifted woman who taught her brother well and so impressed others around her that she was hailed as a reincarnation of Abutsu, sent by Heaven to restore the glory of the house. By this time, women seldom appeared at public events but were often active behind the scenes. Eventually Masatame's sister would go into the service of the shogun Ashikaga Yoshimasa, where she would also be in a good position to further the interests of her family.[11]

Furthermore, Masatame had the support of a host of other allies, among them Shōtetsu, who had benefited as greatly from the removal of Yoshinori as had anyone in the Reizei camp. Whereas his huge personal poetry anthology, *Sōkonshū* (Grass Roots Anthology,

---

10. *Kōen tsugiuta*, poem no. 01136.
11. Inoue, "Reizei-ke no rekishi 9: Tametomi," p. 4.

ca. 1473) records relatively few poems for the late 1430s, the years between 1441 and his death in 1459 show him at the height of his powers—and of his popularity, which he shared with the descendants of his old teacher, Reizei Tamemasa. As a commoner, he practiced primarily among the ranks of the warrior clans, just as the Reizei pursued their Way among the high nobility, but still they were allies against the Asukai and the descendants of Tonna.

In an essayistic work recorded in his last decade, Shōtetsu reveals that he had little use for the poetic houses at court, instead taking only the great Teika as his mentor: "Teika's descendants split into the two factions of Nijō and Reizei. . . . But it is my opinion that a person should pay no attention whatever to these schools. Instead, one ought to cherish the style and spirit of Teika and strive to emulate him even though one may never succeed."[12]

Precisely what inspired this criticism is a mystery. One suspects that it may have been the rather uninspired performance of young Tametomi at poetry gatherings, which various sources record.[13] Not surprisingly, a commoner poet with no special store of secret knowledge and no hoary pedigree would be less impressed than some by the claims of the poetic houses and more demanding on the issue of poetic talent; and one can also imagine that the endless political infighting at court seemed tiresome to one who was in any case denied participation in the highest social circles. Almost certainly, though, Shōtetsu's offhand comments were spoken to disciples in private, the grumblings of an old man tired of the political posturing that was an inescapable feature of court life. In public, he was numbered among Reizei partisans, with whom he was in more philosophical agreement than he was with foes in the Nijō school. Stylistically, his work still revealed the influence of Reizei teachings, as is apparent in a poem from the Eighth Month of 1458, written for a poem sequence composed at the cottage of a fellow monk:

"Dawn at a Traveler's Inn"

Has the day dawned, then?   On the beach
of an inlet   a horse gets moving;

---

12. *Shōtetsu monogatari*. Trans. Brower and Carter, *Conversations with Shōtetsu*, pp. 62–63.

13. See Carter, "Chats with the Master," p. 314. Inoue Muneo notes an incident at a poetry gathering hosted by Yoshimasa in which Tametomi had to plead illness and withdraw because he was unable to read a text written in *Man'yō* script. Inoue, *Chūsei kadanshi no kenkyū, Muromachi kōki*, p. 25.

boats push out, getting afloat— setting the village
athrob.[14]

akenuru ka/irie no iso ni/uma susumi/fune ideukabu/sato doyomu made

Such rustic images and an emphasis on everyday experience were
both hallmarks of Reizei practice. To be sure, the old monk did not
always write in this style. Many of his poems are more reminiscent
of Teika and other poets of the *Shin kokinshū* era. But his poems
reveal that he must have listened to Ryōshun lecture on one point
in particular: the advantages of presenting experience "as it is"—as
evidenced by the poem above and many others like it found
throughout his anthology. A comment to his student Tō no Tsune-
yori (1401–84?) shows that in his teachings he was wont to repeat a
statement of Ryōshun almost verbatim: "The Reizei write in no sin-
gle style . . . whereas the Nijō *do* restrict themselves to one style."[15]
Comments of this sort, which Tsuneyori took as criticism of Nijō
rigidity,[16] suggest that Shōtetsu was not just an ally of the Reizei in
political terms but to a degree an adherent of Reizei teachings.

The headnotes to poems in Shōtetsu's personal anthology show
that his talents were widely appreciated in his time, again despite the
censure of the shogun. In fact, so great was his popularity that one
later text complained that, "Since the Nijō lineage had died out . . .
everyone went following after Shōtetsu, bringing him many disci-
ples."[17] What that criticism fails to say, however, is that Shōtetsu's
students were not from the noble families but from the ranks of war-
rior leaders—the great chieftains Hosokawa Katsumoto (1430–73),
Hatakeyama Yoshitada (d. 1468), and Yamana Sōzen (1404–73), to
name but a few—who sponsored monthly meetings and other gath-
erings in their Kyoto mansions, and by doing so sustained a rela-
tively new and important market for all teachers of poetry. Exactly
what the relationship of these men was to the Reizei is difficult to
determine, but connections meant everything in poetic affairs, as in
politics, and we can be certain that the descendants of Shunzei and

---

14. Shōtetsu, *Sōkonshū*, poem no. 10483.

15. Tō no Tsuneyori, *Tōyashū kikigaki*, p. 346.

16. The sentence immediately following, which we can assume he did
not share with Shōtetsu, is: "Alright, let's suppose they *do* write in just the
one style. Then my question is, what if that style is the correct one [*shōtai*]?"
Tō no Tsuneyori, *Tōyashū kikigaki*, p. 346.

17. *Shimizu Sōsen kikigakii*, (Notes on Statements by Shimizu Sōsen, 1688?),
p. 366. Shimizu Sōsen (1614–97) was a Nijō partisan of the early Edo period.

Teika were as expert in making use of their contacts as their ancestors had been. By the standards of those patriarchs, the Reizei coffers were severely depleted, it must be said, as were those of all the court families in an age of decline for their class; but it would be a mistake to imagine that the Reizei were reduced to penury. All evidence is that at mid-century the two houses were in fact thriving in terms of their poetic activities, that they were still able to find the financial support necessary to support themselves in noble fashion, and that Shōtetsu and his commoner disciples were beginning to play a role in Reizei practice.

WHEN SHŌTETSU died in 1459, Reizei Tametomi, head of the upper house, was in his 30s and well-established at court, along with his cousin, Masatame, who though young was already showing potential as a poet. Even during the most trying of times, during famine, drought, epidemic, or political upheaval, the shogun Ashikaga Yoshimasa sought diversion in his own monthly poetry meetings, to which the Reizei heirs were always invited. Ignoring such activities would have meant denying the long-standing claim that cultural activity was a force for order in the world. Nor were his the only chambers dedicated to such activities on a monthly basis, for the emperor, his father, the heads of many court families, warrior literati, and priests of noble background were similarly involved. As heirs of the Mikohidari line, Tametomi and Masatame were therefore in great demand, not only as poets but as tutors, masters of ceremonies, and judges.[18]

One is not surprised to learn that in such a setting, sentiment for the compilation of a new imperial anthology was quick to emerge. In 1465, a formal commission to begin work on the project came down from Emperor Go-Tsuchimikado (1442–1500; r. 1464–1500), who had ascended to the throne only the year before. Predictably, Asukai Masachika (1416–90), senior member of that lineage and personal tutor to the shogun, was named as compiler. To the delight of the Reizei, however, Tametomi was named one of the fellows of the Poetry Bureau, securing a major role for the family in the proceedings. The shogun, who was by all accounts the primary impetus behind the project, made it known that he would underwrite all expenses, following traditions going back a century and more. Throughout the next year, the calendars of court families were crowded with various

---

18. Inoue, *Chūsei kadanshi no kenkyū, Muromachi kōki*, pp. 157–82.

poetic events, all looking forward to the completion of a collection that would preserve their day in textual memory.[19]

In the Second Month of 1466, 100–poem sequences were requested from prominent poets, most of which were completed and handed in by the fall of that year.[20] Records indicate that everyone involved, from the shogun down, continued actively to pursue plans for the anthology on into 1467. As early as the fall of 1466, however, there had been ominous signs of unrest on the political horizon, involving warrior clans of the shogunate and ultimately the shogun himself. Of course, this in itself was not enough to cause real alarm. Soldiers had congregated in the capital many times before. When fighting began to take place right in the heart of the city in 1467, however, even the most aloof of courtiers had to be concerned.

The immediate cause of the trouble was a series of succession disputes in the Shiba and Hatakeyama clans and in the Ashikaga house itself. In earlier days, the shogun might have been able to control the situation, but far from being true vassals of the Ashikaga, the *shugo* daimyo had by this time, based on regional political alliances and economic interests of their own, become true lords of their own domains. So, as the noble families went about their time-honored duties — one of which was preparations for the Great Thanksgiving Service to be held at the end of the year in honor of a newly ascended emperor — the rest of the city was teetering on the brink of warfare in the streets. Already in the First Month of the year there had been an intense battle fought just north of the city proper, at Goryō Shrine. Five months later, at least 100,000 soldiers were camped all around the shogunal offices, which were located not far from the imperial palace and the homes of most high-ranking courtiers. As the summer rains began, fighting broke out in earnest. It would go on, although with long breaks of relative peace here and there, for the next ten years, reducing the northern half of the city to ashes.

Historians see many reasons for the collapse of authority that followed in the final quarter of the fifteenth century: the corruption of many of the leaders of the imperial court, the criminal negligence of Ashikaga Yoshimasa as shogun, the treachery of some of his generals, the collapse of a power structure that had always been frail, and most of all the growing economic and political influence of various local

---

19. Ibid., pp. 190–93. See also Inoue, "Reizei-ke no rekishi 9: Tametomi," p. 5.
20. Inoue, *Chūsei kadanshi no kenkyū, Muromachi zenki*, pp. 192–93.

groups, from the *shugo* daimyo themselves to vice-constables and peasant leagues. The term used to describe the culture of the time is *gekokujō*—a time when, literally, "those below overthrow those on top." The economic forces that caused the rupture had been putting pressure on the old authority structures since at least the time of Go-Daigo and could not be restrained any longer.

One wonders whether the members of the Reizei house, who still held their traditional ranks, still composed traditional poetry, and still carried on a traditional lifestyle, however truncated at times, ever saw big changes coming. Despite a terrible famine in the early 1460s, earthquakes, and various minor outbreaks of violence, there is no sign that the emperor and his court thought their way of life—as opposed to their own immediate fortunes—was in jeopardy. Traditionally, they had seen themselves as bystanders at such times rather than as full participants. It was not uncommon, in fact, for courtiers and their hangers-on to watch battles going on from the hilltops around the capital. In time, they believed, things would right themselves and ancient rhythms of aristocratic life would be restored.

This time, however, things would be different. For one thing, a new breed of soldier, the dreaded *ashigaru*, or foot-soldier, many of whom were essentially marauders out for booty, had no qualms about bursting in where more class-conscious samurai might have hesitated. Noble estates and temples were taken over and occupied as fortresses; looting and pillaging became commonplace. Before long, the market stalls were all closed and normal commerce virtually ceased. In response, however reluctantly, the high nobility began to abandon the city and seek refuge in temples in the Eastern Hills or in nearby estates where they could do double-duty, watching over their financial interests and gaining safe haven for their families and their treasures. A few officials, such as Ichijō Kaneyoshi, who was still nominally serving as regent, stayed on as long as possible, hoping to serve somehow as mediators to end the disputes that threatened to destroy the imperial city. Finally, though, even they had to capitulate and flee. Even on their own estates, they met resistance from a host of what seemed to them interlopers who demanded large chunks of revenue, but at least there they could escape the fear of being caught between combatants in the capital.

Under such conditions the compilation of a new imperial anthology obviously had to be postponed. At first, the compilers doubtless thought that they would return to finish what they had started when order was restored. In the past, several imperial projects had been interrupted and yet had reached completion later. But on the 11th day of the Sixth Month of 1467, such hopes were dashed when the home of Asukai Masachika, along with all documents of his Poetry Bureau, burned to the ground, a victim of street fighting that had already destroyed scores of noble mansions and would destroy many more before the conflict was over.[21] Masachika and his family escaped to take up residence in Kashiwagi, in nearby Ōmi Province. Other courtiers ended up in places throughout the Home Provinces, from Nara and Sakai in the south to the shores of Lake Biwa in the northeast.

The house of Reizei Tametomi at the intersection of Kitanokōji and Muromachi Streets had been destroyed as well, several weeks earlier.[22] Fortunately, he had sent his library out of the city for safe-keeping. Houses could be replaced; ancient manuscripts could not. Probably because they had relatives there, he and his family took refuge in Sakamoto, at the foot of Mount Hiei, not far from the tempo-rary quarters of the Asukai family in Kashiwagi. Not long after came other nobles, including his cousin Masatame. A small diary-style collection of poems by Reizei Tamehiro (1450–1526), Tametomi's son, from 1469, shows that the refugee community in that area met ofteñ, sometimes at their own houses, sometimes at temples such as the nearby Shōren-in, to compose poems and commiserate. The full moon midway through the Eighth Month, for example, inspired in young Tamehiro thoughts of the past and perhaps hopes for the future:

> Above a troubled world   the sky of
> mid-autumn   is radiant still—
> the moon worthy of the fame   it has had since
> days of old.[23]
>
> *ukiyo o ba / aki no monaka no / sora sumite / tsuki ya mukashi no / na ni tachinuran*

During lulls in the fighting, some courtiers went back to the capital on occasion, meeting in the chambers of the retired emperor. No doubt the chief topic of their conversations was the future—or rather, how they could somehow recapture the past. As time went on, the news brought to them from travelers was not only about events in Kyoto but also about violence in other places, inspiring fear of

---

21. Ibid., p. 193.
22. Nakamura, "Kugyō no ie, suki no ie," p. 186.
23. Reizei Tamehiro, *Tamehiroshū* 1, poem no. 76.

a much larger — and longer — period of uncertainty that now threatened their very existence.

MOST HISTORIANS cite the withdrawal of the warlord Ōuchi Masahiro and his army from Kyoto in the Eleventh Month of 1477 as the last event of the Ōnin War. In reality the worst of the destruction in Kyoto was over by the end of 1470. Thereafter the conflict expanded out into the suburbs of the city and from there into the provinces as the entire nation entered a period referred to with good reason as the Sengoku ("Warring States") era. For the next century and more, the country would be torn apart by warlords competing for territory and power, until finally a kind of political unity was established under the Tokugawa shoguns.

In the first few years of the conflict, the northern area of the city, in particular, had been reduced to a wasteland of burnt-out or abandoned buildings. Gone were the residences of nearly all the high nobility and many of their stewards. Emperor Go-Tsuchimikado was still living in borrowed rooms in the shogun's Palace of Flowers, his own palace in a state of ill-repair. In the Eastern Hills, things were much the same. The great temples and the small shop towns surrounding them, from Nanzenji to Shōren-in, were mostly charred ruins. It would be years before any of these places would be rebuilt.

Despite all this some courtiers again took up residence in the capital. One of them was so confident of a return to peace that on the first day of 1472 he wrote, "Clear skies. Spring arrives, with the heavens peaceful and the four seas calm."[24] While perhaps not so optimistic, many of the old families were no doubt hopeful. Then, the very next year, came three events that seemed to signal a fundamental change: first the death of Yamana Sōzen and then his cohort in the opposite camp, Hosokawa Katsumoto, and the ascension of nine-year-old Ashikaga Yoshihisa (1465–89) as shogun. One of the great issues behind the conflict had been the question of who would succeed Ashikaga Yoshimasa. Now that the matter had been decided, the end of the mayhem — in Kyoto, at least — seemed at hand. In response, some intrepid courtiers returned to the city and rebuilt their homes. But even those who had the resources to reestablish themselves early on would face many trials in the years ahead, a case in point being Konoe Masaie (1444–1505), scion of one of the five houses of the re-

---

24. The quotation is from the diary of Kanroji Chikanaga (d. 1500). See Inoue, *Chūsei kadanshi no kenkyū, Muromachi zenki*, pp. 198–99.

gency, who was burned out three more times after losing his residence for the first time back in the early days of the Ōnin War.[25]

Some were cautious, of course, among them the heirs of the Reizei house, who returned to the capital only for short periods until after 1480 and then only for poetic gatherings, as far as we know. A sequence of poems solicited by the emperor in the summer of 1474, for instance, lists the names of Reizei Tametomi and his son Tamehiro as contributors; and again in 1477 the same two men participated in poetic gatherings sponsored by the emperor.[26] On none of these occasions, however, did they remain in the city for long. Instead they stayed on in Sakamoto, where their possessions—in particular, their library—would be safer.

Sakamoto was not an unpleasant place to be. Standing on the southern shore of Lake Biwa directly east of Kyoto, it was an old city that had served as market and provisioner for the temples of Mount Hiei for centuries. Records indicate that as early as 1211, it contained at least 2,000 residences, a number that must have increased considerably by the time the Reizei family took up life there.[27] It was a lively place full of saké breweries, warehouses, and shipping companies engaged in sending goods overland and by water to and from the Home Provinces.[28] Much of the land around the city was under the direct control of Enryakuji, the great Tendai monastery on the slopes of Mount Hiei, an equally large community that of course included many sons and daughters of the nobility. The expatriate community in the Sakamoto area—and it was a large one—had grown accustomed to their surroundings and were in no hurry to move back to a capital that was little more than a burnt-over field.

Yet the young emperor, Go-Tsuchimikado, needed a court to legitimate his existence. Likewise, the young shogun Yoshihisa, who had been raised as a courtier, was anxious to participate more fully in the noble lifestyle. Encouraged especially by his mother, Hino Tomiko (1440–96), he began to hold poetry gatherings and contests, inviting the nobility, including the Reizei and the Asukai,

---

25. Bruschke-Johnson, *Dismissed as Elegant Fossils*, p. 32. See also Butler, *Emperor and Aristocracy in Japan*, pp. 25–28, 34–36.

26. Inoue, *Chūsei kadanshi no kenkyū, Muromachi zenki*, pp. 203–4 and *Kōen tsugiuta*, pp. 71–74.

27. Yamada, "Sakamoto," p. 288.

28. Souryi, *The World Turned Upside Down*, p. 157.

to attend. Rather than mere diversions, such events signified what seemed like a return to normalcy for all involved, both participants and spectators.

To revive all the activities of the imperial court was an expensive proposition that neither the imperial coffers nor a weakened shogunate could hope to afford. On the first day of 1475, the Obeisance to the Four Directions, one of the most essential New Year's rites, was performed for the first time in nearly a decade. But it was held at the palace of the shogun because the imperial palace was still unrepaired. There would be no grand festivals, no lavish excursions, either at court or at the numerous shrines and temples around the city, which were also in dire financial straits.[29] One thing that could be accomplished at only minimal expense, however, was the restocking of the imperial library. When the palace had gone up in flames, most of the books and manuscripts within its walls had perished as well. Now the emperor and a small group of courtiers around him began to solicit texts of important works from all and sundry, which were carefully copied and stored away. After the degradations of the preceding few years, the need to preserve the documents of court culture was no longer an abstraction but a concrete need. Moreover, with few of the more lavish court rituals and festivals being held, courtiers had time on their hands as they took up the traditional task of attending upon the sovereign. Putting their capabilities as scribes and copyists to use during guard duty must have seemed a reasonable and proper thing to do.

Sources tell us that among the literary texts copied at the time were even some of recent vintage such as a famous critical work by Tonna.[30] In the main, however, the emperor sought out poetic works such as *Tales of Ise* and important collections, which of course meant that the Reizei were involved in the preservation projects from the beginning. As early as 1473, Tametomi had complied with a request to lend the emperor the family manuscript of *Senzaishū*, the imperial anthology for which Shunzei had served as sole compiler 300 years

---

29. For a summary of the fate of *nenjū gyōji* (annual observances) during the early Sengoku period, see Okuno, *Sengoku jidai no kyūtei seikatsu*, pp. 57–74, and Butler, *Emperor and Aristocracy in Japan*, pp. 77–89. Some of the more essential New Year's events and the ceremonies attending advancement in ranks were held even during the late 1400s, but again only with support from the shogunate or daimyo.

30. Inoue, *Chūsei kadanshi no kenkyū, Muromachi zenki*, pp. 215–21.

before.[31] As the process went on, the house was no doubt asked repeatedly to lend out its treasures. For the most part, they cooperated. Restoration of the patterns of the past could only mean increased status for the house, as well as much-needed income. But in 1479, when the emperor was trying to put together a complete set of all 21 imperial anthologies, a conflict arose.[32] Evidently the Reizei were willing to lend out texts from more recent years, but when it came to their most valuable treasures—especially the *Sandaishū*—they balked. These were considered sacred and secret, and access to them was generally granted only to the foremost of disciples as part of their poetic catechism, always accompanied by the oral transmissions of the house, and always under oath. So when the emperor asked to see the house copy of *Shūishū* (Collection of Gleanings, 1005–7; third of the Three Collections), Tametomi refused. In response, the emperor banned him from appearing at court and instructed the shogunate to strip him of his offices. Although the offense listed was "being in the provinces without permission"—a common charge at the time—everyone knew that the real reason was once again the stubbornness of the family when it came to its manuscripts.[33]

The reaction of Tametomi to the emperor's request says a great deal about the order of things in the elite society of the capital at the time. For instead of giving in, Tametomi held his ground and began to lobby with friends in the shogunate and the court elite, and not without success. Rather than being removed from office, he was allowed to resign at the normal time for such acts the following year, and before a full year was out he had been reinstated.[34] It goes without saying that there was a lesson in this for all the court families, which was that their interests and those of the emperor were not always identical. Each house had its own history, its own traditions, and its own survival to consider. All indications are that Tametomi knew that the sovereign's orders could be evaded with the help of those with connections, particularly the warrior elite.

One can argue that there was nothing new in this; for centuries emperors had been dominated by those surrounding them in the

---

31. Inoue, "Reizei-ke no rekishi 9: Tametomi," p. 5.

32. Inoue, *Chūsei kadanshi no kenkyū, Muromachi zenki*, p. 217.

33. Inoue, "Reizei-ke no rekishi 9: Tametomi," p. 5. Many other courtiers during this period were censured for leaving court without formal permission. See Butler, *Emperor and Aristocracy in Japan*, pp. 40–43.

34. Inoue, "Reizei-ke no rekishi 9: Tametomi," p. 5.

civil or military aristocracy. The Reizei themselves had courted the intervention of military men since the time of Tamesuke. In the activities and attitudes of Tametomi and his heir Tamehiro in the days after the Ōnin War, however, there is a perceptible change from even a generation before. In the past, the Reizei held life at the emperor's court as their chief ambition, implicitly recognizing that life as the way to power and privilege, with service as Poetry Master (*waka sōshō*) in imperial gatherings the ultimate honor; now they recognized that their place in the social order could only be maintained by a savvy use of their capital in a broader market, specifically among the warrior elite, from the Ashikaga down. Symbolically, the emperor was still a figure of importance, and would remain so, for ideologically, it could not be denied that the imperial house was still the ultimate legitimizing authority behind all the noble houses. For the time being, however, it appeared that no emperor or retired emperor was likely to be able to exert his own power in the style of Go-Toba, Go-Daigo, or even, more recently, Go-Komatsu. Although Tamehiro would eventually comply with the emperor's wishes to see the treasured Reizei manuscripts after he became head of the house,[35] his father's stubbornness was no mere case of eccentric behavior. When it came to claims on noble families, even the emperor had to be reminded of his place.[36]

Of course, the change went only so far: in order to maintain the position of the Reizei lineage in the social order, the heirs of the old court families still needed court rank and office, which still meant a great deal to the warriors who demanded their services — a fact that would remain unchanged until the late nineteenth century. In itself, though, courtly status was no longer enough. In Tameyuki's time, it had been primarily commoner (*jige*) poets such as Tamemasa's disciple Shōtetsu who served as tutors to men of no standing at court, acting as masters of ceremonies for their monthly poetry meetings, lecturing to them on poetry and the court classics, and providing criticism of their work. In the years to come, this role would be played more and more by members of the family itself. Over time, the Reizei would in fact create a multi-tiered hierarchy of disciples, many of whom were from the ranks of the warrior class or the clergy. All

---

35. Atsuta, "Tamehiro no zenhansei," p. 6.

36. For a fine examination of the "ambivalence" in the attitude of courtiers toward the emperor in this period, see Butler, *Emperor and Aristocracy in Japan*, pp. 58–68.

would swear fealty to the house in much the way a samurai did to his lord. Precedents for this pattern of practice could be traced back to the early medieval period, but it was after the Ōnin War that dependence on disciples—many of whom were patrons in another sense—became essential to the continued survival of the noble lineages.[37]

THE IMMEDIATE reason for this shift in focus was economic. After the dust and ashes of the Ōnin War settled and courtiers began to return to Kyoto, the one thing that became apparent to all was that the revenues from their estates would have to be secured in new ways, if at all. Even before the Disturbance virtually every family had faced difficulties in convincing provincial landlords of their rights as proprietors. Now, Ashikaga Yoshimasa and his son Yoshihisa tried to intervene with the warlords who had direct control of the estates, in many cases even issuing government orders for restoration of fees. But one thing the war years had taught people in the provinces was that the central government often lacked the power to back up its threats, especially in areas distant from the capital. Reizei Tametomi knew about the problem firsthand, having accompanied Ichijō Kaneyoshi in the fall of 1479, as steward of the Ichijō house, on a journey to Echizen Province, where the former regent had tried in vain to convince a prominent warlord to honor Ichijō deeds.[38] Not even the highest officer in the imperial government could hope for a steady flow of income without some sort of credible threat of military force.

Different court families responded to this new reality in different ways. Across the board, they became identified more than ever with their house traditions, in ritual, music, poetry, scholarship, and so on, the practice of which both anchored their identity and brought in some revenue from men anxious to identify themselves with traditional symbols of elite status. When this was not enough—and it seldom was—some families turned to soliciting gifts from warrior patrons or to commercial activities, using properties in the capital or its surroundings to enable them to serve as landlords or partners in business ventures such as the running of markets or shops. Those who did not have such resources often had to take the inevitable step of leaving Kyoto for the provinces. Yonehara Masayoshi has shown that places like Sunpu in Suruga, Ichijōdani in Echizen, Suō in Yama-

---

37. Narita, "Kinsei Tennō to waka," p. 258.
38. Carter, *Regent Redux*, pp. 192–93.

guchi, and Nanao in Noto all served as havens for displaced courtiers during these times.[39] Not a few stayed their whole lives there, becoming in effect clerks, administrators, and paid literati, although most returned to Kyoto occasionally in order to maintain ties with their ultimate source of authority. Just as had been true back in the Kamakura period, a Kyoto accent carried prestige at the time. In addition to providing much-desired literary and artistic services, courtiers were useful in fields as disparate as accounting, clerical work, medicine, costume, etiquette, and architecture.

The Reizei seem to have had little to depend upon in Kyoto proper, which may be one reason why Tametomi continued to live on the generosity of relatives in Sakamoto, along with many other expatriates who, for one reason or another, could not afford to rebuild their homes nearer the imperial chambers. For a time many nobles were able to rely on the support of Hino Tomiko and the young shogun, Yoshihisa, who were making Kyoto into their own fief by collecting tariffs and taxes from all levels of society and who tried to intervene with recalcitrant warriors on behalf of many noble families when it suited their own purposes. But even with such support the years after the Great Disturbance were difficult, as is apparent from the fact that Mochikazu was unable to afford a proper celebration for his son, Masatame, after the latter was elevated to the office of consultant in 1477.[40] No more permanent solution to the challenge of the new economic situation was in sight.

The lament of a courtier written in 1484 shows that things in the capital did not improve with time: "In recent years, brigands rove out of control. There is no shogunal deputy—he's off in the provinces. There is no Board of Retainers (*samuraidokoro*), no lord governor (*shoshidai*), no Office of Retainers. . . . The situation is beyond belief. Truly we are in the Last Days of the Law."[41] The phrase "Last Days of the Law" refers to a Buddhist belief that the world had entered a protracted phase of corruption and devastation, which the state of the capital must have seemed to epitomize. The young shogun, Ashikaga Yoshihisa, and his mother still made attempts to govern the city, but in the end their resources stretched only so far. In a show of support for the nobility, the young shogun even

---

39. See Yonehara, *Sengoku bushi to bungei no kenkyū.*
40. Inoue, *Chūsei kadanshi no kenkyū, Muromachi zenki,* p. 254.
41. Quotation from the diary of Kanroji Chikanaga. See Kuroda, *Chūsei toshi Kyōto no kenkyū,* p. 290.

made plans to put together an imperial anthology of poetry. But when he died in 1489 of illness, the project was abandoned.

So the world through which the heirs of Tametomi and Mochitame would have to make their way was changed from anything the house had known before. Men were still appointed as shoguns but generally did not last long in office; gradually they became difficult to distinguish from other warlords. Ashikaga Yoshitane (1466–1523), for instance, served twice as shogun, the first time being appointed under the patronage of Hino Tomiko and serving just a few years and then again more than a decade later. Yet he spent a great deal of his time, even while in office, outside the capital on various military expeditions, and in truth he was under the thumb of more powerful warlords during virtually his whole tenure as titular head of the government. Much the same could be said for most of the other shoguns who followed him for the next century or so, even down to the last, Ashikaga Yoshiaki (1537–97), who would, strictly speaking, be the last member of the Ashikaga dynasty, serving in that office from 1568 to 1573. What was true of the shoguns was also true of many warlords: their first attention went to their home domains, where they were building up their own resources against conflict with their neighbors. Thus the imperial capital became more and more desolate.

As officers of the imperial court, the heirs of the Reizei houses were affected by all that went on in the capital. By the early 1480s, both men appear to have reestablished residences in the city[42] and to be thoroughly involved in court life, which consisted of standing watch in the imperial residence, participating in the few rituals from the ancient calendar that current budgets could accommodate, attending poetry gatherings, and acting as copyists and editors. But none of these activities produced much in the way of income, and several documents from the 1490s asking for assistance from the

---

42. *Kōen tsugiuta*, a collection of poem sequences composed in the imperial chambers, shows that Tametomi and Tamehiro were present for all of the emperor's monthly meetings in 1481 and fairly consistently thereafter, while Masatame's name does not appear consistently until 1484. Another record indicates that Tamehiro's house burned in a fire in 1492 and another source indicates that Masatame's house was burned some years later, in 1500 (Meiō 9), indicating that both men had houses in the city at the time. Inoue, *Chūsei kadanshi no kenkyū, Muromachi kōki*, p. 27.

shogunate in the restoration of revenues describe the situation of the family as nearly destitute.[43]

The means of resolving the crisis was one that they had chosen many times before: the Reizei had sought out patrons among the military elite in earlier generations, and now they did so again. As a poem recorded in a small collection dating from 1486 verifies, even before Tametomi's death in 1497, his son Tamehiro had attached himself to Hosokawa Masamoto (1466–1507), who held the title of shogunal deputy:

> Fourth Month, 28th day: On "Rice Seedlings Being Planted at Hillside," for a meeting held by Hosokawa Kurō Masamoto
>
> So dense are the pines   that one cannot see
> the paddies   along the hillside;
> but from beneath rising smoke   comes the sound
> of planting songs.[44]
>
> *matsu shigeru / okabe no oda wa / miewakade / kemuri no soko ni / sanae toru koe*

The same collection contains poems written at other places, including the chambers of the shogun, of high-ranking court families, and even of an imperial physician. However, other sources make it clear that Tamehiro went so far as to accompany Masatomo on various excursions and military campaigns, playing the role of courtier to a warlord rather than to the emperor. Thus a record of those accompanying the deputy on a journey to Echigo in 1491 lists among his companions fourteen men on horseback, including a dozen or so samurai and a lone courtier—the Reizei Middle Counselor.[45] For the next fifteen years or so, Tamehiro would follow Masamoto on many journeys and serve essentially as one of his retainers, offering literary services but also acting as confidant and counselor. This of itself is enough to show the great change that had taken place among the old nobility. Whatever income Tamehiro was receiving from the Hosokawa Estate, which appears by this time to have been shared by the upper and lower houses, was evidently not enough to sustain even a modest lifestyle.[46] Help had to be sought elsewhere.

Records show that Tamehiro's fortunes clearly rose and fell with those of his patron. Soon after Masamoto succeeded in securing the

---

43. Atsuta, "Tamehiro no zenhansei," pp. 7–8.
44. Reizei Tamehiro, *Bunmei jūhachinen eisō*, poem no. 102.
45. Owada, "Reizei Tamehiro-kyō no Echigo gekō," p. 3.
46. Inoue, *Chūsei kadanshi no kenkyū, Muromachi kōki*, p. 126.

title of shogun for his candidate, Tamehiro was serving as tutor in poetry to the new leader, but when Masamoto was chased from the capital by a rival in the Ninth Month of 1499, Tamehiro made over all of his possessions to his son and heir and prepared for banishment or death.[47] Again, when Masamoto's forces turned back the opposition and retook the capital in the Eleventh Month of that same year, Tamehiro and his family were rewarded for their loyalty with new estate rights and even with the revenue from several toll gates under the control of the shogun; but when Masamoto was finally assassinated in 1507, Tamehiro was obliged to take the tonsure.[48]

For a time after Masamoto's demise, the shogun served as a protector who could be depended upon to provide resources in the form of social contacts and direct gifts.[49] But it cannot be coincidence that from about this time Tamehiro began to spend a great deal of his time outside Kyoto. By this time, he appears to have lost the rights to most of the old family estates.[50] One place where he still had a claim, however, was the Koshibe Estate in Harima, once owned by the Daughter of Shunzei; and so it was to Harima he went, where he appears to have had many disciples, including the warlord Akamatsu Yoshimura (1472–1521) and many of the latter's vassals.[51] He also cultivated patrons in the provinces of Noto, Echigo, Wakasa, and Suruga, where over time he gained many disciples who hosted him lavishly when he visited and who carried on an active correspondence with him after he returned to the capital.[52] Conceivably, he could have stayed in one place—which is what the head of the lower house would eventually do, becoming resident courtier on their properties in Harima. Instead, Tamehiro sought out disciples wherever he could find them, whom he bound to him by oaths, a number of which have been preserved in the Reizei library.[53] In the provinces, his authority as the heir of Teika was recognized, as were

---

47. Atsuta, "Sōshō to seijō," pp. 6–7.

48. Atsuta, "Tamehiro no yuzurijō," p. 8.

49. Shiba, "Reizei Tamehiro no kenkyū," p. 18, notes that Yoshizumi sent Tamehiro five barrels of saké, a horse, and a sword to congratulate him on a recent literary honor.

50. Atsuta, "Sōshō to seijō," p. 6.

51. Ibid., p. 7.

52. The Reizei library contains "pledges" from eight samurai disciples in service to the Hatakeyama clan from this period. Atsuta, "Tamekazu to montei," p. 8.

53. Atsuta, "Sōshō to seijō,"p. 7.

the authority of his manuscripts and the oral transmissions of the house. Moreover, provincial warriors were wealthy enough to host guests lavishly and to provide their tutors with handsome yearly gifts. Ironically, Tamehiro apparently even began claiming authority as a teacher of *kemari*, the game of kickball that Tameie had mastered—to his father's consternation—centuries before.[54] No doubt the house in fact had texts and teachings on the sport, passed down from Tameie's day.

The income Tamehiro received in the course of his travels is unfortunately only hinted at in most cases. However, a record of his stay in Noto from the autumn of 1514 to the summer of the next year, preserved in the Reizei collection, notes that on a visit to Noto, at least six samurai in the area around Nanao became formal disciples, and also reveals that the individual fee for enrollment was the fairly paltry sum of 100–200 *hiki*,[55] while also referring to disciples in other areas of the domain.[56] Similar records make it clear that he had disciples in Ōmi and Echigo provinces as well.[57] Furthermore, it seems certain that when he attended meetings on his travels he was paid for his services as officiator, lecturer, judge, and so forth, most probably in the form of guarantees of income from estates he had—or had once had—in the various areas. One telling hint about the nature of his relationship with at least one of the great warlords of the time is that Hatakeyama Yoshifusa (1491–1545), of Noto, somehow ended up with a copy of the much-prized *Sandaishū* in the hand of Reizei Tamehide—not one of the texts passed down from Tameie, obviously, but still a treasure.[58] Although all sorts of explanations can be offered as to how he could have received such a boon, the most likely one is that at some point, for either sizable favors or for a hefty price, Yoshifusa simply "purchased" it. Of course, selling off the manuscripts that previous generations had sacrificed so greatly to preserve was a drastic step, but these were drastic times.

---

54. Ogura, "Reizei-ke no rekishi: Edo jidai kara Meiji e," p. 146.

55. Kumakura, "Sanjōnishi Sanetaka, Takeno Jōō, and An Early Form of *Iemoto Seido*," pp. 95–98, records several instances in which Sanetaka, a contemporary of Tamehiro, received gratuities of between 500–1,000 *hiki* from disciples. One hundred *hiki* was the rough equivalent of one measure of rice.

56. Owada, "Reizei Tamehiro-kyō no Noto gekō," p. 4.

57. Owada, "Reizei Tamehiro-kyō no Echigo gekō."

58. Yonehara, *Sengoku bushi to bungei no kenkyū*, p. 138.

IT SHOULD be stressed that regardless of his provincial jaunts, Tame-hiro remained active in the poetic circles of the capital during his entire career, maintaining so high a profile, in fact, that he was grouped with his cousin Masatame and the courtier-scholar Sanjōnishi Sanetaka (1455–1537) as one of the Three Lords (*sanshin*) of poetry at the time. Regardless of recent reversals for the old nobility, men in Tame-hiro's situation knew that it was their status in capital society that ultimately gave them authority in the provinces.

Needless to say, the political and economic realities of life in Kyoto had changed greatly since the days of his youth, but poetic institutions — the master–disciple relationship, rituals and conventions of gatherings, genres and sub-genres, everything down to the old rules on diction and the dominance of composition on set topics (*dai*) — remained remarkably stable nevertheless. One of the few changes that occurred in poetic circles, in fact, was a marked decline in the kind of partisanship that had still dominated things at mid-century, as many scholars have noted. The most likely explanation for this is that in the face of possible annihilation, even the poetic houses were willing to put aside differences in order to present a united front — although never to the point of denying their own specific traditions, particularly in matters of "secret" transmissions and rituals, which were necessary to all noble houses as forms of cultural capital.

In recent years, scholars have often concluded that political détente among the poetic families after the Ōnin War was accompanied by a kind of stylistic détente in which the Nijō orthodoxy finally established hegemony among the poetic houses of the court.[59] However, a close look at poems produced at the time in texts such as *Kōen tsugiuta* (Poem Sequences from the Imperial Chambers) — a record of meetings held in the imperial chambers from the late Muromachi to the Edo period — reveals that this was simply not the case. To the contrary, what actual records from the turn of the sixteenth century reveal is a world in which elements from all three Mikohidari traditions — the Nijō, the Reizei, and even the Kyōgoku — had gained acceptance. From the Nijō came the *ushin* aesthetic and its emphasis on the educated sensibility, from the Reizei the ideal of stylistic variety and a penchant for scenes seemingly taken from everyday life, and from the Kyōgoku an openness — albeit in a limited way — to new diction. If anything, then, it was not the Nijō but the Reizei that finally triumphed, as the following poems by the Three Lords (Tamehiro,

---

59. See, for instance, Shimazu, "Reizei kafū to sono yukue."

Masatame, and Sanetaka, respectively) and one of their most promi-
nent contemporaries, Asukai Masatoshi (1462–1523), show unequivo-
cally. All were composed for imperial gatherings in 1501 or 1502.

"Winter's Voice"

The firewood alone   was heavy enough
without snow   adding to the burden
of one battered by north wind   coming down
a valley path.[60]

sarade dani / omoki takigi no / kaerusa ya / yuki o kozuke no / tani no kitakaze

"Winter Color"

I will look forward   to seeing snow
from here on   —now that winter's blight
has left so little color   in the mountains,
in the fields.[61]

yuki o koso / ima wa machi mime / fuyuzare no / amari iro naki / no ni mo yama ni mo

"Animal"

At autumn's end   mountain winds blow
no fruit   from empty trees;
from far down in a ravine,   monkeys call,
foraging.[62]

aki hatete / ko no mi munashiki / yamakaze ni / asaru mashira no / tani fukaki koe

"Love—in a Sound"

 Could it be him?   I wonder
when I hear   from his direction
the sound of cart wheels turning   —only to then
fade away.[63]

matsukata ni / sore ka to kikeba / oguruma no / todoroku koe zo / yoso ni sugiyuku

All four of these poems may be said to involve evocative concep-
tions that Teika, Tameie, and Tonna gave the name *ushin*, presenting
not scenes but emotional reactions to those scenes from the point of
view of a courtly speaker, which may be what scholars mean when
they talk about the triumph of the Nijō school. However, in their
stark tone and rustic imagery, the first two poems here clearly con-
nect back less to Nijō models than to the works of Reizei Tamesuke
and Tamemasa—and no more so, it should be noted, than Sanetaka's

---

60. *Kōen tsugiuta*, poem no. 05216.
61. Ibid., poem no. 05211.
62. Ibid., poem no. 05087.
63. Ibid., poem no. 05238.

description of monkeys foraging in a bleak winter forest. What is even more significant, however, is the poem by Masatoshi, who as the heir of the Asukai house was one of the standard-bearers of the Nijō school but whose love poem would in earlier times have been attacked by some for qualities associated with the Kyōgoku school — namely, prosaic syntax, simplistic conception, and a complete lack of elegant imagery or poetic devices. Thus even in the most exalted of venues it appears that Reizei and Kyōgoku poetics had a place.

Even when it came to poetic composition, then, court poets around the turn of the sixteenth century seem to have been less divided by factionalism — indeed, they were more eclectic — than had been true for centuries. A further sign of rapprochement was that the Reizei, who until this time had so often been kept from the highest poetic duties at court by the Asukai, were gradually being allowed a greater role in public performances. Indeed, in 1502, Tamehiro was honored with the title of *waka sōshō*, or Poetry Master, on the insistence of the current shogun, Ashikaga Yoshizumi (1480–1511).[64] Again, records do not indicate what direct financial advantage came with this appointment. At the very least, however, it meant that Tamehiro was called upon to perform various ceremonial duties — choosing proper topics for poetic gatherings, acting as judge at contests, and so on — at the imperial palace as well as for shogunal gatherings and perhaps even for meetings in the chambers of other noble families: in other words, the sorts of events that always brought gifts. In addition, some sort of stipend may have been attached.

In recognition of his new status, Tamehiro was singled out in the summer of the very next year as the judge of an old-style poetry contest — *Bunki sannen rokugatsu jūyokka sanjūroku-ban uta-awase* (Poem contest in 36 rounds on the 14th day of the Sixth Month of the third year of the Bunki era), to give the full title of the text as it appears in dictionaries. Topics were chosen by Emperor Go-Kashiwabara (1464–1526; r. 1500–26), who was the formal sponsor of the event, with financial support provided by the shogun. After the requisite banquets, poems were composed by the 36 contestants, put into rounds, and then sent to Tamehiro for him to write out his judgments (*han no kotoba*). More than a month later he presented them to the retired emperor for review. Shunzei, Teika, and Tameie had served as judges before, as had Tamehide back in the 1300s; now Tamehiro had the same opportunity. That Tamehiro managed to work in references both to

---

64. Inoue, "Reizei-ke no rekishi 10: Tamehiro," p. 4.

his dedication to the "occupation of the house" (*kagyō*) and to his own current appointment as *waka sōshō* is perhaps not surprising.[65]

What *is* surprising is that in his judgments Tamehiro allows himself no partisan comments against the two members of the Asukai house involved in the contest or their disciples, any more than he allows himself partisan comments in favor of the four members of the Reizei who participated—himself, his son Tamekazu (1486–1549), his cousin Masatame, heir of the lower house, and the latter's son, Tametaka (1475–1543). A half-century earlier, the famous poetry contest sponsored by Ichijō Kaneyoshi had been a partisan affair through and through, so much so that the members of the Asukai house who were invited to attend chose not to participate at all. Now, however, circumstances had changed. If not unanimity, there was at least a spirit of tolerance and common cause. As noted above, the imperial court in 1502 was a small and frail entity that simply could not afford to be divided against itself. Thus Tamehiro's approach to writing judgments was not to debate any issue but to highlight the court tradition, and in so doing to display his own knowledge and to validate his appointment as Master while also celebrating ancient ways. While he includes a few words of praise, predictably relying on the vocabulary inherited from Shunzei and Teika (*yojō*—"overtones"—in rounds one, two, and nine; *yōen*—"ethereal charm"—in round nineteen; and so on), he uses more ink pointing out allusions and echoes of famous texts of the past—most prominently *Kokinshū* (mentioned ten times), *The Tale of Genji* (six times), the *Poem-Contest in Fifteen-Hundred Rounds* (five times), and *Man'yōshū* (four times). To show his range, however, he also includes references to everything from the Confucian *Analects*, the Chinese *Book of Songs*, *Nihon shoki* (Chronicles of Japan, 720), *Tales of Ise*, *Shin kokinshū*, *Gyokuyōshū*, and *Fūgashū*, and even a poem by Emperor Go-Hanazono from only a few decades earlier. Above all, it appears that Tamehiro wanted to show a firm command of the textual tradition contained in his library, claiming its continuing relevance in the poetic field of his time. Rather than the record of a "contest," the text therefore becomes again a celebration.

In this sense, the character of the contest of 1503—and of much of the poetic discourse during the early sixteenth century—is best summed up by the 34th round, for which poets wrote poems on the topic "Invoking Good Fortune for the Way."

―――――――

65. See rounds 33 and 34. *Bunki sannen sanjūroku-ban uta-awase*, pp. 488–89.

Team of the Left: Middle Counselor Motonaga

Surely everywhere   people will
show their esteem   for the honored way
of the far-flung islands   as it turns
to words of old.

yo ni hiroku / augazarame ya / inishie ni / mata tachikaeru / shikishima no michi

Team of the Right: Consultant Masatoshi

What other Way   but this
of the far-flung isles   makes calm the hearts
of gods and men,   sustaining peace
throughout the land?[66]

kami mo hito mo / yawaragu kuni no / sugata ni wa / izure no michi ka / shikishima no michi

Both poems treat the Way of Shikishima, and neither offers anything too out of the ordinary. Because of its pleasant phrasing, I find myself wanting to award the win to the poem of the Right, but then I wonder whether by referring to "the Way / of the far-flung islands / as it turns to words of old" the author of the poem of the Left truly means only that the poetic conceptions are returning to the past. Given my current status, I have to think the author has more in mind and therefore can't bring myself to decide against the poem of the Left. Instead, I must opt for a draw.

Whether Kanroji Motonaga (1457–1527) truly intended his poem as congratulations to Tamehiro — whose appointment as Poetry Master could indeed be seen as a "return" to the lineage of the past — is moot. The remarkable thing is that Tamehiro's tone should be so conciliatory when it comes to the question of poetic tradition. Masatoshi, who as noted above was the heir of the Asukai house, could easily have been treated as the enemy, and yet Tamehiro has only kind words for his poem. The implication is clear: all are united in their devotion to the Way of Shikishima (the "far-flung islands"), a traditional metaphor for the Japanese islands. As if to emphasize further this same point, Tamehiro awards the win to Masatoshi for the following poem in round ten of the contest with no comment whatsoever about the connotations it must have carried for any member of a poetic house:

"Summer Moonlight in the Trees"

Up in the branches   on nearby mountains
dusk begins   with cicada voices —
faint as the light of the moon   spilling down
through the trees.

naku semi no / hayama no kozue / kuresomete / morikuru tsuki mo / usuki kage ka na

---

66. Ibid., p. 489.

As already noted, in his judgments Tamehiro revealed that he was well acquainted with *Gyokuyōshū* and *Fūgashū*. Evidently he was not the only one, for Masatoshi's poem would have fit perfectly into the pages of either of those Kyōgoku anthologies that, it should be remembered, had been roundly condemned by Nijō adherents of earlier times as unorthodox (*ifū*). Rather than draw attention to this fact, however, in his judgment Tamehiro concentrated on the faults of the poem paired with it and awarded Masatoshi the win. Only two interpretations of such a decision, especially in the case of a formal and highly public setting like a poetry contest, are possible: that as acknowledged leader of the poetic world he was playing the role of conciliator, or that the style of Masatoshi's poem was so well within the mainstream of the time that it demanded neither criticism nor justification. Either way, the validation of Reizei open-mindedness in poetic composition seems undeniable. Tamehiro would provide judgments for a number of other contests, manuscripts of which have just been published in the *Reizei-ke shiguretei sōsho*.[67]

Despite the tribulations of life in the capital after the Ōnin War, then, the Reizei were faring well in poetic circles. Indeed, judging from the following comment made in the 1503 contest, it appears that Tamehiro even had ambitions to succeed in a way no Reizei heir had ever done before: "Having received appointment as Waka Master as in days of old, I cannot help but wonder why in our sovereign's reign no imperial anthology has yet appeared."[68] This was of course not an idle query but a heartfelt plea. No imperial project ensued — but not for lack of interest on the part of Tamehiro, who as Master would probably have been named chief compiler. The reaction of the retired emperor and the shogun to his query, which we can be certain they read because it was presented directly to them, is nowhere recorded. But once again the evidence suggests that despite their poverty the old nobility had not given up on the idea of returning the capital city to the ways of the past.

AT THE same time, however, it is clear that the Reizei were making more and more connections not in Kyoto but in the provinces, and stood ready to make more. Another benefit of Tamehiro's new stand-

---

67. The volume includes six contests judged by Tamehiro and four contests judged by Tamekaze.

68. From round 26 of *Bunki sannen sanjūroku-ban uta-awase*, pp. 480–81.

ing as head of the imperial *kadan*, in fact, was the constant train of paying customers from the provinces it brought to his front gate, seeking his seal of approval. One well-documented example is from the year 1523 when the poet Kenjun (b. 1487), a disciple of the *renga* master Kensai (1452–1510) who was in turn a disciple of Shinkei (1406–75), one of the students of Reizei Tamemasa's student Shōtetsu (connections, once again), asked for an audience with the head of the upper house. Plying his trade in the East Country, where he had a literary practice among local disciples from the samurai class in Aizu, Kenjun seems to have made very few trips to Kyoto. Still, though, the ultimate authority in poetic matters rested in the noble families of the imperial court. So when he did come up to the capital in the fall of 1523, he made up for lost time by copying out various texts not available in his home province, asking for lectures on *The Tale of Genji* from Sanjōnishi Sanetaka and applying for "licensing" as a *daisha*, or one qualified to choose topics for formal gatherings, from Reizei Tamehiro. As might be expected, this process took several months, beginning with an initial meeting to which Kenjun came bearing gifts. The catechism ended with a formal celebration (on the 2nd day of the Fourth Month of 1524) during which the provincial poet received his certificate and a fan, along with the following poem from the master:

> Hurry off, then,   toward your home
> far away!   But pray return again
> and forget not to send word   by the wind
> of this fan.[69]

> *furusato wa / yoshi isogu to mo / mata kaeri / ōgi no kaze no / tayori wasuru na*

Back in the provinces, the fan would serve as a tangible symbol of Kenjun's new authority as a disciple of the Reizei house. The record of course does not mention what gifts he left with Tamehiro, but we can assume that they were both substantial and welcome. A rough contemporary of similar professional standing vis-à-vis his teacher came up with nearly 5,000 *hiki* in gratuities for Sanjōnishi Sanetaka after instruction—a sum far greater than the poet had received from those amateurs in Noto, who had joined as a group, probably to oblige their lord.[70] With payments from estates barely trickling in, revenue from disciples was proving more and more crucial to survival. The

---

69. Inoue, *Chūsei kadanshi no kenkyū, Muromachi kōki*, pp. 303–4.

70. Kumakura, "Sanjōnishi Sanetaka, Takeno Jōō, and An Early Form of *Iemoto Seido*," pp. 99–100.

relative decline in the number of documents in the Reizei library dealing with estate matters and the relative increase in documents involving correspondence with disciples also emphasizes the growing importance of income from paying students at this time.[71]

As in the days before the Disturbance, the upper house still held its own regular meetings, usually on the 16th day of each month. First, poems prepared for the occasion were announced and attendees put their efforts into extemporaneous composition, according to age-old patterns. Like all heirs of the house, Tamehiro had read Ryōshun, who was insistent on the need for constant practice: "In every Way, there are those who are unskilled; but if they study, the Way continues. The truly skillful become so only after accumulating experience. One never hears of a master who did not practice."[72] Required in court poetry were not flights of fancy—a phrase that could not even be applied to Tamekane or Shōtetsu—but the kind of rhetorical polish and dexterity that could only come with submission to discipline. No one hoping to maintain a name in any courtly art could cease regular practice, or *keiko*, which was the primary function of monthly gatherings. Significantly, the word translated as "accumulating experience" here is the same word that in Buddhist contexts is used for "accumulating merit." The association can only have been intended.

For the same reason, Masatame, head of the lower house, was holding meetings, too. Like Tamehiro, Masatame spent some time in the provinces, most frequently at the Hosokawa Estate in Harima; but he maintained a residence in Kyoto, which served as a meeting place for friends and disciples, and he was a devoted attendant at imperial events as well. All three of the following winter poems from different years, for instance, were composed at the monthly meetings held in the imperial chambers:

> "Evergreens in Snow," from a monthly poetry meeting at the palace on the 25th day of the Eleventh Month of 1502
>
> So overburdened   are the branches
> in the groves   that the snow breaks free—
> revealing rows of black pines   looking
> even colder still.[73]
>
> *e o omomi / koboruru yuki ni / makihibara / arawarete nao / samuki iro kana*

---

71. Atsuta, "Sōshō to seijō," pp. 7–8.
72. Imagawa, *Ryōshun isshiden*, p. 178.
73. *Hekigyokushū*, poem no. 740.

"Rain Showers on a Mountain Path," from a monthly poetry
meeting at the palace on the 25th day of the Tenth Month of 1509

After the passing   of a sudden
burst of rain,   I meet a man
on the same mountain path   whose sleeves know nothing
of showers.[74]

murashigure / onaji yamaji ni / au hito no / furu sora shiranu / sode mo koso are

"Year's End at Every House," from a monthly poetry meeting
at the palace on the 25th day of the Twelfth Month of 1517

As the old year ends   no one, not even
the smallest   of the world's households
can help but feel a yearning   for times now
gone by.[75]

yuku toshi wa / yo ni kasuka naru / sumika made / shitau narai ni / morenu koro kana

Thus as late as 1517 the Reizei were writing poems much like those
composed in the imperial chambers two decades earlier. Further-
more, Masatame's personal anthology, which was actually compiled
from a variety of sources hundreds of years after his death, reveals
something else about his practice as well: namely, that he and Tame-
hiro managed to compete in the same market while maintaining sepa-
rate practices. Particularly important for Masatame were a number
of warrior households, the Nikaidō, the Date, and the Ōuchi espe-
cially. Some of the same names appear in Tamehiro's collections,
but so do many others. The crucial fact is that the demand for literary
services was evidently considerable enough to provide support for
both houses—indeed, for both the Reizei houses and for a number
of other houses such as the Asukai as well—that were in a sense in
competition with one another but without the more ideologically
charged rivalries of earlier times.

Masatame was a regular participant at the gatherings of the upper
house as well. A record going back to the Eighth Month of 1490 shows
the upper and lower houses participating together in a memorial ser-
vice—underwritten by a retainer of the Hosokawa clan—at the grave
of Teika.[76] Through the years the houses thus appear to have main-
tained a close relationship based on common interest. When both
Tamehiro and Masatame died within a few years of each other, in
the mid-1520s, they left, among many gifts to coming generations, a

---

74. Ibid., poem no. 676.
75. Ibid., poem no. 804.
76. Inoue, *Chūsei kadanshi no kenkyū, Muromachi kōki*, p. 22.

heritage of cooperation for the good of the lineage that would remain a model for centuries to come. Above all, to their descendants and many disciples they left an example of dedication to the Way of the house — again, a communal enterprise based more in a sense of craft than any more individualistic sense of art — amidst hardships. For by their time, if in fact not much earlier on, it was the great burden of carrying on old traditions rather than the romantic ideal of "creativity" that fell on the shoulders of Reizei heirs. Regardless of political or economic changes, or even larger intellectual or artistic trends, the duty of the descendants of Teika, Tameie, Abutsu, Tamesuke, Tamehide, and now Tamehiro and Masatame was to bear in mind and body always the perpetuation of the house.

SIX

Suruga, Fujisawa, Nara, and Points Between

ONE IMAGE suffices to suggest the financial state of the imperial court in the early sixteenth century — that of Emperor Go-Kashiwabara waiting, because of poverty, in his run-down palace for 21 years, from 1500 until 1521, for his formal ascension ceremony. Of equal significance is the fact that money to support the necessary pageantry came in the end not from the imperial house, not from the nobility, but from wealthy warlords petitioned by the Honganji Temple. The same thing would happen again upon Go-Kashiwabara's death, when Go-Nara ascended the throne, although he would have to wait only 10 years.[1]

Of course this was the situation of the emperor, who by definition could have no patrons per se, except perhaps the shogun himself, who indeed underwrote most activities at court. Not all noble houses were in such a state, partly because their house specialties — scholarship, music, poetry, calligraphy, and so on — gave them some purchase in the cultural market. But even noble families that had such assets were to suffer greatly over the next 70 years or so, until a more stable government structure began to emerge under the direction of Oda Nobunaga (1534–82) and his successors. For much of the time the Reizei houses — upper and lower — were in this number, as well as the Asukai and other noble lineages. It is not coincidence that Tamehiro died,

---

1. Kodama, *Tennō*, p. 226; Kasahara, *Rekidai tennō sōran*, pp. 258–60.

in 1526, not in Kyoto but in Noto, and that Asukai Masatoshi, who had participated in so many meetings with Tamehiro in the imperial chambers, died just a few years earlier in the Ōuchi domains in Suō.

Trouble for the lower house, too, began even before Masatame's death, when his heir, Tametaka, resigned his position as middle counselor in 1521, perhaps due to illness—the records do not say. A decade later, in 1531, Tametaka took the tonsure as a lay monk and thereafter spent much of his time at the Hosokawa Estate in Harima, along with his son Tametoyo (1504–60), who as a result never advanced properly in the court ranks.[2] At the time, many courtiers were being forced to take direct control of their land holdings in order to secure any income at all. For whatever reason, the lower house, while occasionally attending poetic events in the capital, ceased to be a force in literary affairs after Tametaka's retirement to the old estate that Abutsu had fought so hard to keep in the family. Much later, in 1578, Tametoyo's son and grandson would both lose their lives—and many manuscripts, too—when the estate was invaded and ransacked during one of the many military conflicts of the time.[3] A great-great-grandson of Masatame would eventually return to the capital and make a name for himself in the new Edo order, but it would be as a Confucian scholar and not as a poet.

Tamekazu, son of Tamehiro and thus heir of the upper house, also experienced fully the vagaries of life in an age of turmoil. Like his father, he attached himself to a powerful warrior, none other than Ashikaga Yoshiharu (1511–50), the son of one of his father's benefactors, Ashikaga Yoshizumi. No sooner did he secure the support of his patron, however, than he was required to follow him into the provinces on various military adventures. For several years he managed to maintain his profile in the capital despite these interruptions, but the times finally made life in the city impossible, especially with fighting between various warlords going on as close as Ōmi, Settsu, and Izumi Provinces. In 1531, as warfare seemed about to engulf the city once again, Tamekazu moved his family and entourage of stewards, samurai, and servants—more than 100 people, one writer sur-

---

2. He never went beyond junior third rank. At the time, the rule at court was that nobles living in the provinces could not be advanced in rank. See Okuno, *Sengoku jidai no kyūtei seikatsu*, p. 81.

3. Ichiko, "Reizei Tamekage to sono shūhen," p. 2.

mises—to Sunpu, a castle town on the eastern seaboard.[4] Even his library was brought along, it would appear, a sure sign that he was contemplating a long stay.[5] The family treasures had been sent off to temples outside the capital for safekeeping many times; to take them as far as Suruga was a more desperate measure.

As the Reizei had maintained a relationship with the Imagawa since the days of Ryōshun, it was only natural for Tamekazu to look to that quarter in a time of need. Indeed, our first record of Tamekazu's literary activity, which comes from his twelfth year, is from a text by Imagawa Ryōshun that he had copied out by hand.[6] He and his family would spend decades in the Imagawa bastion as part of an expatriate community seeking security in a world of chaos.

Once again, the immediate reason for choosing Suruga over other places was probably economic. Claims against most estates were moot; and the only hope of securing revenue from other estates was to find a strongman willing to offer support. This the Imagawa evidently promised.[7] Imagawa Ujiteru (1513–36), the head of the clan, was one of the most powerful warlords of the day, who held the three provinces of Suruga, Tōtōmi, and Mikawa in fief, within the borders of which the upper Reizei house had estate rights dating back to the days of Tamehide.[8] It was in order to obtain a more steady income from these that Tamekazu gave up life in Kyoto, most likely thinking that the measure would be only temporary. He was not alone in this, for also in Sunpu were a score of noble expatriates, including members of the Ōgimachi Sanjō, Asukai, Nakamikado, Shigenoi, Shijō, Karasumaru, and Sanjōnishi families. Sources indicate that the displaced courtiers, who of course came with their many dependents and servants, even had their own residential quarter in Sunpu, thanks to Imagawa generosity.[9]

Tamekazu quickly found a market for his talents among the many literati in the Imagawa entourage. Ujiteru himself, whose mother was from a noble family, was a very cultured man who composed

---

4. Hotta, *Koen fūraishō*, p. 188.

5. Inoue, *Chūsei kadanshi no kenkyū, Muromachi kōki*, pp. 348–51.

6. Inoue, "Reizei-ke no rekishi II: Tamekazu," p. 4.

7. Atsuta, "Tamekazu to montei," p. 7.

8. Ibid. Three of these (the Odaka, Takabe, and Sagara) were in Tōtōmi, and one (Oyaizu) in Suruga.

9. Nagakura, "Reizei-ke to chihō bunka," p. 4.

poetry not only in Japanese but in Chinese as well.[10] Before long, he became a formal disciple of the Reizei house and had his teacher serving as *daisha* (one licensed to decide on appropriate topics for events) and tutor to himself and a host of his retainers, opening up the way for Tamekazu to travel to other nearby castle towns and port cities to pursue his Way among provincials anxious for a taste of court culture.[11] After Ujiteru's premature death in 1536, Tamekazu continued to enjoy the favor of the new head of the Imagawa, Ujiteru's younger brother Yoshimoto (1519–60).

A number of different sources provide us with these details about Tamekazu's life. Chief among them is his own personal anthology, tellingly known as the *Imagawa Tamekazu shū*—rather than *Reizei Tamekazu shū*—which is in journal form and covers the years 1517 until 1548, just one year before his death. Altogether, the collection contains more than 2,000 of his poems, with headnotes that provide a wealth of information about his activities and affiliations. The poems from countless monthly meetings are recorded, showing once again that the patterns set by earlier generations were being honored. The evidence is that he was on the whole well received, although doubtless he had to be even more entrepreneurial in his lifestyle than his forebears had been. A few poems in fact express his frustration over his financial situation very candidly. One of these, written in 1533, is followed by a note that could not state the crucial problem more directly:

> "Mountain Lament"
>
> Be my witness, gods!   Of how
> for two generations   we have suffered
> beneath the peak of Fuji   and gained nothing
> but more years.
>
> *kami mo shire / futayo wo kakete / fuji no ne no / naranu nageki ni / oi zo shinikeru*

Our house is supposed to hold rights to four properties within the fiefs held by Imagawa Ujiteru and his father Ujichika. Although we lamented our plight to Ujichika and were promised that incomes would be resumed, as of now the ruling has not been enforced.[12]

---

10. For a description of the literary activities of Imagawa Ujiteru and other Imagawa literati, see Horton, *Song in an Age of Discord*.

11. Owada, "Reizei-ke to sengoku bushi no bungei," p. 5.

12. Reizei Tamekazu, *Imagawa Tamekazu shū*, poem no. 1522.

Whether his patrons ever heard his lament is not known. No one reading it would have been shocked, however, for had not Teika and Tameie and Tamehide and Tamemasa all done the same?

Also noted in Tamekazu's anthology are scores of poems submitted to shrines as votive offerings, for either the Reizei themselves or for patrons such as the Imagawa and their vassals, along with numerous others exchanged in correspondence or written on his frequent travels — which brought him into contact with other prominent warriors such as Takeda Nobutora (1494–1574), whose daughter had recently become Imagawa Yoshimoto's wife, a woman who would play important roles in coming conflicts.[13] Unfortunately, he does not record the many poems he received from his students for review and critique. Had he done so, they would no doubt have numbered in the thousands. However reluctantly, he seems to have succeeded very well in making a place for himself and his entourage on the eastern seaboard. In time, the Imagawa do seem to have enforced the Reizei deeds, at least partially, which provided much needed income. In return, Tamekazu seems to have served as an agent for the Imagawa at times, and perhaps even as a negotiator. But he was also involved in two other literary activities aimed at securing financial support. The first was taking in disciples, 20 of whom wrote out oaths that have been preserved in the Reizei collection to this day.[14] The second was copying manuscripts, or even "selling" some, as attested by a poetic text in the hand of Tamekazu himself, the original of which — in Teika's hand — is noted as having been presented to Imagawa Ujichika (1473–1526).[15] Significantly, Tamekazu's copy is written very much in the calligraphic style of Teika, probably in an attempt to create as perfect a copy of the original as possible. Although Teika's original has been lost and is not available for comparison, one can easily imagine that his intent was to produce a version that would pass as Teika's text in some sense.

Tamekazu spent most of his last two decades in Suruga. Late in the year 1540, however, he made a trip back to Kyoto, which was relatively peaceful at the moment. He stayed there for a year before returning to his home in the east. While in the capital, he participated in many poetic activities and also made trips to visit old pa-

---

13. Inoue, *Chūsei kadanshi no kenkyū, Muromachi kōki*, pp. 425–26.
14. Atsuta, "Tamekazu to montei," p. 7.
15. Reizei Tamehito, "Reizei-ke no rekishi to bunka," p. 54.

trons, such as the Hatakeyama in Noto. Yet the purpose of the journey was more than social: for while back "in service" in the capital he was eligible for promotion. This happened in 1541, when he was elevated first to the office of Minister of Popular Affairs and then, some months later, to major counselor. On the 25th day of the Third Month of that year, just after receiving the first promotion, he celebrated his good fortune by attending a monthly poetry meeting at the imperial palace for the first time in years. There he composed four poems, among them this one that hinted at his feelings at being back at court after so many years away:

> "Valley Pine, Standing Many Years"
> While all around   the mountains
> go to blossoms,   at the valley door
> has stood — for oh so long —   a pine log,
> half-buried in spring.[16]
>
> *yomoyama no / hana ni nariyuku / tani no to ni / iku yo ka matsu wa / haru no mumoregi*

The donation of a sizable sum of money to the emperor from the candidate's patrons in Noto around the same time makes it seem likely that essentially he purchased his promotions, or at the very least that he was promoted in recognition of his role in securing the gift.[17] In any case, he seems to have had no intention of actually serving. Maintaining a large household in Kyoto was expensive, as was involvement in court activities, which required expensive clothing and appurtenances and endless gift-giving. So in the Eleventh Month of the same year Tamekazu resigned his offices and left the job of imperial service to his heir, Tamemasu (1516–70), who evidently stayed behind when his father returned to Suruga. Records do not show Tamekazu ever setting foot in the capital again.[18]

For Tamekazu to leave his son in the capital rather than taking him back to the East Country is of course significant as a sign that the old man was not ready to give up all hope of a restoration of imperial culture in the future. No doubt his hope was that in Suruga he could secure enough income to assist his son as he rose in the court

---

16. *Kōen tsugiuta*, poem no. 23558.

17. Inoue, "Reizei-ke no rekishi II: Tamekazu," p. 5.

18. Ibid. See also Inoue, *Chūsei kadanshi no kenkyū, Muromachi kōki*, pp. 347–49. It is not clear whether Tamemasu had been living in the capital or with his father prior to this time.

hierarchy. The upper Reizei still maintained a residence in Kyoto, located at First Avenue and Karasuma Street, just a few blocks from the imperial palace.[19] But Tamekazu would live out the rest of his days in Suruga, supported by his patrons in the Imagawa clan, taking the tonsure in 1549 and passing away the next year, at 64. It would be up to his son to preserve the family Way at court, however slight the prospects of success may have appeared to be.

TAMEKAZU MUST have left other family members behind, of course: sons and daughters for whom there was no room on the noble rolls and therefore about whom we know little. Doubtless in this time as in earlier times there were many sons of the Reizei houses in temples and shrines, as well as daughters who had married into the lower nobility in Kyoto or into warrior clans in the provinces. Such people formed a network for the family, perhaps even contributing resources when the heir of the house was in need. We do know, for example, that Tamekazu had a brother named Ōyū (precise dates unknown) who was a priest of the Jimon sect of Buddhism and who was quite active as a poet and acquirer of manuscripts for the Reizei collection.[20] Even more prominent was an elder brother of Tamemasu—by a mother of low birth, no doubt, which would explain why he did not become heir—known by his Buddhist name Myōyū (1513–82). Myōyū took the tonsure in his youth, eventually becoming prominent in the Time sect, the most powerful of the Pure Land offshoots of the day and one with which Tamekazu is known to have had strong ties. For a time Myōyū lived at Shōjōkōji (more popularly known as Yugyōji) in Fujisawa, Sagami Province, not a great distance from Suruga, but he also traveled widely in the East Country and visited Kyoto at times, where he held his own poetry gatherings and no doubt had considerable contact with his brother. Despite his clerical calling, it appears that he maintained a strong sense of connection to the house. The first character (*myō*, meaning luminous) of

---

19. A map in the diary of Yamashina Tokitsugu (1507–79) locates the upper Reizei house here, next to the Nakamikado, Yanagiwara, and Yamashina lots. The same source shows the lot of the lower house located on Ōgimachi Avenue, right across from the Imperial Palace and next door to the Sanjōnishi house. See Nakamura, "Kugyō no ie, suki no ie," p. 187 and Nakamura, "Waka no ie, kuge no ie," p. 9.

20. Fujimoto, "Reizei-ke no rekishi," p. 10.

his Buddhist name was identical to the one Teika had taken for himself centuries before, and he shared with his illustrious ancestor an interest in *The Tale of Genji*, the evidence for which is a manuscript of the text bearing his name—the *Myōyū Genji*. The existence of manuscripts of *Kokinshū* and several other texts in his hand indicates that he was active in poetic circles and had probably received teachings from either his father or his brother.[21] This in turn suggests a larger web of Reizei relatives of immense importance to the viability of the house as an institution. From what we know of Myōyū's example, we can only conclude that members of Tamekazu's extended family were involved in seeking out disciples and patrons—who were one and the same in many cases—to introduce to the head of the lineage.

What we have from Myōyū's hand, however, is of secondary importance to the manuscripts and sets of teachings that can be traced back to Tamekazu himself, which show the seventh heir of the house in terms of his literary practice to be one of the most important figures in the history of the Reizei lineage. As noted above, the Reizei heir attracted many disciples, whose poems he "marked" and with whom he shared his guidance on composition, which was the primary emphasis with beginners, in particular. To those of high rank or distinguished accomplishment, however, we know from a number of documentary sources of the 1500s and later that he had more precious rewards: highly coveted secrets, often in oral form (*kuden*), bestowed via rites distinctive to the house that involved various levels of initiation, depending on circumstances. As noted in Chapter 3, oral transmissions had played an important role since generations before, in the time of Shunzei, and there can be little doubt that the Reizei had been involved in such matters from the time of Tamesuke on. The question of why this new element of poetic discourse had emerged so strongly in the early medieval period is difficult to answer, but two factors were almost certainly involved: first, the influence of concurrent pedagogical and philosophical developments in esoteric Buddhist thought; and, second, the need of the noble houses to convert their assets into cultural capital.[22] Whatever the historical reasons behind their existence, however, there can be no

---

21. Inoue, "Reizei-ke no rekishi 12: Tamemasu, Myōyū," p. 5. Miyabe no Yoshimasa, *Yoshimasa kikigaki* (p. 712) notes that Myōyū had many disciples of his own and had received the secret transmissions of the house.

22. Klein, *Allegories of Desire*, pp. 78, 98–99.

denying the importance of secret teachings in medieval discourse from that time on. The possession of such secrets, among other things, bound the disciple to the house in a semi-sacred lineage, with the head of the house comfortably at the apex. If nothing else, the *kuden* therefore presented one way for a lineage to maintain control over its own intellectual resources, just as they did over their trove of manuscripts. This last fact in itself is enough to explain why the Reizei house—especially in the 1500s, when hope for steady income from estate rights was diminishing—became so involved in the practice of oral transmissions, which were done under oath and paid for by gifts and favors.

Predictably, the Reizei were not the only ones involved in the burgeoning knowledge industry of the sixteenth century. The proliferation of such oral transmissions is in fact one of the characteristic features of the discursive landscape in general during that period, and not only among the noble families. For in addition to the teachings of the Reizei house and earlier transmissions that could be traced back to Fujiwara no Tameaki and others, there were other *kuden* of commoner origins, specifically, those traced to the *renga* poet Sōgi (1421–1502). Even before the Ōnin War, this *renga* master had begun a campaign to spread what he claimed to be the authentic teachings of the Nijō school, received from the warrior Tō no Tsuneyori, who in turn had received them from a member of the Nijō house before that lineage met its end. About the historical validity of Sōgi's claims, or for that matter the claims of Tsuneyori, there is still some doubt, with some scholars arguing that many of the teachings they claimed to be passing on were actually a product of their own creation—or at least elaboration. But there can be no question that, whatever their derivations, Sōgi passed on his oral transmissions to a number of prominent people—including some of his own commoner disciples and court nobles such as Sanjōnishi Sanetaka—who went on to create their own lineages. At a time of cultural reshuffling and redefinition, the social status granted to holders of ancient knowledge was considerable, as witnessed by the fact that they attracted the interest of even the highest warlords, from Hosokawa Yūsai (1534–1610) to, later on, Tokugawa Ieyasu (1542–1616) and members of the imperial family.

Most of the teachings bestowed in this way dealt with canonical texts, especially *Kokinshū*, and concentrated either on questions of proper pronunciation or on philological problems connected with selected poems or passages from the famous preface to that anthology, which serious poets were always required to study. Indeed, one reason for the development of oral transmissions in the first place was that without some instruction in how to vocalize ancient texts, students could not properly read the treasured texts of the Reizei library that were made available to them as house disciples.[23] But other teachings involved Buddhist or Nativist religious beliefs whose chief appeal was in their mystique and the social status that came from possessing highly coveted secrets. The whole tradition of oral transmissions (*kuden*) and the paper strips (*kirigami*) accompanying them was after all a major feature of Buddhist culture, first of all, and mimicked Buddhist practices in almost every way. It seems entirely fitting, therefore, that a text known as *Reizei-ke kirigami*—"Paper Strips of the Reizei House"—for instance, contains the following passage concerning the "secret" religious identities of the ancient poet Hitomaro, Emperor Shōmu (701–56; r. 724–49), and Sumiyoshi Daimyōjin, the last being the god of the Sumiyoshi Shrine, located on the coast of the Inland Sea in Sakai. Along with 22 other such fragments, the teaching was recorded on its own strip of paper (*kirigami*), with Tamekazu's name and seal affixed to it. Internal evidence makes it certain that some of the strips—including the one quoted from here—originated from teaching sessions between Tamekazu and a disciple in the Time sect to which his son Myōyū belonged.[24]

The Way of *Uta* is the Holy Law [*minori*] of the Japanese Nation, and it was in order to spread the Way that Daimyōjin took corporeal form, becoming Hitomaro. Thus the Original Ground [*honji*] was transformed into the two beings of Shōmu and Hitomaro, which is because they are of the same essence and are therefore said to have joined together. This is a matter of great significance to this house (*tōke no daiji*) and something that other houses do not know. For which reason we keep it as a house secret.[25]

Perhaps the most outstanding thing about this statement is the claim it makes for poetry—and, by logical extension, its practitioners—in the definition of of the Japanese state. It should be noted, however, that in support of this claim Tamekazu employs a mix of

---

23. Ogawa, "Kadōka no hitobito to kuge seiken," p. 204.

24. Kawahira, "Reizei Tamekazu sōden no kirigami narabi ni *Kokin wakashū Fujisawa sōden* ni tsuite," pp. 1–16. Eventually the entire group of paper strips ended up in the possession of the noble Ōgimachi house.

25. Ibid., p. 24.

Buddhist and Shinto syncretist vocabulary that had great currency in the late medieval period—the sort of esoterica that was being passed down in many lineages, despite the Reizei claim of exclusivity. In fact the famous Hitomaro memorial ceremonies of the twelfth century—in which poets of poetic houses treated the sage essentially as guardian deity of their Way—were predicated on precisely such kinds of mystical identifications between Buddhist and Shinto gods, and between gods and men.[26] If the attraction of such teachings for supplicants was the connection the latter made to ancient and sacred traditions of religious authority, however, the attraction they held for the house was that and more. As in this passage, so too in many others are the claims of the house reinforced by explicit reference— "We keep it as a house secret"—and by the authority not just of religious dogma but of *originary* religious dogma.

In a poetry session, such knowledge might be of little practical use, of course—except in the way it gave its possessors authority, which was of course a very practical need for anyone attempting to maintain a reputation in poetic discourse. The whole point of such lore, in fact, was that it could not be derived from any rational methodology applied to texts, but only through transmission. At least since the time of Teika, whom house lore recorded as having had a vision of Sumiyoshi Daimyōjin while spending the night at the shrine,[27] the great shrine at Sumiyoshi was a site sacred to the family. For lore about the place to have come down from generations past must have seemed natural. Thus the pedigree of the house and its long history of involvement in poetic and courtly affairs became one of its chief advantages, making their claims to exclusivity easier to accept than those of many others.

Given the importance of Hitomaro as one of the gods of poetry from the medieval period onward, it should also come as no surprise that the teachings of the Reizei contain much more about the legendary poet, or that Hitomaro would continue to be a focus of interest in coming generations, as witnessed by a number of Kamakura and Muromachi portraits of the poet preserved in the Reizei collection.[28]

---

26. See Klein, *Allegories of Desire*, pp. 80–89.

27. See Brower, "Fujiwara Teika's *Maigetsushō*," p. 422. Arguments exist about the authenticity of the passage and of the whole text, but it is clear that it was accepted as authentic by many poets.

28. *Kyō no miyabi, uta no kokoro: Reizei-ke no shihōten*, pp. 166–68.

Not all of the material on Hitomaro in *Reizei-ke kirigami* draws on eso-
teric religious beliefs, however, which points up an important feature
of Reizei—and Nijō—teachings in general. For, as Susan Klein sug-
gests,[29] the general tone of Reizei teachings of the Muromachi period
and later seems to have been more secular, as well as aimed more
at bolstering their claims of ancient knowledge about the Way of
Poetry than their connections with any particular religious sect. Thus
as an explanation for the meaning behind a statement in the *Kokinshū*
preface—"It was impossible for Hitomaro to excel Akahito, or for
Akahito to rank below Hitomaro"[30]—given by Tamekazu relies not
on any esoteric Buddhist traditions but on a simple, if preposterous
and somewhat fanciful, idea: that the two men were, historically
rather than metaphysically, really one and the same.

As for Hitomaro: In the reign of Emperor Tenmu, in a mountain village in
the Toda district of Iwami Province, Hitomaro appeared—already a 20-year-
old—in the persimmon tree of a man named Katara no Iena. When Iena asked
him if he was human, he replied, "I have no parents, no place that I have come
from, and no talents—except that I am good at poetry." When Iena told the
provincial administrator about this, he in turn informed Emperor Tenmu,
who called Hitomaro into service. He rose as high as senior fourth rank, upper
grade, but then had an affair with the empress, the daughter of the Palace
Minister Sukuru, and was banished to Yamabe in Kazusa Province.

Later, during the reign of Emperor Shōmu, when poems were being
selected for *Man'yōshū*, the emperor lamented that there was no good judge
of poetry at court and Minister of the Left Tachibana Moroe said, "In the
reign of Emperor Monmu, there was a man named Kakinomoto no Hito-
maro who was a true master of poetry, but he was banished to Kazusa after
having an affair with the empress. Perhaps we should recall him and make
him our judge," and proceeded on that course. At that point, however,
Major Counselor Otomaro said that someone who had been banished all
the way to the East Country simply could not return to court and therefore
that recalling Hitomaro would perhaps not be a good idea.

Moroe replied, "During the Tang era, Bai Juyi, who had originally been
named Huang Shuyi, committed an offense, and was banished to Xunyang.
Then later, when he was to be made an imperial tutor, it was also thought
that a man who had been banished as far as Xunyang could not be allowed
into the court again, so a council of courtiers was held and the decision
was made to change his surname from Huang to Bai, his given name from
Shuyi to Juyi, and admit him to court. Why don't we do the same?"

---

29. Klein, *Allegories of Desire*, pp. 271–73.
30. McCullough, *Kokin Wakashū*, p. 6.

So in this case too the man's name was changed, his surname Kakino-
moto becoming Yamabe, after the name of the place to which he had been
banished; and his given name being changed from Hitomaro to Akahito.
Thus Hitomaro was the man's original name, and Akahito his later name.
This is one of the greatest secrets dispensed in the initiation process.[31]

Hitomaro's sudden appearance in an old man's persimmon tree,
full-grown and fully-trained as a poet, may be described as miracu-
lous, of course, but it draws on no particular religious tradition.
Likewise, although the word "initiation" (*kanjō*) is one borrowed
directly from Buddhist vocabulary, the content of the passage has
more to do with legend—presented, in fact, as history—than the
kind of obscure allegoresis of the sort found in the teachings of Fuji-
wara no Tameaki. Most of the names mentioned in the passage are
in fact of actual historical figures, from the two great Man'yō era
poets Hitomaro and Yamabe no Akahito (early eighth century), to
Emperors Tenmu (d. 686; r. 673–86), Monmu (683–707; r. 697–707), and
Shōmu, and the courtiers Soga no Otomaro (precise dates unknown)
and Tachibana no Moroe (684–757).

This is not to claim that the Reizei secret teachings were somehow
completely unaffected by esoteric doctrines. An interpretive com-
ment by Tamekazu from the *Reizei-ke kirigami* on a phrase from *Tales
of Ise*, for instance, seems to draw on precisely the tantric readings
that can be traced to Kamakura poets of Tamesuke's generation. The
phrase comes from what was in conventional terms thought to be
an anecdote about how Ariwara no Narihira kidnapped Fujiwara
no Takaiko (842–910), hiding her away in a ruined storehouse only
to discover later that her brothers—euphemistically described as
"demons" who "ate" her—managed to retrieve her while Narihira
was standing guard outside: "'. . . a dewdrop on a blade of grass.'
There is no way one could see a dewdrop in the darkness of night.
Instead, this refers to a drop of semen falling down after intercourse
between man and woman, forming Heaven and Earth. This is the
beginning of Yin and Yang. There are also profound transmissions
on the meaning of the word 'grass.'"[32] If this interpretation seems
completely bizarre in the context of the story from which the phrase
comes, making it difficult even to integrate into a conventional liter-

---

31. Kawahira, "Reizei Tamekazu sōden no kirigami narabi ni *Kokin waka-
shū Fujisawa sōden* ni tsuite," pp. 20–21.

32. Ibid., p. 32.

ary analysis, it is because the esoteric traditions behind it are concerned less with analyzing than with *generating* new meanings as part of a very explicit religious agenda. The important point for a student of Reizei teachings, however, is simply that so perfect an example of allegorical sleight-of-hand still survived as late as the 1500s, seemingly a remnant from an earlier era.

At least in *Reizei-ke kirigami*, however, such examples of allegorical reading are fairly rare. Furthermore, it is worth noting that the example involved is taken from *Tales of Ise*, which had been one of the more central texts in the esoteric movement of earlier times, the residues of which—especially when backed by the authority of some house—probably continued for many generations. When it comes to *Kokinshū*, the Reizei teachings are more philological in nature, such as the following transmission by Tamekazu on three birds named in that first imperial anthology whose proper identification had been debated for centuries:

On the Matter of the Three Birds of *Kokinshū*

~ *momochidori*. In other houses there are lots of theories about this word. Some say it refers to the *uguisu* [warbler], but the transmission of our house is that it refers to the many birds that sing when spring comes, the *uguisu* not excluded.

~ *yobukodori*. This is said to refer to the gibbon, or again the *kaodori*, or again the box-bird. The teaching of our house is that it refers to the *tsutsudori*. This should be kept secret.

~ *inaōsetori*. There are various theories about this word, some saying it refers to the horse, others to the sparrow, and so on. In the initial stage of instruction, our house teaches that it refers to the wagtail. It is said that the name *inaōsetori* was given to the bird at the time of the two gods, Izanagi and Izanami. There are separate teachings on the three birds, which are secret. Do not show them or speak of them to outsiders, but keep them secret.[33]

Such teachings—which unfortunately for modern scholars produce more questions than they answer—were doubtless elaborated on when presented, with the *kirigami* serving more as assists to memory than as complete records. Moreover, there are several hints that more esoteric teachings are waiting for those privileged to go on to the next level of instruction. In all, however, the answers offered in this installment of the *kuden* are a world apart from those on *Tales*

---

33. Ibid., pp. 24–25.

of Ise, and this is true of most of the teachings contained in the remaining sections of *Reizei-ke kirigami.*

It would be a mistake, however, to conclude that further explanation would make teachings even about three obscure names from ancient times terribly useful in any practical sense. In other words, one of the most important things to understand about the secret transmissions of the more esoteric kind was that although they served a valuable purpose in attracting disciples to the Reizei camp—who were in this sense very clearly in competition with other traditions, as evidenced by comments in the above passage about "other houses"— they were not enough in themselves to sustain the house in its enterprise. Whether powerful in religious terms or not, such teachings were still of little use when it came to teaching poetic composition, which is in the end what a man like Tamekazu spent most of his time doing. Perhaps this explains why the textual record also contains a number of more pedagogical works by Tamekazu, aimed more at students interested in learning how to compose poems. Tameie had stressed not book-learning but training (*keiko*), and so had Tamesuke and Ryōshun; so, for that matter, had generations of poets in the Nijō, Asukai, and other poetic lineages. Initiating students into secrets was no doubt exciting, and profitable within certain limits, but historical tidbits about the identity of Hitomaro or ornithology would not help them produce a proper poem at a gathering.

One of our best sources for understanding the kind of practical teaching Tamekazu passed on to students is one already introduced in Chapter 4 as the source of a comment by Tamemasa, namely, the *Reizei-ke waka hihi kuden,* the substance of which probably dates from the mid-1500s. It was in that work, for instance, that we earlier found Tamesuke's advice on composing in all ten styles, as well as the Reizei dictum about capturing reality "as it is."[34] Also present are Shunzei's definition of poetry as "expressing in words what one feels in one's heart,"[35] Teika's advice about allowing excellent poems to come about naturally rather than laboring to produce them,[36] and Tameie's likening of composing a poem to building a tower, which must start from the bottom (the lower half of the poem) and

---

34. *Reizei-ke waka hihi kuden,* pp. 216–17.
35. Ibid., p. 215.
36. Ibid., p. 219.

work up (the upper half of the poem).[37] Furthermore, the text also contains passages taken from treatises such as *Waka kudenshō* (Selections from Oral Transmissions on Japanese Poetry), *Chikuenshō* (Selections from a Bamboo Grove), and *Sangoki*, dating back to Kamakura days—some of the treatises usually associated with precisely the esoteric teachings discussed above. Yet, when the Reizei text uses such material, it is usually presented in a way that focuses clearly on questions of proper composition, as the following example illustrates. It is taken from an explanation of the Three Modes of Poetry (*waka santai*), a topic that is described as the foremost of all secrets in the Way (*michi ni okite daiichi no hiji*):

A *soku* is a poem in which the author dispenses with explicit links to any word in the first seventeen syllables and proceeds instead in an unexpected direction. Yet, this does not mean that the whole is without logic (*kotowari*). This Way is only for the most skilled of poets.

> On this spring night   my floating bridge
> of dreams   has broken away:
> lifting off a distant peak—   a rack of cloud
> in empty sky.
>
> *haru no yo no/yume no ukihashi/todae shite/mine ni wakaruru/yokogumo no sora*

The poem quoted here is one of Teika's most famous, and one from *Shin kokinshū* (no. 38), a fact that, among other things, puts to rest those claims that the Reizei house in the 1500s was trying to distance itself from part of its heritage. It is also important to note, however, that the passage does not present an analytical concept aimed at readers or scholars, but rather an explication of method aimed at active poets. To clinch this point, the passage also says this about the topic of the Three Modes in general: "This is not easy for a person to master. It should be transmitted only to those who are accomplished in the Way by excelling in training (*keiko*), or to dedicated connoisseurs who show promise of excellence."[38] From this and other statements in *Reizei-ke waka hihi kuden* it is apparent that some of the most coveted secrets of the Way for the Reizei concerned themselves not with lore but with craft and artistic method. The unspoken assumption is that the highest pinnacle of accomplishment

---

37. Ibid., p. 221.
38. Ibid., p. 212.

involves, as the patriarchs had taught, not learning (*saigaku*) — which is what the esoteric teachings amount to — but practice.

This dedication to practice first of all is also visible in a short booklet of answers that Tamekazu provided to questions put to him in 1521 by one Inoue Shōtarō (precise dates unknown), a samurai of the Noto domain. Rather than matters of actual composition, the 1521 text — which from its title, *Reizei-ke hiden* (Secret Transmissions of the Reizei House), we may assume also contained material considered secret — deals primarily with the equally essential topic of social and ritual aspects of composition. Knowledge of such matters, however trivial it may seem to modern readers, was anything but that to medieval devotees of Japanese poetry, for whom the very idea of poetic composition was connected to public performance. With that in mind, one can see how some provincial poet charged with conducting a meeting might find a note like the following supremely useful:

When one is in a gathering with both nobles and warriors, does one record only the offices of the nobles? And does one record only the names of the warriors?

In the case of nobility, if the gathering is a formal one, one records office, surname, and given name. There are various other rules for recording other matters. In the case of the shogun, one records only office and given name. For retainers one records office, surname, and given name. One may exercise discretion when the surnames are the same. For warriors, one also records office, surname, and given name.[39]

If one needs reminding, this passage is sufficient to establish that poetry gatherings were ritualistic affairs that demanded knowledge of etiquette from all participants, especially from the poet in charge, for whom not knowing how to record names properly on the formal transcript could lead to embarrassment or worse. Indeed, it was most likely this kind of knowledge, first of all, that disciples of any social consequence came to Tamekazu to procure. Other entries in the same short text provide instruction on what format to use when recording poems on *kaishi* (pocket paper) in general and for specific occasions — such as when presenting poems as a votive offering to a shrine, or when meeting beneath the blossoms in spring, or when a meeting is being held at a mountain temple. In each case, tradition

---

39. Kawahira, "Honkoku: *Shōkōkanzō-bon Reizei-ke hiden*," p. 19.

required slight variations in custom that it was the business of a master to know. Seating arrangements at gatherings, how to organize furnishings in a room, how to stack papers on the *buntai*, or writing desk, the correct way of reading poems aloud—each topic gets its due. Even the matter of how much space to leave between the headnote and the first line of a poem was carefully prescribed.

While obviously reinforcing existing social hierarchies in a general way, these secret teachings seem to have had one even more explicit purpose: to enunciate the position of the Reizei house—and by extension, competing houses—in the poetic world. Another teaching, this one on the subject of how to choose proper *dai*, from a text attributed to Myōyū, makes the point unambiguously:

> On choosing topics: This is the task of the Master (*sōshō*) alone and is something a normal person (*tada naru hito*) should not undertake. No matter how high in rank or office a person may be, he should not serve in this capacity without the permission of the house. Even when the emperor is going to announce topics, he issues an order to that effect to the house first.[40]

Thus "the house" takes precedence over everything else. Not even an emperor had the authority to usurp the rights of the lineage when undertaking the practice of its own Way. Initiated disciples such as Kenjun could be given leave to act *for the house*, but only as agents bound to the Reizei as disciples.

So the textual record reveals that despite his absence from the capital—or rather, in some ways, *because* of his absence from the capital—Reizei Tamekazu was able to carry on a very active literary practice as teacher of esoteric secrets, poetic composition, and poetic ritual. Like heirs before him, much of his life was dedicated to increasing the store of capital available to the lineage. At a certain point, he even strayed somewhat from the Way of Poetry proper to establish a house style in calligraphy, based on the hand of Teika.[41] As caretaker of many texts in the patriarch's hand, he must have known that Teika had been rather ashamed of his handwriting, which was not praised highly during his own lifetime. By comparison with the elegant, flowing, and restrained lines of Heian

---

40. The text is titled *Daiei no teikin*. See Inoue, *Chūsei kadanshi no kenkyū, Muromachi kōki*, p. 549.

41. Nagoya, "Teika-ryū, Reizei-ryū." See also Nagoya, "Reizei-ke ni okeru sho no keishō," p. 203.

period masters like Ki no Tsurayuki or Fujiwara no Yukinari (972–1027), Teika's style was characterized by thick brush strokes, lines full of gaps—indeed by what might be considered a kind of awkwardness. But the style was Teika's and as such had a certain cachet. Some members of the Nijō line had tried to imitate it, as had Ichijō Norifusa, son of Kaneyoshi.[42] For the head of the Reizei house to do the same seemed an obvious course. This did not make Tamehiro a teacher of calligraphy, to be sure; his purpose was rather to create another distinction between the Reizei and other houses that could be maintained tangibly for generations to come. Already, there were wealthy men collecting scraps of calligraphy to hang in the alcoves of their tea cottages, just as there were collectors of poetic manuscripts—two arts that obviously went together. No harm could come from investment in a collateral art.

KYOTO IN the mid-sixteenth century was a place plagued by floods, fires, famine, epidemic, warfare, and civil unrest. In a real sense, the "city" of olden days no longer existed, having been replaced by several large, fortified communities—Kamigyō, around the shogunal palace and the imperial palace; Shimogyō, around the commercial districts between Third and Fifth Avenues; and finally a few other districts around temples and shrines that had somehow managed to come up with the funds for rebuilding. The *renga* poet Sōchō (1448–1532) had exclaimed that in 1526 "not one in ten" of the houses from before the Ōnin war remained.[43] Now things were, if anything, worse. Inhabited areas were separated by large tracts of abandoned land, some of it being farmed by peasant squatters. A few bold entrepreneurs kept commerce going, but all in all life in the city was a constant labor. From this labor, however, emerged a fairly vibrant culture very unlike anything that had been known in the city before. Within districts (*machi*) formed for self-defense, courtiers, merchants, and commoners worked together to resist intrusions, creating a new city with a population of perhaps 100,000.[44]

Armed with teachings transmitted by his father, Tamekazu's son Tamemasu, eighth head of the upper Reizei house, entered into the literary fray in the capital city in 1540 and managed to hang on some-

42. Nagoya, "Teika-ryū, Reizei-ryū," p. 4.
43. Quoted in Kuroda, *Chūsei toshi Kyōto no kenkyū*, p. 291.
44. Souryi, *The World Turned Upside Down*, pp. 196–98.

how until his death in 1570, a period of 30 long years during which the economic fortunes of the house were at their nadir. Despite difficult conditions, there was still an emperor, who though without much practical power still had a measure of symbolic authority and even some sources of income.[45] Although the grand old festivals and rituals were not being held, life in the Imperial Palace continued, which meant Tamemasu had frequent opportunity to compose poems and act as tutor. Thanks to the support of his warrior patrons in Suruga and elsewhere, the house was still receiving some income from estates, which made life in the capital bearable. Records show that he was living in a house near the intersection of Karasumaru Street and Ichijō Avenue.

Tamemasu was made a middle counselor in 1550 and Minister of Popular Affairs six years later. It appears, however, that he was sickly. In particular, records allude to an "ailment of the eyes." Furthermore, Emperor Ōgimachi (1517–93), who ascended the throne in 1560, was a partisan of the Asukai who had little use for the Reizei cause. Five years later, Tamemasu resigned as middle counselor and stopped appearing at most poetic functions.[46] The immediate reason for his absence was a journey to Suruga, where he stayed from the fall of 1565 until the spring of 1567. Evidently ill, he went to undertake business related to family estates and to renew relationships with his extended family and many disciples in the area, probably in preparation for passing the baton on to his seven-year-old heir. In fact, he begins a letter he left to his wife before leaving Kyoto by suggesting that he may never return: "No one knows what may happen in this world of ours. If I should die, raise our son well."[47] Much else in the letter also indicates that he was imagining a future he would not see. For his chief topic is the proper education of his son, which he outlines in terms that offer us a concrete glimpse of a dimension of noble life barely visible elsewhere, that is, the importance of the larger family network in sustaining the Way.

It goes without saying that anyone hoping to preside over a house enterprise had to be educated. On that score, the family collection of manuscripts was of course a great asset. However, Tamemasu also knew that texts alone were not enough, that much guidance would

---

45. See Butler, *Emperor and Aristocracy in Japan*, pp. 56–63.
46. Inoue, "Reizei-ke no rekishi 12: Tamemasu, Myōyū," p. 4.
47. Atsuta, "Tamemasu no okibumi," pp. 5–7.

be needed to prepare his heir to read, interpret, and use them, and he was very specific about where his wife should look to find it. First of all, he says that the boy should be sent to a temple to learn to read — by which he probably meant learning to read Chinese as well as Japanese, and also to write. Then he says that for poetry lessons he should be sent to a monk named Hōsen, whom we know to be one of Tamemasu's brothers residing at Kōfukuji Temple in Nara, and to "any others available" — a rather enigmatic statement that may mean other Reizei disciples in the area, or perhaps even members of other poetic houses willing to assist. Only after this does he bring up the secret transmissions, which he says are in a leather case. Moreover, since it would not do to pass these on to the boy too readily, he cautions, his wife should have another of Tamemasu's brothers — Tōbō, a monk living in Nara — read the texts to the boy, instructing him as he proceeds. Then he says that his own paper strips on the *kokin denjū* are in a lacquered paper box, there for the boy to study.[48]

The letter contains more that is of interest to a student of the Reizei house as a poetic institution: a note about a manuscript in Abutsu's hand, for instance, as well as others left by Tamehide, Tamesuke, Tameie, Teika, and Shunzei, of which Tamemasu says, "These are treasures without peer under Heaven," and should only be taken out and read with the greatest care. Then Tamemasu goes on to remind his wife about a few things he must have wanted his heir to be taught: that the Reizei were the legitimate heirs of the Mikohidari legacy; that the letters from Tameie deeding properties to Tamesuke in anger over Tameuji's unfilial behavior are also in the leather case; that in a broad sense the Asukai, the Sanjōnishi, and even Sōgi and Tō no Tsuneyori were disciples of the Reizei; and lastly that in more recent years his grandfather, Tamehiro, had been honored with formal appointment as Waka Master at court. Finally, he adds — as a kind of afterthought — that the boy should ask Hōsen about how to write *dai* (which probably is a kind of shorthand for such ritualistic matters generally) and then says a few words about finding places for other children to go.[49]

So while Tamemasu was in Suruga, his son was probably beginning his preparation to take over the house, under the tutelage of his mother, though it is doubtful that he actually got much beyond

---

48. Ibid.
49. Ibid.

reading lessons before his father returned. Furthermore, what we
know about the father's stay in Suruga tells us that, however fatalis-
tic about his long-term chances, he had not gone into retirement yet.
The diary of a famous *renga* master notes that while there Tamemasu
transmitted the house teachings on the conduct of poetry gatherings
to Imagawa Ujizane (1538–1614), Yoshimoto's son, indicating that in
the case of powerful patrons the head of the family still kept some
privileges to himself.[50]

After returning to Kyoto, Tamemasu did not participate in activi-
ties at court. Behind the scenes, however, he remained a player. In
1568, for instance, we know that one of his daughters entered into
service in the imperial palace; and during the same year his son
and heir, Tamemitsu (1559–1619), began his career at court.[51] By the
Seventh Month of 1570, the young man was a gentleman-in-waiting
of junior fifth rank, lower grade.[52] Thus when Tamemasu breathed
his last a month or so later at the age of 54, he could feel that he had
fulfilled his major obligations. Of course, his son was barely into
his teens, but leaving one's heir in such a situation was by that time
almost a tradition of the house. Tamemasu no doubt knew the family
history: Tamesuke, Tamehide, and Tameyuki had also survived the
loss of a father at a young age. His son would have to do the same.
The letter written several years before tells us that he had the re-
sources of a network to call upon in doing so.

Very few poems by Tamemasu survive, probably because he pro-
duced little of note—a lamentable fact but one that is in another way
useful for reminding us that it was less to individual artistic excel-
lence that the heads of the house were committed than to sustaining
the enterprise. However meager his own accomplishments, Tame-
masu did pass on the Way, which involved doing precisely the things
his father had done: marking and editing the work of disciples, lec-
turing, managing library resources, maintaining a profile at the impe-
rial court, and building the family network. Not every heir of the line-
age could be expected to rival the patriarchs in poetic talent. Again,
it was process that mattered more than product, and as his letter to
his wife shows, Tamemasu had been fully dedicated to the process.

---

50. Inoue, "Reizei-ke no rekishi 12: Tamemasu, Myōyū," p. 5. The *renga*
master was Satomura Jōha (1525–1602).

51. Ibid., p. 5.

52. Ibid., p. 4.

Nonetheless, on his deathbed Tamemasu must have known that he was leaving his son to an uncertain fate in the capital. One source says that by the year 1576, the Reizei house was receiving only 26 *kan* (the equivalent of 2,600 *hiki* or just over 5 *koku* of rice) from income-producing lands that in the past had yielded at least ten times that much.[53] That was not all: for after his recent trip to Suruga, Tamemasu probably also realized that his son might have to get along without the aid of the Imagawa as patrons. Ten years earlier, Yoshimoto had been killed on the battlefield by a warrior from the Nagoya area named Oda Nobunaga, and in the years since then, Ujizane had lost out time and again on the battlefield and in negotiations with the rivals who surrounded him. Then, not long after Tamemasu's death, the inevitable happened: the head of the Imagawa lost his position, took the tonsure, and ended up in Kyoto, where he hoped to live the life of a literatus. No longer could he provide the assistance upon which the Reizei had become so dependent over the years. Unlike Utsunomiya Yoritsuna centuries before, Ujizane did not leave the field of struggle with a handsome income and large retinue to support him. His decision to retire from the world was more an act of capitulation than an elegant retirement.

Although Tamemasu cannot have known it, other big changes were coming—changes not unrelated to Ujizane's fate—that would fundamentally affect the future of all court lineages, the Reizei among them. Even before the death of the Reizei headman, the warlord Oda Nobunaga, recently victorious in battles against his neighbors, had advanced on Kyoto, chased out the old shogun and set up a new one in his place. Soon he was sending out edicts designed to restore order and secure the capital as a fortress for the Oda cause. At the time of Tamemasu's passing, the warlord was away from the city, contending with rivals on battlefields to the east. But in the coming years he would return to the capital, where first he would restore peace but also wreak havoc before being cut down himself in a temple on Third Avenue a little more than a decade after he first took command of the city.

---

53. See Butler, *Emperor and Aristocracy in Japan*, p. 33.

SEVEN

Courtiers' Quarter

ODA NOBUNAGA, first of a group of three warlords often referred to by historians of Japan as the Great Unifiers, was a domineering personality who had a volatile relationship with nearly everyone, including the emperor and the old nobility. Nevertheless, after subduing his competition in and around Kyoto in the late 1560s, he left the emperor on the throne and even set workers to the task of repairing the imperial palace. Likewise, he opted not to dispose of the office of shogun, and instead put a man of his own choosing in that office, doubtless because he thought doing so could be turned to his advantage. Lastly, he showed himself willing, at least occasionally, to answer requests for funds from the emperor, noble families, and religious institutions. Since the collapse of the central power structure in the Ōnin War, members of the court had shown little reluctance to beg for gifts from wealthy warriors, and Nobunaga continued the tradition of granting many of their requests.[1] In time, he even arranged modest but stable incomes for many high-ranking noble houses at a time when many were desperate for financial support.[2]

The new palace that Nobunaga constructed for Ashikaga Yoshiaki, his choice for the office of shogun, was a grand structure on Second Avenue, far away from the old site of the Palace of Flowers to the north. A statement was being made: this would not be a mere return

---

1. Butler, *Emperor and Aristocracy in Japan*, pp. 128–39.
2. Ibid., pp. 148–50.

to the old days. The Ashikaga, at least after Yoshimitsu, had maintained an administrative structure that allowed some sharing of power and authority with their own vassals, the ancient nobility, and the great monasteries. Not so Nobunaga, who made it clear that his say would be absolute. Thus when, in 1573, the shogun offended him, Nobunaga simply drove him from the city. Thereafter, though Yoshiaki lived on in exile from the capital for more than 20 years, there was effectively no shogun, because Nobunaga would not deign to appoint one. As further evidence of his power and of his willingness to use it, he burned the recently built Nijō Palace to the ground. Nor was this the first time Nobunaga had shown his resolve. Just two years earlier, when the leaders of the great Enryakuji monastery complex on Mount Hiei defied him, he had also resorted to the torch, razing the temple and putting its entire population—3,000 men, women, and children, it is said—to the sword.

Among the dead on Mount Hiei—and in Sakamoto, where there were also casualties—were of course many people from court families. In other ways, too, the nobility were victims of Nobunaga's ruthlessness in war. On the other hand, no one could deny that the old court families, along with the other inhabitants of the region, were benefiting in other ways from Nobunaga's rule. For one thing, his attempts to reassert class distinctions gave the old houses some hope for a return to higher social status. In the short term, however, the court families were probably most grateful for Nobunaga's efforts toward restoring order. He appointed a lord governor (*shoshidai*), commissioners, and police; and, in all, his soldiers were more disciplined than the dreaded marauders of Ōnin times had been. What's more, his building projects brought thousands of workers into the city, swelling its population and generating commerce, which was further encouraged by his decision to tear down all the toll gates leading into the city—a carry-over from the last century. Before long, the Home Provinces were producing crops regularly, and trade, even foreign trade, was flourishing. In 1576, Nobunaga started building a huge castle for himself not in Kyoto proper but at Azuchi, on the shores of Lake Biwa, some miles away. But even after he moved there in 1579, Kyoto remained firmly under his control. All around the city, especially to the south and east, other warriors built fortresses as well. Far from opposing such developments, the emperor and the noble families—especially in public pronouncements—were among those who looked to Nobunaga with hope for the future.

Records show that Reizei Tamemitsu, although still only a minor captain of fifth rank, was among those able to take advantage of the restoration of order in the capital. Poetry began to thrive again, along with the other courtly arts, first among the nobility but also among the warrior houses. As head of the Reizei house, Tamemitsu was called upon to participate in many events himself. Looking to the future, he made an alliance with the Yamashina house—specialists in court costume and clothing as well as medicine—by marrying one of his sisters to Yamashina Tokitsune (1541–1611), son and heir of Yamashina Tokitsugu, whose journal is one of our most vital sources for the period. Another sister went into service at the imperial palace and produced two children for Prince Sanehito (d. 1586), a son of the reigning emperor, Ōgimachi. Later, the latter sister would be given permission to leave imperial service and become the wife of the head priest of Kōshōji, a sub-temple of Honganji, the great bastion of the True Pure Land sect. Thus Tamemitsu was doing what the heir of a noble house, whatever its special province, must do at all costs: making alliances.[3]

Tamemitsu could therefore afford something that his forebears for the preceding few generations could not—optimism. In the summer of 1582, Nobunaga was obliged to kill himself at Honnōji, a temple on Third Avenue in the capital, when vassals who had turned against him surrounded him there. Needless to say, this sent a perceptible shudder through the city. But the alliances Nobunaga had fashioned held. Toyotomi Hideyoshi (1536–98), the man who succeeded him as dictator, soon proved himself a shrewd politician and administrator. If anything he was even more dedicated to restoring—perhaps refashioning would be a better word—Kyoto than his predecessor. Over time, in fact he created what must be called a truly new city, although one that still retained some of the basic structure of the old one. Around the whole of it, he would eventually construct a huge earthen wall, surrounded by a moat, for defense. Within the enclosure, temples would be gathered together into specified districts, as would the houses of the nobility, around the imperial palace on Tsuchimikado. Not very far away would be the compounds of the warlords of Hideyoshi's own entourage, ranged around the Jurakutei (The Palace of Pleasures), which he built not far from the emperor's palace. This in itself symbolized his desire to enunciate class distinctions, which

3. Inoue, "Reizei-ke no rekishi 13: Tamemitsu," p. 4.

meant high regard for the imperial family and the nobility, an attitude that was evinced earlier by his decision to appoint himself to court rank and office. Nobunaga had adopted court rank and office only after some years in the capital, and then only briefly, but already in 1583 Hideyoshi had himself made consultant, and the next year he rose to middle counselor. A few years later he amazed the city by arranging to be adopted into the regental Konoe house, so that he could be named chancellor and regent. For one whose pretenses to noble pedigree were pure fantasy, his rise was truly extraordinary.

In private, many among the nobility were probably appalled by the notion of an upstart like Hideyoshi serving as imperial regent, including the Konoe, who agreed to the dictator's proposal only under duress.[4] As recipients of his largess, however, they could hardly complain in public. In 1589, Hideyoshi would even set about repairing the imperial palace, which took two full years and amounted to rebuilding almost every structure within the compound.[5] The noble families also benefited in countless other ways, from direct subsidy to the opportunities offered by the new economy, which promised as much to them as it did to textile manufacturers or craftsmen in wood, clay, or iron. Hideyoshi's orders to the residents of various districts of the capital to move their institutions, businesses, or dwellings to different areas caused considerable confusion and financial stress, of course; but the prospect of lasting peace and stability was alluring enough to make many courtiers willing participants.

SO THE mood of the capital under Hideyoshi was upbeat. Sounds of destruction were at last replaced by sounds of construction. Ironically, however, it was just at this time, in the summer of 1585, that Reizei Tamemitsu left the imperial city to take up residence in Izumi Sakai for a few months and then in Osaka. There also he found a thriving economy, for Osaka was a major port, full of warehouses and commercial agents, many of them direct vassals of Hideyoshi or his generals. Indeed, Hideyoshi was building a huge castle there, too, which may be one of the reasons that Tamemitsu ended up settling there rather than somewhere else.

Yet the more immediate motive behind Tamemitsu's arrival in the port city, along with his two colleagues, Yamashina Tokitsune

---

4. Bruschke-Johnson, *Dismissed as Elegant Fossils*, p. 38.
5. *Kyōto no rekishi*, vol. 4, pp. 286–88.

and Shijō Takamasa (1556–1613) — the latter actually being Tame-mitsu's older brother, adopted into the Shijō lineage as heir — was not so positive. For it appears that just as the noble families were beginning to recover from a century of poverty and privation, the three men had gotten into a quarrel with the emperor over income from an estate claimed by the families involved and the imperial house. This in itself was nothing scandalous; quarrels over money were commonplace, even between the nobility and the emperor. The scandal in this case was that instead of pursuing the matter at court, Tamemitsu and his cohorts had appealed to the *shoshidai*, Hide-yoshi's lord governor. In a fit of temper, Emperor Ōgimachi put the three courtiers under imperial censure (*chokkan*). One suspects partisan reasons here, and perhaps collusion with rival families, since the emperor was known to favor the Asukai clan — now the major claimants of the Nijō tradition — in poetic matters. Whatever the reason, the three men had to do something to survive. Rather than trying to stay on in the capital under a cloud, Tamemitsu took refuge in Osaka, with relatives associated with the True Pure Land temple, Honganji.[6]

Tamemitsu was in his mid-20s by the time he departed Kyoto. Whether he had already married before this time is not known, but genealogies show that soon after arriving in Osaka he married the daughter of the chief priest of nearby Sumiyoshi Shrine, of the ancient Tsumori clan. The Tsumori, as was expected of a clan serving Sumiyoshi Daimyōjin, one of the patron gods of poets, had been active in poetic affairs since at least the twelfth century. Moreover, generations before, Tsumori Kunisuke (1242–99) had married one of his daughters to Nijō Tameyo of the Mikohidari line, forging a bond between the two lineages. The alliance was thus a well-established one. After the marriage, Tamemitsu moved into a house in Kitano-shō, near the shrine in Izumi Sakai, provided by his in-laws.[7] Both of his sons, Tameyori (1592–1627) and Tamekata (1593–1653), were born there.

Tamemitsu was able to maintain an active poetic practice in the Osaka area, where he had many patrons among local samurai. One

---

6. Inoue, "Reizei-ke no rekishi 13: Tamemitsu," p. 4. For a narration of the same incident focused on Yamashina Tokitsune, see Butler, *Emperor and Aristocracy in Japan*, pp. 114–23.

7. Nakamura, "Waka no ie, kuge no ie," p. 10.

indication that he assumed that his stay there would be a long one was again that he had his library with him, for which he erected a document storehouse (*bunko*).[8] So when the warrior poet Hosokawa Yūsai came to visit him there in 1586, asking to see the Reizei's precious copy of the *Sandaishū* in Teika's hand, he was able to oblige quickly. Yūsai was the heir of Hosokawa Masamoto, patron of Tamehiro. For these and perhaps other reasons, Tamemitsu seems not to have resisted Yūsai's request. That it was precisely these manuscripts that his great-great-grandfather Tametomi had refused to display at court in the days after the Ōnin War is telling. Not only more powerful than the emperor, Yūsai was also a more highly accomplished poet, a man of taste as well as influence. Never slow to see an opportunity for strengthening the position of the house, Tamemitsu also showed Yūsai three letters from Tameie to Tamesuke—not surprisingly, the same three that had for centuries been used as evidence of Tameie's intent to establish young Tamesuke in his own lineage. Over the years, Yūsai's name has become identified more with the Nijō orthodoxy of the Asukai house than with the Reizei. His interest in the Reizei teachings, however, indicates that at least in some sense he accepted the status of Tamemitsu as the blood heir of Teika and, perhaps more importantly, as inheritor of Tameie's library. In 1594, Tamemitsu would respond in the same way to the request of Tokugawa Ieyasu, Hideyoshi's successor. Then he would go even further, not only showing the dictator the Teika *Sandaishū* but also giving him another manuscript in Teika's hand, the personal poetry collection of the Heian era poet Archbishop Henjō (816–90).[9] As one of Hideyoshi's most powerful generals, the heir of the Tokugawa was a much sought-after patron in his own right and Tamemitsu was careful to take advantage of any opportunity to pique his interest.

In 1591, Hideyoshi ordered Honganji moved from Sakai to Kyoto as part of a general scheme of geographical restructuring intended to reinforce his claims to legitimacy. In the days after the Ōnin War, the great armed leagues (*Ikkō Ikki*) of the True Pure Land sect had been a major force in the Home Provinces, and one that had

---

8. Ibid., p. 10.

9. Inoue, "Reizei-ke no rekishi 13: Tamemitsu," pp. 4–5. In 1592, he also gave a copy of *Kintada Ason shū* in Teika's hand to the warlord Toyotomi Hidetsugu. See Ogura, "Tamemitsu no ryūgū to Reizei-ke zōsho," p. 6.

been subdued by Nobunaga only in 1580 after ten years of fighting. Also aware of the power the sect had over its enormous membership, Hideyoshi evidently wanted the head temple of the sect nearer by, where he could monitor its activities. He also wanted the temple far from Osaka, where any outbreak of violence could interrupt the smooth flow of commerce. Thus it was that the three families that had moved out of Kyoto returned only six years later, taking up life in new quarters annexed to the temple, away from the main courtier community in the north but within the city boundaries.[10]

For a time Tamemitsu's wife stayed in Sakai, near her family, with Tamemitsu commuting back and forth. But when she perished in the great earthquake of 1596—a three-day series of shocks that did substantial damage to Hideyoshi's castle in Fushimi and other buildings all over the Kansai, taking thousands of lives—he brought his sons to Kyoto permanently and built a house near Seventh Avenue with the lumber from his destroyed house in Osaka, complete with another *bunko*.[11] Still under censure by the emperor, he could not do service at court or participate in poetic events there. But he kept his offices and titles and seems to have had enough friends and patrons to do well for himself. Several years later, in 1600, Tokugawa Ieyasu, potentate since the death of Hideyoshi in 1598, intervened on his behalf and Tamemitsu was finally released from censure. For reasons unknown, he had had to wait several years longer than had his compatriots in exile.

In celebration of his reinstatement, Tamemitsu took one of the most treasured texts in the library—Teika's personal anthology, in his own hand—for display before Emperor Go-Yōzei (1571–1617; r. 1586–1611), who had succeeded Ōgimachi in 1586.[12] Even then, however, Tamemitsu did not become a regular at court ceremonies. He did, however, hold his own monthly meetings, inviting not just his own sons and other courtiers but also warriors such as his old patron Imagawa Ujizane, a few priests of the Ji (Time) sect, and tea masters. So even while his status in the eyes of the emperor remained problematic, he prospered in the new Kyoto. Within a few years, Ieyasu arranged for a lot for him just north of the imperial palace, very close

---

10. Nakamura, "Waka no ie, kuge no ie," pp. 10–12.

11. Ibid., p. 12.

12. Ogura, "Tamemitsu no ryūgū to Reizei-ke zōsho," p. 7.

to the site where the residence of the upper house would stand until the present day.[13]

A CONSERVATIVE estimate of the population of Kyoto in 1591 is 500,000. Under the administration of Tokugawa Ieyasu it would continue to grow for some years to come. In 1603, Ieyasu had himself appointed *seii taishōgun* (Subduer of Barbarians), following the example of Minamoto no Yoritomo and the Ashikaga, but it was clear that in other ways there would be no return to the past. Most of the old *shugo* daimyo of the warring states period — including many who had been important patrons of the arts such as the Hatekeyama, the Imagawa, the Ōuchi, and so forth — had been wiped out during the wars of unification. Now shogunal control, at all levels of society, would be more comprehensive than it had ever been under the Ashikaga. The Tokugawa and their vassals were intent on creating an administrative structure that would keep them in power and make any return to the endemic warfare of the last century impossible.

Historians attribute the success of the new regime to a host of factors. One of the most crucial, by all accounts, is the success of Hideyoshi's policies in the area of land reform. Based on a thorough survey of arable land, these reforms did away with the old system of rights to land that had accumulated like layers of paint over centuries. In its place was a new system that gave to daimyo more complete control of domains (known as *ryōbun* at first and later as *han*) — 185 of them in the beginning. Appointment, regional assignment, and political activity of daimyo were controlled by the central government to a degree never dreamt of by the Ashikaga shoguns.

For the country as a whole, and especially for daimyo and their vassals, the new system brought wealth and prosperity, especially in the seventeenth century. At the top of the hierarchy, Ieyasu himself ended up with an income of 2,500,000 *koku* — a *koku* being equal to just over five bushels of rice, which was calculated to be the amount

---

13. See Hayashi, "Go-Yōzei-in to sono shūhen," p. 37. Inoue, "Reizei-ke no rekishi 13: Tamemitsu," p. 5. Nakamura, "Waka no ie, kuge no ie," pp. 12–13. When Tamemitsu moved from his house near Seventh Avenue in 1600, it was to a place just inside Courtiers' Quarter in the north. He did not move to the present lot until expansion of the imperial palace compound in 1606 obliged the Yamashina and the Reizei to locate just outside of Courtiers' Quarter, north of Imadegawa.

needed to support one person for one year. Major daimyo like the Maeda were awarded over 1,000,000 *koku*, while scores of others— the Shimazu, the Yūki, the Date, the Gamō, and so on—received incomes in the hundreds of thousands, and hundreds more in the thousands. With their new riches, the shogunate and daimyo embarked on building projects, both in their domains and in Kyoto, which was highly regarded as a cultural center. By 1637, there would be 66 daimyo of more than 10,000 *koku* maintaining residences in the city, complete with their complements of retainers and servants, and the figure would go up before it went down.[14] The residences were large and well appointed, attesting to the wealth of the new elite, who were drawn to the old city largely for its cultural enticements.[15] With such a ready-made group of consumers to support them, the merchants and artisans of the old city could hardly go wrong. Sales of rice, saké, and all sorts of consumer goods skyrocketed, as did sales of handicrafts, textiles, lacquerware, tea utensils, and a host of other products for which the city remains famous even now.

Under the new government, the imperial family and the nobility would of course have met complete ruin if the new shogunate had not chosen to continue providing them sustenance, as Nobunaga and Hideyoshi had done before. During the Sengoku period, the nobility had managed to claim some revenue by begging help from the shogunate or from warriors in the areas of their estates or by attaching themselves to patrons. Now their old deeds were truly dead letters, and many of their old patrons smoke on the wind. Still, the legitimizing power of the emperor remained great, as did the attraction of old titles, which many warrior chieftains still coveted. Ieyasu and those around him, too, were basically conservative in their attitudes: less reckless than Nobunaga, more patient than Hideyoshi. Hence Ieyasu's decision to continue his predecessors' policy of providing basic financial support for the imperial family and the nobility.

To begin with, the emperor received only 10,000 *koku* from the shogunate, but in time that figure would triple to 30,000 *koku*.[16] The nobility received much less. The men—and usually there were two serving at any one time—appointed as *buke tensō*, liaison officers with the shogunate, were at the top of the list, receiving upwards of 4,000

---

14. Murai, "Jidai gaisetsu," p. 15.
15. *Kyōto no rekishi*, vol. 5, p. 501.
16. Murai, "Jidai gaisetsu," pp. 11–12.

koku in combined income from various responsibilities. Next came imperial princes and the old regental families (the Konoe, the Kujō, the Nijō, the Ichijō, and the Takatsukasa), who received between 1,500 and 3,000 *koku*, while the lowest ranking families were allotted only 100 *koku* or less.[17] Records show that in 1601, the upper Reizei house was awarded an annual income of 200 *koku*, coming from *chigyōchi* (fiefs) in the area around the capital; in 1685 that figure would be raised to 300 *koku*.[18] Compared to what Teika or Tameie or even Tamemasa had received as income from their estate rights, this was not a great sum, but it sufficed to maintain a modest household, with a handful of retainers, samurai, and servants. This was no doubt precisely the outcome envisioned by the shogunate, who wanted the old families to return to a place of honor in the social order but did not want them to be wealthy or powerful enough to be real players in political affairs. Just as it sought to control any other potential challenge to its hegemony, the shogunate was committed to eliminating the old elite from any possibility of true political engagement. Among the nobility, only the *buke tensō*, who swore loyalty to the shogunate with a blood oath, were allowed to exercise any true administrative control in the new regime. It must be said, however, that thanks to the new regime the old families were more financially secure than they had been for more than a century.[19]

There were other ways, too, by which the new shogunate made known its position with respect to the old families. In 1609, for instance, when Emperor Go-Yōzei announced his decision to impose the death penalty on a group of courtiers—some from the most prominent families—after a scandal, Ieyasu intervened and "advised" banishment for most of the offenders, thus making it clear that the shogun had ultimate power even within the court itself.[20] Then the shogun set about rebuilding the imperial palace in grand style, assign-

---

17. Kumakura, *Go-Mizuno'o*, pp. 42–43; Reizei Kimiko, "Bakumatsu no Reizei-ke," p. 293.

18. Inoue, "Reizei-ke no rekishi 13: Tamemitsu," p. 5; Ogura, "Edo jidai no Reizei-ke," p. 9.

19. For a description of the policies of Nobunaga, Hideyoshi, and Ieyasu toward the imperial court and its families, see Butler, *Emperor and Aristocracy in Japan*, pp. 144–53.

20. Kumakura, *Go-Mizuno'o*, pp. 11–22. For a complete treatment of this famous scandal, see Butler, *Emperor and Aristocracy in Japan*, pp. 170–79.

ing men from the shogunal entourage as architects and providing
the labor from levies of his own strongmen so that all would see the
dependence of the imperial family on the new military government.
Finally, at the same time that he was issuing various laws aimed at
regulating the affairs of military households, merchants, the clergy,
and farmers, Ieyasu also issued laws restricting the behavior and
activities of the imperial family and the nobility. The most famous
of these were made public in 1615 in a document titled *Kinchū narabi
ni kuge shohatto* (Regulations for the Imperial Court and the Nobility).
Worked out after exhaustive research and planning, much of it in-
volving Ieyasu himself, these and other regulations promulgated at
the same time clearly put into the hands of the shogunate responsibil-
ity for many court appointments, even appointments to abbacies of
prominent temples long under imperial control. Also enacted were
sumptuary laws aimed at discouraging unruly behavior, which had
been a problem in recent years.

Lee Butler has shown conclusively that much of what went into
the regulations of 1615 had precedent in earlier documents and was
therefore not a matter of surprise to the emperor or the noble families,
who probably saw the guidelines as little more than a restatement
of standards deriving ultimately from their own oldest traditions.[21]
It goes without saying, however, that the new regime met some resis-
tance in Kyoto, first from Go-Yōzei and then from his successor,
Go-Mizuno'o (1596–1680; r. 1611–29), who like most emperors before
them desired some exercise of power. It was partly because of frustra-
tion over his inability to restore more power to the imperial office
that Go-Yōzei finally abdicated in 1611, after being held up by the
shogunate even in his request to leave office. The administration of
Go-Mizuno'o was also marked by a number of conflicts with the new
government. One of the most well-known examples is his resistance
to the idea of taking a daughter of Shogun Tokugawa Hidetada (1579–
1632) as his consort. Rather than refusing outright, he managed to put
the matter off, using various excuses; several times he even threat-
ened to abdicate and put one of his younger brothers on the throne.
When Hidetada insisted, backing up his overtures with "threats and
bribes," as Butler puts it, Go-Mizuno'o relented.[22] In 1620 Empress
Kazuko (also known as Tōfukumon-in; 1607–78) arrived at the impe-

21. Butler, *Emperor and Aristocracy in Japan*, pp. 198–224.
22. Ibid., p. 228.

rial palace accompanied by a grand parade of several hundred attendants, leading ox-drawn carts and carrying chests of treasures that left little doubt about who had won the contest. Although the emperor already had several children by consorts from the noble families—most prominently by a woman named Oyotsu of the Yotsutsuji lineage of the Fujiwara—it would be the daughter of his union with Ieyasu's granddaughter who would go on to reign as Emperor Meishō after Go-Mizuno'o abdicated in 1629—the first female sovereign since the Nara period.[23] That she was chosen over several sons by other wives made the power of the shogunate apparent to all.

Around the same time that he greeted his new wife, however, Emperor Go-Mizuno'o did fully embrace one of the shogun's regulations for the nobility—the first item of the *Kuge shohatto*, which dictated that the true province of the old elite must be the arts (*geinō*) and scholarship (*gakumon*). In effect, this was an endorsement of already existing affiliations, but the imprimatur of the shogun obviously added credibility to the notion of "house Ways" and removed from them any hint of mercantilism. Beginning in the first month of 1619, the Emperor called an assembly of all the nobility and established a monthly schedule of *keiko* for all the courtly traditions, commanding all to dedicate themselves to at least two areas of specialty, according to the following schedule:

2nd Day	Court Lore
6th Day	*Waka* Composition (Japanese Poetry)
10th Day	Confucian Texts
13th Day	Music
19th Day	Japanese Linked Verse (*renga*)
23rd Day	Scholarship on *Kanshi* (Chinese Poetry)
25th Day	*Waka* Scholarship
28th Day	Chinese Linked Verse (*renku*)
29th Day	*Kanshi* Composition

Partly to ensure that meetings did not descend into drinking parties but also to encourage full participation in his plan, the emperor attended many study sessions himself.[24] Unseemly behavior, for which courtiers had achieved a reputation in recent years, could only hurt the noble cause in the long run, while careful attendance to artistic duties could only help. In the new economy of things,

---

23. Kumakura, *Go-Mizuno'o*, pp. 53–64.
24. Ibid., p. 68.

dedication to the old Ways—especially the *uta*, which he regarded as premier among all courtly traditions[25]—was the best hope for political survival, as well as a reliable source of supplemental income.

In addition to ancient arts, Go-Mizuno'o also dedicated much of his time to art forms of less hoary ancestry, such as the tea ceremony and flower arrangement, forming salons of his own and encouraging others to do so as well. In just the first half of 1629, for instance, he participated in no fewer than 30 flower-arranging competitions or meetings himself, often acting as judge.[26] He was determined, it would seem, to establish a firm identity for the old families in the new order that compensated in symbolic capital for what had been lost in political power, devoutly believing that the arts would exercise a "civilizing" influence on his courtiers.[27] Rather than diminishing after his abdication at the end of 1629, his dedication intensified as he began his reign as retired emperor. For obvious political reasons he could not publicly compare himself to Go-Toba, but Go-Mizuno'o's ambitions for his court—in the arena of artistic and scholastic accomplishment, at least—were as high as those of his ancestor four centuries before. When, in 1634, the shogun Iemitsu (1604–51) increased from 3,000 to 10,000 *koku* the stipend of the office of the retired emperor, which Go-Mizuno'o would occupy for nearly five more decades,[28] the once disenchanted sovereign put more effort into preserving and sustaining the courtly arts, poetry chief among them.

COMMON SENSE would seem to dictate that Reizei Tamemitsu should have had a major role in the renaissance of Go-Mizuno'o. After all, he could claim a direct line back to a lineage that had claimed court poetry as its province for more than 400 years. Moreover, we know from the fact that Go-Mizuno'o borrowed texts from the Reizei library for copying that he had esteem for the family's literary holdings and

25. Ōtani, "Go-Mizuno'o-in to Nakano-in, Karasumaru-ke no hitobito," p. 35. The *uta* is in fact the only one of the arts that is explicitly mentioned in the first article of the *Kuge shohatto* as "our country's art" and therefore one that "should not be abandoned" (see Butler, *Emperor and Aristocracy in Japan*, p. 206).

26. Kumakura, *Go-Mizuno'o*, pp. 151–53.

27. See Ōtani, "Go-Mizuno'o-in to Nakano-in, Karasumaru-ke no hitobito," p. 34. In his "Rules for Young Nobles" of 1631, Go-Mizuno'o lists "practice in the arts" as one of his own rules.

28. Butler, *Emperor and Aristocracy in Japan*, pp. 234–35.

that far from losing popularity in the new regime, Teika, for instance, was more highly regarded than ever before, both as a poet and as a calligrapher.[29] Yet for a number of reasons the house did not in fact prosper greatly during Go-Mizuno'o's reign as emperor and then retired emperor, which would continue until 1680.

One reason was that Tamemitsu had evidently been labeled an outsider when he left for Osaka and in various other ways since then. When the shogunate created a Courtiers' Quarter around the imperial palace and the palace of the retired emperor—a sort of castle town within the city—Tamemitsu was given a place only on its fringe; and when expansion of the imperial palace demanded that some families leave the quarter in 1605, it was the Reizei and the Yamashina who were asked to move to a place just outside the walls on Imadegawa Avenue.[30] Whether this action was meant to convey a symbolic rebuff is not recorded, but there is no question that many at court saw the Reizei and the Yamashina as somehow allied with the new shogunate. This charge was undeniable in Tamemitsu's case, since he had traveled to Suruga and Edo to meet with warrior patrons,[31] had gone so far as to give the family teachings to both Ieyasu and Hidetada in 1614—probably in hopes of securing a larger stipend for the house—and often attended Ieyasu at his castle in Fushimi.[32] Tameyori continued in the same fashion, allowing Hidetada to copy the prized Reizei manuscript of *Kokinshū* (for which the house received a gratuity of 203 *koku*[33]), acting as a lector at a poetry gathering at Nijō Castle for the shogun Iemitsu in 1626, and in various other ways allying himself with the government in Edo. It was no wonder, then, that Go-Mizuno'o defined the Reizei as *tozama*, a term used by the shogunate itself in reference to daimyo not numbered among direct vassals. Of course, since the days of Tamesuke, the Reizei had indeed often been outsiders, connected with the warlords of Kamakura, first of all, and then with the Ashikaga, the Hatakeyama, the Imagawa,

---

29. On the "Teika craze" of these years, see Butler, *Emperor and Aristocracy in Japan*, pp. 251–54.

30. Nakamura, "Waka no ie, kuge no ie," p. 13.

31. Kubota Keiichi in his *Kinsei Reizei-ha kadan no kenkyū* (p. 135) notes that Tamemitsu traveled to Edo at least five times that can be documented.

32. Ibid., pp. 32–39. See also Kubota Keiichi, *Kinsei Reizei-ha kadan no kenkyū*, pp. 32, 34, 39, 61–63, 110.

33. Reizei Kimiko, *Tametada-kyō ki 58*," p. 6.

and other daimyo. Their strategy of maintaining a strong relationship with the shogunate while retaining their place in the imperial court had always been a tricky proposition.

Another reason for the shaky status of the house during Go-Mizuno'o's reign was that there was new competition, from several directions. The first was from within the noble brotherhood itself, where a number of families had in the past 100 years or so established themselves as poetic houses, often through identification with various strains of the *Kokin denju*, or secret teachings on *Kokinshū*, and other early poetic texts. Among these were the Konoe, Sanjō-nishi, Nakano-in, Karasumaru, and Mushanokōji houses, as well as the imperial house itself—all of which could provide poetic services with proper authority. Go-Mizuno'o, for instance, had received the secret teachings from his fraternal uncle Prince Toshihito (1579–1629), who in turn had received them from Hosokawa Yūsai; and Go-Mizuno'o passed them on to a number of his courtiers himself. Thus when in 1622 the emperor ordered three imperial poetry gatherings (meaning *tsukinamikai*, intended primarily for practice, or *keiko*) to be held at court, he chose members of the Sanjōnishi, Karasumaru, and Nakano-in families as masters.[34] While the presence of these competitors did not nullify the claims of Tamemitsu and his progeny, it had the effect of expanding the field and intensifying rivalries. The emperor's role in "licensing" certain individuals from noble houses as masters (*sōshō*), moreover, presaged a time when the imperial house would be firmly in control of poetic matters, making the emperors and the retired emperors rivals of the poetic houses as well.[35]

Also of some importance in the competition for students and patrons were competing offshoots of the Reizei house itself, including two lineages formed by Tamemitsu himself: the Nakayama Reizei and the Fujitani. The story of the first of these lineages is a common one in the annals of noble houses. It began when Tamemitsu, who had not produced an heir by his late 20s, took the step of adopting a son from another noble house, only to produce unexpectedly a son of his own a few years later. Loath to allow anyone but a son directly in the bloodline of Shunzei and Teika to inherit the house unless it could not be avoided, Tamemitsu decided quickly to give headship

---

34. Ōtani, "Go-Mizuno'o-in to Nakano-in, Karasumaru-ke no hitobito," p. 28.

35. Morita, "Kinsei Tennō to waka," pp. 260, 271–72.

of the main house to his blood-son. Yet he was also reluctant to leave his ward, known as Tamechika, out in the cold. The solution was to create a new house, known as the Nakayama-Reizei, because the boy had originally been born into the Nakayama lineage. The other offshoot also came about for essentially sentimental reasons, when Tamemitsu could not bear to send his second son, Tamekata, into the priesthood. Thus Tamemitsu created two new lineages, the second known as the Fujitani, harkening back to the district of Kamakura in which Tamesuke had lived centuries before. Each of the new houses (*shinke*—a term generally used in reference to the many new noble lineages established in the early to mid-Edo period) was connected closely to the Reizei but was independently recognized at court. Seeking to find a secure place for itself in the court economy, the Nakayama Reizei became experts at kickball, but poetry remained the primary specialty of the heirs of the Fujitani. Although not as prestigious as the senior house, these junior lineages could quite legitimately be called upon to represent the house when inviting a member of the upper house was politically inexpedient, although in other ways, too, they served the main house by providing wives and sometimes heirs.

Lastly, in addition to rival noble houses and the Fujitani and Nakayama Reizei, the upper house in the 1600s was again obliged to compete with the recently revived lower house. As noted earlier, that lineage had seemed to come to an unhappy end when Tameatsu (1531–78) and his heir Tamekatsu (1557–78) were killed during the seizure of the Hosokawa Estate in Harima Province back in 1578. But there had been another son, born in 1561, who escaped death because he was already living in a temple when the invasion took place. Showing great promise in his studies, this young man, who is known to history as Fujiwara Seika (1561–1619), ended up as one of the major intellectual figures associated with the great Zen temple Shōkokuji. Later, however, he gave up his clerical responsibilities and set himself up as a sort of independent scholar of Chinese thought who would be hailed as the founder of Neo-Confucianism in Japan. As dedicated as he was to continental philosophy, however, Seika was equally determined to restore the lower Reizei house at the imperial court.[36] Although he died in 1619, before seeing his own son enter court ranks, he left behind influential students and patrons who would help the boy, named Tamekage (1612–52), eventually gain

---

36. Ichiko, "Reizei Tamekage to sono shūhen," p. 2.

a place in Go-Mizuno'o's salon. At first, Tamekage was denied the right to use the surname Reizei, instead going by the name Hoso-no—a combination of the areas where the family had traditionally had estates, *Hoso*kawa and *Ono*.[37] But in 1635 he was advanced to senior fifth rank, upper grade, and in time he would be granted the privilege of going by the name of his ancestors again.

From the beginning, then, the upper Reizei were not full participants in Go-Mizuno'o's cultural project, partly because of their affiliations with the new warrior regime and partly because of internecine competition. Go-Mizuno'o was no mere antiquarian to be bowled over by the family pedigree in itself. A serious poet who saw himself as a leader in literary affairs both by disposition and mandate, he demanded hard work and loyalty of his courtiers and brooked no resistance. The upper Reizei could of course claim long service as a poetic house, but the "secret teachings" passed from Sōgi to the San-jōnishi house and Hosokawa Yūsai, which the imperial house now claimed for its own, were of equal prestige at the time. Thus Tame-mitsu's heir faced a daunting challenge in attempting to restore the Reizei to prominence.

However, the fate of the Reizei, at least for the short term, would be decided, as it had been so many times before, less by such factors than by another death. This time it was the death of Tameyori, who passed away at the age of 36, in 1627, leaving as his heir a little boy born just the year before. To make matters worse, the boy seems to have been in some way physically or mentally handicapped, dying at the age of 25 after never even undergoing a coming-of-age ceremony—a sure sign that something was amiss. Just months before his own passing, Tameyori had been advanced to junior third rank, and he had been making progress both as a poet and as a master of the Teika style of calligraphy, which was gaining in popularity.[38] Among his students were men of prominence such as Kobori Enshū (1579–1647), a daimyo who had served as commissioner (*bugyō*) for the construction of Nijō Castle and Tokugawa Ieyasu's castle in Sunpu, as well as the "re-building" of the imperial palace and the palace of the retired emperor. But with his own father gone and his son, Tameharu, not competent to serve as head of the house, Tameyori's death left the lineage in limbo.

---

37. Ichiko, "Reizei Tamekage nenpukō, jō," pp. 102–03.
38. Kubota Keiichi, "Reizei-ke no rekishi 14: Tameyori," p. 5.

This premature death could easily have spelled the end of the upper Reizei house. Many other court lineages had died out under similar circumstances, including the Kyōgoku and Nijō branches of the Mikohidari centuries before and the lower Reizei, for a time, more recently. What saved the day in the mid-1600s was, ironically, one of the junior lineages, namely, the Fujitani, which had been established by Tamemitsu just decades before. If there were dangers in founding junior lineages, then, there were also advantages. Relations with the lower Reizei house at the time were evidently not cordial; Tamemitsu's son, Fujitani Tamekata, on the other hand, was friendlier. Furthermore, he was in his mid-30s and quite prosperous, the records indicate, so wealthy, in fact, that he was able to make substantial donations toward the repair of Kinkakuji, a temple located on the site of Ashikaga Yoshimitsu's villa west of the capital. In a gesture of goodwill, he sent his younger son Tamekiyo (1631–68) to the Reizei house on Imadegawa as heir. It would be some years, of course, before the young man could begin to participate at court, but with an able-bodied infant set on the proper course, there could at least be some hope.[39] Tamekata's elder son, Tameeda, would go on to serve as head of the Fujitani lineage, which would remain closely allied with the parent house for generations to come. Their residence was in fact located just to the west of the Reizei house on Imadegawa, where it would remain until the Meiji era.

On the surface, subsequent heirs of the upper house seem to have much for which to thank Tamekata. Yet records also indicate that there may have been some self-interest in his labors. Tamekata knew that under the Tokugawa regime, which put strict limits on social mobility, his own lineage would find it difficult ever to supplant the main house, which was counted among the *urinke*, houses whose heirs could go as high as major counselor in the court hierarchy, in contrast to heirs of the *meika*, a lower category to which his own "new house" belonged. Placing his son in the main house as heir was thus a way for Tamekata himself to move up in the hierarchy, at least vicariously. Additionally, some scholars believe that there may have been another, more sinister motive behind Tamekata's actions: a desire to gain access to the precious manuscripts of the Reizei library for his own purposes.

---

39. Kawashima, "Fujitani Tamekata shōron."

During the Sengoku period, many noble families had been forced by hard circumstance to part with some of their cultural treasures: paintings by old masters, pots and porcelains, fine kimono, items of furniture, and, of course, manuscripts—especially those in the hands of ancient masters. The traffic in old art objects did not stop with the establishment of peace in the late 1500s. Even with the support of the new shogunate, noble budgets were under stress, and the new wealth of the daimyo and merchant classes created a ready market for antiques. Practitioners of the tea ceremony were always on the lookout for paintings and fragments of calligraphy to hang in the alcoves of their tea houses or to display on the shelves in their meeting halls; warlords and their retainers likewise sought out objects to adorn their residences in Kyoto and Edo. All of this explains the emergence of a new class of cultural entrepreneurs who acted as agents, middlemen, appraisers, and authenticators, a class to which a number of records indicate that Fujitani Tamekata belonged. Hence the theory that he used his son's position as heir of the main house to raid the library, lending out some manuscripts without proper guarantees and selling others outright.[40]

The charge is a very old one that in its earliest form simply says, "In the Reizei house there was a profligate who sold off precious manuscripts handed down for generations."[41] Since we know that Tamemitsu himself had relinquished some manuscripts to patrons, just who the real culprit was in all of this is impossible to tell.[42] There can be no doubt, however, about the eventual result of what was happening, regardless of who was responsible for it. For in 1659, when the monk Hōrin Jōshō records in his diary a visit to the Reizei library, along with the lord governor of Kyoto and one of the current Edo liaison officers, to view the collection at the time it was being aired, he says that he went to the Reizei lot but makes no mention of any member of the house being present: "I saw all of the treasures, and what a joy it was to be able to examine them up close! Works

---

40. Ibid. See also Sugimoto Hidetarō and Reizei Tamehito, "Edo saigo no tōshū, Tametada," pp. 151–52.

41. Quoted in Kubota Keiichi, "Reizei-ke no rekishi 15: Tameharu, Tamekiyo I," p. 5.

42. See Ogura, "Tamemitsu no ryūgū to Reizei-ke zōsho." Manuscript evidence shows that Tamemitsu presented to patrons a number of original texts from the library.

in the hand of Lord Shunzei, Lord Teika, Lord Tameie, the monk Saigyō, the Go-Kyōgoku Regent; Teika's *Meigetsuki*; and a hoard of other texts too numerous to count."[43]

From the monk's effusions we can hazard that the collection was still largely intact but also that the family no longer had access to its own vaults. At some time, between the death of Tameyori in 1627 and the 1650s, the oldest record goes on to say, "an imperial edict was issued sealing the library, so that even the people of the house were not allowed to view its contents."[44] With shogunal approval, no doubt, Go-Mizuno'o evidently had decided to close the library to any use by the Reizei house, perhaps out of real fear that the collection would be lost, perhaps because he wanted to further undermine the authority of a rival constituency.[45] Effectively, the library that so many generations had labored to preserve and protect, the family's chief source of cultural capital, was padlocked. The keys to the treasure house now went to the lord governor of Kyoto and the court liaison officer (*buke tensō*), who would be charged with its care for decades to come.[46] During that time the family may have had some access to the collection, but only with formal approval from above, which meant that they could not readily offer their students one of the privileges for which discipleship in the Reizei house was so highly coveted — the privilege of viewing firsthand the treasures in the storehouse.[47]

SO THE mid-1600s were not easy times for the upper Reizei house. But these were not the 1500s; there would be no point in hying off to the provinces. Though their stipend of 200 *koku* can only be described as meager, especially when compared to that of the regental houses, they also had fewer samurai and servants to support (only ten people altogether, compared with 100 in the employ of one regental house,

---

43. Kubota Keiichi, "Reizei-ke no rekishi 16: Tamekiyo II," p. 4. Ogura, "Tamemitsu no ryūgū to Reizei-ke zōsho," p. 8, suggests 1628 as the probable date for the order to close the storehouse, in order to safeguard the collection.

44. Kubota Keiichi, "Reizei-ke no rekishi 15: Tameharu, Tamekiyo I," p. 5.

45. Kubota Keiichi argues that Go-Mizuno'o may have taken the step to consolidate his own power in poetic circles and to gain secrets of the house. Kubota Keiichi, *Kinsei Reizei-ha kadan no kenkyū*, pp. 38–39.

46. Kubota Keiichi, "Reizei-ke no rekishi 18: Tametsuna II," p. 5.

47. Ogura, "Obunko no fū to Tamekiyo," p. 6.

the Konoe).[48] Furthermore, the surest way for the house to improve its position over time was through attracting fee-paying students, which meant maintaining the proper posture at court. Tamekata's son Tamekiyo maintained a reasonably active profile, especially in the salon of Emperor Go-Sai (1637–85; r. 1654–63). When Tamekiyo too died young, before reaching 40, leaving his young son Tametsuna behind, it was almost as if he was following a family tradition. So too did the women of the house—always there, in the shadows behind documents—follow a family tradition when, after Tamekiyo's untimely death, they did for his heir the only thing that made sense, however difficult it must have been. A genealogy records their decision poignantly: "He [Tametsuna] made progress up the ranks according to family tradition, but without a father to teach him his future in the Way of Poetry was uncertain, and so his mother, caring deeply for him, asked the assistance of Nakano-in Michishige."[49]

In previous generations, some of the daughters of the various Reizei lineages may have had direct knowledge of the house teachings, but with the library off limits there was no hope of properly instructing a new heir. So the dire step had to be taken of sending the young Tametsuna (1664–1722) to another house for instruction. The boy's mother, a daughter of Sono Motonari (also read Moto'oto; 1604–55), a major counselor and one of the finest calligraphers of his day, knew the ways of the noble houses. Her concern was perhaps less with the distinctive traditions of the house than with its survival as part of the larger noble community, for which its affiliation with the Way of Poetry in some form was essential. No courtier was simply a courtier any more; a man always had to have special knowledge, a special province of learning, lore, and practice, all the more so in the new regime. The new economic order offered few opportunities for nobility without a good store of specialized knowledge and expertise.

The choice of Nakano-in Michishige (1631–1710) shows that Tametsuna's mother knew what she was about. The grandson of Michimura (1588–1653), tutor of Go-Mizuno'o, and the most prominent figure of the day, Michishige could be depended on to give the boy guidance and instruction in the areas where it was needed, actual poetic composition being first on the list, followed by some

---

48. Matsuda, "Reizei-ke no keishitachi," p. 2.
49. Kubota Keiichi, "Reizei-ke no rekishi 17: Tametsuna I," p. 4.

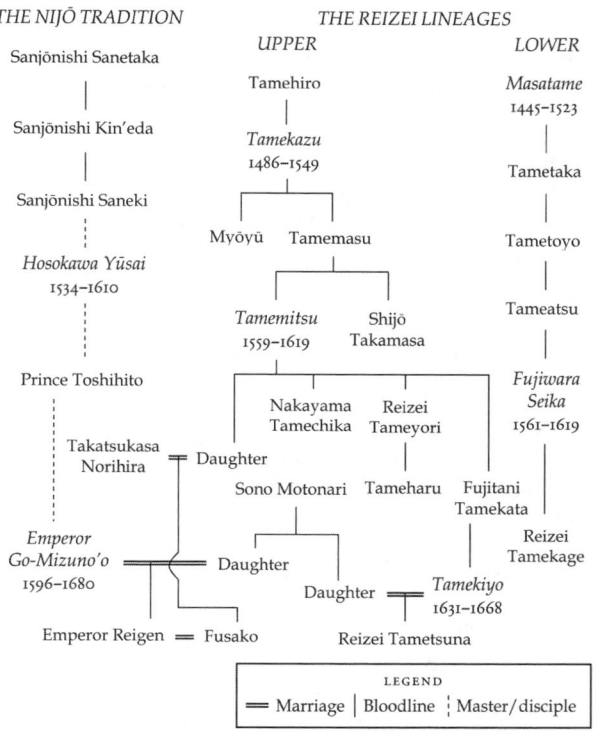

Chart 4 Branches and Rivals, 1500–1700

secret teachings. By the mid-seventeenth century, the transmission of the latter had been routinized, to the extent, in fact, that the central "transmission" was done in various stages and ended in an actual process of licensing. Michishige may not have shared all the secrets of his own traditions with the heir of a rival house, but there must have been a certain satisfaction in being asked to teach a direct descendant of the patriarchs of the court tradition upon whose authority the whole edifice of court poetry rested. Besides, there are many indications in documents that the various houses already knew each other's teachings quite well. Maintaining separate traditions was on one level a choice and not a necessity for the nobility — a choice that allowed all concerned to claim "marketable" distinctions. One may even hazard the guess that Michishige, who may have had access to the Reizei library, passed on what he knew of Reizei teachings to the Reizei heir as an implicit facet of his responsibility in taking Tametsuna on as a student in the first place.

Of course, Michishige's teachings were not the Reizei teachings, scholars are quick to say. In this sense one might argue that in the seventeenth century, the Reizei house was finally overcome by more conservative Nijō attitudes that had been a thorn in their side for centuries. There may be some truth to this contention. More so than in the Sengoku era, the noble families of the seventeenth century formed a tight and insulated community. Yet it should be noted that the claims of the Reizei lineage probably gained rather than lost in prestige. Go-Mizuno'o and his poetic heirs could claim to have received the "secret teachings" from Hosokawa Yūsai, who could trace his poetic lineage back as far as Sōgi and other Nijō poets. Ultimately, however, it was beyond those sources to Teika and Tameie that the entire tradition gestured, to the literal ancestors, in other words, of the Reizei house. Furthermore, any claim that all differences between the noble houses had disappeared is contradicted by contemporary statements such as the following, presented as a critique of a poem by Tamekiyo:

> "Sleeves Scented with Flowering Orange"
>
> The scent of orange   perfumes my sleeves,
> borne along   by evening winds
> that before I've had enough   blow it away
> from my eaves.
>
> *akazu nao/sode ni utsusamu/tachibana no/nioi o kisou/noki no yūkaze*

Reizei poems are coarse [*katashi*], which is no good. . . . By "coarse" I mean that they put conceptions [*kokoro*] too fully into words, cramming everything in. Such poems lack polish (*tsuya*) and do not flow gracefully. [In this case,] it would be better not to include the phrase "before I've had enough" [*akazu nao*], instead allowing that idea to be spontaneously embodied in the poem.[50]

Elsewhere the author of the criticism explains that by *tsuya* he means *hikari*, or "brightness" — "that by which the virtue of the poem is outwardly revealed" (*sono uta no toku ga soto ni arawaretaru tokoro nari*).[51] One is reminded of Shun'e's criticism of Shunzei's poem on the quails crying at Fukakusa and also of those who dismissed Reizei poems of the 1300s as lacking in refinement. No matter how one interprets

---

50. *Waka kikigaki*, p. 816. *Waka kikigaki* is a selection of the teachings of Sanjōnishi Sanenori (d. 1701), one of the chief poets of Retired Emperor Go-Mizuno'o's salon.
51. Ibid., p. 805.

the criticism, however, the point is that it is still criticism — and not just of one poet but of what the author feels comfortable in calling *Reizei uta*, a phrase that serves as shorthand for a particular style or approach to composition.

Such criticisms were probably uttered primarily in private settings, however, and there is no indication that Tametsuna suffered greatly at the hands of his colleagues at court. With the support of the Nakano-in and the Fujitani families, in fact, he was able to make steady progress toward returning the Reizei house to some prominence at the imperial court, as well as toward attracting important disciples among the warrior elite. Documents show consistent attendance at court and frequent participation in courtly events. There were ups and downs, of course, largely in response to the proclivities of emperors, retired emperors, and their hangers-on. But the old *uta* form was as much a part of noble life in the late seventeenth century as it had ever been before. For reasons not entirely clear, there were no new imperial anthologies[52] and few lavish contests, but the heads of most houses still called in poetry teachers to instruct their young men and women in composition; and, in Kyoto especially, there were many wealthy samurai and merchants who sought the same services for themselves and their progeny. Furthermore, the establishment of peace in the kingdom had made communication by correspondence possible in ways not dreamed of for centuries.

That the contents of the Reizei library, still off-limits to members of the house, were still held in high regard is evidenced by the fact that in 1685 Emperor Reigen (1654–1732; r. 1663–87) ordered 320 of its manuscripts loaned to the imperial palace for copying.[53] A great student of courtly traditions, Reigen was responsible for the restoration of many important ancient rites, such as the Great Thanksgiving Celebration and the Kamo Festival.[54] He also was a great patron to Tametsuna. One obvious reason was a blood connection, since Tametsuna's mother and Reigen's mother were sis-

---

52. Retired Emperor Reigen evidently pursued the idea of putting a new imperial anthology together for a time, but the project never reached fruition. Ogura, "Reigen-in to Reizei-ke," p. 139.

53. Kubota Keiichi, "Reizei-ke no rekishi 17: Tametsuna I," p. 5.

54. Ogura, "Reigen-in to Reizei-ke" pp. 135–36.

ters.[55] Another was that the emperor was also an avid poet who actually did obeisances to a portrait of Fujiwara no Teika—placed alongside another of Hitomaro, and later also one of Sanjōnishi Sanetaka—on the first day of every new year.[56] At the time of his own death, he would go so far as to bequeath to the Reizei this portrait, attributed to Fujiwara no Nobuzane (1176–1265?), one of many such artworks that came into the collection in the same way.[57] For the preceding several centuries more material may have been going out of the collection than had been coming in, but now the house began again to acquire.

Reizei Tametsuna died in 1722 at the relatively young age of 59. However, he did leave behind an heir, Tamehisa (1686–1741), who was already in his late 30s. At the very end Tametsuna was able to witness the one thing that he had no doubt been praying for all of his life: the lifting of the imperial censure that restricted access to the Reizei library, which diaries of the time say was allowed specifically because of the great efforts of Tametsuna and Tamehisa to restore the house to its former glory.[58] The order came down from Retired Emperor Reigen in the early fall of 1721, less than a year before Tametsuna's death. This alone meant that the way ahead for Tamehisa would be easier than it had been for himself. An additional dividend came when, just a few months later, in the Tenth Month, Retired Emperor Reigen bestowed the family teachings on Tametsuna in a ceremony at his palace, concluding with the formal opening of the box holding the relevant manuscripts and documents. No doubt by this time Tametsuna already knew something about the coveted teachings, but ritual bestowal of the full corpus of texts and teachings was worth little without the authority to use them as a *sōshō*, or master—which is what the ceremony granted. The Reizei heir must have been proud to realize that his "transmission" was different from most in that it involved showing the retired emperor

---

55. Ibid., p. 137.

56. Ogura, "Reigen Tennō to sono jidai," p. 6 and Ogura, "Reizei-ke no rekishi: Edo jidai kara Meiji e," p. 149.

57. Ogura, "Reigen Tennō to sono jidai," pp. 124, 148–49. See *Kyō no miyabi, uta no kokoro: Reizei-ke no shihōten*, item 185. Most scholars agree that the portrait is not by Nobuzane but they still regard it as the earliest of all extant portraits of Teika.

58. Ogura, "Reigen-in to Reizei-ke," p. 141.

the treasured manuscripts of his own house, brought along for review and then carefully returned to their resting place in the family storehouse.[59]

LOOKING OVER his rather modest record of service at court, one might mistakenly conclude that Reizei Tametsuna's life was all struggle and hardship. These last two events in his later life, however, must have done much to make up for earlier disappointments. Moreover, it so happens that we have another record of the last months of his life that leads one to conclude that he died happy with his lot. Rather than a courtier's diary, the record is from a warrior named Nikki Mitsunaga (d. 1737), a samurai of ancient ancestry in direct service to the shogun Tokugawa Yoshimune (1684–1751). From the ranks of the samurai, Mitsunaga, who is also known by his pen name Shōji, was a paid scholar—and a prominent poet in Edo—who was routinely dispatched to search out important manuscripts and documents in temples, shrines, and houses. In 1721 he was dispatched to Kyoto with the specific task of surveying the "lore" of the Reizei, Yamashina, Hino, and Jimyō-in houses.

We know no concrete details about the relationship between Mitsunaga and the Reizei before his trip to Kyoto in 1721. But a document shows that he had become a disciple of the Reizei in 1715, swearing out an oath to that effect. The full text of the document reads:

From this day forth, I pledge myself a disciple in the Way of Poetry, with the Great Gods [daimyōjin] of Sumiyoshi, Tamatsushima, and my own Clan God [ujigami] as witnesses, that I may never falter in the slightest detail. In recognition of the import of this declaration, I have sworn this oath, as here noted,

Nikki Jingōrō Mitsunaga

On the 5th Day of the Tenth Month of the Fifth Year of the Shōtoku Era

Received at the Reizei Residence

By Lord Nakagawa[60]

Exactly how Mitsunaga was first introduced to Tametsuna is not known, but evidently the immediate go-between was the man whose name appears at the end of the document, otherwise identified as

---

59. Kubota Keiichi, "Jijū-dono no jūsai nari: Kyōhō roku, shichinen no Reizei Tamemura," p. 2. Also, Nikki, Zaikyō zuihitsu, p. 425.

60. Kubota Keiichi, "Reizei-ke no rekishi 18: Tametsuna II," p. 5.

Nakagawa Ukon, a house steward of the Reizei during the time in question.[61] The oath of another samurai disciple—quoted by Mitsunaga himself—from a much earlier period, is identical in wording, showing that the whole process of "applying" for disciple status had been routinized long before.[62] After becoming a disciple, Mitsunaga probably kept up an active correspondence with his teachers by post.

Yet Mitsunaga no doubt traveled frequently between Edo and Kyoto, which held more old manuscripts than any other city in the country, on business of the shogunate. His diary—*Zaikyō zuihitsu* (Jottings on My Time in the Capital)—records his time there from the Ninth Month of 1721 to the Fifth Month of 1722. His "errand" at the time had explicitly to do with the nobility, whose lore he was assigned to survey and collect for the use of the shogun. For decades the Tokugawa government had been engaged in searching out and preserving the records of the past. Mitsunaga was just one of many scholars assisting in this labor.

Mitsunaga arrived in Kyoto in the Ninth Month of 1721 and made his first formal visit to the house on Imadegawa on the 28th day of that month. Thereafter, he came calling frequently and—by what discrete stages the record does not make entirely clear—evidently was given some of the "transmissions" of the house. In the process, he had many meetings with both Tametsuna, as head of the house, and with the latter's heir, Tamehisa, who was already in his mid-30s, and also with Tamehisa's eldest son, Tamemura—thus spanning three generations of the house. Whatever contact he may have had with the family before, his status now was different: he was received very much as a visiting dignitary whose relationship with the shogunate put him among the most valued of disciples. At their first meeting, on the 23rd of the Ninth Month, Tametsuna met with him formally, deciding among other things that his poetic name—the name to be written on *kaishi* and *tanzaku*, etc.—should be Jūchō, the Sinitic reading of Mitsunaga. Then he was taken to see the contents of the library, first the famous texts in the hands of Shunzei, Teika, and Tameie, and later works by Retired Emperor Juntoku, Ichijō Kaneyoshi, and many others. Over the years, the family had gradually added to its collection, and he was privileged—by a directive from the retired

---

61. Ibid., p. 4.
62. Nikki, *Zaikyō zuihitsu*, p. 441. The document dates from 1541.

emperor — to be shown whatever he desired.[63] He was even allowed to take some texts back to his lodgings for copying.

One item in Mitsunaga's journal notes the location of the Reizei compound, on Imadegawa Avenue, at the intersection of Karasumaru Street, on the north side; with the Yamashina compound just to the east.[64] He also jots down a few lines describing the *obunko*, or "manuscript storehouse," itself. His is our first such description: "The Reizei library is two *ma* square, with a tile roof, white-washed walls, and is made up of two stories. The upper floor holds the three gods of Waka, presented by Shunzei, they say. The lower floor holds the boxes of manuscripts."[65] Mitsunaga fails to mention where on the Reizei lot the *obunko* stood. But in other ways what he says could equally describe the building as it would stand for generations to come.[66] Even today, the upper floor of the structure is the place for the various portraits of members of the lineage, which are taken out for memorial services and some other formal occasions.

In his record, Mitsunaga refers several times to secret teachings that he either had not yet received or which he was not at liberty to write down, usually referenced with the elliptical phrase *kuden ari*: "there are oral teachings on this matter." But he also quotes a number of teachings given directly to him by either Tametsuna or Tamehisa on a variety of familiar topics, from definitions of conventional topics (*dai*) to the proper conduct of gatherings, etc. — information of a less secret nature, perhaps, that would be of use to him in his own life as a poet back in Edo. He also alludes to many conversations about poetry (*waka monogatari*) with Tametsuna and Tamehisa, the importance of which should not be overlooked. More informal in nature, these chats were nonetheless important in the instruction of disciples, and had been for centuries.[67] Normally, the theme of such discussions was not set beforehand. Instead, they were desultory conversations during which the master shared his store of knowledge in an intimate setting that did much to cement the relationship,

---

63. Ibid., p. 415.

64. Ibid., p. 431.

65. Ibid., p. 415.

66. Other sources make it clear that the *obunko* and the *shin* (or *nii*) *obunko* both stood in the northeast corner of the lot. See Nakamura, "Waka no ie, kuge no ie," pp. 14–18.

67. For more on this topic, see Carter, "Chats with the Master."

giving the disciple a glimpse into the vast volumes of lore held by the heirs of the house: "Thirteenth day of the Tenth Month: I met with the Commander of the Right Bureau of War, Lord Tamehisa, and we conversed for several hours about poetry. I asked for comments on some of my poems. I was told that in the Reizei house copy of _The Tale of Genji_ there is no "Dew on the Mountain Path" chapter and that the house does not accept that chapter as authentic. Left in the evening."[68] Unfortunately, Mitsunaga does not record the sorts of things a modern reader most wants from a "critical" text, such as the poems he presented for review or any comments Tamehisa made about them or about poetics in general. But this passage does at least reveal that the "conversations" held between master and disciple extended even to topics such as the textual integrity of _The Tale of Genji_. Elsewhere Mitsunaga also notes discussions about interpretation of great poems of the _waka_ canon by past Reizei masters, but also by Saigyō, Sanetaka, and others. Finally, he also records information about matters unrelated to poetry proper, such as the location of rooms in the imperial palace, showing that he looked to his noble teachers not just for instruction in poetry but also in court culture generally.[69]

In all, though, one of the most distinctive characteristics of Mitsunaga's record is that it focuses on the poetic culture of the present, showing that the Reizei were not only scholars but also active participants in the poetic field of their own day. On the 20th of each month, the young Tamemura held his own monthly meeting, which Mitsunaga duly attended, usually recording his poems in his journal. Also mentioned are numerous other poetic gatherings, from a sequence produced as a votive offering for Tamatsushima shrine at the end of the Eleventh Month of 1721 to a meeting held in the imperial palace soon thereafter.[70] The names of participants in these events — including Tame-tsuna, Tamehisa, and ten-year-old Tamemura, but also Tametsune (1654–1722) of the lower Reizei house, Fujitani Tamenobu (1675–1740), Karasumaru Mitsuhide (1689–1748), Fujitani Tameka (1706–57), Higashizono Motonaga (1675–1728), Kazahaya Kiminaga (1665–1723), Mushanokōji Kinya (1688–1743), Sanjōnishi Kinfuku (1697–1736) — and others, show that the upper house, while not the dominant force

---

68. Nikki, _Zaikyō zuihitsu_, p. 421.
69. Ibid., p. 450.
70. Ibid., pp. 433–37.

at the time, was still very much integrated into the poetic life of the nobility.[71] Furthermore, gifts from Reigen, many of them still in the Reizei collection today, attest to ongoing imperial favor.[72]

Mitsunaga also makes comments that reinforce the contention that distinctions from the other houses were still being maintained:

The Reizei Middle Counselor said: On the topic of writing poems on pocket paper: The Nijō house, when recording up to ten poems, writes in two lines plus a third line of seven characters, and in just two lines when writing fifteen or more. In the Reizei house, when recording up to five poems, we write in two lines plus a third line of seven characters, and in two lines when writing seven or more.[73]

When there is no marshall [*dokushi*] present, but only a lector [*kōshi*], there is a way for the lector to go it alone. This is a transmission other houses do not possess; only the Reizei house has it.[74]

As these passages show unequivocally, despite long years of obscurity during which they were denied routine access to the manuscripts in their own library, the Reizei had evidently been able to maintain their separate traditions, at least in the all-important area of etiquette and other discursive practices. That the shogun had sent Mitsunaga to the Reizei specifically meant that the house still had distinctive knowledge to be desired. Closer to home, the noble houses of the capital evidently understood as well, resulting in a steady stream of young courtiers coming to the Reizei house for instruction. Not surprisingly, Mitsunaga does not write much about these other students, but on one day—the 6th of the Eleventh Month—he records that he was even obliged to wait in an adjoining room until one such young man had finished his lesson:

Went to the Reizei residence. This afternoon, Lord Hamuro Yoritane, Controller of the Right, had come to receive the transmission on how to serve as lector [*kōji*] and was meeting with the Commander of the Right Military Guards [Reizei Tamehisa]. While the training was going on, I was in the room immediately adjacent. After Lord Hamuro departed, I went directly in and conversed with his Lordship for some time.[75]

---

71. Ibid., pp. 433–35.
72. Reizei Fumiko, *Reizei Fumiko ga kataru Kyō no miyabi*, p. 150.
73. Nikki Mitsunaga, *Zaikyō zuihitsu*, p. 416.
74. Ibid., p. 464.
75. Ibid., p. 433.

Not all of Mitsunaga's time was spent searching out ancient lore, of course. His noble friends arranged for him to see the sights of the city, got him invited to see several ancient ceremonies at the imperial palace and local festivals, and even gained him permission to view a cockfight held at the Seiryōden, the emperor's private residence.[76] They also arranged for him to see precious poetry manuscripts in other collections, such as a text by Tonna kept in the cloister of a local temple.[77] His time in Kyoto was therefore busy, involving long days perusing manuscripts and receiving instruction, and nights of conversation and social engagements.

As fate would have it, Mitsunaga was in Kyoto when Tametsuna died, on the sixth day of the Third Month of 1722. Tametsuna had been ailing for several months, the journal says, but evidently his death was not expected, as Mitsunaga was on an excursion to Saga to see the cherry blossoms when it came. Upon returning to the city, he immediately went to offer condolences and attended memorial services at the Shinnyodō in the Eastern Hills. For the next month, until his return to Edo, he continued his visits to the Reizei compound, receiving instruction from Tamehisa and getting to know young Tamemura, with whose talents he was greatly impressed. Several times he and the boy went to visit Tametsuna's grave, going once to visit Ginkakuji, Ashikaga Yoshimasa's villa, now a temple.[78]

Mitsunaga left for the East Country in the middle of the Fifth Month of 1722, his assigned duties evidently completed. Although he would visit Kyoto again in the years to come, we have no journal account of his time there. But he did append to his original journal a few items of instruction from a visit in the Fifth Month of 1724. The occasion was the 450th anniversary of the death of Fujiwara no Tameie, a celebration of which was sponsored by Nakano-in Michimi (1668–1739), who as the heir of one of the ministerial lineages was the most senior poetry master (*sōshō*) in terms of family standing.

As might be expected, the event was memorialized by the writing of poems, fifteen of which Mitsunaga records. Among the participants were several of the most prominent noble poets of the day, including Michimi himself and Mushanokōji Sanekage (1661–1738). Understandably, however, the faction most well-represented was the

---

76. Ibid., p. 449.
77. Ibid., p. 456.
78. Ibid., p. 455.

Reizei and its offshoots—Tamehisa and Tamemura, of course, but also Muneie (d. 1769) of the lower house, and two members of the Fujitani line, as well as members of the Takeuchi, Yanagiwara, and Shijō lineages, all of whom in recent generations had adopted Reizei sons into their lines. Also there was the current head of the Higashi-zono family, a descendant of Tametsuna's maternal line. Of the fifteen participants, eight thus had direct ties to the Reizei.

In the spirit of the occasion, many of the poems are openly nostalgic. Michimi's poem, for instance, alludes to Tameie explicitly:

> "Spring Moon Obscured"
>
> A gap lies there   between ourselves
> and the past   he once gazed upon—
> but just the same this hazy night   is the aura 'round
> the moon.[79]
>
> *naki hito no / nagameshi mukashi / hedatete mo / kasumu ya onaji / oboroyo no tsuki*

Across all the years, Michimi suggests, the basics of experience, and of the poetic rendering of experience, have not really changed. There is a gap, yes, but the constancy of the natural world traverses it with ease, as does the constancy of poetic traditions as realized in poems offered up in memoriam.

Young Reizei Tamemura's poem is perhaps less sophisticated than Michimi's, and less colored with sentiment. He too presents a speaker gazing at the moonlight, yet without any direct reference to the past. The conclusion of the others involved in the event may have been that one could not expect much more of a twelve-year-old, even if he had already received approbatory remarks from Retired Emperor Reigen:

> "Snow at Night"
>
> So cold is my bed   that I get up
> to look out late   into the night—
> at moonbeams polishing   a courtyard
> white with snow.[80]
>
> *neya samumi / okiidete mireba / fukaki yo no / tsuki ni migakeru / niwa no shirayuki*

A simple, straightforward description, reminiscent of the Kyōgoku poets and the injunctions of Ryōshun. Had the young man been mak-

---

79. Ibid., p. 469.
80. Ibid., p. 470.

ing good use of the family library, one must ask? No one can know. What later years make certain is that Tamemura, in addition to the qualities that would help him in the profession of poetry—that is to say, the ability to lead at court events, the ability to teach composition, and the judgment necessary to transmit teachings properly—seems to have shown early on something that cannot be taught or easily accounted for: a feel for poetic language. Though perhaps lacking in *ushin*, Tamemura's effort presents a stronger image than Michimi's, and the careful concatenation of repeated vowels (seven *a* sounds, eleven *i* sounds) make for a sonorous effect.

BUT TAMEMURA was still young; for the immediate future, responsibility for the house rested with his father, Tamehisa, who was making steady progress up the court ranks and gaining such a reputation as a poet that he was hailed as "a poet not inferior to Lord Shunzei and Lord Teika."[81] Fortunately, one of his chief admirers was none other than Retired Emperor Reigen, whose patronage of the Reizei was fast making up for the losses of the previous century:

> Lord Reizei Tamehisa wrote this on the topic, "Storm Winds":
>
> Not a single leaf   of autumn color
> remains   among the branches.
> Why then do the winds persist,   storming so against
> the moon?
>
> *aki no iro wa / hitoha no kuma mo / nokoranu ni / nani kogarashi no / tsuki ni fukuran*

It is said that Retired Emperor Reigen praised this poem as the best ever written on the topic "Storm Winds" since the time of *Shin shūishū*. Upon first hearing it, it doesn't seem anything special, but it is truly a superb poem [*shūka*]. People who compose poems should keep this kind of poem in mind as they search for conceptions.[82]

Again, one wishes that the recorder of this statement, the literatus Tada Yoshitoshi (1698–1750), would spell out what about Tamehisa's poem was so impressive that Reigen should call it the finest work on its topic written since 1364—the time of the ninth imperial anthology, *Shin shūishū*. From the vantage point of traditional poetics, however, one can say with certainty that the poem is a superlative

---

81. From *Waka monogatari* (p. 915), a compendium of mid-Edo poetic teachings from various masters.
82. Ibid., p. 891.

example of *ushin* in that it presents an emotional response to a natural scene, foregrounding the consequences of natural forces in the realm of human experience. Moreover, it boasts the same sort of imaginative conception (what is the essence of "storm winds" if not their effect — trees left barren, their ruined form made more stark by the chill of the unchanging but desolate moon, against which the winds seem not to know they have no power?) associated with the poems of Tamesuke, Tamemasa, and Tamehiro.

While he was rising in the ranks — becoming a consultant in 1723 and a middle counselor the very next year — Tamehisa was also making a name for himself in Edo, just at the time when that city was displacing Kyoto as the cultural capital of the nation. During the century since the beginning of Tokugawa rule, the city on the eastern seaboard had gradually grown in population, aided greatly by the influx of capital from the shogunate itself and from daimyo who were required by law to spend a great amount of time there. Now it was clearly surpassing Kyoto not only as a political center, but as a center of the arts and intellectual affairs. Kyoto had not yet become a backwater, to be sure; it was still the center of imperial culture and still attracted the interest — and cash — of samurai. But the future seemed to belong to Edo.

When Tamehisa first came to the shogun's city we do not know. But records show that in 1719 he was one of a group of courtiers who brought gifts to the new shogun, Yoshimune, who over the next decade or so would encourage his personal retainers and vassal daimyo to become disciples of the house, creating a Reizei faction in Edo that would play a conspicuous role in poetic affairs for many decades. Ultimate evidence of Yoshimune's favor came in 1734, when Tamehisa was appointed *buke tensō*, liaison officer with the shogunate, the most coveted because the most lucrative of courtly offices. To hold that position of course meant constant correspondence with Edo, as well as with the officers of the imperial court, making its holder one of the most important figures in Kyoto — a man with whom everyone was free with gifts and favors. It also meant frequent trips to the East Country. Between 1735 and 1741, he made at least seven trips to Edo, staying for at least a month in every case and sometimes considerably longer.[83]

During these visits, much of Tamehisa's time was spent on official duties, one must imagine, but we know that he was constantly

---

83. Kubota Keiichi, "Reizei-ke no rekishi 20: Tamehisa II," p. 4.

visited in his inn by disciples, who brought their poems for review and hoped for a few private moments with their *sensei*.[84] A short travel journal recording poems composed on a pleasure cruise on the Sumida River in the spring of 1740 shows that he was treated well by his Edo hosts. The writer of the journal, Narushima Nobuyuki (1689–1760, of the Hirai clan), was a member of the elite group of counselors surrounding the shogun and de facto head of the Reizei school in the city. Anxious to show his master a good time, he rented a boat and gave a guided tour of the Sumida River, stopping along the way to compose poems beneath the cherry blossoms.[85] In the years to come, Nobuyuki, who is better known by his pen name, Dōchiku, would serve as leader of a group of literally hundreds of high-ranking samurai men and women who advocated the Reizei cause in Edo. In the Kamakura period, the Muromachi period, and the Sengoku period, the Reizei had always managed to make the highest military men their disciples; Tamehisa was doing so again.

In the summer of 1741, the shogunate held formal celebrations marking the coming-of-age of Tokugawa Ieharu (1737–86). Needless to say, Tamehisa was among those invited to the festivities, serving as "imperial messenger"—the court title granted to *buke tensō* in such situations. Now a major counselor of senior second rank, he had achieved the highest office and rank for one of his pedigree and was at the height of his glory as a courtier. After the shogunal celebration, he attended a poetry gathering of his chief disciples in Edo on the 13th day of the Eighth Month, where praise was heaped upon him as the heir of Shunzei and Teika. On the way back home, however, in Ōmi Province, he died—suddenly, it would seem, and without warning. He was 58 years old by the traditional count.[86] He had outlived his own father by less than 20 years.

We have no critical treatise by Tamehisa and far fewer poems by him than by his more famous son, Tamemura. But one compendium of statements by the major courtier poets of the day expresses the tenor of his practice:

For people to do just as they please, not following the houses of their teachers but just writing about whatever comes to mind and proclaiming themselves the disciple of this person or that person—what a lamentable thing that is for

---

84. Ibid., p. 4.
85. Narushima, *Haru no mifune*, pp. 229–34.
86. Kubota Keiichi, "Reizei-ke no rekishi 20: Tamehisa II, p. 5.

the Way of Poetry! Among poems of the noble schools, there may be lots of clumsy efforts that seem downright unsightly, but there will be no hint of transgressing the counsel of the house. Someone who is clumsy may remain so forever and never become skillful, but he will not become unorthodox.[87]

Needless to say, Tamehisa's words remind one of earlier attacks against men such as Kyōgoku Tamekane and Shōtetsu. Tamehisa cannot have forgotten that the word "unorthodox" (*ifū*) had been used to attack the Reizei house and its traditions as well. It is not surprising, however, that during a time when order had once again been restored to the nation, Tamehisa should want first of all to claim a rightful place within that order. To do otherwise would have been to ally the Reizei lineage with the excesses of the Sengoku period, which had put the fate of court civilization in jeopardy. Regardless of their differences, the Nijō and Reizei lineages knew that their best hope was in a regime that aimed for stability in both politics and poetry. In this sense, Tamehisa's position is clearly a political one, and one that in its context must have seemed the obvious stance to take—in public, especially.

Tamehisa's conservative attitude is also apparent in an anecdote contained in a collection of stories about famous poets put together by a scholar named Oyamada Tomokiyo (1783-1847), the disciple of a disciple of the Reizei house in the time of Tamemura:

A Tenryūji monk named Ryūson was very impressed by the style of Lord Reizei Tamehisa and put his whole heart into the labor of composing poems. From the age of six until he was well down the slope of old age he was honored with excellent marks on more than 30,000 of his poems. Never once, however, had he received a "superb" mark (*chōten*)—a distinction reserved only for a poem that was truly a masterwork.

Once when Ryūson was traveling away from Yamato on pilgrimage to Shikoku and the Central Provinces, he visited the mountain grave [of Emperor Sutoku] on White Peak in Sanuki, where he composed this poem:

> Since the distant past   how many hearts
> have paused here   to do oblations!
> —different yet still all the same   in their offering
> of tears.

> *mukashi yori / kokorogokoro no / tamuke ni mo / kawaranu mono wa / namida narikeri*

Tamehisa was kind enough to jot down a note of praise [*hōshi*] next to this poem, but he said that according to custom superb marks were granted only

---

87. *Unjō kakun*, p. 241.

to poems on topics, as opposed to occasional poems [*kotogaki*], which could only be granted a note of praise.[88]

The light humor of this story should not be allowed to disguise an important point—that for Tamehisa the practice of poetry was a highly codified Way that demanded the commitment of all involved, teachers and students alike. Whether the monk mentioned here ever succeeded in receiving a "superb" mark from his Reizei masters is not known, but one feels certain that he at least came away from the incident knowing the importance of precedent in the noble houses.

At the time of Tamehisa's death in 1741, Tamemura was only of junior third rank, and not yet a consultant in the court hierarchy. But Mitsunaga's record shows that even at the age of ten he had been a recognized talent, and the hard work of his grandfather and father left him in a strong position. He was already proving himself a fine poet and teacher; and in addition to many disciples in Kyoto and its environs and in the provinces, he also had the support of partisans in Edo, including the shogun Yoshimune himself. Financially, the house remained in the same category as all noble houses, with a fixed stipend of 300 *koku*. But various offices could be counted upon to bring in more income, and fees from students were also contributing greatly to the family portfolio. More importantly, the prestige of the family, both in Kyoto and in Edo, was at its highest point since the founding of the house by Abutsu and Tamesuke more than four centuries before.

---

88. Oyamada, *Matsunoya sōwa*, pp. 714–15. Oyamada studied under Murata Harumi (1746–1811).

EIGHT

Tōkai Road

MOST HISTORIES of the *uta* in the eighteenth century focus their attention not on the Reizei and other court poets but on the stalwarts of the Nativist movement, from Kamo no Mabuchi (1697–1769) to Tayasu Munetake (1715–71) and Motoori Norinaga (1730–1801). This is mostly because of a tendency among scholars to focus on the newly emerging classes of the Edo period rather than on the old nobility, whose days of political and economic hegemony had indeed passed. Even in the previous century, commoner poets such as Matsunaga Teitoku (1571–1653) and Kitamura Kigin (1624–1705) were doing more inventive work than were their counterparts in the imperial court, the argument goes; besides, this was the age of *haikai* and madcap *uta* (*kyōka*), of popular fiction and drama, and not of the worn and weary genres of the court tradition. As the literate population grew in size and sophistication, poets and scholars of plebeian origins had begun to expand the borders of the reading public by giving open lectures on classics and even by sponsoring the publication of certain canonical texts in book form—something unthinkable among the nobility.[1] Old books, especially literary classics such as *The Tale of Genji*, *Tales of Ise*, and even the most sacred of texts, *Kokinshū*, were being made available to a larger audience. As early as 1700, there were at least half a dozen commoner teachers of *uta* that we know about in Kyoto proper, half of them practicing

---

1. See Keene, "Matsunaga Teitoku and the Beginning of Haikai Poetry," pp. 71–93.

in the northern districts that were the traditional preserve of the nobility.[2]

The name by which such "commoner" writers were known among the residents of Courtiers' Quarter was of course *jige*. It was an old term, referring to those not of court rank, and more descriptive than pejorative in most contexts. In the past it had been used to categorize poets from Tonna and Shōtetsu to Sōgi, who had places of their own in the court canon, despite their low social origins. But such men had never been able to challenge the leadership of the old lineages. They knew that their role in the social scheme of things must always be a subservient one: only men of proper lineage and rank could claim authority in traditional poetic affairs at the imperial court. One courtier in fact declared that even the poems of the great patriarch Saigyō, so highly revered by Shunzei and Teika, still were *jige* in style.[3]

Some *jige* poets of the Edo period, however, were not satisfied with such a role. An anecdote involving Kinoshita Chōshōshi (1569–1649), for instance, shows disdain even for the *Kokin denju*, which were the ultimate expression of noble authority:

Chōshōshi didn't receive the teachings. Once he said this to his son-in-law, Lord Ano:

"I'd like to hear what you make of the *Kokin denju*," he said mockingly. "Do you really think Tsurayuki's goal in putting *Kokinshū* together was to make it difficult for people in later times to understand it?"

Teitoku and Shunshō were in attendance when Chōshōshi made this proclamation. He thought the *Kokin denju* had all been made up.[4]

Significantly, this episode includes no mention of a reaction from Chōshōshi's son-in-law, the court noble Ano Kinnari (1599–1683), or for that matter from the other men involved in the story, Matsunaga Teitoku and his disciple Yamamoto Shunshō (d. 1682). Probably one reason was that far from being a titleless monk in the tradition of earlier *jige* poets, Chōshōshi was a great warlord who had held the title of provincial governor, had been granted court office, and was thus not used to brooking disagreement.[5] Yet still his sympathies

---

2. *Kyōto no rekishi*, vol. 5, p. 126.

3. Shimizudani, *Shimizudani Sanenari dainagon kyō taigan*, p. 43.

4. Shimizu, *Shimizu Sōsen kikigaki*, p. 377.

5. Sources list him as a Provincial Governor (an honorary title at the time) and Lesser Captain in the Gate Guards of the Left, of junior fourth rank, lower grade.

were with *jige* traditions. Although he seems to have been on good terms with Tamekage of the lower Reizei house, Chōshōshi was not strictly speaking a disciple of any noble lineage but rather an independent spirit who kowtowed to no one in poetic matters.[6]

Another man who was openly critical of the ways of the noble poetic lineages was Kada no Arimaro (1706–51), a samurai scholar who, unlike Chōshōshi, was not a connoisseur living in seclusion but a scholar in the employ of Tayasu Munetake, one of the sons of the shogun, Tokugawa Yoshimune. Perhaps because of his high position, he was even more critical of the *kanka* ("houses of court officials"), attacking them for their tendency to regard themselves as unimpeachable authorities, for their practice of disallowing anything but their own highly rarefied vocabulary into poetic discourse, for unbending adherence to old forms of etiquette, and so on. In other words, Arimaro attacked the aristocracy for an attitude that he characterized as proprietary:

Looking at their poems, one sees that they are in a wispy style, as lacking in vigor as willow fronds. What amusement can there be in composing such poems? This may be my own willfulness talking, but I think with a scribe to write for me I could produce several hundred such poems in quick order. Yet those who do nothing but turn out such bland efforts, when confronted with a poem of real power (*chikara aru uta*), say, "Ah, that's in the commoner style (*jigefū*); it's not a poem."[7]

The social system designed by early leaders of the Tokugawa shogunate maintained a place for the old nobility, and in doing so endorsed courtly traditions. But Arimaro saw no need for men of the samurai class, in particular, to feel bound to observe old standards without question.

Not to be left out, the famous Confucian scholar Dazai Shundai (1680–1747), too, took the nobility to task in his *Dokugo* (Talking to Myself) of 1747, lamenting that anyone who wants to get a little learning "unfailingly takes someone from one of the famed houses (*meika*) as a teacher" and that courtier poets limited themselves so exclusively to composition on conventional topics (*dai*).[8] In general, a new generation of scholars and poets with no strong ties to the

---

6. Tamekage is mentioned in the headnotes to several poems in Chōshōshi's personal anthology and also in Chōshōshi's essay, *Ōhara no ki* (p. 41).

7. Kada no Arimaro, *Kokka hachiron*, p. 553.

8. Dazai, *Dokugo*, p. 318.

imperial court was thus asserting its independence in words that could not be misunderstood. Even Ishino Hiromichi (1718–1800), an Edo disciple of the Reizei house who was married to a Reizei woman and who remained loyal to his noble teachers in most ways, complained in an essay that the old houses seemed to have forgotten that Saigyō, Tonna, Sōgi, Tō no Tsuneyori, and Hosokawa Yūsai—poets whose work was often praised by court poets and who had been instrumental in the establishment of the coveted "secret teachings" on *Kokinshū*—had been from warrior families (*bushi*). That his noble teachers thought of the counterparts of these great *jige* poets of the past as somehow unqualified for full participation in the tradition was not easy to accept.[9] For the first time in Japanese poetic history, moreover, the "lower" classes by the first century of the Edo period were not obliged to bow to the judgment of the nobility in all aesthetic matters. Rising rates of literacy, economic growth, and developments in communications, publication technology, and commerce were making it possible for opponents of noble standards and norms to resist the status quo, taking in their own disciples, writing their own handbooks and treatises, and sometimes even disputing the claims of the Reizei and others over the texts and traditions of the past. What Shōtetsu had perhaps wanted to do but could not, some poets of the early Edo period were thus finally able to do—to establish a viable position for themselves within *waka* discourse as "outsiders" with respect to the houses of the court.[10]

Some *jige* poets were persuaded by these critiques of the court houses, which circulated widely among the cultural elite, although not always in written form. As a consequence, they put aside traditional handbooks such as *Eiga no ittei* and began to study other works of criticism. They also read more of anthologies such as *Man'yōshū* and *Shin kokinshū* rather than the blander canon (which by this time tended to champion Tameie, Tonna, and Sanjōnishi Sanetaka as models) recommended by the noble families. In time, some *jige* poets went beyond studying *Man'yōshū* and began to mimic its style, with results that the noble houses condemned as highly mannered and lacking in true feeling.

---

9. Ibi, "Bakushin kajin ni okeru tōshō to kogaku," pp. 264, 277.
10. For more on this topic, see Carter, "Remodeling the Reizei House."

Despite their diatribe against the old houses, however, noble poetic practices were clearly still dominated by courtly categories and conventions. A glance at the personal anthology of the great Nativist advocate Motoori Norinaga, for example, reveals that almost all of his poems are written on traditional *dai*. Poems such as the following, while slightly more "lofty" in overall effect, are really not so different from poems composed by his contemporaries at the imperial court:

> Spring: "Blossoms at Dawn"
>
> A glimpse of blossoms—   there? or not there?
> I wonder,   in those clouds of white
> where spring breezes   shimmer above mountains
> lit by dawn.[11]
>
> *miesomete / hana ka aranu ka / shirakumo ni / harukaze niou / akebono no yama*
>
> Autumn: "Autumn Leaves"
>
> At Mount Tatsuta   rain showers that dyed
> the trees   have all cleared away—
> allowing me to look upon   the first colored leaves
> of autumn.[12]
>
> *tatsutayama / somuru shigure no / ame harete / hatsumomijiba wo / kyō mitsuru ka mo*

Although more famous for a few poems that seem to signal a break with long-standing standards of syntax and rhetoric, Norinaga actually wrote far more poems like these that are slightly archaic in diction but that are unremarkable in other ways. As is so often the case, the bark was worse than the bite: the critiques *jige* poets made of noble traditions were much more extreme than were their own attempts to do something truly different. Even in the way they relied on the master–disciple relationship as their primary mode of instruction, *jige* poets continued to follow the patterns of the noble houses until quite late in the Edo period.

Precisely what noble poets thought of the critical comments of *jige* poets is hard to ascertain. Their usual tactic was to remain above the fray, as a statement by Mushanokōji Sanekage—intended only for his students and not for the general public—makes abundantly clear:

---

11. Motoori, *Suzuyashū*, poem no. 243.
12. Ibid., poem no. 1771.

When showing their poems to other people, some characterize their work as in the commoner style, some the Reizei style, some the Nijō style. I wonder what they mean. Poets should be at one with Heaven and Earth, and it is from individual poets that superb poems come. . . . Whether of the Nijō style, or the Reizei, or the *jige* style, a good poem is just a good poem.[13]

Thus a courtier admits the existence of divisions even while trying to remain above them. To respond in more public terms—if in fact a courtier could even entertain such an option in the first place—would have been to offend against the principle of exclusivity that was fundamental to noble identity. Even when one of Matsunaga Teitoku's noble teachers was scandalized by Teitoku's decision to lecture publicly on *Tsurezuregusa*—a late medieval text that was in some ways not even part of the poetic canon—we read of it only in a text by Teitoku himself.[14] If his noble teacher, Nakano-in Michikatsu (1556–1610), complained at all, he did not do it in a public forum.

This of course leads to the question, Why not? Why did the Reizei and their cohorts in other noble houses not enter more forcefully into a public debate over the proper maintenance of the traditions that were at once the source of their identity and their livelihood? First, one must admit that many sources indicate that they did make comments in private, to their disciples, as noted below. But in more open forums, which were foreign to them as nobles in any case, they kept their own counsel. One reason, already mentioned, was *noblesse oblige*. Their position, still protected by sinecures and by a social system that granted them an arena in which to practice along with considerable wealth and prestige, made it possible for the noble houses to ignore criticisms from the *jige* ranks, among whom, not coincidentally, they still had many admirers.[15] Furthermore, it should be remembered that what put off some potential students attracted others from all social classes. As one samurai student of the Reizei put it, "How can someone understand the proper Way without receiving teachings from a master and accumulating practice?"[16] Five hundred years of precedent stood behind

---

13. Mushanokōji Sanekage, *Shōgaku kōkan*, p. 194.

14. Keene, "Matsunaga Teitoku and the Beginning of Haikai Poetry," p. 80.

15. Kubota Keiichi, "Kaisetsu."

16. Hasegawa Yasuakira (d. 1779). Quoted in Kubota Keiichi, *Kinsei Reizei-ha kadan no kenkyū*, p. 306.

the ways of the noble houses, and for many students this was in itself enough to settle the issue.

Then, too, it is clear that imperial culture and its ideological underpinnings retained its mystique and was still supported by the shogunate for its own ends. In particular, men and women of the samurai classes were anxious to affiliate themselves with the nobility and their arts, which, since long before, had become the fundaments of education for anyone at the top of the social ladder. Pedigree meant a great deal in their world as well; it was not a concept they could question without putting their own privileges in question. Among other things this meant that the Reizei could depend upon their supporters in the warrior clans to speak for them, or, if not for them, at least against the Nativist scholars. It was in this way that even Matsudaira Sadanobu (1758–1829), author of the Kansei reforms and one of the most prominent of all Edo government officials, would end up weighing into the debate in his essay collection, *Kagetsu sōshi* (Flowers and the Moon, 1818):

These days, what people call elegance (*miyabi*) is nothing more than an attempt to gain fame through imitation of what was favored by people of the distant past, even when it is of no interest. They say they are composing poems, but they write with someone else's feelings, imitating someone else's words, thinking only of winning the praise of others. . . .[17]

In the erstwhile reformer's view, the Nativist poets — among whom the archaic term *miyabi* had indeed become a buzzword — were little more than clever mimics of the Man'yō era. Similar attitudes seem to have dominated the thinking of many among the military elite.

So despite the rising influence of poets with little or no connection to court traditions, the court lineages continued in their old ways throughout the eighteenth century, although they were surrounded by some controversy and by artistic and intellectual currents from which they maintained a discreet distance. Gatherings in the old style were still convened in the chambers of the imperial palace, the palace of the retired emperor, the residences of the nobility, the meeting halls of temples and shrines, and often in the chambers of daimyo and high-ranking samurai — places where precedent generally prevailed over the new spirit of philology. In such settings, poems were still recorded on fine paper by the hands of acknowledged practi-

---

17. Matsudaira, *Kagetsu sōshi*, p. 34.

tioners of calligraphy, stored away in boxes, and rarely reduced to the anonymity of print.[18] Notwithstanding the attacks of Dazai Shundai and others, court poets still insisted on the primacy of composing on conventional topics, without apology, following the dictates of men such as Karasumaru Mitsuo (1647–90): "One should compose poems on conventional topics exclusively. This is the first priority in training [*keiko*]."[19] Furthermore, other holdings of the nobility such as the secret teachings—including not only the *Kokin denju* of the imperial house but other esoterica held by the individual houses such as the Reizei—still brought a high price, whether paid in cash or in forms of patronage. The market was large enough to allow for practice of both the old and the new.

ALL OF this is readily apparent in the career of Reizei Tamemura, a rough contemporary of the Nativist scholar Kamo no Mabuchi who was in fact teacher to a host of *jige* poets, among them a few famous ones, such as Ozawa Roan (1723–1801) and Hagiwara Sōko (1703–84). As head of the upper Reizei house, Tamemura lived in the old family compound just outside the northern wall of Courtiers' Quarter, and conducted his affairs in a way that makes it clear that his greatest priority in life was to maintain the position of the house in the cultural world. Indeed, it is not an overstatement to say that it was Tamemura's labor that put the house in a position to survive as a literary institution into the twentieth century.

In his efforts to build up the house, Tamemura not only did much to preserve the treasures of the Reizei library; he also added to our understanding of the house's workings by leaving behind critical commentary of various kinds. Not surprisingly, his statements— which come mostly in the form of notations (*kikigaki*) recorded by disciples—reveal a conflicted attitude toward *jige* poets. One disciple, for instance, quotes him as saying that, "When it comes to disciples of the Reizei house, we hold no one in low regard, making no distinction between Kyoto and the provinces or between so-called noble and commoner styles."[20] Yet when once asked explicitly about

---

18. Ueno Yōzō notes that publishing poetry collections by the emperor and the court was forbidden until mid-Edo. See the *kaidai* to vol. 6 of *SKKT*, p. 967.

19. *Unjō kakun*, p. 238.

20. The quotation is from a text titled *Reizei sōshō ke kikigaki*, by Hagiwara Sōko. See Kubota Keiichi, *Kinsei Reizei-ha kadan no kenkyū*, p. 93.

who among his disciples in Edo—all from the commoner ranks, of course—had truly become masters of the art, he was less gracious: "These people have been undergoing training [*keiko*] for many years, of course; but if I am asked whether they have arrived at the level of true understanding, I am dubious."[21] Thus even the most senior disciples of the house in the shogun's capital, many of whom had been studying for decades, were dismissed out of hand by their master. In the same document, he confided that he had lots of disciples in the provinces, but had never encountered one who was truly worthy of praise.[22]

Such statements bespeak more than personal pride. Most other courtiers of the time would have admitted similar attitudes about their arts, to the maintenance of which they had been born and bred. From the point of view of the aristocracy, commoner masters had a role to play in poetic culture, but only as disciples to whom rather limited roles were allowed, and then only by explicit instruction and licensing. True leadership in courtly fields of knowledge and art was reserved for those with the proper lineage who had imbibed from infancy the atmosphere of the ancient ways. As Tamemura's contemporary Mushanokōji Sanetake (1721–60) unblushingly put it, "Those born into the poetic houses have a natural excellence."[23]

This is not to suggest that the nobility were all lazy or complacent, however; as in previous generations, their privilege still had to be secured and maintained by dedication and hard work. By the time Tamemura came into his own as head of the house at around age 40, for instance, one scholar notes that he had already composed perhaps 100,000 poems.[24] It goes without saying that long before that time he had committed most of the native poetic canon to memory. One of his disciples recorded that Tamemura had memorized the *Sandaishū* (which altogether included nearly 4,000 poems) by the age of thirteen.[25] Only one with such experience could hope to serve as teacher and exemplar in the chambers of the emperor; and only one who could function in that role could ever hope for recognition as a Master of the Way (*sōshō*).

---

21. Miyabe no Yoshimasa, *Yoshimasa kikigaki*, p. 685.
22. Ibid., p. 693.
23. Mushanokōji Sanetake, *Sanetake-kyō kuden no ki*, p. 633.
24. Ueno Yōzō, "Reizei Tamemura," p. 264.
25. Miyabe no Yoshimasa, *Yoshimasa kikigaki*, p. 720.

The parameters of Tamemura's poetic practice—a term that I use here and elsewhere to suggest commonalities with other fields of practice, such as medicine, the law, scholarship, and so on—are well known to us, thanks to numerous documents. Taken altogether, the latter show that Tamemura did what earlier poets had done, only on a larger scale. Namely, he taught students directly, either face-to-face or by correspondence; he worked assiduously to gain and maintain a place at the imperial court; and he made use of the Reizei library and other cultural resources of the house in what can only be called a kind of cultural commerce.

Service as a teacher was of course the prime activity of the head of any poetic house. Sometimes "licensed" agents were used, including, for instance, the stewards of the house, who assisted in bureaucratic matters; but, generally speaking, the master of the house or his heir maintained direct contact with all individuals who had declared themselves disciples, upon whose fees and various acts of favor the house depended greatly.[26] In contrast to the more egalitarian dynamics of *haikai* coteries, as recently analyzed by Eiko Ikegami,[27] the master–disciple relationship as maintained by the Reizei house was anything but egalitarian in its social effects, serving rather to reinforce the authority of the house above all else. Indeed, in a system based on the transmission of special knowledge and practices, the very survival of a house depended upon attracting but also restricting the number of those authorized to do transmissions and the perpetuation of a strong personal bond between the master and each individual disciple.[28] A contemporary source quotes Tamemura as saying that during his lifetime "there was not a single province in which I had no disciple" and surmises that by the time of his death he had more than 1,000 followers.[29] These must have included all the literate classes: the traditional aristocracy, including both those of high rank around the emperor and others of lesser rank who worked in ministries, temples, shrines, and so forth; the military aristocracy and samurai; and even some from the merchant classes. Carrying on an active correspondence with so many disciples was

---

26. Kubota Keiichi, *Kinsei Reizei-ha kadan no kenkyū*, pp. 280–82, describes the various poetic activities of one of the house stewards.

27. Ikegami, *Bonds of Civility*, pp. 171–203.

28. Kubota Keiichii, *Kinsei Reizei-ha kadan no kenkyū*, p. 266.

29. Miyabe no Yoshimasa, *Yoshimasa kikigaki*, p. 726.

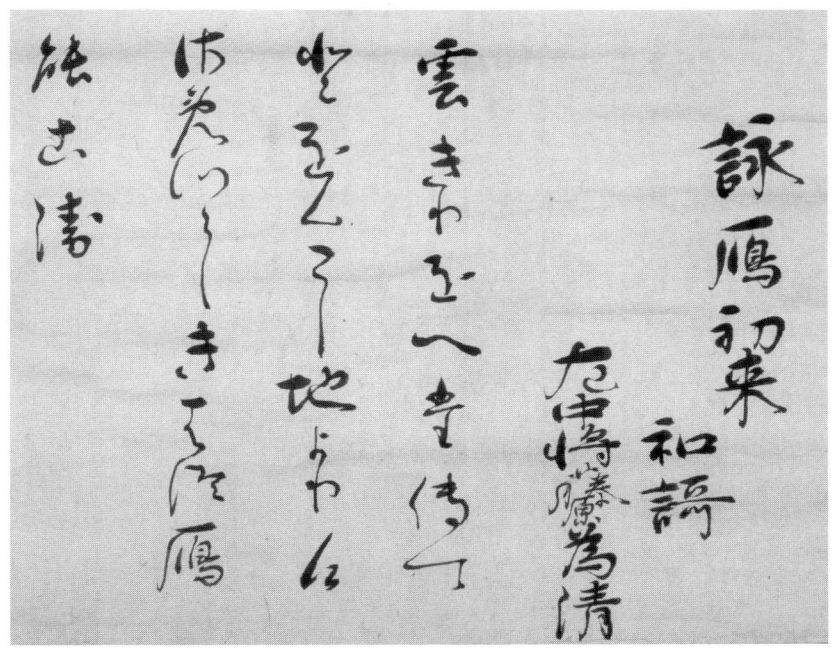

1 *Kaishi* by Reizei Tamekiyo. Used by permission
of the Reizei-ke Shiguretei Bunko.

2　Kamakura-era portrait of Fujiwara no Teika.
Used by permission of the Reizei-ke Shiguretei Bunko.

3 Edo-period portrait of the Mikohidari patriarchs.
Used by permission of the Reizei-ke Shiguretei Bunko.

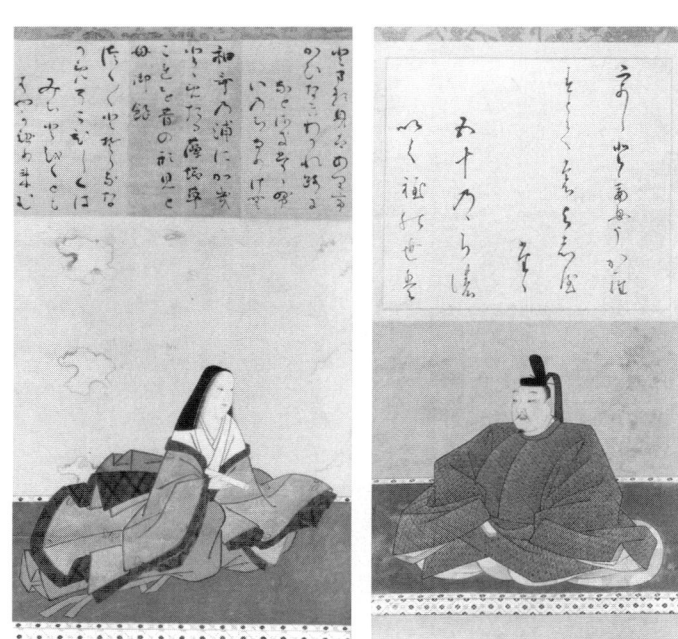

4 Edo-period portraits
of the Nun Abutsu (*left*) and Tamesuke (*right*).
Used by permission of the Reizei-ke Shiguretei Bunko.

5 Page from *Meigetsuki*, the diary of Fujiwara no Teika. Used by permission of the Reizei-ke Shiguretei Bunko.

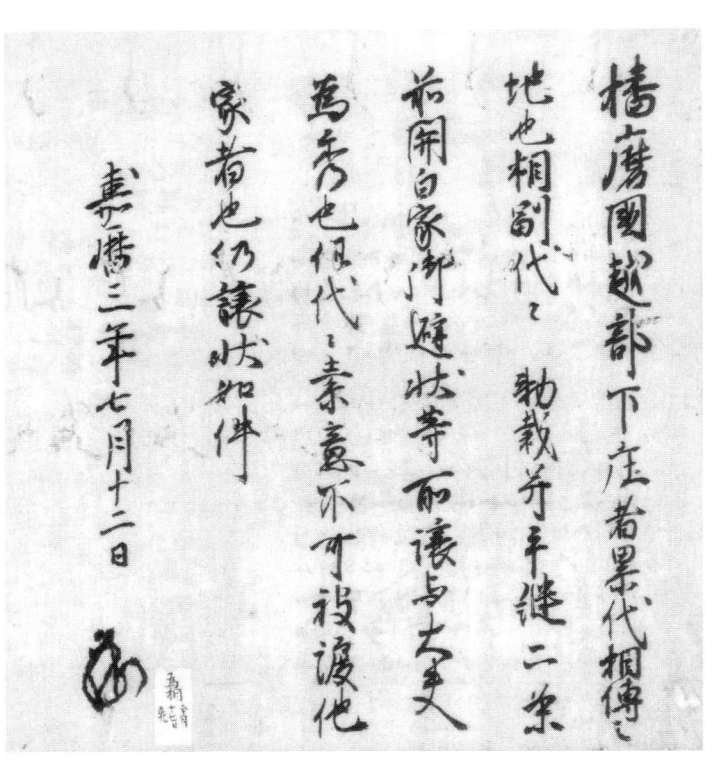

6 Document deeding estate rights to Tamesuke from his father.
Used by permission of the Reizei-ke Shiguretei Bunko.

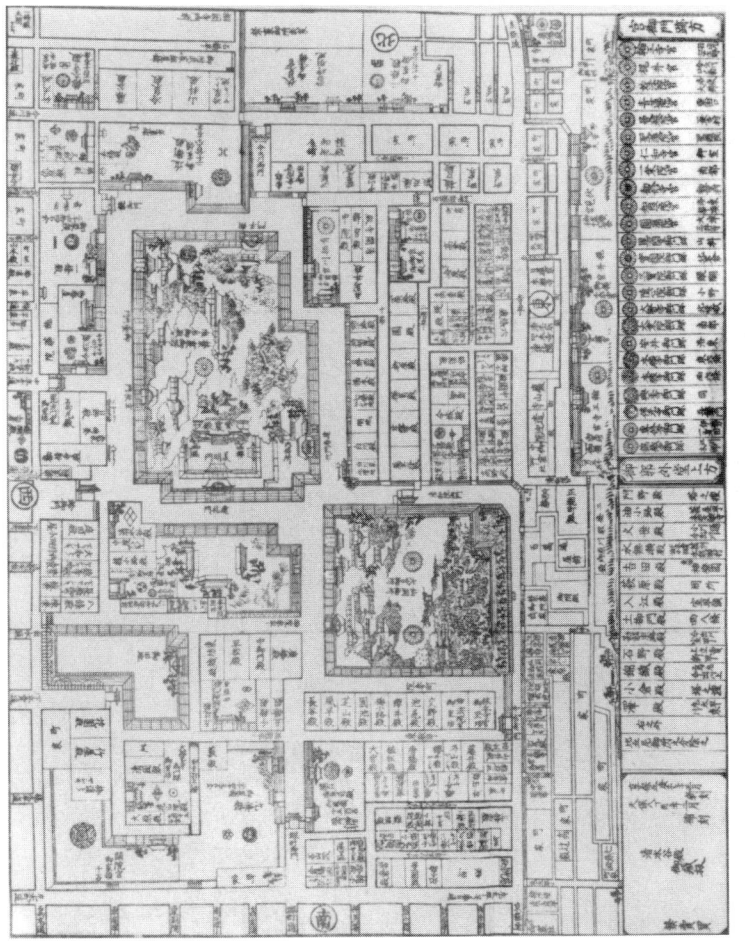

7 Courtiers' Quarter.
Used by permission of the Reizei-ke Shiguretei Bunko.

8 Roster of Disciples of the Reizei house compiled in the time of Tamemura. Used by permission of the Reizei-ke Shiguretei Bunko.

9 Portrait of Reizei Tamemura by Maruyama Ōkyo.
Used by permission of the Reizei-ke Shiguretei Bunko.

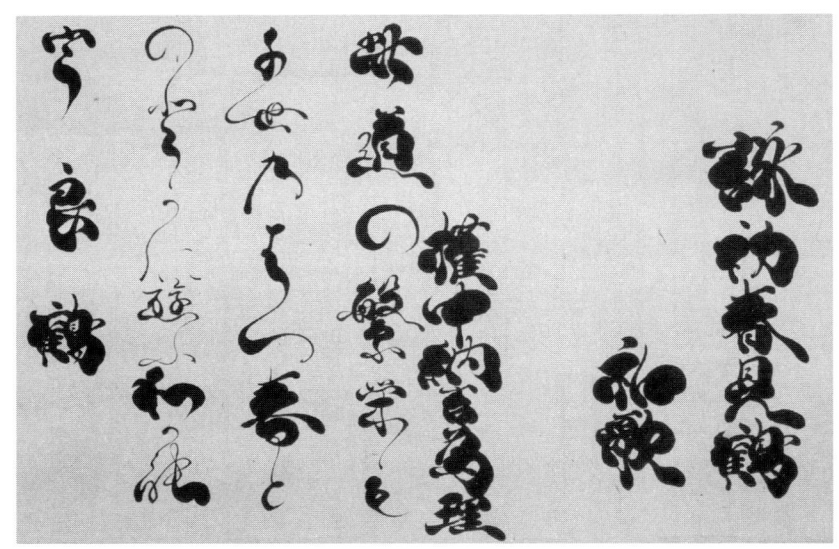

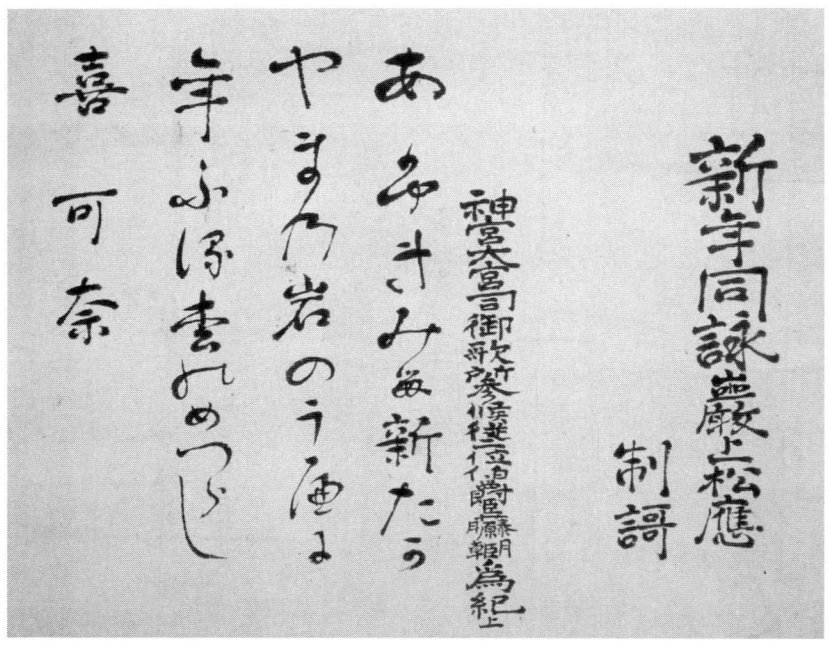

10 Calligraphy in the Reizei style by Tametada (*top*)
and Tamemoto (*bottom*). Used by permission
of the Reizei-ke Shiguretei Bunko.

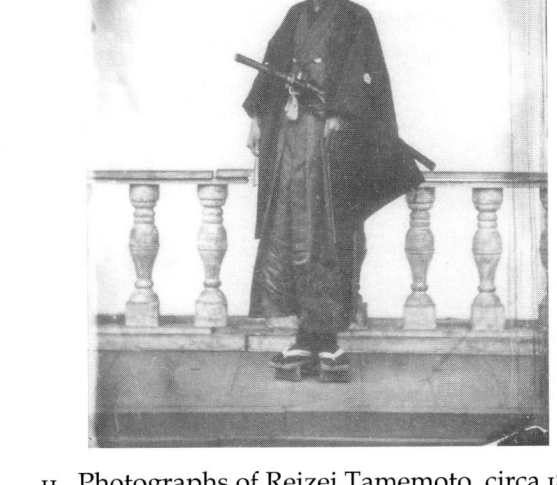

11　Photographs of Reizei Tamemoto, circa 1872.
Used by permission of the Reizei-ke Shiguretei Bunko.

12 Photograph of the Reizei family in the house garden, before the Pacific War. Used by permission of the Reizei-ke Shiguretei Bunko.

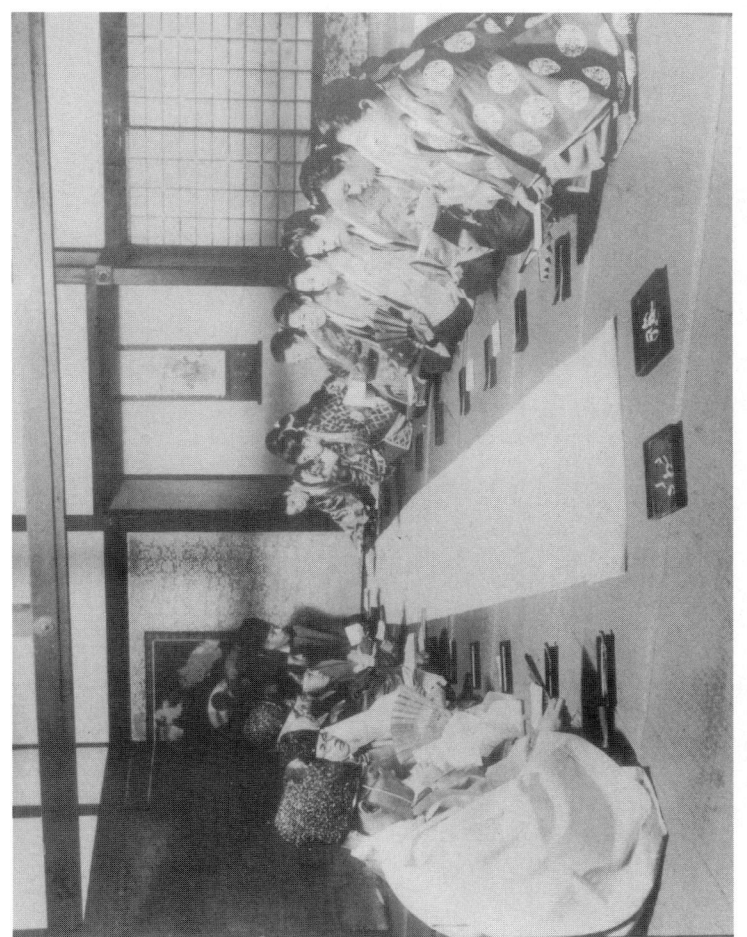

13 Photograph of a Reizei poetry meeting in the late 1920s. Used by permission of the Reizei-ke Shiguretei Bunko.

14 The Reizei Obunko today.
Used by permission of the Reizei-ke Shiguretei Bunko.

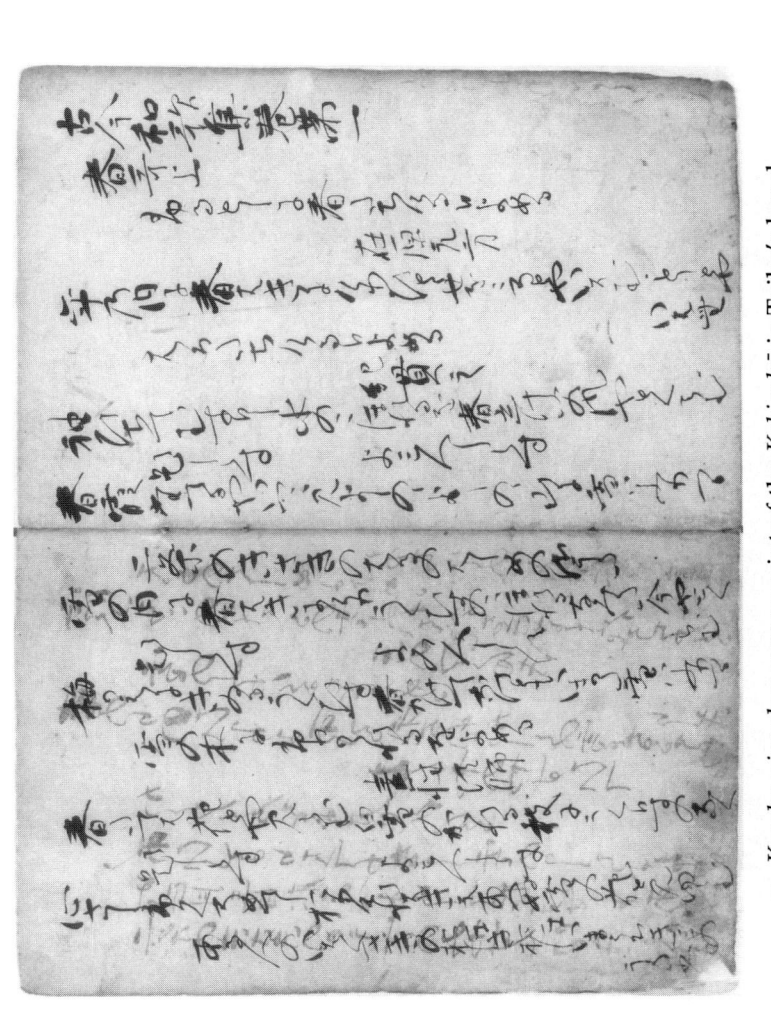

15 *Karoku ninenbon* manuscript of the *Kokinshū* in Teika's hand. Used by permission of the Reizei-ke Shiguretei Bunko.

16   A recent poetry gathering in one of the formal halls of the newly
restored Reizei residence. Used by permission of the Reizei-ke
Shiguretei Bunko.

in itself no small task and goes far in answering the question of how the master spent his time when not in service at court.

The standard mechanisms of instruction in the 1700s were remarkably similar to those of earlier times. Premier place was given to transmitting various levels of house teachings, primarily to advanced disciples. Equally fundamental, however, were the monthly meetings of the house and other formal gatherings, as well as informal meetings in which disciples had opportunities to listen to the master's preaching and homiletic stories (*monogatari*). Next came the "marking" of poems presented for review, either by the master of the house or sometimes by his heir or agents in affiliated houses. Finally, attendance—and later, providing leadership—at court events was also an important facet of poetic practice for Tamemura and later heirs of the house.

Various records indicate that the upper Reizei (along with other poetic houses) held monthly meetings on a regular basis. Standard procedure was to send out some topics, chosen by the master, in advance. After this, participants would prepare poems and then bring them along for a period of "airing" (*hirō*) and critique. In most cases a slightly less formal round of extemporaneous composition would follow this formal period. The role of the master in such meetings was to supervise the choosing and distribution of topics, to act as master or officiator, ensuring that ritual patterns were followed strictly—in other words, to act as a "professional" who served as institutional memory and ultimate authority. Additionally, a master would provide some critique, although there seem to have been broad variations in practice of the last of these roles. Some teachers, lacking either the confidence or the skill to revise poems on the spot, seem to have interfered minimally in such proceedings, while others took a much more active role.

In addition to holding meetings at their house in Kyoto, Reizei teachers also "marked" and corrected the work of poets too distant to attend such affairs, following a process described in some detail by Ogura Yoshio:

The disciple would fold his paper in two, lengthwise (this paper being referred to as *origami*) and then write down the topic he had already received from the Reizei, along with his name, and the poems—two on each topic, as a rule (the second one being called an alternate)—that he had produced on the topics in question. This was the so-called draft, referred to as an *eisō*. It would be sent to the office of the scribe of the Reizei house, where the drafts would be arranged and then taken to the head of the house. The head of the house would look over the poems and put a mark in ink above the better of the two poems on a given topic, just above it to the right. This was a *ten* [mark], sometimes called a *gatten*. For the disciple, receiving a mark next to a poem constituted receiving instruction from the master. Sometimes in addition to marking, the master would also write down suggestions. Then the draft would be returned to the scribe's office, who would send the drafts out to disciples all over the nation. The disciple would look at the marks and comments and derive the master's intent from them. From this experience of learning what made for a good poem and what was good or bad about his own poems, a disciple would accumulate experience. This was the most fundamental form of poetic instruction. Which meant, in other words, that the head of the Reizei house and disciples did not need to meet face to face.[30]

We do not know a great deal about precisely how Tamemura—or any one else, for that matter—conducted himself at actual monthly meetings. At the most, we have headnotes or diary entries here and there that list the date and time of a meeting, perhaps including a list of participants and a few poems. Critical comments—responses to which usually went into the final form of poems as recorded—were doubtless considered private for the most part, and were often not preserved.[31] However, what we know about Tamemura's correspondence with poets in more distant places indicates that he was an ambitious and energetic man who took his responsibilities very seriously. A prime example appears in a number of documents from the Maeda house catalogued in the 1980s by the staff of the Ishikawa Prefectural Museum. Most interesting among these are those that show the high formality of the relationship between master and student, such as the license (*menkyojō*) sent to a high-ranking samurai named Maeda Naomi (precise dates unknown) after the latter approached Tamemura through an intermediary to ask to be accepted as a disciple and the oath that the same man sent in reply. Also of note are documents that show what the Reizei received in payment for their literary services—cash gifts three times a year to Tamemura and his son Tameyasu (1735–1816), as well as to two Reizei stewards—and Tamemura's labor in living up to his students' confidence by timely dispatches of teachings on important matters of etiquette and ceremony, in addition to the marking and correction of poems submitted for review. Relations between samurai in the Noto area and the Reizei had been close since the time of Tamehiro 200 years

---

30. Ogura, "Reizei-ke no rekishi: Edo jidai kara Meiji e," pp. 164–65.
31. Kubota Keiichi, *Kinsei Reizei-ha kadan no kenkyū*, pp. 15, 95.

before, and it is obvious that Tamemura valued his ties with the Maeda highly.[32]

Another source of information on Tamemura's practice as a teacher comes from a manuscript in the vaults of the Mukyūkai Library, a collection of texts generally related to the native religion of Shintō and its institutions. The manuscript records a 100–poem sequence presented for review to Tamemura by one Kimura Seiyō, a samurai in service to the shogunate in Edo. More cogently, it includes not only Tamemura's approbatory marks, but also a number of his interlinear comments and even suggestions for revision. Although not as elaborate as one might hope, these comments offer us a rare glimpse into the practice of a master interacting with a disciple.

Most entries in the manuscript are in the following format, giving first Seiyō's original composition, next to which Tamemura's comments are appended. Finally comes a "revised" version of the poem:

> "Blossoms"
>
> Back into the depths   I do not
> make my way,   my heart enchanted
> already by the blossoms   in the foothills
> of Yoshino.
>
> *oku made wa / wake mo tsukusazu / yoshinoyama / fumoto no hana ni / kokoro todomete*

[Comment:] It makes sense, of course, to enjoy the blossoms in the foothills; but not to press on into the depths would indicate that you are lacking in the proper appreciation of blossoms. Might it not be better to say you wish to go on into the depths after beginning with the flowers in the foothills?

> Back into the depths   I shall now
> make my way,   not surfeited yet
> by the trees in bloom here   in the foothills
> of Yoshino.[33]
>
> *oku made mo / nao wakemibaya / yoshinoyama / akanu fumoto no / hana o hajime ni*

Although delivered delicately, Tamemura's point here is that the poet seems to show too little dedication to the cult of the cherry blossom, which would be a problematic admission to anyone claiming courtly tastes. More important for our understanding of Tamemura's conduct as a teacher is that he has obviously read the poem

---

32. Hamaoka, "Maeda Naomi no nyūmon."
33. Kubota Keiichi, *Kinsei Reizei-ha kadan no kenkyū*, p. 225.

carefully, even going to the trouble of providing a revision—and one that goes beyond technical matters to focus on the issue of proper conception.

Another passage from the text offers further evidence of Tamemura's approach as a teacher.

> "The Moon"
>
> People living here   in the peace
> of the capital   as autumn comes on—
> *they* can gaze up at a moon   shining unclouded
> and clear.
>
> *osamareru / miyako no aki ni / sumu hito ya / omou kuma naki / tsuki o miruran*

[Comment:] Praising autumn in the capital is understandable, but your poem makes it sound as if people living outside the capital are somehow troubled. How would it be to put it this way?

> People living here   in the peace
> of the capital   as autumn comes on
> can gaze up at a moon   looking ever more
> at peace.[34]
>
> *osamareru / miyako no aki ni / sumu hito wa / nao shizuka naru / tsuki ya miruran*

As in the previous case, here Tamemura offers not criticism of poetic structure, or phrasing, but rather of proper—meaning courtly—handling of a topic. It is the whole realm, he hints, that is under the sway (the Japanese word is *osamareru*) of the current regime, not just Kyoto. To imply otherwise would be to miss a chance to praise the accomplishments of the current regime.

A final passage from the sequence shows that Tamemura could also respond to more straightforward problems of style and conception:

> "Cuckoo"
>
> As I lie awake   the cuckoo comes
> a' calling—   right to my pillow,
> crying, "Remember fondly now   the lessons
> of your parents!"
>
> *utatane no / makura toikite / hototogisu / oya no isame o / shinobe to ya naku*

[Comment:] The bottom half of the poem reaches out too far.[35]

---

34. Ibid., p. 226.
35. Ibid., p. 235.

The verb *motomesugu*, "to reach too far," means to make something too explicit, to make things too obvious. Elsewhere, he uses the term in reference to a poem that seems to stray rather far from its topic.[36] In neither case does Tamemura suggest a revision, perhaps because he sees the poems as beyond help. The canons teach that the call of the cuckoo reminds one of those who are away or those who have died. To make the bird appear by one's pillow like a message boy from the netherworld simply "goes too far." Once again, there is a lesson—this time that in court poetry, subtlety should prevail.

HOW MANY sequences of the sort submitted by Kimura Seiyō were reviewed by Tamemura in his lifetime is impossible to say. No one can doubt that the number would have been in the thousands, perhaps even the tens of thousands. By the mid-eighteenth century the roads were far safer than they had been in the late medieval period, and the stewards of the Reizei house spent much of their time dealing with couriers, coming or going. A collection compiled by a Reizei disciple—*Reizei-ke gohōshi eisō* (Poems Praised in the Reizei House)— that records poems by a host of authors singled out for special praise by Tamemura reinforces this conclusion.[37] Unfortunately for anyone interested in the nitty-gritty details of critical practice, the text includes only poems deemed excellent, usually with a few words of praise and no analysis, as in the following example by Ishino Hiromichi:

> "Heron"
>
> So you too remain   above the mud
> all around,   color shining clear—
> you heron standing white   in dead leaves
> on the reeds.[38]
>
> *nare mo mata / nigori ni shimanu / iro miete / ashi no kareha ni / tateru shirasagi*

The commentary attached to this verse says only, "Unusual; very well done" (*mezurashiku yoroshiku sōrō*), adhering to a minimalist strategy that is maintained for nearly every poem in the anthology.

---

36. Ibid.

37. The collection was compiled by Narushima Kazusada and appears in *Go-Hengyokushū*. See Kubota Keiichi, *Kinsei Reizei-ha kadan no kenkyū*, pp. 185–87.

38. *Kinsei wakashū*, p. 188.

Yet if one thinks back to the case of Kimura Seiyō and imagines the number of poems that must have been either rejected or revised before the anthology was put together, one gets a sense of the sheer volume of work done by Tamemura in his lifetime.

To maintain prominence of this sort would of course not have been possible without proper standing at the imperial court, which was still the ultimate legitimizing authority behind the noble lineages and their arts. Tamemura enjoyed this standing beginning in his teens, in the chambers of both the emperor and the retired emperor. He himself admitted that this came about partly because the other poetic families of the time were quite fortuitously in a fallow period.[39] But his own talent and hard work must also have been important in establishing and keeping a prominence that allowed him later in life to note that in 36 years he had only missed imperial *tsukinami* meetings three times.[40] As a statement by Emperor Sakuramachi (1720–50; r. 1735–47) from 1745 attests, by Tamemura's era even the heirs of the old poetic lineages had to gain the approval of the emperor to officiate in poetic affairs: "Even if they are from houses with long pedigrees, those who have not yet received the transmission should not claim themselves disciples and mark the work of students without permission."[41]

Tamemura was clearly among those who came from "houses with long pedigrees" (*ruidai no ie*), which in earlier ages had often been enough to establish a poet's bona fides. But by the time in question, patterns had changed: only those who had become disciples of the emperor by receiving his approval could function as recognized masters of the art under the Tokugawa regime. The very fact that Sakuramachi felt he had to make such a statement is an indication that perhaps some members of the houses were prone to exceeding their authority. By and large, though, the noble families were obliged by common interest to bow to the imperial will.

Although records say nothing about it explicitly, Tamemura of course knew from a young age the importance of imperial approval. Already at age 21 he had been honored to be asked to assist in putting together Retired Emperor Reigen's personal anthology, after the

---

39. Miyabe no Yoshimasa, *Yoshimasa kikigaki*, p. 652.
40. Kubota Keiichi, *Kinsei Reizei-ha kadan no kenkyū*, p. 86.
41. Morita, "Kinsei Tennō to waka," p. 271.

sovereign's death in 1732.[42] (When Reigen's successor, Sakuramachi, died at the young age of 30 in 1750, it would again be Tamemura who was asked to perform the task of compiling the anthology.[43]) By his mid-20s, he was already noted among the most prominent poets, a remarkable achievement in a tradition that revered old age and practice. At age 37, he was granted imperial permission to act as a "marker" for the nobility.[44] Two years later he was made a middle counselor, an office it had taken his grandfather a decade longer to achieve. By the age of 48 he was a major counselor of senior second rank and an acknowledged leader in the imperial kadan.

As had both his grandfather and father before him, however, Tamemura was also careful to cultivate contacts in Edo. Just how calculated were his overtures toward warlords and samurai in the capital of the shogun is a moot point; that he succeeded in attracting hundreds of disciples there, mostly during the time of the eighth shogun, Yoshimune, is beyond dispute. Exactly what circumstances brought Yoshimune into contact with the Reizei is not known, but a passage from a contemporary writing hints that the reason may be as simple as precedent: "He did not abandon the Way of Poetry, often posing queries to the Reizei Major Counselor Tamehisa. In this he followed the example of Tōshōgu [Tokugawa Ieyasu], who had made queries to Tamehisa's ancestor, Major Counselor Tametsuna."[45]

Despite his natural-born arrogance as a court noble, Tamemura evidently realized that Edo was fast becoming the true capital of the empire, and that among its residents were many likely patrons. Some among the court nobility actively shunned contact with their counterparts in the military aristocracy, but the Reizei had more political sense, and of course a long history of activity in the East Country, going back to the founders of the house, Abutsu and Tamesuke.[46]

A poetry gathering held in a temple in Edo in 1746, when Tamemura was in the city as imperial messenger to offer his congratulations to the newly ascended shogun, Tokugawa Ieshige (1711–61),

---

42. Ueno Yōzō, "Reizei Tamemura," p. 264.
43. Kubota Keiichi, Kinsei Reizei-ha kadan no kenkyū, p. 72.
44. Kubota Keiichi, "Reizei-ke no rekishi 23: Tamemura III," p. 5.
45. Quoted in Kubota Keiichi, Kinsei Reizei-ha kadan no kenkyū, p. 110.
46. Watanabe, "Daimyō to tōshō kadan," p. 257.

shows the position of the Reizei in the East Country. Held midway through the Fourth Month, the event was attended by more than 20 local disciples. Most were from the highest ranks of the warrior elite, men such as Narushima Nobuyuki and Isono Masatake (1717–76) who had been disciples of the house since long before. At the same time, however, a number of other men asked to be accepted as disciples.[47] No doubt this was a pattern that would be followed many times.

Over the years, Tamemura would make many trips along the Tōkai Road between Kyoto and Edo, often in official capacities. A roster he made up, which still survives in the Reizei storehouses, includes even the name of Tanuma Okitsugu (1719–88), who eventually went on to become grand chamberlain (*sobayōnin*) and senior councillor (*rōjū*) in the shogunate.[48] Other records show that Lady Okiyo (also known as Gekkō-in; 1685–1752), consort of the shogun Ienobu and mother of Ietsugu, was also a treasured disciple to whom Tamemura gave special attention.[49] By the time of his death, the family rosters would include at least 400 partisans in the East Country.[50] Even in Tamemura's absence, the Reizei disciples thought of themselves as forming a distinct cohort and met often to reinforce their common affiliations. Correspondence between the house and one prominent disciple shows that Tamemura was intimately involved in the supervision of their activities, specifying, for instance, the names of people—including not just men but also their wives and daughters—who should be meeting together for monthly *keiko*, what sorts of topics they should compose on, and the pedagogical goals of such activities.[51] In one document, he even dictated how students should react to approbatory marks, or the absence of them, on their compositions:

Those who receive marks should not boast, but rather concentrate on understanding why the mark was received and giving heed to their companions' criticisms. And those who don't receive marks should be grateful and think to themselves, "The poem was such a clumsy effort that it only makes sense

47. Kubota Keiichi, "Reizei-ke no rekishi 22: Tamemura II," p. 4; Ishino, "Kinsei tōshōha zuisō," p. 322.

48. Reizei Fumiko, *Reizei Fumiko ga kataru Kyō no miyabi*, p. 197.

49. Kubota Keiichi, "Reizei-ke no rekishi 23: Tamemura III," pp. 4–5.

50. Ishino, "Kinsei tōshōha zuisō," p. 327.

51. Kubota Keiichi, *Kinsei Reizei-ha kadan no kenkyū*, pp. 192–93.

that it didn't receive praise. Now, what can I learn from this in order to improve my understanding?"[52]

The record of one Edo meeting of Reizei disciples comes from the Tenth Month of 1763 and records prose and poems in both Japanese and Chinese by seven participants of high samurai status who met at the suburban cottage of Isono Masatake. Attached as a colophon to the record is a comment by Tamemura that thanks his distant disciples for their devotion, concluding with a Chinese couplet of his own:

I spread the scroll out before me and peruse it quietly. Every poem strikes me as so elegant, so refined, that I feel as if I were there with you, enjoying the pleasure of your company. So impressed am I that I am having a copy of the text made, after which I will send the original back to you.

> Among pines and maples—how many springs and autumns?
> Long will last the scroll of our camaraderie in art.[53]

Again, we can only guess at how many such documents Tamemura received by courier. It seems certain, however, that dealing with them was part of an almost daily routine. Not all of them would be copied, of course, but those from important patron-students demanded special care.

Among the disciples of the Reizei house in the eighteenth century, were men (and some women) from virtually all ranks of society. First, of course, came members of the imperial family and the Kyoto nobility and their cohorts in Buddhist monasteries, whose lifestyle virtually required instruction in poetry by an acknowledged master. Then came several of the Tokugawa shoguns, their bannermen and cultural advisors, and members of their families, including their consorts, and daimyo and samurai in provinces all around the country, most of whom were highly literate officials whose dedication to poetry was no less earnest than that of the Kyoto nobility.[54] Next came priests of the Ise, Tamatsushima, Sumiyoshi, and other shrines, for whom the Way of Poetry was intimately connected with native religious beliefs and practices.[55] Lastly, there were even some from among the ranks

---

52. Ibid., p. 63.

53. *Tsunohazu no bessō ni asobu no ki*, p. 491.

54. Ogura, "Reizei-ke no rekishi: Edo jidai kara Meiji e," pp. 172–73 lists several prominent daimyo who were Reizei disciples in the mid-Edo period.

55. Shindō, "Reizei Tamemura no hōnō waka" and "Reizei Tamemura to Sumiyoshi hōnō waka."

of the lower classes—merchants, artists and artisans, and a few tea-house women such as Kajiko of Gion (precise dates unkown). Among all these groups, however, the disciples in Edo were by far the wealthiest and most influential. In 1768, the latter group would even be instrumental in putting together a collection of *tōshō-ha* ("courtly") poems by the warrior class. Titled *Kakanshū* (The Hazy Gate Collection), it included poems by disciples of all the poetic lineages, but the works of Reizei partisans predominated. Although scant records exist to corroborate the fact, many of these students received house teachings of one sort or another, some getting only instruction on mechanics (how to direct meetings, how to record poems on *kaishi*, etc.) and others going on to "higher" poetic truths. All shared a sense of loyalty to Tamemura and to the Reizei house that would serve as a sure foundation throughout the rest of the Tokugawa period. Ogura Yoshio has in fact documented strong relationships spanning several generations with a veritable host of daimyo, from the Matsudaira of Kaminoyama Domain in Dewa, to the Mōri of Hagi Domain in Nagato, to other powerful political figures, such as Yanagisawa Yoshiyasu (1658–1714) and his son and grandson, as well as members of a wealthy merchant clan, the Itō of Nagoya, founders of the Matsuzakaya chain of department stores—all in support of what indeed appears to be an undeniable conclusion: that "the Reizei did not pass through the 200 years [of the Edo period] composing poetry in a realm insulated from the outside world."[56]

This kind of support of course added up to prosperity for Tamemura and his heirs, signs of which are everywhere in the historical record. We know, for instance, that—before she expired from the effort—his second wife, a woman of the Fujitani lineage, had thirteen children (seven girls and six boys), for whom Tamemura was able to find appropriate livings—five of the daughters becoming wives in noble houses. Hints here and there also tell us that he had at least two stewards and a number of samurai and servants, making his house on Imadegawa a lively place.[57] He was no man of leisure, in the tradition of Teika and Tameie, but a salaryman of sorts who in addition to his attendance at court was obliged by circumstance to spend his days bent over a desk correcting the work of his disci-

56. Ogura, "Reizei-ke no rekishi: Edo jidai kara Meiji e," pp. 175–82.
57. Matsuda, "Reizei-ke no keishitachi: *Nakagawa Kiyomoto nikki* shōkai," pp. 2–3.

ples. Still, however, it is safe to agree with Reizei Fumiko, writing in the 1990s, that in the 800 years of the existence of the Reizei house, the time of her great-great-great-great-great-great-grandfather Tamemura was the "most economically well off."[58] In addition to fees and gifts from disciples associated with "marking" poems, the house also received constant requests for authentication of manuscripts, inscriptions on paintings, and samples of calligraphy (written on *tanzaku* or *shikishi*), all of which produced income and helped expand the network of Reizei relations.[59]

TAMEMURA INVESTED most of his wealth back into the house, as Fumiko acknowledges. He repaired buildings, compiled genealogies, did a careful inventory of the library and took great pains to preserve its manuscripts, and held memorial services—even for the Nun Abutsu, the only Reizei woman so honored.[60] He also commissioned portraits—*miei*. Already the storehouse held paintings of Shunzei, Teika, Tameie, and Tamesuke as well as a number of early portraits of Hitomaro, who had become a god of poetry. Now Tamemura added more of these and also portraits of Tamesuke, Abutsu, Tamehide, Tamekuni, Tametsuna, Tamehisa, and his mother. All were done by the finest artists of the day, from the Tosa and Takatsuki lineages.[61] For a likeness of himself, he commissioned the services of the great painter Maruyama Ōkyo (1733–95), who was his disciple in the Way of poetry. Later generations would continue this practice, often arranging for portraits as part of festivities connected with important events, such as the rite of viewing the *Kokin denju* of the house—a privilege granted by the emperor to a Reizei heir, which also marked the day when the head of the house was formally recognized as *sōshō*. Displayed for memorial services, the portraits served as tangible reminders of the long history of the house.[62] Some—in particular, portraits of Teika based on originals owned by the house—were probably produced for sale or as gifts to prominent patrons.[63]

---

58. Reizei Fumiko, *Reizei Fumiko ga kataru Kyō no miyabi*, p. 191.
59. Ogura, "Reizei-ke no rekishi: Edo jidai kara Meiji e," p. 181.
60. Reizei Kimiko, "Abutsu-san," pp. 2–3.
61. Reizei Fumiko, *Reizei Fumiko ga kataru Kyō no miyabi*, p. 189.
62. Ibid., pp. 166–89.
63. Reizei Tamehito, "Reizei-ke no miei," p. 157.

Another project undertaken by Tamemura was the reinstatement
of the so-called Teika-style of calligraphy. In the days of Tamehisa,
Emperor Reigen had objected to the Reizei mimicking that style, on
the grounds that successful copying of the patriarch's manner might
make it difficult for later generations to distinguish Teika originals
from later copies.[64] Following this lead, Tamemura, too, until his
30s, aimed only at gentility in his writing; but thereafter he began
to mimic some aspects of his great ancestor's manner. In particular,
he was taken by Teika's penchant for thick lines and "disconnected"
characters, although only within limits. By this time Reigen was long
gone and the deaths of prominent members of the other poetic
houses had left Tamemura preeminent at court. His new calligraphic
style became known as the Reizei-style[65] and would continue for the
next five generations, playing an important role in the history of
calligraphy. Needless to say, this new "specialty" would play a role
in the economic fortunes of the house in years to come, when stu-
dents of calligraphy began asking for instruction. Many times the
importuners were the same students who had already been studying
poetry under Reizei masters.

It should also be mentioned that Tamemura exerted some effort
in claiming leadership of the various *bunke,* or branch houses, cre-
ated in generations past. Initially the attempt to bring the upper and
lower houses into greater harmony began with the emperor, but
Tamemura was quick to embrace the idea. Around 1750, Muneie,
heir of the lower house, formally became a disciple of Tamemura,
despite the fact that he was ten years his cousin's senior.[66] The Fuji-
tani, their offshoots in the Irie line, and the Imaki (formerly Naka-
yama Reizei) also came to identify themselves more explicitly with
the main house than ever before. In this way, the Reizei developed
from a single house into a bloc, of sorts: a Reizei coalition that could
act in concert in furtherance of common interests.

It should also be noted that in time, the coalition Tamemura
solidified developed into a pseudo-religious institution for which
the *obunko* became a shrine, and its objects — including texts but also

---

64. Ogura, "Reigen-in to Reizei-ke," p. 142; Nagoya, "Teika-ryū, Reizei-
ryū," p. 5.
65. Nagoya, "Teika-ryū, Reizei-ryū," p. 5.
66. Kubota Keiichi, *Kinsei Reizeiha kadan no kenkyū,* p. 90.

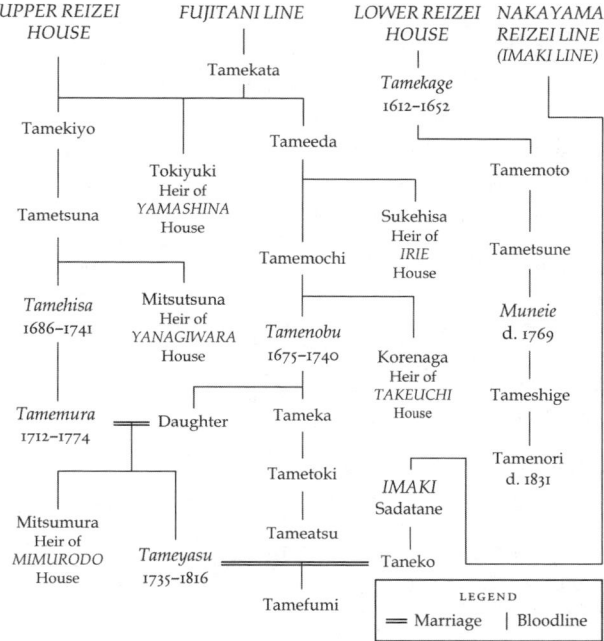

Chart 5   The Reizei Network in the Mid-Edo Period

the portraits and other artworks collected by the family for generations—essentially gods, not just for the house but for its *bunke* and disciples. The beginnings of this process can be traced back centuries, to be sure, but it was in the mid-Edo period that many distinctive annual ritual practices (*nenjū gyōji*) were established, and also during this period that Shunzei, Teika, Tameie, and Abutsu, in particular, were elevated to the status of deities who were worshipped as protectors of the family Way. The founders of the house had long been objects of veneration in literate society more generally, and fragments of their calligraphy fetched high prices among connoisseurs of tea in particular. Although stopping short of selling off items from the library, the Reizei were not slow at capitalizing on this trend in whatever other ways presented themselves.

IN 1769, TAMEMURA resigned his offices at court and took the tonsure with the Buddhist name Chōkaku ("Clear Understanding"). From this time on, while he continued to write poetry and to participate in imperial meetings, he left the mundane details of running the house to his son and heir, Tameyasu. When the father died unexpectedly, in 1774, Tameyasu was already thoroughly ensconced in his position as head of the Reizei clan and its offshoots and was serving as a middle counselor at court. Tamemura had done his job well.

One record of Tamemura's death comes from Miyabe no Yoshimasa (1729–92), a shogun in service to the Matsudaira clan of Takasaki domain in the East Country and disciple of the Reizei. He no doubt heard the details firsthand from Tameyasu:

About the death of the Lay Monk last year. He knew beforehand that he would be dying, and a number of unusual things happened in association with his passing. . . . Beginning in the Fourth Month, he sat in front of a wooden statue of himself, gazing at the character "A" for 100 days, until the end of the Seventh Month. He composed 440 poems during that time. Until the 28th day of that month, he was not even a little ill, indeed not until that very night, when he suffered for only an hour or so before passing on to the next life. What a wonderful master he was! During his life, he had more than 1,000 disciples. Never in the past does one hear of such a master.[67]

Yoshimasa had good reason to praise Tamemura, who had been his own teacher for decades and whose high reputation in Edo was the basis of his own high profile there. By all accounts, he was an excellent student, whose dedication to Tamemura was total. Fortunately, he also left us a record of his interactions with the Master that is as revealing about Tamemura as is Nikki Mitsunaga's about Tametsuna. It is of course a highly respectful, in fact reverential, portrait, but one that tells us a great deal about Tamemura's practice all the same. A colophon tells us that the record was burned once, and then rewritten from memory.[68] The portrait it creates, however, is consistent with other comments made by contemporaries, both in terms of what it says about Tamemura as a poet and about his teachings.

For the most part, the document, titled *Yoshimasa kikigaki* (Yoshimasa's Notes) is either in *mondō* format, in which a master replies to questions put by his student, or in the form of pronouncements directly from the master's mouth. Most items—there are over 200 of them in all—are brief but still substantial enough to give us insights into Tamemura's practice as a teacher. In general, the work represents him as a proponent of the orthodoxy of the time, a topic about which the master does not equivocate, as an exchange from early in the document reveals:

---

67. Miyabe no Yoshimasa, *Yoshimasa kikigaki*, pp. 725–26.
68. Ibid., p. 726.

Question: What should be one's frame of mind (*kokoro*) when composing poems?

Answer: A proper poem (*shōfu*) is one that is composed when one's heart is right. If one focuses one's heart on various things one is writing about, one will achieve poetic concentration, with no distractions. If one keeps one's heart right, the body will have no faults; and of course it will not do to be upright only when one is composing poems.[69]

The attitude revealed here can be traced back at least to the *Kokin-shū* preface, which stressed the power of poetry to "bring harmony to the relations between men and women, and calm the hearts of fierce warriors."[70] More specifically, however, Tamemura's words echo various medieval traditions that connected the practice of courtly arts and rituals to the maintenance of harmony in the community. The recurrent word is *tadashi*, "straight," "upright," "correct" — one of the central terms of Confucian discourse. When the Tokugawa government specified the arts as the preserve of the nobility back in the early 1600s, it was probably with such a conception in mind. Tamemura understood this, as did his one-time teacher Karasumaru Mitsuhide, who articulated the prevailing attitude as clearly as it could possibly be put in a statement to students: "In poetry, the most important thing is to understand the *Analects*. One should never run counter to the Sages."[71] One can of course quibble about which version of Confucian thought had sway in noble poetic discourse, but there can be no doubt that its rhetoric is dominated by ideas of social order. Indeed, this may be one reason for Tamemura's tendency to dismiss all but the aristocracy from consideration as "serious" poets, in passages like the following: "The Way of Poetry is nothing other than this: to be completely filial and to do one's proper duty. It is this that one should concentrate on. Specifically, one who is born into a military house should not be lax in learning the Ways he should know — the bow and the horse. Only after this should he compose poems."[72] The proper role of a military man, according to Tamemura, is thus to dedicate himself to his own social station and not to spend most of his time in the courtly arts. For a warrior, the latter must always be a secon-

---

69. Ibid., p. 653.
70. McCullough, *Kokin Wakashū*, p. 3.
71. *Unjō kakun*, p. 252.
72. Miyabe no Yoshimasa, *Yoshimasa kikigaki*, p. 714.

dary concern, no matter how intense his feelings and devotion. Real achievement was only possible for those born to that privilege.

It appears, then, that Reizei Tamemura accepted the notion that the role of poetry was to support the dominant social order, which not coincidentally was the order that vouchsafed him his social position. To a great extent, this order was inherited from the past, or at least conceived of in that way. Attesting to this concern, nothing stands out more sharply in Tamemura's responses than the importance of studying poems from the old anthologies—the heritage of the court—and of traditional training. "The first principle of training (*keiko*) is to study old poems carefully," he tells Yoshimasa,[73] and not just once but many times. Three different passages make the point:

By reading through the *Sandaishū* of the house over and over again, one comes to understand poems that are difficult to interpret. One must read them any number of times, so that one comes to comprehend them naturally—that is the best way. What one doesn't understand one should ask about. There is no better training (*keiko*) for poetry than poring over old poems.[74]

I was also told when asked about how young people should practice (*keiko*) that the main thing is to memorize old poems. Poems learned when one is young infuse one's heart and are not forgotten. One should study carefully the *Sandaishū*, of course, and also the *Sandaishū* of this house, and Tameie's personal collections. Even if one doesn't understand them, one should first of all memorize them, he taught. And the poems one composes one should learn to do correctly from the very beginning, he said.[75]

How many poems Lord Chōkaku has committed to memory! He once told me that he had memorized the *Sandaishū* by the age of thirteen. The current middle counselor has also memorized lots of old poems. He always says that you cannot compose poems if you have not memorized old poems.[76]

Such statements remind us that the elite literate society of eighteenth-century Japan was still by and large a memory culture in which powers of recollection were more highly valued than powers of creativity. These memories, as codified in various poems, teach-

---

73. Ibid., pp. 713, 718.

74. Ibid., p. 695. "*Sandaishū* of the house" evidently refers to *Senzaishū*, *Shin chokusenshū*, and *Shoku gosenshū*—the three imperial anthologies for which Mikohidari men (Shunzei, Teika, and Tameie, respectively) served as sole compilers. *Shirin shūyō* (p. 210) and *Takamatsu Shigesue kikigaki* (pp. 118–19) says the same thing.

75. Miyabe no Yoshimasa, *Yoshimasa kikigaki*, p. 714.

76. Ibid., p. 720.

ings, and practices, were in fact the cultural capital of the nobility, whose assets were in that sense as prodigious as anything claimed by their competitors among the ranks of the Nativist scholars.[77]

Not all of Tamemura's advice to Yoshimasa was so didactic, however. On the subject of how to produce excellent poems—obviously a concern of those coming to him for instruction—he was very practical: "One should not strive to compose a good poem, but rather not to compose a bad poem. It is because people want to compose poems that will be praised that they end up with bad poems. The point is to compose a poem that will not be laughed at."[78]

Tameie and others had said the same thing, and for the same reasons. Steady effort and long years of practice, even in the absence of great individual talent, could eventually lead to good poems—but only if one learned the lesson of self-restraint. Discipline was the key. Evidently discipline was a quality that Tamemura displayed to a great degree:

Looking on Lord Chōkaku as he was about to compose a poem, poised over his paper and inkstone, you somehow felt that a fine poem was bound to result. When he was putting an inscription on a painting, too, he would look at the painting just a few moments, then quickly pick up the brush and write without further ado, always coming up with an interesting poem of his own. He was so swift in doing this that I asked him about it. "The conception is there in the painting," he said, "I just look at it and the poem appears." It came to him quite freely.[79]

The sort of "freedom" (*jiyū*) alluded to here should not be confused with modern notions of the term. Rather, what is implied is the "facility" of the craftsman or practitioner of the martial arts or the gymnast or figure skater whose life of long discipline is a preparation for every such performance. The seemingly natural aspect of the master's posture is not natural at all but rather a result of painstaking conditioning of body and mind.

Yet Tamemura was no philosopher but a teacher and pedant who could also offer a good deal of concrete instruction on specific problems of composition. Some dozen or so pages of Yoshimasa's text, for instance, show drawings of how to record poems on various sizes of paper for various kinds of occasions, according to the time-honored

77. Carter, "Remodeling the Reizei House," p. 38.
78. Miyabe no Yoshimasa, *Yoshimasa kikigaki*, p. 709.
79. Ibid., p. 722.

stipulations of the Reizei lineage. Tamemura also gives Yoshimasa a long list of "prohibited" words and responds to a number of more specific questions, such as these:

Question: In a poem on "The Autumn Moon," is it permissible if the word "autumn" does not appear in the poem?

Answer: Even if the idea of autumn is there, you must compose in such a way that the moon is not treated as if in the "miscellaneous" category: then it is permissible.[80]

Question: Is there any difference in meaning between [the topics] "Old Love" and "Past Love"?

Answer: "Old Love" refers to not having met in a long time. "Past Love" means the meeting took place a long time ago.[81]

As in the time of Shōtetsu, who also left replies to many such questions that he had probably learned from his Reizei masters, so too in the mid-Edo era specific bodies of knowledge were necessary for anyone attempting to compose poetry in traditional venues — without knowledge of which one could be almost certain to end up with a "bad poem," to harken back to Tameie. More than half the items in *Yoshimasa kikigaki* deal with knowledge of this sort.

Needless to say, the opportunity to ask such questions was one of Yoshimasa's primary reasons for seeking interviews with Tamemura. But similar answers could have been given by almost any court poet of the time. To take full advantage of the association, he also needed to ask questions concerning the Reizei house more specifically. This explains his queries on matters of genealogy, for instance, and on various texts, as in the following example:

Question: How much of the *Meigetsuki* does the house own?

Answer: The journal was kept by Lord Teika from his sixteenth year until his old age. It is a national treasure, and a mirror to this house. More than 60 fascicles in Teika's own hand have been passed down to this house. Soon I will show them to you.[82]

To those interested in Teika's diary, it may be the third sentence in this statement that is of greatest interest, telling us how much of the original work the Reizei possessed in the eighteenth century. How-

---

80. Ibid., p. 649.
81. Ibid., p. 702.
82. Ibid., p. 651.

ever, Tamemura's last sentence—a direct comment to Yoshimasa, no doubt recorded with some pride—should not be passed over without comment. For by the eighteenth century, the manuscripts of the Reizei library were already museum pieces that attracted interest as much for their antiquity and courtly provenance as for anything else. Centuries earlier, Tameie had chided his progeny for not adequately revering his father's voluminous diary, but Tamemura had no need to do the same. The value of such artifacts was now beyond dispute. Yoshimasa cannot have been the only disciple who came hoping to get a glimpse of the cultural treasure of the Reizei house, which in the years to come would only gain in significance. Already in Tamemura's time the old storehouse was functioning as not just a library but as a proto-museum. Needless to say, the opportunity to get a glimpse of such house treasures was something for which many were doubtless willing to pay.

Elsewhere in the text, Tamemura also promises to show Yoshimasa other texts, fragments of calligraphy, an old writing desk (*buntai*), and even to take him on a tour of the gravesites of Shunzei, Teika, and Tameie, and to the Niitamatsushima Shrine, which appears to have been under the jurisdiction of the family—all for the same reason. The opportunity to see such things with one's own eyes was doubtless a major attraction for disciples, and Tamemura was not one to miss opportunities to take advantage of family assets.

When praising the holdings of the family library, Tamemura could afford to be forthright. Inevitably, however, there were some questions directed to him as the head of the Reizei lineage that demanded more tact. Chief among these were those that dealt with the troubled history of the Mikohidari house. Specifically, the old conflict with Nijō traditions was still very much alive in other houses, from the Nakano-in to the Asukai. In every one of his statements, however, Tamemura downplays conflicts, presenting a "united front," as might be expected in answering the questions of a disciple who is, after all, a commoner:

Question: What was the cause of disharmony between Tameuji and Tame-suke?

Answer: One feels bad about having to say this, but it appears that Tameie and Tameuji were not on good terms, and Tameie's bequest therefore came to this house. Homes, books, and many estate rights were deeded to Tamesuke. For that reason, after Tameie's death, Abutsu-ni went down to the East Country to plead her case concerning the estate rights, and it appears that that is why the relations between the brothers became strained. One also hears that at that time, Tameuji was also not getting along with his young brothers Tamenori and Tamekane, who were very kind to Tamesuke. Of course, among Tamesuke's siblings by the same mother were Tamemori, later called Kyōgetsubō, and Dharma Eye Genshō, and two or three girls. And then there were a number of other siblings of Tameuji, by the same mother. Now the lineage of Tameuji has died out; only the descendants of Tamesuke remain. That is why even those of Tameuji's lineage come here for instruction.[83]

The conflict happened long ago, Tamemura says, and then argues that it was really a problem between Tameie and Tameuji—a matter of personalities rather than politics. In another passage, he goes even further, arguing that ultimately the Way of Poetry is one:

Question: Is it true that Tamesuke and Tamehide were actually involved as compilers at time of *Gyokuyōshū* and *Fūgashū*?

Answer: This is an unfortunate contention that comes from later disciples of the Nijō house who wish to speak ill of the Reizei. To be sure, Tamekane and Tamesuke were on very good terms, and Tamehide was called upon during the two reigns of Fushimi—that is how the idea came to be. But Tamekane's style was one style, while Tamesuke's and Tamehide's style were each different. The notion that the Mikohidari [Tameyo], Bishamondō [Tamekane], and Fujigayatsu [Tamesuke] divided up into three separate styles is something the later disciples argue about. However, the late major counselor wrote a poem:

> All of a whole   are the teachings
> of the way   of Many Islands.
> Who was it that strayed away   and began
> the division?[84]
>
> *shikishima no / michi no oshie wa / hitosuji o / ta ga mayoi yori / wakaresomeken*

Both these passages amount to posturing, as any student of the Reizei past must know: if Tamesuke and Tamehide could not technically count themselves among the compilers of imperial anthologies, it had not been for want of trying. Moreover, the heads of the house in the medieval period had never complained of "feeling bad" about owning up to the conflicts that had after all been responsible for their very existence. In earlier times, distinctions between the houses had always served as forms of cultural capital. This was still true, up to a point; but it was equally true that the noble families of the mid-Edo period had a common interest in maintaining at least an

---

83. Ibid., p. 717.
84. Ibid., pp. 717–18.

outward display of harmony, especially as *jige* "outsiders" became more and more numerous.

Tamemura's conciliatory comments are thus a reflection of the political situation of his own day, when the noble houses—a small and insulated community whose only province was now the traditional arts—found it useful to emphasize commonalities rather than differences. One indication of this is that elsewhere Tamemura does admit differences, with the qualification that they tend to occur only in the realm of textual transmissions and ritual practices, as a way for the houses to distinguish themselves from one another *as distinct lineages* within noble society that are nevertheless dedicated to the same basic traditions:

> The Nijō house, the Reizei house—all descend from Tameie, and their teachings are not different. Because there was disharmony long ago, however, people think that their teachings were different too. In recent times, all, including this house, have sought imperial recognition, and there is no difference between the Nijō and the Reizei in terms of the proper way of composition (*shōfū*). It is just that the various tenets of the houses have continued down from ancient times, and in this the Reizei and the Asukai, for instance, are indeed different.[85]

Just what are the tenets (*setsu*) that Tamemura is willing to admit? Not surprisingly, they are precisely the ones that most benefit the house in competition for students. Chief among them are textual transmissions:

> Question: Are there any differences between Nijō and Reizei transmissions on *Kokinshū*?
>
> Answer: In this house, we have texts and fragments in the hands of Lord Shunzei, Lord Teika, and Lord Tameie, all of which are stored in the Library. . . . When it comes to *Kokinshū*, we use the textual line of the Karoku Era, whereas the Nijō house has received the Jō'ō era text. Further details are kept secret, so I cannot say anything about them.[86]

The text of *Kokinshū* Tamemura mentions here (dating from the second year of the Karoku era, 1226), which is in Teika's own hand and includes some interlinear notes by both Teika and Tameie, is still in the Reizei storehouse today. In fact, it is one of five texts that have been designated by the Japanese government as National Treasures

---

85. Ibid., p. 691.
86. Ibid., pp. 691–92.

(*kokuhō*).[87] Even 200 years ago Tamemura knew that it was an impor-
tant asset that the other houses could not claim to have. Tameyuki had
refused even to show it to the Asukai in the dark days of the shogun
Ashikaga Yoshinori, but now Tamemura could show it to anyone—
even a commoner—if it suited his purposes. The challenge was thus
to maintain ownership and access, to control circulation. Inheritors
of the old Nijō traditions in the Asukai, Nakano-in, Mushanokōji, and
other lineages could claim possession of their own secrets on *Kokinshū*
and other texts, but the Reizei were still the only house that could
claim the Mikohidari bloodline, as well as the largest trove anywhere
of manuscripts from the hands of Shunzei, Teika, and Tameie.

Yoshimasa lists a few other differences noted by Tamemura as well.
In the very first section of the document, for instance, he says that
the houses differ in the way they read certain titles, the Reizei way
of course being the right way. There are other minutiae as well, rang-
ing from discrepancies between the background colors of poem strips
(section 163) to interpretations of lines from old poems (section 161)
to shapes and styles of writing desks (section 76). In every case, he
suggests that Reizei practices are superior in one way or another.
His tone, however, is basically light and congenial. He wanted to be
accepted as the head of all the poetic houses of the court, after all;
it only made sense to try to unite rather than to divide. Nakano-in
Michishige had nurtured Tametsuna in his youth, as he explains in
section 82, and his feelings of gratitude for that generosity were no
doubt sincere. This demanded not the bravado of some of his an-
cestors, but modesty, a trait that Yoshimasa is careful to document:
"When I asked for a sample of his calligraphy, perhaps recording
a poem of his that he liked, what he said was, 'I'm 60 now, but I've
yet to compose a poem that truly stands out.'"[88]

Such self-effacement was of course expected of a true master,
which he evidently tried to be at all times, even when he was en-
gaged in activities that most would have seen as outside the realm
of poetic practice:

Often he would go for a stroll in the suburbs of the capital on which I would
accompany him, listening to his stories. On every occasion, he talked about
poetry and poetry alone. One time, as he was talking, a group of women car-
rying charcoal came toward us down a narrow path. When they saw him,

---

87. Reizei Fumiko, *Reizei Fumiko ga kataru Kyō no miyabi*, pp. 98–99.
88. Miyabe no Yoshimasa, *Yoshimasa kikigaki*, p. 722.

they all stepped off the path and stopped to let him pass, but then he stepped off the path and waited, saying that we must let them be on their way. After they had passed, he said to me, "We are in no special hurry, just enjoying a stroll; but if the women are held up for even a moment they may be too late to sell their charcoal. To have proper consideration for the feelings of others in such situations — that is the Way of Poetry." A very gracious attitude.[89]

For one who represents the Way, there can be no rest, especially with students, so the master says. As he had declared earlier, "It will not do to be upright only when composing poems."[90]

JUST HOW many poems did the most famous of Edo-period Reizei poets compose, in the end? If modern scholars are correct, a conservative estimate would be perhaps 200,000 to 300,000.[91] Most of these, of course, were composed as *keiko* and were not permanently recorded, a fact that reinforces the idea of process over product that so informs his teachings to Yoshimasa. Only those that he thought would be most useful in instruction, just over 2,000 of them, made it into his personal anthology. There they are organized in the traditional manner by category (spring, summer, autumn, winter, love, miscellaneous) and topic. Almost no long headnotes are recorded, indicating that he wanted his works to be considered primarily in terms of their handling of convention and not as statements of "self-expression" or personal circumstance.

Kubota Keiichi argues that some of Tamemura's statements reveal impatience with the rigidity of his cohorts in the Nijō line and also sees stylistic nuances that set Tamemura apart from his contemporaries.[92] It is true that in comments such as the following from *Reizei sōshō-ke kikigaki* concerning syntactical prohibitions on the use of certain grammatical particles (*kana* and *tsutsu*) Tamemura presents himself as less narrow in his thinking than his competitors were:

In the Reizei school (*Reizei-ryū*) we have no transmission on this matter. Speaking in broad terms, if the particles work in a given poem, we don't prohibit anyone from using them — although in the Nijō house of our time those who have not received the transmissions are indeed not permitted to use them. Our position in the Reizei house is that while one should not be

---

89. Ibid., p. 724.
90. Ibid., p. 652.
91. See note 15 above.
92. Kubota Keiichi, *Kinsei Reizei-ha kadan no kenkyū*, pp. 280–88.

too ready to defy this convention, we don't dictate any syntactical placement, provided only that the poem turns out well. Setting out to compose a poem [that defies convention] is of course bad, but if a poem with those particles comes about naturally, we make no distinction between beginners and mature practitioners.[93]

The circumlocutions that Tamemura employs in delivering this critique reduce its rhetorical impact considerably. In another statement made to the same disciple, however, he reveals his breadth of vision—as well as his gracious attitude toward a student, who was basically complaining about the difficulty of learning all the rules of the art—more unequivocally: "I understand, of course. No matter what your question may be about, you must just ask me. If you represent your feelings uprightly [*tadashiku*], you will not go contrary to the Way. You need not be directed on every little detail. The Way of Poetry is after all like the Great Way. The best thing is to proceed straight ahead, openly and uprightly."[94]

No one reading this last statement, which was circulated among disciples, could fail to appreciate Tamemura's forthcoming attitude. A final statement in the same text settles the issue once and for all. The context again is a technical one, involving which texts the Nijō school allowed to be used to establish precedent, but the answer needs no further interpretation: "In our school we have no such regulations. . . . This is the happy thing [*arigataki tokoro*] about the teachings of the Reizei house."[95] While as the head of a noble house he could not, with Kinoshita Chōshōshi, suggest abandoning the *Kokin denju* altogether, he could insist—against the mounting attacks of *jige* poets—that the old teachings were not meant to be "constricting."[96] For him, as for Reizei poets in the time of Tamekazu and Tamehiro, secret transmissions were less central to the Way of Poetry than composition was.

There is indeed evidence, then, that in his attitude toward the *Kokin denju*, and probably toward the tyranny of convention in general, Tamemura was a progressive of sorts. One must admit, however, that finding any sign of a true departure from the basic aesthetics of the court tradition in his poetry is difficult—as one would

---

93. Ibid., pp. 286–87.
94. Ibid., p. 92.
95. Ibid., p. 288.
96. From *Yoshimasa kikigaki*. Quoted in Kubota Keiichi, *Kinsei Reizei-ha kadan no kenkyū*, p. 287.

expect, given the discursive circumstances in which he pursued his career. This does not mean, however, that the slight innovations in his work should be discounted, especially since it was to the idea of slight innovation that the Reizei poets had been dedicated for nearly 500 years. In the following poem from a 30-poem sequence, for example, we can identify a kind of new and clever phrasing (*haru furu wa/haru o uzumanu*) that draws attention to itself rather than to what it describes:

> In spring they descend   yet still leave spring
> unburied —   fine flakes of snow
> piling up, one thinks at first,   'til they swiftly
> melt away.[97]
>
> *haru furu wa/haru o uzumanu/awayuki no/tsumoru to miru mo/kiyuru hodo naki*

The following two examples show an imaginative power that helps transcend the limits of timeworn topics:

> "Blossoms in the Rain"
>
> Wet now, the branches   of the cherries
> in full bloom   are heavier still —
> leaving one no need to fear rain   unaccompanied
> by wind.[98]
>
> *nurete nao/sakari no hana no/eda o omomi/kaze naki ame wa/furu mo itowazu*

> "In Sympathy with the Moon"
>
> Is that a reason   to stop enjoying
> its light?   No, I won't complain
> that every autumn moon   adds to my burden
> of years.[99]
>
> *shikari tote/misutemu mono ka/akigoto no/tsuki ni tsumoramu/oi wa nagekaji*

By Tamemura's time, hundreds of thousands of poems on cherry blossoms and the moon had been composed, making the task of creating a new poem on such topics a particular challenge. Tamemura meets the challenge not by innovations in phrasing, wordplay, or even metaphor, but by delicate nuances in conception. Neither poem describes a scene so much as a state of mind evoked by a scene,

---

97. Kubota Keiichi, *Kinsei Reizei-ha kadan no kenkyū*, p. 74.
98. *Kinsei wakashū*, p. 156 (poem no. 33).
99. Ibid., p. 165 (poem no. 69).

showing Tamemura to be a descendant not only of Tamesuke and Tamemasa but also of Teika.

It must be reiterated, however, that viewed in the larger context of poetic history such nuances are very slight, which is no doubt the way a "practitioner" like Tamemura wanted it. For him the best poem was not necessarily one that generated questions and analysis. Flawlessness was what was wanted, as Tameie had taught, and not novelty—or at least not novelty for its own sake. He could not endorse the excesses of his sometime student Ozawa Roan, who wrote poems such as this one in what he called "everyday language":

> Summer: "Melons"
>
> You peasant women,   go bring in
> those melons   drying on the gate!
> The wind's raising thunder clouds;   rain will be
> pouring down soon.[100]
>
> *shizu no me ga / kado no hoshiuri / toriireyo / kaze yūdachite / ame koborekinu*

The language here is too colloquial and the tone too intimate for the head of a noble poetic house to accept. Indeed, the topic "Melons" itself is too common for noble taste, making one suspect that Roan wrote the poem first and then assigned it a "false" topic in an attempt to hide the fact. When Tamemura writes of peasant women, it is in more elegant language and from what he would have considered a proper remove.

> Autumn: "Fulling Block"
>
> The peasant women   in the cold air
> of a night chilled   by autumn wind
> beat robes on blocks that echo   far and near
> throughout the sky.[101]
>
> *shizu no me ga / koromo yosamu no / akikaze ni / uchi mo tayumanu / ochikochi no sora*

Here the peasant women are reduced to a sound in the distance—the echo of mallet on fulling block, an image long sanctioned by poetic practice. The autumn setting too is appropriate for the topic.

Tamemura's own focus in composition was of course precisely on the proper handling of topics. This allowed for a certain degree of creativity: a new turn of phrase, a different vantage point, an

---

100. Ozawa, *Rokujō eisō*, poem no. 515.
101. Reizei Tamemura, *Tamemura shū*, poem no. 1011.

image not used in that context before, a slightly new conception, but always within well-known bounds. More substantial departures would amount to abandoning the tradition that provided his sustenance. So "Snow" in Tamemura's poems must still be snow, indeed, snow in its very essence; a "Coal Fire" must still be a real coal fire; a "Friend in the Snow," must in some way articulate the idea of friendship while also including the required image:

Winter: "Snow"

Beneath snow piled up   through the course
of a night   the path has vanished;
this morning, no one yet   has visited
my mountain home.[102]

furitsumishi / yo no ma no yuki ni / michi taete / kesa yamazato wa / tou hito mo nashi

Winter: "Coal Fire Late into the Night"

Has it grown so late?   As I chat
with myself,   how faint is the light
of my small coal fire   in the cold
of my bedchamber.[103]

fukenuru ka / hitori katarau / uzumibi no / hikari mo usuki / neya no samukesa

Winter: "A Friend in the Snow"

I wait for no one   to disturb
my garden—   taking as a friend
the snow that is piling up   at the break
of a new day.[104]

tou hito mo / mataji yo niwa ni / furitsumu o / tomo to nagamuru / yuki no akebono

All three of these poems present winter as it appears in countless other poems by court poets. Never a crowd of people caught in a blizzard or an ice storm, always a solitary figure surrounded by a chilly yet beautiful landscape; never a warming blaze, but always faintly glowing embers; never dirty slush, always pure powder. Only the last poem offers something slightly new in the form of the conceit that makes the snow into a friend. But making the best of one's loneliness was a very old idea by the eighteenth century. If anything is new, then, it is the topic itself, although unlike Roan's "Melons," it does little more than combine two topics sanctioned long before.

---

102. Ibid., poem no. 1313.
103. Ibid., poem no. 1334.
104. Ibid., poem no. 1437.

If there is anything else "distinctive" about Tamemura's poetry, it is the variety of styles he employs, as one would expect of a master who had to display his competence as such. Needless to say, among these is the "realistic" style that engenders bucolic scenes that had been a Reizei tradition since the time of Tamesuke:

> Miscellaneous: "Birds around a House in the Fields"
>
> After the harvest   they still gather
> together —   flocks of sparrows
> chirping as they forage   for rice dropped
> in gate paddies.[105]
>
> *kariageshi / nochi mo murekite / murasuzume / kadota no ochiho / asaru koegoe*

> Miscellaneous: "Woodcutter"
> Is he forgetting   the pains of his
> daily lot   cutting wood for fires?
> On his way home from the hills   the mountain man
> is singing.[106]
>
> *tsumagi toru / mi no uki waza mo / wasurete ya / kaesa no michi ni / utau yamabito*

Such views abound in his personal collection. Also present, however, are poems in other styles that present lofty imagery of the sort that earlier critics had accused the Reizei line of being unwilling or unable to master:

> Miscellaneous: "Vista"
>
> As I gaze afar   at where evening sun
> casts light   on the fields' far edge —
> a lone column of herons   crosses over
> the mountain rim.[107]
>
> *yūhi sasu / tazura no sue o / nagamureba / yama no ha wataru / sagi no hitotsura*

> Miscellaneous: "Many"
>
> All across Heaven   the clouds have cleared
> away,   night after night
> leaving stars shining brightly   in numbers
> beyond knowing.[108]
>
> *ōzora no / kumo wa harewataru / yona yona ni / kagayaku hoshi wa / kazu mo shirarezu*

> Miscellaneous: "A View of the Sea"

---

105. Ibid., poem no. 1874.
106. Ibid., poem no. 2089.
107. Ibid., poem no. 1849.
108. Ibid., poem no. 1910.

Seagulls rise high   above wave paths
that stretch out far,   so far away —
while here before my eyes   skies clear above
the Sea Plain.[109]

kamome tatsu / namiji no sue mo / harubaru to / miru me haretaru / kesa no umibara

Even Tamemura's poems in the lofty style do not employ the kind of archaic diction so favored by the Nativist poets, however. When he gestured toward the past, it was from within the confines of the present, and always with restraint. He was particularly harsh about "stealing" too much from old poems:

The best practice for beginners is to memorize old poems. But when one is composing a poem, it is best to work through it without looking [directly] at examples from the past. . . . If you decide to look at the poems of others every time you compose a poem, in order to steal from them, you will never be able to produce a poem from your own heart. Those who steal the words and conceptions from poems already written by others will have difficulty ever understanding the Way of Poetry.[110]

Three hundred years before, Shōtetsu had complained that a prominent member of the Asukai house — adherents of the Nijō school — "seems to have taken phrases from many other people and incorporated them into his own poems."[111] The technique of *honkadori*, or allusive variation, of course, entailed just that, in a sense; but Tamemura made it clear that there was such a thing as "borrowing" too much — the sort of offense against which it was the duty of men in the houses, whose job it was to memorize the canon, to protect the Way. The question was not one of plagiarism in the modern sense but of not rising to the challenge. Consequently, when Tamemura alluded to a famous poem from the past, it was in order to respond to it creatively and not simply to repeat or mimic. A good example is this autumn poem on the topic "Snipes in the Marshes":

Somewhere out there   snipes rise up
into flight   while still the moon
takes lodging in the marshes   where daybreak
lights the sky.[112]

izuku ni ka / shigi no tatsuran / tsuki wa nao / yadoru sawabe no / akegata no sora

---

109. Ibid., poem no. 1944.
110. Miyabe no Yoshimasa, *Yoshimasa kikigaki*, p. 718.
111. Brower and Carter, *Conversations with Shōtetsu*, p. 64.
112. Reizei Tamemura, *Tamemurashū*, poem no. 1010.

Any student of court poetry will of course recognize this as an allusion to one of the most famous poems of Saigyō:

Autumn: Topic unknown

Even those of us   who claim to be
beyond feeling   sense this sad beauty:
snipes rising up from marshes   on an evening
in autumn.[113]

kokoro naki / mi ni mo aware wa / shirarekeri / shigi tatsu sawa no / aki no yūgure

Saigyō's poem presents a monk who, despite his vow to have extinguished normal human feelings, finds himself startled by the beauty of snipe suddenly rising before him into the autumn dusk. Taking this as a backdrop, Tamemura goes beyond this conception by focusing on snipes not seen but unseen, and on how the moon, a conventional symbol for Buddhist Law, still shines down on the waters of the marshes in the light of dawn, suggesting perhaps that despite a momentary lapse in concentration, the speaker remains devout. Dusk has passed and a new dawn—both literal and symbolic—is approaching.

The final impression one is left with after reading through Tamemura's critical comments, quips to disciples, and personal anthology of poems is therefore of a man who is every bit the master or *sōshō*, in the old sense of the term. For the glimpses we get of him, whether sitting in front of a Buddhist image while confronting his own demise, or poised over paper before composing a poem, or even out walking in the hills with a disciple, is always of a man who is "right" in both heart and body, and always ready to proceed: not a modern "artist" dedicated to his "works" but a craftsman or practitioner of sorts, a man dedicated to a larger enterprise who asks to be recognized less as an individual talent than as the agent of an ongoing discourse. Like Tameie, he shunned anything that might be called "strikingly new" and sought for "freshness and originality" only within the strictest limits.[114]

In this sense, Tamemura represents the culmination of a tradition in which the head of a lineage is clearly more invested in the role of master—and the activities of instruction—than in the creation of an individual style. What Mushanokōji Sanekage says to his students

---

113. *Shin kokinshū*, poem no. 362.
114. Brower, "The Foremost Style of Poetic Composition," p. 429.

goes for Tamemura as well: "First, ponder the books your teacher says you should study, then carefully look at any other books and ask your teacher whenever you come across anything questionable."[115]

Above all, the teacher must be poised for the gaze of those who look to him for guidance. The image of Tamemura as master, sitting in the proper posture, prepared to perform his duties, is thus meant to instruct, just as were images of Shunzei and Teika and the other forebears in the family storehouse. In the final analysis it was Tamemura's ability to serve quite literally as a model (to perform, critique, and instruct) that was most crucial to his success in his occupation, rather than the quality of any one or even any group of his own poems — that and his authority as the descendant of Shunzei and Teika with a trove of manuscripts and practices to prove it. Perhaps this had been true even in earlier generations, but now the fact was inescapable: the Reizei house had become something akin to an *iemoto* in which the tradition invested as much in process as in product.[116]

If Tamemura's poems are calm and sedate, then, we should understand that those adjectives would have had the most positive connotations among most of those in his social circle. A short quotation from one of his contemporaries, Takamatsu Shigesue (1698–1745), shows that despite Tamemura's conciliations the old criticisms were still circulating among those of rival houses: "All the Nijō collections are fine, but the Reizei collections are in unorthodox styles [*ifū*], so don't study them."[117] In all, however, Tamemura was able to avoid contention, practicing his art and providing for his family in a time of peace and plenty. The concept of orthodoxy was a double-edged sword that could easily be turned to the house's favor.

Tamemura's was not a long life, by comparison with the patriarchs; but when at 63 he passed away, he left Tameyasu, nearly 40 and a middle counselor at court, in a position of considerable strength. True talent of the sort we are used to associating with literary accomplishment cannot be passed on, but lineage, knowledge, and technique, along with the heirlooms of the old storehouses — these, once again, were tangibles that a father in Edo court society could in fact hand down to his progeny with considerable hope that the tradition, and the fortunes of the house, would indeed carry on.

---

115. Mushanokōji Sanekage, *Shōgaku kōkan*, p. 203.
116. Smith, "Transmitting Tradition by the Rules," pp. 37–39.
117. *Unjō kakun*, p. 955.

NINE

Abandoned Capital

BY THE turn of the nineteenth century, Kyoto had become a sleepy town, outpaced by Edo in virtually every way. One writer, in a travel record published in 1781, cut the city to the bone: "Two hundred years ago it was 'the flowery capital'; now it's a flowery backwater."[1]

Yet some things did not change. The city still boasted scores of religious institutions, which drew pilgrims and sightseers; and still it was a cultural and educational center, where traditional arts and crafts flourished. Writer Takizawa Bakin (1767–1848), another visitor to the city, complained that the people were stingy, the food was bad, and the water transport inconvenient — what one might expect an Edokko ("child of Edo") to say. But he also listed three things he liked: the women, the water of the Kamo River, and the temples and shrines.[2]

Needless to say, Courtiers' Quarter remained an enclave for the old aristocracy, the Reizei among them. Their place in the scheme of things, however reduced when compared to the times of their ancestors, remained secure. Emperor Kōkaku (1779–1840; r. 1778–1817), who was dedicated to poetry and the other arts, sponsored a lively salon that provided abundant opportunity for the members of the poetic houses to display their talents. Relatively speaking, the houses also remained wealthy. One of the largest of the noble residence compounds in Courtiers' Quarter — that of the Kujō house — was spacious

---

1. *Kyoto*, p. 322. The writer was Kimuro Bō'un (d. 1783), known best for his madcap *uta* (*kyōka*).
2. Ibid.

enough to accommodate several large halls, garden space, an ornamental lake, and numerous small cottages and teahouses, which the house was able to maintain on their stipend of 2,043 *koku* and the income from other business ventures, a distillery among them.[3] Houses such as the Reizei, which were much further down the scale, were obviously not as prosperous but clearly had enough to live up to the demands of a noble lifestyle. Even the 60 new branch houses (*shinke*) that had been added to the noble rolls in the time of Go-Mizuno'o were able to hold their own.[4]

Thus the sixteenth head of the lineage, Tameyasu, took over the house in a time of prosperity and prominence. Unfortunately, however, quotations such as the following from a *bushi* disciple suggest that he had a difficult time living up to the expectations of the many students that he inherited from his father: "Compared to his father, Lord Tameyasu was noticeably more restrained, and never showed a lively spirit. So diligent was he in being truthful and proper that he seldom gave words of praise and was rather punctilious in all he did. He was often slow in marking work."[5]

The author goes on to say that some impatient students began to take their fees to other noble teachers, most prominently Hino Sukeki (1737–1801). Among the defectors were even old, established disciples such as Miyabe Yoshimasa, dedicated disciple and recorder of *Yoshimasa kikigaki*, who was subsequently sent a formal writ of excommunication by Tameyasu for betraying his oath.[6]

It should be noted, however, that for students to shift their allegiances from one house to another was not uncommon at any time, especially after the death of the head of a house. Besides, rifts were routine. In 1773, Tamemura himself had excommunicated Ozawa Roan, for instance, probably over disputes about poetic philosophy. Roan had been a disciple for more than 20 years, but over time, it seems, he had become more and more dissatisfied with the narrowness of *kuge* rules and conventions and the exaggerated importance given to secret teachings, until finally he began to compose poems and to propound standards of a sort that his teacher could not countenance. Rather than defecting to another noble family, though, he

---

3. Ponsonby-Fane, *Kyoto: The Old Capital of Japan*, pp. 372–74.
4. Ibid., pp. 366–72.
5. Kubota Keiichi, "Reizei-ke no rekishi 24: Tameyasu," p. 3.
6. Ibid., p. 3.

ceased contact with the *kuge* coteries altogether. After Tamemura's death, Roan developed friendships with a number of *jige* poets, including Motoori Norinaga, Ban Kōkei (1733–1806), Ueda Akinari (1734–1809), and the young Kagawa Kageki (1768–1843). In time, he had a number of disciples himself. As a *jige* master with his own school, he had scarcely any further connection with any of the old houses.

The problem of defections did not begin with Tameyasu, nor would it end with him. By the end of the eighteenth century, *jige* poets were routinely challenging the privileged place of the noble houses. Yet it appears that there were still plenty of disciples left for the Reizei and other court houses, for whom quality still mattered more than quantity. Noble and priestly lineages, shogunal officials and daimyo, as well as many commoners still lured by the mystique of the imperial court, were still happy to call a Reizei man their teacher. One scholar even suggests that the real reason for Tameyasu's difficulties was that his father had simply left him too many disciples to deal with, each of whom expected personal attention. Every month, scores of compositions came to the house by mail, so many that he could not keep up with the job of commenting and marking.[7] Far from panicking at the thought of losing a few students, Tameyasu may have welcomed a reduction in his workload.

To those who insist that Tameyasu was less successful than his father had been, then, one can reply that there is little sign that the house truly suffered much during his time, except perhaps in the sense that all the old families of Kyoto suffered in comparison with *jige* poets in Edo and the provinces. He was elevated to senior second rank in 1776, was licensed by the emperor to serve as a master in 1781, and became a major counselor in 1787. Like Tametsuna, Tamehisa, and Tamemura before him, he too was called upon to provide *dai* for imperial gatherings and to act as *sōshō* for imperial poetic events. Furthermore, he continued to instruct students in the house style of calligraphy. Every indication is that he lived in relative comfort, supported by the family stipend, revenues from students, and the various incomes that accompanied courtly appointments. His days were spent correcting the work of students and obeying the demands of the calendar for various rights and customs, including memorial services for the many generations of Reizei. He held monthly poetry gatherings, as well as sponsoring and responding to

---

7. Ibid., p. 2.

calls for votive sequences. His other primary concerns were the care of the library and, of course, his obligations toward his immediate family, branch families, stewards, samurai, and servants. In other words, he continued in every way the traditions of his father, even in the way he maintained a close association with the Tokugawa government, despite the criticisms of some of his court colleagues.[8]

One crisis of the sort his father had never had to face came in 1788, the year of the Tenmei Conflagration, one of the greatest urban fires in Japanese history.[9] It began toward dawn on the last day of the First Month, in a few uninhabited houses on the east bank of the Kamo River. By dawn the next day, virtually the whole city, from Shōkokuji in the north to the Honganji temples on Seventh Avenue in the south, had been destroyed.[10] Not since the Ōnin War more than 300 years before had the city suffered such devastation. Standard sources say that as many as 36,000 homes were burned in the fire, and the Reizei house on Imadegawa did not escape. Thanks to the ingenuity of its design, however, the contents of the *obunko* remained untouched. Its earthen walls and the earthen roof were designed to protect the structure after the wooden roof collapsed onto it, and indeed the structure proved impregnable. Among the Reizei, then, there was cause for celebration. The house could be rebuilt — indeed, as a wood structure it was constantly being repaired in any case. The contents of the library, on the other hand, were irreplaceable. The shogunate immediately sent money to assist in recovery, as did wealthy Osaka merchants and others. Most *kuge* houses received cash gifts according to their status in the hierarchy that went far toward the cost of rebuilding.[11] In addition, many no doubt received considerable help from wealthy disciples and well-wishers.[12]

It took several years for the nobility to rebuild their homes. By 1790, the imperial palace had been completed, at shogunal expense. The finest artists of the day, including the painter Maruyama Ōkyo, a Reizei disciple, had been commissioned to produce new screen paint-

---

8. Ogura, "Reizei-ke no rekishi 25: Tamefumi," p. 5.

9. Ponsonby-Fane, *Kyoto: The Old Capital of Japan*, p. 406.

10. Shimosaka, "Tenmei no taika," pp. 102–4.

11. Ponsonby-Fane, *Kyoto: The Old Capital of Japan*, p. 408; Nakamura, "Waka no ie, kuge no ie," p. 17.

12. Reizei Tamehito and Sugimoto Tarō, "Edo saigo no tōshū, Tametada," p. 152.

ings.[13] As a final touch, Tameyasu, his son, and his grandson were privileged to be among those asked to provide poems to adorn the sliding panels of the Seiryōden (the private living chambers of the emperor), a sure sign of the respect they commanded among their peers. Thus one of the poems of his heir Tamefumi (1752–1822) ended up on one of the sliding partitions in the Kokiden chambers of the new imperial living quarters, next to a painting of the Katsura River:

> No village in sight—　just the faint moon
> shimmering　on Katsura River
> where even its light fades off　into willows'
> murky glow.[14]
>
> *sato miede / honomeku tsuki no / katsuragawa / yanagi ni niou / kage mo usumeru*

Poems recorded in books, even those of the new printed variety—a kind of publication the Reizei of course shunned—often collected dust on the shelf. The most elite of spectators would often view a poem adorning the palace walls, at least until the next fire.

Around the same time, the rebuilding of most of the other houses in Courtiers' Quarter was also completed. The layout of the quarter was the same as it had been before the fire, with the imperial palace at the center and the palace of the retired emperor to the southwest. The five regental houses still boasted the largest compounds, as did those of the princely lineages, such as the Fushimi, the Arisugawa, and the Kan-in. Next in size came the *seigake* (whose heirs could rise as high as chancellor) and the *daijinke* (who could go as high as minister of the left) and the lower ranks of the nobility—made up of *urinke* houses such as the Asukai and the Reizei and *meika* houses such as the Hino and the Hirohashi. In most cases, these governing hierarchies strictly dictated the size of lots and the houses that stood on them. The regental Konoe house, for instance, was 4,000 *tsubo* in area, while the Tokudaiji (one of the *seigake*) was only 670.[15]

The Reizei house was rebuilt on the same old lot, outside the quarter proper, on the north side of Imadegawa Avenue. As if in compensation for what seemed like *tozama* status, the lot was slightly larger than those of many assigned to *urinke* houses within. Next door to the

---

13. Sasaki Jōhei and Sasaki Masako, "The Formation and Development of Japanese Painting Schools," p. 53.

14. Ogura, "Reizei-ke no rekishi 25: Tamefumi," p. 4.

15. Kawakami, "Kuge jūtaku no hensen ni tsuite," p. 176.

east was the compound of the Fujitani; to the west, that of longtime allies, the Yamashina. The Irie, another branch family, descended from the Fujitani, was several blocks to the north. The lower Reizei and Imaki both occupied lots inside the quarter. The main house also maintained a secondary residence just southeast of the palace of the retired emperor, for servants, perhaps, or for confinement of women during childbirth, and so on.

The new residence, which one assumes was similar in basic design to the one that preceded it, again stood within a walled compound facing Imadegawa, a concrete embodiment that expressed its identity in most features of its layout and design. In front of the formal entryway and its broad wooden porch (*shikidai*, slightly raised so that riders in palanquin could step directly into the house) of zelkova wood was a traditional trelliswork screen, called a *tatejitomi*—a carryover from the architecture of an earlier time that was designed to provide privacy when the front gate was open. To the west of the entry were the kitchen areas and office spaces for stewards; on the east were the more formal rooms, the Envoy Room (*shisha no ma*, eight mats in size),[16] the Middle Hall (*naka no ma*, twelve mats), and the Great Hall (*hiro no ma*, thirteen mats), the latter two fronting on garden space. Day-to-day living quarters, which included interior gardens and rooms for women, children, and maids, were behind these rooms, running along the back of the building from the northeast corner to the kitchen area. The *kura*, or storehouses—and there were as many as eight at one time—were in the western back corner of the lot, while the *obunko* and the new library (*oshinbunko*) created by Tamemura to house copies of rare manuscripts and more recent acquisitions, were in the northeast, nearly up against the back wall and close by the living quarters of the master of the house. On the southwest corner of the compound stood a carriage house and guards' quarters, while in the southeast corner there was a small hut that evidently served as a teahouse, testifying to the prominence this relatively new art form had managed to achieve even among the old nobility.[17]

---

16. In his diary, Tametada indicates that in the 1460s, at least, there appears to have been no *shisha no ma*, although the details he provides don't indicate what that space was being used for. See Reizei Kimiko, "*Tametada-kyō ki 74*," p. 6. Nakamura, "Waka no ie, kuge no ie," p. 30, indicates that the *shisha no ma* was added in the reconstruction of 1790.

17. Nakamura, "Kugyō no ie, suki no ie."

The Great Hall, which was used only for the most important meet-ings and rituals, boasted an ornamental alcove (*tokonoma*) and the inner rooms were covered with *tatami* mats, following the patterns of *shoin* style architecture, although there were no bookshelves—an indication that the space was designed for the performance of various rites and not just for private pleasures.[18] The entire inner area of the living wing was partitioned with sliding doors that could be removed to enlarge the space for various kinds of events. In contrast to the sliding panels in other noble houses, those in the formal spaces of the Reizei house were not adorned with landscape paintings so as not to become a distraction during poetic events.[19] Fronting on the formal rooms was a large lawn space, complete with rose plum and orange trees flanking the old-style stairway leading up to the porch of the Great Hall, a feature carried over from ancient times.[20] In front of the *tatejitomi* was a courtyard space covered with white gravel. A special gate led from the courtyard into the garden area and the entries to the formal rooms. It was used only by imperial messengers, who would be carried by palanquin and who would disembark directly onto the stairway.

On the surface, the residence showed few vestiges of the old *shin-den* style, but still there were wooden verandas, inner gardens, and so forth, as well as other traditional features. The basic structure, for instance, involved an entry area (*ōgenkan* and *naigenkan*) at the center, with "wings" to the west and east, the former being the pub-lic (*hare*) side, the latter the private (*ke*). While the *genkan* was a later development in architecture, then, the way it led, on the east, into a building that was essentially one large structure, divided up into four major rooms by partitions that could be taken out, was much like the old *shinden* style.[21] Rather than by the covered walkways of olden days, however, the main structure was connected to the living spaces by interior hallways that were in turn linked by more hall-ways to the "business" end of the house on the west, which con-tained the stewards' offices and kitchen areas. While not retaining nearly as many features of old court architecture as, say, the Toku-daiji house just to the west or the Konoe house across the street,

---

18. Nakamura, "Waka no ie, kuge no ie," pp. 32–33.
19. Ibid., pp. 35–36.
20. Ibid., p. 33.
21. Nakamura, "Kugyō no ie, suki no ie," pp. 203–8.

the new Reizei house still contained a few concrete gestures toward the courtly past.[22]

In his new house, surrounded by his progeny and kept busy by his many literary and family obligations, Reizei Tameyasu, sixteenth head of the lineage, lived a long, peaceful, and uneventful life, dying at the age of 82. He saw his son, Tamefumi, move up through the ranks at court, eventually taking over the more onerous of administrative burdens, and then in turn looked on as his grandson Tamenori (1777–1848) did the same. Even his great-grandson, Tametake (1802–45), had advanced into the court ranks before Tameyasu finally passed away in 1816.

REIZEI DESCENDANTS followed in the patterns that had been set by Tamemura. All were raised to revere their ancestors as gods and to sustain the Way of Poetry. This was no mean task, for by the mid-Edo period almost every activity, including even the most trivial of everyday duties, was hemmed in by precedent, the maintenance of which itself became the family occupation. In almost everything—from what to wear on a particular day, to what words of address to use in speaking with people of various ranks and stations—a Reizei man (or woman) had to be guided by standards handed down for generations. This was of course a burden; but it was also a strong ground for identity and the chief means of reinforcing the seemingly "natural" place of the lineage in society.

Tamefumi survived his father by only six years, leaving responsibility for the house to his heir Tamenori, who managed to work his way into the affections of Kōkaku—now retired emperor—early on, as well as succeeding at recruiting new disciples. Still, then, the house held its own, maintaining its place in the elite economy, virtually oblivious to movements in poetry outside the noble houses. Lamentably, Tamenori's son Tametake died in his early 40s in 1845, three years before his father. Family lore says that the culprit was alcohol.[23] But a premature death in the nineteenth century was not as serious a matter as it had been centuries before. Stipends were secure and social positions fixed and stable. Furthermore, the other noble families, knowing that the same could happen to any one of them, gathered round to lend support in the crucial area of poetic training.

---

22. Kawakami, "Kuge jūtaku no hensen ni tsuite," pp. 170–78.
23. Reizei Fumiko, *Reizei Fumiko ga kataru Kyō no miyabi*, p. 201.

Because he died so young, Tametake never went beyond the office of consultant at court and we know little of his practice except that he served as *daisha* at court and had many disciples in Edo.[24] About his son Tametada (1824–85), on the other hand, we know a great deal, largely because he kept a diary, from 1841 until just before his death more than 40 years later. To date, the record has not been published in any form, but for the past two decades or so Reizei Kimiko, daughter of Fumiko and Tametō, has been introducing its contents to readers of *Shiguretei*, the newsletter of the Reizei Corporation. So far, around 100 installments of her "summary" have appeared, taking the story of her great-great-grandfather up until just before the Meiji Restoration of 1868.

Kimiko is somewhat apologetic about Tametada's diary, which she characterizes very much as a courtier's journal, like *Meigetsuki*, that was kept not to reveal the "inner self" in the manner of diaries written for different reasons. "It records the quiet days of just one courtier who dedicated himself to the family enterprise [*kagyō*] of the Way of Poetry [*kadō*] and strove to preserve the library for coming generations."[25] From her summaries, however, it is apparent that the diary is a rich record that reveals much about the workings of the house if not so much about the private thoughts of the man.

From the diary we learn, for instance, that the stipend of the family in the mid-1800s was still 300 *koku*, and also where most of that income came from—200 *koku* coming from one place, Ichijōji village at the foot of Mt. Hiei.[26] The family apparently maintained a very close relationship with this village over the years, sending children there for rearing, taking in village maids and servants, and sending family treasures there for safety during fires or times of unrest. No doubt the same pattern had persisted for centuries, but it is only in Tametada's jottings that we get verifiable details. Also noted is the stipend of the Fujitani, which was set at 200 *koku*, considerably more than that of the lower Reizei, who received only 150 *koku*, and much above that of another branch family, the Irie, at only 30 *koku*. Among other things, Tametada's recording of such details shows that he thought of these lineages as very much connected to his house. Plainly he was considered the head of an expanded Reizei

24. Ogura, Reizei-ke no rekishi 27: Tametake," pp. 4–5.
25. Reizei Kimiko, "*Tametada-kyō ki 1*," p. 3.
26. Reizei Kimiko. "*Tametada-kyō ki 4*," p. 6.

lineage, which included the lower Reizei, the Fujitani, the Irie—and also perhaps the Yanagiwara, the family of his wife, Yoshi (1824–1909).[27] One sign of this is that he never failed to invite them to his poetic gatherings. But the relationship went well beyond that. When he had good or bad news to announce, he always sent messages to them.[28] He did ritual cappings for their heirs.[29] And when Fujitani Tamesaki (1830–58) died, he quickly arranged for a fifteen-year-old in the Irie house to be taken in as heir.[30] We also know that for a time Tametada served the Takatsukasa house—one of the five houses of the regency—as a kind of *keishi* as in generations past.[31] In this sense, one can say that much of the structure of social relations at court in medieval times still persisted in the late Edo period, although probably in truncated form.

Tametada's diary also tells us a good deal about the size of the Reizei household and the nature of its daily activities. Genealogies show that by a daughter of Yanagiwara Takamitsu (1793–1851) and several women of lesser rank, Tametada sired fifteen children, five of whom died as infants.[32] In 1854, however, Kimiko estimates that the household on Imadegawa consisted of only six family members, two stewards (*zasshō*, whose primary responsibility was relations with the imperial palace and other noble families), one senior clerk (*yōnin*, who was similar to a steward but who had responsibility primarily for formal visits to temples), two guards (*omotezamurai*), one more manservant, and five or six serving women (*shimobe*, *jochū*, and *nakai*)—from fifteen to twenty people in all, although not all of them were actually living in the house.[33] Young children were often sent to Ichijōji village to be raised and some of those not destined for life at court were sent to temples or shrines. One son was sent to the Irie family as a ward and three daughters were married into

---

27. Reizei Kimiko, "Bakumatsu no Reizei-ke," pp. 289–93. The relationship between the Reizei and the Yanagiwara went back to the time of Yanagiwara Mitsutsuna (1711–60), who was actually a son of Reizei Tametsuna.

28. Reizei Kimiko, "*Tametada-kyō ki* 18," p. 6.

29. Reizei Kimiko, "*Tametada-kyō ki* 21," p. 6.

30. Reizei Kimiko, "*Tametada-kyō ki* 18," p. 6 and Reizei Kimiko, "*Tametada-kyō ki* 21," p. 6.

31. Reizei Kimiko, "*Tametada-kyō ki* 9," p. 6.

32. Reizei Kimiko, "*Tametada-kyō ki* 2," p. 6.

33. Reizei Kimiko, "Bakumatsu no Reizei-ke," pp. 276–77; and Matsuda, "Reizei-ke no keishitachi," p. 2.

other, lesser court families.[34] There were two stewards (*zasshō*), it seems, from the Kondō and Taira Shimizu families, while another man, of the Nakagawa house, is described as a clerk (*yōnin*). All of these were hereditary positions given to low-ranking men who did much of the day-to-day administrative work of the house and who stood in for the master of the house at certain ceremonies. Yet the expectation was that they would also be involved in the world of poetry, as disciples, first of all, but also as clerks, copyists, and librarians.[35]

This is in fact one of the things that emerges most unequivocally in Tametada's record: that everything in the house — or at least everything that he felt it appropriate to record — had to do with composition or teaching or rituals dedicated to memorializing ancestors and the Way. Tametada was a courtier, of course, who was obliged to do his rounds of attendance at the imperial court.[36] Yet in an era when the court had virtually no real role in governance, such duties were formalities; his real energy went into poetic activities. For instance, every year on the 1st day of the month, in the evening, Tametada had all the portraits of past heads of the house taken down from the second floor of the *obunko* for display in the Great Hall, where incense and flower offerings were made before the assembled household. This was a religious service, essentially; as Kimiko notes, the portraits were felt to embody the spirits of the departed. As noted before, the family had been commissioning portraits for this purpose since the time of Tamemura, at least. Tametada himself commissioned a painter of the Tosa school to do a portrait of Tamenori, which then joined the rest in memorial serves.[37]

Such events literally filled much of the family calendar. Any remaining time went to poetic duties, some private, some more public. His primary personal obligation, of course, was the instruction of his own son, Tamemoto (1855–1905). This began very early in the boy's life, when he was five years old, and involved not only poetry composition but also the study (and memorization) of classic texts, be-

---

34. The Toyooka, Kitanokōji, and Yamashina. Reizei Kimiko, "*Tametada-kyō ki 2*," p. 6.

35. Reizei Kimiko, "*Tametada-kyō ki 5*," p. 6. See also Reizei Kimiko, "*Tametada-kyō ki 9*," p. 6.

36. Reizei Kimiko, "*Tametada-kyō ki 3*," p. 6.

37. Reizei Kimiko, "*Tametada-kyō ki 17*," p. 6.

ginning with *Hyakunin isshu*, and training in calligraphy.[38] Other noble students (and we know from the diary that after his father's death, sons of the Kanroji, Sonoike, Yamashina, Mibu, and Takatsukasa families, as well as the daughters of the Takatsukasa and Kujō lineages, were almost immediately lining up to become disciples[39]) were catechized in the same way. Commoner disciples—and he had many, particularly in Edo and closer by in Naniwa—were instructed according to similar patterns, although in separate gatherings. Mixing the classes would not do.[40]

Being still relatively young and inexperienced when his father died, in the beginning Tametada asked for the assistance of the Asukai house for direction in his poetic duties.[41] But within a few years he was functioning on his own. Needless to say, he also composed poetry himself, on a daily basis. By the end of his life, he had accumulated 36 volumes of his poems, beginning with the year 1858 and ending in 1883. In any given year he generally recorded more than 2,000 poems, and that includes only the ones he saved. All 36 volumes are currently in the Reizei library, as yet unpublished in any form.[42]

In the more public arena, Tametada of course provided various poetic services for the emperor, involving everything from providing topics for gatherings to acting as officiator at them. In addition, though, he had other, less obvious obligations, such as those associated with his appointment as the liaison officer (*tensō*) of the Niitamatsushima Shrine. Originally founded by Fujiwara no Shunzei centuries before, this small shrine was dedicated to the god of Tamatsushima Shrine in Kii Province, one of the patron deities of poets. In the 1600s, the *jige* poet Kitamura Kigin had been the caretaker of the shrine. Since then, it had fallen into disrepair and had been restored several times. Most recently, it had been destroyed in the fire of 1788, after which it was rebuilt by Emperor Kōmei (1831–66; r. 1846–66), who appointed Tametada as *tensō*. On the 13th day of every month, Tametada composed a votive sequence for the shrine, and held a festival on that day in the Eleventh Month every year.

---

38. Reizei Kimiko, *"Tametada-kyō ki 27,"* p. 6.

39. Reizei Kimiko, *"Tametada-kyō ki 6,"* p. 8.

40. Reizei Kimiko, *"Tametada-kyō ki 6,"* p. 8; Reizei Kimiko, *"Tametada-kyō ki 7,"* p. 6.

41. Reizei Kimiko, *"Tametada-kyō ki 6,"* p. 8.

42. Reizei Kimiko, *"Tametada-kyō ki 5,"* p. 6.

For his duties, he received a small yet not insignificant annuity. Like most courtiers, he depended heavily on such supplementary incomes to augment a rather meager yearly stipend. Nearly all duties associated with the imperial house could be turned to a profit in one way or another.[43]

Family tradition says that Tametada, sobered by the example of his father, never touched alcohol, and that he demanded the same of his son.[44] He seems to have been an energetic and multitalented man who enjoyed his position as head of a noble house. In addition to composing poetry, he also painted, dabbled in the tea ceremony, and practiced both the Teika and Tameie styles of calligraphy—acting thoroughly the part of the *bunjin*, or literatus.[45] That he was able to indulge himself in these ways is itself an indication of relative prosperity. As one scholar argues, by Tametada's time the court families "functioned as the highest expression of *iemoto*, the hierarchical, hereditary, and house-centered pattern of secret tradition and transmission of skills" that was at the very heart of traditional education in virtually all arts and fields of learning.[46] Evidently Tametada was comfortable with his role as the leader of an artistic Way that was still considered first among all the courtly arts, despite the flourishing of poetry in various forms—*uta* and *haikai*—among *jige* poets operating beyond the reach of noble authority.

Tametada's priorities are made clear in what he says about himself in a record of another fire, in 1854. This was the worst fire to hit the city since 1788. It burned the imperial palace, the palace of the retired emperor, and the mansions of the Ichijō, Imadegawa, Hino, Karasumaru, Kajūji, Daigo, and Saionji families—all within Courtiers' Quarter. The Reizei house, however, was spared, to Tametada's great relief: "That the palace has been burned down is an awful turn of events, of course, but I can't help weeping tears of

---

43. Reizei Tamehito and Sugimoto, "Edo saigo no tōshū, Tametada," pp. 153–54, explain that when Emperor Meiji ascended the throne, Tametada was appointed one of three "commissioners" (*bugyō*) to provide him with a new set of personal effects, which included, among other things, standing screens adorned with paintings. As was the custom, he had paintings made up for himself at the same time—at no cost.

44. Reizei Kimiko, "Kindai no hito," pp. 2–3.

45. For a discussion of Tametada's talents as a painter, see Reizei Tamehito, "Fude no nishiki."

46. Marius Jansen, *The Making of Modern Japan*, p. 161.

gratitude to know that my house has escaped, thanks to the mercy of Kannon."[47]

The library had survived the fires of the Ōnin War, the Great Fire of 1788, countless other smaller fires, and now another conflagration that had destroyed many of the treasures of imperial and court culture. Properly vigilant, Tametada had arranged to send his family and his most precious manuscripts to Kaimyōji Temple before running off to attend the Emperor Kōmei in his flight from the city.[48]

EIGHT MONTHS after the fire, the imperial palace had been rebuilt, just as it had been a few decades earlier.[49] Following precedent, Tametada was asked, along with members of the Asukai house, to suggest topics for poems for *shikishi* to adorn the sliding panels in the imperial living quarters, and to present poems himself.[50] Rather than on a panel in the Seiryōden, one of his poems appeared next to a painting of Tagamigawa in the emperor's daytime quarters (*kogosho*):

> In cold moonlight   I gaze up—and hear
> plovers   crying as they pass
> over Tagami River   in the faintly
> dawnlit sky.[51]
>
> *tsuki samuku / mireba chidori no / nakiwataru / tagamigawa no / ariake no sora*

In recognition of his service in the rebuilding of the palace, Tametada—still a captain in the Gate Guards—was allowed the rare privilege of attending at court in the sort of formal robes that were usually reserved for those above the office of middle counselor.[52] In other ways too, he was scrupulous as a court official, taking his turn at attendance in the imperial chambers and living up to all his other official obligations, from those associated with his formal offices to ad hoc appointments.

One of his most important appointments came in 1859, when he was called for an interview with the current liaison officer and was appointed imperial messenger for the festival of Nikkō Shrine—funeral shrine of the ruling Tokugawa clan in the East Country—which was

---

47. Reizei Kimiko, "Bakumatsu no Reizei-ke," p. 304.
48. Ibid., pp. 304–05.
49. Takinami, "Shōshi: Kyōto gosho," p. 226.
50. Ogura, "Reizei-ke no rekishi 28: Tametada I," p. 4.
51. Ibid.
52. Ibid.

to be held midway through the Fourth Month. No doubt the prospect excited him greatly, not least because it would give him an opportunity to join a long line of poets in going out on the road and later writing about it in a diary. Many poets, nobles and commoners alike, had penned such works in the past; it was only natural that he should want to do the same. Since the journey was a formal affair, however, it involved a large group of attendants, guards, and bearers—even a physician and his staff—and was in this sense rather unlike the medieval sojourns that he had read about.[53] His record, too, is much more detailed and "realistic" in its descriptions than were the travel records of medieval monks or even those of his ancestor Tamemura, who had left a record of one of his trips to Edo on an imperial errand many decades before.[54]

As a court official, he and his three stewards traveled by palanquin, accompanied by 30 men on horseback and 50 on foot. Surrounded by onlookers, the entourage left on the 1st day of the Fourth Month. On the way east, the group took not the more popular coastal road but the Nakasendō, the mountain route to their destination, which passed through Mino, Shinano, Kōzuke, and on to Ueno and Nikkō. While stopping at inns along the road, he was often greeted by local disciples or approached by suitors, much like Matsuo Bashō (1644–94) had been on the journey made famous by his *Oku no hosomichi*. Usually, the disciples brought gifts, in return for which participation in a poetry meeting was expected. Before leaving Kyoto, he had prepared boxes of gifts himself—mounted poems (*shikishi*) and poem strips (*tanzaku*)—to dispense to well-wishers.[55] In this sense, the journey was a way to propound the family Way, even to gain new disciples—a working tour.[56] One result was that the journey was wearing, as he quipped in a poem:

> With no time to rest   night after night
> after night,   it is at inns
> and not out on the road   that I learn the pains
> of travel.[57]

nuru hima no/yona yona nakuba/michi yori mo/yadori ni tabi no/uki o shirinuru

---

53. Reizei Kimiko, "Ōtsu made," p. 1.
54. See Carter, "Travel as Poetic Practice."
55. Reizei Kimiko, "*Tametada-kyō ki 23*," p. 6.
56. Reizei Kimiko, "*Tametada-kyō ki 35*," p. 6.
57. Reizei Kimiko, "*Tametada-kyō Nikkō gekōki 9*, Kutsukake made," p. 2.

This is not to suggest, however, that he found no pleasures along the way. He did, for instance, occasionally stop to get a taste of local varieties of tea. At Shimosuwa, after exhausting himself climbing to a vantage point with a good view of Mt. Fuji, he even caught a few hours to enjoy the waters of a local hot spring.[58] He also enjoyed the scenery, his reactions to which he dutifully recorded in both prose accounts and poems:

The Kiso area was no different from what I had heard. Damson blooms both red and white, cherry blossoms, globeflowers, wisteria, camellia, pear, red and white peach, azalea, mustard flower—all were in their glory at the same time.

I heard warblers, pheasants, and larks, and also saw them frolicking beneath the cherry blossoms and young leaves. A most unusual sight.

The degree of cold in Kiso must depend on the year. This year it is about the same as what is usual in Kyoto in the Fourth Month. In the daytime, I am using my fan, but here and there it is a little chilly.

Today must be the real height of the blossom season.

> Cherries, damson,   wisteria
> and globeflower—   all in their glory.
> Truly summer in Kiso   is a rich
> brocade.[59]
>
> *sakura momo/fuji yamabuki mo/hanasakari/kisoji no natsu wa/nishiki narikeri*

Even on an official errand, Tametada was still a poet conscious of his heritage. Any list of places famous in the court tradition included Kiso, making it a virtual requirement for the head of the Reizei house to record his impression of the place in poetry. While his account departs from ancient standards in the way it includes much about the day-to-day experience of travel, it is well within the traditions of the past in the place it gives to poems.

Tametada arrived at Jōdō-in Temple, near Nikkō, on the 15th day of the Fourth Month of 1859, after two exhausting weeks on the road. The next several days were given over to various rites associated with the festival, during which he represented the emperor and his court, without incident, it would appear, thanks to the initiation he had received in the appropriate rituals from the Shirakawa house

---

58. Reizei Kimiko, "*Tametada-kyō Nikkō gekōki 8*, Shiojiri kara Wada e," p. 2.

59. Reizei Kimiko, "*Tametada-kyō Nikkō gekōki 6*, Nezame no Sato, Kiso no san," p. 1.

back in Kyoto before departing on his journey.[60] The day began with a long procession of more than 40 men arriving at the ornamental gate (*torii*) of the shrine. There Tametada got out of his carriage and began the process of paying his respects at various sites, the particulars of which he records in some detail, no doubt as a favor to any of his progeny who might be called upon to perform the same offices in the future.[61]

True to the pattern of things along the way, at least one man—identified as the former Major Archbishop of Nikkōzan Shugaku-in—came asking to be accepted as a disciple while Tametada was still at Nikkō. On the 17th, though, Tametada was off again, headed toward Edo, to pay his respects at the shogunal offices. One night he stopped at Mibu station, where two disciples waited to greet him, with two more men wanting to take the oath; the next day, he arrived in the shogun's city, with the intent of passing through rather quickly. Stopping at Asakusa, however, proved a mistake: he and his cohorts enjoyed the sights there so much, and got so taken up with buying gifts to take home, that they stayed longer than expected. It was late afternoon when the procession arrived at Shinagawa. Still, though, there was no rest. Fifteen disciples were at his inn awaiting his arrival. That night, he presided at a poetry meeting, and afterwards several disciples kept him up with questions.[62]

Early in the morning, on the 20th day of the Fourth Month, Tametada set off down the Tōkaidō toward home. At the time, he was only miles away from Kamakura, where Abutsu and Tamesuke, founders of the Reizei lineage, had lived centuries before. Yet he did not visit, evidently because he had been forbidden to do so by government authorities, who insisted that such private concerns had no place when he was on imperial business. Visits from disciples were one thing; going out of one's way to travel to a site that had no connection whatsoever to the errand at hand was evidently another. In his diary, Tametada recorded his frustration: "What a disappointment it is that I am not able to pay my respects in person. Will I ever have another occasion to visit the East Country?"[63] But

---

60. Reizei Kimiko, "*Tametada-kyō Nikkō gekōki 1*, Tabi no shitaku kara shuttatsu made," p. 3.

61. Reizei Kimiko, "*Tametada-kyō ki 30*," p. 6.

62. Reizei Kimiko, "*Tametada-kyō ki 31*," p. 6.

63. Reizei Kimiko, "*Tametada-kyō ki 32*," p. 6.

there was nothing he could do but send money and some incense to the temple where Tamesuke's gravemarker stood—Jōkōmyōji—for a memorial service. He also sent a poem:

> From the foothills   of Kamakura's
> mountains   that I cannot visit
> I look back in reverence   toward grave markers
> grown old.[64]

mōde senu / kamakurayama no / fumoto yori / ato mo harubaru / augu furutsuka

The return trip, though on a different road, was similar in every other way to the trip there: long days on the road, short nights at inns, where disciples usually gathered to greet him. There were exchanges of gifts, oaths, and endless bowls of tea. Near the Katsura Detached Palace, just east of Kyoto, his son Tamemoto was waiting for him, with news that all was well at home. The two arrived in Kyoto on the 1st day of the Fifth Month. Immediately, he went to pay his respects to the *buke tensō*, the governor general, the emperor, the retired emperor, the regent, and his noble patrons of the Takatsukasa house. Even after this, however, there was no rest, for the 2nd day of the Fifth Month was by tradition a day set aside for celebrating the gods of the *obunko*. As Kimiko says after reading the passages of the diary that describe the rites exhaustively, her great-great-grandfather was *mattaku isogashii*—as busy as ever.[65] Just a few months later, he would petition to fill a vacancy at court among the middle counselors, winning after a short lobbying campaign in which he defeated four competitors.[66] Since he had only served as a consultant for two years, appointment to counselor status was a high honor. Teika, as he well knew, had had to wait nearly 20 years for the same promotion.

ALTHOUGH THERE is no hint of it in Tametada's travel record, any student of Japanese history knows that the mid-nineteenth century was a time of momentous change, beginning with foreign ships trespassing in Japanese waters and ending in a series of treaties that opened the country to commerce with the outside world of a sort that had not been allowed for two centuries. Of course such changes

---

64. Ibid.
65. Reizei Kimiko, "*Tametada-kyō ki 35*," p. 6.
66. Reizei Kimiko, "*Tametada-kyō ki 36*," p. 6.

were accompanied by debate, controversy, and some bloodshed. Emperor Kōmei, as might be expected, argued against opening the Land of the Gods to foreign barbarians, no matter what the cost.[67] Most courtiers agreed with their sovereign, as they were bound to do, but some felt that to resist what seemed inevitable given what was happening elsewhere in Asia would be folly in the long term; others, particularly those of lesser rank, simply fretted and waited for events to decide the matter. In March of 1860, not a full year since Tametada's return from the East Country, one of the major political players in the maneuvering of the time—a daimyo named Ii Naosuke (1815–60) of the Hikone Domain, not far from Kyoto—was assassinated outside one of the gates of Edo Castle by those who opposed his decision to sign an important commercial treaty with the United States. Such acts of violence left many wondering what the future would bring.

Unfortunately, Reizei Kimiko's study of Tametada's diary takes us only to 1863. She makes it clear, however, that Tametada says relatively little about political matters outside the court itself. As one might expect, he seems to have been a royalist, whose natural instinct was to preserve the imperial institution at all costs and to keep the doors closed against the Western barbarians—a firm believer in the slogan *sonnō jōi*, "Honor the Emperor and Expel the Barbarians!"[68] Yet in his position he could be little but a bystander in political affairs. Although a few courtiers would play a role in coming events, for the most part power was in the hands of the samurai class, from whom leadership for the new nation would come.

Nevertheless, political events did have a direct impact on his life, even on the practice of poetry. Since 1853, for example, after the arrival of Commodore Perry's Black Ships, monthly poetry meetings (*tsukinamikai*) at the imperial palace had been discontinued on the grounds that such activities had no place in a time of national crisis, and they had never been reinstated. Formal poetry meetings, on the other hand, were still held, since they were an important part of court ritual, as were meetings of a votive (*hōraku*) nature, which were offered to religious establishments as prayers.[69] The feeling of crisis was thus accompanied by an attitude of retrenchment, which in some ways seemed effective. Another important event of 1860, for example,

---

67. Keene, *Emperor of Japan*, pp. 7–8.
68. Reizei Kimiko, "*Tametada-kyō ki 22*," p. 6.
69. Reizei Kimiko, "*Tametada-kyō ki 15*," p. 6.

was the arrival of a box from the governor general confirming the estate rights of the family, as was always the case when a new shogun—this one was named Iemochi (1846–66)—took office.[70] Such reinforcements helped to strengthen the resolve of the Kyoto nobility to persevere. They had all read the annals, which taught that they had weathered political storms in the past; there was no reason to believe they would not do so again.

Tametada's priorities are immediately apparent in his diary for the year 1860, which records in detail two important family events: the coming-of-age ceremony of his now six-year-old son, which took place in the Ninth Month of that year; and a high point in his own life— his invitation, by the reigning emperor, to receive the secret teachings on *Kokinshū* in the Eleventh Month. As in previous generations, the reception had been reduced to a rite; not a true "transmission" from teacher to student but the ritual opening of a box containing the teachings (*kaiken denju*). In the case of the Reizei, the box was in the family library, a treasure box since the time of Go-Mizuno'o that evidently no one could open without explicit permission of the emperor.

Tametada's diary gives us one of the most complete accounts of how the ritual—founded on ancient precedents, one must believe— was performed, at least in the Reizei house. On the 25th day of the Fourth Month, a messenger from the palace came with a summons for Tametada's attendance in the imperial chambers. Tametada immediately went and was told by the sovereign himself that because of his "constant endeavors in the Way of Poetry" the time had come for him to open the box containing the sacred teachings on *Kokinshū*. At first the poet demurred, as was only polite, saying that he was not worthy of the honor, that since there were others now who had received the teachings there was no need to rush, and so forth. But doubtless this was posturing. In the end, after several more shows of modesty, he gave in and agreed and quickly hurried round to offer his thanks to his patrons, including the current regent, the Takatsukasa, and the other major poetic houses—the Sanjōnishi, the Karasumaru, and the Asukai.[71]

The date decided upon for the event was the 18th day of the Eleventh Month. The Great Hall of the house on Imadegawa was pre-

---

70. Reizei Kimiko, "*Tametada-kyō ki 47*," p. 6. The shogun had taken office in 1858.

71. Reizei Kimiko, "*Tametada-kyō ki 39*," p. 6

pared. Shintō priests came to purify the site on the 16th. On the 18th, Tametada, having abstained from sexual contact since the night before and having in other ways purified himself, awoke before dawn, groomed himself, did ablutions, donned formal robes, and then with Tamemoto in tow, went into the Great Hall—alone, it would seem—to view the contents of the box. In the alcove, a painting of Kakinomoto no Hitomaro attributed to Fujiwara no Nobuzane was hung,[72] with a portrait of his grandfather, Tamenori, suspended from a standing screen. After doing obeisance to each of these, he opened the box and viewed its contents. To conclude, he invited Tamemoto in for a brief repast of food and rice wine. After that it remained only for father and son to climb into an old-style carriage, accompanied by two outriders, two samurai guards, and a few servants, and offer their thanks to the usual list of high officials and shrines. That night, a banquet was held at the house and several days later a large poetry meeting was held, with 21 disciples from among the nobility in attendance. The pattern followed was thus the usual one for noble events: private ceremony, public spectacle (although only a modest one in this case), and private celebration.[73]

While the Reizei were preoccupied with such ritual concerns, the country around them was in turmoil over constant pressure from outside its own shores and over conflict among leaders concerning how best to respond. It goes without saying that most of the old families steadfastly opposed the notion of opening the country to the Western barbarians, as well as any fundamental change in government that would endanger their sinecures. Early on, some argued for consolidation of the imperial and shogunal governments (*kōbu gattai*) through intermarriage, which was partially accomplished in 1862. However, as more and more daimyo lost patience with the shogunate's inability to do anything consequential about the foreign threat, its future seemed in jeopardy. In 1862, this inspired several courtiers to cooperate with a group of daimyo to make certain demands against the shogunate that would cede more power to their own coalition.[74]

Early the next year, several acts of violence against courtiers—duly noted by Reizei Tametada in his diary—shocked the people of Kyoto and must have made those conniving in politics think twice about the

---

72. *Kyō no miyabi, uta no kokoro: Reizei-ke no shihōten*, p. 166.
73. Reizei Kimiko, "*Tametada-kyō ki 39*," p. 6.
74. Beasley, *The Meiji Restoration*, pp. 179–84.

wisdom of their acts. The first took place in the Second Month of the year, when a steward of Chigusa Arifumi (1815–69) was captured, carved up, and, along with threatening letters, sent in pieces to various members of Arifumi's "consolidation" faction—the head to one, one arm to another, another arm to another. Following this, another man, a Confucian scholar with close connections to a court faction, was murdered in Osaka, his ears sent to two court officials, who promptly resigned their posts. The third act was somewhat less grisly: this time it was wooden statues of three of the Ashikaga shoguns on display at Tōji-in that were beheaded and then stuck on pikes in the Kamo River bed—obviously a threat aimed at the current shogun. The final event was perhaps more frightening than all the rest, because it involved the murder of a courtier, the young Anega-kōji Kintomo (1839–63), a staunch royalist who had been greatly involved in recent political affairs, serving among other things as an imperial envoy to the shogunate. When he too was assassinated, on his way back to his house on the night of the 20th day of the Fifth Month of 1863, courtiers realized that such activities involved great risks. Kintomo's killers, or at least those strongly suspected of being so, were captured and dealt with. The dead courtier was elevated to the office of consultant and senior second rank, posthumously.[75]

Ironically, then, the imperial court, which had been denied any substantive role in government for more than three centuries, would have a more pivotal part to play in the events leading up to what we know as the Meiji Restoration. Since the early 1850s, the shogunate had itself approached the court for counsel on matters of national defense, and now it had to obey precedent, however much doing so complicated the process of developing and carrying out policy.[76] One result was renewed interest in the imperial institution, which to many seemed to offer an alternative to Tokugawa authority. As the shogunate lost the allegiance of some daimyo, those same daimyo began to build houses in Kyoto, especially after suspension of the old *sankin kōtai* rule of attendance on the shogun in Edo.[77] One source describes the influx of military men as astonishing:

---

75. Reizei Kimiko, "*Tametada-kyō ki 72*," p. 6. See also Keene, *Emperor of Japan*, pp. 67–68.

76. Keene, *Emperor of Japan*, p. 36.

77. Beasley, *The Meiji Restoration*, pp. 182–83. The old rule had dictated that daimyo spend six months of every year in Edo. After October 1862, the pe-

The prestige of the Court had become so great that every daimyo tried to obtain an official residence in the capital. . . . All the . . . clans, both great and small, and even the *hatamoto*, cleared land both within and without the city, to the number of more than a hundred, and erected mansions for themselves. As all these places were filled with troops, the town assumed a very busy and flourishing aspect. Shops were opened everywhere, and the whole population down to the lowest classes began to get rich.[78]

Even allowing for some exaggeration, it is clear from such descriptions that by the mid-1860s, Kyoto was once again a bustling place. Daimyo residences brought with them large contingents of samurai and servants, as well as horses, pack animals, and other kinds of transport. Soon the streets were athrob with activity.

As a way to legitimate their various claims to leadership in the newly developing order, the military aristocracy often turned to the old nobility, who were old hands at behind-the-scenes plotting and conniving. It was in this way, for instance, that a young gentleman-in-waiting (*jijū*) of junior fourth rank named Nakayama Tadamitsu (1845–64) who also happened to be the brother of Emperor Kōmei's consort, Yoshiko (1835–1907), and thus uncle of the Crown Prince, became the nominal leader of a coup attempt in the summer of 1863, known as the Tenchūgumi no Ran.[79] Although the conspirators succeeded in taking the shogunal offices at Fifth Avenue and killing the chief shogunal officer (the *daikan*) there, forces loyal to the military government put the rebellion down swiftly, and without major damage to the city. Still the perilous days were not over. In the summer of the following year, zealots of the Chōshū domain succeeded in attacking the imperial palace, intending to force the emperor to call for immediate expulsion of all foreigners. They came close to seizing the emperor, and the fires they set destroyed 28,000 buildings in the capital before troops of the shogunate could stop them.[80]

Despite the success of the Tokugawa government in putting down these uprisings, the fact was that old opponents of the Tokugawa

---

riod was reduced to 100 days in every three years. Various restrictions on travel to and residence in Kyoto were also relaxed around this time.

78. The source is *Ganji Yume monogatari*, quoted in Ponsonby-Fane, *Kyoto: The Old Capital of Japan*, p. 384.

79. Tadamitsu was the son of Nakayama Tadayasu (1809–88), a major counselor in the imperial government. After the failed coup attempt, he fled the capital but was assassinated the next year.

80. Keene, *Emperor of Japan*, pp. 80–82.

were gaining strength. Thus the stage was set for further armed conflict, perhaps again within the streets of the old imperial city. Once again, as at so many times in the past, the imperial standard became a rallying point. Members of the Konoe, Kujō, Sanjō, Takatsukasa, Nakayama, and Iwakura lines in particular were involved in the political infighting that would go on for the next four years. As in ancient times, the basis for the noble–daimyo affiliations was often marriage — this time between noble houses and daimyo — but more was at stake than the fate of a few heirs.

IN THE end, three events proved crucial in forcing the hand of the government. First came the shelling of Shimonoseki by warships from America, France, England, and Holland in 1864, which made it clear that the pressure to open the country would never cease and that Japanese defenses could not stand against foreign firepower. Then came the death of the frustrated shogun Tokugawa Iemochi, in August 1866, at the age of 20, followed just five months later by the death of Emperor Kōmei, also a young man at 35. The shogun had threatened to resign several years earlier and had already lost much of his effectiveness. But Kōmei was still a vital player in the politics of the time and his death came as a shock. The official cause of death was announced as smallpox, but records do more than hint that he was in fact poisoned. Certainly there were many around him who felt that his obstinacy on the issue of relations with foreign powers was making progress toward resolution of the national problems impossible. In the charged atmosphere of the time, his death may have seemed a practical necessity. In any case, 1867 became a year of mourning, as young crown prince Mutsuhito (later Emperor Meiji; 1852–1912; r. 1867–1912) prepared for his coronation as 122nd emperor of Japan. Although he, too, favored expelling the barbarians, so young a man of course had little influence. It would be those around him, nobles and samurai, who would wield power from now on.

Finally, in 1867, the new shogun, Tokugawa Yoshinobu (1837–1913), who had only been in office a year or so, resigned under pressure from within and without. For years, even before his appointment as shogun, Yoshinobu and his advisors had tried to placate the royalists and still live up to treaty commitments, but without success. In effect, he was forced to leave office because of a vote of no confidence. To make it clear that there could be no appointment of a new shogun, troops under the standard of the Satsuma domain surrounded the

imperial palace in Kyoto in the First Month of 1868, obtained an im-
perial edict that did away with all existing offices, and set up a coun-
cil of imperial princes, announcing an "imperial restoration" (*ōsei
fukko*). Rather than accept defeat readily, the remnants of the Toku-
gawa government at first made ready to fight. Yoshinobu and those
loyal to him tried in various ways to turn events in their favor. Even-
tually, they barricaded themselves in Edo and awaited attack by an
imperial army led by a prince of the Arisugawa lineage, the first time
that an imperial figure had been involved in warfare since late me-
dieval times. Seeing that there was no hope for triumph, however, the
Tokugawa forces capitulated, and Edo was spared destruction of the
sort Kyoto had known so many times. Some pro-shogunate forces
still held out in the north, but by June of 1869 that part of the conflict
was over. In a sense, the hopes of many courtiers had been fulfilled.
Iwakura Tomomi (1825–83), imperial chamberlain and one of the chief
architects of the new order, was unequivocal on the issue, even sev-
eral years before the "restoration" finally took place: "For the country
to be united, policy and administration must have a single source.
And for policy and administration to have a single source, the Court
must be made the center of the national government. Thus may the
will of the gods and the wishes of the people be observed."[81]

In this spirit, a new government was formed, made up of samurai
and some court nobles. The Imperial Restoration had begun. How-
ever, rather than destroy their former enemies, as might have been
expected, the new government almost immediately pardoned Yoshi-
nobu and the men around him. They were talented men of great
experience whose efforts would be needed in the great challenges
that lay ahead for the new Japanese nation.[82]

THROUGH ALL these years the Reizei were of course involved in the
endless conversations that went on at court about how to respond
to events. When Takatsukasa Sukehiro (1807–78) was serving as re-
gent, the entire Reizei entourage was more involved in court politics,
as stewards of that regental line.[83] But Sukehiro's tenure was very

---

81. Quoted in Beasley, *The Meiji Restoration*, p. 261.
82. Ibid., p. 299.
83. Reizei Kimiko, "*Tametada-kyō ki 59*," p. 6; Reizei Kimiko, "*Tametada-kyō
ki 60*," p. 6. Takatsukasa Masamichi (1789–1868) served as regent from 1823–56
and his son Sukehiro from 1863–64.

short, and Tametada seems to have avoided trouble. When it was over, the poetry master returned to his normal position as a counselor in the court ranks.

Yet as a counselor he was witness to many events. He was in the imperial chambers, for instance, when shogun Tokugawa Iemochi came to Kyoto with an army of 3,000 retainers — the first time a shogun had visited the city in 230 years — to try to win allies for consolidation in the Third Month of 1863.[84] Tametada merely watched from the wings, however, and remained aloof from direct involvement. When a shogunal messenger visited the Reizei house on Imadegawa with gifts from Iemochi, he was not greeted warmly. Rather than meeting with the man personally, Tametada sent out one of his stewards, without even preparing the room with good ashtrays, the diary says.[85] Partly this was no doubt a way of insisting that imperial rank put him above any shogunal representative, but politics was involved as well. Along with everyone else, the head of the Reizei lineage was grateful to the shogun for a substantial gift of cash that came to the court families after the shogun's visit,[86] but that was not enough to buy his goodwill. By the fall of 1863, anyone with eyes could see that the future of the shogunate, at least in its current form, was in jeopardy. When Tametada was dispatched to convey the condolences of the court to the governor general upon Iemochi's death in 1866, he can only have wondered about what the future would bring.[87]

More important at this time to Tametada, in any case, were private matters such as the marriage of one of his daughters, which he describes in some detail, ending with the usual celebratory visits to the *buke tensō* and the Takatsukasa.[88] He was in attendance upon Emperor Kōmei, however, when the latter made trips to the Kamo shrines in the late spring of 1863, to offer prayers for the nation, with the shogun in tow.[89] He was also there when the emperor visited Iwashimizu Shrine a short time later, this time without the shogun, who had pleaded illness but who was probably actually fearful of

---

84. Reizei Kimiko, "*Tametada-kyō ki 63*," p. 6; Reizei Kimiko, "*Tametada-kyō ki 64*," p. 6.
85. Reizei Kimiko, "*Tametada-kyō ki 64*," p. 6.
86. Reizei Kimiko, "*Tametada-kyō ki 76*," p. 6.
87. Ogura, "Reizei-ke no rekishi 27: Tametake," p. 5.
88. Reizei Kimiko, "*Tametada-kyō ki 65*," p. 6.
89. Reizei Kimiko, "*Tametada-kyō ki 66*," p. 6.

an assassination attempt.[90] Over the next five years, until a conclusion to all the conflicts was reached, this was the pattern of Tametada's life. Private life continued on, almost unchanged, while public issues worked themselves out. A number of courtiers, including members of the Konoe and Takatsukasa regental lines, became greatly involved in politics at the time, occasionally ending up under censure. Nothing so severe happened to anyone in the Reizei house, whose dedication was still to poetry.

Tametada was, however, greatly honored to serve as a herald at the enthronement ceremonies of the new emperor, known as Meiji, which took place in the Eighth Month of 1868. In many ways, the rites were rather different from those of previous ages, which powerful men such as Iwakura Tomomi considered to be antiquated and sullied by Chinese influence. But still there was much pomp, and Tametada was part of it. After the emperor was seated in his throne chamber in the Hall of State of the imperial palace, it was Tametada who read the official proclamation of the imperial succession, as well as prayers for his reign. He can only have been greatly gratified, too, that the new leaders had decided that traditional poetry should remain very much a part of imperial culture. A Japanese poem was read aloud as part of the ceremonies. Later, at the first formal poetry gathering of the new emperor's reign, Tametada would serve as an officiator. As crown prince the young emperor had already been studying poetry for some years, under the guidance of Tametada and others. He would compose 100,000 poems in his lifetime.[91]

The new emperor showed signs of intelligence and ambition, but it was mostly the new leaders around him who made the decisions. Almost immediately, it became clear that the idea of "expelling the barbarians" anytime soon was delusional. The new leaders realized that it was *their* survival and not the survival of their overseas competitors that was at stake. Once they had lifted the burden of the old shogunal administration from their backs, they quickly set about creating policies and institutions that would serve their cause of "strengthening the nation" for competition with the imperialist powers of the West. Rather than looking to their own past, or even to China, the new lead-

---

90. Reizei Kimiko, "*Tametada-kyō ki 70*," p. 6. See also Keene, *Emperor of Japan*, pp. 71–72.

91. Ogura, "Reizei-ke no rekishi 29: Tametada II," p. 4; Keene, *Emperor of Japan*, pp. 36, 157–59.

ers looked to Europe for models and ended up creating a modern nobility on the foundation of the old—including the imperial family, *kuge*, and daimyo. In 1869, four new designations were adopted: *kō-zoku* (the imperial family), *kazoku* (the nobility), *shizoku* (former samurai), and *heimin* (commoners). Old titles were dispensed with and more than 400 court families and daimyo were merged into one noble class, with stipends still coming from the government. Some were appointed to offices in the government or in government-controlled institutions, and all were ordered to reside in Tokyo, the new seat of government, where the emperor would dwell in a huge new palace constructed within the grounds of the old shogunal compound.

The reason for relocation to Tokyo, which was first represented as a mere procession but which finally became a true removal, was explicitly political: no longer would the emperor dwell apart from other government institutions. His residence would by contrast be in the very heart of the city that was already the center of finance, commerce, and government for the nation, albeit still separated from the public by four miles of moats and walls that symbolized his sacred status within the body politic. Fortuitously, a series of fires had destroyed many of the shogunal structures that had occupied the huge compound in the 1860s. New buildings, for both the emperor and his attendants, were built to correspond with the needs of a new age. The new nobility followed, building homes not too far away. In his diary Tametada notes that imperial officials at first asked that the order to proceed to the new capital be rescinded, arguing that to go to such lengths with the future still unsettled was unwise, but their petition was denied.[92]

Thus the 200 or so houses that had made up the old Courtiers' Quarter in Kyoto simply vanished after more than two and a half centuries. The emperor left in the Third Month of 1869 and most court families followed soon after. Left behind were a few buildings here and there—the Shūsuitei, a teahouse on the west bank of the ornamental lake on the old Kujō lot, the Shirakumo Shrine on the Saionji lot, and so on. Before long, the other houses, except for the imperial palace and the palace of the retired emperor, were all torn down, the space they had occupied becoming a park called the Gyoen. The transfer of the emperor and his court to Edo, arguably the single most significant event in the history of the Kyoto nobility

---

92. Ogura, "Reizei-ke no rekishi 29: Tametada II," p. 4.

since the city's founding a millennium before, took only a few years.[93]

By 1870, then, the nobility had left Kyoto — except, that is, for a few houses, including the upper Reizei. For, almost alone among all the court families, they did not follow the emperor to the new capital in the East Country. Various explanations are given by the family, among them Tametada's strong commitment to protect the library at all costs and the claim that he was actually asked by the new emperor to remain behind as a caretaker of the Quarter.[94] One scholar adds another, more explicitly literary, reason: that the advisors of the emperor were all "progressives" who were rather critical of the old poetic houses.[95] Thus when an office of poetry (first called the *kadō goyōgakari* and later the *ōutadokoro*) was established as part of the central government in 1871, its officers were all primarily adherents of *jige* schools from Satsuma and Chōshū and not disciples of the old noble houses of Kyoto.[96] The consequences of the change were immediate: between 1862 and 1869, for instance, Tametada had been a central figure in the *utakai no hajime*, or "first imperial poetry gathering," held annually on the 24th day of the First Month of each new year; but after 1870 — when the meetings began to be held in Tokyo — he was no longer even on the guest list.[97] What was being called an "imperial restoration" was for the Reizei, at least, nothing of the sort.

As most other noble families abandoned their old lots and sought new living quarters in Tokyo, the Reizei and their comrades the Fujitani stayed behind.[98] The population of Kyoto, which had reached perhaps 1,000,000 before the move, plummeted to less than half that

---

93. Ponsonby-Fane, *Kyoto: The Old Capital of Japan*, pp. 372–82.

94. Reizei Kimiko, "*Tametada-kyō ki 1,*"p. 3; Reizei Fumiko, *Reizei Fumiko ga kataru Kyō no miyabi*, pp. 198–99.

95. Ogura, "Reizei-ke no rekishi 29: Tametada II," p. 5.

96. The first head of the office was Hatta Tomonori (1799–1873), a man from Satsuma who was a disciple of Kagawa Kageki (1768–1843), and after Hatta's death in 1873 one of his students, Takasaki Masakaze (1836–1912), took over. It was not until a decade later that a Reizei man would hold office in the bureau, and then only at a low level.

97. See Aoyagi, "Meiji shōnen no kakai no hajime."

98. Reizei Kimiko, "Yomigaetta komonjo," p. 1, says the Fujitani were there until before the Pacific War. The lower Reizei went to Tokyo along with the vast majority of noble houses (see Ueno Takeshi, "Hosokawa shō, sono ni," p. 5).

number in a few short years.[99] Artistic traditions still survived there, but increasingly it was not traditional court culture but *chōnin bunka* — the culture of merchants — that dominated the city.

Yet the Reizei still had reason to feel encouraged by recent events. The nobility had survived another threat to their ancient privileges, emerging with a financial base that seemed to insure survival. While no longer a middle counselor, Tametada was still a member of the nobility and still had a stipend confirmed at 310 *koku*.[100] All the same, however, the command to stay in Kyoto also must have been a shock for Tametada and his family. The other families would of course have to face the task of establishing life in a new city that had no experience in accommodating *kuge* ways, but the Reizei had to get used to living in what for them, with the departure of the imperial family and the nobility, must have seemed a ghost town. Nor would they be immune from changes even in Kyoto. Tametada notes in his diary, for instance, that one day in the late 1860s he discovered that his son and heir had cut his topknot and had had his hair cropped, modern style. One can only imagine the older man's feelings when, upon chiding the young man, he was told simply, "I was ordered to do so by the Regent."[101] Soon most courtiers would be putting aside their formal kimono for top hats and tails.

WRITING IN the 1990s, Reizei Fumiko said the decision to stay in Kyoto was the single greatest "accomplishment" of Tametada's life, a rather strange compliment.[102] She was right, however, if one thinks ahead to the Kantō earthquake of 1923 and the bombing raids of the Pacific War, from which it is unlikely the house and library would have emerged unscathed if the Reizei had followed the emperor to Tokyo. It is equally true that while some noble families managed to gain a place for themselves in the Meiji order, most did not. In this sense, staying in Kyoto did indeed work to the benefit of the family and its traditions in the long run. In the short term, however, one can only imagine the feelings of abandonment Tametada and his household experienced as they said goodbye to relatives, colleagues, friends, and of course many of the students who had provided much

99. Ponsonby-Fane, *Kyoto: The Old Capital of Japan*, p. 425.
100. Ogura, "Reizei-ke no rekishi 29: Tametada II," pp. 4–5.
101. Ibid., p. 5.
102. Reizei Fumiko, *Reizei Fumiko ga kataru Kyō no miyabi*, pp. 198–99.

of their income. Nearly 140 *kuge* families left the city. Only the Reizei residence remained standing, hidden away on a narrow lane in the shadow of the trees on the vacant imperial palace lot.[103]

The next two decades were tumultuous ones for the new nation of Japan. Foreigners walked the streets of Edo, while Japanese traveled to Berlin, London, Paris, and Washington, D.C. Treaties changed the face of commerce and diplomacy. The old calendar was done away with, along with many other traditions. Endless conferences and commissions studied the best ways to meet the challenges of modern statehood. Ministries were formed; laws involving everything from education to military readiness were promulgated; new institutions, including a representative assembly, were established. Public opinion was not always united on all issues, and there were some bloody days along the way, but no one can deny that the social, industrial, techno-logical, and military accomplishments of the time were remarkable.

Many changes involved the privileges of the nobility directly. In 1884, for instance, another new social system replaced the one put in place in 1869. Now the social elite — meaning the imperial family, the court nobility, daimyo, and samurai — were divided into five ranks. At the top were dukes (*kōshaku*), followed by marquis (*kōshaku*), counts (*hakushaku*), viscounts (*shishaku*), and barons (*danshaku*). In general the gradations followed ancient precedents. The heads of *go-sekke* houses were made dukes; the heads of *seigake* houses, marquis; the heads of *daijinke* and *urinke*, counts; and all other nobles, viscounts. Thus Reizei Tametada was designated a count in the new hierarchy, although in formal terms the office apparently went to his son, since Tametada was essentially in retirement. His stipend, and even his ties with old villages, remained intact, as did his employment of lower-ranking nobility as stewards and servants. The branch families were also included in the new hierarchy: the Yanagiwara as counts, the lower Reizei, the Fujitani, and the Irie all as viscounts.

In Tokyo, a number of new institutions arose to support the nobil-ity. Kazoku Kaikan, or Peers' Hall, a clubhouse of sorts, was opened there, with an imperial prince at its head. Iwakura Tomomi, its second president, put it under the jurisdiction of the Kunaishō, or Imperial Household Ministry, one of the ministries in the Council of State (*Dai-jōkan*), as a way to enunciate the role of the nobility as protectors of

---

103. Ponsonby-Fane, *Kyoto: The Old Capital of Japan*, p. 372. A list of all the families, broken down into their status categories, is found on pp. 366–72.

imperial traditions.[104] Likewise, an imperial university, Gakushū-in, established for the children of the imperial family and the nobility, opened in 1877 under the direction of Peers' Hall. Later, in 1889, the House of Peers was established by the Meiji constitution. In contradistinction to the House of Representatives, whose members were elected, members of the House of Peers were appointed from among the most capable men in the elite ranks. Since a provision allowed for the appointment of men to peerage on the basis of merit (*kunkō*), many new barons were added over time, eroding the power of the old nobility.[105] Most bearers of old names thus became men of leisure, still associated with the arts of poetry, calligraphy, music, ritual, scholarship, costume, and so forth. At first, they were supported by stipends, but these were converted to bonds in 1877.[106] Many invested in banks and markets and lost their wealth over time. Some were reduced to actually teaching their arts for a meager living, becoming something like the heads of *jige* houses, who taught the tea ceremony and popular music.[107]

Back in Kyoto, however, apparently the Reizei maintained their old ways with little difficulty. Happily for them, the old Tokudaiji lot, next door to the west, became a Peers' Hall for Kyoto, a place that boasted a billiard table but also a *kemari* court and rooms where Japanese arts from painting to tea ceremony were taught.[108] Tametada continued to act as poetry master, regardless of his official title. The house still had its old traditions to attend to, and it still had the library with its treasures. Geographical distance shielded them from political conflicts in Tokyo, which Tametada was probably beyond caring about in any case. Evidently ill much of the time, in 1875 he had turned over the family fortunes to his son, Tamemoto.[109] He must have watched with some concern, however, as the imperial palace and its precincts were allowed to fall into disrepair. A drawing of the time shows the area around the palace as open space, as if to testify directly to the absence of the old families.[110]

---

104. Lebra, *Above the Clouds*, p. 49.
105. Ibid., pp. 53–54.
106. Ibid., p. 100.
107. Ibid., p. 87.
108. Reizei Fumiko, *Reizei Fumiko ga kataru Kyō no miyabi*, p. 219–21.
109. Ogura, "Reizei-ke no rekishi 29: Tametada II," p. 5.
110. Takinami, "Shōshi: Kyōto gosho," p. 194.

The founding that same year of a new Christian college — later called Dōshisha — on the lot just to the east of the Reizei house, where the Yamashina house had stood just years before, must also have been disquieting. The barbarians, fended off for so long, had finally moved in next door. At first the school had only a few small buildings and offered only courses in English and theology, but within a decade generous donations, mostly from Americans, allowed the construction of more buildings and the addition of law and politics to the curriculum. Enrollment grew from a handful of students to several hundred. By 1895, 600 students were walking by the front gate of the Reizei house every day on their way to and from classes in everything from nursing to Latin and Greek, in tall buildings with Western names, such as Byron-Stone-Clarke Hall. By the same date, the library of the college included 16,543 volumes, many of them in foreign languages. Needless to say, all were open to the use of faculty and students, without elaborate preparation, without licensing, and without oaths of secrecy.[111] Over the years, the college would eventually buy up all the land surrounding the Reizei lot, finally acquiring the Fujitani residence in 1939. Though tempted to sell their lot several times, the Reizei continued to refuse.[112]

WHEN REIZEI Tametada breathed his last in 1885, after serving for just a year as a count in the new social order, his son Tamemoto was 30 years old and his grandson, Tametsugi (1881–1946), was just four. As dictated by the new system, Tamemoto, now head of the Reizei lineage, was advanced immediately to the title of count. Already he was serving as an official in the Imperial Household Ministry, formed back in 1869. A few years later, in 1888, he was appointed as a consultant (*sankō*) to the Poetry Bureau in that same ministry — a modest appointment, but no doubt welcome nonetheless. While those with little talent or inclination to work in administrative offices were often left to live as dilettantes, the Meiji government tried to make use of talent even among the *kuge* when it was discovered. It appears that Tamemoto was a capable man. Nor was he alone in representing the Reizei line in the new government, for his younger brother Tamemori (1868–1936) who had been adopted into the Irie clan as heir,

111. *The Official Guide-book to Kyoto and the Allied Prefectures*, pp. 209–10.
112. Tanaka Masato, "Dōshisha — Reizei-ke no tonari."

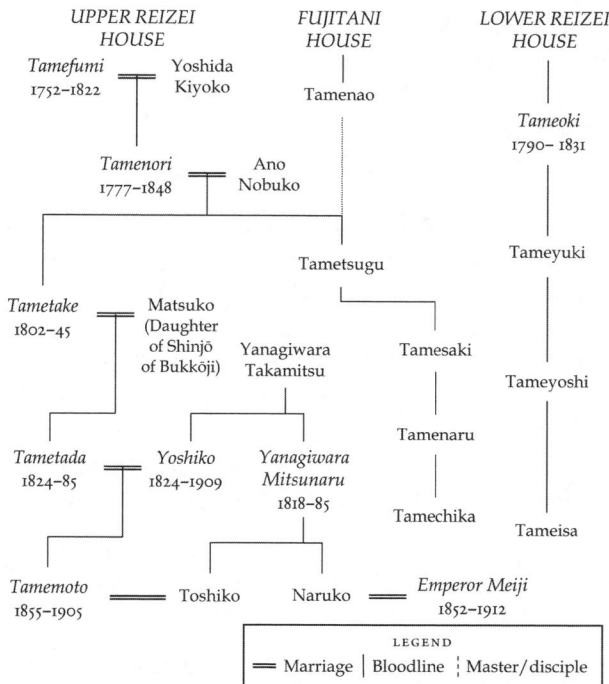

Chart 6   The Reizei Lineages in the Nineteenth Century

was also appointed to various offices, serving ultimately as Grand Chamberlain to the crown prince—a position his son, Sukemasa, would also hold during the days of the Pacific War and on into the postwar era. Even after the Restoration, the old alliances still held, at least for a time. Close ties among the upper and lower houses, the Fujitani, and the Irie have continued until the present day.

Tamemoto's mother Yoshiko (1824–1909) was from another "allied" lineage, the Yanagiwara, and the woman chosen as his wife was from the same family, the fourth daughter of Mitsunaru, named Toshiko (d. 1882). As was the custom of the day, she came to the house as a child and essentially was trained for her role as wife by Tamemoto's mother until her mid-teens. However, she died young, after giving birth to an heir, and Tamemoto spent virtually all of the rest of his life without a wife. Whether for that reason or some other, he started frequenting the Gion pleasure quarter about this time. His status as virtually the only member of the old nobility left in the city gave him a special standing in the abandoned capital, which it was in his best interest to embrace. He also appears to have been a very amiable man of diverse interests and abilities. Kimiko says he did not drink but amused himself in other ways. He was evidently a creative sort who not only wrote poems but also dabbled in painting, chanted *nō* librettos, and became a tea enthusiast and a connoisseur of various arts and crafts—a Kyoto connoisseur (*bunjin*) through and through, just as his father had been.[113]

In the Kyoto of mid-Meiji times engagement in such activities was the norm. The city, now abandoned altogether by the political elite, was obliged more and more to rely on the culture business for its survival. In 1888 the city was incorporated, with the governor of Kyoto municipality holding power, along with a city council. In an official guidebook the new officials made their strategy for renewal of the city's fortunes clear:

> The removal of the capital robbed the city of much of its former grandeur; but its natural attractions, its ancient temples, and the artistic skill of its inhabitants remain, making Kyoto a city full of interest, not only to the people of the land of which it was once the political, literary, and artistic center, but also to increasing numbers from foreign lands who are attracted thither by its fame.[114]

Hope for the future of Kyoto was thus once again in its past—its old buildings, old artworks, and the traditions behind them.

Obviously the Reizei could fit into such a scenario. Indeed Tamemoto was very active in civic affairs, as evidenced by his authorship of a proposal (*ikenshō*) to the prefectural educational administration to include reading and calligraphy in the education of women—who, coincidentally, for some time had dominated the student rosters of the house.[115] The Meiji government considered the education of future mothers of paramount importance to the building of a viable state, which was the great project of the day, and popular sentiment was that classical poetry in particular had an elevating effect on female emotion.[116] More and more, the Reizei devoted their time to the instruction of young women who requested "finishing." That Abutsu was listed in a popular women's magazine along with Murasaki Shikibu, Sei Shōnagon, and Lady Ise as among the great Japanese women writers of the past signified that once again the

---

113. Reizei Kimiko, "Kindai no hito," pp. 2–3.
114. *The Official Guide-book to Kyoto and the Allied Prefectures*, p. 52.
115. Ogura, "Reizei-ke no rekishi 30: Tamemoto," p. 4.
116. Copeland, *Lost Leaves*, pp. 10–13, 19, 28, 41.

Reizei were being granted a place—albeit a peripheral one—in the canon.[117]

Tamemoto was also involved in one of the most important events in the Meiji era for the former capital: the anniversary celebration of the founding of the city by Emperor Kanmu (737–806; r. 781–806). Having succeeded in their request to host the Fourth National Industrial Exhibition in Kyoto in 1895 as a way to boost the city's profile, the leaders of the time decided to hold a sort of grand birthday party as well. Since Kanmu had first occupied his palace in 796, the year 1895 was reckoned as the 1100th anniversary year. His Imperial Highness Prince Arisugawa Taruhito (1835–95) was nominally in charge of the festivities, with Duke Konoe Tadahiro (1808–98) as chairman. But other notable citizens were also much involved in planning, Tamemoto evidently among them. Moreover, his contribution to the celebration, if family records are correct, was perhaps most significant of all. For he is said to have been the person who suggested the idea of commemorating the founding of the city by building a huge new shrine, modeled on the Daigokuden of the imperial palace compound in ancient times, which still stands today as one of modern Kyoto's most prominent tourist attractions.[118] The site of the new shrine occupied twelve acres in the Okazaki area of the city, on which were erected a shrine to the memory of Emperor Kanmu, the memorial hall itself, eastern and western wing-corridors, two towers, and a large ornamental gate (Ōtenmon). The walls of the memorial hall were painted white, the woodwork of the buildings was painted a bright vermillion red, while the roof tiles were glazed a dark green. In scale, the buildings are much smaller than were the originals they are patterned upon, but the site, known as Heian Shrine, is still impressive today, and must have been doubly so for visitors in 1895. Dedicatory services included prayers and congratulatory messages from dignitaries, and artistic performances.[119]

Another event of the anniversary year in which Tamemoto was evidently involved was the *jidai matsuri*, or Festival of the Ages. Essentially a procession of people dressed in period costume representing various eras of Japanese history, this festival was first held in the anniversary year, on October 22nd, the day of Kanmu's entry into the

---

117. The magazine was *Jogaku zasshi*. See Copeland, *Lost Leaves*, p. 33.
118. Reizei Kimiko, "Kindai no hito," p. 3.
119. *The Official Guide-book to Kyoto and the Allied Prefectures*, pp. 58–59.

capital in 794. It has been held on the same day every year since then, except for a few lapses during wartime. Making up the parade were a number of discrete groups, for instance, representatives of the three great unifiers, Nobunaga, Hideyoshi, and the Tokugawa. More important for the Reizei were the groups that represented the emperor, the Fujiwara, and court women. Then as now, the procession, which involved thousands of participants, began at the Heian Shrine and made its way to the old imperial palace, then returned the same way. Reizei Kimiko notes that, as evidence of Reizei involvement, the parade Abutsu-ni, as it still does today.[120]

At the time of the anniversary celebration, Tamemoto was serving a seven-year term—some of which he probably spent in Tokyo—in the House of Peers (Kizoku-in), the legislative body of the elite, having been elected in 1890.[121] Even after his term in office, he continued to be very active in various public roles. In 1897, he was appointed head priest of Heian Shrine, after having served already in the administration of Go-Toba Shrine in Shiga and elsewhere; then, after a year, he was made chief priest (*gūji*) of Ise Shrine, in 1898. At the time, the Meiji government was attempting to bring the old religion of Shinto into direct identification with the state, as both ideological support and as a ready source of spectacle in the form of rites and celebrations. Tamemoto's position, then, was one of some importance, as well as a needed source of income. Although his duties did not require constant attendance in Ise, he appears to have spent a good deal of time there, leaving his heir, Tametsugi, in charge in Kyoto. Among other things, the family credits him with developing the marriage ceremony that is still practiced today at various shrines.[122]

Tamemoto's association with Shinto shrines should not be taken as evidence of a waning interest in poetry, however. He put together several collections of his poems and supported his son in his pursuit of the family Way. Far from being mutually exclusive, the native Way of Poetry and the Way of the gods had been associated fields for centuries, as evidenced by the close relationship of the Reizei with the Sumiyoshi, Tamatsushima, and other shrines since medieval times. Like most noble families, the Reizei still maintained ties with

---

120. Reizei Kimiko, "Kindai no hito," p. 3; Reizei Fumiko, *Reizei Fumiko ga kataru Kyō no miyabi*, p. 200.

121. Ogura, "Reizei-ke no rekishi 30: Tamemoto," p. 5.

122. Reizei Kimiko, "Kindai no hito," p. 3.

various Buddhist temples, even during the years when the government seemed hostile toward the old sects for a variety of reasons. But it was the Way of the native deities that offered the most support in the years after the Restoration, and the Reizei were not slow in taking advantage when it was offered.

Tamemoto died, suddenly, in 1905, at the age of 52. At the time he was attending to duties in Ise. Kimiko describes how his mother and her servants, who had been the real power in the household in his absence, waited in the formal entry of the house on Imadegawa, dressed in white, for the return of his remains. As had happened so many times before, an heir only in his 20s would now have to take on the obligations of the Reizei house. Recently, Tametsugi had greeted his new bride, Yukiko, of the noble Minase lineage. The small group held a funeral service for Tamemoto at the Reizei house and then went in procession to his gravesite at Shinnyodō Temple, about one *li* away, where many members of the family had been memorialized. Because of his Shinto affiliations, his headstone bears only the name Fujiwara Ason Tamemoto, with no Buddhist name—as would be true of his son, who also served as the head of a Shinto shrine.[123]

Kimiko notes that as a final sign of his popularity in the old city, when the first members of the entourage arrived at the temple, the line stretched all the way back to the house, without a break.[124] This in itself was a sign that the Reizei had managed to make a place for themselves in the new Japan. Although no one at the time could have known it, however, Tamemoto's heirs would not bask in such public attention for many decades to come, in Kyoto or anywhere else.

---

123. Reizei Fumiko, *Reizei Fumiko ga kataru Kyō no miyabi*, pp. 123–24.
124. Reizei Kimiko, "Kindai no hito," p. 4.

TEN

Kyoto

THE EARLY 1900s were a time of great growth for the new Japanese state, which in 1904 fought and won a war with Russia and in 1905 succeeded in annexing Korea as a protectorate, just two signs of its growing profile among the industrialized nations. New technologies were being introduced almost daily; businesses of all sorts flourished. Other signs of revolutionary change were evident in most other aspects of society, including literature. Western writers, from Shakespeare to Bulwer-Lytton, were being introduced to Japanese audiences for the first time, in Japanese translation, and the emergence of a larger and more sophisticated reading audience also provided a market for new kinds of poetry and a whole procession of Japanese "novels" (shōsetsu). In the decade from 1900 to 1910 alone a number of publishing events signified fundamental changes in the literary world: the founding of the poetry journal Myōjō (Bright Star); the publication of groundbreaking vernacular fiction by Mori Ōgai (1862–1922), Natsume Sōseki (1867–1916), Shimazaki Tōson (1872–1943), and Nagai Kafū (1879–1959); and the appearance of an unconventional tanka collection, Ichiaku no Suna (A Handful of Sand, 1910), by Ishikawa Takuboku (1886–1912). To be sure, there were some echoes of Edo-period literature in all these modern works, but no one could doubt that along with all the political and economic changes of the new era had come changes in the trajectory of Japanese literature as well. To a great extent, progress was being measured in terms of distance from the past.

Even in this environment, interest in traditional forms of Japanese poetry never died out altogether. Many of the most famous novelists of the Meiji period in fact composed *uta* (Mori Ōgai) or *haikai* (Natsume Sōseki and Nagai Kafū). Some of these called for more fundamental change than did others. But the pages of most new books were dominated by the works of poets such as Yosano Akiko (1878–1942), who in her *Midaregami* (Tangled Hair, 1901) wrote poems that gestured toward a world apart from anything ever contemplated by the Reizei or other poetic families of the court. No student of a Reizei master, for instance, would ever have accepted a poem as unrestrained as this one addressed by Akiko to her husband:

> Must you lecture me?
> Must you expound your way?
> Enlighten me?
> Put your karma away now—
> I offer you hot blood.[1]

isamemasu ka/michi tokimasu ka/satoshimasu ka/sukuse no yoso ni/chi o meshimase na

While the most obvious way in which this poem offends against traditional standards is in its explicit sensuality, it flies in the face of virtually every other ancient convention as well. In its staccato syntax, abstract diction, passionate tone, and lack of a proper *dai* sanctioned by centuries of usage, the poem simply turns its back on noble norms of subtlety and understatement. Moreover, Akiko made it clear that this was not by happenstance. She wrote that when she looked at the supposedly great women's poems of the imperial anthologies, she saw only clumsiness.[2] Like many other poets of the time, she would define her own work in a spirit of opposition to the courtly heritage.[3]

Not all readers appreciated Akiko's poetry. Sasaki Nobutsuna (1872–1963), a professor at Tokyo Imperial University who had been trained in traditional ways, voiced the views of many when he dismissed such explicit eroticism as "no more than *shunga*" (pornographic woodblock prints).[4] Moreover, traditional poetry was still being written. For while old-style *waka* no longer played the kind of ritual role it had played in elite culture, it still had a place in another area: education. For many parents of the social elite still wanted the

---

1. Quoted in Carter, *Traditional Japanese Poetry*, p. 450.
2. Beichman, *Embracing the Firebird*, p. 65.
3. Ibid., p. 66.
4. Ibid., p. 178.

prestige attached to proper "breeding" for their children, especially, in the new age, for their daughters, whose cultural accomplishments (dress and comportment, entertainment and communication skills, in particular) would be important in maintaining a proper profile in society. Even among the elite, however, expectations were changing as "modern" became the prevailing buzzword. Hence a collection appeared in 1908 titled *Shindai kashū* (Poems on New Topics) that contained poems by court ladies with names such as Yanagiwara, Chigusa, Sono, Anegakōji, Ogura, and Irie. While a far cry from Akiko's explicit sexuality, the poems recorded in the book just as certainly declared the advent of a truly new age:

> "Telephone"
>
> Such a world is ours!   That though oceans
> and mountains   may separate us
> still we can exchange words   one with
> another.[5]
>
> *umiyama o/hedatete sumedo/morotomo ni/kataraikawasu/yo to narinikeri*

This poem was composed not by a commoner but by Yanagiwara Naruko (1859–1943), concubine of Emperor Meiji and mother of Emperor Taishō (1879–1926). Doubtless she had received traditional training in poetic composition from poetic masters in Edo, as was still the custom. The structure, syntax, diction, and tone of the poem are conventional, in other words; but the topic is so unusual—or would have seemed so to the Reizei, at least—that it quite overpowers everything else. To the old houses, traditional topics were central to the whole enterprise of Japanese poetry. To do away with them, along with the social contract their existence represented, was quite literally to do away with the role of the house as a licensing authority. In this sense, the appearance of such poems by children of the nobility may have been more of a shock to the old poetic families than were avowedly modern works by Yosano Akiko and Ishikawa Takuboku that openly advertised themselves as new.

REIZEI TAMETSUGI was a teetotaler, as were his father and grandfather, and he spared no effort when it came to the affairs of the house. Upon his father's death he went daily to the temple for 50 days, adhering to conventions that few even among the old nobility still maintained.

---

5. *Shindai kashū*, p. 703.

On the way back, Fumiko says, he even did ritual purifications at the riverbed, a sign that he took his Shinto offices very seriously.[6] He was not a man whose spirits were easily ruffled, at least according to his daughter. When the new trends gained so much in popularity that even the teahouses of Kyoto ceased to appreciate the old ways, he pursued his hobbies (which included the *shō*, or flute, and the *biwa*, a kind of lute) at home, in a little *omonomi* ("lookout") that he also used as a private teahouse, and in which he also pursued his profession, on the southeast corner of the Reizei lot.[7]

The income from his various offices in Shinto shrines, which he had inherited from his father, augmented by proceeds from estates, allowed Tametsugi to live comfortably pursuing his elegant hobbies and practicing his profession as a poetry master, a pursuit that he approached with reverence.[8] Right up until the Pacific War, there were stewards (*zasshō*) to take care of many routine matters, just as there were maids to do most of the cooking and cleaning. The Reizei calendar was crowded with poetic events and other activities that, along with his students, were his primary concern. Monthly poetry meetings, several photographs of which from the late 1920s have survived, show students lined up in formal dress in the Great Hall, kneeling before inkwells and paper.[9] Such things demanded constant coordination and planning. The routine honoring of all past heads of the house on their death anniversaries, for instance, in itself occupied 27 days every year. On each occasion, the portrait of the ancestor (or a *tanzaku* in the case of the earliest generations, for which no portraits exist) was brought from the storehouse for a service in the Great Hall, where the family would assemble for a memorial service.[10]

While the rest of the world donned Western clothing, Tametsugi continued to wear old-fashioned *hakama*, every day, all day.[11] Also

---

6. Reizei Fumiko, *Reizei Fumiko ga kataru Kyō no miyabi*, p. 101. Tametsugi succeeded his father in his offices at Heian and Ise shrines. Brower, "The Reizei Family Documents," p. 453.

7. Fumiko refers to the place as a teahouse, but Ponsonby-Fane (pp. 377–78) calls it an *omonomi*, noting that many noble residences had such a small cottage designed to allow the nobility to get a view of what was going on outside on the street without exposing themselves to view.

8. Reizei Fumiko, "Uta no Reizei-ke," p. 32.

9. See *Reizei-ke no rekishi*, pp. 68 and 212.

10. Reizei Fumiko, *Reizei Fumiko ga kataru Kyō no miyabi*, pp. 14–15.

11. Ibid., p. 139.

every day, he did obeisance at the *obunko*, the protection of which he
held as his most solemn duty. Because it held portraits of the deities
of the house — including the gods of Sumiyoshi, Tamatsushima, and
other shrines, but also of Teika (always referred to as Teika-san) and
the other heads of the house over the centuries — the library was a
holy place. During periods of mourning, he did not enter the building
at all, and after any kind of pollution he always purified himself be-
fore venturing inside. Following traditions that had been established
in the early Edo period, no other member of the family — except the
heir of the house, his son Tameomi (1911–44) — was ever allowed en-
trance.[12] When Tametsugi took anything from the collection to peruse
in the house, he treated it with the utmost respect. Fumiko has memo-
ries of him sitting in proper robes in *seiza* position, after washing his
hands, and gently turning the pages of a manuscript from the library,
"as if it held the spirit of the one who wrote it."[13]

Tametsugi's diligence was rewarded in the public arena, if only to
a limited extent. From 1900 on, for example, he served as poetry mas-
ter for a Kyoto-based cultural organization (first called the Shōyōkan
and then the Shōkōkan) that held meetings and published a maga-
zine on the courtly arts.[14] In 1914 he was chosen to act as imperial
lector (*gosei no kōji*) for newly ascended Emperor Taishō in the first
poetry gathering of the new reign, an office he again fulfilled at the
ascension of Emperor Shōwa fourteen years later. In both the latter
cases he probably owed his appointment to his uncle, Irie Tamemori,
who also had him made a consultant in the Poetry Bureau in 1918.[15]
But maintaining a high profile in Tokyo affairs while staying on in
Kyoto was a virtual impossibility. Perhaps as a way to counteract
this problem, he took steps to showcase the Reizei heritage in other
ways. The most important of these was the publication of selected
items from the library, the texts of which he recognized might still
have some purchase among academics and poets, who in a time of
nation-building could not fail to be curious about Reizei holdings.
Within months of his father's death, Tametsugi had arranged for
publication of photostatic copies of five texts from the library, to
which he attached an introductory note that reveals much about his

---

12. Ibid., pp. 128–29, 147.
13. Reizei Fumiko, "Reizei-ryū no uta no kokoro," p. 60.
14. Takayuki, "Reizei-ke to Keimeishū, Keikō," pp. 2–3.
15. Ogura, "Reizei-ke no rekishi 30: Tamemoto," p. 4.

thinking at the time: "As the current reign is bringing things into the light of day, this is no time to keep things hidden. So out of concern that these days so few people know anything about ancient poetry, I decided to approach my father for permission to publish some of the writings and teachings passed down from our forefathers."[16]

The treasured "secrets" of the Reizei house were still reserved for disciples, of course. But Tametsugi saw the wisdom in letting the world get at least a glimpse inside the family library. Some years later, in the midst of the Pacific War, he would also arrange the first public display of portions of Teika's famous diary in conjunction with that poet's 700th death anniversary.[17] In the past, the Reizei had always managed to make a place for themselves in any new cultural order, and Tametsugi seems to have been intent on carrying on that tradition.

Despite these attempts at maintaining a public profile, however, it is clear that Tametsugi spent most of his time and energy at home, which was his place of business. Unfortunately, he left no diary of the sort kept by his grandfather. But his elder daughters Sugako (1907–94) and Hideko (1909–2001) left reminiscences of him in a book published in 1987 — the record of an interview, essentially — that tell us much about his practice as head of the household and master of traditional poetry. Born in 1907 and 1909, respectively, the daughters stayed in the house until their marriages in the mid-1930s and were very much a part of their father's poetic practice. Ostensibly, the focus of the book is on *nenjū gyōji*, or annual rites and observances, but in the Reizei house such matters were often associated with poetry. Remembering New Year's activities, for instance, the sisters describe decorations but also their father's routine:

Hideko: After arising, Papa, as head of the house, would put on his formal hunting robes [*kariginu*] and go do obeisance at the *obunko*. The door was left closed; he just did the honors from the outside. Meanwhile his breakfast would be prepared.

Sugako: We were children, of course, so we just watched from the kitchen. . . .

Hideko: After his obeisance at the *obunko*, we would have our family celebration.

Sugako: For the celebration, Papa would change from his hunting robes into a kimono and crested skirt [*hakama*]. The crests on skirts differed according

---

16. Ibid.
17. Ibid.

to court rank. Mama would wear a white kimono and an overgarment [*kai-dori*]. At some point later on, Mama began wearing just a crested coat.

Hideko: Between Papa and Mama would stand a four-legged charcoal brazier. My older brother would sit in the foremost place, with the other children following him in order of age, and there would be a four-legged brazier between my older brother and sister, too. There were normal earthenware braziers, one for each two of the people present. These braziers were used especially for New Year's. . . .

Hideko: We really got nothing very delicious to eat. Papa had to go pay his respects at the imperial palace, so he had no time for a leisurely meal. Moreover, it appears that there were daimyo at the time who had no stacked boxes at all, and since they would be going to the palace too, Papa couldn't take time to celebrate with the family.

Sugako: After finishing breakfast, Papa would write his first poem of the New Year [*kakihajime*] — he had to have it finished since he would be recording it when he went to the imperial palace. He would grind the ink with new water [from the well] and write the poem out.

Hideko: Then off to the palace. I think it was around 10 o'clock. And he would have changed into his frock coat. He had a very busy morning![18]

The life the daughters describe is indeed a busy one, and not only at New Year's. In addition to the celebrations marking the death dates of all the previous heads of the house noted previously, there were big affairs with poetry and religious services at Tanabata time and on the death dates of Shunzei and Teika. Most of Tametsugi's time, however, was taken up with the day-to-day activities of his many students. The core of his work in this regard took place on a monthly basis, as the daughters explain. How much of the schedule was based directly on precedent is hard to say, but at least some of the meetings appear to have their origins in the twentieth century, showing that Tametsugi was able to adapt to the demands of a new market.[19]

Sugako: Then there were the poetry meetings.

Hideko: On the 4th was "airing" practice. More than ten people would come and practice together.

Sugako: On the 10th came the National Style Group — the men's gathering. I think about seven or eight men came, perhaps. Only men who had completed the beginner's course would attend.

---

18. Arao and Kodera, *Reizei-ke no saijiki*, pp. 57, 61–63.
19. Ibid., p. 225.

Hideko: On the 12th was the women's meeting. Just under 20 people would come. This was like the National Style Group, only for women.

Sugako: The beginner's course was on the 18th. This was the day they would listen to a lecture on how to compose poems—for people just entering the Way of Poetry. About 30 people would come to study.

Hideko: On the 22nd came the specialists' course. This was a meeting for a select group from among the women. I think there were six or seven of them.[20]

In addition to attending to all the other ritual demands of the Reizei calendar, then, Tametsugi thus held five different meetings every month. The first was for truly advanced students who needed practice in the conduct of poetic rituals, followed by meetings for advanced poets and finally one for beginners. That the last meeting was for a "select" group of women, according to Hideko, is probably evidence that some of his most important students were women—a trend that had started decades before and would continue down to the present, which makes sense in a culture that tends to define women as the perpetuators of traditional ways.[21] Each of these meetings was several hours long and each demanded considerable preparation time, since topics had to be chosen and sent out in each case, and poems marked before the meetings took place. In addition, a tea gathering was held on the 20th of each month in the family teahouse; and every summer all the students of the house were required to write two poems a day each day for 100 days, beginning on the 1st day of June—all of which Tametsugi had to read and critique. More informal meetings among family members and some other students were evidently also routine.[22] Thus Tametsugi did all that he could to attract and keep students. In 1917, he went so far as to announce in the Shōkōkan magazine that he was inviting participation in the extemporaneous portions of meetings (*tōza*) by telephone—and without the usual expectations concerning demeanor: "You can compose your poems in the most relaxed way, lying on the floor upstairs to take the cool air in summer, or sitting in your *kotatsu* in winter."[23] His own position required a more dignified posture, perhaps, as Teika and Ryōshun and

---

20. Ibid., pp. 211–12.

21. Copeland, *Lost Leaves*, p. 13.

22. Arao and Kodera, *Reizei-ke no saijiki* (pp. 225–26), for instance, note that when they were girls they had "competitions" with their friends once a month or so, where students would compete for marks.

23. Matsuda, "Reizei-ke to Keimeshū, Keikō," p. 3.

others had counseled. In the case of cash-paying students, however, allowances could be made.

Tametsugi also encouraged the whole family to be involved in poetry as much as possible. Instruction for his son and heir, Tameomi, began when the boy was an infant, and the older sisters were also required to listen to lectures and do their *keiko* from the time they were just learning to write.[24] Sugako, in fact, says she went through the beginner course a full three times, perhaps because she felt a special responsibility as eldest daughter.[25] His attitude in teaching his own family was evidently quite liberal: attendance was mandatory, but expectations were not terribly high. Whether poems were outstanding or not was a secondary consideration with him, Fumiko says. "As long as you enjoy it," he would say, "that's enough."[26] Often the children would compete with each other in composing on set topics, with sweets as rewards.[27] In the autumn, the family would gather on the night of the full moon to compose poems, afterwards dining on traditional *soba* (buckwheat noodles).[28] The daughters insist that stylistically their father favored an approach that Sugako refers to ironically as *shasei*—"sketching from life," a term usually associated with the poetics of Masaoka Shiki (1867–1902), one of the harshest critics of the courtly tradition. But it is clear that the sisters are not thinking of Shiki when they use the term, or for that matter any other term used in modern criticism, with which they are unfamiliar. What they are referring to is something like "unpretentious":

Hideko: Papa liked plain poems—he quoted what Teika said in his first lecture on the Way of Poetry, that a poem is something composed naturally about what comes into your mind.

Sugako: Yes. It's sketching from life. Obscurities are not necessary.[29]

The poems left behind by Tametsugi show that for the most part he followed his own advice. Virtually all of his poems were written on traditional topics, which he approaches in ways of which Tameie would have approved:

---

24. Arao and Kodera, *Reizei-ke no saijiki*, p. 222.
25. Ibid., p. 225.
26. Reizei Fumiko, *Reizei Fumiko ga kataru Kyō no miyabi*, pp. 153–54.
27. Ibid., p. 157.
28. Ibid., pp. 143–44.
29. Arao and Kodera, *Reizei-ke no saijiki*, pp. 139–40.

"Autumn Village"

How long has it been   since the sound
of fulling blocks   ceased for the season?
Quiet now is autumn   at Toichi
Village.[30]

koromo utsu / oto wa itsu yori / taenikemu / toichi no sato no / aki shizuka nari

"Lamps in a Distant Village"

From where I am   the lamps seem
not so far away,   'til walking on I see
how distant still is the town   at the foot
of the mountains.[31]

tomoshibi wa / chikaku miyuredo / ayuminaba / nao tōkaramu / yamamoto no sato

One could easily connect such rustic scenes back to many earlier
poets of the Reizei lineage. But even to begin a discussion of them
in that way seems almost an evasion, since the most important thing
one can say about such poems in historical terms is that writing them
in the 1920s obviously meant something different than it had even
100 years earlier. Put simply, Reizei Tametsugi, as he filed sheaves
of his poems away in the *obunko*, was refusing engagement with the
larger literary world of his own day and instead withdrawing into
a small circle of intimates, first among whom were the members of
his own immediate family. Somehow one is not surprised, therefore,
to find among his published poems one that reveals his home life
more directly than does perhaps any poem in the entire Reizei tradi-
tion. The scene is a touching one that probably illustrates precisely
what his daughters meant by *shasei*:

"People in Winter"

On a day when snow   just keeps piling up
outside   even my children
come gathering around me   as I sit
by my coal fire.[32]

shirayuki no / furitsumoru hi wa / kora made mo / tsudoikinikeri / uzumibi no moto

By Tametsugi's time, the old Reizei networks were largely defunct. In
earlier ages, small children had generally been sent off to rural vil-

---

30. *Reizei-ke no waka*, p. 151.
31. Ibid., p. 157.
32. Ibid., p. 152.

lages to be raised.[33] But now the house was a nuclear family whose leader taught poetry in the way that other *iemoto* houses taught *samisen* or flower arrangement, surrounded by a world for which its ancient ways and noble affiliations had ceased to have much public significance. Old claims of transcendence—aesthetic or religious—were no longer a major feature of Reizei discourse, and while Tametsugi still probably believed in the poetry as a moral force in Confucian terms, his own practice treated training as little more than finishing.

A PHOTO of the whole Reizei family taken in the early 1930s shows them in the garden of the house on Imadegawa. The mother and four daughters, flanking the two men of the house, are clad in *kimono* and *tabi*. Tametsugi, bespectacled and in formal kimono, looks rather stern, as does his son, in school uniform. Fumiko's reminiscences, however, indicate that they were very much a nuclear family that did many things together. Tametsugi had no mistresses and sired only five children, all of whom were raised at home. Even the girls were sent to public schools, where they were surprised to learn that teachers had heard of their great ancestors Shunzei and Teika. Fumiko remembers that in third grade she began wearing Western-style clothing to her school, named Muromachi Elementary, and believes that the clothes had been hand-sewn by her mother, who had studied sewing at the nearby Kazoku Kaikan.[34]

Tametsugi's heir, Tameomi, graduated from the Third Middle School of Kyoto municipality at eighteen and then enrolled at Koku-gaku-in—the Academy of National Studies—where he entered the literature division, evidently with the assistance of his uncle, Irie Tamemori, who was head of the Poetry Bureau and an influential man in academic circles.[35] Tameomi's own desire had evidently been to study the sciences, but this his father could not allow; as the only son of the current head of the house, he would one day succeed his father. If he resisted at all, it was not for long. At Kokugaku-in, where the curriculum concentrated very specifically on Japanese imperial culture, he concentrated on traditional poetry, writing his graduation thesis on the work of his ancestor, Fujiwara no Shunzei. By 1936 he was out of school and working in the library of Kyoto

---

33. Reizei Fumiko, *Reizei Fumiko ga kataru Kyō no miyabi*, p. 207.
34. Ibid., p. 207.
35. Ogura, "Reizei-ke no rekishi 32: Tameomi," p. 4.

University. Two years later, he was advanced to upper fifth rank and heavily involved in the family Way.

Evidently with his father's consent, Tameomi began to apply some of his university and library training directly to the family collection. First, he did a thorough inventory. Labels were attached to the texts of the *oshinbunko*, while *tanzaku* inscribed with identifying numbers were inserted into the texts of the older *obunko*. Then, in 1940, he published *Teika zenkashū* (The Complete Poems of Teika), followed by a volume of reproductions of Teika's calligraphy the next year, in commemoration of the 700th anniversary of the poet's death. Soon after, in 1942, came the first volume of a series titled the *Shiguretei bunko*, or Shigure Pavilion Library. Hopes were high among scholars of classical literature that he would go on to publish more treasures from the storehouse. His sister reports that his desire was to follow the pattern of Yōmei Bunko, the library of the Konoe house, which since 1938 had been housed in its own building in Kyoto, under the administration of a corporation formed to preserve its holdings; but there was no money to further such grand ideas. So he decided to put things into print gradually and somehow to raise enough money to make at least some of the family treasures available.[36]

While Tameomi was engaged in his literary pursuits, however, most other young Japanese men were of course serving in the armed forces. Since the 1930s the Japanese had been pursuing an expansionist policy in Asia and the Pacific, which required soldiers for its execution. The days of samurai elitism were long past; now all men in reasonably good health were pressed into service. Perhaps because he was slight of build, rather weak of constitution, and myopic, according to Fumiko, Tameomi was not called up as soon as many others were. For two more years, he was able to pursue his literary studies. By the spring of 1944, however, the situation in the Pacific had become so desperate that virtually anyone who could carry a rifle was being drafted. Even the sons of the nobility were obliged to obey the call of duty. By that time Tameomi was 33 years old and serving as a lecturer at Dōshisha, and he would of course have rather served the emperor in the Way of Poetry, Fumiko notes; but that option was not open, and so he accepted his fate, declaring: "In the past, the many generations of the Reizei house have served the court in letters (*bun*), but from today I will serve the Emperor

36. Reizei Fumiko, "Uta no Reizei-ke," p. 32.

in arms *(bu)*."[37] Even after he was called up, the family evidently hoped that he would not get through the physical exam. When he passed, they were obliged to watch him go off to the front in China, with the 6213 Infantry Corps.[38]

As air raids brought the reality of the war closer and closer to home, Tametsugi continued to function as usual, as much as was possible. After news of the bombing at Pearl Harbor in 1941, the monthly poetry meetings of the house had been discontinued; and the little teahouse also gradually went to ruin, unused and unoccupied.[39] He still composed poetry and taught some students, discreetly, and did research on the Way of the gods. Since public display of any kind was being discouraged, he and his own stayed at home, maintaining the family traditions inconspicuously. Even when things were at their worst, he managed to hold onto the family servants and maids, to avoid sullying his own hands with menial tasks. When the family had to resort to the black market, it was his daughters who did the deed, Fumiko says.[40] Likewise, he did not dirty his hands when the ornamental garden was dug up and planted with squash, cucumbers, eggplant, tomatoes, and daikon radish, or when chickens were introduced to the lot, for eggs and to produce fertilizer.[41]

By the time Tametsugi saw his son off to the Chinese front, the U.S. Pacific fleet was gradually closing in on the Japanese islands. Guam and Saipan were lost by the summer of 1944, and MacArthur regained Manila in February of the next year, before going on to defeat the Japanese forces at Iwo Jima and Okinawa that next spring. In mid-March of 1945 American bombers were beginning to reduce Japanese cities to rubble. Within a few months, Kobe, Osaka, Nagoya, Yokohama, and Tokyo were in ruins. When Kyoto's turn would come no one could know. Fumiko says that her father declared that he would not evacuate to the countryside under any circumstances, but would stay and burn with the library if it came to that. Otherwise, he felt he could not face his ancestors with a heart free of guilt.[42]

----

37. Reizei Fumiko, *Reizei Fumiko ga kataru Kyō no miyabi*, pp. 142–43.
38. Ibid., p. 142.
39. Ibid., pp. 77–78.
40. Ibid., pp. 138–40.
41. Ibid., pp. 95–97.
42. Ibid., p. 139.

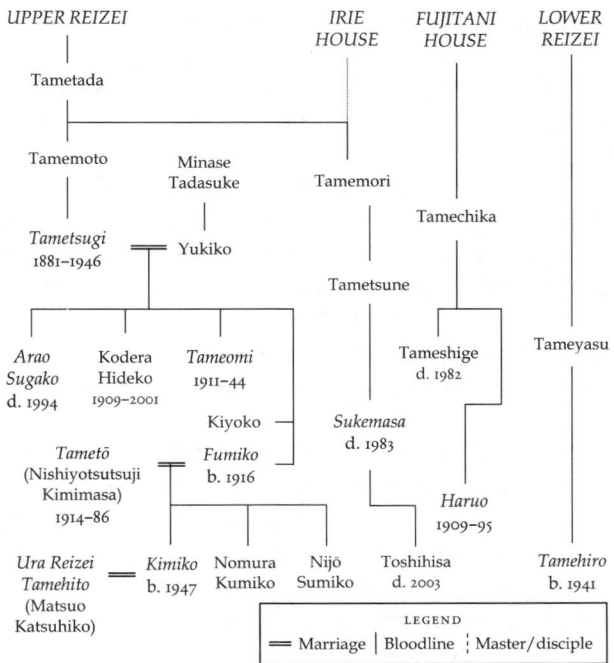

Chart 7   The Reizei Lineages in the Twentieth Century

As it turned out, lobbying from various fronts in the U.S. kept Kyoto off the bombing list, despite the fact that munitions factories surrounded it. So Tametsugi and his family were shielded somewhat from the worst degradations of the war years. But in the summer of 1945 came two blows that they could not be spared. The first came on the 6th day of June, when a letter from the Army arrived in the mail, informing the family that Tameomi was dead—had been dead, in fact, for nearly a year. Though he did not give in to tears in front of the family, Fumiko says, he muttered, "This I hadn't expected; I guess the male line ends here."[43] As always, his thoughts were on the fate of the house.

The second shock came in August, when the Emperor announced the end of the war over the radio. Sitting in proper *seiza* posture, Tametsugi sat in front of the radio, with his wife and daughters behind him, as in convoluted language that most people could not understand, the sovereign accepted defeat. Tametsugi, long schooled

---

43. Ibid., p. 141.

in court language, of course had no trouble understanding what the emperor was saying but perhaps could not grasp what it would all mean in the end. During the broadcast, he sat in silence and then without saying a word withdrew into his private quarters at the back of the house.[44]

It would be several years before a funeral stone was erected in Shinnyōdō cemetery honoring Tameomi's memory. In the meantime, like most families, the Reizei were occupied mostly with keeping body and soul together at a time when food and fuel and other necessities were scarce. Yet still Tametsugi was thinking of the future—which meant somehow securing an heir. Fumiko would have preferred that he opt for taking in one of the sons of the collateral lineages, the lower Reizei or the Fujitani.[45] But for some reason Tametsugi did not agree. Through intermediaries, a match was instead arranged between Fumiko and one of the younger sons of the Nishiyotsutsuji lineage (a branch of the Yotsutsuji that had been granted *kuge* status in the early Edo period), a graduate of Gakushū-in who had worked in a bank before serving as an army officer in the war.[46] Since the older daughters were all married, the youngest daughter and her husband as adopted heir would have to do their best to carry on the family Way. Years later, Fumiko would say that as the fourth daughter of the house she was considered as "something akin to garbage" (*gomi mitai na mono*)—perhaps meaning something disposable—as a child.[47] Although she had studied the tea ceremony, flower arrangement, and calligraphy,[48] she had not truly been educated in the Way of Poetry, beyond composing poems on occasions when the whole family was expected to participate. Nonetheless, her father chose to leave the house in her hands. On a February day in 1946, the couple was married in the Great Hall of the house on Imadegawa.[49] He was 32; Fumiko was two years his junior. Immediately, Tametsugi began to instruct his new son-in-law in the poetic and other matters that he would have to know in order to conduct himself as head of

---

44. Ibid., pp. 139–40.
45. Reizei Fumiko, "Uta no Reizei-ke," p. 29.
46. Amano, "Kamoku na chichi no namida," p. 3.
47. Reizei Fumiko, *Reizei Fumiko ga kataru Kyō no miyabi*, p. 206.
48. Ibid., p. 213.
49. Ibid., p. 135.

the house. Perhaps to make his expectations of the young man clear, Tametsugi chose a character denoting "responsibility" for the second character in the young man's name — Tametō.

Evidently Tametō got the message, for Fumiko says that on the day after their marriage he set about breaking up wood to stoke the fire for the bath — the sort of menial task to which her father would not stoop.[50] From the beginning, then, Tametō took as his first obligation the survival of the house. He quickly took on other duties, including going to pawnshops to pawn Fumiko's and her mother's *kimono* and trading on the black market. Every day was divided between study and scheming. He made some mistakes, such as when he used a post from the teahouse — which had been neglected until it became a hazard, and then torn down — to stoke the fire for the family bath, not realizing the value it had because of three sword marks by members of the famous Meiji-era Shinsengumi band of samurai.[51] All in all, however, he took his new responsibility very seriously. As the son of a noble lineage, he had been given some instruction in traditional poetry, but he had never expected to become the heir of a lineage dedicated wholly to that art.

No doubt Tametsugi had high hopes of passing on all of his teachings to his son-in-law, fulfilling his own obligations to his ancestors. But before 1946 came to a close he fell ill and died — in October — at the age of 66, his duty largely unfulfilled. Again the family faced a crisis, indeed the most serious one since Muromachi times. For in some ways Tametō's lack of experience in poetic matters was the least of their problems. More pressing was the need to put rice in the pot after the postwar government, in 1947, disenfranchised the old nobility entirely, doing away with the estate rights that still provided their stipends. Tametsugi had been able to survive as a poetry teacher, but his heir would not be able to do the same.[52] Thus it was that Tametō, twenty-fourth head of a noble courtly lineage, went to work as a "salaryman" in a bank.[53] Even this was not enough to pay off the inheritance and property taxes that came due after Tametsugi's death. To raise the money, he and Fumiko decided to sell off what properties the family still held, except for the house

---

50. Ibid., p. 138.
51. Ibid., p. 138.
52. Reizei Fumiko, "Uta no Reizei-ke," p. 32.
53. Ogura, "Reizei-ke no rekishi 33: Tametō," p. 4.

on Imadegawa, and some things from their storehouses: not books, but perfume implements, lacquerware, and tea utensils. Tametō had no time for tea, and he had been breaking up the old *omonomi* in the corner of the Reizei lot for firewood for some time in any case.[54]

Not long after the end of the war, the Kazoku Kaikan, located on what had once been the Tokudaiji lot just to the west of the Reizei residence, became Kyoto GHQ—General Headquarters of the Allied Forces.[55] Once again, the barbarians had moved in next door. Going off to work every day so close to the symbol of the defeat must have had a profound effect on Tametō's state of mind. He and his new wife decided to cut back on many of the old rites that Tametsugi had maintained so religiously, partly because the head of the house no longer had Shinto affiliations, but mostly because neither they nor Tametsugi's widow knew how some of them should be done and because there was not enough time or money to continue them. No longer, for example, could the family hold memorial services for every head of the house. Instead, Tametō created a scroll with the words "The Spirits of the Generations of the Reizei House" that was hung in the alcove once a year, before which the family gathered for prayer.[56] Other customs or rites that involved considerable expense or labor were likewise truncated or eliminated altogether. In some cases, Fumiko and her mother persisted in practicing simpler and less expensive rites even when they had no idea of their purposes and promised effects.[57] Fumiko says that her mother told her explicitly, "When your time comes, you can quit performing all these rites, if you wish."[58]

However, neither Tametō nor Fumiko dared touch the contents of the *obunko*—so insistent had Tametsugi been in his pronouncements and so adamant was his widow, who lived on for another 25 years, until 1970. Especially in the immediate postwar years, when many noble families sold off their heirlooms, the temptation to raid the library must have been great. But on this they held firm, even when they had to tear down several of the other storehouses that were in bad repair or when there was not enough money to do

---

54. Reizei Fumiko, *Reizei Fumiko ga kataru Kyō no miyabi*, pp. 137–39.
55. Ibid., p. 220.
56. Ibid., pp. 14–15.
57. Ibid., pp. 36, 42, 47.
58. Ibid., p. 133.

routine maintenance. As Fumiko's daughter Kimiko would later put it, "Just as no one considers melting down the Great Buddha in Nara for money, we never thought of selling our library to get our hands on some cash."[59] As head of the lineage, Tametō did his daily obeisances there, as in previous generations; and Fumiko and her mother, also as in the past, gave the place a wide berth, obeying the old rules about women and their pollutions.

DESPITE THEIR difficult economic situation, the family did return to poetic affairs as soon as normalcy returned to the city. Responsibility for supervising the monthly poetry meeting, called Shōkōkan, that had been supervised by Tametsugi until his death, went first to Tametsugi's younger brother, then to Tametsugi's widow, and then to Sugako, Fumiko's eldest sister, who had studied poetry along with Tameomi.[60] But as political changes eliminated the old nobility from positions of influence in public life, the Reizei came to seem more like families involved in the *iemoto* system that dominated many traditional arts and crafts, such as flower arrangement, music, and the tea ceremony, none of which had direct connections to the old nobility.[61] The old affiliations associated with noble lineage were of little force in the new world. In 1946, the Ōutadokoro at the imperial court in Tokyo had been disestablished, replaced by a committee of poets—mostly commoners—whose only duty was to choose appropriate poems for New Year's festivities.[62] While the modern *tanka* movement continued to thrive, any interest in the courtly traditions seemed to have disappeared.

The three children born to Tametō and Fumiko, all girls, went to nearby public schools, where they were indistinguishable from other middle-class children from Kyoto merchant households. Indeed, as the years went on and Japanese society reshaped itself, the identity of the family seemed more and more tied up with the city of Kyoto itself and less with the aristocracy that had once dominated its landscape. While Fumiko and her husband tried their best to live up to the demands of the ancient calendar, neither had the confidence

---

59. *ST* 3, p. 5.

60. Reizei Fumiko, "Uta no Reizei-ke," p. 38.

61. Fumiko makes this comparison very explicitly in a 1981 interview. Reizei Fumiko, "Uta no Reizei-ke," 35.

62. Irie, *Jijū to paipu*, p. 101.

to supervise in poetic matters except in the most superficial way—
keeping the form alive for its own sake, but giving up all pretensions
of broader relevance in the context of modern Japanese literature.
The old secrets no longer held any attraction, except as subjects of
academic study, and the couple did not know most of them in any
case. So the Reizei turned their attention to other things—Tametō
to the task of scraping money together to keep the roof of the decay-
ing old house from leaking and Fumiko to her duties as the mother
of three daughters. She spent her time in the antiquated kitchen,
cooking, and, after the hard postwar days were over, planting the
old garden space with flowers.

During the 1960s and 1970s, Fumiko and her husband maintained
time-honored routines as best they could, still holding monthly
poetry meetings and still honoring some days of the old calendar,
now with the sense that they were quite literally the only family in
Japan, outside the imperial house, that was doing so.[63] During this
time, the family had virtually no public profile whatsoever outside
of Kyoto; and even there their only claim to fame was the old house on
Imadegawa, which the travel guides all identified as the only example
of *kuge* architecture left from the Edo period, although they did not
mention that it was gradually descending into a profound state of
disrepair. Remarkably, however, the family continued to cling to its
traditions, insisting especially on the sanctity of the *obunko*, as a quota-
tion some years later from Fumiko's eldest daughter, Kimiko, reveals:

The *obunko* was handed down to the eldest son only, and other children were
never allowed to enter it. Gradually, because of the mystical aura associated
with it, it evolved into a site of religious significance. This religious identity
was necessary to the survival of the house, of course, but at the same time it
served to preserve the *obunko* as a cultural property.

In the past, then, we never once considered the documents and manu-
scripts as worldly wealth [*zaihō*]. It was as the gods of our house that we
preserved them, just as temples preserve their buddhas. Even now, when
we stand before the *obunko* it is with hands together and heads bowed. Even
my aunts, who left the house to marry, never set foot inside the *obunko*.[64]

As eldest child, evidently Kimiko was also taught to compose
poetry and to honor the lore of the house, not only by her mother
but by her aunts Sugako and Hideko. Rather than majoring in litera-

---

63. Reizei Fumiko, *Reizei Fumiko ga kataru Kyō no miyabi*, p. 99.
64. Reizei Kimiko, "Bunkazai mamoru ketsui ni kandō," p. 3.

ture in college, however, she majored in Japanese history, completing a Master's course at Kyoto Women's College, and after finishing her academic program, she began a career not as a poet but as a schoolteacher. This thoroughly middle-class trajectory, and the lack of a male heir, evidently went far toward convincing Tametō that there was really no hope in saving the family Way in any form. When the younger daughters married and left the house to start lives of their own, Tametō spent more and more time worrying about days to come—especially with regard to financial matters. Feeling the pressure of new tax laws that might require partitioning of the estate upon his death, he had many long discussions with his wife, in which a number of options for the library and the house were entertained. For years, scholars had been encouraging Tametō to allow access to the library's manuscripts. Finally, he was convinced. An announcement was made in April of 1980 that the Heian Museum would begin to catalogue the collection.[65] Fumiko describes how she, her husband, and Kimiko entered the *obunko* to clean it up, before it was opened to visiting scholars. Feeling that after 800 years of steadfastly denying access to virtually everyone except the head of the house, there ought to be some ritual act performed before taking so important a step, Fumiko stood before the little building and announced simply, "Tomorrow, we open you to the public."[66]

As for the house, one idea discussed by the family was to tear it down and put up an apartment complex that would continue to serve as a source of income.[67] Capital-poor, land-rich farmers and merchants were doing the same thing all around the nation. No one could blame the Reizei for taking the same course. Kimiko, the oldest child and the one with the strongest ties to family traditions, was reluctant but basically agreed.[68] Keeping the house in repair was becoming a greater burden all the time. Tametō had retired in 1979 and had more time, but his advancing age made doing endless chores a burden.

What finally saved the building from demolition was intervention from the outside, which came in an unexpected form with the an-

---

65. Brower, "The Reizei Family Documents," p. 445.

66. Reizei Fumiko, *Reizei Fumiko ga kataru Kyō no miyabi*, p. 132.

67. Reizei Fumiko and Reizei Kimiko, "Haha kara musume e tsugu mono: Reizei-ke happyakunen no shihō o mamoru," p. 172.

68. Ibid., pp. 171–72.

nouncement in 1981 that the decrepit house on Imadegawa itself had been classified as an Important Cultural Property (*jūyō bunkazai*) under a national law concerned with preserving cultural treasures, which was followed in spring of the next year by news that ten items in the library would be given the same status. Kimiko narrates the sequence of events:

We had heard by way of friends the rumor that the house would be designated an Important Cultural Property. But we had never thought that even things in the storehouse would be objects of such attention. One day, a professor who had come to undertake a survey took a quick look into the storehouse, and a reporter from *Asahi shinbun* accompanying him took a photo—and then they just left. We heard nothing from them until one day the picture appeared in the newspaper, as an exclusive, no less. Thereafter, we didn't exactly get overrun with reporters, but helicopters flew over the house and there was a big to-do in the newspapers and on television.[69]

Significantly for the family, one of the texts granted "protected" status was the *Kokinshū* in Teika's hand that had been recognized as a treasure so many times in earlier history, the same text that Tamehiro had refused to share with the Asukai, the same text that had attracted the interest of men like Hosokawa Yūsai and Tokugawa Ieyasu. Also honored were Teika's personal diary, Shunzei's history of Japanese poetry, *Korai fūteishō*, and other documents that the lineage had spared no effort in preserving over the centuries.

Designation under the Cultural Properties Law in itself carried little direct financial advantage, but it drew public attention. Within a short time, a number of prominent figures from the business world were offering support. Not by chance, Japan was entering a period of economic growth and prosperity that was accompanied by an intense re-evaluation of the past. In such a market, the Reizei again could find a place, as they had done so many times in the past. Keeping their holdings only for the few had been the strategy in the past; now the strategy would be to make them the property of the nation.

A committee had already been formed to deal with the library, which would be known as the Shiguretei Bunko, the name that Tameomi had decided upon decades before. First a survey of its contents was undertaken; then came a plan for *Asahi shinbun* to publish photostatic copies of the most treasured of the countless texts passed down from ancient times, to be titled *Reizei-ke Shiguretei sōsho*. (The first vol-

---

69. Ibid., p. 172.

ume—which appropriately turned out to be the family's treasured copy of *Korai fūteishō*, in Shunzei's own hand—would appear in 1992.) In the meantime a corporation was formed to manage the family assets and to make them available for public scrutiny. "We had been told that forming a corporation was out of the question because it cost so much money," Kimiko says, "but within just the space of a year, it was established."[70] The eldest Reizei daughter—who had no brothers—quit her job as a schoolteacher and began to work full time in the family interest, in time identifying herself as a historian specializing in the nobility of the Edo period.[71]

THE CORPORATION newsletter is a ready source for the history of all that has gone on since 1981, as well as a repository of much scholarly work on the history of the Reizei house. The first issue came out in March of 1982, with a picture of the front of the house and its famous *tatejitomi* on the cover, above a short congratulatory statement by Sakamoto Tarō (1901–87), member of the Japan Academy and emeritus professor of history at Tokyo University. Inside was a floor plan of the house and notes on the parts of it that had been designated Important Cultural Properties (the *zashiki*, the *obunko*, the kitchen, and the front gate). Also included were words of thanks from Reizei Tametō, along with words of goodwill from Irie Sukemasa (1905–83), Grand Chamberlain in the Imperial Household Agency and first president of the corporation, making clear the connection with imperial culture. Finally, congratulatory remarks from the heads of two big Japanese companies—Kyōcera Corporation and Wakōru—were solicited to claim the Reizei treasures for Japanese culture. Inamori Kazuo, representing Kyōcera, put the matter emphatically, saying that the Reizei family deserves credit for aiding in the campaign to "guard against the fragmenting of the heritage of the nation's people" (*kokumin*) in general and for efforts to "pass on the culture of Kyoto and indeed the heart of the Japanese people to later generations."[72] What had once been an unapologetically elite discourse that would always remain obscure in some ways was now being claimed to represent the entire heritage of Japan. To overemphasize the relationship of the house to imperial culture was

---

70. Ibid.
71. See "Kyōto Gyoen," p. 50.
72. Inamori, "Nihon no kokoro o kōsei ni," p. 7.

to risk falling under the shadow still cast by the militant nationalism of the Great East Asia Co-Prosperity Sphere. Identifying the house with "Japanese" culture, or even with the culture of Kyoto, was the more prudent course.

At the end of the inaugural newsletter came a calendar of events, followed by a roster of officers. Listed as advisors were the mayor of Kyoto City and the mayor of Kyoto Municipality, along with Matsushita Kōnosuke (1894–1989), founder of the mammoth Matsushita electronics empire. Reizei Tametō was noted as Chairman of the Board of Directors (*rijichō*), while Fumiko was managing director (*jōmu riji*), working with a board that included the directors of companies (Suntory, Kansai Electric Company, etc.) and the presidents of several Kansai-area universities. On the Board of Trustees were more such leaders of the culture industry, including some specialists in Japanese poetry, Kubota Jun, Shimazu Tadao, and Taniyama Shigeru, who would play a major role in surveying and publishing manuscripts, as well as the leaders of the Sen and Ikenobō schools of the tea ceremony. Arao Sugako, Kodera Hideko, Reizei Kimiko, and Fujitani Tameshige (d. 1982) were listed as representatives of the Reizei family and its offshoots. At the very end of the newsletter was a roster of all dues-paying members of the corporation, more than 700 of them. To show that the corporation would always be glad to welcome new members, the issue ended with a request for funds to help sustain its activities.

There were a few poems, too, produced by what is identified as the Reizei-ryū *kadan*, the coterie of the Reizei school. Among the ten poems listed, chosen by Fumiko from work sent by family and students, were one each by Tametō, Fumiko, and Kimiko, as well as by Fumiko's sisters Arao Sugako and Kodera Hideko. In later issues, the work of students would be given preference, rather than poems by the family, but at the beginning a display of the qualifications of the Masters must have seemed in order. Fumiko's poem expressed the mood of the time:

> Kindly protected   by the generous
> hearts   of people of the world,
> it will prosper all the more —   the Way
> of Shikishima.[73]
>
> *yo no hito no / atsuki kokoro ni / mamorarete / iyoiyo sakaeyuku / shikishima no michi*

---

73. Ibid., p. 7.

Just a few years earlier, the fate of the house and its poetic traditions had been anything but certain. Now "the people of the world" — primarily the Japanese cultural elite, of course, as the various rosters document—were lining up to preserve what they obviously thought of as not just Reizei customs but the foundations of Japanese culture. Once again patronage played a great role in the survival of the house.

Every issue of the newsletter since the inaugural number has contained the same basic kinds of material. On the front is a photo of a text or artwork from the Reizei collection, above a short column by Tametō and later by his successor; then come short scholarly articles by academics and by Kimiko; followed by reports on activities of the corporation, announcements of upcoming events, and so on. Special attention is given to information concerning the status of texts in the library. Broadly speaking, the *obunko* has yielded items—more than 1,000 of them—in three categories: historical documents; literary manuscripts, almost all from the first three centuries of the family's history; and works of art, many of which come from later periods. So far, five texts have been moved up from designation as "important cultural properties" to the law's highest category, that of *kokuhō*, or "national treasures": three of those already mentioned above (Shunzei's *Korai fūteishō*, Teika's *Kokinshū*, and Teika's diary); a copy of *Gosenshū*, another early imperial anthology, recorded in Teika's hand; and Teika's personal anthology of poetry, *Shūi gusō*.[74] As if in compensation for an honor long overdue, in 2002 all the storehouse's many personal poetry anthologies, which had been collected over the years in order to prepare the house for the responsibility of compiling an imperial anthology—a hope never realized—were designated as important cultural properties. In all, the *obunko* held 258 such works, mostly from the Heian and Kamakura periods. Rarely, however, have the editors of the newsletter been able to report on a truly "new" discovery. Among the few exceptions are a poetic collection whose title had been known but no text of which had ever

---

74. This is an ongoing process. Every year the Bunkachō undertakes studies of various texts or artworks, designating some as National Treasures, others as Important Cultural Properties, etc. *Meigetsuki* was only elevated to the higher category in 2000 (see *ST* 73, p. 2) and *Shūi gusō* only in 2003 (see *ST* 84, p. 1). *Shiguretei* 74 (October 2000) lists 28 texts of imperial poetry anthologies in the library that had as of that date received designation as Important Cultural Properties.

before been unearthed, and a partial copy of the famous *oki-bon* text of *Shin kokinshū*, a version of that anthology emended by Emperor Go-Toba while he was in exile.[75] Instead, what they can claim is to have some of the earliest extant texts in scores of categories.

The newsletter pays attention to nothing as much as the library and its treasures. But also standing out in its pages are reports on notable visitors to the house, from Prime Minister Nakasone Yasuhiro (b. 1918) in 1984 to Crown Prince Akihito (b. 1933; now reigning as Emperor Heisei) and his wife in 1988—both of whom are occasional poets, although not in the Reizei style. Black and white photographs of various other items from the various storehouses, from kimono to furnishings, also appear regularly. Every issue ends with a list of *shin kaiin*, new dues-paying members.

At the back of each issue is an invitation for devotees of *waka* to join the association and instructions about how poems should be recorded on *kaishi* and sent for review, in anticipation of poetic gatherings. For a time, two groups were maintained: the Shōkōkan, which traced its roots back nearly 100 years to the mid-Meiji period, and the Tamano'o kai, which Fumiko began herself in the mid-1970s,[76] although more recently the former has been collapsed into the latter. In addition, an inaugural event is held every January and two others in early autumn, commemorating the old Tanabata festival—one for family members only and another for disciples. Equally important, however, are events held to memorialize Fujiwara no Teika and Fujiwara no Shunzei. The first is now held in late spring, near Mount Ogura, and the second in autumn, at Tōfukuji, not far from Shunzei's grave. There are fees for participation in all events, but not onerous ones; the money charged can do no more than cover expenses. Collections of poems from the various meetings are published—but at cost, it would seem, and not as a way to make money. However, no opportunity for soliciting donations is allowed to pass. Some income no doubt comes in from the sales of the *Reizei-ke Shiguretei sōsho*, but the need for capital to keep all the activities of the corporation going is constant.

---

75. On the first text, titled *Gen'yōshū*, see *ST* 39. The *Oki-bon Shin kokinshū* is described in *ST* 73.

76. Reizei Fumiko, *Reizei Fumiko ga kataru Kyō no miyabi*, p. 155. The word *tamano'o* (jewel string of life) refers to a famous poem from *Shin kokinshū* (no. 1034).

The family began one very specific campaign in the early 1990s, aimed at raising money to restore the old house, which was in great need of repair. The project started in the spring of 1992, with the aim of restoring the structure to the form it had had back when it was first constructed in the Edo period. Restoration began with the *obunko*, which meant its deities had to be transferred to the *oshin-bunko*. Fumiko describes how she stood watching from the garden as the treasured portraits, covered in white silk, were moved from one storehouse to the other by Shinto priests who had told her that it simply would not do for women to be involved in so sacred a task.[77] Earlier, in March of that year, the head of Kami Goryō Shrine had pronounced a blessing in the garden space in front of the *obunko*.[78] Seven years later, at the end of 1999, the house had been restored, inside and out, with a new roof of Japanese cypress covering the "public" buildings. The garden and outbuildings were finished by the autumn of 2000. Needless to say, the new structures are impressive: everything is clean and polished, shining brightly thanks to new coats of paint and varnish. The new *obunko*, in particular, stands out now in a way that it did not before. In an old picture of Tametō offering his prayers for the New Year before the residence of the family gods, the building looks rustic, surrounded by overgrown bushes and standing on a rough foundation. Now the bushes have been cut back, leaving the new building, radiantly white, standing in the open in a gravel courtyard.[79]

As many updates in the newsletter attest, throughout the process of rebuilding, Fumiko insisted on the proper observance of rites of various sorts. Indeed, it appears that rather than following her mother's advice to do away with the onerous "yearly rituals" (*nenjū gyōji*), over the years she has become even more committed to preserving them. She has also insisted that the old ways be maintained in poetic events. At all Reizei meetings, poems are composed on the old *dai* of the court tradition. On the last page of every newsletter, topics for various meetings are noted, along with instructions on how the poems should be recorded on proper *kaishi* ("pocket paper").

Inevitably, the newsletter also tells the story of the family, sometimes including rather intimate details. One reads there, for instance,

---

77. Ibid., p. 131.
78. *ST* 40, p. 12.
79. See *ST* 39, p. 8, and Reizei Tamehito, "Reizei-ke toki no emaki," p. 39.

about the marriage of Kimiko to a man named Matsuo Katsuhiko (b. 1944) in 1984. Then a college professor at Ōtemae Women's University specializing in Japanese painting, he was described by a speaker at the wedding banquet as a true *inakamono* ("country bumpkin" is perhaps too harsh a translation but is close in its connotations) from Hyōgo Prefecture, who really only discovered the aesthetic traditions of his own nation in college and knew nothing about Japanese poetry— although of course he was now committed to learning about it.[80] A bigger problem was that he was a commoner, for which reason Kimiko's mother at first would not approve of the marriage. Even Crown Prince Akihito had married a commoner, back in 1959, but that was not enough to convince Fumiko. Fortunately for Kimiko, her father, however, was not opposed, and he won out. A friend at the time of his death from cancer in 1986 notes that Tametō, who of course knew what it was like to be adopted into a lineage as son-in-law, had once said that he would do anything to see that Kimiko's happiness was not sacrificed on the Reizei altar. "For her happiness, I will do anything, even if it means abandoning the Reizei house."[81]

In an interview for a women's magazine in 1999, Kimiko was even more forthcoming. While her mother had had to get permission from the Imperial Household Bureau to marry, she quips that in her generation that was not necessary, thereby putting her mother in her place.[82] But Fumiko's reply shows that she was not won over easily. "Had the two of them proceeded to destroy the house I would have remained angry," she says, "but they have restored the residence that had come down from our ancestors, with money gathered from I don't know where. Maybe the new head of the house is the sort who knows how to raise money."[83] A love marriage will do, in other words, as long as the couple remains dedicated to preserving the family ways. Just to make it clear what those ways demand, Fumiko insisted that Katsuhiko form his own new house, called the Ura Reizei, making him a member of a branch family.[84] Later, his first name was changed to Tamehito. By 1986, he had learned enough to

---

80. *ST* 11, p. 3.

81. Fukui, "Nyūin to taiin to no aida: sore wa sei to shi no aida datta," p. 3.

82. Reizei Fumiko and Reizei Kimiko, "Haha kara musume e tsugu mono: Reizei-ke happyakunen no shihō o mamoru," pp. 171–72.

83. Ibid., p. 172.

84. *ST* 11, p. 8.

assist his wife in officiating at one of the annual poetry meetings—
the two acting as a *konbi,* or "companionship," as the newsletter put
it.[85] Although he has never given up his day job as a college profes-
sor—first at Ōtemae, then at Ikenobō Junior College in Kyoto, and
more recently as a guest professor at Dōshisha Women's University
and Ritsumeikan University—he was made Chairman of the Board
of Directors of the Reizei Corporation in 2002 and continues to be
very active in house affairs.

In poetic matters, however, Fumiko and Kimiko are still clearly
seen as the de facto heads of the house. Despite the deficiencies of
her education in her youth, Fumiko has been practicing the family
Way for more than 50 years. Moreover, she has a strong sense of
the importance of women, beginning with Abutsu but also including
herself, in the history of the lineage:

> I have to believe that the Reizei women, from my grandmother and mother
> down to myself and Kimiko, have the strength of Abutsu running through
> our veins.
>
> Looking back, I see that my grandmother lived through the upheavals of
> the last days of the Tokugawa shogunate. Then it was my mother and I
> who preserved the house through the Second World War and fought
> through the storms attending upon inheritance taxes when our income was
> cut off by the disestablishment of the nobility system and land reforms after
> the war was over. And I also believe that the spirit of Abutsu was at work
> in the establishment of the Reizei Shiguretei Corporation. My daughter and
> I have now restored the dilapidated old family residence and taken charge
> of the nationwide "Treasures of the Reizei House" exhibition. . . . I can't help
> but conclude that the women of the Reizei house have walked forward to
> this day with a resolve similar to that of Abutsu, who put the survival of
> the house on the line when she went off to Kamakura.[86]

However deficient in knowledge and lacking in formal training,
Fumiko obviously believes that something from her ancestors has
come down in her blood. Through all the generations, Reizei
women—almost all of them nameless, as she notes—have perse-
vered. In this she is determined to emulate them, and to pass on that
same spirit to her daughter.[87]

Fumiko's "teachings"—although that is probably a grander term
than she would use for them—are straightforward. As there are no

---

85. *ST* 19, p. 2.
86. Reizei Fumiko, *Reizei Fumiko ga kataru Kyō no miyabi,* p. 190.
87. Ibid.

longer any noble poetic houses to compete with, she instead empha-
sizes differences with modern poetry, especially in the *tanka* form,
which seems traditional in some ways. Above all, she insists that
the Way of the Reizei house is an expression of ancient court civiliza-
tion and that composing poems according to the old conventions
is always an explicitly religious act in which poems are presented
as offerings to the gods. In this sense, she argues, the poems of the
house must remain different from modern *tanka*, which are funda-
mentally secular and are written on all sorts of topics that do not
have the sanction of precedent.[88] Writing on anything but the time-
honored topics of the old anthologies is simply unthinkable. For ad-
vice on how to compose on topics, one would do better to read
Tameie's *Eiga no ittei* than any modern text—a tradition that her
daughter Kimiko has followed.

Beyond these basics, Fumiko says little in public about her practice
as a poetry teacher. At meetings, where she and more recently Kimiko
preside now that her older sisters have passed away, one may assume
that there is some critique of individual poems by students, but Fumi-
ko stresses that the house no longer engages in formal "marking" or
even giving grades and that it does not require oaths from disciples.[89]
The atmosphere at gatherings is formal but it is not charged with the
sort of competitive spirit that characterized many medieval meetings.
Rather, the emphasis is on maintenance of ritual and conservative
diction. Like her father, Fumiko suggests that poets today cannot
hope to be compared with a genius like Teika-san. In fact, she goes
so far as to say that the strength of the Reizei house is in the way it has
produced "poets of outstanding mediocrity" (*idai naru bonjin*) who
concentrated on dedicated practice rather than on flights of fancy. The
thing is to help disciples to "write poems on things as they are, the
natural world as you feel it," she says. "I am always telling disciples
that what they need is to refine their emotions and build up their
powers of observation and concentration."[90] Technique is only a fa-
cilitator, a way to bring forth the feelings of the heart: "To put one's
heart into one's poems is one of the most basic teachings of the Reizei
house. But putting one's heart into things is truly a challenge. Of

---

88. Ibid., pp. 176–77.

89. Ibid., p. 230, p. 155. Hideko died at age 91 in February of 2001 (*Shiguretei* 76, p. 8).

90. Reizei Fumiko, *Reizei Fumiko ga kataru Kyō no miyabi*, p. 79.

course it depends partly on a person's inborn talent, but it takes time until one is able to put one's heart into a poem."[91]

Even in the modern world, such an approach attracts some students—in the hundreds, at least. The fees they pay are not enough to produce income, but the point of the meetings is of course less to make a profit than to maintain a profile. As in the tea ceremony or in flower arrangement, all who attend invariably dress in formal attire, and all the niceties of etiquette are strictly observed. *Keiko* is still the way to advancement and recognition, although only within a very small circle of intimates. Money changes hands, of course, unapologetically but always inconspicuously.

Those who have joined the ranks as students seem pleased with the experience that affiliation with the house affords. In the spring of 1989, a group of seven of them met to discuss their feelings about the Reizei-style Way of Poetry (*Reizei-ryū kadō*) in a *zadankai*, or round-table discussion—one of many that has taken place at the Reizei house in recent years. Six of the participants were women, one a man—an unsurprising ratio that reflects the overall pool of students and a general identification of classical court literature with the feminine in recent Japanese history. The comments the students make about their motivations are equally predictable. Takeichi Tsuneko, from Kyoto, for instance, says that she joined the group after finding that Japan had been too "Americanized" while she was away in London.[92] Kobashi Yoshiko, of Himeiji, says that she joined after seeing the Reizei house art exhibit at the Kyoto National Museum. "'Can this kind of world really exist in today's Japan?' I wondered."[93] Fujita Kyōko, also of Kyoto, makes the desire for an identification with the old ways even more explicit: "As I watched the funeral of the Shōwa Emperor, I was struck by the beauty of Japanese ritual, and very impressed. The way the forms sustain one spiritually, you know. When I am dressed in court costume, I feel as if I have truly become a person of the court. And I think to myself how much I want to preserve these traditions."[94]

What seems to appeal to Reizei disciples now is thus a connection to the "Japanese" past and to imperial culture, free of foreign ele-

---

91. Ibid., p. 174.
92. *ST* 28, p. 2.
93. Ibid.
94. *ST* 28, p. 3.

ments, all through the medium of an aesthetic practice that is taught as a craft rather than as an "art" only for the artistically gifted. More important than the work itself is the act of participation—in traditional dress, with traditional tools, according to traditional etiquette, and with goals that stress the harmony of the group rather than the ambition of its individual members. "How grateful I am that I was taught, 'It's better to leave the paper blank than to produce something strange [*hen na uta*],'" Ms. Kobashi says.[95] Even one who cannot produce a poem of any excellence can dress properly, sit properly, and enjoy the reassurance that comes from participation in a long tradition that can be fairly described as emphasizing precisely such an approach to poetic training.

THE REIZEI have therefore succeeded in establishing a version of the ancient ways even in the post–World War II era. One obvious measure of their success is the continued existence of the house on Imadegawa, marvelously restored, and at considerable expense (the *Kyōto shinbun* offers the figure of 630,000,000 yen).[96] In the standard tourist guidebooks, it receives only a few lines of attention but it is always there. Unlike many temples, it is not open to the general public. Only members of the poetry coteries are allowed in for their meetings and, once a year, for a guided tour. But the fact that the house is in such a prominent place, right across the street from the Imperial Park, means that it will always get some attention, especially now that it has an eye-catching new roof. Imadegawa Avenue was widened to accommodate a trolley line back in 1917, making it a broad thoroughfare, which since the war and the demise of the trolleys has become busy with car and bus traffic.

Another measure of success is the acclaim garnered by a traveling exhibition of Reizei treasures that made the circuit of major Japanese cities (Tokyo, Himeji, Nagoya, Sendai, Fukuyama, Fukuoka, and Kyoto) in the late 1990s. The exhibit featured manuscripts prominently: the national treasures and many other poetic texts from early periods, but also holdings of other sorts that give a view of court civilization: calligraphy, scroll paintings, teaware, dolls, paintings, kimono and other forms of court dress, and even the *miei*, or portraits of the fam-

---

95. *ST* 28, p. 3.
96. "Kokerabuki yane 'kuge yashiki' fukugen," accessed 3 November, 2006.

ily heads, all in superb condition because they were stored away almost immediately after acquisition and were seldom touched even by members of the family. Once again, the house has succeeded in creating a profile before the public, claiming the role of preserver of Japanese traditions. As Kimiko puts it, the desire at the heart of such projects is to show people—especially the Japanese themselves—the "heart of Japan" at a time when they are seeking for "truly Japanese culture" (*honmono no Nihon no bunka*).[97] A catalogue of the exhibit was published by NHK, the Japan Broadcast Corporation. Among other things, it displays portraits of the various gods of the house that in former times were viewed only by the family during memorial services. So successful was the first tour that another was immediately undertaken, this one emphasizing Edo-period manuscripts, artworks, and household furnishings that reflect the daily life of the Reizei during that time.[98] Also recently, an exhibition of the family text of Teika's diary, now fully restored and preserved thanks to support from the Japanese government, attracted interest as well. Abutsu might be scandalized at the idea of showing the treasure of the house to the public, but at least she would be satisfied that it was not being ignored.

For the time being, then, the fortunes of the Reizei house seem again to be on the rise. In recent years, Fumiko has received several public awards, the most recent being from the Japanese Ministry of Culture, citing her for her "long years of unstinting labor in preserving the cultural holdings of the Reizei house and contributions thereby to the preservation of our national cultural heritage."[99] Now in her early 90s, she is less directly involved in day-to-day affairs than she once was, leaving such matters to her son-in-law and Kimiko. The latter's study of the diary of Tametada continues on. And Tamehito has learned, he says, how to get along in his new world. "Just know your part," he says, "and as long as you don't depart from it, things will be fine."[100] He announced a few years ago that the decision has been made to produce more volumes for the publication series, raising the count to 84 volumes, with publication expected to continue

---

97. Reizei Fumiko, *Reizei Fumiko ga kataru Kyō no miyabi*, p. 231.

98. *ST* 75, p. 8.

99. *ST* 79, p. 1.

100. Reizei Tamehito and Sugimoto, "Edo saigo no tōshū, Tametada," p. 162.

until at least 2009.[101] In recent years, he has also educated himself enough about courtly poetic traditions to declare his gratitude that the Reizei house has managed to "get through to the present" without being sullied by what he terms "Americanized pragmatism."[102] In the continuation of this task, he is assisted by a board that now includes a new group of prominent business, academic, and government leaders, including Itō Jirōzaemon, leader of the Matsuzakaya department store empire, as well as heirs of the Yamashina, Irie, Nishiyotsutsuji, and lower Reizei lineages.[103] In this sense, the old network seems to have sprung back to life. Following Fumiko's lead, he attributes the good fortune of the lineage to the relative obscurity of the house, particularly in the modern era, when many more prominent noble lineages died away or were absorbed into the larger cultural trends of the day.[104] Once again, the current good fortune of the house is attributed to the decision to stay in Kyoto at the beginning of the Meiji period.

One great challenge of course still confronts the family, for Kimiko and Tamehito have produced only two children, both girls. While the Reizei Corporation will no doubt survive as part of the culture industry, it is not certain that the lineage will actually continue on at all, let alone that it will persevere in teaching poetry in the tradition of Teika and Tamemura.[105] There is also the question of whether the modern world will continue to produce students interested in the Reizei Way. As early as 1993 Kimiko was saying that the poetry meetings of recent years were like "old folks' gatherings."[106] But one cannot tell; one thing that the past teaches is that there are always ways to carry on. Tamehito, in a poem written for the first issue of the newsletter in 2001, at least seemed hopeful as he looked out on the resurrected Reizei house:

> Shingles of cypress,   newly put down,
> reflect light   from the New Year sun;

---

101. *ST* 74, p. 1.

102. Reizei Kimiko and Reizei Tamehito, "Nijū seiki ni mukatte," in *Reizei Fumiko ga kataru Kyō no miyabi*, p. 235.

103. A new roster is printed in *ST* 81, p. 8.

104. Reizei Tamehito, "Katari," p. 235.

105. Personal interview with Reizei Kimiko, November 16, 2005.

106. "Zadankai: Shōkōkan to tomo ni," p. 5.

for a thousand years of glory   the garden
celebrates.[107]

fukiageshi / kokera ni hatsuhi no / terihaete / chiyo no sakae o / iwau kono niwa

An article on the Reizei New Year celebrations published in the *Japan Times Online* on the first day of 2004 seems to justify his optimism.[108] Written by a reporter who admits to knowing little about the traditions the Reizei represent, it gives a brief history of the lineage, complete with obligatory references to Shunzei, Teika, Tamesuke, and a reference to the Reizei Family Shiguretei Library—and spreads precisely the message that Reizei Kimiko would most want to transmit to English readers, even down to a final claim that the Reizei Way of poetry is "the essence of Japanese culture." Even the photo adorning the article has been chosen with great care. For what it shows is a group of poets, six women and one man (Tamehito), all in kimono, seated in the Great Hall of the house on Imadegawa, in exactly the seating order that has been prescribed for such ritual gatherings since at least the time of Tamemura. Just as predictable is the topic chosen for composition that day—"Pines in Early Spring"—about which it is almost impossible to conceive a negative thought. Pines may not last forever, it may be said, but still they suffice as a symbol of what persists against vicissitudes in the world of men.

---

107. *ST* 75, p. 1.
108. Kamiya, "Time Travel the Reizei Way," accessed 3 November, 2006.

Conclusion

IN JANUARY of 2000 a new issue of the magazine *Subaru* appeared on the stands with a portrait of Fujiwara no Teika on its cover. He was seated, in black robes with just a hint of red underlining here and there, in high court cap, baton in hand. At his right was the title of the piece inside to which the cover alluded: a "special New Year conversation" involving Tanabe Seiko, a prominent historical novelist, Reizei Kimiko, and Kubota Jun, one of Japan's most distinguished scholars of traditional poetry.

The *zadankai*, or round-table discussion, is a very popular journalistic form in Japan. A few such discussions have even appeared in the Reizei house newsletter, involving scholars discussing the history of the house, manuscripts, and so on. Thus Reizei Kimiko was not unfamiliar with the demands of such a venue. That she was very much a willing participant is obvious from the fact that the event took place in her own house.

As usual, much of the preliminary talk amounted to posturing and positioning, clarifying social status, and so forth. Tanabe made the proper effusions on visiting the house—how it had the sweet smell of tradition, how amazing it is that the family has succeeded in preserving texts by Shunzei and Teika for so many centuries, how when coming through the gate she was impressed again with the cultural accomplishment of the family and its associates, who in "an attitude of reverence" (*agamete*) dedicated themselves to keeping the past alive. Then, she made the predictable jump to the central role of the Reizei family in preserving Japanese culture: "That these priceless treasures have been passed down, through times of warfare and natural disaster and everything else, bad and good, is to the good fortune of the Japanese people (*Nihon minzoku*), and something for which we are grateful."[1] Now that court culture is essentially defunct, the importance of the house must be linked to a broader constituency. None of this is new, of course; it has become very much the party line to all associated with the house since the end of the Pacific War. Imperial culture, court culture—in other words the socioeconomic worlds that actually sustained the whole Reizei poetic enterprise until Meiji—are seldom mentioned, their place taken by more vague but equally powerful notions of nation, race, or culture.

Much of the discussion was therefore predictable. The conversation contains a few statements, however, that are of interest to those who want to know more concrete details about the current state of the Reizei fortunes. For instance, Kimiko says that there are at least some young people among the 100 or so members of the Tamano'o kai.[2] To this extent, Tamehito and Kimiko deserve credit for attempting to maintain the most fundamental tradition of the house—which, as I hope this book has shown, is not so much the writing of poetry as the teaching of poetry, the maintenance of a Way. Kimiko also says, however, that the family has no money to hire people to do the clerical work necessary to run the corporation, but that graduate students, working half as volunteers, are working on the library collection under the supervision of scholars.[3] Doubtless the corporation has not made the family wealthy, at least in cash terms, or prominent in intellectual terms. Lectures on poetry are still given, and books of poems by the Reizei-ryū *kadan* are still published and advertised for sale on the last page of the newsletter. But the goal in all of this is obviously not to turn a profit. If the corporation is in some sense a business, then, poetry is taught now as a kind of public service, a way to carry on the traditions of the past for their own sake. To the extent that the Reizei-ryū in poetry has any kind of institutional support, in fact, it is in the academic world rather than in the world of contemporary poetry and poetic discourse,

---

1. Kubota Jun, Reizei Kimiko, and Tanabe, "Fujiwara Teika no sennen," p. 63.

2. Personal interview, November 16, 2005.

3. Kubota Jun, Reizei Kimiko, and Tanabe, "Fujiwara Teika no sennen," p. 63.

which rarely even recognizes the Reizei's existence. In this sense, the historical assets of the house — nicely incarnated in the remodeled dwelling on Imadegawa — still outweigh its more monetary ones, and probably always will.

Kimiko knows that this makes the role of Reizei traditions in the modern world a small one. Yet she is not convinced that there is no hope for the future. Indeed, taking advantage of the most "highbrow" venue ever offered her — for *Subaru* is one of the most prestigious of intellectual monthlies — she makes a case for old-fashioned poetry in the contemporary world. Not surprisingly, this place is defined in direct opposition to more modern poetry, indeed, to modern "Western" society:

Modern *tanka* is after all a genre of modern literature in which — perhaps because its founding concepts are individualism and the ego — one writes about how you and I are different, but our poetry meetings are not like that.

At New Year's time, one writes on spring topics . . . and the underlying assumption is that one is happy. Now, there are many people who are not happy even when spring comes, people who may be physically ill, for instance, and in modern *tanka* it is alright to write about one's unhappiness; but for us that is not allowed (*sore wa ikemasen*). When the topic is celebratory, one expresses one's happiness, no matter how sad one may be as an individual.[4]

One can of course wonder how the ever "egotistical" Teika, who wrote some decidedly unhappy poems, would react to such a statement. To be fair, however, one must remember that it is not Teika so much as Tameie who is the great founder of the Reizei house. And Tameie, both in his poetry and in his critical writings, does seem to argue always for a safer approach, a Way that has as its goal a subtle harmony in both the aesthetic and social worlds. It is this safer, more "communal" approach, based on shared attitudes and conventions and emphasizing participation in a long tradition, that Kimiko explicitly recommends:

The atmosphere of a Reizei poetry meeting has the same qualities as the tea ceremony. Perhaps it's because you are sharing the same space, sharing the same topic and the same feelings in common. In this aspect it is very different from modern *tanka*. Yet, it seems that recently there are more and more people who seem to enjoy [our way of doing things].[5]

---

4. Ibid., p. 64.
5. Ibid.

Such a description might not do for a poetry contest at the time of Retired Emperor Go-Toba, or even perhaps for a monthly gathering in the imperial chambers at the time of Retired Emperor Reigen, where egos were certainly involved. But in most ways the Way of Poetry for the Reizei house has indeed gone the way of the tea ceremony, which is to say the way of ritualization and formalism, in modern times. At a time when there are no rewards available, except the distinction of being part of an exclusive group, any but the most ornamental competition within the ranks would serve little purpose. For Fumiko and Kimiko, who never had the benefit of true instruction in the art they felt obligated to preserve, this affiliation with the *iemoto* system has become a way of making a virtue of necessity.

One is therefore not surprised to hear Kimiko disagree with Tanabe on the most crucial of issues—the nature of *daiei*, composition on set topics. Since the time of Teika and before, court poets have composed most of their poems on these pre-established topics, as Tanabe of course knows. But still she persists in connecting poetry to "individual" expression, in an effort, one supposes, to allow it some relevance in the modern literary field:

Tanabe: But certainly even among traditional poems written on topics (*daiei*), there are some poems of differing shades and colors, revealing the sensibility of the individual.

Reizei: A very difficult point. I think my conception of literature is rather different from what people mean today. Perhaps I would call it a kind of craft (*gijutsu*). I feel that it is close to something like that.[6]

The obverse of this is of course that the poems produced by the Reizei approach, on set topics and according to rhetorical conventions that predate even Teika, all seem the same. "In some ways," Kimiko admits, "one can't tell who wrote one poem and who another." But there are compensations. "When such a poem is read aloud in a meeting, it sounds beautiful to the ear, and when one writes it down, it is beautiful—that's what is so good."[7] Again, what is vital is communal experience in an ongoing enterprise by people sharing a store of what they would call cultural memory but which critics today might term a cultural imaginary.

----

6. Ibid., p. 67.
7. Ibid., p. 68.

However small the number of Reizei disciples there may be, Kimi-
ko thus argues that there ought to be room in the world of poetry
for those tired of modern individualism and competition. On this
point Tanabe is willing to agree: "Ever since Western literary theory
was imported in during the Meiji period, everything has been going
in that direction, but now that a whole century has passed, I wonder
if people aren't beginning to realize that's not all there is to litera-
ture; in Japanese traditions there may be a different kind of literary
climate (*bungaku fūdo*)."[8]

If this seems to come very close to the kind of neo-conservative
rhetoric of Umehara Takeshi, Shiba Ryōtarō, Nakano Kōji, and count-
less other contemporary Japanese culture critics, it is because there
is an inevitable intersection between those interests and the Reizei
cause. Kimiko and her circle are indeed allied with them in lamenting,
for instance, what they see as the ignorance of the Japanese people
about their own past and their mindless mimicry of the West.

In another recent interview, however, Kimiko makes it clear that
she wants nothing to do with overtly political causes, conservative
or otherwise, and resents the way the Reizei house is often associ-
ated with the right wing. In this one area, she devoutly hopes that
the activities of the house are regarded as in the realm of art, and
thus above sectarian squabbles:

> It's unfortunate that this country so often faces outward. For some reason,
> things get tied to ideology, and then cultural treasures don't get preserved.
> In France and other places, they adopt the posture of setting philosophical
> matters aside when it comes to preserving culture. Things get difficult when
> people try to press *Kokinshū* and *Genji* — which are neither left wing nor right
> wing — into absurd uses.[9]

Of course it is inevitable that a corporation with such close ties
to the leaders of the business world, government officials, and others
in the culture industry should be associated in the public mind with
conservative forces. But that is equally true of virtually all museums
and other artistic organizations, which would never survive without
support from just such quarters. In this one respect, the plight of the
Reizei at the beginning of the twenty-first century is in fact very

---

8. Ibid., p. 66.

9. Reizei Fumiko and Reizei Kimiko, "Haha kara musume e tsugu mono:
Reizei-ke happyakunen no shihō o mamoru," p. 173.

much like its plight in all eras of Japanese history. As noted in the introduction, they have always had to convert their social and cultural capital into income in the form of patronage, gifts, or cold cash. Dependence on the powerful—emperors, regents and higher-ranking nobles, shoguns, daimyo, samurai, and so on down through the ages—is a constant of the Reizei story, as is the frustration of those whose role it is to secure support for an activity that, on the surface, at least, seems apolitical indeed:

Kubota: Do your disciples these days still use words from ancient times?

Kimiko: Now the first thing I do is give a lecture—teaching what kind of words there are to express the idea of "the moon," that is if "the moon" has come up as a topic. This is a kind of secret transmission (*hiden*)—if that's not too grandiose a term—of the words that have been employed down through the ages. Around any one word are many other beautiful words, and to put them to proper use—that is the poetry of the Reizei house, I think.[10]

In the absence of the old "secret teachings" of the house, the whole vocabulary of the *uta* tradition thus must serve as a substitute, a sacred language. Whether teaching a handful of people the special vocabulary of an ancient verse form is enough to sustain one aristocratic house after the official demise of the aristocracy of course remains to be seen. It is worth noting, however, that the effort is not unlike efforts in earlier times, when the cultural "stock" of the house went through periods of devaluation. There may be no way to give relevance to the old "secret teachings" of the house in the larger literary world, but the general vocabulary of *waka* may continue to prove to be marketable as the basis of a traditional craft—a word from which, as noted above, Kimiko does not shy away.

SO THERE is no reason to count the Reizei out. What they do is anachronistic, almost by definition, and will probably never attract large or powerful disciples from the broader literary world. The teaching end of their enterprise will continue to be a small one, especially as compared with generations past. But after all is said and done the house still controls the library, which, barring some cataclysmic disaster, will doubtless survive, whether in its new storehouse on Imadegawa Street in Kyoto or eventually in the vaults of some univer-

---

10. Kubota Jun, Reizei Kimiko, and Tanabe, "Fujiwara Teika no sennen," p. 66.

sity. Its continued existence is the one undeniable contribution of the Reizei family to history—as recent members of the lineage have always understood. For as long as the library continues, the story of the house, too, will remain alive on some level, a monument to the dedication of those who struggled to keep their past alive in more than a dry and academic way. Whether the lineage survives— and Kimiko is somewhat doubtful that it will, as noted earlier—is in that respect a moot point.[11]

A poem by Fumiko's elder sister, Hideko, composed on the 750th anniversary of Teika's death in 1990, expresses well the attitude of all recent Reizei men and women, an attitude of nostalgia, perhaps even of loss, but not quite of pessimism:

> For the waning moon   shining above
> in mid-air   I would ask questions:
> about distant ancestors   who once lived
> on Saga Moor.[12]

> *nakazora no/hatsuka no tsuki ni/koto towamu/tōtsumioya no/mashishi sagano o*

The distance between past and present is always immense, of course, perhaps more vast than the space between earth and moon, which has now been traversed. Moderns may find this fixation on engagement with a long tradition—especially one that is embodied in a kind of conventionality rather than in a properly sanctified lineage of geniuses—curious for this very reason. But there is more at stake in refusing to learn from the Reizei story than the story itself. For to overlook conventionality, in the case of *waka*, at least, is to refuse to engage the record of the past as an ongoing project that cannot be reduced to the accomplishments of a few canonized "masterpieces" or sanctified "geniuses"—to allow the reputation of a few individuals and texts, in other words, to obscure the contours of a much larger discourse. Furthermore, it is to ignore one of the fundamental assumptions that is at the heart of much Japanese poetry in all forms, namely, that the literary is always social. Matsuo Bashō—who had no affiliation whatsoever with the Reizei but who was still part of the same "memory culture"—is reported to have

---

11. Personal interview, November 16, 2005.
12. "Fujiwara no Teika-kyō nanahyakugojūnenki," p. 2.

said: "Poetry is to be enjoyed while you are producing it. Once it's written down on paper, it's no more than garbage."[13]

No amount of obfuscation can get around the position that Bashō takes in this quotation, which is that it is in the social moment that the text has its primary being. This does not mean that texts do not survive that social moment, which they certainly do; nor does it mean that texts never receive exalted status in the Japanese case, which is patently untrue. Bashō's words and the attitude they represent do serve, however, to remind us of what the sociologist S. N. Eisenstadt characterizes as the typical Japanese approach to semantic structuration, which "is characterized by the minimization of the importance of the subject relative to the environment and emphasis on relational and indexical criteria (as against abstract, linear principles) as the regulating principles of the discourse."[14] Whatever excels in traditional Japanese poetic discourse must do so within the limits of strict convention and not outside of them.

The Reizei may be relatively unaware of these larger philosophical issues. But they are not unaware that their Way offers an alternative, more participatory tradition that has too long been stigmatized because it does not measure up to Western ideals of originality and monumentality. In this they have much in common with other literary genres that also receive short shrift from modern critics, a list of which would include everything from *haiku* to historical fiction. In addition to its own innate interest, then, perhaps the story of the Reizei house has something else to offer students today, namely, an opportunity to reconsider Tsubouchi Shōyō's famous dismissal of so much in Japan's past literature that to him seemed the work of "adaptationists" (*yakinaoshika*).[15] For certainly adaptation is at the heart of all that we call craft and indeed much that we call art. Is not adaptation, after all, the word scientists give to strategies of survival? Whether the Reizei meet the challenge of adapting to new cultural demands may be a questionable proposition, perhaps; but

---

13. Quoted in *Haikai mondō* (*Haikai* dialogues), by Bashō's disciples Morikawa Kyoriku (1656–1715) and Mukai Kyorai (1651-1704), p. 114.

14. Eisenstadt, *Japanese Civilization*, p. 319.

15. See *Shōsetsu shinzui* (The Essence of the Novel), p. 79, where Shōyō dismisses Edo- and mid-Meiji-period writers of fiction as dominated by "adaptations, translations, and revisions" and sees no sign of a true creator, or *sakusha*.

that adaptation is a fundamental feature of all discourse — including those dismissed by elitist critics as formulaic — is not.

Finally, a study of the Reizei Way also gives us a view of a peculiar aesthetic that it shares with many other traditional arts and crafts and without an account of which no description of Japanese culture can be complete. How to characterize this aesthetic is no easy matter, but a modern poet from another traditional lineage, Sasaki Yukitsuna (b. 1939), makes the attempt:

One senses that the way classical poets got enjoyment from *uta* is different from the way poets of modern *tanka* who value individualism get their enjoyment. It is an enjoyment based on recognizing foundation poems [*honka*] and poems very similar to each other. Aware of the poems that have come before, one aims to come as close as one can to them and then enjoys the thrill [*suriru*] of the near miss [*niamisu*].[16]

It goes without saying, of course, that the pleasures of the "near miss" are only for those with a sure knowledge of the canon. "In order to taste this thrill, one must memorize whole catalogues of earlier poems, word for word, rigorously, accurately," as Sasaki says.[17]

Ultimately this is why the future of Reizei poetic practices, as distinct from the library and its treasures, must be in doubt. Even the emperor, who still composes poetry in 5-7-5-7-7 format, has given up on pursuing the erudite thrill of the near miss in favor of more transparent referentiality.[18] Few people these days have the time or the inclination to memorize thousands of old poems. Even among poems composed in Reizei gatherings are many like the following — on the topic "Bedclothes" from a recent publication of the Tamano'o Group — that are closer to modern *tanka* than Kimiko's statements about Reizei teachings might lead one to believe:

> So soft on my skin   are the quilts
> of muted red   I have used all year

---

16. Sasaki, "Koten jidai no kajin no jōken," p. 53.

17. Ibid.

18. See Philomène and Saito, eds., *Tomoshibi, Light*. Each of the poems quoted in this anthology does include a stated topic, but a look at the nature of the topics — "Yachts," "The Return of Okinawa," "In Zaire," to name a few — indicates the distance between Reizei practices and those of the imperial couple.

that beneath them I forget   the cold
on a frosty night.[19]

toshi nareshi / usubeniiro no / atsufusuma / hada ni yasashiku / shimoyo wasururu

Through the deep snow   that surrounds
my little cottage   no one comes to visit;
cold beneath my bedclothes   I lie waiting
for my husband.[20]

yuki fukaku / tou hito mo naki / waga iori / fusuma tsumetaku / otto o machiiru

In the poetics of Kyōgoku Tamekane—which the Reizei can legitimately claim as part of their own heritage—there is perhaps precedent for such poems, as there is in Tametsugi's encouragement simply to "say what you feel." Whether future Reizei teachers will call upon those sources for justification in support of another necessary adaptation is one of the many things about the future of the Reizei house that remains to be seen.

---

19. *Heisei jūninen Tamano'o kai shū*, p. 137. The author of the poem is Reizei Michiko, wife of Tamehiro, current head of the lower Reizei lineage.
20. Ibid. The author of the poem is one Ohara Mieko.

APPENDIX

One Hundred Poems
of the Reizei School

As NOTED above, Teika's famous *Hyakunin isshu* has inspired many poets and scholars to create their own small collections of representative poems. In the latest of these, put together by the novelist Maruya Saiichi at the turn of the millennium, only one poem by a member of the Reizei lineage appears. Predictably, it is one by Tamesuke:

> In a mountain home   the hazy night sky
> intrudes   right through the window —
> tinging a spring lantern   with the hues
> of moonlight.[1]
>
> *yamazato wa / mado no uchi made / kasumu yo ni / tsuki no iro naru / haru no tomoshibi*

The headnote to the poem notes that it was a *byōbu uta* — a poem written on a painted screen. As Maruya suggests, the screen in question, which has not survived, probably featured the moon on a hazy spring night and a person looking out at the moon through his open window.[2]

Doubtless the main reason Maruya did not include more Reizei poets in his collection is that he restricted his selections to the period

---

1. Maruya, *Shinshin hyakunin isshu*, p. 67. The poem originally appeared in *Rokka wakashū*, poem no. 77.

2. Maruya, *Shinshin hyakunin isshu*, pp. 67–68.

of the imperial anthologies, thus eliminating the possiblity of honoring Tamemura or other Reizei devotees of the late medieval, warring states, and Edo periods. For whatever reason, it is unfortunate that the Reizei have been overlooked again.

My purpose in the remaining pages of this book is to introduce 100 poems by poets of the Reizei "persuasion" (my attempt to translate the Japanese term *Reizei-ha*). Needless to say, I have not been able to include all the poets who in one way or another may be identified with the Reizei house. The major ones, however, are all represented. Following the injunctions of Tamesuke and his heirs, I have not restricted my selections to any one style, instead aiming for variety in topic, technique, theme, and aesthetic effect. The moon, cherry blossoms, autumn leaves, and snow all abound, to be sure, but so they must if one is to mirror honestly the habits of the Reizei poets over the centuries. As I hope the pages above have shown, the word *Reizei-ha* usually implied social affiliation rather than any clearly definable style, and my efforts have therefore been to represent the variety of the Reizei tradition as fully as possible. It is safe to say that few of the poets whose work appears here claimed to have a truly individual style, and I have not taken any such consideration into account when choosing which poems to translate.

I have tried to include representatives from all the standard venues of poetic composition: meetings and parties of various sorts, often recorded in collections, large and small, private and public; contests, real or staged; decorations for standing screens and sliding door panels; letters and diaries; inscriptions; votive offerings; and so on. My hope is that anyone reading the sequence will get a sense of the social contexts in which poetry in the traditional *uta* form has been produced, from the eleventh century until today.

Some of the early poems, especially those by the founders of the lineage, are quite famous. The rest, however, are relatively unknown even among scholars. Unfortunately, many collections of the late Edo period are still unavailable in print and are likely to remain so for some time to come. The newsletter of the house and other resources quoted here and there in scholarly articles have therefore been very important in providing examples of the *Reizei-ha* in recent times.

Readers will notice that four of the last five poems in the sequence are by women. My design in making these choices was not to slight the poetic efforts of men such as Fumiko's husband, Tametō, or the current family head, Tamehito, but rather to emphasize the importance of women to the survival of the house and to try to make up for the paucity of poems by women from earlier periods, who certainly must have written much that has either not been preserved or has yet to emerge from the *oshinbunko*.

1. *Fujiwara no Michinaga (966–1027)*

> Parting: When Shikibu was going down to Ueno, he received a fan from the Empress, on which was painted a roadside inn, next to which Michinaga wrote this:

> On a grass pillow   at an inn
> by a roadside   heavy with dew —
> that is when one wants a breeze   to gently brush
> the drops away.

> *kusamakura / tabi no yadori no / tsuyukeku wa / harau bakari no / kaze mo fukanan*

FUJIWARA NO Michinaga was chieftain of the Fujiwara clan, minister, regent, and grandfather to three emperors, and as such his arena was the Hall of State and not the salons of literati. Men in his position were expected to specialize in only one thing, and that was politics.

Yet even a regent was expected to be able to produce a poem when custom required. The one above was inscribed by Michinaga on a fan that had been presented to Ki no Shikibu (precise dates unknown) by Michinaga's daughter, the Empress Akiko (also read Shōshi; 988–1074), when Shikibu was embarking on a trip to the East Country. On such an occasion, poems expressing the proper sentiments were appreciated if not expected. Michinaga breaks slightly from tradition by producing a sentiment that is more cheerful than is usually the case with travel poems. But in the way it works in the suggestion that the fan may be useful in brushing away dew — a metaphor for tears — it is an appropriately courtly effort. The whole incident serves to remind us that poetry at court was from the beginning as much a social as an artistic enterprise.

Strictly speaking, the Mikohidari line begins not with Michinaga but with his sixth son, Nagaie. But the three houses have always been proud of their descent from the greatest of Heian political figures, who reigned over the golden age of court culture — the age that produced *The Tale of Genji*, *The Pillow Book of Sei Shōnagon*, the diary of Izumi Shikibu, and other court classics.

The poem is recorded in the parting book of *Shin senzaishū* (no. 742), eighteenth of the imperial anthologies.

2. *Retired Emperor Go-Reizei (1025–68)*

Miscellaneous: Written during the time he was living at Kayano-in, on the 13th of the Ninth Month, when he was looking out at the waterfall he had had stones brought in to create

Water flowing out   from gaps between
boulders   races swiftly by.
How steady, though, is the light   reflected there
by the moon!

iwama yori / nagaruru mizu wa / hayakeredo / utsureru tsuki no / kage zo nodokeki

KAYANO-IN WAS a palace built by Fujiwara no Yorimichi (992–1074), eldest son of Michinaga, which later served as the residence of various notable figures, including Retired Emperor Go-Reizei. Contemporary records describe the grounds of the palace as spacious and well appointed. The flowing water of Go-Reizei's poem is doubtless a reference to the stream flowing out into an ornamental pond.

By this time, certain sites—Naniwa, for example, known for its reeds; or Tatsuta, for its autumn leaves—had already gained the status of *nadokoro*, or "famous places" that virtually demanded a poem from visitors. The scene of Go-Reizei's poem, however, is in some sense not "natural" at all but a human construct, and he seems to play on the distinction. The contrast is an old one: the world below versus the world above. The palace, however imposing, is temporary; the waterfall is artificial, the stones real enough but clearly imposed on the landscape by human hands. The poem thus presents via the image of the flowing water a metaphor for the world of constantly shifting appearances. Only the moon, distant and cold, is steady by comparison. Even its light, however, is a reflection and in that sense another phenomenon of the floating world. This play of shifting images will remain a theme of court poetry for all the ages to come.

The poem appears in the first miscellaneous book of *Goshūishū* (no. 846), fourth of the imperial anthologies of the genre.

3. *Fujiwara no Nagaie (1005–64)*

Winter: Written for a *shōji* painting depicting hawking on a snowy morning

A mottled hawk   freed from its cage
for the hunt   finds nowhere to perch:
soaring off in search of prey   into skies portending
snow.

toyakaeru / shirafu no taka no / koi o nami / yukige no sora ni / awasetsuru kana

THE CONNECTION between painting and poetry was forged early in the history of the imperial Japanese court. As early as the ninth century, Chinese poems were being inscribed on paintings, providing a means of commentary and counterpoint. By the time of Emperor Daigo (885–930; r. 897–930), who commissioned the first imperial collection of Japanese poetry, the practice had been extended to poems in the native language, referred to as *byōbu-uta*, or "screen poems." Records show that all the major poets of that time left examples of the genre, although we have only the poems and not the paintings as evidence.

Headnotes indicate that the paintings were generally on seasonal themes, sometimes depicting famous landscapes, sometimes court festivals or rites, as in the case of the earlier poem by Michinaga. In this sense, the paintings functioned much as would conventional topics, or *dai*, in later times, providing the poet with a pre-established pattern of treatment within which to conceive his or her work. How prominent the form had become by the mid-tenth century is suggested by the fact that nearly two-thirds of the poems in the personal collection of Ki no Tsurayuki were written for paintings.[3]

Nagaie's poem was composed for a painting on a sliding door panel rather than a standing screen, but the dynamic involved was the same. Since he knew his poem would survive as an independent artifact, he was obliged to make it complete on its own terms — a straightforward winter scene, showing men on a hunting field setting their hawks to work beneath skies that threaten snow. Yet we can also assume that Nagaie attempted to respond to the work of the (unnamed) visual artist. The scholar Kenshō (ca. 1130– ca. 1210) goes so far as to suggest that the poem makes a witty comment on the painting, which "must not have contained a tree for the hawk to perch on."[4] In other ways, too, the poem may be read as a depiction of the scene on the door it helped adorn. The play of light and dark, the contrast between the small bird and the broad expanse of the sky, the idea of a "blending" of elements — all were probably inspired by the painting first of all.

The poem is recorded in the winter book of *Goshūishū* (no. 393).

---

3. McCullough, *Brocade by Night*, p. 236.
4. *Goshūishō chū*, pp. 350-351.

4.   *Fujiwara no Tadaie (1033–91)*

Miscellaneous: Composed when courtiers at the Palace presented
poems on the idea of "Enjoying Artificial Cherry Blossoms,"
at the time of Retired Emperor Go-Reizei

Not so different   from those one picks
from the trees   are these cherry blossoms—
standing out but in the way   they will never
fade and fall.

sakurabana/orite mishi ni mo/kawaranu ni/chiranu bakari zo/shirushi narikeru

MOST POEMS on cherry blossoms appear in the spring section of an-
thologies. But probably because it celebrates not real but artificial
blossoms, the editors of *Shin kokinshū* put this one in the miscellane-
ous section, among other poems that likewise employ the image of
cherry blossoms while being chiefly about something else.

The original was composed for a gathering in the emperor's living
quarters, the Seiryōden, on the 27th day of the intercalary Third
Month of 1056. At the time, artificial cherry blossoms were placed in
the *hirobisashi* (peripheral chambers) of the building for all to enjoy.
To courtiers in later days, when such extravagant displays were no
longer possible, events like these became the stuff of fantasy and
nostalgia.

Tadaie, second son of Nagaie, was a major counselor at the time of
the event and was very active in the entourage of Retired Emperor
Go-Reizei. His poem is clearly congratulatory, a prayer that, like the
blossoms, the sovereign's glory will never end.

The poem appears as no. 1462 in *Shin kokinshū*.

5.   *Fujiwara no Toshitada (1073–1123)*

Summer: "On Orange Blossoms," written for a poem contest
at his home

Out there in the gloom   of a night
in the Fifth Month   are orange blossoms,
their whereabouts proclaimed   through the skies
by passing wind.

satsukiyami/hanatachibana no/arika o ba/kaze no tsute ni zo/sora ni shirikeru

IT WAS during the mid-Heian period that poetry contests first took
place in the meeting halls of the imperial palace and at the homes
of court nobles. Thereafter they were a constant feature of poetic
culture until the late Muromachi period. Needless to say, the contest

format was ideally suited to the purposes of court poetry. Contests were public spectacles that allowed for display of competence but also the reinforcement of social hierarchies and the spectacle of a community united by a common sensibility and a shared canon.

Usually participants were divided into two sides, the left and the right, competing in pairs against each other. In the early days, a judge might simply award the win to one contestant on the spot; later, participants often decided the matter by vote, usually after discussion. Later it was also common for *han no kotoba*, "words of judgment," to be appended to each round, offering criticism and exegesis. Sponsorship of poetry contests was often undertaken by patrons with the financial resources to provide the finest of accoutrements. Sometimes, though, the poetic houses took the obligation upon themselves, as was the case with the contest that produced the poem above, the full title of which reads *Poem Contest at the Home of the Middle Captain in the Left Guards*. At the time of the meeting—the Fifth Month of 1104—Toshitada was active in the salon of Retired Emperor Horikawa (1079–1107; r. 1086–1107). By comparison with the more famous contests, Toshitada's was a modest affair, only thirteen rounds in all, and involved only sixteen participants. After a period of open critique, Minamoto no Toshiyori served as final judge.

In keeping with the season in which the contest was held, the topics were nearly all in the summer category— "Cuckoo," "Summer Grasses," "Fireflies," and so on. Though quite conventional in the way it treats its subject, Toshitada's poem won its round. Toshiyori praised it for the witty phrasing of its last two lines.

The poem is recorded in the summer book of *Kin'yōshū* (no. 148), fifth of the imperial anthologies.

6. Fujiwara no Shunzei (1114–1204)

Miscellaneous: Written on the idea of "The Moon
at a Mountain Home"

Tired of my old life   I came
into the mountains   to hide myself away—
and found too radiant, almost,   the moon shining
in the night.

sumiwabite / mi o kakusu beki / yamazato ni / amari kuma naki / yowa no tsuki kana

A TEACHER must provide models for his students; hence the existence of one of Fujiwara no Teika's earliest critical works, *Kindai shūka*, "Superior Poems of Our Time." Evidently intended explicitly for instruction, the treatise—if one can call so slight a work by so grand a name—begins with a short preface on the history of Japanese poetry and then goes on to offer words of encouragement on various dimensions of composition.

Kindai shūka ends with a list of exemplary poems, among which are a half dozen by his father, including the one above. Since it appears in *Senzaishū*, an imperial anthology compiled by Shunzei himself, we can assume that Shunzei had regard for it as well. The topic is one that often evokes the image of a recluse lamenting his decision to leave the world behind. Shunzei's poem expresses a related idea, i.e., that even those who claim to have left the world have not truly done so, as he complains in another poem included in *Kindai shūka*:

> Ah, this world of ours—   it leaves no path
> of escape.   For even back here
> in the mountain recesses   I hear the call
> of a stag.[5]

> *yo no naka yo / michi koso nakere / omoiiru / yama no oku ni mo / shika zo naku naru*

The world—meaning the world of human affairs—cannot be escaped. Even in the deepest mountains, moonlight illuminates the dark of one's hiding place; even there one hears the call of a stag yearning for its mate, bringing unwanted memories to mind. A student of Tendai doctrine, Shunzei knew the Buddhist tenet of the universal in the particular, the world in a grain of sand—a doctrine that can easily be inflected to mean that the world is the same wherever one goes.

The poem appears in the miscellaneous book of *Senzaishū* (no. 988).

7.   *Fujiwara no Teika (1162–1241)*

From *The 30-Poem Sequence of the Provisional Major Counselor,* on "Pines at a Mountain Home"

> With never a thought   that I might
> be remembered,   I let time go by—
> accustomed to Ogura's pines   standing right here
> at my eaves.

> *shinobaremu / mono to wa nashi ni / ogurayama / nokiba no matsu zo / narete hisashiki*

OUR FIRST extant *hyakushu uta* (100-poem sequences) date to the late tenth century. By the time of Teika the form was one of the chief

---

5. Fujiwara no Teika, *Kindai shūka*, p. 109.

genres of court poetry, as important as the poetry contest. Prominent figures of all sorts commissioned such works on a variety of occasions, including the announcement of plans for a new imperial anthology. Virtually all sequences were in fact imperial anthologies in miniature, beginning with seasonal poems and going on to love and miscellaneous topics.

Smaller collections were also produced. The 30-poem sequence from which the poem above is taken, for instance, was commissioned by Kujō Motoie, son of Teika's old patron and friend Yoshitsune, for presentation at a gathering at Motoie's house on the 29th day of the Third Month of 1225. Other participants included Fujiwara no Ietaka, Jien, and Teika's son and heir, Tameie, as well as a handful of others. All wrote on 30 topics according to the usual pattern. Teika's diary notes that he worked on the poems for months before the meeting, sending them to Motoie just a week or so before the date scheduled for formal presentation. The completed sequences were copied by a calligrapher, stored in a fine box, and placed in the library of the Kujō house, alongside other manuscripts that attested to their dedication as patrons.

Many of Teika's poems for the set are melancholy in mood, as is his meditation on the passing of time at Ogura. On the surface, the musing may seem disingenuous; any poet in Teika's position knew that he would be remembered, after all. But does that reduce the poem to empty posturing? At the time, Teika was 64 and certainly old enough to be thinking about a future he would never see. As it happened, he would live on for 15 years, during which time he would visit his retreat in Saga often. But he knew that the pines would outlive him. The theme is no less touching for being of ancient vintage. As death approaches, an old man wonders where all the time went, and how he could have taken so much for granted for so long.

The poem appears in Teika's personal anthology, *Shūi gusō* (no. 1982).

8. *Shunzei's Daughter (precise dates unknown)*

Spring: On "Blossoms," from *The 100–Poem Sequences at the Home of the Tō-in Regent*

I know, of course, that flowers
in our floating world bloom only to fall —
yet still I cannot bring myself to despise
the mountain cherries.

sakeba chiru / hana no ukiyo to / omou ni mo / nao utomarenu / yamazakura kana

THE EARLY sixteenth-century poet Junsō says that Abutsu admired this poem.[6] Perhaps that is why it was included in *Shoku gosenshū*, tenth of the imperially commissioned anthologies, for which her husband Tameie was sole compiler. Originally, the poem came from a sequence commissioned nearly 30 years earlier, in 1230, by Kujō Michiie, father of the Tō-in Regent Norizane (1210–35). Participants in the project included both those men, Teika, Shunzei's Daughter, and others. Among the poems is a famous one by Teika:

> To have grown old— with the snow
> all around me I know what it means.
> No one comes to visit and I have no place
> to go.[7]

oiraku wa / yuki no uchi ni zo / omoishiru / tou hito mo nashi / yuku kata mo nashi

While not so somber, the poem by Shunzei's Daughter hints at a similar sadness over the inevitability of decline.

By the 1230s, Shunzei's Daughter, born sometime in the 1170s, would have been well along in years. Though known as his daughter, she was actually his grandchild, the child of his daughter Hachijō-in Sanjō. Shunzei took her in as a foster child and arranged a marriage to a prominent courtier, and when the marriage failed sent her into Go-Toba's service. She took the tonsure in 1213, and lived for a time in Saga. After Teika's death in 1241, she moved to Koshibe Estate in Harima Province (modern Hyōgo Prefecture), where she died at past 80. Later, deeds for her estate rights there would come down to the Reizei house. To this day, a small shrine there—named Tenka-san, a corrupted form of Teika-san, it would seem—keeps her memory alive.[8]

The poem appears in the spring book of *Shoku gosenshū* (no. 122), tenth of the imperial anthologies.

9. *Archbishop Jien (1155–1225)*

> Buddhism: "Too Empty for Thought"
> Everywhere around the sky above
> is empty, or so I had thought—

---

6. *Ungyokushū*, poem no. 95.
7. *Fujiwara Teika zenkashū*, poem no. 1446.
8. Reizei Kimiko, "Tenka-san."

until I saw wisteria   blooming in clouds
of purple.

oshinabete / munashiki sora to / omoishi ni / fuji sakinureba / murasaki no kumo

POEMS ON Buddhist topics, known as *shakkyōka*, go as far back as the court tradition. It was only in *Goshūishū* (1086), however, that a place for them was set aside within the miscellaneous section of an imperial anthology. The designation is very broad, including poems about basic Buddhist themes such as impermanence, poems on lines from sutras, poems written at or about temples, poems on doctrines, and poems by monks and nuns.

Jien's poem, composed on a phrase from *The Lotus Sutra*, is an allegory in which the sky signifies the emptiness of life in the world and the wisteria, salvation in the Paradise of Amida. A gloss would read, "Looking out at the sky, I at first thought it was empty, but now I see wisteria in bloom—clouds of purple like those that bring Amida from the Pure Land to greet us. In this sense, temporary illusion is no more than a revelation of ultimate truth." According to tradition, the savior Amida was believed to come forward to welcome the faithful on a purple cloud.

Jien's is one of more than 60 *shakkyōka* included in the twentieth and last book of *Shin kokinshū*. It also appears in a "mock" poetry contest put together around 1198, which is titled *Jichin oshō jika-awase* ("The Personal Poetry Contest of Revered Jichin"). Made up mostly of poems by Jien, but also by some members of his family, the manuscript of this contest was presented to the seven shrines of Hiyoshi as a votive offering, fifteen rounds going to each. Judgments were written by Shunzei. The "mock" contest format would continue as a sub-genre throughout the medieval period, functioning as a way to solicit commentary by a prominent master. It was particularly popular during the *Shin kokin* period.

Jien, a son of Kujō Kanezane, was not a member of the Mikohidari lineage. As a major patron of Shunzei and Teika, however, he has been highly venerated by their descendants, who also credit him for discouraging Tameie from giving up the Way.

The poem appears in the Buddhism book of *Shin kokinshū* (no. 1944).

10.   *Fujiwara no Tameie (1198–1275)*

Miscellaneous: Written on the 22nd day of the Fourth Month
of the Eighth year of the Bun'ei era (1271). From a 100-poem sequence

The hour has grown late.   For a moment
I doze off   into fitful sleep—
hearing still from time to time   the tolling
of the bells.

fukenikeri / shibashi madoromu / utatane ni / tabitabi kane no / koe zo kikoyuru

IN THE year 1271, when this poem was written, Tameie was in his 74th year. Tamesuke was 8 years old, Tamemori just 6. With those facts as a backdrop, one is tempted to conclude that in his fitful sleep the old man is worrying over the future of the children of his old age. Conflicts with Tameuji over estate rights that Tameie wanted to assign to Tamesuke had begun several years before. One can easily imagine such matters keeping the old man from restful sleep, even on a tranquil spring night.

Yet such a reading must remain tentative, for by the thirteenth century the persona of the wakeful old man was already well established. In many cases, the cause of wakefulness was not worry over the present but memories of the past. What is keeping the old man awake, then, must be left to the imagination.

What initially wakes him from his fitful sleep, on the other hand, is clearly stated: a temple bell, or perhaps bells. This tells us that it is indeed late, nearly dawn. The bells call the monks to their prayers and tell everyone around that a new day is about to begin. Metaphorically, they also summon believers from the dreamworld, the realm of illusion, back to the reality of the Buddhist Law. The speaker in Tameie's poem is caught in between, dozing off repeatedly, seemingly reluctant to heed the call and to join the world of the awakened.

The poem is recorded in Tameie's personal anthology, *Tameie shū* (no. 1212).

11.   *Abutsu (d. ca. 1283)*

Autumn: Written in Saga

All these years, never   did a night go by
when I heard no call   from a stag—
beset in my mountain home   by autumn
wakefulness.

toshi o hete / shika no ne kikanu / yowa mo nashi / kono yamazato no / aki no nezame wa

THE POEMS of *Shūi fūtei wakashū*, an early fourteenth-century compilation usually attributed to Tamesuke, are organized just like an imperial anthology. Abutsu's poem is from the autumn book, where it appears alongside the poems of a number of poets of the anti-Nijō coalition of those days, from Tameaki and Tamekane to Keiyū (precise dates unkown), one of Tameie's cleric sons. But Tameie, Shunzei's Daughter, Go-Toba, and even Tameyo are also represented. One purpose of such collections was to make a statement, and Tamesuke's whole purpose in putting the collection together was to claim the right of full participation in poetic affairs, including the compilation of anthologies for the court as a whole. To list only the poems of his cohorts in the East Country would have been to admit defeat.

No one knows the precise date of Abutsu's poem, which is recorded nowhere else. Since it was written in Saga, however, one may hazard that it comes from before her travel to Kamakura, perhaps even before Tameie's death. The headnote mentions no *dai*, or "fixed topic," which may mean that it was not written for a contest or some other social gathering, or may simply mean that the topic had been forgotten. Certainly one could put the poem in any collection under either of several topics—"Stag," "Autumn Wakefulness," "Autumn Night," and so on—without doing damage to it or to the collection.

In court poetry, the call of a stag nearly always evoked thoughts of a lost or absent mate, an appropriately melancholy thought to occupy the mind of a person of advanced years lying awake on a long autumn night. Although it was the place where she became Tameie's lover and wife, Abutsu must have had mixed feelings about Saga. She had competitors, and despite her best efforts she was unable to secure the future she wanted for her sons when she was still living there before Tameie's death.

The poem is recorded in *Shūi fūtei wakashū* (no. 92).

12. Ta'a (1237–1319)

"Winter"

Only this morning   did the leaves begin
to fall from trees   in my garden.
Can it really be that the wind   sounds different
from yesterday?

kesa yori zo / niwa ni ko no ha wa / chirisomuru / kinō ni kawaru / kaze no oto ka wa

MANY CLERICS were of noble birth. This was particularly true of the abbots of temples of the great aristocratic sects, such as Tendai and Shingon. But noble sons also led some of the newer sects.

One of these was Ta'a (short for Ta-Amidabutsu; also known as Shinkyō), who appears to have been a descendant of the Mibu lineage. He became second patriarch of the Time sect (Jishū) founded by Ippen (1239–89). Especially popular among the warrior class, the Time sect—so called because its practitioners believed in salvation for all beings as a single and timeless event—had a great following in the East Country, where Ta'a spent most of his time pursuing the duties of his office, which included extensive travel. The 1,460 poems of his personal poetry collection, however, show that he had time to compose poems along with his many acquaintances, among whom were Tamesuke, Tamekane, and Tamemori. In this he was not alone among members of his sect, which would later include prominent masters such as Tonna and the *renga* master Zenna (precise dates unknown). In his last years, Ta'a founded a temple in Sagami, on the eastern seaboard just west of Kamakura. It was there that he died.

Ta'a's poem alludes to the first poem in the autumn section of *Kokinshū* (no. 169), by Fujiwara no Toshiyuki (d. 901):

> Autumns' arrival   is not something
> that is clear   before our eyes,
> but rather a jolt that comes   with the sound
> of the wind.
>
> *aki kinu to / me ni wa sayaka ni / mienedomo / kaze no oto ni zo / odorokarenuru*

Toshiyuki claims it is the sound of the wind that announces Autumn's arrival, but Ta'a gently begs to differ, noting another effect of the wind's passing—falling leaves. The poem is no. 910 in *Ta'a Shōnin kashū*, the monk's personal anthology. Included in a sequence presented to Reizei Tamesuke for judgment, it is one of the poems Tamesuke honored with a mark (/).

13. *Retired Emperor Fushimi (1265–1317)*

> Miscellaneous: On "Summer Grasses," from a 50-poem sequence
>
> Caught in the tangles   of a world
> where troubles crowd 'round   like summer grasses,
> my heart has lost all sense   of which way
> it should go.
>
> *natsugusa no / koto shigeki yo ni / midasarete / kokoro no sue wa / michi mo tōrazu*

IN COURT poetry, summer is a time of luxuriant green growth but also of long rains and oppressive heat, a time when the summer grasses quite take over the landscape. To Retired Emperor Fushimi, however, the topic "Summer Grasses" suggests something more: the nature of life in a world of troubles.

The man we know as Retired Emperor Fushimi knew a great deal about worldly conflict. Born to a lesser consort of Emperor Go-Fukakusa, Fushimi became crown prince in his teens in the context of political complications and eventually ascended the throne, where he served as sovereign for more than a decade. Expecting a more leisurely sort of life as an imperial prince, he had developed aesthetic interests early on, particularly in the sister arts of poetry and calligraphy. While serving as emperor from 1287 to 1298, he sponsored a lively court and did the same when he was made senior retired emperor in 1308. It was with his support that Kyōgoku Tamekane compiled *Gyokuyōshū*. In 1313, he took the tonsure. He died in 1317, having lived just long enough to see Tamekane sent into his second exile.

Both *Gyokuyōshū* and *Fūgashū*, the latter compiled by one of Fushimi's sons, were attacked by Nijō poets as unorthodox (*ifū*), as were Tamekane and Fushimi himself. Yet there are few poems in either collection that might have invited censure. Fushimi's poem on summer grasses, for instance, might be taken to task for straying somewhat from its topic. But in its diction, syntax, and theme it offers nothing truly unorthodox. One is tempted to read it as a commentary on the challenges of court polilitics, but that is probably too narrow an interpretation. The poem aims to say something about the human condition, suggesting that to be crowded round with troubles, like encroaching summer grasses that obscure the path ahead, is the predicament of all.

The poem appears in *Fūgashū* (no. 1516).

14. *Prince Hisaakira (1276–1328)*

Travel: Topic Unknown

By some traveler   used and then tossed
to roadside —   a torch of pine tar
still smoldering forlornly   in the faint glow
before dawn.

tabibito no / tomoshi sutetaru / matsu no hi no / kemuru sabishiki / noji no akebono

PRINCE HISAAKIRA, a son of Emperor Go-Fukakusa, was the third imperial prince to serve as shogun under the watchful eye of the Hōjō regents in Kamakura. Having received a proper education in the courtly arts, he gathered about him others of similar interests, Reizei Tamesuke among them.

Unlike many imperial princes before him, who lived their whole lives in Kyoto, Hisaakira may have known life on the road firsthand.

When he traveled, however, it would have been with a large entourage rather than alone. The scene he presents in his poem, then, serves less to represent his personal experience than to display his knowledge of the topic of travel in the poetic tradition.

Here, the traveler is walking alone along a path across the fields, in the first light of day, when he comes upon a torch cast aside by someone on the path ahead — someone who set out even earlier, even before dawn. Since a lone traveler would probably not be carrying a torch, perhaps the speaker imagines a group: a man of some standing, guarded by samurai. In any case, the point is that the sign of others on the road makes the speaker feel all the more alone. Straining his eyes to see into the distance in the murky light of dawn, he wonders who the traveler might be, wishing for some kind of companionship on the road ahead.

Hisaakira's scene is very much in the Reizei tradition in that it presents no metaphor, no wordplay, but a straightforward description "as is" — *ari no mama*, to borrow the phrase that would later be used by Imagawa Ryōshun. Its rustic imagery, presented close-up rather than from a distance as in the pastorals of the Nijō school, is also typical of the Reizei approach. No vague plume of smoke in the distance, the smoldering torch of pine tar is an image meant to represent "reality" without other mediations.

The poem appears in *Shūifūtei wakashū* (no. 256).

15. Hōjō Sadatoki (*1271–1311*)

Autumn: On the Idea of the "The Moon Rising Late," written for a poem contest at his house

Does it know somehow   that the nights
linger longer   when autumn comes?
How unhurried is the rise   of the moon
on the mountain rim!

aki no yo no / nagaki hodo o ya / tanomuran / idete isoganu / yama no ha no tsuki

HŌJŌ SADATOKI, ninth regent (*shikken*) of the Kamakura shogunate, was a great patron of artists and Buddhist sects. The Hōjō had been supporters of the Minamoto clan early on, and after the premature death of the first shogun, Yoritomo, the Hōjō gradually became the real power in Kamakura. By Sadatoki's time, the regents were clearly more powerful than the shogun, who in effect served at their pleasure. An avid poet, Sadatoki was encouraged in his interest by Tamesuke, who was a member of his salon. Twenty-four of Sadatoki's poems would eventually be included in imperial anthologies, a testament to his prominence as a patron but also to his mastery of poetic conventions.

"The Moon Rising Late," is what is called a "compound topic" (*musubidai*). In the early days, topics often consisted of just one word, "Blossoms," for instance, or even "Spring." Later, most topics involved at least two words—"Snow in the Fields," and so on. By the late 1200s, even more lengthy topics began to appear.

It has to be said that more detailed topics make the task of composing somewhat easier: a simple topic such as "Moon" demands much more of a contribution on the poet's part. "Moon Rising Late" demands only that the poet answer the question, "Why?" Several answers immediately suggest themselves. One is to attribute the tardiness to weather—showers or clouds—or to some other physical impediment; another is to attribute the perceived tardiness to the psychology of an over-anxious viewer, a lover looking forward to a meeting, for instance.

Sadatoki takes neither of those courses, relying instead on straightforward personification. The moon is taking its time, he says, because it knows that autumn nights are long and it chooses to respond accordingly. The unspoken suggestion is that this decision makes those waiting for the moon's appearance appreciate its beauty all the more.

The poem is recorded in *Ryūfū wakashō* (no. 75)

16. *Reizei Tamesuke (1263–1328)*

Spring: Written for a screen at the residence of Lord Sadatoki

From the plum at my eaves I should like to pick
a sprig of glowing red
now muted on its branch by a dusting of white
snow.

orite mimu / nokiba no ume no / kurenai o / usuku furinasu / yuki no hitoeda

MANY OF the poems produced by medieval poets were stored away in boxes as memorials of specific events that could later be taken out for perusal. Screen poems, on the other hand, were on constant display, at least for as long as the screens on which they were recorded survived.

When the above poem, recorded in Reizei Tamesuke's personal anthology *Fujigayatsushū* (poem no. 9), was composed we do not know, although it was almost certainly produced to adorn the residence of his patron, Sadatoki, in Kamakura. Once again, the screen for which it was composed has not survived, leaving the poem as our only evidence of its existence. Ironically, then, the poem had a seemingly more stable and permanent corporeal existence in its inscribed form than in its purely textual form—but only temporarily. So vulnerable were residences of the day to fire and the elements that none lasted very long.

The heirs of the Reizei lineage were constantly called upon by patrons to produce poems as decoration, which helps to explain why they considered it important to be skilled calligraphers as well as poets. In modern times, a huge gap has opened up between the poem itself as a kind of mental or aural artifact and the representation of the poem in physical form. For medieval Japanese poets, however, this gap was obviously not so large. Perhaps it was on screen paintings more than anywhere else that the "physicality" of the poem became evident, so much so that in the aesthetic economy of the time poetic composition could be characterized as in some sense truly a decorative art. Among other things, this may have been a reason why the aesthetic preoccupations of traditional Japanese poetry have been more fixed on visual experience than on propositional truth or abstract philosophy, on matters of design and presentation rather than on more semantic factors. What Sadatoki wanted on his screen was doubtless a beautifully rendered poem that complemented the painting on the screen and not a conundrum—a vision, not an essay or treatise. Tamesuke obliged.

17. *Musō Soseki (1275–1351)*

Spring: Written when he was looking at flowers in his garden court
Were it left to me   I would find a way
to keep them   from the wind's knowledge—
these flowers by my hermitage   that have become
my friends.

onajiku wa / kaze ni shirarenu / yoshi mogana / waga tomo to naru / kakurega no hana

Musō Soseki is one of the most prominent figures in the history of Zen in Japan. Born in the province of Ise into a lineage descended from Emperor Uda, he studied esoteric Buddhism (*mikkyō*) in Nara but later trained under a Chinese Zen master at Kenchōji Temple in Kamakura, and quickly rose to prominence for his administrative abilities. He was abbot of Nanzenji Temple in Kyoto twice and founded Tenryūji, in Saga. He was patronized by Emperor Go-Daigo, Ashikaga Takauji, and many other political leaders and was influential in the establishment of the *gozan* — the name given to the network of Zen temples patronized and governed directly by the Ashikaga shogunate.

Some of the more rigid Zennists of the day dismissed poetry as a frivolous pastime, "idle words and fancy phrases." The fact is, however, that Zen monasteries were centers of learning that attracted many men of literary ambition. Musō wrote poetry in both Chinese and Japanese and was acquainted with most of the leading literati of his day. Records show that Reizei Tamesuke, particularly during his final years, maintained a close relationship with Musō, who spent a great deal of time in Kamakura, where the influence of Zen temples was considerable.

Although many of Musō's poems are on Buddhist themes, his education included the composition of court poetry as well. The above poem articulates no strong doctrinal theme, instead expressing a commonplace sentiment via the commonplace device of personification. Only the image of cherry blossoms — often used to symbolize the ephemerality of existence — suggests an underlying Buddhist theme.

The image of a man living in solitude with only the blossoms as friends is nothing new, of course. In all, then, the poem is a straightforward statement of a conventional theme, showing that Musō was well schooled in the niceties of court culture, a monk who could participate in the salons of the court nobles with no fear of embarrassment. The world-weariness implied in the line, "Were it left to me . . ." is perhaps all that suggests a Buddhist attitude.

The poem appears in Musō's collection *Shōkaku Kokushi shū* (no. 29).

18. *Kyōgoku Tamekane (1254–1332)*

Travel: Written on the idea of "Traveling in the Rain"

Out under the sky   on a day
when rain is falling   I conclude too soon
that night is on its way—   when still there is
far to go.

tabi no sora/ame no furu hi wa/kurenu ka to/omoite nochi mo/yuku zo hisashiki

KYŌGOKU TAMEKANE, son of Tamenori, was more successful at court than his uncle, Tamesuke, had been. Thanks to the patronage of Emperor Fushimi and others, he rose to the junior second rank and achieved the office of major counselor, enjoying prosperity much of the time. Yet not all of his life was spent in Kyoto. He was exiled twice, to Sado in the Japan Sea and to Tosa; and records also indicate that he journeyed between Kyoto and Kamakura often. Clearly he traveled widely enough to understand the experience of life on the road.

For many medieval poets, the topic of travel offered a way to speak of something else, usually the vicissitudes of life in the world, or ruminations on the passage of time inspired by famous sites. Here, though, Tamekane describes the feeling of being on the road in more immediate terms. On a rainy day, as a traveler makes his way along a path in the countryside, the skies turn so dark that he thinks the sun must be going down and he begins to look for a place to rest. But soon he realizes that he has been deceived: the impinging darkness is no more than the effect of rain clouds, and dusk is in fact hours away. Relief must be replaced with resignation and somehow the traveler must fight back the feeling of fatigue that inevitably descends with anticipated rest.

Many poems in the court tradition present confusion of the senses: what looked like blossoms turn out to be snow; what looked like torches turn out to be fireflies. Here the confusion is not so elegant or whimsical, partly because the consequences are more physical and the psychological impact more profound. For rather than describing rain on the road, the poem really concentrates on the mind of the traveler in a moment of heightened awareness of what travel is — exposure to the elements. An unidentified partisan of the Nijō house dismissed the poem as "the work of a juvenile,"[9] no doubt because to him it read too much like prose. Yet one can hardly imagine a more straightforward — or effective — treatment of its topic.

The poem appears first in the *Kingyoku uta-awase* (The Kingyoku Poetry Contest), a mock contest dating from 1303 that presents 60 poems each by Tamekane and Fushimi, probably put together by Tamekane or someone close to him. Twenty-two of Tamekane's poems from the contest were later put into *Gyokuyōshū*, this one (no. 1204) among them.

19. *Reizei Tamenari (d. 1330)*

Winter: "Fallen Leaves, in Moonlight"

------

9. Given as *osanaki mono no uta* in the original Japanese. *Kaen renjō kotogaki* (Joint Signatories of the Garden of Poetry, 1315), p. 118.

All to no avail   showers fall
then pass away—   barely dampening
a garden strewn with fallen leaves   whose colors
rain won't change.

itazura ni / nurasu bakari no / murashigure / niwa no ochiba ni / sou iro wa nashi

GENEALOGICAL CHARTS often show Tamehide as the second head of the Reizei house. But in fact Tamehide had an older brother, known as Tamenari (alternatively read Tameshige), who would have succeeded Tamesuke had he not died in his 30s. Tameshige went as far as the third rank in the court hiearchy, with the office of captain in the Gate Guards. He appears to have been at least ten years Tamehide's senior and was quite active in poetic circles until the time of his death.

In court poetry, the changing of leaves in the autumn is conventionally attributed to passing showers that supposedly "dye" leaves red and gold. Since the topic assigned to Tamenari (under what circumstances, we do not know) asks for treatment of leaves at night and in a winter context, however, the poet must provide something more than the obvious. Tamenari responds first with a rhetorical tease ("all to no avail"); then he goes on to present an aural scene—a brief shower passing in the night, following which he adds the image of leaves already covering the ground, gray and lifeless, quite beyond the power of showers to dye—a final answer to the tease of the first line. If there is any color in the poem, then, it is only there as a kind of potential latent in the topic, an image briefly suggested only to be quite literally washed away. In this sense, the poem truly offers a winter scene in which the delights of autumn remain only as a memory brought back by the shimmering moonlight.

The poem appears in *Ryūfū wakashō* (no. 105).

20. *Eifukumon-in (1271–1342)*

Love: From among her Love poems

The hour has grown late.   If even by the clouds
above,   crisscrossing the sky—
if only somehow I could ask him   what he is doing
tonight.

kurenikeri / ama tobu kumo no / yukiki ni mo / koyoi ika ni to / tsutae teshigana

EMPRESS EIFUKU was the daughter of Saionji Sanekane, one of the most powerful politicians of the late Kamakura period. She was made consort to Emperor Fushimi in 1288 and participated in all the activities leading up to compilation of *Gyokuyōshū* (1313).

After Fushimi's death and the banishment of Kyōgoku Tamekane on her own father's order, Eifukumon-in held the Jimyō-in lineage together, at the same time providing support for Saionji Sanetoshi (1335–89), whose father had been killed during the fighting surrounding Go-Daigo's abortive attempt to restore imperial rule. After years of discouragement, she was able to play a role in the events that led to the compilation of *Fūgashū*, although the collection did not appear until 1346, several years after her death.

The custom of court society was that men visited women, and not vice-versa. The poem above thus presents a well-established scenario: a lonely woman, waiting for her man long after there is any hope that he will appear, if indeed he made any promise to come at all. Tired and dejected, the woman looks to the sky just before dawn and sees clouds moving back and forth, whimsically imagining that somehow they might act as couriers and bring her word about where her man might be. To pin one's hopes on anything so ephemeral and unpredictable as clouds is of course an admission of despair. The unspoken fear, of course, is that he may be visiting another woman, oblivious to her feelings of abandonment.

The poem appears in one of the love books of *Fūgashū* (no. 1046).

21.   *Tamesuke's Daughter (precise dates unknown)*

Miscellaneous: Topic Unknown

On a rocky shore   in the shade
of the pine trees   bobs a fishing boat,
tethered there but tossed about   by the motion
of the waves.

araiso no / matsu no kage naru / amaobune / tsunaginagara zo / nami ni tadayou

THE WOMAN known only as Tamesuke's daughter went to the East Country with her father, and no doubt participated actively in poetic activities associated with the Reizei household. That Tamesuke was successful in marrying her into the harem of the shogun Prince Hisaakira suggests that she was both beautiful and talented. She produced a son for him—Prince Hisayoshi. Unfortunately, though, apparently she died young, perhaps even before Hisaakira was deposed in 1308.

Eleven of the poems of Tamesuke's daughter appear in imperial anthologies, again only in *Gyokuyōshū* and *Fūgashū*. The poem above, which appears under the topic heading miscellaneous, presents a scene very much "as it is." None of the images in itself offends against the standards of courtly decorum, but taken together the rough shore, the pine shadows, and the boat being tossed about by the waves present a stark picture of the sort not usually favored by Nijō poets. Rather than prettifying it with traditional metaphor or wordplay, the poet offers a natural scene on its own terms.

If on the surface the poem presents a harsh scene, the connotations of the phrase *tsunaginagara zo* ("tethered there but . . .") add an even more ominous suggestion. For who can notice a tethered fishing boat without wondering about the fisherman who depends on it for his livelihood? Lurking in the shadows behind the "realistic" scene, then, is the figure of a lone man tossed about on waves that will be even higher out in the offing. Perhaps for now the fisherman is waiting out a storm; but in time he must resume his perilous life along the rocky shore.

The poem appears in *Fūgashū* (no. 1720).

22. *Nijō Tameakira (1295–1364)*

Summer: "Evening Shower"

More intense, it seems   grows the bustle
of merchants   at Abe Market:
for approaching over the pass   come clouds
of an evening shower.

itodoshiku / abe no ichibito / sawagu rashi / saka koekakaru / yūdachi no kumo

IN 1356, soon after the reigning emperor issued the order to the head of the Nijō house for compilation of an imperial anthology, he also ordered the major court poets of the day to submit 100-poem sequences for review. In this he followed a pattern that had been established with the *Shoku gosenshū* a century before and that would continue until the end of the court tradition. Knowing that poems submitted in such a context stood a good chance of making it into the coming anthology, poets often spent months preparing their contributions.

In this case 33 court poets were invited to present their works. From the Reizei faction, only Tamehide was included in the request, and he refused to participate on the grounds that the project was so clearly partisan. Not all those who submitted 100-poem sequences were outright enemies of the Reizei, however. Tameakira, for instance, was so well disposed toward Tamehide that eventually he would take in the latter's son Tamekuni as his own heir, sharing with him many of the treasured family teachings of the Nijō line. Although his poems show no strong affinity for the Reizei style, he is usually counted as an ally.

The lists of topics for such formal sequences included only the major topics of the court tradition — haze, blossoms, returning geese, and so forth for spring; dew, the moon, colored leaves for autumn; and so on. One- or two-word topics prevailed, and no unusual combinations were allowed. "Evening Shower" (*yūdachi*), for instance, is one of the oldest of summer topics. To his credit, Tameakira gives it fresh treatment by choosing an interesting setting. Situated on the eastern road out of Kyoto, just west of Ausaka Barrier, Abe was a market town to which farmers and merchants brought their wares for sale on certain days of every month. One imagines stalls set up at the roadside, displaying everything from fresh produce to farm tools and housewares. On this summer day, however, what looms up over the pass is not more customers approaching but the dark clouds of a thunder shower, news of which sends shopkeepers scurrying to cover their wares and customers seeking cover.

The title of the 100-poem sequences in which the poem appears is the *Enbun hyakushu* (no. 2633), "The 100-Poem Sequences of the Enbun Era."

23. *Ashikaga Takauji (1305–58)*

Miscellaneous: On "Mountain at Dusk"

In pines on the peak　　the voice
of the mountain wind　　has faded away;
clouds of evening settle　　calmly
in the valley.

yamakaze wa / takane no matsu ni / koe yamite / yūbe no kumo zo / tani ni shizumaru

ASHIKAGA TAKAUJI was the first of the Ashikaga shoguns. Educated for participation in elite society from a young age, he had cordial relations with both the Nijō and Kyōgoku camps, tending to favor the ascendant group at any particular time. As shogun, he initiated the process that would result in the compilation of *Shin senzaishū* (1359), eighteenth of the imperial anthologies. His successors would follow him in this and in other practices of patronage.

The poem above is very much in the Kyōgoku style in the way it captures a moment of change in the natural landscape. As if announcing the coming of evening, a mountain wind blows through the pine boughs, drawing the eyes of the speaker to the darkening sky. Then the wind dies as evening clouds settle calmly in the valley.

The poem makes no attempt at a more philosophical statement but simply presents a brief moment of natural movement on its own terms. In its syntax and logic, it gestures toward a famous poem by Tamekane:

> In a sudden gust   the wind blew through
> the trees   and faded away —
> the blossoms it left behind   now fluttering down
> in peace.[10]

> *hitoshikiri / fukimidashitsuru / kaze wa yamite / sasowanu hana mo / nodoka ni zo chiru*

The Miscellaneous category includes topics that either do not fit into other categories or that combine elements of several other categories. Here none of the images indicates a clear seasonal context. This does not mean that Takauji's poem is in any way unconventional, however; all of its images are in fact traditional. In this sense, the miscellaneous category, which might in some other historical situation have offered a way out of the strictures of tradition, did nothing of the sort. In time, the category would in fact be divided up into many subcategories (Buddhism, lamentation, parting, travel, and so forth) that were themselves further examples of conventionalization.

Takauji's poem appears in *Fūgashū* (no. 1656).

24. *Reizei Tamehide (d. 1372)*

"Love"

Only after one   has been
quite forgotten —   that is when one learns
that life is not so fragile   as one had always
thought.

wasurarete / nochi koso sara ni / omoishire / hakanakaranu wa / inochi narikeri

THE FIRST obligation of the head of the Reizei house was to preserve its traditions and its place in the scheme of things: to achieve high office, to serve as master at court, to maintain the reputation of the house, and so on. Though all had to be good teachers, not all were great poets. Tamehide, the records say, was both a fine teacher and an estimable poet. Only about 60 of his poems survive, but records of his time show the high esteem in which he was held among Nijō

---

10. *Fūgashū*, poem no. 228.

poets, Kyōgoku poets, and courtiers such as Nijō Yoshimoto, who were in some ways above the fray.

In his *Kinrai fūtei*, Nijō Yoshimoto singled out a number of poets for brief comment. Of Tamehide, he said that his style was of course "something quite apart" (*kakubetsu*) from the prevailing Nijō style and that some accused him of being vulgar, but that in fact he had an inborn talent and wrote many poems that were gentle and peaceful (*yasashiku odayaka naru*), quoting as an example the one above. Yoshimoto also says that the poem represents one of the more interesting (*omoshiroki*) styles of his own day.[11]

The topic of Tamehide's poem, which appears only in *Kinrai fūtei*, is not known. Although the love topics were often compounds ("Love, with the Moon as an Image," etc.), there were still many occasions when poets were asked to compose without the help of a guiding image. That may have been the case here.

Like many love poems, this one deals with a discovery. Once, the speaker suggests, he said that he would rather die than be rejected, so bitter was the prospect of being cast aside. But it is only after he has in fact been rejected and forgotten that he realizes how truly awful is the state of one lost in love. For even when one thinks the pain unendurable, even when one wishes for death, life goes on. From rejection one thus learns that life is stronger than love, even when there is little happiness in the thought.

25.   *Tamehide's Daughter (precise dates unknown)*

Love: Topic Unknown

Words too are fickle   in this world
of uncertainty —   this I realize.
Yet still I wish to live on   til we exchange
a pledge of love!

koto no ha mo/sadamenaki yo to/omoedomo/chigirishi made no/inochi to mogana

WE KNOW very little about Tamehide's Daughter. Evidently she lived with her father in the East Country as a girl, and came to the capital with him in the early 1330s. She was one of the participants in the Niitamatsushima Poetry Contest of 1367 and shared in her father's good fortune under Ashikaga patronage at that time. We have no record of her after Tamehide's death.

---

11. Nijō Yoshimoto, *Kinrai fūtei*, p. 185.

Since the topic of the poem above is listed as unknown, there is a chance that the poem comes from actual correspondence. The abstract nature of the sentiment expressed, on the other hand, suggests that the poem was indeed written for some poetic venue. Rather than expressing the feelings of someone actually in the throes of love, the lines seem to offer a conclusion about the nature of love itself.

The upper half of the poem presents what in another context could be a statement of Buddhist truth: that words are as unreliable as any other worldly phenomena. They are in the world and of the world, not separate from it, which means that the world in the end mocks the things they express — promises, hopes, dreams. But the last lines express an idea that a devout Buddhist would be unlikely to embrace. "Let me meet with him," the speaker says, "even if it means heartache in the end!" Despite knowing that a lover's pledge is by nature unreliable, the speaker wants at least once to hear these words, even if it means being deceived.

The poem appears in *Shin shūishū* (no. 1213), nineteenth of the imperial anthologies, which was compiled by Nijō Tameakira and Tonna, both members of the Nijō camp who were nevertheless friends of Tamehide.

26. *Retired Emperor Hanazono (1297–1348)*

Love: On "First Love," from a 6-poem poetry contest

To find oneself   moved
so unexpectedly   is moving in itself —
knowing that if not for love   one would not feel
this way at all.

uchitsuke ni / aware naru koso / aware nare / chigiri narade wa / kaku ya to omoeba

RETIRED EMPEROR Hanazono was one of the most learned men of his time, a student of Buddhist doctrine, Chinese thought, and the courtly literary tradition. After the death of his father, Retired Emperor Fushimi, he took over as patron of the literary progeny of Kyōgoku Tamekane. The *Fūgashū*, second of the imperial anthologies compiled by partisans of the Kyōgoku faction, was put together under his order. He was more personally involved in the process of compilation than any emperor had been since Go-Toba at the time of *Shin kokinshū*.

The poem above, which Hanazono selected for inclusion in *Fūgashū* (no. 1015), offers a classic reflection on the nature of love. The essence of love is to move us, even at the most inconvenient of times, the poem says — a fact that is in itself moving. A dictionary definition of the word repeated in the phrase—*aware naru koso aware nare* (literally, "to be moved itself—that is moving")—is a tender feeling of love tinged with sadness, resignation, knowledge of the transience of the emotion itself and the circumstances that inspire it. The conception is very much a courtly one that assumes a sensibility fine-tuned by education and long habit.

The poem is philosophical in that it offers not just the experience of love but analysis of that experience. We make vows of love (*chigiri*), the speaker says, and then are impressed that we have the ability to do so. In this way the poem becomes a comment on the circularity of the emotional process. The implication is that those who love are as much in thrall to love itself as to each other. Such a thought can lead to various dark conclusions, of course, but Hanazono takes us only so far.

The "6-poem sequence" for which this poem was first composed was commissioned by Hanazono himself in 1343, from 32 poets. Such little anthologies were stored away in boxes in noble houses, temples, and shrines, to serve as raw material for anthology projects in the future.

27. *Yoshida no Kenkō (b. 1283)*

Written by request for a woman, when the man she had relied upon to come that night went to someone else instead

Such a waste of time!   To continue
to rely   on a fickle pledge
and wait on for an evening   that for me will yield
nothing.

hakanaku zo / adashichigiri o / tanomu tote / waga tame naranu / kure o machikeru

THE PERSONAL anthologies of most medieval poets organize their poems by topics—first the four seasons, then love, then miscellaneous. But there are a few exceptions. One is the anthology of Yoshida no Kenkō, whose 286 poems are organized in journal fashion. Many are still composed on topics, of course; but he includes more "occasional" poems than do most poets of his era.

The poem above is an example, and one that is doubly interesting because it is what is called a *daisaku*, a poem written on request for someone else. References to poems written by proxy are rare, for obvious reasons. Those who requested them probably did not want news of their lack of skill or confidence to get around. But since Kenkō doesn't mention the name of the woman (or the man she is waiting for), the woman's secret was no doubt secure. To write such poems was one of the duties of professional poets—and probably one that generated some income.

The headnote does not record whether the poem had any effect on her man. Rather than anything elaborate or hyperbolic, Kenkō produced for his client a straightforward expression of frustration— a complaint, in fact. For a woman in love the approach of evening is always an anxious time; but for one who worries that her lover will probably not appear, the anxiety is even more intense. In the end she is unable to restrain feelings of hope that are almost certain to be dashed, knowing all the while that she is wasting her time. In a very unpretentious way, the poem thus offers a textbook definition of the nature of love as defined in traditional poetry: a feeling that persists against reason, almost against even self-interest.

The poem is no. 32 in *Kenkō Hōshi shū*.

28. *Retired Emperor Kōgon (1313–64)*

Winter: "Dog in the Snow"

Not getting up,   still within
my bedchamber,   I hear a dog bark—
and feel in the sound the snow   of a day breaking
with snow.

okiidenu / neyanagara kiku / inu no koe no / yuki ni oboyuru / yuki no asaake

THE CONTOURS of Retired Emperor Kōgon's life are no less stark than are the images of his poetry. Born into the Jimyō-in line of the imperial family, he was enthroned by Ashikaga Takauji in 1331 only to be deposed two years later by his cousin Go-Daigo, whose imperial restoration put the whole future of the Jimyō-in line in question. When Go-Daigo's government failed, Kōgon was appointed to serve as retired emperor for the Northern Court, which he did until 1351. Soon thereafter, he took the tonsure.

For most emperors, retirement from the political world meant days of peace and artistic pleasure. What followed for Kōgon, however, was a protracted period of uncertainty during which he was escorted from place to place in the provinces under either "protection" or arrest while rival political factions battled for supremacy in Kyoto. Finally, in 1357, he returned to the capital. For the rest of his life, he devoted himself to religious devotions, particularly the study of Zen. He died in 1364 in a rustic cottage in Tamba Province, entirely cut off from court culture.

Kōgon was the grandson of Emperor Fushimi and was close to his uncle, Emperor Hanazono—two stalwarts of the Kyōgoku style; and he himself played a major role in the compilation of *Fūgashū*. In many ways, though, his poems go beyond those influences to show elements of Zen thought. In the poem above, for example, one is presented with the scene of a man lying in bed on a winter morning, surmising from the muffled sound of a dog's bark that snow must have fallen but not wanting to brave the cold to get up and see—not the sort of image one expects from the brush of a former sovereign. On the other hand, it is precisely what one expects of a Zennist dedicated to finding interest and meaning in everyday experience. The topic itself is an uncommon one; and the final two lines, "to feel in the sound the snow / of a day breaking with snow" almost sound like a Zen conundrum.

The poem appears in the retired emperor's personal anthology, *Kōgon-in gyoshū* (no. 88).

29. *Tonna (1289–1372)*

Miscellaneous: "Skies Clearing—Snow Falling from Tall Pines"

From branches lit   by morning sun
on the peaks,   clumps of snow fall—
revealing the green of pines   against skies
shining clear.

asahi sasu / mine no kozue no / yuki ochite / matsu wa midori ni / haruru sora kana

IN ADDITION to the imperial collections of Japanese poetry, most courtiers also studied Chinese poetry, although often only in snippets. Most well known to all was the early eleventh-century *Wakan rōeishū* (Songs in Japanese and Chinese), an anthology of *uta* and selected lines from Chinese poems (*kanshi*) by both Chinese and Japanese poets. But some poets, especially Buddhist priests for whom the ability to read Chinese at an advanced level was a professional necessity, went far beyond such anthologies. Tonna, who studied on Mount Hiei in his teens and early 20s and spent his whole life as a priest of the Time sect, was in the latter category.

The line quoted in the headnote to Tonna's poem—which serves as his topic—is from a poem recorded in a relatively obscure collection of the Southern Song dynasty.[12] Along with others, it was

---

12. See Inada, *Waka Shitennō no kenkyū*, pp. 870–81.

chosen by Tonna as a topic for 100-poem sequences composed by himself and four of his disciples—all priests—in 1361. The practice of using lines from Chinese poems as topics was by then a very old one, going back to the tenth century. Other lines chosen by Tonna for the sequences come from that same Southern Song collection but also from more well-known works such as the poems of Bai Juyi.

The Chinese line to which Tonna's poem responds presents an image of clear skies after a snowstorm, when melting snow starts to fall from pine boughs. His treatment reverses the order of the images and thus the process of discovery, presenting a speaker whose eyes are first drawn by the sound of snow falling and who then sees the green of the pines and the clearing sky above. The variation is a subtle one, but of course in classical poetry subtle change is usually the whole point.

Tonna's lines contain no direct statement of human sentiment, unless the "clearing" is interpreted in very broad terms. In this sense, it is rhetorically akin to the poems of the Kyōgoku school, for whom the poetry of the Song was a major influence. Although he was most clearly allied with Nijō Tameyo in his lifetime, Tonna also had a congenial relationship with Reizei Tamehide and in the Edo period was claimed as a member of the Reizei school.

The poem appears in *Tonna kudai hyakushu* (no. 236).

30. *Reizei Tamekuni (precise dates unknown)*

Spring: "Haze on the Bay"

All hazed over,   the Great Plain
of the Ocean   is more boundless still—
as the eightfold seaways   swell in the light
of a spring dawn.

kasumite zo / nao kagiri naki / wata no hara / yae no shioji no / haru no akebono

ALTHOUGH NOMINALLY organized by Tonna and other poets of the Nijō camp, the *Niitamatsushima uta-awase* (New Tamatsushima Shrine Poetry Contest) of 1367 also involved Reizei Tamehide—who chose the topics for the contest and acted as judge—as well as Tamehide's son, Tamekuni, and daughter. There appears to have been no formal meeting attended by all the participants, but apparently a formal *hirō*, or "airing," of the poems did take place in the Third Month of that year. In addition to composing poems, Tamekuni also acted as lector (*kōji*) for the public event.

The poem above comes from the twentieth round of the contest. Its topic, one of only three for the entire contest (the others being "In Search of Blossoms" and "Gods"), calls to mind Waka Bay in Kii Province, where the Tamatsushima Shrine, parent shrine of the smaller building in Kyoto, stood. Tamekuni's lines, then, are probably intended as a description of that famous place, albeit in very idealistic terms.

Traditionally, haze is the harbinger of spring, the vapor that indicates the end of winter bleakness. Rather than showing haze spreading out over a landscape, however, Tamekuni creates a seascape in which the ocean at Waka Bay, metaphorically rendered as a great plain, extends off in the imagination even farther than the barrier presented by morning haze. In keeping with the tone of the whole, the phrase "eightfold seaways" is of ancient origin, appearing earliest in *norito*, ancient Shinto prayer texts. The imagery, diction, and syntax — the latter leading to a final "opening" to the light of a spring dawn — are thus all approbatory. In terms of style, the poem may be aptly described as an example of the lofty manner (*taketakaki yō*) of *Shin kokin* days — a style that Reizei poets were often accused of overlooking.

31. *Nijō Yoshimoto (1320–88)*

"Spring"

After going home   surely they will
yearn again   for the capital —
spring geese flying away now   to a land
without flowers.

kaerite wa / mata ya miyako o / shinoburamu / hana naki sato no / haru no karigane

THE POEM above is from a 100-poem sequence (*Go-Fukō'on-in-dono onhyakushu*, no. 8) dating from 1352, which evidently brought together poems composed by Nijō Yoshimoto over the previous several years. As was the custom of the time, he celebrated his accomplishment by presenting copies of the collection to some of the masters of the time for approbatory "marks" (*ten*). Rather surprisingly for a man who was of the highest court rank, Yoshimoto chose as his patrons not courtiers but the commoner masters Tonna, Keiun, and Kenkō — three of the four so-called Deva Kings of Poetry at the time.

This poem got marks from all three men. Unfortunately, no comments accompany their brush strokes, but the agreement of all three indicates a strong affirmation and a certain consistency in critical judgment.

No doubt one of the things the masters liked about the poem was
the way it alludes to a famous poem by Lady Ise:

> Turning away   from the spreading haze
> of spring   the wild geese depart —
> accustomed, perhaps, to life   in a land
> without flowers.[13]
>
> *harugasumi / tatsu o misutete / yuku kari wa / hana naki sato ni / sumi ya naraeru*

Every year, after wintering in Japan, wild geese return to the
continent or to the northern islands in the spring, leaving just as
the flowers begin to appear. Ise asks how they can stand to live in
a place — the word is *sato* in Japanese, and means something like
"home" — without flowers. Yoshimoto quotes only one line ("a land
without flowers") from the original poem directly but clearly as-
sumes that his readers will know the earlier work. His use of the
capital instead of *sato* may imply not just the natural beauties of
central Japan, but the beauty of the court itself, where spring is
celebrated in an endless round of ceremonies.

32.   *Imagawa Ryōshun (1326–1420)*

> Among poems that came to mind as he was lamenting the state of
> the world:
>
> If I did not stop   to gaze up
> into the blue   of Heaven above
> how could I make my way   in a world so fraught
> with trials?
>
> *tsukuzuku to / midori no sora ni / augazu wa / yo no uki tabi ni / ikade sugusamu*

THE FIRST of the great Japanese travel diaries is *Tosa nikki* (945), a short
work by the courtier Ki no Tsurayuki, which sets down the story
of his return to the capital after service as a provincial governor.
Several more examples of the genre appeared in the Heian period,
but the golden age of the genre was the medieval period, when any
major poet who went on the road was expected to leave a record of
his journey.

Many of these travel records simply list poems composed along the
way, with a few words in prose to set the scene. Not so *Michiyukiburi*
(Thoughts Along the Way, 1371), which chronicles the journey of Ima-

---

13. *Kokinshū*, poem no. 31.

gawa Ryōshun from Kyoto to northern Kyushu at the time he took up the office of *tandai*, or governor general, of that southern island. In addition to poems, Ryōshun's work includes fairly detailed prose descriptions of scenes along the way, along with his ruminations.

On the surface, Ryōshun's poem (written as he was passing through Bingo Province) praises the restorative power of nature. Modern scholars point out, however, that the phrase *midori no sora*, or "blue sky," probably refers also to the Way of Heaven — a metaphor for the rule of the gods, which is represented on earth by the imperial institution. At the time, Ryōshun was on his way to subdue the last opposition to Ashikaga rule, and along the way he made numerous references to worldly strife. There can be no doubt that his hope was to draw on the powers of Heaven to bring peace to the realm. Whether the blue of the sky in itself was enough to give him hope is a moot point, but for a man of his time and education to identify the imperium with the power of the natural world would itself have seemed "natural."

33. *Asayama Bontō (b. 1349)*

Miscellaneous: Topic unknown

As it rises high   how pristine are the rays
it casts!   Above the cascade
at Mifune Mountain —   the moon
of an autumn night.

sashinoboru / hikari mo kiyoshi / taki no ue no / mifune no yama no / aki no yo no tsuki

BORN INTO a prominent military lineage, Asayama Morotsuna, better known by his priestly name Bontō, ended up in service to Ashikaga Takauji and later Ashikaga Yoshimitsu. In later life he took the tonsure as a lay monk and spent a great deal of time on pilgrimage in the provinces. He studied poetry under both Reizei Tamehide and Nijō Yoshimoto and gained a reputation in both *uta* and *renga*.

The above poem, one of several of his appearing in imperial anthologies, was classified in the miscellaneous category by contemporaries despite the presence of the "moon of an autumn night" because it includes more than autumn imagery. Neither the word "waterfall" nor the place name Mifune Mountain has a distinct seasonal connotation.

Mifune Mountain is located in Yoshino, one of the most famous of all Japan's many mountainous regions and a favorite haunt of poets. Nearby is Miyanotaki (Palace Falls), so named because an im-

perial retreat was located there in ancient times. Most likely it
was a place that Bontō had visited in his travels and would in any
case have known about through the scores of poems written about
it. Many temples were—and still are—located in the area. Here the
sound of the waterfall draws the speaker's eyes upward, where
he sees the play of light on the white water. Above it all, rising high
into the clear autumn sky, is the moon. Since "Mifune" means
"boat," there may also be a suggestion that the vantage point is very
like that of a boat riding a cascade of moonlit water.

The poem appears in *Shin shokukokinshū* (no. 1717), last of the im-
perially commissioned anthologies.

34. *Reizei Tamemasa (1361–1417)*

Winter: "Leaves Falling in the Mountains"

Not even sunlight   would get through,
or so I thought,   in forest so deep—
until leaves fell on a path   cleared above
by withering winds.

hikage dani / morazu to mieshi / miyamaji no / ochiba ni haruru / kogarashi no kaze

REIZEI TAMEMASA's *Thousand Poems*, from which this poem (no. 518)
is taken, was produced on the request of the shogun Ashikaga
Yoshimochi at a time of great hopefulness for the house. Recently
promoted to major counselor, with the rank of junior second and
the concurrent post of minister of popular affairs, Tamemasa could
congratulate himself on achieving the greatest honors possible for
one of his lineage.

He approached the task of putting the poems together in a spirit
of celebration. So impressed was Yoshimochi with Tamemasa's
performance in this and other venues that he restored to the house
the old rights to Hosokawa and Ono Estates, providing the financial
stability that the house had lacked for more than half a century.
For these and other reasons, the sequence holds a special place in
the Reizei oeuvre.

The way Tamemasa handles a rather conventional topic is in-
genious: presenting a speaker on a path in mountains so thickly
wooded that even the sunlight can't get through—that is, until a
gust of winter wind tears enough leaves from the trees to allow a
glimpse of sky. If the task of the poet is to handle his topic in a
way that is faithful to Teika's old dictum, "old words, new heart,"
Tamemasa succeeds well. Rather than the usual landscape of fallen

leaves beneath a cold winter sky, he builds his final scene around the sudden appearance of sunlight. In the process, he presents a dynamic scene of natural change, showing not just effect but *both* cause and effect.

It goes without saying that Tamemasa had studied the Kyōgoku poets, many of whose poems also present such scenes of dynamic change that function as records of sensory (as opposed to intellectual) revelation. His poem also serves to define the essence of travel as well as any of theirs do, which is a subtext of the poem regardless of its inclusion in the winter section of the *Thousand Poems*. Out on the road, the poem suggests, one is at the mercy of the elements. Even the seemingly solid canopy of the forest, which from the outside looks so dense and impenetrable, is subject to the ravages of passing winds.

35. Shōtetsu (1381–1459)

Miscellaneous: "People Going over a Bridge"

On Yodo River   someone on the bridge
above   asks a question
a man in a boat can't answer   before he is
too far gone.

yodogawa ya / hashi yuku hito no / koto tou o / kotae mo aezu / tōzakaru fune

AS A worshipper of Teika, the Zen monk Shōtetsu did not share Nijō reservations about the *Shin kokinshū*, as articulated by Nijō Yoshimoto: "There is no collection as interesting as *Shin kokinshū*, but it is no good for beginners."[14] Instead he encouraged his own students to study this work above others, and he tried personally to emulate its style of *yūgen*, or "mystery and depth."

Yet Shōtetsu also wrote many poems that show other influences, including that of his earliest teachers, Imagawa Ryōshun and Reizei Tamemasa. The poem above is an example. There is nothing dreamy or mysterious about it, nothing to suggest hidden depths. The scene it presents is in fact as plebeian as anything one will find in medieval Japanese poetry. The men—one on a passing boat and one on a bridge above—are most probably not courtiers, but commoners, and whatever they are trying to communicate is likely of a mundane order. The backdrop is the bucolic landscape of the Yodo River, which flows

---

14. Nijō Yoshimoto, *Kinrai fūtei*, p. 187.

from Fushimi to Osaka Bay and serves as the primary commercial waterway between Kyoto and the port city of Sakai.

If one wishes, one may tease some deeper interpretive possibilities from the poem. Both men are journeying on paths that cross so briefly that true communication is impossible—perhaps a figure for the nature of all acquaintances in the phenomenal world. As a Zen monk, Shōtetsu would have been acutely aware of the idea of evanescence, which the poem can be said to express. But there is nothing in the poem to overtly suggest such a reading. Perhaps it is better to take it as another quotidian scene in the style of Tamemasa or Tamesuke. The gentle humor of the scene should not be overlooked, either.

The poem appears in Shōtetsu's anthology, *Sōkonshū* (no. 9367).

36. *Reizei Tameyuki (1393–1439)*

Winter: On "Mountain Snow," from a 30-poem sequence commisioned by the Minister of the Left for presentation to New Tamatsushima Shrine

The skies grow so dark   that one can barely
make out   the mountain rim
until things seem to clear   and one sees —
a fall of snow.

kakikurete / sadaka ni mo naki / yama no ha no / haruru to mireba / tsumoru yuki kana

IN 1434, the New Tamatsushima Shrine, then located within the precincts of the Jōkō-in Temple, burned to the ground. Since the mid-fourteenth century, proprietorship of the shrine had rested with the descendants of Tonna, who appealed to the shogun, Ashikaga Yoshinori, for funds to rebuild the structure. When construction was completed, it was celebrated with a *hōraku*, or votive offering of poems. The "airing" of the poems took place on the 21st of the Twelfth Month of that same year, at the shogun's residence.

All of this happened while compilation of *Shin shokukokinshū*, 21st of the imperial anthologies, was underway, with the financial support of the shogunate and under the leadership of Asukai Masayo. Neither the upper or lower Reizei—to their great chagrin—were asked to serve among the compilers, despite their pedigree. This snub so angered them that a few years later Tameyuki refused to allow Masayo any access to the family library. In return for his stubbornness, Tameyuki was stripped of his rights to the Ono Estate and was denied advancement at court.

In 1434, however, Tameyuki may still have had some hope that he would be allowed to participate in the project. Hence his involvement in the votive offering, from which he must have assumed that at least some poems would be chosen for the anthology. Though he died before ever seeing the anthology, two of his poems were included in the end. His brother, Mochitame, was less fortunate: none of his poems was included.

Tameyuki's poem offers another example of "confusion of the senses"—a very old rhetorical technique. The skies above grow dark, the speaker says, so dark that one can barely make out the silhouette of the mountains above. Then one suddenly sees what looks like light striking the mountain rim but which turns out instead to be snowfall. From an image of warmth and light one goes back to dark and cold, a beautiful scene but also a forbidding one.

The poem appears in the winter book of *Shin shokukokinshū* (no. 695).

37. *Ninagawa Chikamasa (Chiun; d. 1448)*

"Lamp in a Mountain Home"

After the sun sets,   that is when
one discovers huts   where people live.
In the shade of a mountainside —   windows lit
by lamplight.

kurete koso / hito sumu io mo / shirarekeru / kata yamakage no / mado no tomoshibi

THE NINAGAWA was an old samurai family with a history of distinguished service to various warlords going back to the 1100s. Chikamasa, better known by his pen-name Chiun, served the Ashikaga shogun Yoshinori, after whose death in 1441 he took the tonsure and dedicated himself to the study of Zen Buddhism and poetry in both the *uta* and *renga* forms. He was among the many students of Shōtetsu.

In modern times, Chiun is better known as one of the Seven Sages of Linked Verse than as a master of the *uta*. The poem above reads much like a *renga* link, in which the first lines offer a riddle and the last an answer. How is it that one discovers where huts are after dark? Because that is when one sees the lamps go on in windows. The scene is a rustic one entirely in keeping with a Zen commitment to the quotidian.

The poem appears in a text titled *Shūgai sanjūroku kasen* (Thirty-Six Poetic Sages Not Represented in the Anthologies). The original "Thirty-Six Poetic Sages" (*Sanjūroku kasen*) was compiled by Fujiwara no Kintō (966–1041), who included among his sages the *Man'yō-shū* poets Kakinomoto no Hitomaro and Yamabe no Akahito, as well as poets close to his own time such as Ki no Tsurayuki. This was followed in the late-Kamakura period by "Thirty-Six Women Poetic Sages." *Shūgai sanjūroku kasen*, also called "Thirty-Six Poetic Sages of Modern Times," was compiled either by Retired Emperor Go-Mizuno'o or his son Go-Sai. Records say that the poems were first displayed on standing screens in the Tōfuku-in. Later, a member of the Kanō School did portraits of each poet, which have become famous. The poets are alike in that none is represented in any imperial anthology and that all are commoners. Prominent on the list are Shōtetsu and his students (Shinkei, Chiun, and Kensai) and a host of *renga* masters, from Sōgi to Matsunaga Teitoku.

38. *Reizei Mochitame (1401–54)*

Love: "Love, with 'Painting' as an Image"

To be rejected — is to see maiden
flowers in a painting:
beckoning brings no response, never a hint
of swaying.

tsurenasa wa / tada e ni kakeru / ominaeshi / kou to mo nabiku / kage ya nakaramu

LOVE IS one of the most fundamental themes of the court tradition in poetry, or for that matter in painting and in many other arts. Some of the earliest recorded poems are love poems, and love has remained a prominent topic down to the present.

In some of the earliest collections, the single word "love" often appears as a topic, with no elucidation. Judging from headnotes, we can assume that in fact many poems in the early periods were written for actual correspondence rather than as works of art. By the twelfth century, however, other, more explictly literary topics such as "First Love," "The Morning After," and "Love on the Road" began to appear, in the same way that "compound topics" ("The Moon at Midnight," "Autumn Travel," etc.) began to dominate books on the seasons.

The poem above is an example of a particular kind of compound topic, which follows the formula, "Love — with X as an image or theme." The requirement for dealing with such topics was that the poet produce a poem that was identifiably a love poem but one that also prominently displayed the prescribed image or theme.

Mochitame's poem is an ingenious example of the technique that goes somewhat beyond the topic by introducing a second image, in addition to the painting itself: the maidenflower, no doubt employed because of its obvious association with love as a topic. Along with other flowering plants, the *ominaeshi* was a common subject for painters working on standing screens or door panels.

"Rejection" is a frequent theme in love poems, for obvious reasons. Mochitame's poem gives the term concrete definition by alluding to flowers seen in a painting—beautiful, needless to say, and alluring, but beyond our grasp. On the canvas they seem so real that one imagines them swaying in one's direction as one beckons. But the painting is a cruel illusion: there is no real swaying any more than there are real flowers. The further implication is that love is just such an illusory experience.

The poem appears in a small collection of Mochitame's poems from the year 1432 (*Eikyō yonen eisō*, no. 135).

39. *Ichijō Kaneyoshi (1402–81)*

Written at the the ruins of Fuwa Gatehouse

Broken, all a ruin   are the eaves
of the roof   at Fuwa Gatehouse—
but ah for how long a time   they have kept
its name alive!

arehatsuru / fuwa no sekiya no / itabisashi / hisashiku mo na o / todomekeru kana

ONE OF the most prominent court officials of the fifteenth century, Ichijō Kaneyoshi was also a scholar of great erudition who lectured on everything from *The Tale of Genji* to the Chinese classics. As such, he was dedicated to the poetic traditions of the court, including especially the Reizei family. He married his son to a Reizei woman, took on several members of the family as *kerai*, or stewards, and championed the cause of the lineage at court.

During the Ōnin War, Kaneyoshi—who was in his third term as imperial regent at the time—abandoned his home in Kyoto and took up residence in Nara. There, for ten years, he spent his time in scholarly pursuits and in trying to find a source of financial security for himself and his progeny. It was for the latter reason that he traveled to Mino in 1473, to visit family members who had found refuge there and to ask for help from the warlord Saitō Myōchin. The record of his journey is called *Fujikawa no ki*.

Following ancient traditions, Kaneyoshi wrote poems at the famous sites along his way. The poem above (p. 390) is one of these, composed at the site of the Fuwa Barrier, "The Gate Indestructible," which had been erected by an emperor in the seventh century. In writing his poem, Kaneyoshi alluded directly to a famous poem by his own ancestor, Kujō Yoshitsune, written on the topic, "Autumn Wind at a Barrier":

> No one lives now   beneath the
> broken-down eaves   of Fuwa Gatehouse;
> for years the only passerby   has been
> the autumn wind.[15]
>
> *hito sumanu / fuwa no sekiya no / itabisashi / arenishi nochi wa / tada aki no kaze*

Kaneyoshi's poem is also a rumination on the vanity of human ambition, but it strikes a hopeful note in suggesting that at least those who compose poems are keeping the name of the gatehouse alive.

40. *Shinkei (1406–75)*

> Autumn: From a 100-poem sequence composed in 1468,
> on the topic "Moon"
>
> Tell me your tales, moon!   For surely night
> after night you must see   the sorrows
> of the distant capital   from your place
> in the sky.
>
> *katare tsuki / tōki miyako no / aware o mo / miruran mono o / yona yona no sora*

ALTHOUGH BETTER known as a *renga* master, Shinkei studied *uta* under Shōtetsu for 30 years and clearly wanted a reputation in the more prestigious form. He argued that *uta* and *renga* should be one and the same in terms of aesthetic goals.

In 1468, when the poem above was composed, Shinkei was in the East Country, having fled the capital at the time of the hostilities leading up to the Ōnin War of 1467–77. There he played the role of poetry master to locals and other expatriates, including two men who would later became equally famous as *renga* masters—Sōgi and Kensai. He died there in 1475.

Shinkei never got over being separated from the capital and its culture, and often made alienation the theme of his poems, including

---

15. *Shin kokinshū*, poem no. 1601.

the one above. In poetry the bright, shining moon is often cast as indifferent to human concerns: a symbol of the Buddhist law lighting the way to extinguishing of emotion and release from worldly concerns. But Shinkei confronts it with heated emotion, beginning with an abrupt command and then going on to say, "Surely night after night as you look down on the earth from above, you must see the degradations going on in the capital. Can't you tell us how people are faring?" Of course, there is no answer; the moon remains aloof in the sky, a Buddhist symbol for emptiness.

Centuries before, the hero of *Tales of Ise,* as he traveled in the East Country, had asked a bird fortuitously named the Capital Bird to give him news of home. So famous was the poem that Shinkei must have had it in mind:

> Are you indeed   what your name
> says you are,   Oh Capital Bird?
> If so, I have a question: "Do things go well
> for my love?" [16]
>
> *na ni shi owaba / iza koto towamu / miyakodori / waga omou hito wa / ari ya nashi ya to*

Shinkei's poem appears in his personal anthology of *uta, Shinkei shū* (no. 235).

41.   *Ashikaga Yoshimasa (1436–90)*

Spring: "Halting Spring That Will Not Stay"

> As I fret and yearn,   the days all go
> slipping by   and spring moves away—
> while I wish idly for a weir   to trap clouds
> that won't return.
>
> *shitau ma ni / hi tsugi utsurite / yuku haru no / kaeranu kumo no / shigarami mogana*

ALTHOUGH THE Reizei suffered harsh treatment at the hands of Ashikaga Yoshinori, succeeding shoguns in the Ashikaga line were kinder. Yoshimasa, who took office in 1469, in fact counted a Reizei woman among his consorts and looked to Reizei Tamehiro as a poetry master.

The date of the 100-poem sequence in which the poem above appears is not known, although internal evidence suggests that it was after 1484, when the shogun was in his late 40s and Tamehiro in his late 30s. As was the custom of the time, the master returned his

----

16. *Kokinshū,* poem no. 411; section nine of *Ise monogatari.*

student's work with approbatory "marks" brushed in. Tamehiro marked only sixteen of the poems, including this one—not a high number considering Yoshimasa's social position.

The shogun's poem on "Halting Spring That Will Not Stay" renders the sky as a river in which spring is coursing away; appropriately so, since it is the next to last poem in the spring category. The clouds that the speaker wants to trap with a weir—a device made of wooden stakes placed in a river to trap fish—may suggest spring flowers, which are often compared to clouds. In any case, the clouds represent the glories of spring.

The poem does not make clear precisely what the direct object of the verb *shitau* is, which I have translated as to "fret and yearn." Probably it is the springtime itself, the beauties of which are always touched with sadness because we all know they cannot stay. Summer has its virtues and beauties, too, of course; but rain and heat are judged to make the season less pleasant overall. Perhaps as an indication of this, Tamehiro honors six of his patron's spring poems with marks and not a single one of his summer poems.

The poem appears in *Ei hyakushu waka* (no. 19).

42. *Kido Takanori (1434–1502)*

> Written when a certain Archbishop planted cherry trees around the residence of the Ishiyama Abbot
>
> Years in the future   no one will
> even know   who so long ago
> planted trees in a garden   where the blossoms
> will remain.
>
> *toshi o heba / taga ueokishi / kozue to mo / shirarenu hana ya / niwa ni nokoran*

KIDO TAKANORI lived in Kōzuke Province, in the East Country, where his family long served as retainers of the shogunal deputy (Kantō Kanrei). There he came into contact with Shinkei and other students of the Reizei house. Eventually, he became a disciple and corresponded with Mochitame for years while maintaining his own literary practice among the warrior elite of his own region.

One normally associates poetic diaries with earlier times. But many later poets kept diary-like records of the places and occasions of their compositions. Takanori's personal anthology is one such work, which includes long prefaces and even in some cases notations about which poems he sent for review to his Reizei master in Kyoto. The poem above is among that number.

The poem is on an ageless theme — the transience of human life. The blossoming trees are not natural, the headnote reminds us; someone planted them. But even they outlast those who put them in the ground.

A poem by Ki no Tsurayuki begins with a headnote that tells a similar tale:

> On seeing plum blossoms at a house where the owner had died
>
> The hue is as rich   and the perfume
> as fragrant   as in days gone by,
> but how I long for a glimpse   of the one who
> planted the tree.[17]
>
> *iro mo ka mo / mukashi no kosa ni / nioedomo / uekemu hito no / kage zo koishiki*

Tsurayuki is remembering someone in the past, while Takanori is looking forward to the future. Both take some comfort in the beauty of the blossoms.

The poem is no. 37 in Takanori's personal anthology, *Takanori shū*.

43. *Ashikaga Yoshihisa (1465–89)*

> "Transience"
>
> In this world of ours   of what
> can we be sure?   A sky that yesterday
> seemed full only of sorrows   does not look the same
> today.
>
> *yo no naka o / nani to tanoman / uki koto no / kinō ni mo ninu / kyō no sora*

YOSHIHISA, NINTH of the Ashikaga shoguns and son of Ashikaga Yoshimasa and Hino Tomiko, was carefully trained for leadership. The best scholars of the time, including Ichijō Kaneyoshi, were called in to lecture him and no expense was spared in teaching him everything from the martial arts to statecraft. His instruction in Japanese poetry began when he was just a boy and he would remain a devotee all of his life — which turned out to be short, as he fell victim to illness at the age of 25.

The poem above was composed when he was only thirteen years old (in 1477), as part of a 100-poem sequence composed at the rate of one a day for a 100 days — a so-called *chakutō uta*. The first examples of this sub-genre appear in the previous century, but it is in records

---

17. *Kokinshū*, poem no. 851.

of the 1400s that it becomes most prominent. Originally used for composition practice, by the time of Yoshihisa it was more than that. The topics chosen for the sequence in this case are those of the famous *Horikawa hyakushu*. A line at the beginning of the text says that the first poem was composed on the 9th day of the Ninth Month. The usual scenario was that the poet—or poets, for sometimes a number were involved—would deliver a poem every day to the person who had commissioned the work.

Since he was only a teen when he wrote the poems, one wonders if the young shogun had help in composing his poems. Yet the way the poem handles its topic—*mujō* (transience)—makes one wonder if perhaps he really wrote the poem on his own. A more experienced poet, with a more thorough grounding in the court tradition, would almost certainly have taken the poem in the opposite direction, noting how the *happiness* of yesterday, rather than its sorrow, has been quick to fade away. Yoshihisa's poem is less somber. Of course, one need only think through the implications of the poem to realize that the two options are sides of the same coin: the whole point is that the skies above, symbolizing the state of the world, are changeable. Nonetheless, Yoshihisa's rather childish conception at least puts the emphasis on the positive, which in itself is noteworthy in a tradition that tends to emphasize the opposite.

The poem appears as no. 98 in a text titled *Chakutō hyakushu waka*.

44. *Shimo Reizei Masatame (1445–1523)*

"Thinking of the Capital While on the Road"

To be far away   when one hears
of the capital   is all the more sad—
there being no way to ask   how things turned out
in the end.

tōku kite / miyako no tsute no / kanashiki wa / mata ika ni to mo / kikiaenu hodo

EARLY IN the Third Month of 1511, Emperor Go-Kashiwabara issued an order for seven poets—eight including himself—to compose one poem per day over the course of the next 100 days—a *chakutō hyaku-shu*. The first poems were to be presented on the 3rd day of the Third Month, the last on the 14th day of the Sixth Month. Among those asked to participate were Tamehiro of the upper Reizei and Masatame of the lower Reizei.

The early years of the sixteenth century were some of the darkest the imperial court would ever know. The shogunal government,

although it persisted on paper, had lost the ability to control its so-
called vassals, which left those dependent upon its power with no
way to demand revenues from their estates. In such circumstances,
most traditional events — festivals, rites, and so forth — could not be
held. Thus courtiers had lots of time on their hands but little ready
cash.

Fortunately, the composition of poetry cost very little. As long
as there was no fighting going on in the streets, the emperor held
his monthly meetings, one of which Masatame attended in the same
month (on the 25th day) in which the *chakutō* sequence began (see
poem no. 820 of *Hekigyokushū*). Grand poetry contests and other public
events were of course out of the question, but to hold small gatherings
required only paper, ink, brushes, a little food, and whatever saké
servants could obtain. Even less expensive was a *chakutō* sequence,
which involved no meetings per se, except perhaps a final celebration.

The topic of the poem above is not a common one. One suspects
that it was chosen, in fact, because it was something of which every-
one in the project could claim experience, having been burned out
of their homes in the capital at the time of the Ōnin War. Masatame,
for instance, spent a great deal of his time at Hosokawa Estate even
after the war years had passed. There is a certain irony, though,
in the poem's last line. No doubt all the poets had experienced
the frustration of not knowing for a while what was going on back
home, but everyone knew how things had turned out in the capital
in the end.

The poem appears as no. 288 in *Dairi chakutō hyakushu*.

45. *Kensai (1452–1510)*

Miscellaneous: On the idea of "Dawn"

Wakeful in the night   I listen
for a sound   within the silence —
echoes from a temple bell   on a distant
mountainside.

nezame shite / shizuka ni kikeba / kikoyu nari / tōyamadera no / kane no hibiki mo

WHAT IS the essence of dawn? Here we have a poem that attempts
to answer this question in a concrete way. A man lies in bed, unable
to sleep, engulfed in silent loneliness. Then, off in the distance, he
hears something and listens again, carefully, finally recognizing the
sound as a bell from a far temple, announcing the beginning of an-
other day.

On the metaphorical level, the temple bell is of course the voice of the Buddha. Ironically, though, the man listening so intently is already awake. We don't know why, of course. In court poetry, wakefulness is associated with various real-world problems: frustration over rejection in love, worries over the state of the world, or the onset of old age. Any one of these or all of them may be implied here.

Whatever the reason for his wakefulness, the fact that the speaker is far away from the mountain temple symbolizes alienation. A new dawning has come, yes; but is there any awakening in him? The echoes continue on, but whether something in him responds is not clear. The poet, Kensai, wore Buddhist robes, like many literati of his day. And as a student of Shinkei, he must certainly have taken the Way of Poetry seriously as a religious avocation. The last line leaves the outcome hanging in mid-air. The bell announces dawn, but what kind of dawn it will be is not settled.

It is as a master of linked verse that Kensai is known, but in his day he was also active as a poet in the *uta* form, as Shinkei had been. As a disciple of Shinkei, who had been a disciple of Shōtetsu, he was affiliated with the Reizei house, although he also had a close relationship with the Asukai.

The poem appears as no. 279 in *Kanjinshū*.

46. *Reizei Tamehiro (1450–1526)*

From a meeting at Hidenao's place on the 17th of the Fifth Month, on "Fan"

To cool myself   I take up a fan
and find   a picture of fields
and mountains I've never seen   — right in the palm
of my hand.

suzushi tote / narasu ōgi no / utsushie ni / shiranu noyama zo / tanagokoro naru

BY 1486, the ravages of the Ōnin War were fading into memory. The Reizei had returned to the city, as had many noble heirs. Tamehiro's personal anthology records 139 poems for the year 1486, some composed at his own dwelling but many also at the homes of friends, at temples and shrines, at the imperial palace, and at the mansions of various warrior chieftains. Ashikaga Yoshihisa was holding his monthly meetings on the 25th day of each month, and Tamehiro was a regular participant.

The poem above was written for a meeting at the home of Tanba Hidenao (precise dates unknown). Two of the three formal topics (*kendai*) for the gathering were summer topics—"Fan" and "Long Rains"—that fit the season. The diary of another courtier—Konoe Masaie (1444-1505)—reveals that it had in fact rained every day for the past week or so, and would continue to do so for some weeks to come.[18] The city was in the throes of the long and sultry season known as *tsuyu*.

Poets writing of this time of year often cast about for a way to reduce the heat. In Tamehiro's poem, it is a fan that offers relief. But rather than just the fan itself, the poet says, it is the scene inscribed on it that brings a moment of coolness in its scenes of mountains and fields where the winds blow. In this sense, it is the imagination that offers respite from oppressive heat.

Fans were often adorned with poems as well, although there is no indication of that here. Because the Chinese reading of the character for fan (read *ōgi* in the poem) is homophonous with the second character of the name Reisen (a non-standard reading of Reizei), the house has always prized fans, some of which have been handed down to modern times. Like poem strips, they served as gifts for visitors to the house on Imadegawa or for patrons on the road. Small and light yet thought of as legitimate art objects and useful utensils, the fan itself also became a motif in larger paintings, illustrating again the interplay of various traditional arts and crafts in Kyoto culture.

The poem appears in *Tamehiro shū 1* (no. 109).

47. *Shōkō (1412–93)*

> When the cherries were in full bloom, we composed linked verse beneath the branches, and Nōa and I and some others all went to the shrine. We composed a lot of poems but didn't bother to record them, instead just presenting ten each as a votive offering.

> "The Way of the Gods, with 'Blossom' as an Image"

> Sustain me, gods!   The pains
> of advancing age   make lifting one foot
> a weighty endeavor   on the path
> beneath the flowers.

> *mamore kami / oi wa kurushiku / hitoashi mo / aguru ni omoki / hana no shitamichi*

AS CHIEF disciple of Shōtetsu, Shōkō took over his master's practice after the former's death in 1459 and maintained a prominent place

---

18. *Go-Hōkō-in no ki*, volume 2, pp. 100–1.

there until his own death more than 30 years later. His relationship with the various members of the Reizei family was cordial, although as a *jige* poet his market was more the middle classes of warrior society than the court elite.

Like Shinkei and others of Shōtetsu's disciples, Shōkō was driven from the capital at the time of the Ōnin War, going to Nara for safety. His personal anthology records excursions to see the sights there with the *renga* master Nōa (1397–1471) in the spring of 1470. Eventually, the two men and other companions made their way to Yoshino to see the cherry blossoms. As the headnote to the poem above notes, the group composed many poems there in a rather casual spirit, not even bothering to record them, something that must have happened quite often. Shōkō records only the ten poems that were written up in proper style for presentation to Zaō Gongen, chief deity of Kinbusen Temple in Yoshino, as a votive offering celebrating their visit.

While wearing the robes of a Zen monk (who had resided at both Nanzenji and Tōfukuji in Kyoto), Shōkō was a firm believer in the native gods, whose support for the Way of Poetry was a major tenet of belief in poetic discourse. Here he asks for sustaining power in his old age, no doubt also asking for protection of his Way. The poem is built on contrasts, the most obvious one being the old man and the new blossoms. Shōkō could not know that he would live on to witness the frail beauty of the cherry blossoms for another 23 years.

The poem is recorded, along with the other nine Shōkō composed on his visit to the shrine, in his personal anthology, *Shōkashū* (no. 766).

48. *Emperor Go-Kashiwabara (1464–1526)*

Love: "Forgotten in Love"

Surely you still have just one
of those letters I wrote to you;
so look at that, at least —and think again
of me!

kakiyarishi / waga hitofude mo / nokoruran / so o dani mite mo / omoiidete yo

EMPEROR GO-KASHIWABARA lived in hard times, ascending to the throne in 1500 and dying in 1526 without ever becoming retired emperor. Anecdotes of his time claim that he was forced to sell his calligraphy to keep body and soul together. The walls of his palace were in such disrepair at times that passersby could catch glimpses of the royals going about their daily routines. Stones from the imperial gardens were stolen in the night.

Nevertheless, Go-Kashiwabara was a strong devotee of courtly arts such as music, kickball, and poetry. For teachers, he looked to the Asukai house and Sanjōnishi Sanetaka primarily, but he was also on good terms with both the upper and lower Reizei houses. His personal anthology of *uta* includes nearly 5,000 poems.

Love poems about being abandoned or forgotten abound in the court tradition. Often they are lugubrious. Go-Kashiwabara's poem takes a different approach. As he thinks of one who has abandoned him, he recalls meetings in the past and wonders what became of the love letters he had sent. Surely she cannot have destroyed them all, he reasons, and if not, then there is some chance that someday she will peruse them again and remember him. Thus the poem answers the question of how one who has been forgotten may hold out some hope of being remembered.

The poem does not say that the lover will come calling again, of course; that would be asking too much. But she might send a letter herself. Failing that, the existence of his letters somewhere in her closets at least saves him from oblivion. The letters attest to his existence.

The poem appears in *Hakugyokushū* (no. 2181).

49. *Shimo Reizei Tametaka (1474–1543)*

"Winter"

Not knowing even   which pathway
I should use   I travel onward
aimlessly, beneath a sky   darkening toward
year's end.

tsukau beki / michi mo shirade / itazura ni / tabi no sora ni mo / kururu toshi kana

REIZEI TAMETAKA, third head of the lower house, left behind no personal anthology. Several 100-poem sequences, however, show that he was quite active in his day. He rose to the office of middle counselor in the court bureaucracy before retiring from public life in his early 60s.

The sequence from which the poem above was taken bears the approbatory marks of Sanjōnishi Sanetaka, one of the most prominent nobles of the day. Although this poem is not among those singled out, Sanetaka did write next to it, "Very delicately phrased" (*yasuraka ni iinashite kikoesōrō*).

Any court poet had to be able to handle the topic of travel. But Tametaka probably knew life on the road better than most. Especially after his retirement, he spent much of his time at Hosokawa Estate in Harima, the property that Abutsu and the Nijō house had fought over centuries before. Tametaka lived a life of relative obscurity there, though no doubt he was well aware of troubles back in the capital.

The poem presents an extreme statement on the topic of travel. By definition, the road was a lonely place where one longed for home. Here the traveler is truly lost, not even knowing which path to take. The last two lines indicate that not only is it the end of the day but the end of the year as well. As daylight fades away, he presses on through a bleak landscape, hoping that he will soon find a place of shelter. Off in the distance waits the promise of the new year, one might argue; but the suggestion of happier days in the future does little but make the loneliness of the current moment seem even more severe.

The poem is no. 70 in *Ei hyakushu waka*, a sequence dating from 1511.

50. *Reizei Tamekazu (1486–1549)*

"Wild Geese"

As I gazed out,   the colors faded
away from   the clouds at dusk —
though still bright are the voices   from a flock
of passing geese.

nagamenuru / yūbe no kumo no / usuiro ni / koe sayaka naru / kari no hitotsura

IN THE Eighth Month of 1518, Reizei Tamekazu was in the imperial capital trying to succeed as a poetry master. His personal anthology shows him attending gatherings at the imperial palace, at various temples, and at the homes of other nobles and patrons among the warrior elite.

The poem above, however, is different from the ones he wrote for most gatherings in one important respect. For it is one of two poems introduced with the headnote, "Written in place of someone." While it is Tamekazu's own work, then, it was doubtless presented as the effort of an anonymous student or patron who wanted to be sure to impress.

As noted above in the commentary on a poem by Yoshida no Kenkō (no. 27), any poetry master would be asked to provide such services, which came with a fee. In the earlier case, the poem was included in a love letter evidently sent directly to a man. Tamekazu's poem, by contrast, was probably composed for an upcoming social event of some sort. One can easily imagine a gathering of warrior chieftains in which most of the poems were actually written by various teachers.

Again, references to such matters in headnotes are very rare, since the party requesting the poem would not want his lack of confidence in his own abilities known, at least in a way that caused public embarrassment. Though it was a common practice, proxy work had to be undertaken with discretion. That Tamekazu recorded the poems in his personal anthology shows first of all that personal anthologies did not circulate widely until well after the poet was dead. But it must also indicate that he was pleased with the poems himself, which he felt free to claim as his own for posterity.

The poem presents no new image, but at least combines old materials in a new way. Its success rests on its witty contrast between the murky color of the dusk sky and the "clear" voices of the wild geese passing above, producing something close to synesthesia.

The poem appears in *Imagawa Tamekazu shū* (no. 260).

51. *Fujiwara Seika (1561–1619)*

"Alone, Looking at the Moon"

No exchange of words   can one expect
with the moon,   yet still I must ask:
of people of long ago,   of people
of long ago.

iikawasu / mono naranaku ni / tsuki ni tou / inishie no hito / inishie no hito

ALTHOUGH BETTER known now as one of the founders of Neo-Confucian thought in Japan, Fujiwara Seika was one of the younger sons of Tameatsu of the lower Reizei house. As was often the case with younger sons, he was sent off to a temple at a young age, to be prepared for a career in the Buddhist priesthood. This was fortuitous, as it turned out, for it allowed him to escape the fate of his father and elder brother, who were killed when rivals invaded the Hosokawa Estate in Harima in 1578. Soon thereafter, Seika ended up going to the capital, where he studied at Shōkokuji, one of the most important intellectual and artistic centers of the time. He never formally became a monk, however, and never held any official position, instead living a modest life as a scholar.

Seika of course read and wrote Chinese—prose and poetry. But he also left behind more than 200 *uta*. The one above is from a collection put together by Tamekage, his son. The anthology also contains poems by acquaintances such as the poet Kinoshita Chōshōshi, showing that the scholar had a broad variety of affiliations.

Many of the poems have long headnotes, indicating that they were primarily occasional in nature. Moreover, they are not organized according to the usual pattern. In these ways, Seika departed from the usual traditions in ways that the head of the house would perhaps not be free to do.

Hitori miru tsuki ("Alone, Looking at the Moon") is an old topic. "People of long ago" may refer to the sages of the past (especially famous poets), or perhaps to his own lineage. Looking at the moon, one inevitably thinks of others who have gazed up at it, in different times, different places, different circumstances. From a distance, the moon seems more permanent and unchanging than the world below, on which it has been shining down for generations. The men of long ago truly belong to a time that is now gone forever. One after another, they appear in the mind, only to fade off into nothingness in a process that never stops, never rests.

The poem appears in *Seika shū* (no. 59).

52. *Reizei Tamemitsu (1559–1619)*

"Love"

And if I *do* pray,   will my efforts
in the end   not come to nothing?
That is what I would ask the god   who brings lovers
together.

inorite mo/kai nakaru beki/yukue ka to/chigirimusubu no/kami ni towaba ya

THE *TENSHŌ dairi uta-awase* (Poetry Contest at the Imperial Palace during the Tenshō Era) was held by Emperor Ōgimachi, most likely in either 1579 or 1580. Among the 20 nobles requested to submit poems were the leaders of the two most important poetic houses of the time, Asukai Masanori (1520–94) and Reizei Tamemitsu. There were 30 rounds of poems in all, on three topics—"Insects," "The Moon," and "Love." The latter fact and internal evidence suggest that the contest took place in the autumn, although there is no indication that it was anything but a "paper" event. Short "words of judgment" (*han no kotoba*), most likely by Asukai Masanori, are included in the text.

Tamemitsu was barely out of his teens at the time of the contest, but his poem shows considerable skill. As a prayer for success in love it may seem blasphemous, since the whole point of Buddhist teaching is to deliver believers from their passions. Here the gods referred to are not Buddhist deities but native Japanese *kami*, who demanded ritual but not adherence to a strict moral code. Prayers to them for success in love were commonplace.

Interestingly, the speaker here does not ask for quick success in realizing his desires so much as a guarantee of no pain in the end (*yukue*)—a much more difficult request to grant. For love, at least as it is defined in the court tradition of poetry, is by its very nature characterized by insecurity and risk. Indeed, one might say that to be in a state of constant doubt about the future is the very essence of love: it is a state of almost permanent anxiety. In this sense, Tamemitsu's poem is not naïve at all. The question it asks—which of course the gods cannot answer—is to that extent not a question so much as a statement.

The poem appears in *Tenshō dairi uta-awase* (no. 56).

53. *Kobori Enshū Masakazu* (*1549–1647*)

"Cold Moon over an Inlet"

The wind turns cold   and there is no spray
from waves   coming into shore.
On a frozen inlet shines   the moon
of a winter night.

kaze saete/yosekuru nami no/ato mo nashi/kōru irie no/fuyu no yo no tsuki

THE WORD "daimyo" conjures up images of martial valor. In fact, though, many men to whom this title was assigned in the Sengoku and Edo periods were much more than military leaders. A case in point is Kobori Masakazu, also known as Enshū. Born into a warrior lineage of some prominence in Ōmi Province, he followed his father into service to Toyotomi Hideyoshi, eventually inheriting a domain of over 12,000 *koku*. Most biographies of the man, however, note first his accomplishments as a designer of castles (including Nijō Castle and Fushimi Castle in Kyoto) and gardens when he served as commissioner of public works (*fushin bugyō*) under the first three Tokugawa shoguns. He also studied calligraphy and poetry, the latter under Reizei masters, including Tamemitsu and Tameyori.

The poem above shares much with the spare but elegant aesthetic of *wabicha* that Enshū favored as a student of Furuta Oribe (1543–1615), another daimyo of great artistic accomplishment. Late on a night on the coast, the winter moon shines down on the frozen surface of an inlet—frozen so solid, in fact, that there are no waves to disturb the frigid surface at all. The utter silence of the scene adds to the chill.

Along with Chiun (poem 37), Enshū is one of the commoner poets represented in *Shūgai sanjūroku kasen*, compiled either by Retired Emperor Go-Mizuno'o or by his son Go-Sai. The poets are alike in that none is represented in any imperial anthology. Enshū left only a few small collections of poems behind, none of which rises to the level of a personal anthology. As a tea master, however, he had to be proficient in the *uta* form and legends of his prowess as a poet abound in Edo-period texts.

The poem is no. 35 in *Shūgai sanjūroku kasen*.

54. *Kinoshita Chōshōshi (1569–1649)*

Written in the autumn, when he visited the remains
of Teika's Ogura retreat

To Ogura I go   in search
of a past   now all a ruin—
though from the peak a stag calls,   still, it seems,
remembering.

ogurayama / toeba kotauru / ato furite / mine ni wasurenu / saoshika no koe

IT WOULD be hard to exaggerate the reverence with which poets of the late medieval and early modern eras regarded the founders of the Mikohidari lineage, particularly Teika, fragments of whose calligraphy were in high demand among poets and tea masters. No doubt many of these same people visited sites associated with the patriarch's name, including Mount Ogura.

The Reizei were not slow to recognize this kind of interest, which they fostered in any way they could. Indeed, one of the the primary attractions of becoming a disciple of the house was the opportunity to get a glimpse of treasures from the Reizei library and to be given the chef's tour of important sites in the Kyoto area by Reizei heirs or their stewards.

There is no indication that a member of the Reizei house accompanied Kinoshita Chōshōshi when he composed the poem above (*Kyohakushū*, no. 1616). We do know from the headnotes to poems such as the following (*Kyohakushū*, no. 1614) that he was close to the head of the lower house at the time, Tamekage:

Written in the Sixth Month, after Lord Tamekage
had come by for a chat

What need could one have   to visit
Mount Himuro?   —when friends of like mind

can forget about summer   as they share
conversation.

himuroyama / nani ka tazunen / omou dochi / natsu o wasururu / mutsugatari shite

Mount Himuro refers to a place where ice was stored — an obvious
refuge from summer's heat, but one for which Chōshōshi says he has
no need since he is with a true friend.

At Ogura, Chōshōshi was not able to chat with his Reizei friend.
His poem, however, does recall one of those by Tameie quoted ear-
lier in which, four centuries before, the father of the founder of the
Reizei lineage spoke of how he too communed there with spirits of
old, hearing through his years there always "the same feeling in the
call of the stag."[19]

55. *Retired Emperor Go-Mizuno'o (1596–1680)*

Miscellaneous: "Transience, with the image 'Boat' "

How long must my boat   be tossed about
in the waves   of this world of ours,
I ask myself — but then reply: let be whatever
will be.

yo no naka wa / nami no sawagi mo / itsumade no / mi no ukibune yo / sa mo araba are

THE YOUNG emperor Kotohito, whom we know as Go-Mizuno'o,
was evidently not always happy with the role of the emperor and
his court in the Tokugawa social order. Without vassals of his
own or even a strong imperial guard, however, military resistance
was impossible. While resisting as best he could in the symbolic
realm, he embraced the role of artistic preserver as dictated by the
shogunate.

He was on the throne for 19 years and thereafter served as retired
emperor until his death nearly 50 years later, in 1680 — through the
reigns of his daughter, Meishō, and his sons, Go-Kōmyō (1633–54;
r. 1643–54), Go-Sai, and Reigen. He was a patron of all the arts, in-
cluding old ones such as poetry and new ones such as the tea cere-
mony. In poetic matters he seems to have favored members of the
Nakano-in, Karasumaru, and Asukai lineages more than those of the
upper Reizei house. He was patron, on the other hand, to members
of the Reizei "network" in the Fujitani and Imaki lineages, and the

---

19. *Tameie shū*, no. 4959. Quoted in Chapter 1, p. 52.

fact that he ordered texts from the Reizei library copied in order to preserve them for posterity shows that he had respect for the holdings of the Mikohidari lineage.

The poem above comes from a large collection called *Shin meidai wakashū*, which was compiled in the mid-eighteenth century as a resource book for poets. Rather than memorializing any particular poet or faction, the anthology brings together exemplary poems organized by topic. Thus an old, well-established topic such as *natsukusa* (Summer Grasses) is represented by 21 poems, while a less common topic such as the one Go-Mizuno'o writes about in the poem above (no. 4487) is one of only two examples. The other, also by Go-Mizuno'o, comes to a similar conclusion about life in the floating world:

> There, then not there;   not there, then there
> again: a moving boat appears
> briefly between the waves   that are the world
> of men.[20]

aru wa naki / naku wa namima ni / arawarete / kogiyuku fune ya / hito no yo no naka

56. *Fujitani Tameeda (1620–80)*

Autumn: "Early Autumn"

The autumn wind   begins to blow
through my sleeves   more coolly now;
even its sound seems different   in the reeds
of my garden.

akikaze no / sode ni suzushiku / fukisomete / oto koso kaware / niwa no ogiwara

ONE OF the many anthologies published in the Edo period designed as reference works for poets is the *Burui genyō wakashū*. Containing more than 10,000 poems by members of the imperial family and courtiers, it offers scores of examples of poems written on almost every known conventional topic (*dai*), arranged according to the standard order. Poets in training must have found it an invaluable resource.

Fujitani Tameeda was the son of Tamekata, founder of the Fujitani lineage, and as such would have remained under normal circumstances in a subservient position with respect to the main Reizei house. Yet the untimely death of Reizei Tameharu left a vacancy that Tameeda's brother, Tamekiyo, was asked to fill, putting the Fujitani

---

20. *Shin meidai wakashū*, poem no. 4488.

at center stage for a time. It was probably this rather than anything else that explains Tameeda's success in the court of Go-Mizuno'o. In 1669, he was made a middle counselor and in 1673 he was given senior second rank, creating a pattern that several generations of Fujitani after him would follow.

The topic "Early Autumn" obviously calls first of all for a response that emphasizes the *early* stages of the season. Tameeda accomplishes this by drawing attention to the way the wind blowing through his sleeves suddenly seems cooler. In summer, of course, a cool breeze is always welcome; but here the wind is a little too cool for comfort — a sign that the warmth of summer is fading away. Another sign, again articulated by the wind, comes in the form of another sensation: hearing. For as summer fades away, the leaves gradually become more dry and brittle, making for a different sound when the wind blows through them. Thus with subtle signs the change of seasons is announced.

The poem appears as no. 3359 in *Burui genyō wakashū*.

57. *Ima Shikibu (1630–68)*

Autumn: "The Night of the 15th Day, in the Eighth Month"

On this very night   in Cathay
and Yamato   people will make poems.
Oh that I could ask the moon   the thoughts of each
and every heart!

koyoi shi mo/kara ni yamato ni/yomu uta no/kokorogokoro o/tsuki ni towaba ya

WHEN EMPRESS Meishō ascended the throne in 1629, it was the first time that a woman had served as sovereign since the eighth century. Comparisons with the great Heian courts being inevitable, her father, Go-Mizuno'o, immediately set about finding lady literati to place around her. Eventually, this brought to court a woman known to us by the name Ima Shikibu — "the Shikibu of the Age," an explicit comparison to the great Murasaki Shikibu, lady-in-waiting to Empress Akiko and author of *The Tale of Genji*.

Although Ima Shikibu did little else to justify comparison with Murasaki Shikibu, references here and there in Edo texts indicate that she did leave behind a collection of poems, which one of her sons published as *Ima Shikibu shū*. Unfortunately, the text is not extant. In all, only a handful of her poems have survived.

We know that Ima Shikibu was born to a *renga* master with the family name Yamada, that her given name was Kameko, and that for a time she was married to one Andō Sadatame, who had been a student of Tamekage of the lower Reizei house. She served Go-Mizuno'o, Meishō, and Go-Mizuno'o's consort, Tōfukumon-in.

The topic of the poem above is really "the full moon in autumn," which occurs on the 15th day of the Seventh, Eighth, and Ninth Months. Yet rather than concentrate on the moon itself, Ima Shikibu draws attention to the people looking up at it. "Moon viewing" (*tsuki-mi*) was one of the favorite leisure activities of autumn, which meant that as she gazed on it she knew that many others all around — at court and elsewhere — would be doing the same. Such events inevitably included poetry.

The poem appears in *Ima Shikibu shū* (p. 102).

58. *Shimo Reizei Tamekage (1612–52)*

"Lamp in Seclusion"

For no real purpose,   not even
to provide light   for perusing books —
still in the window remains   a lamp burning
in the night.

miru fumi no/tame to shi mo naki/mado no naka ni/munashiku nokoru/yowa no tomoshibi

THOSE WHO abandon the secular world often have the most laudable of reasons for doing so: to cast off worldly attachments and live a simpler and purer life, to undertake religious devotions with no distractions, and so on. But there were other reasons people went into seclusion, some of them not happy ones. Political difficulties, economic reverses, physical ailments, even government censure — these too could lead a person into retirement.

Why the subject of this poem by Tamekage of the lower Reizei house has chosen a life of quietude is not clear. But that he is unable (or unwilling) to find joy in the one thing such a life allows — time to pore over old books, making friends with poets and scholars of the past — is an indication that he is not pleased with his lot. The most important word in the poem is *munashiku*, "emptily," or "to no purpose." Whatever high-minded intentions others may have in choosing to live the simple life, the speaker here disavows them. For whatever reason, his life in seclusion is bitter.

The futility of existence is an old Buddhist theme. In Tamekage's poem, however, one senses something more mundane at work. Perhaps within, beyond the window, the occupant of the house is ill, or even dead. To make the matter clear might seem on the surface to make a better poem, but leaving the matter unresolved allows room for the imagination. That the lamp is still burning seems to offer some reason for hope.

The poem appears in *Reizei Tamekage Ason kashū* (no. 151).

59. *Nakano-in Michishige (1631–1710)*

Spring: "Blossoms at a Mountain Home"

They all come to see: people you know, people
you don't,   making the mountains
no good for hiding yourself   when the cherries
are in bloom.

shiru shirazu / hito mo toikite / mi o kakusu / yama no kai naki / hana no koro kana

MICHISHIGE OF the Nakano-in lineage, descended from Emperor Murakami (926–67; r. 946–67), was the most prominent poet of the court of Go-Mizuno'o. For his service, he was rewarded in 1704 with the office of Palace Minister, the first time anyone in his line had achieved ministerial status since the 1200s. The next year he was advanced to junior first rank, a rarity in any age. He was known not only for his knowledge of court lore (*yūsoku kojitsu*), but also for his poetry and calligraphy.

The Nakano-in house had been prominent in poetic affairs since the late 1400s. Traditionally the house was affiliated more with Nijō traditions than with the Reizei. But by the 1600s the Nijō bloodline no longer existed, leaving the Reizei as the only actual descendants of Shunzei and Teika. For this reason, Michishige, while he maintained a commitment to the "orthodoxy" of Nijō teachings, also chose to assist the Reizei in carrying on their traditions. Thus Tametsuna, who lost his father at the age of 4, became Michishige's student.

Michishige's poem presents the predicament of a recluse, who has come into the mountains to escape human contact and to enjoy the beauties of nature. Blossoms attract scores of people in places like Edo or Kyoto, but the same is true even in the mountains. All kinds of people come to see. Those you don't know are a nuisance; and even the ones you know may overstay their welcome. You came to the mountains to hide yourself from the world, but the world comes to you.

The poem appears as no. 894 in *Shin meidai wakashū*.

60. *Reizei Tamekiyo (1631–68)*

"Blossoms on Peaks"

So taken is my heart   with cherries
now in bloom   that again today
I push ahead, not knowing   how many peaks
I just crossed.

saku hana ni / kokoro ukarete / kyō mo mata / shirazu ikue / mine o koeken

ON THE 16th day of the Third Month of 1662, Emperor Go-Sai held a poetry gathering in the imperial chambers. Poems were composed extemporaneously (*tōza*), on topics all involving blossoms, as was appropriate given the season. In all, 20 poems were composed by those assembled, three by Reizei Tamekiyo.

The first draft of Tamekiyo's poem ended with the phrase *mine ya wakekoshi* ("unaware / of the many peaks I passed by") rather than *mine o koeken*. The change was penned in by the emperor himself, with no explanation. Perhaps he preferred the softer and more tentative *koeken* to the more confident *wakekoshi*.

Perhaps in the back of Tamekiyo's mind was a famous poem by his ancestor, Shunzei, written at an imperial gathering on a similar topic:

"Going after Blossoms in the Distance"

How many times now   have I crossed
mountain crests   with the image
of blossoms leading me on—   toward nothing
but white clouds?[21]

omokage ni / hana no sugata o / sakidatete / ikue koekinu / mine no shirakumo

Shunzei's poem says nothing definite about how long the speaker has been lured on by the beauty of the blossoms, while Tamekiyo makes it clear with the phrase "again today" that he has been in the mountains for some days. Furthermore, Tamekiyo's speaker is not deceived into forging on by any illusion: his heart is taken by the real thing. Both poems present a man so sensitive that he can put worldly demands aside as he hikes through the mountains in search of blossoms. The only thing that will bring him back, we surmise, will be the end of the blossom season, which will come too soon.

The poem is quoted in the foundation newsletter, *ST 66* (p. 5).

------

21. *Shin chokusenshū*, poem no. 57.

61.   *Imaki Sadanori (1635–89)*

Love: "Being Told a Lie about Where to Go"

How am I to know   which of all these places
is hers?   There is no sign at all
of what she said to watch for—   just house after house
all the same.

ikade sono / yado to wa shiran / oshietsuru / shirushi wa miede / nitaru ieie

THE STORY of the Imaki lineage is a common one in the annals of the court nobility. It begins with the decision of Reizei Tamemitsu to allow his younger son Tamechika to establish a branch family, known early on as the Nakayama Reizei. Three generations later (Tamechika — Tamehisa — Sadanori), Sadanori took the name Imaki in order to distinguish his line from the Reizei. Although lower in status, the new lineage managed to maintain a place for itself in poetic circles throughout the rest of the Edo period. As time went by, their affiliation with the Reizei faded, in contrast to the Fujitani, for instance, another branch family that maintained a strong sense of connection to the parent house.

The topic of Sadanori's poem is unusual, to say the least. To be rejected in love is nothing new; nor is it out of the ordinary for a speaker to be unable to meet with his or her lover. But to go out and to be unable to find her house? The image of a man walking the streets, looking for the directions some woman gave him (a tree of some kind? a distinctive fence? the possibilities are endless), is almost comical. If he does not even know the way to her house, the relationship must be just beginning. One cannot help but wonder if the woman is having a laugh at his expense.

The poem appears as no. 3690 in *Shin meidai wakashū*. Needless to say, it is the only poem listed under its topic. There is even the possibility that the topic was made up after the fact, in order to maintain the pretense of following convention.

62.   *Fujitani Tamenori (also Tamemochi; 1654–1713)*

Summer: "Evening Faces on a Fence"

Already aglow   with a sprinkling
of dewdrops,   the evening faces
shine more coolly on the fence   in the light
of the moon.

oku tsuyu no / hikari o soete / yūgao no / kakine suzushiku / yadoru tsukikage

FUJITANI TAMENORI, son of Tameeda, was the third head of the Fuji-
tani house, which occupied the lot just to the west of the Reizei lot
on Imadegawa Avenue. The relationship between the two houses
has remained strong down to the present day.

Like Imaki Sadanori, Fujitani Tamenori was highly favored in the
time of Retired Emperor Go-Mizuno'o. As a token of his success, he
was appointed major counselor just before his death. One of his
younger sons became the head of the Takenouchi house, and two
other sons became wards of the Irie house. Intermarriage among all
of these "related" houses—the upper Reizei, the lower Reizei, the
Fujitani, the Imaki, the Irie, and the Takenouchi—was routine, and
young sons were often adopted into one branch from another when
vacancies occurred.

Tamenori's poem cannot help but bring to mind the famous scene
in *The Tale of Genji* when the hero first goes by the house of the
woman who is subsequently called Yūgao ("evening faces") after the
flowers of that name that cover her fence. A vine-like plant, the *yūgao*
produces tiny white blossoms whose delicate beauty first attracts
Genji to their owner. When one of his men goes over to pick a few
blossoms for his lord, a servant girl gives him a fan, the initiating act
in a romance that will develop between the young lady of the house
and Genji.

The first lines of Tamenori's poem, with their image of dew
sparkling on evening faces, are probably meant as a direct allusion
to *The Tale of Genji*. Rather than go on to deal in some way with
the story of Genji and Yūgao, however, he simply adds the light of
the moon shining coolly on the little flowers. Thus the romance—one
of the saddest stories in the tale, which ends with Yūgao's death—
remains in the background.

The poem is no. 1571 in *Shin meidai wakashū*.

63. *Imaki Sadatsune (1656–1702)*

Summer: "Summer Grasses"

Thick though they may grow   I will not
cut them back: for in no time
I will see autumn flowers   on my garden's
summer grasses.

shigeru to mo / yoshi ya harawaji / aki ni min / hana hodo naki / niwa no natsugusa

SUMMER IN the Kyoto basin is hot and humid, beginning with endless
rains (*samidare*; modern *tsuyu*) and ending with sweltering heat. As

if in compensation, the poetic tradition tends to focus more on relief from the oppression of sunlight. Nocturnal scenes tend to dominate, a reflection of both poetic tradition and actual life practices, since most summer activities were held at night.

In the natural world, summer is associated with excess and profusion: sheets of rain, clouds of fireflies, irises in endless rows at pondside, frogs croaking in chorus in rice paddies. It is a time of dense and luxuriant growth, leading on toward a bountiful harvest.

The topic of the poem above by Imaki Sadatsune (son of Sadanori; poem 61 above) is "summer grasses," which are rich and luxuriant by nature, so much so that they quickly obscure a pathway or take over a garden. Metaphorically, they stand for whatever is excessive, whatever dominates or overwhelms.

One way to deal with the thick summer growth is to cut it back. When contemplating this option, however, the speaker of the poem thinks better of it, reasoning that the thicker the grasses grow in summer, the more numerous will be the wildflowers of autumn. A further suggestion is that those same grasses, and their flowers, will inevitably die in late autumn. Nature will tend its own garden if allowed to progress on its own.

The poem is no. 1536 in *Shin meidai wakashū*.

64. *Kajiko of Gion (precise dates unknown)*

> Once when there was a picture of a boat hidden in the reeds
> inscribed on a fan, someone asked to her to write a poem about it:
>
> My body too   may end up
> rotting the same way: hidden in the reeds
> of the bay at Naniwa,   a discarded
> fishing boat.
>
> *kakute mi mo / kuchi ya hatenan / naniwae no / ashimagakure no / ama no suteobune*

GION IS the name given to the area around Yasaka Shrine in Kyoto. Festivals were held there in ancient days, but it was in the Edo period that Gion became a truly lively district, full of shops, teahouses, bars, restaurants, and government-licensed brothels.

Generations of Reizei men frequented the teahouses of Gion. It was there that the proprietor of one of those establishments became a disciple, of sorts. The preface to her small personal anthology tells the basic story: "In the Gion area there was a woman named Kaji who ran a teahouse. She was of gentle disposition, was not at all vulgar, and from her youth up was filial toward her parents. In her spare time, she became enamored of tales and romances and asked any customer who seemed to know about such things questions about old poems."[22]

A woman of such background could not attend formal gatherings, but in the past, several poems by "women of pleasure" had even been included in imperial anthologies. There could be nothing wrong with encouraging her in private and occasionally looking over her poems. While she may not have attended formal functions at the Reizei house, then, she did participate in votive sequences sent to shrines and so forth.

Kajiko left behind a small anthology, *Kaji no ha*, which contains just 148 poems, published in 1707. Predictably, most are occasional pieces or love poems, such as the one above (no. 123 in the collection). The bay at Naniwa was famous for its reeds, and abandoned boats rotting at waterside appear frequently in late medieval *uta* as well. The directness with which she speaks of her body in the first two lines, however, is somewhat unusual. As the proprietor of a teahouse, she was a woman of the world who knew its ways.

65.　*Irie Sukehisa (1655–1716)*

Autumn: "The Moon at Dawn"

Who else besides me　　might still be up
so late,　　into dawn's first light —
looking to the moon above　　to purify
his heart?

mata mo tare / akatsuki fukaku / okiitsutsu / kokoro o tsuki ni / sumashite wa miru

THE IRIE family, descended from Sukehisa, a younger son of Fujitani Tameeda, was another of the branch families of the Reizei. Their house was located north of Courtiers' Quarter, near Shōkokuji, and their stipend of only 30 *koku* put them far down on the list of courtiers, but their strong affiliation with the parent house continued into the twentieth century.

"The Moon at Dawn" was an old topic long before Sukehisa was asked to compose a poem on it, for what occasion we do not know. The challenge with such a topic was to do something new and yet stay within the bounds of tradition in diction and imagery. He makes the attempt by asking who "besides himself" may be sharing

---

22. Gion Kajiko, *Kaji no ha*, p. 331.

the same experience, "deep into dawn's first light" (*akatsuki fukaku*), thus opening the borders of the poem up to include other moon viewers imagined all around. Then, closing things up again, he wonders how many of those gazing up at the moon are doing so to "purify" their hearts.

What the speaker means by "purify" here is not clear. Certainly moonlight often stands for the message of the Buddhist Law (a light shining in the darkness of the world) in many canonical texts, which opens up one possibility. Another is that the speaker is involved in preparation for some rite, steeling himself physically and spiritually by gazing into the pure light from above. The first half of the poem, however, makes answering this question less important, shifting the focus from the speaker to countless others caught in the same human predicament—caught in a world of dirt and toil that makes the moon seem even purer by comparison.

The poem appears as no. 4408 in *Burui genyō wakashū*.

66. *Shimo Reizei Tametsune (1654–1722)*

Miscellaneous: "River Bridge"

How cold in the sleeves   of people going
back and forth   looks the morning wind
as it passes over the bridge   across the river
and away.

yukikayou / sode ika bakari / samukarashi / asakaze wataru / tō no kawahashi

TAMETSUNE OF the lower house was a rough contemporary of Tametsuna who was active in the imperial salons. At the time, relations between the houses were strained. Philosophically, however, the houses remained quite similar in approach, as this poem shows. In the emphasis on a moment of change in the natural landscape and the absence of any "emotive" words or any explicit persona, Tametsune shows the influence of dispositions inherited from the founders of the Reizei style—Tamesuke, Tamehide, and Tamemasa.

The poem presents us with the image of a bridge passing over a river—no place of note, it would appear, just a nondescript bridge across which some anonymous people are making their way. Rather than focus only on the people, however, the poet draws our attention to another natural element—the morning wind, visible as it blows the sleeves of the travelers. Though the season is not identified, we are told that it is a cold wind, which makes us imagine the people on the bridge being assailed by it. The last line, drawing our attention to the speed of the wind going on its way, leaving the people of the bridge laboring far behind, is a fine finishing touch that cinematically opens up the landscape and reduces the men in the scene to insignificance. The poem thus provides a fine enunciation of its topic, helping the reader to "feel" the essence of a bridge in human terms. The bridge is of course a human creation made to traverse water—one of the most powerful of nature's devices; but the morning wind passing quickly by the travelers also shows how puny man's powers truly are.

The poem appears as no. 4008 in *Shin meidai wakashū*.

67. *Nikki Mitsunaga (d. 1737)*

"Saga"

Oh, if I could live   back in the depths
of Saga!   —even if not
at the time of spring blossoms   or the season of
fall leaves.

sumaba ya na/saga no no oku no/hana no haru/momijiba no aki no/ori narazu to mo

IN 1721, Nikki Mitsunaga, an Edo samurai, was in Kyoto an on errand from the shogun to collect knowledge and materials from a number of court families, the Reizei among them. His diary says that during his time in Kyoto, he visited the Reizei house on Imadegawa often, attending poetry gatherings, copying out texts from the family collection, and interviewing family members.

While in Kyoto, Mitsunaga also did a great deal of sightseeing, including some "guided tours" by the Reizei or their stewards, who showed him the gravesites of prominent ancestors. The old city was full of historical sites, beautiful gardens, and its outskirts were of course famous for their views of mountains, forests, rivers, and streams.

On the 12th day of the Tenth Month, Mitsunaga was among those asked to participate in composition of a votive sequence to be presented to Tamatsushima Shrine, under the supervision of nine-year-old Tamemura—referred to by his title of *jijū*, "gentleman-in-waiting." That evening, he stayed on to converse with Tametsuna—"chatting for several hours," he says, "about nothing but poetry." That same night, he recorded the poem above, probably composed with his Reizei hosts.

Mitsunaga of course knew that Saga was a place of special importance to the Reizei house. Teika had lived there, in his Ogura cottage, and so had Tameie. To say that he too would like to live there is probably an indication that he had visited the place and found it to his taste, but more than that, it is an avowal of loyalty to the Way of Poetry, and specifically to Reizei traditions. Declaring that he would be happy to live there in any season, even without the blessing of the spring and autumn foliage for which the site was famous, is probably his way of saying that one of low social rank would be pleased to have any standing in the house.

The demands of his duties as a samurai in shogunal employ of course left no possibility for Mitsunaga to realize his dream of living the life of a poet-recluse in Saga or anywhere else, at least until retirement. He would visit Kyoto again, but when he died it was in Edo.

The poem is quoted in *Zaikyō zuihitsu* (p. 420).

68. *Retired Emperor Reigen (1654–1732)*

Miscellaneous: "Green Bamboos in the Rain"

As the rain comes down   it washes once
again   over new green growth.
Of a deeper hue when wet   is my grove of
tall bamboos!

furu ame ya / midori o sara ni / arauramu / nururu iro koki / niwa no kuretake

RETIRED EMPEROR Reigen, son of Go-Mizuno'o, was as dedicated to the courtly arts as his father was. In addition to sponsoring a lively poetic salon, especially after he became retired emperor in 1687, he also lectured to the members of his court on *Kokinshū* and other poetic works.

In 1685, Reigen issued an order for the Reizei to lend 320 manuscripts from the house library to his own librarian's office in order to have them copied for safekeeping. The texts he most wanted to preserve were mostly poetry collections from the Heian and Kamakura periods rather than works by the Reizei themselves, but still he became a great patron of the house. In fact, it was under his administration, in the year 1722, that the century-long censure against family use of the *obunko* was lifted. Tametsuna, Tamehisa, and Tamemura were all highly favored by Reigen, whose patronage was a great factor in the flourishing of the house in the 1700s. In recognition of his importance in Reigen's court, Tamemura was asked to put together a comprehensive personal anthology of his patron's poems, an honor that symbolized the Reizei heir's preeminent place in the poetic hierarchy of the day.

The poem above comes from a *chakutō* sequence (100 poems composed one a day for a 100 days) composed in 1721. Because no word in the topic is strictly affiliated with one season rather than another, the poem is classified in the miscellaneous category. Most probably, though, the scene is set in summer, the time of new green growth, the rich color of which is enhanced by a rain shower—and even more so when one shower is followed by another.

The poem appears as no. 365 in *Reigen Hōkō gyoshū*.

69. *Reizei Tametsuna (1664–1722)*

"Wild Geese Going with Clouds"

As they pass above   the peaks begin
to brighten —   a flock of wild geese
following trailing clouds   in one
solitary line.

koete kuru / mine akesomete / yokogumo ni / nabiki tsuretaru / kari no hitotsura

THE JOURNAL of Nikki Mitsunaga, *Zaikyō zuihitsu* (see poem 67 above) lists six poems composed for a poetry meeting held at the imperial palace in the Twelfth Month of 1721, which he says he copied from the text of the gathering. Three of the poems are by Reizei Tametsuna, current head of the Reizei house, two are by his son and heir Tamehisa, and the last one by Karasumaru Mitsuhide. All are on different topics. No doubt there were many other poems composed as well, but Mitsunaga concentrates on those by his patrons.

At the time, Tametsuna was in his late 50s, a middle counselor at court, and in his prime as a poet. The topic of his poem is a conventional one that brings a conventional response. Mitsunaga adds no note of commentary or criticism, instead simply listing the poem as he lists other things, from titles of texts in the library to items of genealogy. In this sense, the poem is presented less as an example of excellence than as an example of conventionality: a typical performance.

The poem is straightforward: off in the distance, just as daylight begins to light the peaks, a flock of geese crosses over the ridge, as if trailing after racks of cloud drifting horizontally across the sky. The last line reduces the scene to a single column of geese, making their way overhead and away.

The poem is quoted in *Zaikyō zuihitsu* (p. 460).

70. *Fujitani Tamenobu (1675–1740)*

Love: "Love Increasing the Morning After"

Now that he has gone,   he cannot know
what I feel   the morning after —
not even if my love for him   is even stronger
than before.

okiideshi / ato ni wa hito no / yo mo shiraji / kesa iyamashi no / omoi sou to mo

ANOTHER LARGE collection of *uta*, arranged according to topic and intended for use as a reference work, is the *Shin dairin wakashū*, published in 1716. It includes 9,415 poems on 3,772 topics by Go-Mizuno'o, Reigen, Karasumaru Mitsuhiro (d. 1638), Nakano-in Michi-mura, and others of the early to mid-Edo period.

As arranged in imperial anthologies and other collections, most love poems are on topics such as "Love from Afar," "Loving in Secret," "Love Unrequited," "Rejection," "Abandonment," and so on. There are few poems on consummation, and almost none on the idea of lasting love.

Those who embark on the courtly way of love must therefore prepare for nights of longing, wishing, waiting, and despairing. Even when things seem to be going well, periods of separation can easily lead to doubt. In the above poem by Fujitani Tamenobu, for instance, a woman has just spent the night with her man — whether husband or lover the poem does not say. Rather than enjoying warm memories, however, the woman soon finds herself wishing that he had not had to leave. Now that he is gone, she muses: "I wonder how he is feeling. Does he miss me the way I miss him? If only I could somehow tell him how his departure has made me want him all the more. But of course, he cannot read my mind. Expressions of the way I feel will have to be communicated in a letter or await our next meeting. And when will that be?"

According to old convention, based on the social realities of earlier times, it is men who visit women at their homes and not vice versa in court poetry. Thus the point of view here is that of a woman who is obliged to stay at home wringing her hands. When — or whether — the man comes again depends entirely on his fickle heart. Even if he does reappear, his visit will inevitably be followed by another time of longing and doubt.

The poem is no. 6148 in *Shin dairin wakashū*.

71. *Emperor Nakamikado (1701–37)*

"Spring View of a Bay"

Waves in the offing   stretch into the
distant haze   of Naniwa Bay
where the wind is not chilly   and the plums are rich
with scent.

uranami wa / haruka ni kasumu / naniwae ni / kaze samukarazu / ume mo kaorite

ONE OF the traditional roles of poetic houses such as the Reizei and the Asukai was to choose topics for imperial poetry gatherings, as well as to serve in various supervisory or ritual offices. Especially after the fifteenth century, when for a variety of reasons large imperial anthologies were no longer produced, officiating in such capacities became the primary way of ratifying one's identity as the head of a courtly tradition.

After meetings in which a family member had played a crucial role, the emperor (or retired emperor) would often send the *kaishi* on which one of his poems had been recorded as an indication of his gratitude. These would quickly be mounted on cloth—sometimes from imperial robes that had also been received as gifts—and stored away in the family storehouses, along with their treasured manuscripts from ancient times. The head of the house would typically note the relevant details of the event on a piece of paper placed in the paulownia box, or sometimes write the details on its lid. Needless to say, these gifts became some of the most prized possessions of the house. They would be taken out only for brief display in the alcove of the Great Hall on the most formal of occasions.

The poem above, by Emperor Nakamikado, is inscribed on a *kaishi* still stored in the Reizei library. It was composed in 1721, on the 24th day of the First Month, on the occasion of the first poetry meeting of the new year in the imperial palace. Reizei Tametsuna had chosen the topic, which was no doubt judged to be perfect for such a meeting. The spreading hazy, mild winds, gentle waves, and fragrant plum blossoms are all harbingers of spring. To put all of them together, especially in a poem set in the storied Bay of Naniwa, would in itself be considered a kind of prayer for mild weather during the coming year.

The *kaishi* is displayed in issue 59 of *ST* (p. 3).

72. *Karasumaru Mitsuhide (1689–1748)*

"Love on the Road"

Back home, she will be   gazing at it
all alone.   For how many nights
on the road have I looked up,   seeking her face
in the moon?

furusato ni / hitori miruramu / omokage o / ikudo tabine no / tsuki ni koitsutsu

THE KARASUMARU lineage, a branch of the older Hino clan that was founded in the 1400s, was one of the poetic houses most favored by the imperial house in the early Edo period. Mitsuhide was held in particularly high regard as both a poet and a critic, and in recognition of his literary contributions, he was appointed Palace Minister just before his death.

The affiliations of the Karasumaru were not with the Reizei but with Nijō orthodoxy, as represented also by the Asukai, the Sanjō-nishi, and Go-Mizuno'o and his heirs. Yet probably out of respect for the boy's bloodline Mitsuhide took in the young Reizei Tame-mura as a student, supervising his *keiko*. No doubt he also recognized the young man's talent and was happy for the chance to steer him toward Nijō orthodoxy.

The above poem was written in 1729, for a 100-poem sequence commissioned by Retired Emperor Reigen. The topics for the sequence were those of one of the most famous of all such sequences, the *Horikawa hyakushu* of the early 1100s. Reigen jotted down a few critical comments here and there about Mitsuhide's poems. Next to the one above, however, he simply drew in a "long mark" (*chōten*), indicating his approbation. Indeed, the poem is a worthy example of what poetic treatises praise as the style of *ushin*, or "deep feeling."

In Mitsuhide's poem we are not sure where the speaker is — actually out on the road or in an inn. The focus of the poem is not on the landscape but on the moon above and on the thoughts the moon inspires. Back home, he reasons, the one I long for will be alone looking up at the moon just as I am now, thinking of me as I am thinking of her. While the lovers are apart, they cannot help searching the moon's surface for something they know is not there and feeling disappointment. And the ordeal will go on: for though the "how many" must refer to the past, it also makes one think of the future. The journey is not yet over; on coming nights the moon will serve again as an almost unwelcome reminder of loneliness.

The poem is quoted in *Nihon meika shūsei* (p. 339).

73. *Reizei Tamehisa (1686–1741)*

Love: "Love, with 'Dream' as an Image"

All that I saw —   it was nothing
but a dream!   But still that image
lingers on above my bed   as if somehow
it were real.

mishi wa tada / yume no chigiri o / utsutsu ka to / hakanaku tadoru / toko no omokage

THIS POEM was probably written for a gathering of some sort. The basic challenge to the poet implied in such a topic is straightforward: to compose a love poem that uses the word "dream" in its conception. One encounters virtually every kind of image imaginable — at least within the limits of decorum — in such topics: "Love, with the image of 'the Moon,'" "Love, with the image of 'Driftwood,'" "Love, with the image of 'Fallen Leaves.'" Obviously, the purpose behind such assignments was to tax the talents of masters, to test their competence in coming up with a convincing connection between the abstract idea of love and a given image.

The relation between dreams and love had been defined long before. Typically, lovers who cannot meet in reality meet in dreams, although there are other variations. Tamehisa chooses to stick close to the usual conception. His speaker has been asleep and has literally just awakened to realize that all he had just experienced — which in the Japanese text strongly suggests sexual union — must have been a dream and no more. But no sooner does he come to this conclusion than he sees something in the darkness above his bed, something lingering there. The image of his lover, perhaps?

Whatever was there for a moment in the darkness fades quickly, as does the dream. As in so many other poems, here love itself is as fleeting and insubstantial as a dream and a dream's ephemeral traces. One gazes into the darkness for a glimpse of it, but in vain.

The poem appears as no. 10324 in *Shinshoku dairin wakashū*.

74. *Gekkō-in (1685–1752)*

Miscellaneous: "Feelings on Old Age"

How can it be   that I have lived
to such an age?   — when every time
that I was faced with trials   I doubted
I would survive!

kabakari no / oi to naru made / uki tabi ni / ikeran mi to mo / omowazarishi o

SOME OF the finest poets of the classical Japanese canon were women serving in the imperial courts of the Heian and Kamakura periods. Thereafter, there were still women at court, and many still composed poems, but as the court lost political power they lost their social prominence and ceased to be such a force in the literary world. As time went on, the number of women participating in even the most formal courtly events—poetry contests, and so forth—declined greatly.

This does not mean, however, that poetry by women ceased altogether. Even in the Muromachi period, texts reveal the names of a handful of women poets, although very few of their works have survived. In the Edo period, not only women at the imperial court but also women in the courts of the shogun were active participants in poetic life. One example is a woman known informally as Gekkō-in (whose personal name was Okiyo), a woman of the Katsumata clan who was the wife of the shogun Ienobu and the mother of Ietsugu. A student of Reizei Tamemura, she was a central figure among the Reizei partisans in Edo during her last years. Her personal anthology contains over 370 poems.

The poem above could have been written by a lady of the Heian era. Looking back on a long life, the speaker wonders how she weathered the many storms of the past. So many times she thought she would not survive the perils of human existence, from physical illness or emotional upheaval to political conflict, natural calamity, or social unrest. Yet somehow the time has gone by, and she is old. There is some pride in the declaration, perhaps, but it is tempered by the knowledge that one day a test will come that she cannot outlast.

The poem is no. 1023 in *Kakanshū*.

75. *Narushima Nobuyuki (1689–1760)*

Miscellaneous: "Old Age"

Think about it,   you who despise
those grown old —   for your recompense
may be to live to an age   when you are despised
in turn.

omoe hito / oi o itoishi / mukui yori / itowaruru mi to / tsui ni naru yo o

THE LAST imperial *waka* anthology was compiled in the 1430s, although others were planned some decades later. After the degradations of the Sengoku period, there seems to have been a feeling of distance between the present and the past that precluded returning to many old practices, imperial anthologies among them. At various times, the suggestion to put together a new collection was bruited about, but nothing ever materialized.

Yet still there were anthologies, as noted before. The largest were essentially reference works, usually organized by topic and intended for the instruction and inspiration of young poets. *Shin dairin waka-shū* — "The New Collection of Poems on Clustered Topics" of 1716 — and *Shinshoku dairin wakashū* — "The New Later Collection of Poems on Clustered Topics" of 1764 — are outstanding examples in which poems by a number of Reizei poets are represented. Then there were personal anthologies, which were put together by and sometimes for any poet of prominence. Finally came a host of anthologies put together by groups, in order to memorialize their activities.

The *Kakanshū* (Hazy Gate Collection) was a member of the last group. About 1,200 poems by 200 poets, all of them active in Edo and affiliated with one or another noble lineage, make up its pages. The first version of the text was compiled by Ishino Hiromichi, a shogunal official and disciple of the Reizei house, around 1768. There are several textual lines, the latter one deleting a number of poets who were excommunicated from the house later. Poets of the Nativist persuasion are shunned altogether.

Narushima Nobuyuki, also known by his sobriquets Dōchiku and Kinkō, was one of the leaders of the Reizei faction in Edo. Originally from the Shirakawa area, he was adopted into a prominent Edo house and eventually became a personal attendant in the shogunal entourage. He left behind a personal anthology and several other poetic works. His poem does no more than state common sense: the old may be forgotten, even by those who care for them, but the law of retribution is absolute — somehow all will be repaid.

The poem appears in *Kakanshū*, no. 1064.

76. *Gion Yuriko (d. 1757)*

Love: "Love as an Impediment to Study"

Though far from finished   I put aside
my lesson book   and waste my time
on a missive from a man   whose feelings come
as a surprise.

mimohatezu / manaberu fumi wa / okotarite / aranu omoi no / hito no tamazusa

NOT SURPRISINGLY, the foster daughter of Kajiko of Gion, a woman known as Yuriko, inherited her mother's literary inclinations. Taking over Kajiko's teahouse on the latter's death, she submitted work for review to Reizei Tamemura and gained considerable acclaim in her circle. She too left behind a personal anthology, called *Sayuriba*, which was published in 1727.

The topic of the poem above is quite unusual, although in some ways it reminds one again of the old days of Murasaki Shikibu and the other ladies of the imperial court's golden age. The subject of the speaker's lesson books (*fumi*) is not clear: it could be a Chinese book, or even a classical poetic text of some sort—in any case, some kind of formal instruction of the sort intimated by the verb *manabu*. The crucial point is the contrast with *tamazusa*, an old and elegant term for "letter" that refers to some kind of private correspondence. The first represents the world of duty, the second the world of leisure and sentiment—a classic dichotomy that informs many Edo-period plays and stories.

Since the poem appears in the love book of her anthology, we are safe in assuming that Yuriko's intention was to suggest that the letter was a love letter of some sort, although whether from the present or the past is not made clear. Thus we have a young woman preparing for her roles as wife and mother by doing her lessons, who in a moment of boredom picks up another kind of reading material that soon has her enthralled. The poem is on a topic, of course, and thus makes no overt claim to represent real experience. Still, the temptation is strong to see it as a moment of respite for the author from the chores of everyday existence.

The poem appears in *Sayuriba* (p. 390).

77. *Fujitani Tameka (1706–57)*

Summer: "Orange Blossoms by Eaves"

Gone far away now   are memories
of the past   that I call to mind —
but close by, right at my eaves   is the scent
of orange blossoms.

omoiizuru / mukashi wa tōku / hedatete mo / chikaki nokiba ni / niou tachibana

AS THE senior Reizei house prospered in the mid-Edo period, so did its branch lines, the lower house, the Fujitani, the Irie, and indeed all other houses that were in one way or another close associates. Records of court events of the time show them participating together often.

Tameka's poem articulates an old association between the scent of orange blossoms and memories. As is so often the case in the court tradition, the relationship was established by a poem in *Kokinshū*:

Catching the scent   of orange blossoms
that await   the Fifth Month's coming,
I recall the scented sleeves   of someone
from long ago.[23]

satsuki matsu / hanatachibana no / ka o kageba / mukashi no hito no / sode no ka zo suru

Scores of poets in the ages after *Kokinshū* alluded to this poem, establishing incontrovertibly the notion that the blossoms of the orange tree, more than any others, evoked memories, especially of loved ones who have passed on. Tameka's poem is thus a variation on a theme. The past is now remote, his speaker says; as I call to mind memories, they seem beyond reach. But when I catch the scent of orange blossoms, the *feelings* of those times return, immediate and sure. In a sense, this adds to the frustration (and the irony), since the feelings hover in the air somewhere, intangible and thus also beyond reach. Yet there is some comfort in the idea that every year the blossoms will send out that same fragrance again, calling forth the feeling of memories that in that sense will never fully die.

The poem appears as no. 3059 in *Shinshoku dairin wakashū*.

78.   *Isono Masatake (1717–76)*

"Fallen Leaves at a Mountain Home"

Even the harsh blasts   of winds over
fallen leaves   to me sound peaceful
as I listen with calm heart   from my hut
in mountain shadows.[24]

kaze araki / ochiba no oto mo / kokoro kara / sumu yamakage wa / shizuka ni zo kiku

ISONO MASATAKE was one of the Edo samurai in service to Tokugawa Yoshimune who was virtually required to become a disciple of the Reizei house, first under Yoshihisa and then under Tamemura. After the death of Narushima Nobuyuki in 1760, he became the leader of the Reizei camp in Edo, although he fell out of favor some years later.

---

23. *Kokinshū*, poem no. 139.
24. *Kinsei wakashū*, p. 184.

The poem above is one of those contained in the *Reizei-ke gohōshi eisō*, a compilation of poems with words of praise by Reizei masters. The comment attached to the poem, however, is very terse—*yoroshiku sōrō*, or "very fine." In effect, then, the poem probably ranked only slightly above one that received a mark without commentary—a word of encouragement from a coach, rather than concrete criticism or instruction.

Masatake's poem echoes one by Tonna, written on the topic, "Lament," three centuries earlier:

> Had there been no place   to escape
> into the calm   of mountain shadows,
> what would I have to console me   amid the world
> and its woes?[25]
>
> *nogarekite / sumu yamakage no / nakariseba / nani o ukiyo no / nagusame ni sen*

Both poems—written by men who were very much involved in worldly affairs—involve posturing, but also the claim of aesthetic sensitivity that is so central to the court tradition and was so crucial a requirement in courtly poetics. One suspects, in fact, that it is this display of proper sensibility toward which the Reizei note of praise is directed as much as to the poem's conception or technical artistry.

79. *Hagiwara Sōko (1703–84)*

Summer: "Cuckoo Calling in a Dream"

> Was it a dream, then?   Even my lover
> pillowed   here by my side
> did not hear the season's first call   from a mountain
> cuckoo.
>
> *yume nare ya / makura narabete / neshi hito mo / kikanu hatsune no / yamahotogisu*

HAGIWARA SŌKO (lay name: Sadatoki) was born into the Suzuki house in Edo but as a young man was adopted as heir of another house known as the Hagiwara. He served as a samurai of *yoriki* rank in the Edo government. Retiring early because of illness, he dedicated his declining years to the arts. He studied poetry under Karasumaru Mitsuhide, Mushanokōji Sanekage, and Reizei Tamemura and was one of the most prominent poets in the shogun's city.

---

25. Tonna, *Sōanshū*, poem no. 1221.

The theme of Sōko's poem is very old. The cuckoo, whose song was felt to be especially beautiful, is notoriously stingy with its calls, which are among other things considered harbingers of summer. Thus when the speaker thinks he heard the bird call out—just once— he concludes that perhaps he has dozed off a moment and heard the call in his dream. His lover, lying next to him in the summer night, says that she did not hear the call.

Following this poem, which appears in *Kakanshū* (no. 236), is a note: "They say Tamemura gave this an 'excellent' mark, but one wonders. Perhaps the person who heard this misunderstood. Am I being narrow-minded to think that the idea and the words are vulgar?" One of the editors of the anthology thus had reservations about the poem, although including it at all implied some degree of approval.

No doubt the offending phrase is "even my lover pillowed / here by my side," which gestures too directly toward the physical realities of erotic love for aristocratic taste. While this directness may be what appeals most in the poem now, it may indeed have rankled some with courtly sensibilities. Whether Tamemura gave the poem high marks or not is of course unknowable, although we can say that he occasionally departed from the strictest standards of decorum himself.

80.   *Reizei Tamemura (1712–74)*

The Reizei Middle Counselor, Lord Tamemura, carried on the traditions of his house splendidly and succeeded in gaining a fine reputation. He wrote this poem when someone asked him to inscribe a poem on a fan depicting Kumagai Jirō Naozane pursuing the fleeing Atsumori at Suma Bay. The poem was one that everyone talked about.

How harsh the winds   coming down
relentlessly   from the cliffs behind!
— wrecking the flower of youth   on a tree
at Suma Bay.

fukitaenu / ushiro no yama no / kaze mo ushi / suma no wakaki no / hana no chirigata

THE TALE of how the young Taira warrior Atsumori (1169–84) was killed attempting to flee to the boats after the Battle of Ichinotani during the Genpei War of the 1180s is one of the most poignant and popular stories of the classical canon. As the story is told in *Tales of the Heike* and in the Nō play *Atsumori*, the warrior Kumagai no Naozane (1141–1208) rides a fleeing warrior down, throws him from his horse, and is about to take his life when he realizes that his opponent is just a boy — too late to spare him, however, since he knows that the rough East Country warriors behind him will never let the boy live. Reluctantly, Kumagai takes the boy's head and makes sure that the flute he finds on the body is returned to the Taira camp. Later, he becomes a monk and dedicates himself to a life of prayer for the repose of Atsumori's spirit.

Reizei Tamemura was a court aristocrat most of whose time was spent with people of his own class and whose poems were probably not as widely known as, say, the poems of Matsuo Bashō. Yet what Oyamada Tomokiyo says about this poem in his essay collection *Matsunoya sōwa* (p. 719) — literally, that people "made it a topic of conversation" (*kataraigusa ni nan shikeru*) — indicates that even an elite poet like Tamemura had a larger public profile. Since Tomokiyo studied under Murata Harumi, a Reizei disciple, it may be that he heard the story from his teacher, but his final comment makes it clear that the poem was being talked about outside noble circles.

Poetic dogma in Tamemura's time and class regarded poems written on topics (*dai*) as the highest articulations of poetic art, consigning more occasional poems to a strictly secondary status. Anecdotes such as the one above are valuable in that they suggest a broader world of poetic practice in which even poets of the court classes were inevitably involved. In addition to composing poems for the screens or sliding partitions of rich patrons, then, a man in Tamemura's position also had to be ready to dash off something appropriate for a fan, an inscription, a painting, a poem strip, whatever occasion required.

81.   *Shimo Reizei Muneie (1702–69)*

Love: "Love, with 'Cloud' as an Image"

This body of mine   that does not fade
like a cloud —   how long must it drift
so aimlessly through the sky   with no sure
destination?

mi wa kumo to/kie mo hatenade/itsu made ka/yukue mo shiranu/sora ni mayowamu

ALTHOUGH IN the beginning the upper and lower houses of the Reizei lineage were regarded as roughly equals in court society, by the mid-Edo period the upper house was clearly ascendant. As an expression of this fact, Muneie, twelfth head of the junior lineage, was formally made a disciple of Tamemura. Over time, he gained the master's trust, to the point where he was given permission to "mark" the texts of *jige* poets, although only under the direction and supervision of the upper house.[26] This was the highest honor available to a subordinate in such a situation and indicates that Tamemura had high regard for his cousin's judgment.

In the poem above, Muneie shows his knowledge of the court canon by alluding to a famous poem by Saigyō:

> As smoke that drifts   from the peak
> of Mount Fuji,   fading into sky
> with no sure destination—   such is the trend
> of my passion.[27]

> *kaze ni nabiku / fuji no keburi no / sora ni kiete / yukue mo shiranu / waga kokoro kana*

Saigyō's poem—one of his own favorites, the tradition says—was written when he was visiting the east and was meant to express the Buddhist attitude toward human passions, which are regarded as the chief impediment to enlightenment. Although not a love poem per se, the idea of the heart being as much at the mercy of the passions as is smoke drifting from Fuji's peak can easily be interpreted as an expression of that topic. "Fire" and "smoke" are common images in love poems, suggesting the intensity of passion and its tendency to consume and destroy those it possesses.

Muneie's poem is more explicitly a poem about love. His reworking of the theme emphasizes that the cloud symbolizing his body refuses to fade, drifting on endlessly, with no end in sight.

The poem appears in *Shinshoku dairin wakashū*, no. 9730.

82.   *Miyabe no Yoshimasa (1729–92)*

Miscellaneous: "Mountain"

> From Fuji's peak   the smoke no longer
> rises—   though remaining on
> since the age of the gods   shines the light
> of the snow.

> *fuji no ne no / kemuri wa taete / kienokoru / yuki ni kamiyo no / hikari misu rashi*

MOUNT FUJI is one of the most prominent of "famous places" (*na-dokoro*) of the court tradition. Yet, perhaps because it is so far from

---

26. See Miyabe no Yoshimasa, *Yoshimasa kikigaki*, p. 693.

27. *Shin kokinshū*, poem no. 1615.

Kyoto, it was not nearly as prominent in classical and medieval times as, say, Yoshino or Naniwa.

On a clear day, however, the loftiest of lofty Japanese peaks was visible from Edo, which may explain why it was so important a topic for painters and poets of that area beginning in the seventeenth century and has continued to be an icon of Japanese culture until the present day.

Tradition dictated that Fuji be treated with reverence, which often meant a poem in the "lofty style" (*taketakaki yō*). It is not surprising, then, that Miyabe no Yoshimasa, shogunal official and stalwart of the Reizei cause, should have produced a poem of elevated diction that draws attention to the timelessness of the peak, lit always by the pure light of snow.

Yoshimasa also includes a detail that reveals his allegiance to Reizei teachings. For according to the secret teachings on a much-debated passage in the preface to *Kokinshū*, Yoshimasa's teachers argued that smoke "does not rise" over the mountain, whereas the Nijō took the opposite position, that the smoke "never stops."[28] The poem thus might be glossed to read: "The smoke that once rose over Mount Fuji does so no more, it is true; but still showing us that the mountain has existed since the age of the gods is the timeless snow that never melts away."

Yoshimasa's poem appears in *Kakanshū*, no. 899.

83. Yōren (1719–74)

Spring: "Plum Blossoms"

Ah, how gently blows   the morning wind
that carries   a scent of plum
from groves in their full glory   in the shadow
of spring hills.

nodoka ni mo/fuku asakaze no/nioi kite/umezakari naru/haru no yamakage

YŌREN IS the priestly name of a man from Ise, a member of the Takada branch of the True Pure Land sect who studied poetry under Reizei Tamemura. Evidently a committed recluse, he spent most of his days in a hut he called the Lion's Cliff in Saga, where he lived a simple life dedicated to Buddhist devotions—and, it would seem,

28. Miyabe no Yoshimasa, *Yoshimasa kikigaki*, p. 713. See also the note appended to poem no. 729 in *Kakanshū*.

to poetry. Perhaps out of a desire to admit no worldly attachments, he recorded none of his own poems. It was only after his death that a friend put together an anthology of his work, the *Shishigan wakashū* (The Lion Cliff Collection), which contains just over 1,000 poems. He also left a calligraphy primer and a travel record entitled *Yoshino kikō* (A Trip to Yoshino).

Yōren was a friend of Ozawa Roan and Ban Kōkei, both commoner poets of renown in the Kansai area, and was somewhat influenced by Roan's *tadagoto*—or "plain-language"—style. In the main, though, he followed the teachings of the Reizei school. His anthology records a number of poetic exchanges between himself and Tamemura, indicating an intimate relationship.

The poem above is a good example of the courtly style that Yōren learned from his Reizei master. By the eighteenth century, thousands upon thousands of poems had of course been written on the topic of plum blossoms, making any truly original treatment next to impossible. Rather than attempting anything truly new, then, Yōren aims to treat the topic in its essence. The time is morning, the season spring, which we know from the scent of groves in full bloom in the shadow of spring hills—unseen, as yet, but abundantly present. The scene is one of utter tranquility, a scene of peace with no hint of dissonance as natural forces combine to express the essence of a topic that is itself the essence of the court style.

The poem is quoted in *Kinsei waka no sekai*, p. 43.

84.   *Ishino Hiromichi (1718–1800)*

Love: "Waiting for Love in Secret"

"We must be careful!"   he said, and promised
to come   only well into night—
as if one could sleep awhile   and later on
wake again!

shinobureba / fukete to iishi / chigiri tote / yoru no ma bakari / nerare ya wa suru

ISHINO HIROMICHI served variously as governor of Tōtōmi Province and commissioner of the island of Sado. Like many other samurai poets, he studied under several noble teachers, including Reizei Tamemura and his son Tameyasu. He was one of the chief compilers of *Kakanshū*, the premier Edo-period anthology of courtly *uta* composed in Edo. His own poem noted here comes from this collection (no. 769).

One Hundred Poems

Hiromichi's poem evokes the kind of love affair that was the staple of courtly literature in the golden age of *The Tale of Genji* and other romances. True to convention, he adopts the position of the "waiting woman" in order to deal with the topic of pining away for someone who is late in appearing. The characteristically "feminine" complaint the poem expresses about a man who seems oblivious to the anguish of those who must sit and wait is also a common one in court poetry. The man, who is free to move around at will and may have relationships with many women at the same time, does not properly understand the predicament of a woman left to wait for his attentions—especially one who must do so in secrecy, not giving away her true feelings to those around her. The idea of sleeping in such an emotional state is absurd. "Does he think that I can sleep awhile," she muses, "and wake later on to greet him?" Desire is not something so easy to turn off and on. The last line of the poem, which in a more literal translation reads as a rhetorical question, "How could one possibly sleep?" is the litany of many lovers waiting in similar circumstances.

The concern for reputation and the corresponding need for secrecy is also a theme of many court poems. Just why secrecy must be maintained in this case the text does not disclose. Perhaps the man is married and is trying to keep his philandering from his wife; perhaps political considerations make it impossible to admit their union openly. Any number of scenarios is possible. One thinks again of stories found in *Tales of Ise* or *The Tale of Genji* in which lovers are forced by various circumstances to avoid prying eyes.

85. *Yoshimasa's Wife (d. 1788)*

Autumn: Written on the 15th day of the Eighth Month

From far in a past   I never saw
into a future   I shall not witness—
unchanging ever is the light   of the renowned
autumn moon.

minu mukashi/mizaran nochi mo/kawaraji na/nadataru aki no/tsuki no hikari wa

THE WIFE of Miyabe no Yoshimasa (known as Manjo), originally from the Asai clan, no doubt had a conventional upbringing for the daughter of a samurai household, which would have included instruction in the tea ceremony, flower arrangment, calligraphy, and poetry. Along with her husband and later her son, she was one of the supporters of the Reizei cause in Edo.

For those who lived by the ancient lunar calendar, the moon of the 15th day was the full moon, and the fullest of all moons was that of mid-autumn — the Eighth Month, which corresponds to sometime in mid- or late September in the Western calendar.

The full moon of course deserves praise, but how to come up with a new superlative? Yoshimasa's wife begins by alluding to the short span of a human life, which exists between a past and a future that we can never know but can only imagine — while the moon goes on, waxing and waning, revolving on its course. Since the beginning of time, the poem suggests, the moon has witnessed all the past, and it will go on witnessing into the future — but with no reaction, only a cold glare. It truly does not change, no matter what the state of affairs in the world.

So there is irony in the poem, but only of the gentlest sort. The most lasting image comes in the last line, with a vision of enduring light that provides some comfort in a world in which little else can be depended upon.

The poem appears as no. 469 in *Kakanshū*.

86. *Yoshiaki's Wife (precise dates unknown)*

Love: "Love, with 'River' as an Image"

Had I any hope   that our streams
would meet again   after drifting apart,
I would gladly cast myself   into the River
of Tears.

nagarete mo / nochi ni au se no / tanomi araba / namida no kawa ni / mi o ya sutemashi

TAZAWA YOSHIAKI (1693–1750) served as a hunting master under the shogun Tokugawa Yoshimune and later went into the service of an imperial prince. He was a prominent member of the Reizei coterie in Edo. As was often the case, his wife — whose personal name we do not know — shared his interest. By the period in question, poetic composition — along with calligraphy, the tea ceremony, and music training — was one of the subjects involved in "finishing" for women of any social standing, a pattern that would remain true into the early twentieth century.

A famous poem by Retired Emperor Sutoku from *Hyakunin isshu* (no. 77) provides the imagery and conception for the one Yoshiaki's wife composed centuries later, under what circumstances we do not know:

In a swift current   a boulder may block
the rush   of falling water
and split streams that in the end   will join together
again.[29]

se o hayami / iwa ni sekaruru / takikawa no / warete mo sue ni / awamu to zo omou

Sutoku's speaker is at least hopeful that those who part may someday come together again. Obstacles — symbolized by a great boulder — are inevitable in the course of human events, he suggest, but they may not last. Streams may come together again.

Yoshiaki's wife is less sanguine, and more tentative. Before beginning a love affair, she realizes the innate changeability of the River of Tears, which is full of dangerous currents. For a time lovers may be together, but so strong are the forces that they may drift apart. There is no guarantee that streams will ever meet again. Throwing oneself into such a current, she says to an insistent suitor, is a fateful step that may not lead to happiness in the end.

The poem appears in *Kakanshū* as no. 763.

87. *Machiko of Gion (1728?–84)*

Summer: "Fireflies"

On a summer night,   down along
the bottom   of a shallow marsh,
another tangle appears —   this one made
of firefly light.

natsu no yo no / asasawanuma no / minasoko ni / kage mo midarete / hotaru tobikau

YURIKO, THE foster daughter of Kajiko of Gion, married a shogunal official and spent ten years with her husband before divorcing and returning to work in her adopted mother's teahouse. The unsuccessful marriage yielded a child known as Machiko (or Machijo). Unlike her mother, Machiko never worked in the tea trade, but instead was married young to a very prominent literatus named Ike no Taiga (1723–76). She herself took the artistic name Gyokuran and was very much a partner with her husband in his artistic pursuits.

Although most well known as a painter, Taiga was an avid poet who studied under Reizei Tamemura. His wife, too, who as a child had no doubt studied poetry and the court canon under her mother, also became Tamemura's student. Together, the two worked

---

29. *Shikashū*, poem no. 229.

as painters, primarily, but they were also involved in calligraphy and poetry.

The poem above is from Gyokuran's personal poetry collection, *Hakufuyō* (*NWT*, volume 3, p. 102). It brings to mind a poem by Tonna on the topic "Fireflies in the Fields":

> On Miyagi Moor   in the gloom beneath
> the trees,   fireflies dart about—
> more numerous than dewdrops   in their tangle
> of light.[30]

miyagino no / ko no shita yami ni / tobu hotaru / tsuyu ni mo masarite / kage zo midaruru

The conventions of the Way disallowed direct allusion (*honkadori*) to a poem from so late in the tradition. What we have here, then, is only an "echo" of sorts, but one that any trained poet would hear. Gyokuran chooses not to include any reference to the famous place Miyagino, with its many associations. Instead, she paints a scene "as it is" of fireflies creating a tangle of light among already dense tangles of summer grasses.

88. *Yokose Sada'on* (*1733–1800*)

Travel: "From among his Travel poems"

> What was I thinking   to say life was hard
> to bear   when I was back home?
> —compared to the misery   of brief nights
> spent at inns.

furusato o / nani sumiushi to / omoiken / karine ibuseki / yado ni kurabete

YOKOSE SADA'ON was another of the Reizei cadre in Edo. Although his elder brother became a disciple of the Nativist scholar Motoori Norinaga, Sada'on favored the aristocratic tradition. He was a shogunal retainer who also received court appointment as governor of Suruga and went as high in the court hierarchy as a gentleman-in-waiting of junior fourth rank—a purely ornamental title of course, but still of symbolic importance. He began his studies under Reizei Tamemura and was among many Edo poets who continued their studies under Hino Sukeki after Tamemura's death.

There are scores of court poems that involve the question, "What could I have been thinking?"—usually as part of an emphatic state-

---

30. Tonna, *Sōanshū*, poem no. 382.

ment of some new understanding or feeling, suddenly obvious in ways it was not before. One of the most famous is by Go-Toba, opining on the beauty of spring evenings at Minase, the site of one of his many palaces:

> Looking far, I see　　the haze move low
> on the slopes　　along Minase River —
> and wonder how I could have thought　　autumn the season
> for dusk.[31]
>
> *miwataseba / yamamoto kasumu / minasegawa / yūbe wa aki to / nani omoikemu*

Sada'on's poem is the opposite of Go-Toba's in everything but rhetorical technique: for besides putting the question at the beginning rather than the end, it deals with a less lofty scene and communicates misery rather than elation. In lamenting life on the road he is part of a very long tradition, extending back to the beginnings of Japanese poetry in the *Man'yōshū*. *Karine* ("brief nights") spent at inns were by definition lonely, and were often unpleasant because of a lack of the usual comforts of home.

The poem appears as no. 1126 in *Kakanshū*.

89.　*Jien (1748–1805)*

Spring: "Returning Geese, in Scattered Flocks"

> One flock already　　has vanished
> into the haze　　when in their wake
> — seeing them on their way —　　more geese head off
> through the sky.
>
> *hitotsura wa / kasumi ni kiete / yuku ato o / miokuru sora ni / kaeru karigane*

RECORDS TELL us that Jien — not to be confused with Archbishop Jien of the Kamakura period — was born in Kawanakajima, Shinano Province, the youngest son of a physician and younger brother of Tsukada Taihō (1745–1832), a prominent Confucian scholar. As a young man he went to Kyoto and studied at the great Tendai monastery on Mount Hiei, but early on he moved into a cottage in the Eastern Hills and took up the life of a literatus. He studied poetry under Tamemura and was numbered, along with Ozawa Roan, Ban Kōkei, and Chōgetsu (1714–98), as one of the Four Commoner Deva Kings (Heian Jige Waka Shitennō) of Poetry.

------

31. *Shin kokinshū*, poem no. 36.

Jien was a staunch defender of the courtly tradition against those he considered to be interlopers, particularly Nativist scholars but also some of his cohorts—Roan chief among them—whose style seemed to him to tend too much toward the colloquial.

The poem above shows that Jien followed his own advice. The central idea, which follows rather naturally from the second half of the topic, "Wild Geese, *in Scattered Flocks*," is somewhat original in the way it describes one flock appearing as if "seeing off" another flock just disappearing into the haze on their journey north, but any creativity the verse can claim ends there. In this sense, Jien follows Teika's old dictum, "old words, new heart." The vocabulary, syntax, imagery, and overall conception of the poem are all well within the orthodox standards that Jien learned from Tamemura.

Jien left no personal anthology, but many of his poems are included in *Ruidai wakanashū* (1827), a collection of poems by Kyoto poets such as Roan, Chōgetsu, Ueda Akinari, Ike no Taiga, and others. This poem appears in the spring section of that anthology.

The poem is quoted in *Kinsei waka no sekai*, p. 55.

90. Okun (*1715–81*)

"Bedclothes"

In my old age   I pile on
layers of bedclothes,   and yet still I feel
through the walls of my chambers   the cold
of the passing wind.

oiraku wa/yoru no fusuma o/kasanete mo/neya no hima moru/kaze zo samukeki

OKUN IS the name of a woman from a samurai household in Nagoya who became the consort of Tokugawa Muneharu (1696–1764), ninth lord of Owari, one of the most important of all Edo-period domains. She studied poetry first under Reizei Tamemura and later Tameyasu and also had her work marked by Muneie of the lower Reizei house. She left behind more than 4,000 poems.

The poem above is one of twelve submitted to Okun's Reizei masters for comment. Next to most of the poems is written the simple phrase *yoroshiku sōrō*—"very good." Next to this one, however, we read: *jitsujō ka*, "Your real feelings, perhaps?" Traditionally, the task of writing on a topic was seen as more objective, i.e., to capture something in its essence (*hon'i*). But speaking from "real" experience was also allowed, within certain limits. The comment thus is intended as approbation and not criticism. "This one has the ring of truth," the master suggests.

The topic of "Bedclothes" is not a common one, which perhaps explains why it elicited a more subjective response. When one could not call on precedent, only personal experience remained. It reads as a wonderful example of capturing an experience "as is" (*ari no mama*), although a conservative critic might argue that it strays somewhat from the topic in that what it really defines is old age.

The poem appears in *Okun shū* (p. 38).

91.   *Murata Harumi (1746–1811)*

Miscellaneous: "On Seeing Clouds Clear Away from Mount Fuji"

The place I guessed   at as I gazed
into white clouds   was only foothills!
Higher up in clearing skies   is the peak
of Mount Fuji.

kokoro ate ni / mishi shirakumo wa / fumoto nite / omowanu sora ni / aaruru fuji no ne

MURATA HARUMI was born into a prominent merchant house in Edo. His father and older brother were both literati and he began studying poetry in his youth. When he showed promise, his father arranged to have him adopted into the house of the *renga* master Saka Shōshū (d. 1784), who had no heir. Later, however, when his own older brother died, he returned to his own house and took over the family business. Evidently his training as a *renga* master did net prepare him well for the commercial world, for he soon destroyed the business with profligate living.

Harumi is generally thought of as a disciple of Kamo no Mabuchi of the Nativist faction. In his early years, however, as head of the Saka lineage, he was associated with the Reizei house. A number of his poems appeared in the first edition of *Kakanshū* (circa 1768), which was compiled by the Reizei partisan Ishino Hiromichi, and other evidence also shows a cordial relationship. That none of his poems were included in the second edition of that same work (which appeared in 1799), however, is a strong indication that by that time he had cut his ties to the Reizei and, indeed, to the court tradition of poetry. He went on to become one of the primary figures of what is called the "Edo School" (Edo-ha), along with Katō Chikage (1735–1808).

Harumi's personal anthology, titled *Kotojirishū* (Behind the Zither) was put together by his daughter and published in 1813. The poem above, no. 1051 in that work, is one of his most famous. Many poems about Mount Fuji of course preceded his, and the topic was particularly popular with poets of the East Country. His poem succeeds as well as any in getting across the essence of Fuji as a topic, which is the way it towers alone over the landscape. At first the speaker looks up into the clouds in search of the storied mountain's peak, but then realizes that the peak is above even the clouds, hovering as if in open space.

92.   *Reizei Tameyasu (1735–1816)*

Miscellaneous: "Birds in a Grove at Dusk"

As darkness comes down   on the trees
of a grove,   a throng of crows
in search of a roosting place   goes cawing
noisily by.

yūgure wa/kigi no hayashi no/muragarasu/negura motomuru/koe sawagu nari

EDO-PERIOD court poets were taught that the works of Kyōgoku Tamekane and his patrons, from Retired Emperor Fushimi to Retired Emperor Hanazono, represented an unorthodoxy (*ifū*) that should be shunned. The very fact that they were still mentioned in handbooks and treatises, however, is proof that they were still read. There seems to have been an openness to Kyōgoku poetics among Reizei poets in particular.

From the Nijō point of view, this poem by Reizei Tameyasu is unconventional in two ways: first, because it presents the inelegant image of a "throng of crows" (*muragarasu*), and second, because it contains no word that directly represents the sensibility of the poet, nothing that would qualify it as embodying the idea of *ushin*, or "intense feeling."

The poem is on a conventional topic, which in a way makes it even more striking: for rather than as mere description, it can be taken as an insistence that even the quotidian is a proper subject for poetry. Tameyasu could have chosen many other birds, from wild geese to cranes or warblers; to choose crows instead was to make a statement.

One cannot help but wonder if Tameyasu may have had a famous *hokku* by Matsuo Bashō in mind when he chose to treat his topic in the way he did:

On a bare branch
crows have settled down to roost.
In autumn evening.[32]

kareeda ni / karasu no tomarikeri / aki no kure

Scholars argue about whether the *karasu* of Bashō's poem should be
singular or plural. If one takes it to be the latter, Tameyasu's poem
may be taken as an echo of the *haikai* master's creation. Socially, *hai-
kai* and courtly *uta* existed in largely separate worlds, of course, but
nothing precluded their meeting in the world of the imagination.

Tameyasu's poem appears in *Shinshoku dairin wakashū* (no. 11897).

93. *Reizei Tamefumi (1752–1822)*

One of two inscriptions on his portrait:

As those before me,   I too labor
to offer up   my meager part —
knowing that I bask in light   cast by
generations past.

rei no mama ni / oroka naru mi mo / tsutomekite / yoyo no megumi no / hikari to zo shiru

THE TRADITION of leaving one's final words in a death poem (*jisei
no uta*) goes back to very ancient times. On his visit to the Reizei
house in the 1700s, Nikki Mitsunaga was even shown a death poem
in Teika's own hand, which he recorded.

If I must pass on   I will not
lament my fate —   so long as the moon
lights the long way before me   toward distant
Vulture Peak.[33]

irinu to mo / nagekazaranamu / tsukikage wa / washi no takane ni / tōkute teraseba

Scholars are dubious about the authenticity of these supposed last
words, but the poem is still instructive in the way that it contrasts
with Tamefumi's. For at death, Teika is looking forward to Vulture
Peak, the site of one of the Buddha's most famous sermons, while his
descendant eighteen generations later looks backward, and not to the
moon — a conventional symbol for the Buddhist Law — but to previous
generations. So powerful had the heritage of the lineage become.

---

32. Matsuo, *Matsuo Bashō shū*, no. 48.
33. Nikki, *Zaikyō zuihitsu*, p. 418.

Though still believers in the Buddhist Law, by the mid-Edo period, worship in the Reizei house focused on ancestors in the Way of Poetry. The word *tsutomeru* (translated here as "to labor") in this context in fact means very specifically "to accumulate effort" in pursuing the family Way.

Tamefumi probably did not write his poem on his deathbed, but at some time just after he sat for a portrait by Hara Zaichū (1750–1837), the upper-right-hand corner of which contains a *shikishi* version of the poem.[34] Zaichū had also done a portrait of Tamefumi's father, Tameyasu. Furthermore, Zaichū's teacher, Maruyama Ōkyo, had done a famous portrait of Tameyasu's father, Tamemura. Zaichū and Ōkyo were some of the most prominent painters of their day.

94. *Reizei Tamenori (1777–1848)*

Written for a sliding door in the Bush Clover Room
of the Imperial Palace

In the night breeze   on the shore
at Hirosawa   the reeds freeze;
cold is the sheen of moonlight   on ripples
in pond water.

sayokaze no / ashibe kōrite / hirosawa no / tsukikage sayuru / ike no sazanami

THE GREAT fire of 1788 destroyed the imperial palace, along with most of the other buildings of Courtiers' Quarter. Rebuilding began soon, supported by funds from the shogunate. As the process drew to a close, a group of courtiers was asked to produce poems to adorn the sliding doors (*shōji*). Three generations of the Reizei (Tameyasu — Tamefumi — Tamenori) were among the courtiers included in the request. Their assignment was to compose poems to be mounted on *shikishi*, square paper, for the Seiryōden, the private living quarters of the sovereign.

Within the Seiryōden was a room called the *hagi no to*, the "bush clover door," just north of the night chamber. It was here that the poem above would remain. The painting was evidently of Hirosawa Pond, a famous site to the west of the capital — one of the famous places that could trace its history back for 1,000 years.

---

34. *Kyō no miyabi, uta no kororo: Reizei-ke no shihōten*, p. 189; see also Ogura, "Reizei-ke no rekishi 25: Tamefumi," p. 5.

Records say that Tamenori had a part in choosing the topics for the poems. Since he was barely in his teens at the time, however, one suspects that the task was actually left to his father and grand-father, who probably chose from a list provided by the palace. One also suspects that Tamenori may also have had help with this poem, which is one of the first we have recorded for him. The four *sa* sounds in the original—one in each line of the poem except one—give the poem a unifying aural structure, just as the uniformly chilly images of frozen reeds, cold moon rays, and ripples on the broad expanse of the lake come together to form a striking winter scene.

The poem is quoted in *ST* 76, p. 2.

95. *Reizei Tametada (1824–85)*

From *Tametada-kyō Nikkō gekō ki*

From people back home   arrives
a speedy reply   to my last letter—
setting my heart at ease   as I face the road
ahead.

furusato no / fumi no irae no / toku tsukite / yasuku kokoro no / tabiji to wa nare

IN THE late spring of 1859, Reizei Tametada was on his way to the shogunal shrine at Nikkō as imperial messenger. Before leaving, he had been busy with preparations since early in the new year. In ad-dition to making travel arrangements and preparing appropriate gifts and provisions, he set himself to studying the appropriate ritu-als he would have to perform as the emperor's representative at the shrine and purified himself at various shrines. He, his stewards, and a large group of porters and servants left Kyoto on the 1st day of the Fourth Month.

The poem above, which comes from a record he kept of the journey, was written on the 5th day of the Fourth Month, when he received a letter from home—a reply to a letter that he had dispatched only three days before, at Moruyama. In medieval times, such a quick response would have been impossible. For one on an official errand in the late Edo period, however, there were few impediments to rapid transit, especially on the well-traveled roads between Kyoto and Edo.

Along the way, Tametada and his entourage stayed in comfort-able quarters—inns or quarters offered by local officials—and were feted regularly. The only genuine complaint Tametada could make was that he had trouble getting enough sleep. There was no danger from thieves or brigands, and the weather was generally pleasant.

If the poem can be taken as sincere, even bouncing along in his palanquin on one of the few trips he would ever make to the East Country, Tametada was evidently thinking of home—a theme of most travel poems, to be sure, but one that rings true to a student of Tametada's life. Tamemura and his son and grandson had been frequent guests in the shogun's city, but not so the family heads since then. Their province was the old capital and its environs. Even when the rest of the families of the court moved to the new capital at the beginning of the Meiji era, the Reizei stayed behind.

Reizei Kimiko quotes the poem in *RSSG* 29.

96. *Reizei Tametsugi (1881–1946)*

Autumn: "Rain in the Night"

The floating bridge of dreams   that I had
just traversed   breaks and drifts away —
dashed by the sound of rain   tapping on my eaves
above.

musubitsuru / yume no ukihashi / todaekeri / nokiba o tataku / ame no oto shite

TAMETSUGI, 22nd head of the Reizei house, wrote poems daily, but like his ancestors preserved only those in which he felt some confidence. This is one chosen for a book entitled *Reizei-ke no waka*, compiled in the mid-twentieth century. One hundred of Tametsugi's poems are included in the book, all on standard topics: 20 on each of the four seasons and 20 on miscellaneous topics. Interestingly, the topic love is absent. Whether this is because of a Shinto connection or a sort of Victorian prudishness is hard to say, but the same is in fact true of Reizei meetings today. In an interview published in January 2000, Kimiko declared that poems on the four seasons were at the center of poetic activity for the house, and admitted that few love poems are written by Reizei devotees today.[35]

Tametsugi's poem (p. 155) thus seems to be representative of the modern Way of the house. But appearances are deceiving, for the famous poem by Teika to which Tametsugi's openly alludes is one of the most famous love poems of the entire court tradition:

On this spring night   my floating bridge
of dreams   has broken away:

---

35. Kubota Jun, Reizei Kimiko, and Tanabe, "Fujiwara Teika no sennen," pp. 66–67.

lifting off a distant peak — a rack of cloud,
in empty sky.[36]

haru no yo no / yume no ukihashi / todaeshite / mine ni wakaruru / yokogumo no sora

Teika's poem itself alludes to at least two love stories: first, to the last chapter of *The Tale of Genji* and the saga of Ukifune and her suitors, and next to a Chinese story about a king who met a heavenly maiden in a dream, who when she departed told him to think of the clouds trailing away from Mount Wu as a keepsake of their love. So even in a modern seasonal poem, love lurks in the background as a force that cannot be completely denied.

97. *Reizei Yukiko (d. 1970)*

"Pines on the Shore"

How many times now   have the waves
crashing against   Sumiyoshi's shore
washed over the roots of pines   — ever steadfast
and secure?

ikutabi ka / kishi utsu nami no / araite mo / nezashi ugokanu / sumiyoshi no matsu

THE WIFE of Reizei Tametsugi, Yukiko, lived for nearly a quarter of a century after his death, and bore the primary burden of maintaining the family traditions. If there is one person who deserves credit for the survival of house traditions in the difficult postwar years, it is she.

As the daughter of a Shinto priest at the Minase Shrine, Yukiko would of course have been well acquainted with the importance of the Sumiyoshi Shrine (located on Osaka Bay in modern Sakai) in the history of court poetry. By the late Heian period, the god enshrined there, known as Sumiyoshi Myōjin, was already established as a patron deity of poets. Moreover, according to one medieval text, the connection of the family to the place had been strong ever since Teika, while in retreat there, had a dream that ratified his status as a poet.

The import of Yukiko's poem, one of just ten of her works recorded in *Reizei-ke no waka* (p. 159), is straightforward: the Sumiyoshi pines represent the vitality and longevity of the Way of Poetry, whose roots

---

36. *Shin kokinshū*, poem no. 38.

had withstood the storms of time for 22 generations. Among those generations were of course many women, beginning with Abutsu. Unfortunately, we have little poetry from any woman after Abutsu. It is certain, however, that in every age Reizei women participated in meetings with their fathers, husbands, and sons; and it is equally certain that since Tametsugi's death it has been the women of the house — Yukiko and her daughters and grandaughters — who have sustained the Way, and indeed women who have made up the majority of those who call themselves disciples.

98. *Arao Sugako (1907–94)*

"Fallen Leaves in a Garden"

There is no one   I am waiting for
and no one   coming to visit;
but in my rain-soaked garden   leaves fall, covering
the ground.

matsu hito mo / toikuru hito mo / nakeredomo / shigururu niwa wa / ko no ha chirishiku

AS THE eldest daughter and eldest child of the house, Reizei Sugako, according to Fumiko, was given considerable instruction by her father, Tametsugi, and even after her marriage in 1935 continued to be greatly involved in family affairs. From early on she was ex-pected to compose poems, and after her father's death she continued to play a central role in the poetic activities of the house. This continued until the founding of the Reizei Corporation in the early 1980s. In particular, she had responsibility for running the monthly poetry meetings her father had established decades before. In the first issue of *Shiguretei*, Sugako's name is listed among the Board of Trustees, along with her younger sister Kodera Hideko and Fujitani Tameshige (d. 1982), head of one of the junior Reizei lines — a sign that the family would still be at the heart of the Reizei enterprise.

The poem above was written for the anniversary of Fujiwara no Shunzei's death held at Shōkaku-an, a small temple within the large Tōfukuji complex in southeast Kyoto, on the 30th day of November, 1982. Tametō, Fumiko, Kimiko, Hideko's husband Kodera Masatarō, and some disciples were there as well. Poems by all are recorded in *ST* 4 (p. 3).

Sugako died in 1994. Her duties were taken over by Fumiko, after an apprenticeship of more than 40 years.

99. *Reizei Fumiko (b. 1916)*

Written upon receiving the Dawn Prize from the City of Kyoto

For eight hundred years   Izumi River
has flowed   down to our time—
and for thousands of years more   we pray it will
course as strong.

izumigawa / yaho no toshitsuki / nagarekite / nao iku chiyo no / sakae noramu

IN THE spring of 1998, Reizei Fumiko, then 82, spent time in the hospital with back trouble. Before long, however, she was back at work. That same fall, the city of Kyoto awarded her the Akebonoshō ("Dawn Prize"), which is given yearly to a woman for outstanding accomplishment. In her case, praise was given for her work as de facto head of the Reizei Corporation in making the contents of the family library available to a broader public. "It made me very happy," she said, "because it seemed a recognition of my having preserved the library."[37]

Over her years as mainstay of the house, Fumiko has written many poems, about which she is generally apologetic. The one above, however, which served as frontispiece to the catalogue of the Reizei-ke no Shihōten Exhibition (1997) and also ends a chapter of her book *Kyō no miyabi*, is one for which she evidently has some affection. In the book, she quotes it immediately after mentioning her gratitude for having received the Dawn Prize, the only high praise she has received since grade school, she quips.

Quite appropriately, the poem is explicitly about the house. Izumi River is the ancient name of Kizu River in southern Kyoto. Teika wrote a poem about it:

Written on "Great Oaks" at a poetry contest at Yoshitsune's
house when Yoshitsune was still a Guard's Captain

The seasonless waves   are displaying
colors now   in Izumi River.
Up in the Hahaso Groves   storm winds
must be blowing.[38]

toki wakanu / nami sae iro ni / izumikawa / hahaso no mori ni / arashi fuku rashi

---

37. Reizei Fumiko, *Reizei Fumiko ga kataru Kyō no miyabi*, p. 205.
38. *Shin kokinshū*, poem no. 532.

Every year the leaves emerge green and lush in the summer only to turn red or gold in the autumn and then fade away and fall. But the river — Fumiko asserts — always courses on.

100. *Reizei Kimiko (b. 1947)*

Written at the Ogura Mountain Meeting on the 25th day of October, 1986, on the topic "Autumn View"

Raising my eyes   to gaze
at Mount Ogura   I see crimson leaves
and the first geese passing by   on an evening
in autumn.

ogurayama / furisakemireba / momiji shite / hatsukari wataru / aki no yūgure

ON THE 25th of October, 1986, Reizei Fumiko, Kimiko and her husband Katsuhiko, along with relatives and disciples, met at the Enri Cottage in Saga to honor the memory of Fujiwara no Teika. Normally, the festivities were held on the anniversary of Teika's death in August, but this year various impediments — including the death of Tametō — had required that the meeting be postponed.

The festivities began with a Buddhist memorial service. Then came the obligatory poetry meeting, where the poem above (in *ST* 19, p. 3) and others by Fumiko, Tamehiro, current head of the lower Reizei house, and others, were presented in a formal "airing" (*hirō*). For the first time, Katsuhiko served as *dokushi*, or marshal, very much in the shadow of his absent father-in-law. Kimiko did the more demanding work of serving as *kōji*, or lector, the one reading the poems aloud.

Memories of Tametō's passing no doubt made the mood of the occasion somewhat somber. Kimiko's poem hints at her own sadness rather obliquely, through allusion to a poem she knew all in the gathering would recognize.

Raising my eyes   to the broad plain
of heaven   I see the same moon
that shone at Mount Mikasa   in Kasuga,
far away.[39]

ama no hara / furisakemireba / kasuga naru / mikasa no yama ni / ideshi tsuki ka mo

---

39. *Hyakunin isshu*, poem no. 7; *Kokinshū*, poem no. 406.

The poem, one of those chosen by Teika for *Hyakunin isshu*, was written by Abe no Nakamaro in China, when he was planning to return to Japan after many years away. In fact, however, circumstances prevented his journey, and his hopes for seeing Mount Mikasa again were never realized. His poem—full of hope when he wrote it—thus became a poignant statement of the sadness of separation to which Kimiko alludes.

Reference Matter

Works Cited

Place of publication for Japanese works is Tokyo unless otherwise noted. The following abbreviations are used for titles of collections:

KKSH   *Karon kagaku shūsei.* 10 vols. In progress. Miyai shoten, 1999–.
MN   *Monumenta Nipponica.*
NKBT   *Nihon koten bungaku taikei.* 102 vols. Iwanami shoten, 1956–68.
NWT   *Nyonin waka taikei.* 6 vols. Kazama shobō, 1978–91.
RSSG   *Reize-ke Shiguretei sōsho geppō.* Asahi shinbunsha, 1992–.
SKKT   *Shinpen Kokka taikan.* 10 vols. Kadokawa shoten, 1983–92.
SNKBT   *Shin Nihon koten bungaku taikei.* 100 vols. Iwanami shoten, 1989–2000.
ST   *Shiguretei.* Zaidan hōjin Shiguretei Bunko, 1982–.

Akase Shingo. "Reizei-ke no so, Tameie to Abutsu-ni." In *Reizei-ke toki no emaki*, ed. Reizei Tamehito, pp. 92–121. Shoshi furōra, 2001.

Amano Yukihiro. "Kamoku na chichi no namida." Special issue of *ST* (July 1986): 3.

Aoyagi Takashi. "Meiji shōnen no kakai no hajime." *Waka bungaku kenkyū* 85 (December 2003): 1–16.

Arao Sugako and Kodera Hideko. *Reizei-ke no saijiki.* Kyōto: Kyōto shinbun-sha, 1987.

Ashikaga Yoshihisa. *Chakutō hyakushu waka.* In *Chūsei hyakushuka* 8, pp. 177–94. Koten bunko, 1990.

Ashikaga Yoshimasa. *Ei hyakushu waka.* In *Chūsei hyakushuka* 8, pp. 157–76. Koten bunko, 1990.

Atkins, Paul S. "Fabricating Teika: The Usagi Forgeries and Their Authentic Influence." *Proceedings of the Association for Japanese Literary Studies* 1 (Summer 2000): 249–58.

Atsuta Kō. "Bannen no Tamehide." *RSSG* 38 (December 1999): 5–8.

———. "Reizei-ke ryō no seiritsu," *RSSG* 35 (April 1999): 5–8.

———. "Shimo Reizei-ke no bunritsu." *RSSG* 41 (June 2000): 6–8.

———. "Sōshō no seijō." *RSSG* 45 (April 2001): 5–8.

———. "Tamehide no futatsū no mōshijō." *RSSG* 37 (August 1999): 5–8.

———. "Tamehiro no yuzurijō." *RSSG* 44 (February 2001): 6–8.

———. "Tamehiro no zenhansei." *RSSG* 43 (December 2000): 6–8.

———. "Tamekazu to montei." *RSSG* 46 (June 2001): 5–8.

———. "Tamekuni to Tamemasa." *RSSG* 39 (February 2000): 6–8.

———. "Tamemasa to shōen." *RSSG* 40 (April 2000): 5–8.

———. "Tamemasu no okibumi." *RSSG* 47 (August 2001): 5–8.

Beasley, W. G. *The Meiji Restoration.* Stanford, CA: Stanford University Press, 1972.

Beichman, Janine. *Embracing the Firebird: Yosano Akiko and the Birth of the Female Voice in Modern Japanese Poetry.* Honolulu, HI: University of Hawai'i Press, 2002.

Brower, Robert H. "Ex-Emperor Go-Toba's Secret Teachings: *Go-Toba no In Gokuden.*" *Harvard Journal of Asiatic Studies* 32 (1972): 5–70.

———. "The Foremost Style of Poetic Composition: Fujiwara Tameie's *Eiga no Ittei.*" *MN* 42.4 (Winter 1987): 391–429.

———. "Fujiwara Teika's *Maigetsushō.*" *MN* 40.4 (Winter 1985): 399–425.

———. "The Reizei Family Documents." *MN* 36.4 (Winter 1981): 445–61.

——— and Steven D. Carter. *Conversations with Shōtetsu.* Ann Arbor, MI: University of Michigan, Center for Japanese Studies, 1992.

——— and Earl Miner. *Japanese Court Poetry.* Stanford, CA: Stanford University Press, 1961.

Bruschke-Johnson, Lee. *Dismissed as Elegant Fossils: Konoe Nobutada and the Role of Aristocrats in Early Modern Japan.* Leiden: Hotei, 2004.

Bunki sannen sanjūroku-ban uta-awase. In *Chūsei waka shū,* vol. 49 of *Shin Nihon koten bungaku zenshū,* ed. Inoue Muneo, pp. 451–95. Shōgakukan, 2000.

Bunpō hyakushu. In volume 4 of *SKKT,* pp. 504–39.

Burui genyō wakashū. In vol. 1 of *Kinsei waka senshū shūsei,* ed. and comp. Ueno Yōzō. Meiji shoin, 1985.

Butler, Lee. *Emperor and Aristocracy in Japan, 1467–1680: Resilience and Renewal.* Cambridge, MA: Harvard University Asia Center, 2002.

Carter, Steven D. "Chats with the Master: Selections from *Kensai Zōdan.*" *MN* 56.3 (Autumn 2001): 295–347.

———. *Regent Redux: A Life of the Statesman-Scholar Ichijō Kaneyoshi.* Ann Arbor, MI: University of Michigan, Center for Japanese Studies, 1996.

———. "Remodeling the Reizei House." *Early Modern Japan* 9.2 (Fall 2001): 30–39.

———. " 'Seeking What the Masters Sought': Masters, Disciples, and Poetic Enlightenment in Medieval Japan." In Thomas Hare, Robert Borgen, and Sharalyn Orbaugh, eds., *The Distant Isle: Studies and Translations of Japanese Literature in Honor of Robert H. Brower,* pp. 35–58. Ann Arbor, MI: University of Michigan, Center for Japanese Studies, 1996.

———. *Traditional Japanese Poetry, An Anthology.* Stanford, CA: Stanford University Press, 1991.

———. "Travel as Poetic Practice in Medieval and Early Modern Japan." *Journeys: The International Journal of Travel and Travel Writing* 5.1 (2004): 23–46.

Copeland, Rebecca L. *Lost Leaves: Women Writers of Meiji Japan*. Honolulu, HI: University of Hawai'i Press, 2000.

Dairi chakutō hyakushu. Ed. Hayashi Tatsuya. In *Chūsei wakashū, Muromachi hen*, vol. 47 of *SNKBT*, pp. 353–415.

Dazai Shundai. *Dokugo*. In vol. 1 of *Meika zuihitsushū*. Yūhōdō shoten, 1928.

Enbun hyakushu. In vol. 4 of *SKKT*, pp. 539–96.

Enkyō ryōkyō sochinjō. Ed. Ogawa Takeo. In vol. 10 of *KKSH*, pp. 61–105.

Eisenstadt, S. N. *Japanese Civilization: A Comparative View*. Chicago, IL: University of Chicago Press, 1996.

Fuboku wakashō. In vol. 2 of *SKKT*, pp. 477–858.

Fūgashū. In vol. 1 of *SKKT*, pp. 553–99.

Fujigayatsushū. In vol. 7 of *SKKT*, pp. 674–80.

Fujimoto Kōichi. "Kami Reizei-ke to Shimo Reizei-ke: obunko o tsūjite." *ST* 4 (February 1983): 4–5.

———. "Reizei-ke no rekishi." In *Kyō no miyabi, uta no kokoro: Reizei-ke no shihōten*, pp. 8–13. NHK, 1997.

———. "Reizei-ke to Nijōke-bon." *ST* 34 (September 1990): 4–5.

———. "Shōen to Reizei-ke." In *Reizei-ke no rekishi*, ed. Reizei Tametō, pp. 221–54. Asahi shinbunsha, 1981.

Fujiwara no Tameie. *Tameieshū*. In vol. 7 of *SKKT*, pp. 417–55.

Fujiwara no Teika. *Kindai shūka*. Ed. Hisamatsu Sen'ichi. In vol. 65 of *NKBT*, pp. 99–111.

———. *Shūi gusō*. See *Fujiwara Teika zenkashū*.

"Fujiwara no Teika-kyō nanahyakugojūnen ki." *ST* 35 (December 1990): 2–3.

Fujiwara Seika. *Seika shū*. In vol. 8 of *SKKT*, pp. 805–11.

Fujiwara Tameie zenkashū. Ed. Satō Tsuneo. Kazama shobō, 2002.

Fujiwara Teika zenkashū. Ed. Kubota Jun. 2 vols. Kawade shobō shinsha, 1985–86.

Fukui Keiichi. "Nyūin to taiin to no aida: sore wa sei to shi no aida datta." In special issue of *ST* (July 1986): 1–2.

Gion Kajiko. *Kaji no ha*. In vol. 3 of *SKKT*, pp. 331–34.

Gion Yuriko. *Sayuriba*. In vol. 3 of *NWT*, ed. Nagasawa Mitsu, pp. 385–92.

Go-Hōkō-in no ki. Vols. 5–8 of *Zōho Shiryō taisei*. Kyoto: Rinsen shoten, 1967.

Go-Kashiwabara Tennō. *Hakugyokushū*. In vol. 8 of *SKKT*, pp. 480–521.

Goshūishū. In vol. 1 of *SKKT*, pp. 108–41.

Gyokuyōshū. In vol. 1 of *SKKT*, pp. 421–81.

Hamaguchi Hiroaki, ed. *Asukai Masaari nikki chūshaku*. Ōfūsha, 1990.

Hamanaka Osamu and Nagasaki Ken. *Kōdō suru josei Abutsu-ni*. Shintensha, 1996.

Hamaoka Nobuya. "Maeda Naomi no nyūmon." *ST* 20 (March 1987): 4–5.

Hashimoto Fumio. "Chokusenshū senshin to shikashū." *ST* 11 (December 1984): 4–5.

Hayashi Tatsuya. "Go-Yōzei-in to sono shūhen." *Kinsei dojō waka ronshū*, comp. Kinsei dōjō waka ronshū kankōkai, pp. 21–38. Meiji shoin, 1989.

Heisei jūninen Tamano'o kai shū. Comp. Reizei Fumiko. Kyoto: Reizei-ke Shiguretei Bunko, 2000.

Horton, H. Mack. *Song in an Age of Discord: The Journal of Sōchō and Poetic Life in Late Medieval Japan.* Stanford, CA: Stanford University Press, 2002.

Hotta Yoshie. *Koen fūraishō.* Shūeisha, 1999.

Huey, Robert N. *Kyōgoku Tamekane: Poetry and Politics in Late Kamakura Japan.* Stanford, CA: Stanford University Press, 1989.

———. "Warrior Control over the Imperial Anthology." In *The Origins of Japan's Medieval World: Courtiers, Clerics, and Peasants in the Fourteenth Century,* ed. Jeffrey Mass, pp. 170–91. Stanford, CA: Stanford University Press, 1997.

Ibi Takashi. "Bakushin kajin ni okeru dōjō to kogaku." In *Kinsei dōjō waka ronshū,* comp. Kinsei Dōjō Waka Ronshū Kankōkai, pp. 259–77. Meiji shoin, 1989.

Ichijō Kaneyoshi. *Fujikawa no ki.* Ed. Fukuda Shūichi and Tsurusaki Hiro. In *Chūsei nikki kikō shū,* vol. 51 of *SNKBT,* pp. 383–403.

Ichiko Natsuo. "Reizei Tamekage nenpu kō, jō." *Ochanomizu joshidaigaku jinbun kagaku kiyō* 46 (1993): 99–113.

———. "Reizei Tamekage to sono shūhen." *Kinsei bungei* 30 (1979): 1–11.

Ikegami, Eiko. *Bonds of Civility: Aesthetic Networks and the Political Origins of Japanese Culture.* New York: Cambridge University Press, 2005.

Ike no Gyokuran. *Hakufuyō.* In vol. 3 of *NWT,* p. 103.

Imagawa Ryōshun. *Michiyukiburi.* Ed. Inada Toshinori. In *Chūsei nikki kikō shū,* vol. 48 of *SNKBT,* pp. 389–426.

———. *Nigonshō.* Ed. Yamamoto Tokurō. In vol. 11 of *KKSH,* pp. 65–85.

———. *Rakusho roken.* Ed. Takanashi Motoko. In vol. 10 of *KKSH,* pp. 87–127.

———. *Ryōshun isshiden.* In vol. 5 of *Nihon kagaku taikei,* ed. Sasaki Nobutunsa, pp. 177–89. Kazama shobō, 1957.

———. *Shisetsu jikenshū.* In vol. 5 of *Nihon kagaku taikei,* ed. Sasaki Nobutsuna, pp. 213–19. Kazama shobō, 1957.

Ima Shikibu shū. In vol. 3 of *NWT,* pp. 101–2.

Imatani Akira. *Kyōgoku Tamekane: wasurarenubeki kumo no ue ka wa.* Minerva shobō, 2003.

Inada Toshinori. *Waka shitennō no kenkyū.* Kasama shoin, 1999.

Inamori Kazuo. "Nihon no kokoro o kōsei ni." *ST* 1 (March 1982): 7.

Inoue Muneo. *Chūsei kadanshi no kenkyū, Muromachi kōki.* Revised edition. Meiji shoin, 1987.

———. *Chūsei kadanshi no kenkyū, Muromachi zenki.* Revised edition. Kazama shobō, 1984.

———. *Chūsei kadanshi no kenkyū, Nanbokuchōki.* Revised edition. Meiji shoin, 1987.

———. "Reizei-ke no rekishi 1: Michinaga, Nagaie, Tadaie, Toshitada." *ST* 51 (January 1995): 2–3.

———. "Reizei-ke no rekishi 2: Shunzei, Teika." *ST* 52 (April 1995): 4–5.

———. "Reizei-ke no rekishi 3: Tameie, Abutsu-ni." *ST* 53 (July 1995): 4–5.

———. "Reizei-ke no rekishi 4: Abutsu-ni, Tamesuke." *ST* 54 (October 1995): 2–3.

———. "Reizei-ke no rekishi 5: Tamesuke no shūhen to Tamehide." *ST* 55 (January 1996): 4–5.

———. "Reizei-ke no rekishi 6: Tamehide." *ST* 56 (April 1996): 4–5.

———. "Reizei-ke no rekishi 7: Tamekuni, Tamemasa." *ST* 57 (July 1996): 4–5.

———. "Reizei-ke no rekishi 8: Tamemasa, Tameyuki." *ST* 58 (October 1996): 4–5.

———. "Reizei-ke no rekishi 9: Tametomi." *ST* 59 (January 1997): 4–5.

———. "Reizei-ke no rekishi 10: Tamehiro." *ST* 60 (April 1997): 4–5.

———. "Reizei-ke no rekishi 11: Tamekazu." *ST* 61 (July 1997): 4–5.

———. "Reizei-ke no rekishi 12: Tamemasu, Myōyū." *ST* 62 (October 1997): 4–5.

———. "Reizei-ke no rekishi 13: Tamemitsu." *ST* 63 (January 1998): 4–5.

———. "Reizei-ke no rekishi: Ōchō kara chūsei e." In *Kyōto Reizei-ke no happyaku-nen: waka no kokoro o tsutaeru (rekishi hen)*, pp. 81–138. NHK shuppan, 2004.

Irie Sukemasa. *Jijū to paipu.* Chūkō bunko, 1979.

Ishida Yoshisada. *Fujiwara Teika no kenkyū.* Bungadō shoten, 1957.

Ishii Susumu. "The Distinctive Characteristics of the Environs of Kamakura as a Medieval City." *Acta Asiatica: Bulletin of the Institute of Eastern Culture* 81 (September 2001): 53–71.

Ishino Masao. "Kinsei tōshō-ha zuisō." In *Kinsei no gakugei: shiden to kōshō*, ed. Sankokai, pp. 317–28. Yagi shoten, 1976.

Jansen, Marius. *The Making of Modern Japan.* Cambridge, MA: The Belknap Press of Harvard University Press, 2000.

Junsō. *Ungyokushū.* In vol. 8 of *SKKT*, pp. 573–96.

Kada no Arimaro. *Kokka hachiron.* Ed. Fujihira Haruo. In vol. 50 of *Nihon koten bungaku zenshū*, pp. 531–66. Shōgakukan, 1975.

Kaen renjō kotogaki. Ed. Sasaki Takahiro. In vol. 10 of *KKSH*, pp. 107–29.

Kagen hyakushu. In vol. 4 of *SKKT*, pp. 461–504.

Kakanshū. In vol. 6 of *SKKT*, pp. 813–43.

Kamiya Jun. "Time Travel the Reizei way." *The Japan Times Online*, 1 January 2004. http://www.japantimes.co.jp/cgi-bin/nn20040101o2.html (registration required).

Kaneko Shigeru. "Fujiwara Tameuji no shōgai." *Rikkyō Daigaku Nihon bungaku* 31 (March 1974): 36–47.

Karasumaru Mitsuhide. *Karasumaru Mitsuhide-kyō kuden.* In vol. 2 of *Kinsei kagaku shūsei*, ed. and comp. Kinsei waka kenkyūkai, pp. 475–609. Meiji shoin, 1997.

Kasahara Hidehiko. *Rekidai tennō sōran: kōi wa dō keishō sareta ka.* Chūkō shinsho, 2001.

Katayama Jun. "Shoku shūiwakashū." In vol. 3 of *Nihon koten bungaku daijiten*, pp. 410–11. Iwanami shoten, 1984.

Kawahira Hitoshi. "Honkoku: Shōkōkanzō-bon Reizei-ke hiden." *Atomi Gakuen Joshi Daigaku kiyō* 26 (March, 1993): 1–23.

———. "Reizei Tamekazu sōden no kirigami narabi ni Kokin wakashū Fujisawa sōden ni tsuite." *Atomi Gakuen Joshi Daigaku kiyō* 24 (March 1991): 1–53.

Kawakami Mitsugu. "Kuge jūtaku no hensen ni tsuite." In *Reizei-ke no rekishi*, ed. Reizei Tametō, pp. 133–78. Asahi shinbunsha, 1981.

Kawashima Masao. "Fujitani Tamekata shōron." *Kyōto-shi rekishi shiryō-kan kiyō* 10 (1992): 369–87.

Kazari Takehiko. "Fujigayatsushū ni tsuite." *Waka bungaku kenkyū* 88 (June 2004): 28–40.

Keene, Donald. *Emperor of Japan: Meiji and His World, 1852–1912.* New York: Columbia University Press, 2002.

———. "Matsunaga Teitoku and the Beginning of Haikai Poetry." In *Landscapes and Portraits: Appreciations of Japanese Culture.* Kodansha International, 1971.

Kensai. *Kanjinshū.* In vol. 8 of *SKKT,* pp. 447–54.

Kenshō. *Goshūishō chū.* In Kawamura Teruo, ed., *Goshūi wakashū,* pp. 330–52. Osaka: Izumi shoin, 1991.

Kidō Saizō. *Rengashi ronkō.* 2 vols. Revised edition. Meiji shoin, 1993.

Kido Takanori. *Takanori shū.* In vol. 8. of *SKKT,* pp. 421–23.

Kinoshita Chōshōshi. *Kyohakushū.* In vol. 9 of *SKKT,* pp. 53–85.

———. *Ōhara no ki,* ed. Ueno Yōzō. In vol. 67 of *SNKBT,* pp. 39–45.

Kinsei kagaku shūsei. Ed. and comp. Kinsei waka kenkyūkai. 3 vols. Meiji shoin, 1997.

Kinsei waka no sekai. Ed. Murakami Akiko and Yanase Mari. Ōfūsha, 1989.

Kinsei waka senshū shūsei. Ed. and comp. Ueno Yōzō. Meiji shoin, 1988.

Kinsei wakashū. Vol. 73 of *Shin Nihon koten bungaku zenshū,* ed. Kubota Keiichi. Shōgakukan, 2002.

Kin'yōshu. In vol. 1 of *SKKT,* pp. 141–58.

Klein, Susan Blakeley. *Allegories of Desire: Esoteric Literary Commentaries of Medieval Japan.* Cambridge, MA: Harvard University Asia Center, 2002.

———. "Fujiwara no Tameaki." In *Medieval Japanese Writers,* ed. Steven D. Carter, pp. 26–34. Vol. 203 of the *Dictionary of Literary Biography.* Detroit, Washington, D.C., London: The Gale Group, 1999.

Kobayashi Kazuhiko. "Karonshi no yami: Reizei Tamehide no shūhen." *Nihon bungaku* 47:7 (1998): 24–32.

———. "Kyōgoku-ha kajin to wa ikanaru hitobito of sasuka." *Kokugo to kokubungaku* 966 (May 2004): 83–97.

———. "Tameie, Tameuji, Tameyo." *Kokubungaku, Kaishaku to kyōzai no kenkyū* 42.13 (November 1997): 77–83.

Kodama Kōta. *Tennō.* Vol. 8 of *Nihonshi kohyakka* series. Kondō shuppansha, 1978.

Kōen tsugiuta. Comp. Kōen tsugiuta kenkyūkai. 2 vols. Osaka: Izumi shoin, 2000.

Kōgon-in. *Kōgon-in gyoshū.* In vol. 7 of *SKKT,* pp. 730–33.

Kokinshū. In vol. 1 of *SKKT,* pp. 9–33.

"Kokerabuki yane 'kuge yashiki' fukugen." *Kyōto shinbun,* 20 December 2000, evening edition. Archived at http://telecom21.nikkei.co.jp (member account and access fee required).

Kubota Jun. *Ransei ni hana ari: Fujiwara Teika.* Shūeisha, 1984.

———. "Shoku kokin wakashū." In vol. 3 of *Nihon koten bungaku daijiten,* pp. 406–7. Iwanami shoten, 1984.

———, Reizei Kimiko, and Tanabe Seiko. "Fujiwara Teika no Sennen." *Subaru* (January 2000): 63–78.

Kubota Keiichi. "Kaisetsu." In *Kinsei wakashū,* vol. 73 of *Shinpen Nihon koten bungaku zenshū,* pp. 375–404. Shōgakukan, 2002.

——. "Jijū-dono no jūsai nari: Kyōhō roku, shichinen no Reizei Tamemura." *ST* 56 (April 1996): 2–3.

——. *Kinsei Reizei-ha kadan no kenkyū*. Kanrin shobō, 2003.

——. "Reizei-ke no rekishi 14: Tameyori." *ST* 64 (April 1998): 4–5.

——. "Reizei-ke no rekishi 15: Tameharu, Tamekiyo I." *ST* 65 (July 1998): 4–5.

——. "Reizei-ke no rekishi 16: Tamekiyo II." *ST* 66 (October 1998): 4–5.

——. "Reizei-ke no rekishi 17: Tametsuna I." *ST* 67 (January 1999): 4–5.

——. "Reizei-ke no rekishi 18: Tametsuna II." *ST* 68 (April 1999): 4–5.

——. "Reizei-ke no rekishi 19: Tamehisa I." *ST* 69 (July 1999): 4–5.

——. "Reizei-ke no rekishi 20: Tamehisa II." *ST* 70 (October 1999): 4–5.

——. "Reizei-ke no rekishi 21: Tamemura I." *ST* 71 (January 200): 4–5.

——. "Reizei-ke no rekishi 22: Tamemura II." *ST* 72 (April 2000): 4–5.

——. "Reizei-ke no rekishi 23: Tamemura III." *ST* 73 (July 2000): 4–5.

——. "Reizei-ke no rekishi 24: Tameyasu." *ST* 74 (October 2000): 2–3.

Kumakura Isao. *Go-Mizuno'o*. Asahi shinbunsha, 1982.

——. "Sanjōnishi Sanetaka, Takeno Jōō, and An Early Form of *Iemoto Seido*." In *Literary Patronage in Late Medieval Japan*, ed. Steven D. Carter, pp. 93–105. Ann Arbor, MI: University of Michigan, Center for Japanese Studies, 1993.

Kundoku meigetsuki. Ed. and trans. Imagawa Fumio. 6 vols. Kawade shobō shinsha, 1977–79.

Kuroda Kōichirō. *Chūsei toshi Kyōto no kenkyū*. Azekura shobō, 1996.

Kyōgoku Tamekane. *Tamekane-kyō wakashō*. Ed. Hisamatsu Sen'ichi. In vol. 65 of *NKBT*, pp. 153–64.

Kyō no miyabi, uta no kokoro: Reizei-ke no shihōten. Ed. Reizei Tamehito et al. NHK, 1997.

Kyoto. Ed. Naramoto Tatsuya et al. Yama to keikokusha, 1973.

"Kyōto gyoen." *Serai* 17.19 (Special autumn issue, 2005): 50.

Kyōto no rekishi. Comp. Imaizumi Atsuo et al. 10 vols. Gakugei shorin, 1968–76.

Kyūan hyakushu. In vol. 4 of *SKKT*.

Lebra, Takie Sugiyama. *Above the Clouds: Status Culture of the Modern Japanese Nobility*. Berkeley, CA: University of California Press, 1993.

Man'yōshū. In vol. 2 of *SKKT*, pp. 7–179.

Maruya Saiichi. *Shinshin Hyakunin isshu*. Shinchōsha, 1999.

Matsuda Takayuki. "Reizei-ke no keishitachi: *Nakagawa Kiyomoto nikki* shōkai." *ST* 72 (April 2000): 2–3.

——. "Reizei-ke to Keimeishū, Keikō," *ST* 86 (October 2003): 2–3.

Matsudaira Sadanobu. *Kagetsu sōshi*. Ed. Matsudaira Sadamitsu and Nishio Minoru. Iwanami bunko, 1939.

Matsumura Yūji. *Hyakunin isshu: Teika to karuta no bungakushi*. Heibonsha, 1995.

Matsuo Bashō shū. Ed. Imoto Nōichi et al. Vol. 41 of *Nihon koten bungaku zenshū*. Shōgakukan, 1972.

McCullough, Helen Craig. *Brocade by Night: 'Kokin Wakshū' and the Court Style in Japanese Classical Poetry*. Stanford, CA: Stanford University Press, 1985.

——. *Kokin Wakashū: The First Imperial Anthology of Japanese Poetry*. Stanford, CA: Stanford University Press, 1985.

——: *Taiheiki, A Chronicle of Medieval Japan*. Rutland, VT: Charles E. Tuttle, 1979.

Meigetsuki. See *Kundoku meigetsuki*

Miyabe no Yoshimasa. *Yoshimasa kikigaki*. In vol. 2 of *Kinsei kagaku shūsei*, pp. 645–734. Meiji shoin, 1997.

Morikawa Kyoriku and Mukai Kyorai. *Haikai mondō*. In vol. 10 of *Koten haibungaku taikei*, pp. 101–70. Shūeisha, 1972.

Morita Teiko. "Kinsei Tennō to waka." In *Waka o rekishi kara yomu*, pp. 257–74. Kasama shoin, 2002.

Motoori Norinaga. *Suzuyashū*. In vol. 9 of *SKKT*, pp. 455–93.

Munemasa Iso'o. *Edo jidai no waka to kajin*. Dōhōsha, 1991.

Murai Yasuhiko. "Jidai gaisetsu." In *Raku: Chōtei to bakufu*, vol. 5 of *Kyō no rekishi to bunka*, pp. 7–17. Kōdansha, 1994.

Murata Harumi. *Kotojirishū*. In vol. 9 of *SKKT*, pp. 544–78.

Murayama Shūichi. *Fujiwara Teika*. Yoshikawa kōbunkan, 1962.

Mushanokōji Sanekage. *Shōgaku kōkan*, ed. Matsuno Yōichi. In vol. 67 of *SNKBT*, pp. 185–208.

Mushanokōji Sanetake. *Sanetake-kyō kuden no ki*. In vol. 2 of *Kinsei kagaku shūsei*, ed. and comp. Kinsei waka kenkyūkai, pp. 611–64. Meiji shoin, 1997.

Musō Soseki. *Shōkaku Kokushi shū*. In vol. 7 of *SKKT*, pp. 704–6.

Nagakura Chieo. "Reizei-ke to chihō bunka." *ST* 26 (September 1988): 4–5.

Nagoya Akira. "Reizei-ke ni okeru sho no keishō." In *Reizei-ke toki no emaki*, ed. Reizei Tamehito, pp. 184–217. Shoshi furōra, 2001.

——: "Teika-ryū, Reizei-ryū." *ST* 22 (September 1987): 4–5.

Nakamura Toshinori. "Kuge no ie, suki no ie." In *Reizei-ke no rekishi*, ed. Reizei Tametō, pp. 179–219. Asahi shinbunsha, 1981.

——: "Waka no ie, kuge no ie." In *Reizei-ke no toki no emaki*, ed. Reizei Tamehito, pp. 8–43. Shoshi furōra, 2001.

Narita Teiko. "Kinsei Tennō to waka." In *Waka o rekishi kara yomu*, ed. Kanechiku Nobuyuki and Tabuchi Kumiko, pp. 257–74. Kasama shoin, 2002.

Narushima Nobuyuki. *Haru no mifune*. In vol. 1 of *Kinsei kikō nikki bungaku shūsei*, ed. Tsumoto Nobuhiro, pp. 229–34. Waseda Daigaku shuppanbu, 1993.

Nawa Osamu 1993. "Yōmei bunko." In vol. 14 of *Kokushi daijiten*, p. 352. Yoshikawa kōbunkan, 1993.

Nicolson, Adam. *God's Secretaries: The Making of the King James Bible*. New York: HarperCollins, 2003.

Nihon kagaku taikei. Ed. Sasaki Nobutsuna et al. Fourth edition. 10 vols., 5 supplementary vols. Kazama shobō, 1977–81.

Nihon meika shūsei. Comp. Akiyama Ken et al. Gakutōsha, 1988.

Niitamatsushima uta-awase. In vol. 5 of *SKKT*, pp. 726–30.

Nijō Tameyo. *Waka teikin*. Ed. Sasaki Takahiro. In vol. 10 of *KKSH*, pp. 131–43.

Nijō Yoshimoto. *Go-Fukō'on-in-dono onhyakushu*. In vol. 10 of *SKKT*, pp. 179–80.

——: *Kinrai fūtei*. Ed. Ogawa Takeo. In vol. 10 of *KKSH*, pp. 181–204.

Nikki Mitsunaga. *Zaikyō zuihitsu*. In vol. 2 of *KKSH*, pp. 413–73.

Nojima Jusaburō. *Kugyō jinmei daijiten*. Nichigai asoshiētsu, 1994.

Nomori no kagami. In vol. 4 of *Nihon kagaku taikei*, ed. Sasaki Nobutunsa, pp. 64–96. Kazama shobō, 1962.

Ogawa Takeo. "Kadōka no hitobito to kuge seiken." In *Waka o rekishi kara yomu*, ed. Kanechiku Nobuyuki and Tabuchi Kumiko, pp. 193–217. Kasama shoin, 2002.

Ogura Yoshio. "Edo jidai no Reizei-ke." In *Reizei-ke ten: Kinsei kuge no seikatsu to dentō bunka*, ed. Reizei-ke Shiguretei Bunko, pp. 68–77. Asahi shinbunsha, 2002.

———: "Obunko no fū to Tamekiyo." *RSSG* 51 (June 2002): 6–7.

———: "Reigen-in to Reizei-ke." In *Reizei-ke toki no emaki*, ed. Reizei Tamehito, pp. 122–49. Shoshi furōra, 2001.

———: "Reigen Tennō to sono jidai." *RSSG* 48 (December 2001): 5–8.

———: "Reizei-ke no rekishi 25: Tamefumi." *ST* 75 (January 2001): 4–5.

———: "Reizei-ke no rekishi 26: Tamenori." *ST* 76 (April 2001): 2–3.

———: "Reizei-ke no rekishi 27: Tametake." *ST* 77 (July 2001): 4–5.

———: "Reizei-ke no rekishi 28: Tametada I." *ST* 78 (October 2001): 4–5.

———: "Reizei-ke no rekishi 29: Tametada II." *ST* 79 (January 2002): 4–5.

———: "Reizei-ke no rekishi 30: Tamemoto." *ST* 80 (April 2002): 4–5.

———: "Reizei-ke no rekishi 31: Tametsugi." *ST* 81 (July 2002): 4–5.

———: "Reizei-ke no rekishi 32: Tameomi." *ST* 82 (October 2002): 4–5.

———: "Reizei-ke no rekishi 33: Tametō." ST 83 (January 2003): 4–5.

———: "Reizei-ke no rekishi: Edo jidai kara Meiji e." In *Kyōto Reizei-ke no happyakunen – waka no kokoro o tsutaeru (rekishi hen)*, pp. 139–93. NHK shuppan, 2004.

———: "Tamemitsu no ryūgū to Reizei-ke zōsho." *RSSG* 49 (February 2002): 5–8.

Okun. *Okun shū*. In vol. 3 of *NWT*, pp. 18–46.

Okuno Takahiro. *Sengoku jidai no kyūtei seikatsu*. Gunsho ruijū kanseikai, 2004.

Ōtani Shunta. "Go-Mizuno'o-in to Nakano-in, Karasumaru-ke no hitobito." In *Kinsei no waka*, vol. 8 of *Waka bungaku kōza*, ed. Ariyoshi Tamotsu, pp. 29–46. Benseisha, 1994.

Owada Jun. "Reizei Tamehiro-kyō no Echigo gekō 1." *ST* 12 (March 1985): 3–5.

———: "Reizei Tamehiro-kyō no Echigo gekō 2." *ST* 13 (June 1985): 3–5.

———: "Reizei Tamehiro-kyō no Noto gekō." *ST* 7 (December 1983): 4–5.

———: "Reizei-ke to sengoku bushi no bungei." *ST* 2 (June 1982): 5–6.

Oyamada Tomokiyo. *Matsunoya sōwa*. In vol. 2 of *Nihon zuihitsu zenshū*, 689–762. Kokumin tosho kabushikigaisha, 1928.

Ozawa Roan. *Rokujō eisō*. In vol. 9 of *SKKT*, pp. 406–47.

Philomène, Marie and Masako Saito, eds. *Tomoshibi, Light: Collected Poetry by Emperor Akihito and Empress Michiko*. New York: Weatherhill, 1991.

Ponsonby-Fane, R. A. B. *Kyoto: The Old Capital of Japan (794–1869)*. Kyoto: The Ponsonby Memorial Society, 1956.

Reigen Tennō. *Reigen hōkō gyoshū*. In vol. 5 of *SKKT*, pp. 239–57.

Reizei Fumiko. "Fujiwara no Teika-kyō nanahyakugojūnenki." *ST* 35 (December 1990): 2–3.

———: *Reizei Fumiko ga kataru Kyō no miyabi, Reizei-ke no nenjū gyōji*. Shūeisha, 1999.

——. "Reizei-ryū no uta no kokoro." In *Reizei-ke no rekishi*, ed. Reizei Tametō, pp. 55–69. Asahi shinbunsha, 1981.

——. "Uta no Reizei-ke, Reizei-ke Shiguretei Bunko no koto, Reizei Fumiko-shi ni kiku." Interview in *Kokubungaku kaishaku to kyōzai no kenkyū, Fujiwara Teika to hyakunin isshu* 26.16 (December 1981): 28–38.

—— and Reizei Kimiko. "Haha kara musume e tsugu mono: Reizei-ke happyakunen no shihō o mamoru." Interview in *Fujin kōron* (November 22, 1999): 170–73.

Reizei-ke no rekishi. Ed. Reizei Tametō. Asahi shinbusha, 1981.

Reizei-ke no waka. Kyoto: Hayakawa Jishō, 1960.

Reizei-ke toki no emaki. Ed. Reizei Tamehito et al. Shoshi furōra, 2001.

Reizei-ke waka hihi kuden, ed. Nakagawa Hiroo and Sasaki Takahiro. In vol. 11 of *KKSH*, pp. 207–23.

Reizei Kimiko. "Abutsu-san." *RSSG* 8 (February 1994): 1–5.

——. "Bakumatsu no Reizei-ke." *Reizei-ke no rekishi*, pp. 255–317

——. "Bunkazai mamoru ketsui ni kandō: michi no kata kara kaiin mōshi-komi." *ST* 17 (June 1986): 2–3.

——. "Kindai no hito." *RSSG* 14 (February 1995): 1–4.

——. "Shigure no chin." *RSSG* 4 (June 1993): 1–3.

——. "*Tametada-kyō Nikkō gekōki* 1, Tabi no shitaku kara shuttatsu made." *RSSG* 24 (February 1997): 1–3.

——. "*Tametada-kyō Nikkō gekōki* 2, Ōtsu made." *RSSG* 25 (April 1997): 1–3.

——. "*Tametada-kyō Nikkō gekōki* 6, Nezame no Sato, Kiso no San." *RSSG* 30 (April 1998): 1–3.

——. "*Tametada-kyō Nikkō gekōki* 8, Shiojiri kara Wada e." *RSSG* 32 (August 1998): 1–3.

——. "*Tametada-kyō Nikkō gekōki* 9, Kutsukake made." *RSSG* 33 (December 1998): 1–3.

——. "*Tametada-kyō ki* 1." *ST* 1 (March 1982): 3.

——. "*Tametada-kyō ki* 2." *ST* 2 (June 1982): 6.

——. "*Tametada-kyō ki* 3." *ST* 3 (October 1982): 6.

——. "*Tametada-kyō ki* 4." *ST* 4 (January 1983): 6.

——. "*Tametada-kyō ki* 5." *ST* 5 (May 1983): 6.

——. "*Tametada-kyō ki* 6." *ST* 6 (September 1983): 8.

——. "*Tametada-kyō ki* 7." *ST* 7 (December 1983): 6.

——. "*Tametada-kyō ki* 9." *ST* 9 (June 1984): 6.

——. "*Tametada-kyō ki* 15." *ST* 15 (December 1985): 6.

——. "*Tametada-kyō ki* 17." *ST* 17 (June 1986): 6.

——. "*Tametada-kyō ki* 18." *ST* 18 (September 1986): 6.

——. "*Tametada-kyō ki* 21." *ST* 21 (June 1987): 6.

——. "*Tametada-kyō ki* 22." *ST* 22 (September 1987): 6.

——. "*Tametada-kyō ki* 23." *ST* 23 (December 1987): 6.

——. "*Tametada-kyō ki* 27." *ST* 27 (December 1988): 6.

——. "*Tametada-kyō ki* 30." *ST* 30 (September 1989): 6.

——. "*Tametada-kyō ki* 31." *ST* 31 (December 1989): 6.

——. "*Tametada-kyō ki* 32." *ST* 32 (February 1990): 6.

———. "Tametada-kyō ki 35." ST 35 (December 1990): 6.
———. "Tametada-kyō ki 36." ST 36 (March 1990): 6.
———. "Tametada-kyō ki 39." ST 39 (January 1992): 6.
———. "Tametada-kyō ki 47." ST 47 (January 1994): 6.
———. "Tametada-kyō ki 58." ST 58 (October 1996): 6.
———. "Tametada-kyō ki 59." ST 59 (January 1997): 6.
———. "Tametada-kyō ki 60," ST 60 (July 1997): 6.
———. "Tametada-kyō ki 63." ST 63 (January 1998): 6.
———. "Tametada-kyō ki 64." ST 64 (April 1998): 6.
———. "Tametada-kyō ki 65." ST 65 (July 1998): 6.
———. "Tametada-kyō ki 66." ST 66 (October 1998): 6.
———. "Tametada-kyō ki 70." ST 70 (October 1999): 6.
———. "Tametada-kyō ki 72." ST 72 (April 2000): 6.
———. "Tametada-kyō ki 74." ST 74 (October 2000): 6.
———. "Tametada-kyō ki 76." ST 76 (April 2000): 6.
———. "Tenka-san." RSSG 9 (April 1994): 1–4.
———. "Yomigaetta komonjo." RSSG 15 (April 1995): 1–4.
——— and Reizei Tamehito. "Nijū-isseiki ni mukatte." In Reizei Fumiko, Reizei Fumiko ga kataru Kyō no miyabi, Reizei-ke no nenjū gyōji, pp. 225–35. Shūeisha, 1999.
Reizei Mochikazu. Mochikazu-kyō ei. In vol. 8 of SKKT, pp. 28–31.
Reizei Mochitame. Eikyō yonen eisō. In vol. 8 of SKKT, pp. 23–28.
———. Mochitame shū 3. In vol. 8 of SKKT, pp. 32–34.
Reizei Tamehiro. Bunmei jūhachinen eisō. In vol. 8 of SKKT, pp. 526–29.
———. Tamehiro shū 1. In vol. 8 of SKKT, pp. 522–26.
Reizei Tamehito. "Fude no nishiki." In Reizei-ke ten: Kinsei kuge no seikatsu to dentō bunka, ed. Reizei-ke Shiguretei Bunko, pp. 68–77. Asahi shinbunsha, 2002.
———. "Reizei-ke no miei." In Kyō no miyabi, uta no kokoro: Reizei-ke no shihōten, pp. 157–61. NHK, 1997.
———. "Reizei-ke no rekishi to bunka." In Kyōto Reizei-ke no happyakunen, rekishi hen, pp. 7–80. NHK shuppan, 2004.
——— and Sugimoto Hidetarō. "Edo saigo no tōshū, Tametada." In Reizei-ke no toki no emaki, pp. 150–65. Shoshi furōra, 2001.
Reizei Tamekazu. Imagawa Tamekazu shū. In vol. 7 of Shikashū taisei, pp. 519–84. Meiji shoin, 1976.
Reizei Tamemasa. Tamemasa senshū. In vol. 4 of SKKT, pp. 632–50.
Reizei Tamemura. Tamemura shū. In vol. 9 of SKKT, pp. 356–88.
Reizei Tametō. "Kadō no shinan ni ikiru." ST 1 (March 1982): 2.
Rokkashū. In vol. 6 of SKKT, pp. 334–70.
Ryūfū wakashō. In vol. 6 of SKKT, pp. 268–71.
Sakai Shigeyuki. "Reizei Tamesuke no Kaidō yadotsugi hyakushu." Kokugo to kokubungaku 943 (June 2002): pp. 32–44.
Saki no sesshō-ke uta-awase. In vol. 5 of SKKT, pp. 760–81.
Sanjōnishi Sanenori. Waka kikigaki. In vol. 1 of Kinsei kagaku shūsei, ed. and comp. Kinsei waka kenkyūkai, pp. 705–846. Meiji shoin, 1997.

Sasaki Jōhei and Sasaki Masako. "The Formation and Development of Japanese Painting Schools." In *Fenway Court: Competition and Collaboration: Hereditary Schools in Japanese Culture*, pp. 46–59. Boston, MA: Isabella Stewart Gardner Museum, 1992.

Sasaki Yukitsuna. "Koten jidai no kajin no jōken." *Kokubungaku kaishaku to kyōzai no kenkyū* 34.13 (November 1989): 52–53.

Satō Tsuneo. "Kagaku to teikin to karon—Tameie karon kō." In *Waka bungaku ronshū: karon no tenkai*, pp. 225–58. Kazama shobō, 1995.

Senzaishū. In vol. 1 of *SKKT*, pp. 184–215.

Shiba Mikiko. "Reizei Tamehiro no kenkyū." *Shinwa kokubun* 7 (1973): 15–38.

Shimazu Tadao. "Reizei kafū to sono yukue." *Waka bungakushi no kenkyū (waka hen)*. Kadokawa shoten, 1997.

Shimizudani Sanenari. *Shimizudani Sanenari dainagon kyō taigen*. In vol. 2 of *Kinsei kagaku shūsei*, ed. and comp. Kinsei waka kenkyūkai, pp. 41–84. Meiji shoin, 1997.

Shimizu Sōsen. *Shimizu Sōsen kikigaki*. In vol. 1 of *Kinsei kagaku shūsei*, ed. and comp. Kinsei waka kenkyūkai, pp. 319–426. Meiji shoin, 1997.

Shimo Reizei Masatame. *Hekigyokushū*. In vol. 8 of *SKKT*.

Shimo Reizei Tamekage. *Reizei Tamekage Ason kashū*. In *Kinsei shoki shokashū* 2, pp. 5–70. Koten bunko, 1996.

Shimo Reizei Tametaka. *Ei hyakushu waka*. In *Chūsei hyakushuka* 1, pp. 207–18. Koten bunko, 1982.

Shimosaka Mamoru. "Tenmei no taika." In *Shō, Seijuku suru miyako*, vol. 5 of *Kyō no rekishi to bunka*, ed. Murai Yasuhiko, pp. 91–124. Kōdansha, 1994.

Shin chokusenshū. In vol. 1 of *SKKT*, pp. 259–88.

Shindai kashū. In vol. 5 of *NWT*, pp. 691–713. Kazama shobō, 1978.

Shin dairin wakashū. In vol. 1 of *Kinsei waka senshū shūsei*, ed. and comp. Ueno Yōzō. Meiji shoin, 1985.

Shindō Munenori. "Reizei Tamemura no hōnō waka." *Tezukayama gakuin tanki daigaku kenkyū nenpō* 43 (1995): 37–59.

———. "Reizei Tamemura to Sumiyoshi hōnō waka." *Kōgakukan ronsō* 28.3 (June 1995): 1–24

Shinkei. *Shinkei shū*. In vol. 8 of *SKKT*, pp. 256–63.

Shin kokinshū. In vol. 1 of *SKKT*, pp. 216–58.

Shin meidai wakashū. In vol. 6 of *SKKT*, 723–813.

Shin senzaishū. In vol. 1 of *SKKT*, pp. 599–650.

Shinshoku dairin wakashū. In vol. 1 of *Kinsei waka senshū shūsei*, ed. and comp. Ueno Yōzō. Meiji shoin, 1985.

Shin shokukokinshū. In vol. 1 of *SKKT*, 722–67.

Shin shūishū. In vol. 1 of *SKKT*, pp. 650–90.

Shōkō. *Shōkashū*. In vol. 8 of *SKKT*, pp. 315–81.

Shoku gosenshū. In vol. 1 of *SKKT*, pp. 288–317.

Shoku kokinshū. In vol. 1 of *SKKT*, pp. 317–57.

Shōtetsu. *Sōkonshū*. In vol. 8 of *SKKT*, pp. 82–256.

Shūgai sanjūroku kasen. In *Chūsei waka shū*, vol. 49 of *Shin Nihon koten bungaku zenshū*, ed. Inoue Muneo, pp. 513–24. Shōgakukan, 2000.

Shūifūtei wakashū. In vol. 6 of *SKKT*, pp. 258–68.

Smith, Robert J. "Transmitting Tradition by the Rules: An Anthropological Interpretation of the Iemoto System." In *Fenway Court: Competition and Collaboration: Hereditary Schools in Japanese Culture*, pp. 37–45. Boston, MA: Isabella Stewart Gardner Museum, 1992.

Smits, Ivo. "The Poet and the Politician: Teika and the Compilation of the Shinchokusenshū." *MN* 53.4 (Winter 1998): 427–72.

Souyri, Pierre Francois. *The World Turned Upside Down: Medieval Japanese Society.* New York: Columbia University Press, 2001.

Ta'a. *Ta'a Shōnin kashū.* In vol. 7 of *SKKT*, pp. 644–63.

Tabuchi Kumiko. *Abutsu-ni to sono jidai.* Kyoto: Rinsen shoten, 2000.

———. "Nyōbō kajin no ie ishiki: Abutsu-ni made." *Nihon bungaku* 52 (July 2003): 12–22.

Takenishi Hiroko. *Hyakunin isshu.* Chūnichi shinbun, 1983.

Takinami Sadako. "Shōshi: Kyōto gosho." In *Shō: seijuku suru miyako*, vol. 6 of *Kyō no rekishi to bunka*, ed. Murai Yasuhiko, pp. 189–228. Kōdansha, 1994.

Tanaka Masato. "Dōshisha—Reizei-ke no tonari." *ST* 80 (April 2002): 2–3.

Tanaka Noboru. "Reizei-ke ga tsutaeta kotenseki." *Kyōto Reizei-ke no happyakunen (waka hen)*, pp. 79–150. NHK shuppan, 2004.

The Official Guide-book to Kyōto and the Allied Prefectures. Comp. The City Council of Kyōto. Nara: Meishinsha, 1895.

Tenshō dairi uta-awase. In vol. 10 of *SKKT*, pp. 369–74.

Tonomura Nobuko. *Kamakura no kajin.* Kamakura: Kamakura shunjūsha, 1986.

Tonna. *Tonna kudai hyakushu.* In vol. 10 of *SKKT*, pp. 184–93.

Tonna. *Sōanshū.* In vol. 4 of *SKKT*, pp. 166–93.

———. *Seiashō.* In vol. 5 of *Nihon kagaku taikei*, ed. Sasaki Nobutsuna, pp. 18–122. Kazama shobō, 1962.

Tō no Tsuneyori. *Tōyashū kikigaki.* In vol. 5 of *Nihon kagaku taikei*, ed. Sasaki Nobutsuna, pp. 329–89. Kazama shobō, 1957.

Tsubouchi Shōyō. "Shōsetsu shinzui." In vol. 1 of *Gendai nihon bungaku zenshū*, pp. 79–131. Chikuma shobō, 1956.

Tsukamoto Kunio. "*Meigetsuki*: Hito no ko no chichi, Teika." *Kokubungaku kaishaku to kyōzai no kenkyū* 26.16 (1956): 20–27. See *Meigetsuki*, Kenpo 1.5.16.

Tsunoda Bunpei. "Fujiwara Teika no Ichijō-Kyōgoku tei." *Kokubungaku kaishaku to kyōzai no kenkyū* 26.16 (December 1981): 6–11.

Tsunohazu no bessō ni asobu no ki, ed. Matsuno Yōichi. In 67 of *SNKBT*, pp. 457–92.

Ueno Takeshi. "Gokurakuji to Tsukikage no Yatsu." *ST* 93 (July 2005): 4–5.

———. "Hosokawa shō, sono ni." *ST* 88 (April 2004): 4–5.

———. "Jōkōmyōji to Tamesuke-bo." *ST* 94 (October 2005): 4–5.

Ueno Yōzō. "Reizei Tamemura." In vol. 6 of *Nihon koten bungaku daijiten*, pp. 264–65. Iwanami shoten, 1985.

———. "Kaidai." In volume 6 of *SKKT*.

Unjō kakun, comp. Hagiwara Sōko. In vol. 67 of *SNKBT*, pp. 209–56.

Waka monogatari, comp. Tada Yoshitoshi. In vol. 2 of *Kinsei kagaku shūsei*, ed. and comp. Kinsei waka kenkyūkai, pp. 875–918. Meiji shoin, 1997.

Wallace, John R. "Fitful Slumbers: Nun Abutsu's *Utatane*," *MN* 43.4 (Winter 1988): 391–416.

Watanabe Kenji. "Daimyō to dōjō kadan." In *Kinsei dōjō wakaronshū*, pp. 235–58. Meiji shoin, 1989.

Yamada Takemaro. "Sakamoto." In vol. 6 of *Kokushi daijiten*, p. 288. Yoshikawa kōbunkan, 1985.

Yanase Kazuo. *Kōchū Abutsu-ni zenshū*. Enlarged Edition. Kazama shobō, 1981.

—— and Takei Kazuto. *Izayoi nikki, Yoru no tsuru chūshaku*. Osaka: Izumi shoin, 1986.

Yonehara Masayoshi. *Sengoku bushi to bungei no kenkyū*. Ōfūsha, 1976.

Yoshida no Kenkō. *Kenkō Hōshi shū*. In vol. 4 of *SKKT*, pp. 161–65.

"Zadankai: Shōkōkan to tomo ni." *ST* 44 (April 1993): 2–5.

Character List of Japanese Names

Abe no Nakamaro　安部の仲麻呂
Abutsu-ni　阿佛尼
Akamatsu Yoshimura　赤松義村
Akazome Emon　赤染衛門
Akihito Shinnō　明仁親王
Andō Sadatame　安藤定為
Anegakōji Kintomo　姉小路公知
Ankamon-in　安嘉門院
Ano Kinnari　阿野公業
Ano Nobuku　阿野宣子
Arao Sugako　荒尾須賀子
Arisugawa Taruhito　有栖川熾仁
Ariwara no Narihira　在原業平
Asayama Bontō　朝山梵燈
Ashikaga Tadayoshi　足利忠義
Ashikaga Takauji　足利尊氏
Ashikaga Yoshiaki　足利義昭
Ashikaga Yoshiakira　足利義詮
Ashikaga Yoshiharu　足利義晴
Ashikaga Yoshihisa　足利義尚
Ashikaga Yoshimasa　足利義政
Ashikaga Yoshimitsu　足利義満
Ashikaga Yoshimochi　足利義持
Ashikaga Yoshinori　足利義教
Ashikaga Yoshizumi　足利義澄
Asukai Masaari　飛鳥井雅有
Asukai Masachika　飛鳥井雅親
Asukai Masanaga　飛鳥井雅永
Asukai Masanori　飛鳥井雅教
Asukai Masatoshi　飛鳥井雅俊

Asukai Masatsune　飛鳥井雅経
Asukai Masayo　飛鳥井雅世
Asukai Masayori　飛鳥井雅縁
Asukai Norisada　飛鳥井教定

Bai Juyi　白居易
Ban Kōkei　伴蒿蹊
Bifukumon-in no Kaga
　　美福門院の加賀

Chigusa Arifumi　千種有文
Chigusa Tadaaki　千種忠顕
Chiun　智蘊
Chōgetsu　澄月
Chōkaku　澄覚

Daigo　醍醐
Dainagon no Suke
　　大納言典侍
Dazai Shundai　太宰春台
Dōchiku　道筑

Eifukumon-in　永福門院
Eisai　栄西

Fujitani Haruo　藤谷治雄
Fujitani Hideo　藤谷英雄
Fujitani Tameatsu　藤谷為敦
Fujitani Tamechika　藤谷為寛
Fujitani Tameeda　藤谷為條

Fujitani Tameka　藤谷為香
Fujitani Tamekata　藤谷為賢
Fujitani Tamemochi　藤谷為茂
Fujitani Tamenao　藤谷爲脩
Fujitani Tamenaru　藤谷為遂
Fujitani Tamenobu　藤谷為信
Fujitani Tamenori　藤谷為教
Fujitani Tamesaki　藤谷為兄
Fujitani Tameshige　藤谷為隆
Fujitani Tametoki　藤谷為時
Fujitani Tametsugu　藤谷為知
Fujiwara Nagakiyo　藤原長清
Fujiwara no Ietaka　藤原家隆
Fujiwara no Kamatari　藤原鎌足
Fujiwara no Kintō　藤原公任
Fujiwara no Michinaga　藤原道長
Fujiwara no Mitsuie　藤原光家
Fujiwara no Mototoshi　藤原基俊
Fujiwara no Muneie　藤原宗家
Fujiwara no Nagaie　藤原長家
Fujiwara no Nariie　藤原成家
Fujiwara no Nobuzane　藤原信実
Fujiwara no Sanemune　藤原実宗
Fujiwara no Shunzei　藤原俊成
Fujiwara no Sueyoshi　藤原季能
Fujiwara no Tadaie　藤原忠家
Fujiwara no Tameaki　藤原為顕
Fujiwara no Tameie　藤原為家
Fujiwara no Tameko　藤原為子
Fujiwara no Tamemori　藤原爲守
Fujiwara no Tameuji　藤原為氏
Fujiwara no Tamezane　藤原為実
Fujiwara no Teika　藤原定家
Fujiwara no Toshitada　藤原俊忠
Fujiwara no Yorimichi　藤原頼通
Fujiwara no Yukinari　藤原行成
Fujiwara Seika　藤原惺窩
Fujiwara Takako　藤原高子
Furuta Oribe　古田織部
Fushimi　伏見

Gekkō-in　月光院
Gen'e　源恵
Genshō　源承
Gion Kajiko　祇園梶子
Gion Machiko　祇園町子

Gion Yuriko　祇園百合子
Go-Daigo　後醍醐
Go-Fukakusa　後深草
Go-Fushimi　後伏見
Go-Hanazono　後花園
Go-Horikawa　後堀川
Go-Kameyama　後亀山
Go-Kashiwabara　後柏原
Go-Kōgon　後光厳
Go-Komatsu　後小松
Go-Kōmyō　後光明
Go-Mizuno'o　後水尾
Go-Murakami　後村上
Go-Nara　後奈良
Go-Nijō　後二条
Go-Reizei　後冷泉
Go-Saga　後嵯峨
Go-Sai　後西
Go-Shirakawa　後白河
Go-Toba　後鳥羽
Go-Tsuchimikado　後土御門
Go-Uda　後宇多
Go-Yōzei　後陽成
Gusai　救済
Gyōjin　堯尋
Gyōkō　堯孝

Hachijō-in no Sanjō
　　八条院の三條
Hagiwara Sōko　萩原宗固
Hamuro Mitsutoshi　葉室光俊
Hanazono　花園
Hara Zaichū　原在中
Hasegawa Yasuakira　長谷川安卿
Hatakeyama Yoshifusa　畠山義総
Hatakeyama Yoshitada　畠山義忠
Hatta Tomonori　八田知紀
Heisei　平成
Henjō　遍照
Higashizono Motonaga
　　東園基長
Hino Sukeki　日野資枝
Hino Suketomo　日野資朝
Hino Tomiko　日野富子
Hino Toshimoto　日野俊基
Hirohito　裕仁

Hisaakira Shinnō　久明親王
Hōjō Masako　北条政子
Hōjō Sadatoki　北條貞時
Hōjō Takatoki　北條高時
Hōnen　法然
Horikawa　堀川
Hōrin Jōshō　鳳林承章
Hosokawa Katsumoto　細川勝元
Hosokawa Masamoto　細川政元
Hosokawa Yūsai　細川幽斉
Hosono Tamekage　細野為景
Huang Shuyi　黄淑易

Ichijō Kaneyoshi　一條兼良
Ichijō Norifusa　一條教房
Ichijō Sanetsune　一條実経
Ichijō Yoshiyasu　一條能保
Ii Naosuke　井伊直弼
Ike no Gyokuran　池玉瀾
Ike no Taiga　池大雅
Imagawa Ryōshun　今川了俊
Imagawa Sadayo　今川貞世
Imagawa Ujichika　今川氏親
Imagawa Ujiteru　今川氏輝
Imagawa Ujizane　今川氏真
Imagawa Yoshimoto　今川義元
Imaki Sadanori　今城定淳
Imaki Sadatane　今城定種
Imaki Sadatsune　今城定経
Imaki Taneko　今城種子
Ima Shikibu　今式部
Inoue Shōtarō　井上小太郎
Ippen　一遍
Irie Sukehisa　入江相尚
Irie Sukemasa　入江相政
Irie Tamemori　入江為守
Irie Tametsune　入江為常
Irie Toshihisa　入江俊久
Ise　伊勢
Ishikawa Takuboku　石川啄木
Ishino Hiromichi　石野広通
Isono Masatake　磯野政武
Iwakura Tomomi　岩倉具視
Izumi Shikibu　和泉式部

Jichin　慈鎮

Jien (b. 1155)　慈円
Jien (b. 1748)　慈延
Jōkaku　定覚
Junsō　馴窓
Juntoku　順徳

Kada no Arimaro　荷田在満
Kagawa Kageki　香川景樹
Kajiko　梶子
Kakinomoto no Hitomaro
　　柿本人麻呂
Kameyama　亀山
Kammu　桓武
Kamo no Mabuchi　賀茂真淵
Kaneyoshi Shinnō　懐良親王
Kanroji Chikanaga　甘露寺親長
Kanroji Motonaga　甘露寺元長
Karasumaru Mitsuhide　烏丸光栄
Karasumaru Mitsuhiro　烏丸光広
Karasumaru Mitsuo　烏丸光雄
Katara no Iena　語の家命
Katō Chikage　加藤千蔭
Kazahaya Kiminaga　風早公長
Kazan-in Nagachika　花山院長親
Kazuko　和子
Keiun　慶運
Keiyū　慶融
Kenjun　兼純
Kensai　兼載
Kenshō　顕昭
Kido Takanori　木戸孝範
Kimura Seiyō　木村正容
Kimuro Bō'un　木室卯雲
Ki no Shikibu　紀式部
Ki no Tsurayuki　紀貫之
Kinoshita Chōshōshi　木下長嘯子
Kitabatake Chikafusa　北畠親房
Kitamura Kigin　北村季吟
Kobori Enshū　小堀遠州
Kōchō　公朝
Kodera Hideko　小寺比出子
Koga Michimitsu　久我通光
Koga Michitada　久我通忠
Kōgon　光厳
Kōkaku　光格
Kōmei　孝明

Konoe Masaie　近衛政家
Konoe Tadahiro　近衛忠熙
Koreyasu Shinnō　惟康親王
Kujō Ieyoshi　九条家良
Kujō Kanezane　九条兼実
Kujō Motoie　九条基家
Kujō Norizane　九条教実
Kujō Yoritsune　九条頼経
Kujō Yoshisuke　九条良輔
Kujō Yoshitsune　九条良経
Kusunoki Masanori　楠木正儀
Kyōgetsu　暁月
Kyōgoku Tamekane　京極為兼
Kyōgoku Tameko　京極為子
Kyōgoku Tamemoto　京極為基
Kyōgoku Tamenori　京極為教
Kyōken　経賢

Madenokōji Nobufusa
　万里小路宣房
Maeda Naomi　前田直躬
Maruyama Ōkyo　円山応挙
Masaoka Shiki　正岡子規
Matsudaira Sadanobu　松平定信
Matsunaga Teitoku　松永貞徳
Matsuo Bashō　松尾芭蕉
Matsuo Katsuhiko　松尾勝彦
Matsushita Kōnosuke
　松下幸之助
Meiji　明治
Meishō　明正
Michitsuna no haha　道綱の母
Mimurodo Mitsumura
　三室戸光村
Minamoto no Kaneuji　源兼氏
Minamoto no Sanetomo　源実朝
Minamoto no Toshiyori　源俊頼
Minamoto no Yoritomo　源頼朝
Minase Tadasuke　水無瀬忠輔
Minbukyō no Tenji　民部卿典侍
Miyabe Manjo　宮部万女
Miyabe no Yoshimasa　宮部義正
Mongaku　門覚
Monmu　文武
Morikawa Kyoriku　森川許六
Mori Ōgai　森鴎外

Moriyoshi Shinnō　護良親王
Motoori Norinaga　本居宣長
Mukai Kyorai　向井去来
Munetaka Shinnō　宗尊親王
Muneyoshi Shinnō　宗良親王
Murakami　村上
Murasaki Shikibu　紫式部
Murata Harumi　村田春海
Mushanokōji Kin'ya
　武者小路公野
Mushanokōji Sanekage
　武者小路実陰
Mushanokōji Sanetake
　武者小路実岳
Musō Soseki　夢窓疎石
Mutsuhito　睦仁
Myōyū　明融

Nagai Kafū　永井荷風
Nakagawa Kiyosada　中川清貞
Nakamikado　中御門
Nakano-in Michikatsu　中院通勝
Nakano-in Michimi　中院通躬
Nakano-in Michimura　中院通村
Nakano-in Michishige　中院通茂
Nakayama Tadamitsu　中山忠光
Nakayama Tadayasu　中山忠野
Nakayama Tamechika　中山為親
Narushima Kazusada　成島和鼎
Narushima Nobuyuki　成島信遍
Natsume Sōseki　夏目漱石
Nijō Michihira　二條道平
Nijō Tameakira　二條為明
Nijō Tamefuji　二條為藤
Nijō Tamefuyu　二條為冬
Nijō Tameko　二條為子
Nijō Tamemichi　二條為道
Nijō Tamemigi　二條為右
Nijō Tameo　二條為雄
Nijō Tamesada　二條為定
Nijō Tameshige　二條為重
Nijō Tametada　二條爲忠
Nijō Tametō　二條為遠
Nijō Tameyo　二條為世
Nijō Yoshimoto　二條良基
Nikki Mitsunaga　仁木充長

Ninagawa Chikamasa
蜷川親当
Nishiyotsutsuji Kinmasa
西四辻公尹
Nitta Yoshisada
新田義貞
Nōa 能阿

Oda Nobunaga 織田信長
Ōe no Hiromoto 大江広元
Ōe no Masafusa 大江正房
Ōgimachi Kinkage
正親町公陰
Ōgimachi Tenno 正親町
Okiyo おきよ
Okun 阿薫
Ōuchi Masahiro 大内政広
Oyamada Tomokiyo
小山田与清
Ōyū 応猷
Ozawa Roan 小沢蘆庵

Reigen 霊元
Reizei Fumiko 冷泉布美子
Reizei Kimiko 冷泉貴実子
Reizei Kiyoko 冷泉清子
Reizei Kiyoko 冷泉伎与子
[Shimo] Reizei Masatame
下冷泉政為
Reizei Matsuko 冷泉松子
[Shimo] Reizei Michiko
下冷泉実智子
[Shimo] Reizei Mochikazu
下冷泉持和
[Shimo] Reizei Mochitame
下冷泉持為
[Shimo] Reizei Muneie
下冷泉宗家
Reizei Nobuko 冷泉宣子
[Shimo] Reizei Tameatsu
下冷泉為純
Reizei Tameeda 冷泉為條
Reizei Tamefumi 冷泉為章
Reizei Tameharu 冷泉為治
Reizei Tamehide 冷泉為秀
Reizei Tamehiro 冷泉為広

[Shimo] Reizei Tamehiro
下冷泉為弘
Reizei Tamehisa 冷泉為久
Reizei Tamehito 冷泉為人
[Shimo] Reizei Tameisa
下冷泉為勇
[Shimo] Reizei Tameka
冷泉為香
[Shimo] Reizei Tamekage
下冷泉為景
[Shimo] Reizei Tamekatsu
下冷泉為勝
Reizei Tamekazu 冷泉為和
Reizei Tamekiyo 冷泉為清
Reizei Tamekuni 冷泉為邦
Reizei Tamemasa 冷泉為尹
Reizei Tamemasu 冷泉為益
Reizei Tamemitsu 冷泉為満
Reizei Tamemoto 冷泉為紀
Reizei Tamemura 冷泉為村
[Shimo] Reizei Tamenaka
下冷泉為栄
Reizei Tamenari 冷泉為成
Reizei Tamenori 冷泉為則
[Shimo] Reizei Tamenori
下冷泉為訓
[Shimo] Reizei Tameoki
下冷泉為起
Reizei Tameomi 冷泉為臣
Reizei Tamesuke 冷泉為相
Reizei Tametada 冷泉為理
[Shimo] Reizei Tametaka
下冷泉為孝
Reizei Tametake 冷泉為全
Reizei Tametō 冷泉為任
[Shimo] Reizei Tametō
下冷泉為柔
Reizei Tametomi 冷泉為富
[Shimo] Reizei Tametoyo
下冷泉為豊
Reizei Tametsugi 冷泉為系
Reizei Tametsuna 冷泉為綱
[Shimo] Reizei Tametsune
下冷泉為経
Reizei Tameyasu 冷泉為泰
Reizei Tameyori 冷泉為頼

Reizei Tameyuki　冷泉為之
[Shimo] Reizei Tameyuki
　　下冷泉為行
Reizei Toshiko　冷泉俊子
Reizei Yoshiko　冷泉良子
Reizei Yukiko　冷泉恭子
Renjō　蓮生
Rokujō Kiyosuke　六條清輔
Rokujō Yukiie　六條行家
Ryūben　隆弁
Ryūson　龍尊

Saien　西円
Saigyō　西行
Saionji Kinmune　西園寺公宗
Saionji Kinsuke　西園寺公相
Saionji Kintsune　西園寺公経
Saionji Sanekane　西園寺実兼
Saionji Sanemune　西園寺実宗
Saionji Sanetoshi　西園寺実俊
Saionji Saneuji　西園寺実氏
Saka Shōshū　阪昌周
Sakuramachi　桜町
Sanehito Shinnō　誠仁親王
Sanjōnishi Kin'eda　三條西公條
Sanjōnishi Kinfuku　三條西公福
Sanjōnishi Saneki　三條西実伎
Sanjōnishi Sanenori　三條西実教
Sanjōnishi Sanetaka　三條西実隆
Sasaki Dōyo　佐々木道誉
Sasaki Nobutsuna　佐々木信綱
Sasaki Takahide　佐々木高秀
Sasaki Yukitsuna　佐々木幸綱
Satomura Jōha　里村紹巴
Sei Shōnagon　清少納言
Sesonji Yukiyoshi　世尊寺行能
Shiba Ryōtarō　司馬遼太郎
Shijō Takafusa　四条隆房
Shijō Takamasa　四条隆昌
Shimazaki Tōson　島崎藤村
Shimazu Tadao　島津忠夫
Shimizu Munekawa　清水宗川
Shimizu Sōsen　清水宗川
Shimizudani Sanenari
　　清水谷実業
Shinkan　真観

Shinkei　心敬
Shōkō　正広
Shōmu　聖武
Shōtetsu　正徹
Shōwa　昭和
Shun'e　俊恵
Shunzei no Musume　俊成女
Sōchō　宗長
Soga no Otomaro　蘇我の乙丸
Sōgi　宗祇
Sono Motonari　園基音
Sugawara no Michizane
　　菅原道真
Sukuru　勝
Sutoku　崇徳

Ta'a　他阿
Tachibana no Moroe　橘諸兄
Tada Yoshitoshi　多田義俊
Taira no Atsumori　平敦盛
Taira no Munemori　平宗盛
Taishō　大正
Takakura　高倉
Takamatsu Shigesue　高松重季
Takasaki Masakaze　高崎正風
Takatsukasa Fusako　鷹司房子
Takatsukasa Masamichi
　　鷹司政通
Takatsukasa Norihira　鷹司教平
Takatsukasa Sukehiro　鷹司輔熙
Takayoshi Shinnō　尊良親王
Takeda Nobutora　武田信虎
Takeuchi Korenaga　竹内惟永
Takizawa Bakin　滝沢馬琴
Tamehide no musume　爲秀女
Tamesuke no musume　爲相女
Tanabe Seiko　田辺聖子
Tanuma Okitsugu　田沼意次
Tayasu Munetake　田安宗武
Tazawa Yoshiaki　田沢義章
Tenchi　天智
Tenmu　天武
Tō Dainagon no Tsubone
　　藤大納言局
Tōfukumon-in　東福門院
Tokugawa Hidetada　徳川秀忠

Tokugawa Ieharu　徳川家治
Tokugawa Iemitsu　徳河家光
Tokugawa Iemochi　徳河家茂
Tokugawa Ienobu　徳川家宣
Tokugawa Ieshige　徳河家重
Tokugawa Ieyasu　徳川家康
Tokugawa Muneharu　徳川宗春
Tokugawa Yoshimune　徳川吉宗
Tokugawa Yoshinobu　徳川慶喜
Tō no Tsuneyori　東常縁
Tonna　頓阿
Toshihito Shinnō　智仁親王
Toyotomi Hideyoshi　豊臣秀吉
Tsubouchi Shōyō　坪内逍遥
Tsukada Taihō　冢田大峰
Tsumori Kunisuke　津守国助

Uda　宇多
Ueda Akinari　上田秋成
Uemon no suke　右衛門佐
Umehara Takeshi　梅原猛
Utsunomiya Yoritsuna
　宇都宮頼綱

Yamada Dōmu　山田道夢
Yamada Kameko　山田亀子
Yamamoto Shunshō　山本春正
Yamana Sōzen　山名宗全
Yamashina Tokitsugu　山科言継
Yamashina Tokitsune　山科言経
Yamashina Tokiyuki　山科言行
Yanagisawa Yoshiyasu　柳沢吉保
Yanagiwara Mitsunaru　柳原光愛
Yanagiwara Mitsutsuna
　柳原光綱
Yanagiwara Naruko　柳原愛子
Yanagiwara Takamitsu　柳原隆光
Yokose Sada'on　横瀬貞臣
Yōren　涌蓮
Yosano Akiko　与謝野晶子
Yoshiaki no tsuma　義章の妻
Yoshida no Kenkō　吉田の兼好
Yoshimasa no tsuma　義正の妻

Zeami　世阿弥
Zenna　善阿

General Index

Harvard-Yenching Institute Monograph Series
(titles now in print)